Ignorance and Moral Responsibility

Ignorance and Moral Responsibility

MICHAEL J. ZIMMERMAN

OXFORD
UNIVERSITY PRESS

Great Clarendon Street, Oxford, OX2 6DP,
United Kingdom

Oxford University Press is a department of the University of Oxford.
It furthers the University's objective of excellence in research, scholarship,
and education by publishing worldwide. Oxford is a registered trade mark of
Oxford University Press in the UK and in certain other countries

© Michael J. Zimmerman 2022

The moral rights of the author have been asserted

First Edition published in 2022

Impression: 1

All rights reserved. No part of this publication may be reproduced, stored in
a retrieval system, or transmitted, in any form or by any means, without the
prior permission in writing of Oxford University Press, or as expressly permitted
by law, by licence or under terms agreed with the appropriate reprographics
rights organization. Enquiries concerning reproduction outside the scope of the
above should be sent to the Rights Department, Oxford University Press, at the
address above

You must not circulate this work in any other form
and you must impose this same condition on any acquirer

Published in the United States of America by Oxford University Press
198 Madison Avenue, New York, NY 10016, United States of America

British Library Cataloguing in Publication Data
Data available

Library of Congress Control Number: 2022936162

ISBN 978–0–19–285957–0

DOI: 10.1093/oso/9780192859570.001.0001

Printed and bound in the UK by
TJ Books Limited

Links to third party websites are provided by Oxford in good faith and
for information only. Oxford disclaims any responsibility for the materials
contained in any third party website referenced in this work.

Preface

There is a long tradition, stemming from Aristotle, according to which one bears moral responsibility for some event just in case one satisfies two conditions. The first condition is that the event's occurrence must have been within one's control. The second is that its occurrence must have been within one's ken. It is the first condition that has received the lion's share of attention from philosophers. Much of this attention has been devoted to the puzzle posed by the apparent fact that satisfaction of this condition is consistent with neither determinism nor indeterminism. Indeed, it was my introduction to this puzzle in an undergraduate course that I took over 50 years ago that first sparked my curiosity about moral responsibility, and my interest in the concept has never waned since.

It was in part because I despaired of ever finding a satisfactory solution to the puzzle about control that I turned, some 10 years later, to a consideration of the second condition of responsibility. But I quickly ran into another puzzle here, too, which is simply that many of our everyday ascriptions of responsibility apparently fail to conform to this condition. For although we often treat ignorance as an excuse for wrongdoing, we also often don't. We don't when we judge that the person in question "should have known better." Even if this judgment is accurate, though, how is it supposed to suffice for responsibility for the wrongdoing in question? This puzzle struck me as likely to be more tractable, and so I decided to look into it. I came to the conclusion that ignorance provides an excuse for wrongdoing far more often than is commonly thought, and hence that many of our everyday ascriptions of responsibility are mistaken. I took a first stab at presenting my argument for this conclusion in the mid-1980s, and I have offered various versions of it since then in a continuing effort to improve on it.

The epistemic condition of moral responsibility is no longer neglected. On the contrary, it has come under increased scrutiny in recent years, some of which has been devoted to my argument. Although some of those who have considered the argument are prepared to accept its conclusion, many are not—which is hardly surprising, given its revisionary nature. To begin with, much of the resistance to the argument pretty much took the form of, "That can't be right." I felt entitled to ignore this reaction, since no attempt was made to identify just where the argument supposedly went wrong. More recently, however, there have been several critical discussions that purport to provide reasons for rejecting one or other of the premises in the argument, and it became clear to me that I needed to revisit it and the issues surrounding it. This book is the result of my doing so.

In Chapter 1 I present a case—"based on a true story," as the saying goes—in which a tragedy occurs, one that it seems could easily have been prevented. In cases of this sort the question naturally arises, "Who is to blame?" In this case the tragedy would not have occurred, had one or more of many people behaved differently. These people thus appear to satisfy the control condition of moral responsibility. (In so saying, I am of course putting the puzzle about this condition to one side.) But the vast majority of these people had no idea that such a tragedy might occur, and so it's not clear how they could properly be said to satisfy the epistemic condition. The common view is that, if any of these people could and should have foreseen the tragedy, then the fact that they didn't foresee it affords them no excuse. But this claim raises the question how foreseeability in the absence of foresight is possible and why, if it is, it undermines an excuse that one would otherwise have. Consideration of this question leads me to my argument—which in this book I call the Argument from Ignorance—that ignorance provides an excuse for wrongdoing far more often than is commonly thought. I present a first draft of this argument toward the end of the chapter and note that it applies not only to what I call incidental moral ignorance (ignorance of wrongdoing that is rooted in some non-moral mistake) but also to what I call fundamental moral ignorance (ignorance of wrongdoing that is rooted in some moral mistake).

The Argument from Ignorance is, of course, an argument about the relation between ignorance and moral responsibility, and in the chapters immediately following the first I undertake an extended inquiry into these concepts. In Chapter 2 I distinguish between various kinds of responsibility, both moral and non-moral, and home in on that particular kind—moral blameworthiness—with which the Argument is concerned. My discussion prompts a reformulation—a refinement—of the Argument, after which I embark on a lengthy investigation into the nature of moral blameworthiness, attending separately to both the blame and the worthiness involved. In Chapter 3 I turn to a consideration of the nature of ignorance and explain why it is that, for the purposes of this book, we should focus in particular on the failure to believe that one is doing wrong and on cases in which the wrongdoing in question is to be attributed to such a failure. This discussion prompts several further reformulations of the Argument. Then, in Chapter 4, I turn my attention to the control condition of moral responsibility, since this condition plays a key role in the Argument, despite the fact that it is the epistemic condition that occupies center stage in the book.

Once these preliminaries are out of the way, I investigate the implications of the Argument from Ignorance regarding culpable ignorance (Chapter 5), negligence (Chapter 6, in which I offer two further reformulations of the Argument), recklessness (Chapter 7), and fundamental moral ignorance (Chapter 8). My purpose in doing so is, first, to reveal the nature of these much-discussed but, I believe, often-misunderstood phenomena and, second, to explain just how it is that the

Argument's implications regarding them are revisionary. Finally, in Chapter 9, I address a number of challenges to the Argument to be found, either implicitly or explicitly, in the recent literature. I concede that many of these challenges have merit but contend that the Argument, reformulated one last time, survives them.

My overarching aim in the book is simply that of improving our grasp of the nature of moral responsibility. The outline that I have just provided is very meager, but it should provide some idea of the contents and the purpose of the book. A perusal of the Table of Contents should also be of some help, as would taking a look at the opening paragraphs in each of Chapters 2 to 9, where a summary is given of what is to come in the chapter.

Finally, I should perhaps say something about the relation between this book and my last book, whose title is *Ignorance and Moral Obligation*. That book was concerned with how it is that ignorance affects our obligations regarding how the future is to unfold—a topic on which I began work a mere 20 years ago. This book is concerned with how ignorance affects our responsibility for how the past has unfolded. For reasons that I give in Chapter 2, these two issues are largely independent of one another; as a result, there is very little overlap between the two books, although my findings in the earlier book do play an important role in my discussion of recklessness in Chapter 7 of this book.

Contents

List of Charts and Figures   xiii
Acknowledgments   xv

PART I: INTRODUCTION OF THE ARGUMENT FROM IGNORANCE

1. The Argument from Ignorance   3

PART II: EXAMINATION AND REFINEMENT OF THE ARGUMENT FROM IGNORANCE

2. Moral Responsibility   27
   2.1 Varieties of responsibility   29
      2.1.1 Some key distinctions   29
      2.1.2 The relation between blameworthiness and wrongdoing   32
      2.1.3 Agent-evaluation and act-evaluation   37
      2.1.4 Three kinds of moral judgments   38
   2.2 Blameworthiness   41
      2.2.1 The basis of blameworthiness   41
      2.2.2 Diverse mental qualities   43
      2.2.3 Control   45
      2.2.4 The relation between the object and the basis of blameworthiness   45
   2.3 The blame in blameworthiness   48
      2.3.1 Thin blame (and praise)   48
      2.3.2 Thick blame (and praise)   51
      2.3.3 Thick blame (and praise) and the reactive attitudes   57
      2.3.4 Thick blame as essentially emotional   60
      2.3.5 Thick blame as essentially involving certain dispositions   62
      2.3.6 Thick blame as essentially calling for an answer   62
      2.3.7 Thick blame as essentially conversational   66
      2.3.8 Thick blame as essentially involving a moral community   69
      2.3.9 A conceptual circle   74
      2.3.10 Breaking the circle   78
   2.4 The worthiness in blameworthiness   81
      2.4.1 From fittingness to worthiness   81
      2.4.2 The ethics of blame   84
      2.4.3 Between blameworthiness and blamelessness   87

2.5 Degrees of blameworthiness	89
2.5.1 Maximal blameworthiness	89
2.5.2 The two dimensions of blameworthiness	91
2.5.3 Comparing and aggregating degrees of blameworthiness	92
2.5.4 The basis of blameworthiness	93
2.5.5 Full blameworthiness	96
3. Ignorance	**101**
3.1 Knowledge and ignorance	102
3.2 Believing and failing to believe	106
3.2.1 Knowledge and belief	106
3.2.2 Beliefs and dispositions	108
3.2.3 Occurrent beliefs	112
3.2.4 Degrees of belief	117
3.2.5 Conflicting beliefs	122
3.2.6 Failing to believe	124
3.3 Acting from ignorance	126
3.4 Blameworthiness without wrongdoing	128
3.4.1 Accuses	128
3.4.2 Moral realism	133
3.4.3 Suberogation	133
4. Control	**137**
4.1 Volitional control	138
4.1.1 Doing something at will	138
4.1.2 The bilateral nature of volitional control	139
4.1.3 Direct *vs.* indirect control and immediate *vs.* remote control	141
4.1.4 Complete *vs.* partial control	143
4.1.5 Basic *vs.* enhanced control	144
4.1.6 Simple *vs.* intentional control	145
4.1.7 AB-conditionals and indirect control	146
4.1.8 AB-conditionals and direct control	148
4.1.9 Control *vs.* freedom	153
4.1.10 Possessing *vs.* exercising control	154
4.2 Simple *vs.* intentional control	156
4.2.1 Control and awareness	156
4.2.2 Reasons-responsiveness	161
4.3 Direct *vs.* indirect control	166
4.4 Control over omissions	169
4.4.1 Acts of omission	169
4.4.2 Can control be purely passive?	173
4.4.3 The locus of direct control	176
4.5 Degrees of control	177
4.5.1 The extent of control	177
4.5.2 Whole control	178
4.5.3 Awareness of circumstances	179

	4.5.4	Reasons-responsiveness	180
	4.5.5	Difficulty	181
	4.5.6	Freedom	182
	4.5.7	The relation between degree of blameworthiness and degree of control	182
4.6	Control over beliefs		183
	4.6.1	Doxastic voluntarism	183
	4.6.2	Indirect control over beliefs	184
	4.6.3	Direct control over beliefs	186
	4.6.4	Believing at will	188
	4.6.5	The Argument against Believing at Will	195
	4.6.6	The Argument against Considering at Will	206

5. Culpable Ignorance — 209

5.1	Tracing blameworthiness		210
	5.1.1	Tracing and tracking	210
	5.1.2	Does tracing require tracking?	211
	5.1.3	Foreseeability	214
	5.1.4	Moral luck	217
	5.1.5	Tracing culpability for ignorant wrongdoing	225
5.2	Exculpatory culpable ignorance		232
	5.2.1	Does ignorance of wrongdoing ever provide an excuse for wrongdoing?	233
	5.2.2	The shadow cast by the benighting act	234
	5.2.3	Inculpatory ignorance	236

6. Negligence — 237

6.1	Inadvertent wrongdoing		238
6.2	Morally substandard inadvertence		244
	6.2.1	Substandard inattention to what one already knows	244
	6.2.2	Substandard ignorance	252

7. Recklessness — 256

7.1	Conscious wrongdoing		256
	7.1.1	Conscious negligence and inadvertent recklessness	257
	7.1.2	Acting recklessly *vs.* acting knowingly	260
	7.1.3	Conscious risk-taking *vs.* conscious wrongdoing	261
	7.1.4	Risking harm *vs.* risking wrong	264
	7.1.5	Purposely doing wrong	271
7.2	Motivated ignorance		273
	7.2.1	Varieties of motivated ignorance	274
	7.2.2	The law on willful ignorance	276
	7.2.3	The duty to inquire	278
	7.2.4	Motivated non-moral ignorance	283
	7.2.5	Motivated moral ignorance	286

xii CONTENTS

8. Fundamental Moral Ignorance — 289
   8.1 Psychopathy — 290
   8.2 Evil — 294
   8.3 Amoralism — 298

PART III: CHALLENGES TO THE ARGUMENT FROM IGNORANCE

9. Varieties of Blameworthiness — 301
   9.1 Negligence — 303
     9.1.1 Inadvertence and blameworthiness — 304
     9.1.2 Agent-regret and remorse — 306
     9.1.3 Morally substandard inadvertence — 311
   9.2 Blameworthiness and quality of will — 312
     9.2.1 Caring for morality *de re vs.* caring for morality *de dicto* — 313
     9.2.2 Conscientiousness and doing something for the right reason — 318
     9.2.3 Moral fetishism — 325
     9.2.4 Ill will — 328
   9.3 The unique moral significance of voluntary wrongdoing — 333
   9.4 Blameworthiness without responsibility — 345

Postscript — 347

Bibliography — 349
Index of Names — 365
Index of Subjects — 370

List of Charts and Figures

Charts

1.1	Sally *vs.* Heinrich	14
1.2	Sally *vs.* Heinrich *vs.* Karl	16
2.1	A Taxonomy of Responsibility	31

Figures

2.1	BILL AND JILL	46, 142, 211
4.1	BILL AND THE CLOCK	145, 166, 177, 186
4.2	BILL'S ACTIVE OMISSION	169, 187
4.3	BILL'S INEFFICACY	171
4.4	BILL'S PASSIVE OMISSION	173, 188
4.5	BILL AND THE BIRD	177, 219
4.6	BILL'S PERSISTENCE	178, 220
5.1	DOT AND PAT	212

Acknowledgments

For me, as for many, the practice of philosophy is in large part a solitary enterprise, but, in my case at least, it is one that is fueled by frequent interaction—conversation, correspondence—with others. Those with whom I have had the good fortune to interact and who have had a direct impact on what I have to say in this book include the following: Craig Agule, Santiago Amaya, Robert Audi, Steve Bero, Nathan Biebel, Gunnar Björnsson, Krister Bykvist, Yenni Milena Castro, Randy Clarke, Angelo Corlett, Oisin Deery, Benjamin De Mesel, John Eriksson, Rick Gallimore, Pete Graham, Ish Haji, Liz Harman, Wilson Herrera, Doug Husak, Mats Ingelström, Zoë Johnson King, Riin Koiv, Sara Magrin, Ellie Mason, Hans Mathlein, Michael McKenna, Michael Moore, Christian Munthe, Alexander Narváez, Dana Nelkin, Jonas Olson, Carlos Patarroyo, Rik Peels, Derk Pereboom, Dario Perinetti, Ingmar Persson, Andrew Reisner, Anna Rez, Sam Rickless, Simon Rippon, Phil Robichaud, Mauro Rossi, Carolina Sartorio, Holly Smith, Caj Strandberg, Matt Talbert, Torbjörn Tännsjö, Bas van der Vossen, Martin van Hees, Alejandro Velasco, Alejandro Vesga, and Jan Willem Wieland. My thanks to all!

Of those people just mentioned, six deserve special recognition.

Pete Graham and Jan Willem Wieland were the readers for OUP. I am very grateful for their advice and encouragement.

Several years ago, Rik Peels invited me to contribute to a volume he was putting together on the moral and social significance of ignorance. I replied that I doubted I had anything new to say on the topic, but he kindly persuaded me otherwise. He turned out to be right. I am grateful for his persistence.

Over the course of many years, on occasions too numerous to count, Randy Clarke, Doug Husak, and Holly Smith have all helped me in my efforts to develop and refine my view of moral responsibility (among other matters). Each of them has, in his or her own way, been unfailingly supportive of these efforts. In each case, both our professional association and our personal friendship mean a great deal to me.

During the writing of this book I received financial support in the form of research leave from the University of North Carolina at Greensboro. I am grateful for this support. I am grateful, too, for permission to include snippets of the following works of mine, recorded in the bibliography as Zimmerman (1995), permission granted by the Philosophy Documentation Center; (1996) and (2008), permission granted by Cambridge University Press; (1997b), permission granted by the University of Chicago Press; (2002), permission granted by the *Journal of Philosophy*; (2006), permission granted by the *Canadian Journal of Philosophy*; (2010), (2016), and (2017d), permission granted by Springer Nature; (2015a), (2015b), (2017b), (2017c), and (2020), permission granted by Oxford University Press; and (2017a), permission granted by Taylor and Francis.

PART I
INTRODUCTION OF THE ARGUMENT FROM IGNORANCE

1
The Argument from Ignorance

On October 1, 1957 a promising new drug, manufactured by Chemie Grünenthal and marketed under the trade name Contergan, was made available to the general public for the first time in West Germany. Sold over the counter, it was lauded for its sleep-inducing and anxiety-reducing properties. This same drug was introduced into the UK in April 1958 under the trade name Distaval, and eventually it was sold under a variety of names in 46 countries world-wide.

One claim made in support of the drug, and its chief selling-point, was that, unlike other somnifacients and sedatives that were in use at the time, no dosage, no matter how large, could prove hazardous. A representative advertisement that ran widely in the UK in 1961 featured a picture of a toddler peering into an open bottle of Distaval, accompanied by the following text:

> [T]his child's life may depend on the safety of 'Distaval'. Consider the possible outcome in a case such as this—had the bottle contained a conventional barbiturate. Year by year, the barbiturates claim a mounting toll of childhood victims. Yet it is simple enough to prescribe a sedative and hypnotic which is both highly effective... and outstandingly safe. 'Distaval' [...] has been prescribed for over three years in this country, where the accidental poisonings rate is notoriously high; but there is no case on record in which even a gross overdosage with 'Distaval' has had harmful results. Put your mind at rest. Depend on the safety of 'Distaval'.[1]

Like many other drugs, however, this drug eventually proved to have some undesirable side effects. Among those effects initially reported were dizziness, low blood pressure, constipation, and other relatively minor conditions. However, in late 1959, suspicions arose that Contergan might be the cause of polyneuritis in some patients, and pressure grew to make the drug available only with a physician's prescription. Then, in mid-1961, an Australian doctor, who had discovered that Distaval was especially effective in treating morning sickness, began to question whether its use by women in the early stages of pregnancy might be responsible for the dramatic increase that he had observed in the incidence of phocomelia in newborns, an otherwise extremely rare condition. Later that year, a

---

[1] Among other places in which this advertisement appeared: *The British Medical Journal*, Vol. 1, No. 5242 (June 24, 1961), front matter p. 12.

German doctor also noted a significant association between the use of Contergan by pregnant women and phocomelia in newborns. He brought this to the attention of Grünenthal in November 1961 and, by the end of that month, the drug was withdrawn from the German market, although it remained available elsewhere in the world for some time after that.

Polyneuritis is an inflammatory disorder of the peripheral nerves that can be very painful and even crippling. Phocomelia is a congenital disorder in which the limbs are grossly underdeveloped or even absent. The generic name of the drug that turned out indeed to have these extremely serious side effects is, as I suspect you have already surmised, thalidomide. It is estimated that, in all, around 10,000 infants were born with malformations, and that many others died *in utero*, as a result of their mothers' ingestion of the drug. "Outstandingly safe"![2]

The tragedy of thalidomide, as it is often called, is one of the most infamous episodes in the annals of medicine. When such a tragedy occurs, it is both common and natural to seek to pin responsibility for it on someone. "Who is to blame?" we ask. "Someone must be."

* * *

Imagine that it is December 1961. Sally is a woman living in the UK who has just given birth to her first-born child. She has basked in the delights and endured the tribulations of pregnancy and childbirth and now, filled with a mixture of joy and relief, eagerly anticipates taking her baby into her arms for the first time. She notices, though, that a pall has fallen over the attending medical personnel and that they are reluctant to pass her baby to her. She turns inquiringly to her husband, who has just entered the room, and sees, much to her consternation, a look of horror on his face. Upon her repeated insistence, her baby is handed over to her, and she discovers the source of the hesitation and horror. Her baby's arms and legs are terribly stunted and twisted.

Actually, as a parent myself, I find it impossible to imagine, in any detail, what it must be like to undergo such an experience, let alone to try to come to terms with what has happened and with what lies ahead. It seems likely that Sally would be overwhelmed with all manner of emotions. I won't venture to explore these emotions in all their variety and complexity. There is just one on which I wish to focus: guilt.

I expect that almost all parents of so-called thalidomiders have, at one time or another, felt crushing guilt over their child's plight. I also expect that almost everyone else, while sympathizing with these parents, would declare their guilt misplaced. What is it that they are supposed to be guilty of? In order to regiment the discussion, let us suppose that her baby's phocomelia has been traced to Sally's

---

[2] The historical and medical data cited both above and below are drawn primarily from Brynner and Stephens (2001). It should be noted that birth defects related to thalidomide also included deafness, blindness, and a variety of other very serious disorders.

having taken thalidomide the previous April in order to ward off morning sickness.[3] She feels terribly guilty about her child's condition, saying that she ought never to have taken the drug. Her friend Jane protests, saying, "You mustn't blame yourself! You couldn't possibly have known that Distaval would have this effect!" Apparently, Jane is claiming that Sally's ignorance relieves her of any responsibility for taking the drug or for her child's resulting condition. Is she right about that?

Given that her child's condition (call it C) is indeed a causal consequence of Sally's having taken a dose of thalidomide, there is clearly a sense in which she *is*—or better, *was*—responsible for it. That sense is simply this: she committed an act that contributed causally to C. This is the same sense of "responsible" as that which is at issue when we say things like "The drought was responsible for the wildfire," "The dog was responsible for the mess on the floor," and so on. Of course, it is not only Sally who was responsible, in this sense, for C. Many other people also contributed causally to C—a point to which I will return shortly. But I think it's clear that, when Jane denies that Sally bears responsibility for what has happened, it is not *causal* but *moral* responsibility that she has in mind. More particularly, she is concerned with that negative form of moral responsibility that consists in *blameworthiness*. When Jane says that Sally mustn't blame herself for what has happened, it's because she thinks that her doing so is inappropriate, inasmuch as she's not blame*worthy* for it, even though she did indeed help bring C about. The claim that Sally is not blameworthy for what has happened (or, equivalently, that she's not *to* blame for it), despite the fact that she helped bring C about, implies that one's being, or having been, causally responsible for some outcome is not sufficient for one's being morally responsible for it—and surely that's right. To be morally responsible for bringing about, or helping to bring about, some outcome, one must have been in a certain *state of mind* regarding that outcome. But which state, or states, are the ones that count?

Clearly Jane thinks—as does anyone, like me (and you?), who endorses her position—that that particular state of mind that consisted in Sally's being *ignorant*, at the time at which she took the drug, of the fact that Distaval was teratogenic[4] lies at the heart of the reason why she is not to blame for what happened. Taken at face value, this idea suggests the following principle:

(A) If a person P committed an act A, which resulted in an outcome O, but P was ignorant, at the time at which he or she committed A, that O would occur as a result, then P is not to blame for either A or O.

---

[3] Contrary to popular belief, this was not in fact the most common use of the drug in pregnant women. In many cases, thalidomide was prescribed for women with anxiety or insomnia who were not yet aware that they had become pregnant.

[4] This is an awful term for an awful property, a term that I would eschew were it not standard. It stems from ancient Greek, with the literal meaning of "monster-making."

Put less formally and more roughly: ignorance always renders one blameless. Applied to Sally's case, this principle yields the desired, intuitively correct conclusion: she is not to blame either for taking the drug or for its outcome, C.

An appeal to Principle A might rely on one or the other of two possible underlying rationales. The first is this. If, when P committed A, he or she was ignorant of the fact that O would occur as a result, then it was not morally wrong for P to commit A; and, if it was not morally wrong for P to commit A, then P cannot be to blame either for A or for its outcome, O. This might well be what Jane had in mind when trying to console Sally. She might have thought that, given her ignorance of the properties of Distaval, Sally did nothing wrong in taking the drug and, since one can only be to blame if one has done something wrong, she is therefore not to blame for taking it or for the plight of her child. (In the last sentence, and henceforth, by "wrong" and "to blame" I mean, unless otherwise stipulated, "*morally* wrong" and "*morally* to blame.")

The second possible rationale is this. In taking the drug, Sally did indeed do wrong (unwittingly), but, in light of her ignorance, she nonetheless has an excuse, and so is once again not to blame, either for her act or for its outcome.

In the next chapter, I will take up the question whether Sally did anything wrong when she took the drug. For present purposes, though, what matters is that the verdict, that her ignorance of the fact that thalidomide was teratogenic renders her blameless for what has happened, seems clearly correct. (Matters would have been considerably different had she *not* been ignorant of this fact. Almost everyone would agree that it would have been wrong for her to take the drug and that she would be to blame for doing so, and for her child's resulting condition, if, despite knowing of the dangers of Distaval, she had gone ahead and taken it anyway in order to get some relief from her morning sickness. Under those circumstances, her feeling guilty may well have been entirely appropriate.)

* * *

Although Principle A yields the intuitively correct verdict in Sally's case, the fact is that it cannot be accepted as it stands. One problem with it is this. Although it is true that one can be to blame for an outcome only by way of being to blame for doing something that resulted in that outcome, still it is possible that, when P does A and O occurs as a result, P is to blame for A but *not* for O, and it is also possible that P is to blame for O but *not* for A. Consider the following example. Dave drives into town, goes to a bar, has several drinks, and becomes very drunk. He then leaves the bar, gets into his car, drives out of the parking lot, and promptly crashes into another car parked just around the corner. At that point, he stumbles out of his car, takes a cursory look at the damage he has caused, sits down on the sidewalk, keels over, and falls asleep. In this sordid little story, Dave commits several acts that have several outcomes. The acts include his driving into town (call this A_1), going to the bar (A_2), drinking heavily (A_3), leaving the bar (A_4), getting into his car (A_5), driving out of the parking lot (A_6), crashing into the other car (A_7), getting out of his car (A_8), glancing at the damage (A_9), and sitting down on the sidewalk (A_{10}). The outcomes include his being drunk (O_1), the damage to the other car (O_2), keeling over (O_3), and falling asleep (O_4). (Notice that the outcomes *also* include many of his acts. For example, each of A_2 through A_{10} is itself an outcome of A_1.) For which of these acts and outcomes is Dave to blame? Well, that depends on further facts about the case that I haven't provided, but it would be odd if Dave were to blame for O_4, say, even though it was an outcome of A_3, for which he might well be to blame. And it would be odd if he were to blame for A_1, even though he might well be to blame for O_2, which was an outcome of A_1.

This problem is easily corrected. Principle A should be amended as follows (the amendment appearing in bold type):

(B) If P committed A, which resulted in O, but P was ignorant, at the time at which he or she committed A, that O would occur as a result, then P is not to blame, **in virtue of the fact that A resulted in O,** for either A or O.

Applied to Sally's case, this principle once again yields the intuitively correct verdict, namely, that she is not to blame, in virtue of the fact that her taking Distaval resulted in her child's condition, either for her act or for its outcome.

* * *

It is important to note, though, that Principle B needs amending, too. When Jane tried to console Sally, she didn't simply say, "You *didn't know* that Distaval would have this effect." What she said was, "You *couldn't have known* that Distaval would have this effect." This is important because, if Jane thought that Sally *could* and *should* have known that the drug was teratogenic, she presumably would not have been so quick to declare her blameless. The underlying idea here is that, contrary to what Principles A and B say, ignorance does *not* always render one blameless—not if one is to blame *for one's ignorance*. It seems, therefore, that Principle B should be rejected and replaced by the following principle:

(C) If P committed A, which resulted in O, but P was ignorant, at the time at which he or she committed A, that O would occur as a result, then P is not to blame, in virtue of the fact that A resulted in O, for either A or O, **unless P is to blame for his or her ignorance**.

On the plausible supposition that, like other people who are or were parents of thalidomiders, Sally could not have known that thalidomide was teratogenic, it seems to follow that she is not to blame for her ignorance of this fact. If so, Principle C once again yields the intuitively correct verdict in this case: she is not to blame either for her act or for its outcome.

Yet Principle C seems problematic, too, because still too strong. Knowing that thalidomide is teratogenic doesn't require knowing that, if one is in the early stages of pregnancy, then taking a dose of it *will* cause phocomelia in one's fetus, since in some such cases phocomelia *didn't* result. Rather, it involves knowing that taking a dose of it *might*, to a significant degree of probability, have this result. (What counts as a "significant" degree is a complex question, one that I will address in Chapter 7 when discussing recklessness. Here I will simply use the phrase "might well" to capture this idea.) If Sally *had* had such knowledge, then, again, almost everyone would agree that she *would* be to blame for taking the drug and her child's resulting condition. So it seems that Principle C should be replaced in turn by the following principle:

(D) If P committed A, which resulted in O, but P was ignorant, at the time at which he or she committed A, that O would **or might well** occur as a result, then P is not to blame, in virtue of the fact that A resulted in O, for either A or O, unless P is to blame for his or her ignorance.

Again, given the plausible supposition that Sally, like other parents of thalidomiders, could not have possessed the relevant knowledge and therefore is not to blame for her ignorance, this principle, too, implies that she is not to blame either for her act or for its outcome.

* * *

Although Principle D lets Sally off the hook, morally, it leaves open the possibility that *others* are nonetheless to blame for her child's condition. As noted above, she is obviously not the only one who was causally responsible for C. Might there be reason to say that some of those other people who were causally responsible for C are also morally responsible for it?

The list of people other than Sally who were causally responsible for C is very long. It includes all her ancestors, for example, and many others besides. But presumably the list of people who are plausible candidates for being morally responsible for C is much shorter. Given the foregoing considerations, it might seem that what we should say is this. Among those who were causally responsible for C, only those who either did know or should have known that thalidomide was teratogenic can properly be declared morally responsible for C. Who might these people be? I expect that many who consider the question would put on their list of suspects some or all of the following: those who developed or manufactured or promoted or distributed or administered Distaval.

It is pretty clear, however, that, if these people are to remain on the list of suspects, Principle D must once again be qualified since, as it stands, it would in all likelihood require striking most of them off the list. This is because, in all likelihood, most of them could not possibly have known that *C in particular* would or might result from their activities, whether as developers or manufacturers or promoters of the drug—although it might be that someone who distributed the drug (Sally's pharmacist, say) or administered it (her physician) could have known this. The reason is simple. In all likelihood, none of these other people either did know or should have known that Sally existed at all, let alone that she was pregnant and was considering taking Distaval for her morning sickness. Thus, in order to capture the idea that they might nonetheless be to blame for *C*, we must say something along the following lines: they either did know or should have known that their activities would or might well result in an outcome *of a certain, sufficiently narrowly specified type*, a type of which *C* was an instance. For even if, being unacquainted with Sally and her situation, they could not have foreseen that *C* itself would or might result from their activities, it seems reasonable to think that perhaps they either did foresee or should have foreseen that their activities would or might well result in an undesirable outcome of some such type.

What should be said to count as "some such type" of outcome, though, is a tough question. To appreciate the difficulty, compare the following two possible scenarios.

Suppose, first, that more thorough research by the employees at Grünenthal would have revealed both that thalidomide was a potential cause of polyneuritis and that it was a teratogen. Many would say in this case that it is reasonable to blame those employees for *C*, even if they did not and could not have known about Sally or her morning sickness in particular, since *C* was an instance of the type of undesirable outcome that they could and should have foreseen and thus (as it is sometimes put[5]) "fell within the risk" created by the decision not to carry out this research.

Now suppose, second, that further research would have revealed only that thalidomide was a potential cause of polyneuritis and *not* also that it was a teratogen. I suspect that in this case most would say that, even though the failure to carry out this research would have rendered the employees blameworthy for any cases of polyneuritis that resulted from use of the drug, they would *not* have been to blame for *C* itself, since *C* did *not* "fall within the risk" created by the decision not to pursue further research.

But why should we agree with this verdict in the second scenario? After all, if further research would have revealed that thalidomide was a potential cause of polyneuritis, then, since polyneuritis is a harmful condition, this research would have revealed that thalidomide was a potential cause of harm. Indeed, it's precisely *because* polyneuritis is a harmful condition that it seems reasonable to blame the employees for failing to prevent it, if their failure to carry out further research resulted in it. But of course phocomelia is *also* a harmful condition, one that would

---

[5] Cf. H. M. Smith (1983), p. 551; Husak (2016), pp. 185 f.; Robichaud and Wieland (2019), p. 22. See also the American Law Institute (1985), §2.03(3).

also have been prevented if, as a result of further research's revealing that thalidomide was a potential cause of harm, the drug had not been put on the market in the first place. So why not blame the employees for *C* after all, even in the second scenario?

The answer can only be that, although *C* is an instance of a type of outcome, harm, that occurred as a result of the failure to carry out further research, nonetheless this type is not sufficiently narrowly specified to qualify as grounds for blame in this case—which is something of a mystery, I think, inasmuch as, as I have just indicated, it would seem that it's the harmfulness both of polyneuritis and of phocomelia that raises the question of blameworthiness in the first place. In any case, some more narrowly specified type is required, one of which a particular case of polyneuritis that resulted from the use of thalidomide would have been an instance but of which *C* itself is not.

Just *how* narrowly specified, though—well, there's the rub. Again, it seems correct to say that the type must be specified sufficiently narrowly so as to exclude *C* in the second scenario (but not in the first), but presumably it must not be specified so narrowly that, in the first scenario, had Sally's baby been born with slightly longer limbs, this condition—call it *C**—would *not* have been an instance of the relevant type. On the contrary, the type should be specified sufficiently broadly so as to encompass in the first scenario not only *C* but also *C** and any other condition in that "vicinity." The correct specification, then, must constitute a kind of compromise reminiscent of the one achieved by Goldilocks. It must not be too broad or too narrow. It must be "just right."

In light of these considerations, it seems that Principle D should therefore be replaced in its turn by the following principle:

(E) If *P* committed *A*, which resulted in *O*, but *P* was ignorant, at the time at which he or she committed *A*, that **an outcome in the vicinity of** *O* would or might well occur as a result, then *P* is not to blame, in virtue of the fact that *A* resulted in *O*, for either *A* or *O*, unless *P* is to blame for his or her ignorance.

Given the vagueness of both "in the vicinity of" and "might well," Principle E is of course itself in need of refinement, but let us pretend for the moment that such refinement has been successfully accomplished. Call the resulting principle Principle E*. The question would still remain whether any of those who were in fact involved in the development or manufacture or promotion or distribution or administration of Distaval either knew or should have known that an outcome in *C*'s vicinity (as established by Principle E*) would or might well (as established by Principle E*) result from their activities. This is, of course, a hypothetical question, since Sally's case is a hypothetical case. But the corresponding question in actual cases in which a child's phocomelia resulted from its mother's ingestion of thalidomide is (or was) for many people one of the most important questions raised by the whole sorry episode. It is (or was) important not only to those engaged in the activities in question but also, of course, to the children and their parents, as well as to many other people besides (including members of the legal profession). Despite its importance, however, this is *not* a question with which I will be concerned. Answering it correctly would require all kinds of information that I do not have and have no hope of obtaining. What I wish rather to do is to pursue the *moral implications* of the correct answer to this question, supposing we had this answer.

* * *

Let us continue, then, with the example of Sally and her child, and let us now suppose the following. One of the employees in Grünenthal's department of research and development—call him Heinrich—had learned early on, in 1956, that thalidomide posed a serious risk of birth defects, and so knew that failing to reveal this fact to others might well have disastrous consequences, but he nonetheless kept the information to himself. I suspect that almost everyone would want to say that, under these circumstances, Heinrich was guilty of *recklessness* and that, since the tragedy that ensued fell within the risk that he created by his decision not to divulge the pertinent information, he is to blame (along with others, perhaps) for that tragedy, including that part of the tragedy that consisted in C in particular. I submit, though, that this verdict would be premature.

I have noted that one's being causally responsible for some outcome is not sufficient for one's being morally responsible for it. One's being in a certain state of mind is (also) required. (I have put "also" in parentheses, because it is an interesting question—one that I won't pursue here but will address in Chapter 4—whether causal responsibility is in fact required for moral responsibility.) Does Heinrich's knowing that, in deciding not to reveal the pertinent information, he was running the risk of some outcome in the vicinity of C satisfy this requirement? I think that, on reflection, it's clear that it does *not*. Let me explain.

Risk is a function of two factors: how bad an outcome would be, if it occurred, and how likely it is that that outcome will occur. The worse the outcome, or the more likely it is to occur, the greater the risk. Now, there's no doubt that C was very bad. On the assumption that Heinrich was aware that it was highly likely that failing to reveal the pertinent information would result in an outcome in the vicinity of C, it's clear that the risk he ran was indeed very serious and, we may assume, that he knew that it was. But—and this is crucial—that fact, by itself, does *not* support the charge of recklessness, and this is simply because it can be perfectly morally *justifiable* to take a risk, even a very serious risk, of harm. (Think, for example, of a case of very risky but nonetheless warranted surgery.) Knowing that one is running a risk, even a very serious risk, of harm therefore does not itself constitute a state of mind that renders one susceptible to censure. It is knowing that one is *unjustifiably*, i.e., *wrongly* running such a risk that does so. (It would, of course, be quite surprising if Heinrich *didn't* know that it was wrong of him to run the risk he ran. Let me now stipulate that he did indeed know this.) By the same token, what can provide one with an excuse for running a risk of harm is not simply that one doesn't know that one is doing so but, more particularly, that one doesn't know that one is *wrongly* doing so. It's also worth noting that, in Heinrich's case, the risk in question is one that was incurred, not, strictly speaking, in virtue of any *act* that he committed, but in virtue of an *omission*. It was his *failing* to reveal the pertinent information that was the problem. We should therefore make yet a further adjustment and move from Principle E to the following:

(F) If *P* committed act **or omission** *A*, which resulted in *O*, but *P* was ignorant, at the time at which he or she committed *A*, that **it was morally wrong to commit *A* in virtue of the fact that** an outcome in the vicinity of *O* would or might well occur as a result, then *P* is not to blame, in virtue of the fact that *A* resulted in *O*, for either *A* or *O*, unless *P* is to blame for his or her ignorance.

* * *

Like Principle E, Principle F of course requires refinement. Imagine now that we have successfully carried out this refinement and that the resulting principle—call it Principle F*—is one that, finally, needs no further amendment and is therefore one that we should accept. If, as we have supposed, Heinrich *did* know that, for the sort of reason specified in Principle F*, his failing to reveal the pertinent information was morally wrong, would we then, finally, be in a position to conclude that he is indeed to blame for *C*?

The traditional answer given by philosophers to this question is "No." Ever since Aristotle,[6] it has been held that, to be blameworthy, one must satisfy *two* conditions. One of these—the one that we have been investigating up to this point—is an *epistemic* condition having to do with what one *knows* about the nature of one's act and its possible outcomes. This is what Principle F* concerns. The other is an *agential* condition having to do with whether one is or was in *control* of one's act and its outcomes. We need a second principle, one that spells out this second condition.

To see what is at issue here, suppose that Alice slings racial slurs at Ben, offending him deeply. We would normally assume that Alice was in control of her act and its outcome—that it was *up to her* whether she maligned Ben, and thus up to her whether Ben was offended—so that, on that score at least, there is no reason to deny that Alice is to blame for what happened. But if we knew that Alice

---

[6] Aristotle (1941), bk. III, ch. 1.

suffered from a condition such as Tourette Syndrome that rendered the impulse to utter slurs irresistible, so that it was *not* up to her whether she maligned Ben, then we would surely hesitate to blame her for what happened, *even if* she had been fully aware that her slurs were deeply offensive and wholly unwarranted.

In addition to Principle F*, therefore, it seems that we should accept the following principle:

(G) If P committed A, which resulted in O, but P was not in control of either A or O, then P is not to blame for either A or O.

I suggest that, if you are inclined to blame Heinrich for C, this is because you think that he was not only *aware* of the wrongness of the risk he was taking but was also in *control* of taking this risk.

Principle G implicitly relies on two distinctions that, in light of the important, indeed crucial role that they will play in the argument to follow, should be noted explicitly. The first is the distinction between *direct and indirect* or, equivalently, *original and derivative control*. The second is the distinction between *direct and indirect* or, equivalently, *original and derivative blameworthiness*. Suppose that Alice *had* been in control of whether she maligned Ben. Then, as far as the agential condition for blameworthiness is concerned, she would have had no excuse after all either for her behavior or for Ben's consequent umbrage. Notice that in this case her control over Ben's umbrage would have been indirect or derivative; it would have *stemmed from* her control over her behavior, over which, we may assume (for the time being—I will examine the question more closely in Chapters 2 and 4), she exercised direct or original control. To put the point another way: she would have been in control of Ben's umbrage *by way of* being in control of whether she maligned him. Because her control over Ben's umbrage would have been indirect, *so too* would her blameworthiness for it have been indirect. She would have been blameworthy for it *by way of* being blameworthy for her behavior.

I observed earlier, when discussing the case of Dave driving drunk, that an act can have several outcomes and an outcome can stem from several acts. Suppose that Alice had been suffering for some time from her condition and had sought medical help, and that her physician had prescribed a drug to help her manage the impulses associated with her condition. The drug proved successful, but unfortunately it rendered Alice listless, a side effect that she disliked intensely. She was therefore reluctant to take it, even though she knew that not doing so raised the risk of embarrassing incidents such as the episode involving Ben. In this case, we might well be less hesitant to blame her for her behavior and for Ben's consequent umbrage. This is because, even if, at the time at which she maligned Ben, she was not in *direct* control of what she was doing, it seems that she had, at some earlier time at which she chose not to take the drug, been in direct control of her decision and thus in *indirect* control of her subsequent behavior and, thereby, also of Ben's umbrage. If we blame her for his umbrage, then, this will be because we *do* blame her, indirectly, for maligning him, by virtue of blaming her, directly, for deciding not to take the drug.

In light of these considerations, the agential condition for blameworthiness can be more fully rendered by replacing Principle G with the following principle:

(H) If P committed A, which resulted in O, but P was not in control **at any time, either directly or indirectly**, of either A or O, then P is not to blame, **either directly or indirectly**, for either A or O.

* * *

My inquiry so far has focused on two agents, Sally and Heinrich, who contributed to the condition, C, of Sally's child, and on two possible excuses, captured in Principle F* (having to do with ignorance) and Principle H (having to do with control), that they might have had for contributing to C. I have assumed that neither agent has an excuse grounded in lack of control, but that Sally does have an excuse grounded in ignorance, whereas Heinrich does not. On the further assumption, which I will accept here for the sake of argument, that Principles F* and H exhaust the rationales for declaring someone blameless for wrongdoing, the pertinent differences between Sally and Heinrich are captured in Chart 1.1.

Heinrich is, of course, a figment of my imagination. As I have said, I am in no position to determine whether any actual employee of Grünenthal had knowledge of the sort that I have attributed to Heinrich. Even so, I should add that it strikes me as highly unlikely that anyone *did* in fact have such knowledge *at the time relevant to my example*. Remember that, in this example, Sally took Distaval in April 1961, *before* any suspicion was raised by anyone outside of Grünenthal

	Sally	Heinrich
Contributed to C, but could have avoided doing so	Yes	Yes
Knew that she/he was risking contributing to an outcome in the vicinity of C	No	Yes
Knew that she/he was wrongly risking contributing to an outcome in the vicinity of C	No	Yes
Should have known that she/he was risking contributing to an outcome in the vicinity of C	No	N/A
Should have known that she/he was wrongly risking contributing to an outcome in the vicinity of C	No	N/A
Is to blame for C	No	Yes

Chart 1.1 Sally *vs.* Heinrich

about thalidomide's being a teratogen, and I know of no evidence that indicates that anyone inside the company already had such a suspicion. Thus, if some employee of Grünenthal were nonetheless to blame for C, it seems that this must be the case *despite* his or her being ignorant of thalidomide's being teratogenic.

So let us for the time being dismiss Heinrich from the scene and imagine instead that Karl, another employee in Grünenthal's department of research and development, had stumbled in 1955 upon the fact that thalidomide was highly effective as a hypnotic and a sedative and had immediately recognized its huge commercial potential. After conducting a few experiments on animals and observing no undesirable side effects, he made his findings known to his colleagues in manufacturing and promotion, and the drug was rushed to market. I suspect that, in this case, many would be inclined to say that Karl and his colleagues were guilty of *negligence* and thus to blame them for C, on the grounds that, even though none of them knew that an outcome in the vicinity of C would or might well occur as a result of their activities, they *should* have known this and *would* have known it if Karl had, either on his own initiative or at his colleagues' insistence, conducted more thorough research on the properties of thalidomide. I submit, however, that this verdict, too, would be premature.

For the sake of simplicity, let's leave Karl's colleagues aside and focus on Karl in particular. (Similar remarks would pertain to his colleagues.) The charge that, in helping to bring C about, Karl acted negligently rests on the claim that it was morally wrong of him to engage in such slipshod research. He should have investigated thalidomide more thoroughly. Had he been more cautious, more conscientious, and more diligent, he would have discovered that thalidomide was a teratogen and the ensuing tragedy would then have been averted. He is therefore to blame both for his failure to research the drug more thoroughly and (again, along with others, perhaps) for the consequences of this failure, consequences that of course include his remaining ignorant of the fact that thalidomide was teratogenic and the consequences in turn of this ignorance, among the most important of which were his failure to inform others of the dangers of thalidomide, the subsequent use of thalidomide by people such as Sally, and the ensuing tragedy, of which C was a part.

Suppose that, for the sake of argument, we grant the following key points, whether explicit or implicit, in the charge just made: that Karl could and should have investigated thalidomide more thoroughly; that, had he done so, he would have discovered that the drug was a teratogen; and that he therefore not only could but should have known both that thalidomide posed a grave risk of phocomelia and that his failure to alert others to this fact might well result in an outcome in the vicinity of C. (Whether we should make such concessions regarding those of Grünenthal's employees who were in fact engaged in research is a question that I will not pursue.) Suppose, that is, that Chart 1.2 captures the pertinent differences between all three of the agents we have discussed.

	Sally	Heinrich	Karl
Contributed to C, but could have avoided doing so	Yes	Yes	Yes
Knew that she/he was risking contributing to an outcome in the vicinity of C	No	Yes	No
Knew that she/he was wrongly risking contributing to an outcome in the vicinity of C	No	Yes	No
Should have known that she/he was risking contributing to an outcome in the vicinity of C	No	N/A	Yes
Should have known that she/he was wrongly risking contributing to an outcome in the vicinity of C	No	N/A	Yes
Is to blame for C	No	Yes	___

Chart 1.2 Sally *vs.* Heinrich *vs.* Karl

Even with all this granted, the reasoning behind the charge, just presented, that Karl is to blame for negligently contributing to C is flawed. It requires that we fill in the blank in the bottom right-hand corner of Chart 1.2 with "Yes," but that might be a mistake. The reason is simple. Karl *might not have known* that he ought to investigate thalidomide more thoroughly. If Karl *did* know that it was wrong of him not to do so, then, as with Heinrich, Principle F* would *not* afford him any excuse for his behavior or for its consequences. But if Karl *didn't* know this, then of course this principle might indeed afford him such an excuse. For it implies that he is *not* to blame, *unless* he is to blame for his ignorance.

So the key questions in the case of Karl are these. Did he know that he ought to carry out more thorough research on the drug? If not, is he to blame for not knowing this?

Since Karl, like Heinrich, is a figment of my imagination, it is up to me how to answer these questions. In answer to the first, let me simply stipulate that he did *not* know that he ought to carry out further research. (How likely is it that those of Grünenthal's employees who were in fact engaged in research on thalidomide didn't know that they ought to investigate the drug more thoroughly? Well, as before, I won't venture an answer to this question, although the following two points are relevant to such an answer. First, the standard for testing new drugs that was generally accepted at the time was far lower than the rigorous standard that is generally accepted today. Indeed, it was partly in response to the thalidomide tragedy that the standard was raised. Second, it was generally, though not universally, believed at the time that no drug taken by a pregnant woman could pass across the placental barrier and harm the fetus she was carrying.) Given this stipulation, Principle F* again implies that Karl is not to blame for his failure to investigate the drug further or for the consequences of this failure—unless, of course, he is to blame for not knowing that he ought to investigate the drug further.

And so we are down to one question. Is Karl to blame for his ignorance, that is, for not knowing that he ought to conduct a more thorough investigation into the properties of thalidomide? There are just two possibilities. At this point, I won't simply stipulate an answer to the question. Instead, I propose to investigate what is to be said on each possibility.

The first possibility is that Karl is not to blame for his ignorance. In this case, Principle F* implies that he is not to blame for his failure to investigate thalidomide more thoroughly or for the consequences of this failure, consequences that of course include C in particular (unless, he could have avoided these consequences in some way other than by engaging in further research—but we may safely assume that this was not the case). The verdict that Karl is not to blame is not the verdict endorsed by those who would accuse him of negligence. Their verdict therefore requires that the second possibility be the case, namely, that Karl is to blame for his ignorance. Let's now pursue this possibility.

According to Principle H, if one is to blame for something, one must have been in control of it. Thus, if Karl is to blame for his ignorance, he must have been in control of it. How can one control whether one is ignorant of some fact? Well, consider this example. At the moment, as I write this sentence, I don't know what the capital of Kazakhstan is. But bear with me for just a moment... [Brief pause.] OK, now I know (or think I know). I just consulted Wikipedia, according to which the capital of Kazakhstan is a city called Astana. (I don't think I'd ever heard of this city before. It looks pretty impressive.) On the supposition that Wikipedia hasn't misled me, I now know something that I didn't know a short time ago, and my coming to know it was something over which I exercised control. How? By making an inquiry. This is one of the most common ways in which one can control whether one remains ignorant of some fact. There are other ways. One can go to school, for instance, and passively receive new information, rather than actively engage in some inquiry. Or one can simply, and literally, turn on a light and see what there is to be seen. And so on. All these ways of overcoming or eliminating ignorance have a crucial component in common: they all involve engaging in some behavior *by means of which* one comes to learn some new fact or facts. Indeed, it seems clear that no one can control whether he or she is or remains ignorant of some fact except by some such means. That is, if one is ever in control of one's ignorance, one's control over it must be *indirect*. By the same token, if one is ever to blame for one's ignorance, one's blameworthiness for it must be *indirect*.

But if one is only indirectly in control of and only indirectly blameworthy for something, that thing must be a consequence of something else for which one is directly blameworthy and over which one has, or had, direct control. In the present case, what might this something else be? The answer seems plain:

failing to engage in that behavior in which one could have engaged and by means of which one would have eliminated one's ignorance. (Thus, if I had promised someone to find out what the capital of Kazakhstan was but failed to keep my promise, then I would, or might well, have been to blame for failing to make the relevant inquiry and for my remaining ignorant about the matter.) So, in particular, if Karl is to blame for not knowing that he ought to investigate thalidomide more thoroughly, there must have been *something else* that he could and should have done that would have eliminated this ignorance, something that he is to blame for *failing* to do. What might this something else have been?

Well, there are any number of things that he could have done. He could have made an inquiry (he could have asked one of his colleagues whether he ought to look further into thalidomide); he could have gone to school (he could have taken a class in the ethics of scientific research); etc., etc. Let us suppose, for the sake of argument, that at least one of these things is something that he ought to have done, that is, that it was wrong of him not to have done it. Call whatever this thing is X. If Karl is to blame for X and, thereby, for the consequences of X (consequences that include his ignorance about the wrongness of not undertaking further research on thalidomide, his failure to carry out such research, his failure to alert others to the dangers of the drug, Sally's taking a dose of it, and C), then, given Principle F*, he must either have been aware of the wrongness of X or, if not aware of this, be to blame for not being aware of it. But now, as I hope has become plain, we are set on a regress, a regress that can only be stopped at some point at which Karl is to blame for some piece of behavior of whose wrongness he was *not* ignorant. If this piece of behavior was not X itself, then we must look for some prior piece of behavior, Y, of which X was a consequence and for which Karl is to blame. If he knew that Y was wrong but did it anyway, then that's the stopping-point. But if he didn't know that Y was wrong, then we must look back even further into his history and find yet some other piece of behavior, Z, for which he is to blame and which constituted the basis of his blameworthiness for all that followed.

The upshot is this. If Karl is to blame for C, his blameworthiness for it can only be indirect. That is, this blameworthiness presupposes that, at some point in his (and C's) history, there was some piece of behavior for which he is directly to blame. Whatever this piece of behavior was, it must have been something of whose wrongness Karl was aware.

This argument can be generalized, for the conditions that Karl must satisfy to be blameworthy are the conditions that anyone must satisfy. It will be easier to examine this argument, which I will call the Argument from Ignorance, if I give a formal rendition of it. Here is a first stab at doing so (where, as before, "P" refers to a person and "A" refers to an act or omission):

The Argument from Ignorance (Draft 1):

Suppose that

(1) (a) P committed A and (b) A was wrong, but (c) when P committed A, P was ignorant of the fact that A was wrong.

In general it's true that

(2) if one committed some act or omission that was wrong while ignorant of the fact that it was wrong, one is to blame for it, and thereby to blame for any of its consequences, only if one is to blame for one's ignorance.

Thus

(3) P is to blame for A, and thereby to blame for any of its consequences, only if P is to blame for P's ignorance (call it *I*) of the fact that A was wrong.

It's also in general true that

(4) one is to blame for something only if one was in control of that thing.

Thus

(5) P is to blame for *I* only if P was in control of *I*.

Three further general truths are that

(6) one is never directly in control of whether one is ignorant of something— that is, any control that one has over being ignorant is always only indirect,

(7) if one is to blame for something over which one had only indirect control, then one's blameworthiness for it is itself only indirect, and

(8) one is indirectly to blame for something only if that thing was a consequence of something else for which one is directly to blame.

Thus

(9) P is to blame for A, and thereby to blame for any of its consequences, only if there was something else (call it *X*) for which P is directly to blame and of which *I* was a consequence.

But

(10) whatever *X* was, it cannot have been an act or omission such that (a) P committed it and (b) it was wrong and (c) when P committed it, P was ignorant of the fact that it was wrong, since otherwise the foregoing argument regarding A would apply all over again to *X*.

Thus

(11) whatever *X* was, it was either (a) not some act or omission that P committed or (b) not wrong or (c) something such that, when P committed it, P was not ignorant of the fact that it was wrong.

Two further general truths are that

(12) one has direct control over something only if that thing is an act or omission, and

(13) one is to blame for an act or omission only if that act or omission was wrong.

Thus

(14) whatever X was, it was an act or omission such that, when P committed it, P was not ignorant of the fact that it was wrong.

This is a pretty long and complicated argument. It may help you to digest it if I point out that, at bottom, it reaches its conclusion by way of the two conditions for blameworthiness—the epistemic condition and the agential condition—that I have discussed above.[7]

As for the epistemic condition: this is contained in Premise 2, which is a restatement of Principle F* shorn of any reference to the question whether the consequences of P's behavior "fell within the risk" of that behavior. As it stands, Premise 2 is broader than is required for the argument to go through. Consider Karl. In order for him to be absolved of responsibility for C due to his failure to conduct further research on thalidomide, he needn't have been ignorant *tout court* of the wrongness of this failure; he need only have been ignorant of it insofar as an outcome in the vicinity of C was concerned. (Had he known that it was wrong not to engage in further research because failure to do so risked an outcome in the vicinity of polyneuritis, he would still have remained blameless for C.) But, as it stands, Premise 2 is much simpler to deal with than Principle F*, so let's stick with it.

As to the agential condition of blameworthiness: this is what Premises 4, 6, 7, 8, and 12 all have to do with, and together they cover, indeed extend beyond, what is stated in Principle H. Premise 4 states the condition in its most general form. Premises 6, 7, and 8 concern the distinction between direct and indirect control and the attendant distinction between direct and indirect blameworthiness. It's important to note, though, that Premises 6 and 12 go beyond simply the claim that control is required for blameworthiness. They make substantial claims about what we can control and how.

The remaining two premises serve a different purpose. Premise 10 is the recursion clause that involves the repeated application of the argument made up

---

[7] Gideon Rosen has proposed a very similar argument in several places. (See Rosen (2003), (2004), and (2008).) His argument is explicitly concerned with the epistemic condition for moral responsibility. However, even in the most precise rendition of his argument, presented in Rosen (2004), Rosen makes no explicit mention of the agential condition. I suspect, though, that it is an implicit concern with control that underlies one of the premises in this argument, namely: "X is culpable for failing to know that P only if his ignorance is the upshot of some prior culpable act or omission" (2004, p. 301, in italics). On the next page, he elaborates on this, observing that "in the normal case, belief revision is a *passive* matter." Again, this strongly suggests that he is concerned with how one might exercise control, indirectly, over one's beliefs. Cf. Rosen (2008), p. 608, where Rosen is concerned, this time explicitly, with whether we have direct control over what we care about. Cf. also Levy (2011), ch. 5.

to that point. And Premise 13 makes the claim that blameworthiness presupposes wrongdoing.

It is of course true that an argument is only as strong as its weakest premise, and all of the premises in the argument just presented are open to question. Indeed, this entire book will in effect be devoted to an examination of them. I submit, though, that each of them has considerable initial plausibility, and that, when they are conjoined as they are, the result is pretty surprising. The result is this. If one is blameworthy for some act or omission that one committed while ignorant of the fact that it was wrong, and thereby blameworthy for some of its consequences, then that act or omission was a consequence of some other act or omission that one committed, and for which one is blameworthy, while *not* ignorant of the fact that it was wrong. What's surprising about this result is that it amounts to saying that, in order to be justified in blaming someone, it's not enough to point out that that person *should have* known better than to do what he or she did. One must also establish that, somewhere back down the "chain" of acts or omissions and their consequences for which that person is to blame, there is some act or omission, some piece of behavior, for which he or she is blameworthy in virtue of the fact that he or she *did* know better. Thus, if ever one is blameworthy for some piece of behavior, either one knew better at the time than to engage in it, or one knew better at some earlier time than to engage in some earlier piece of behavior to which the later piece of behavior can be traced. I will call this the Origination Thesis, a first formulation of which may be put as follows:

The Origination Thesis (Draft 1):
Every chain of blameworthiness is such that at its origin lies a piece of behavior for which the agent is directly blameworthy and which he or she knew, at the time at which he or she engaged in it, to be wrong.

To put the point succinctly: *all* blameworthiness rests on, or is rooted in, *non-ignorant*, that is, *witting* wrongdoing. This is, I think, a pretty radical idea,[8] even though it follows from premises that seem far from radical.

The idea is radical because it runs counter to many of the ascriptions of blameworthiness that we typically make in our everyday lives. Many, but certainly not all. It doesn't affect what I assume we want to say about Sally. She's not to blame for C precisely because, as her friend Jane said, she couldn't have known that Distaval would have such an effect. Nor does it affect what I assume we want to say about Heinrich, since he knew that it was wrong to keep quiet about the dangers of thalidomide. But it does affect what I assume many would want, at least

---

[8] Radical, but not unprecedented. It's an idea that has been endorsed in one form or another not only by myself but also by, among others, Douglas Husak, Neil Levy, Rik Peels, and Gideon Rosen. See Husak (2016), Levy (2011) and (2014), Peels (2017), and Rosen (2003), (2004), and (2008).

initially, to say about Karl. For unless some episode of witting wrongdoing—more particularly, witting with respect to an outcome in the vicinity of *C*—occurred at some point in Karl's history, then the Origination Thesis implies that Karl is *not* to blame for *C*. Thus, if such an episode cannot be found, then the charge that he is to blame for having acted negligently would be mistaken. Even if such an episode can be found, however, a charge of negligence would still seem misguided, inasmuch as (as with Heinrich) it should be replaced by a charge of recklessness. The Origination Thesis is radical, therefore, in that it threatens to undermine *all* charges of negligence.

But it is radical in another way, too. To see how, imagine that the reason why Karl thought that he didn't need to engage in further research on thalidomide was that he didn't know that it was possible for a drug to pass across the placental barrier and harm the fetus. In this case, his ignorance about the wrongness of not engaging in further research will have stemmed from his being ignorant about some *non*-moral matter, namely, what happens, or can happen, during pregnancy. Given that his ignorance about the wrongness of his behavior cannot be traced to some episode of witting wrongdoing on Karl's part, the Origination Thesis implies that he is not to blame for his behavior or its consequences. But now imagine that the reason why Karl thought that he didn't need to engage in further research was that he subscribed to the standard for testing new drugs that was generally accepted at the time, a standard which, we may assume, was mistaken because far too lax. In this case, his ignorance about the wrongness of his behavior will have stemmed from his ignorance about a general *moral* principle, a principle to the effect that people ought to be treated with a degree of caution that surpasses the degree embodied in the standard in question. Each of these cases involves a morally significant kind of ignorance. Philosophers often call ignorance of the first kind "factual" ignorance and ignorance of the second kind "moral" ignorance, but this terminology is doubly misleading. First, both cases involve a kind of moral ignorance, since both involve Karl's being ignorant of the fact that he ought, morally, to engage in further research. Second, distinguishing moral ignorance from factual ignorance suggests that moral ignorance doesn't involve ignorance of facts—which is odd, since ignorance can only be ignorance of some fact or facts. It is preferable, therefore, to use a different pair of labels. I will say that, in the second case in which Karl was ignorant of the wrongness of his behavior due to his ignorance of some governing *moral* principle, his ignorance was an instance of *fundamental* moral ignorance. And I will say that, in the first case in which his ignorance about the wrongness of his behavior stemmed from ignorance about some *non*-moral fact, his ignorance was an instance of *incidental* moral ignorance.

It should now be clear just how radical the Origination Thesis is. The Argument from Ignorance concerns moral ignorance *generally*. It applies *equally* to both incidental and fundamental moral ignorance. Since this argument issues in the Origination Thesis, this thesis also applies *equally* to both kinds of moral ignorance. The idea that fundamental moral ignorance is exculpatory (unless it can itself be traced to an episode of witting wrongdoing) is, I think, very radical. We are accustomed to excusing people like Sally who exhibit incidental moral ignorance, but we are certainly not accustomed to excusing people who exhibit fundamental moral ignorance. Consider Sam, a member of ISIS, who routinely engages in atrocities. In so doing, he is conscientiously adhering to a moral code that is horribly twisted. But, of course, he is ignorant of the fact that it is twisted. The moral ignorance that underlies his actions is therefore fundamental. Unlike Sally, he knows full well that these actions cause great suffering, and yet he nonetheless believes that what he is doing is right—indeed, righteous; he is doing what he takes to be God's will. According to the Origination Thesis, unless Sam's awful ignorance can be traced to an episode of witting wrongdoing on his part (something that I think we can agree is highly unlikely in cases such as his), he is *blameless*. To many people, this verdict will be repugnant. Yet it is the verdict mandated by the Argument from Ignorance.

* * *

The Argument from Ignorance thus warrants careful examination, which it is my purpose in this book to carry out. I will begin in the next chapter with an inquiry into the concept of moral responsibility, a concept which, in the form of blameworthiness, lies at the heart of the argument.

PART II
EXAMINATION AND REFINEMENT OF THE ARGUMENT FROM IGNORANCE

2
Moral Responsibility

In the last chapter, I presented an argument, the Argument from Ignorance, from which I derived a thesis, the Origination Thesis, according to which all blameworthiness is rooted in witting wrongdoing. This thesis poses a challenge to many of our everyday ascriptions of moral responsibility, inasmuch as it appears to imply that we frequently blame the blameless. For this reason, both argument and thesis merit scrutiny. A thorough assessment of them will require an investigation of the key concepts involved: moral responsibility, ignorance, and control. I will address these concepts in turn in this and the next two chapters.

My procedure in this chapter is as follows. In §2.1 I note that there are many different kinds of responsibility, and I draw a number of distinctions with a view to identifying that particular kind of responsibility, moral blameworthiness, with which the Argument from Ignorance and the Origination Thesis are concerned. I examine the relation between such blameworthiness and moral wrongdoing, explaining how they are not necessarily coextensive. Whereas doing wrong has to do with how one's behavior is to be judged, being blameworthy has to do with how one oneself is to be judged, and these judgments can come apart. Judgments of the former kind are commonly called deontic judgments. There is no common term for judgments of the latter kind; I call them hypological judgments, and I explain how they are to be distinguished from judgments of yet a third kind, commonly called aretaic.

In §2.2 I turn to the question of what it is that makes someone morally blameworthy for something. A popular answer is that it is a person's quality of will when engaged in certain kinds of behavior that accounts for that person's being blameworthy for that behavior and its consequences. This is an answer that, given considerable qualification, I claim should be endorsed, although I note that, unless quality of will somehow comprises control, it won't constitute the entire basis of blameworthiness. I then explain why we should reject the claim, made by some philosophers, that one is to blame for something only if one is to blame on the basis of that thing.

To be blameworthy is to be worthy of blame. In §2.3 I undertake an extended investigation into the nature of blame. The road is long and winding. I begin by distinguishing between two kinds of blame: thin and thick. Roughly, the former consists in judging that the person one is appraising has failed to measure up to some pertinent standard (this is akin to what several philosophers appear to have in mind when discussing a form of responsibility that they call "attributability"),

Ignorance and Moral Responsibility. Michael J. Zimmerman, Oxford University Press. © Michael J. Zimmerman 2022.
DOI: 10.1093/oso/9780192859570.003.0002

whereas the latter consists in reacting to the person in a way that incorporates or reflects this judgment (this is akin to what several philosophers appear to have in mind when discussing a form of responsibility that they call "accountability"). Given this rough distinction, it might seem that the most straightforward procedure would be to (try to) give a precise account of what thin blame is, followed by a precise account of what thick blame is (one that explains how thick incorporates thin), followed by an account of what blameworthiness is, whether thin or thick. But this is not my procedure in this chapter, since I know of no way to give an illuminating account of thin blame that is independent of either thick blame or blameworthiness. Instead, I turn first to the source of almost all recent discussions of moral responsibility in general and of blameworthiness in particular, namely, P. F. Strawson's highly influential treatment of the matter. On Strawson's account, moral responsibility has essentially to do with what he famously calls "the reactive attitudes," although it's not entirely clear either just what he means by this term or just how he conceives of the relation between the attitudes he has in mind and moral responsibility. On one common interpretation, Strawson is to be understood as offering an analysis of the concept of moral responsibility in terms of the reactive attitudes, but even here there is disagreement about just what the proposed analysis is. I mention a couple of candidates and discuss challenges to them, with a view to homing in on that particular reactive attitude (or set of attitudes) in which thick blame may plausibly be thought to consist. En route I criticize recent proposals according to which it is essential to such blame that it be emotional, or that it involve certain dispositions, or that it call upon the person blamed to answer for his or her behavior, or that it be a form of conversation, or that it involve a moral community. I then make a proposal of my own of what it is that blame(worthiness), both thin and thick, consists in. Regrettably, the account I give is circular, and so its capacity to illuminate is severely curtailed, but I know of no better alternative.

In §2.4 I address the question of what it means to say that a person is worthy of blame. I argue that alternative expressions that are often used in this context (such as that it is fitting to blame the person) may not be equally fitting. This is brought out by the fact that it can be fitting to blame someone who is not blameworthy and unfitting to blame someone who is blameworthy. This observation leads to a brief discussion of the ethics of blame. I end the section by noting the importance of distinguishing between blamelessness and the absence of blameworthiness. The former implies the latter, but the converse implication does not hold. Failure to appreciate this point can be dangerous, in that it can render one oblivious to the fact that the blameless positively deserve to be protected from certain forms of treatment.

Finally, in §2.5 I inquire into what is involved in ascribing a degree of blameworthiness to someone. I ask, first, whether there is in principle a cap on the degree to which someone might possibly be to blame. My answer is "No." I then address a seldom-noted ambiguity in the phrase "more blameworthy." On one reading, it means: worthy of more blame. On another reading it means: more worthy of blame. Since these two dimensions of blameworthiness are independent of one another, the notion of "the" degree to which someone is to blame is threatened, but I propose a way to handle this problem. I turn next to the question of how the degree to which one person is to blame can be compared to the degree to which another person is to blame, and I point out how such comparisons are often highly problematic. Problematic, too, is the kind of aggregation of blameworthiness in which we often engage when we make judgments about someone's responsibility for extended courses of action. I then turn to the question of what the basis is for one's being blameworthy to a greater or lesser degree for some piece of behavior. I end the chapter with a discussion of what it is to be fully to blame for something, as opposed to having an excuse, whether total or partial, for that thing.

2.1 Varieties of responsibility

2.1.1 Some key distinctions

I will start with a very common but very important observation. The terms "responsibility," "responsible," and so on are ambiguous. They have *many* different senses. It is one thing to acknowledge this fact, however, and another thing to heed it. In this section I will embark on the task of drawing several fundamental distinctions, ones that we ignore at our peril.[1]

First there is the distinction between *causal* responsibility, which I mentioned in the last chapter, and *personal* responsibility. Causal responsibility arises when one *event* or *state* causes another. For example, a hurricane might be responsible in this sense for a flood, a drought for a wildfire, and so on. Personal responsibility, by contrast, involves a *person's* being responsible for something. (Sometimes we ascribe such responsibility, not to a person directly, but to a group of persons, such as a crowd, or to some other entity, such as a corporation, that is in some way composed of persons.)

Personal responsibility comes in two main varieties: *prospective* and *retrospective*. To be prospectively responsible, or to have a prospective responsibility, is to have an obligation or duty. Steve, for example, may be responsible in this sense for the swimmers' safety—i.e., it is his responsibility to see to it that they remain safe. Such responsibility is prospective in that it concerns what is supposed to happen in the future. Retrospective responsibility, by contrast, concerns what

---

[1] A classic discussion of many of the distinctions with which I will be concerned is to be found in Hart (1968), pp. 211 ff.

has happened in the past. Dave, for example, may be responsible in this sense for the swimmers' deaths. (We wouldn't say that Dave *has a* responsibility for their deaths—that would be gruesome, inasmuch as it suggests that the swimmers haven't yet died and Dave has a responsibility to see to it that they do—but we might well say that he *bears* responsibility for them.)

It is easy to confuse causal responsibility with personal responsibility, in part because there is a sense in which persons can be causally responsible for something. Suppose you say to me that Susie caused a sensation. I reply, "Why? What did she do?" and you tell me that she finally told Jim what she thought of him and then stormed out of yesterday's meeting. "Everyone's jaw dropped," you say, "and then cheers erupted." In this case, your statement that *Susie* caused a sensation is simply short-hand for the more particular statement that her *behavior* caused a sensation. This is just an ordinary instance of one event's causing another. In general, when we say that some individual caused an event, what we mean is that some event *involving* that individual caused the event in question. And instead of saying that the individual *caused* the event, we might say that the individual was *responsible* for the event. But notice two things. First, the individual in question might not be a person at all. (Consider the example in the last chapter of the dog being responsible for the mess on the floor.) And so, second, the kind of responsibility in question is not personal responsibility of the sort that I ascribed to Dave in the last paragraph.

Personal responsibility, whether prospective or retrospective, may be either *non-moral* or *moral*. It may be a CEO's responsibility to maximize profits, or a citizen's responsibility to report a crime, but these non-moral (professional, legal) prospective responsibilities may not align with any moral duties possessed by either CEO or citizen. Moreover, the fulfillment or the failure to fulfill such non-moral responsibilities may be the occasion for the incurrence of a corresponding form of non-moral retrospective responsibility. Certainly CEOs and citizens are often *held* responsible, by shareholders and legal authorities, for what they have or have not accomplished by way of carrying out their non-moral duties.

Retrospective responsibility, whether moral or non-moral, may be either *positive* or *negative*. The terms most often used in this context are "praiseworthiness" and "blameworthiness," respectively, although "laudability" and "culpability" are also common. The possibility of an intermediate, neutral form of retrospective responsibility is seldom discussed but sometimes acknowledged. There is no standard term for it—perhaps "indifference-worthiness" will do.[2] Such a form of responsibility may seem rather unexciting but, for reasons that I will give in §2.4.3, it is in fact very important.

---

[2] This is a term I used in Zimmerman (1988), pp. 61 f. Cf. Fischer and Ravizza (1998), p. 8, n. 11; Haji (1998), p. 8; McKenna (2012), pp. 15 ff.

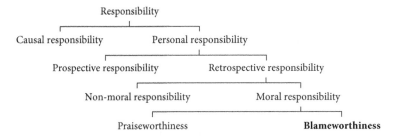

Chart 2.1 A Taxonomy of Responsibility

Chart 2.1 represents the process of specification in which I have just been engaged. Three points should be noted. First, I have highlighted "blameworthiness," since that will be the form of responsibility on which I will tend to focus in this book, although I will also have more to say about moral responsibility generally. Second, as I will discuss below, the category of blameworthiness itself admits of subdivision. Third, the chart is incomplete, in that some of the categories of responsibility mentioned above are not represented in it. As just noted, prospective responsibility may be either non-moral or moral, and there are non-moral forms of praise- and blameworthiness. (Indeed, we often engage in a kind of praise and, especially, blame of non-persons. We might blame the weather for the poor crops, for example. What we have in mind here is simply the fact that the weather is *causally* responsible for something *bad*.)

Chart 2.1 is incomplete for another reason, too. There are moral, or morally relevant, uses of "responsible" that it does not and cannot capture. The chart is designed to account, more particularly, for various uses of the term "responsible *for*," but "responsible" can be used differently. We often talk of someone as being "responsible" period—with no "for" attached. There are two senses in which we do so. In one sense, a responsible person is someone who is conscientious, that is, someone who takes his or her prospective responsibilities *seriously* and endeavors to meet them. The contrary of "responsible" in this sense is "irresponsible," and the trait in question is scalar; for one can be more or less (ir)responsible. In another sense, a responsible person is someone who is *capable* of being morally responsible for something, whether prospectively or retrospectively. There is no common contrary of "responsible" in this sense, although sometimes the term "non-responsible" is used for this purpose. We tend to treat responsibility in this sense as an all-or-nothing affair—one either has the capacity in question or not—but matters tend to get murky when the moral status of children and other "marginal" individuals is in question.[3]

---

[3] Cf. Shoemaker (2007) and (2015b).

2.1.2 The relation between blameworthiness and wrongdoing

The failure to heed the distinctions between the various senses of "responsible" just identified can cause considerable confusion. Consider the tragedy of thalidomide discussed in the last chapter. There is no doubt that many of the employees of Grünenthal were *causally* responsible for this tragedy (or, rather, no doubt that this is so unless omissions cannot be causes—an issue on which I will comment in §4.4.1). Many people seem prepared to leap from this observation to the accusation that these employees were therefore *morally* responsible, in particular *blameworthy*, for this tragedy. But this simply doesn't follow. (Nor, of course, does it follow that they *weren't* to blame for the tragedy. The question is an open one.)

Or consider the distinction between prospective and retrospective moral responsibility. Some people appear to embrace, implicitly or explicitly, the following thesis:

The Equivalence Thesis:
Necessarily, one is (retrospectively) morally responsible for having committed some act or omission if and only if one had a (prospective) moral responsibility not to commit it but committed it nonetheless.

If one omits the terms in parentheses, this thesis may have an initial superficial plausibility, but there are a number of problems with it that including these terms helps us to avoid.

One problem is this. The Equivalence Thesis appears to confuse retrospective responsibility in general with blameworthiness in particular; it overlooks praiseworthiness (and indifference-worthiness). Whereas it may seem plausible to say that one is blameworthy for having done something if and only if one had an obligation to do it that one did not fulfill, there is no plausibility at all in tying praiseworthiness to unfulfilled obligations in this way.

A second problem with the Equivalence Thesis is that it overlooks the distinction between *pro tanto* or *prima facie* obligation, on the one hand, and overall or all-things-considered obligation on the other. In general, the failure to fulfill a moral obligation constitutes the commission of a moral wrong.[4] There are accordingly two types of moral wrongdoing: *pro tanto* wrongdoing and overall wrongdoing. The distinction between these two types of moral wrongdoing consists roughly in this: one commits a *pro tanto* moral wrong just in case there is *some* moral reason not to do something which one nonetheless does, whereas

---

[4] There may be some exceptions to this general claim. If one can have an obligation now to do something later, and if such an obligation can be extinguished before its fulfillment becomes due (as when, for example, someone releases you from a promise that you have made before the opportunity to keep that promise arises), then *failing to fulfill* an obligation need not involve *violating* that obligation.

one commits an overall moral wrong just in case there is a *conclusive* or *decisive* moral reason not to do something which one nonetheless does.[5] (Here "do" is to be construed liberally, so as to cover not only acts but also omissions.) Since one can have a moral reason not to do something that is overridden by a stronger moral reason to do it, it's clear that it can be overall morally right to commit a *pro tanto* moral wrong. (For example, even if lying is always *pro tanto* morally wrong, it seems very reasonable to think that it can nonetheless sometimes be overall morally right.[6]) For that reason, it's also clear that it is the commission of an overall morally wrong act or omission that raises the question of whether one is morally to blame for what one has done. This observation should be explicitly accommodated in both the Argument from Ignorance and the Origination Thesis. We should therefore amend the first drafts of both argument and thesis as follows (the amendments once again appearing in bold type):

The Argument from Ignorance (Draft 2):
Suppose that

(1) (a) P committed A and (b) A was **overall morally** wrong, but (c) when P committed A, P was ignorant of the fact that A was **overall morally** wrong.

In general it's true that

(2) if one committed some act or omission that was **overall morally** wrong while ignorant of the fact that it was **overall morally** wrong, one is **morally** to blame for it, and thereby **morally** to blame for any of its consequences, only if one is **morally** to blame for one's ignorance.

Thus

(3) P is **morally** to blame for A, and thereby **morally** to blame for any of its consequences, only if P is **morally** to blame for P's ignorance (call it I) of the fact that A was **overall morally** wrong.

It's also in general true that

(4) one is **morally** to blame for something only if one was in control of that thing.

Thus

(5) P is **morally** to blame for I only if P was in control of I.

Three further general truths are that

---

[5] For a classic discussion, see Ross (2002), ch. 2.

[6] Kant famously thought, or at least is famously thought to have thought, otherwise. (See Kant (1949), pp. 346 ff.) Others frequently speak as if they think otherwise, too, but I doubt that they really do. For example, when I ask students whether they think it is always wrong to lie, they often respond, "Yes, but sometimes it's necessary." I suspect that in almost all cases what they mean by "wrong" is what I mean by "*pro tanto* morally wrong," and what they mean by "necessary" is what I mean by "overall morally right."

(6) one is never directly in control of whether one is ignorant of something—that is, any control that one has over being ignorant is always only indirect,

(7) if one is **morally** to blame for something over which one had only indirect control, then one's blameworthiness for it is itself only indirect, and

(8) one is indirectly **morally** to blame for something only if that thing was a consequence of something else for which one is directly **morally** to blame.

Thus

(9) *P* is **morally** to blame for *A*, and thereby **morally** to blame for any of its consequences, only if there was something else (call it *X*) for which *P* is directly **morally** to blame and of which *I* was a consequence.

But

(10) whatever *X* was, it cannot have been an act or omission such that (a) *P* committed it and (b) it was **overall morally** wrong and (c) when *P* committed it, *P* was ignorant of the fact that it was **overall morally** wrong, since otherwise the foregoing argument regarding *A* would apply all over again to *X*.

Thus

(11) whatever *X* was, it was either (a) not some act or omission that *P* committed or (b) not **overall morally** wrong or (c) something such that, when *P* committed it, *P* was not ignorant of the fact that it was **overall morally** wrong.

Two further general truths are that

(12) one has direct control over something only if that thing is an act or omission, and

(13) one is **morally** to blame for an act or omission only if that act or omission was **overall morally** wrong.

Thus

(14) whatever *X* was, it was an act or omission such that, when *P* committed it, *P* was not ignorant of the fact that it was **overall morally** wrong.

The Origination Thesis (Draft 2):
Every chain of **moral** blameworthiness is such that at its origin lies a piece of behavior for which the agent is directly **morally** blameworthy and which he or she knew, at the time at which he or she engaged in it, to be **overall morally** wrong.

A third problem with the Equivalence Thesis is that, even when it is understood restrictively so as to concern only blameworthiness and wrongdoing, there still seems to be reason to declare it false, and false in both directions. (Here and henceforth, unless I stipulate otherwise, I am using these terms to refer to *moral* blameworthiness and *overall moral* wrongdoing in particular.) It seems reasonable to deny that, necessarily, one is to blame for having committed some act or omission *if* one had an obligation not to commit it, since it seems possible to have an *excuse* for having done something wrong. This is a common observation. It also seems reasonable to deny that, necessarily, one is to blame for having committed some act or omission *only if* one had an obligation not to commit it, since it seems possible to have what I call an *accuse* for having done something wrong. This is a far less common observation (one that puts Premise 13 of the Argument from Ignorance into question). I will discuss excuses more fully later in this chapter and accuses more fully in the next, but let me say something briefly about the former here, since doing so will help explain not only the distinction between prospective and retrospective responsibility but also the at-least-partial independence of one from the other.

In order not to succumb to the confusion against which I have been inveighing, I will henceforth largely eschew the term "prospective responsibility" and use "obligation" instead, reserving "responsibility," unqualified, to refer to retrospective responsibility. Philosophers are divided on the question just what conditions are necessary and sufficient for someone to have a moral obligation to do something. Many embrace what I will call an objective view according to which (to put the point very roughly but nonetheless, I think, adequately for present purposes) one's moral obligations have only to do with what *would in fact* happen if one were to make one choice rather than another.[7] For example, if one has a choice between doing something that would in fact prove harmful and doing something else that would in fact prove harmless, then (*ceteris paribus*) one is morally obligated not to choose the former; doing so would be morally wrong. It is easy to see how, given such a view, it is possible to have an excuse for wrongdoing, and thus how the question of what one is (retrospectively) morally responsible for is, to that extent at least, independent of the question of what one's moral obligations are or were. Consider Sally from the last chapter. By taking a dose of Distaval, she caused great and avoidable harm to the fetus she was carrying. Many of those who subscribe to a purely objective view of moral obligation and wrongdoing would say that what Sally did was therefore morally wrong, but I suspect few would blame her for what she did. Under the circumstances, her ignorance excuses her.

---

[7] A classic example of such a view is to be found in G. E. Moore (2005).

Many other philosophers, however, do not subscribe to an objective view of moral obligation. Some among them would say that, since Sally had no *reason to believe*, indeed no reason even to suspect, that taking Distaval would harm her fetus, she did nothing wrong in taking it.[8] On such a view, one's moral obligations are at least in part a function of one's epistemic situation—of the *evidence* that one has. Compare Sally with Heinrich. Heinrich knew that thalidomide posed a serious risk of birth defects but nonetheless kept this information to himself. In so doing, he was (given that he knew that it was wrong not to divulge the information) being egregiously reckless. But we cannot accuse Sally of such recklessness, precisely because she didn't have, and had no reason to think that she should acquire, the kind of information that Heinrich had. On the view that one's moral obligations depend in part on one's evidence, it is perhaps not so easy to see how wrongdoing and blameworthiness can come apart. Nonetheless, they can indeed do so for two reasons. First, unless the only excuses one could have concerned one's epistemic status, declaring moral obligation to be determined in part by this status clearly leaves room for excuses stemming from some other kind or kinds of consideration (having to do, say, with compulsion, or duress, or incapacity). Second, it is very important to note that, even on this epistemically constrained approach to moral obligation, there is room for ignorance to provide an excuse for wrongdoing; for one may fail to believe what one has good reason to believe and be blameless for this failure. Gideon Rosen gives this example:

> Suppose Dr. Feldman consults a chart that would lead any competent doctor to conclude that her patient is diabetic, but that Feldman fails to draw this conclusion and harms her patient as a result. Feldman acts from ignorance...: she is unaware that her conduct has the features that make it wrong. Moreover her ignorance is not justified. Given her evidence and background knowledge, the only reasonable thing for her to think is that the treatment will harm her patient. And yet it does not follow that she is morally culpable for the harm she causes. Suppose that Feldman fails to draw the obvious conclusion only because her blood pressure medication has temporarily addled her judgment. If the effects of the medication are severe enough and in no way foreseeable, we should conclude that Feldman is not responsible for her mistake or for the harm it causes.[9]

In this passage, it seems that Rosen implicitly subscribes to an objective view of moral obligation; he says that Dr. Feldman is unaware that her conduct has the features that make it wrong, and the pertinent feature that he seems to have in mind is that the treatment she has chosen will in fact harm her patient. But the example also serves perfectly well for present purposes, inasmuch as the pertinent

---

[8] One example: Zimmerman (2014).   [9] Rosen (2008), p. 599.

feature could be said to be that, given her epistemic situation, the treatment that Feldman has chosen poses an unwarranted risk of harm to her patient. She is unaware of that fact, too, and blamelessly so.

Many philosophers subscribe to both views of moral obligation just outlined. They do so by drawing a distinction between what one's "objective" moral obligations are and what one's "subjective" moral obligations are.[10] Thus it might be said that, in taking the pill, Sally did something objectively wrong but subjectively right. I have some misgivings about drawing such a distinction, but they need not detain us here. I do think, however, that one can subscribe to both views only if one draws some such distinction. Some philosophers appear to overlook this point, saying, for example, that both harming and risking harm are wrong-making features of action, yet drawing no distinction between the kinds of moral wrong at issue.[11] The problem with such a position can be illustrated by a variation on Sally's case. Suppose that, in addition to there having been no reason to think that taking the pill would be harmful to her fetus, there was very good reason for her to think that *not* taking it *would* be harmful. In this case, Sally's evidence would have been diametrically opposed to the facts. The objective view implies, as before, that it would have been wrong (*ceteris paribus*) for Sally to take the pill; the subjective view implies that it would have been wrong for her *not* to take it. Unless these two kinds of moral wrong are distinguished from one another, the conjunction of the two views implies that Sally was in what is often called a moral dilemma. I submit (but will not argue here) that that is an untenable result.

2.1.3 Agent-evaluation and act-evaluation

The distinction between moral obligation and moral responsibility can be captured in another way. It is often said that judgments about the former have to do with the evaluation of *acts* (or omissions), whereas judgments about the latter have to do with the evaluation of *agents*. This is essentially correct, I think, although stated thus baldly the observation is slightly misleading. After all, both kinds of judgment concern both acts and agents; for it is *agents* that are obligated to act in certain ways, and it is for their *acts* (and omissions, and the consequences thereof) that agents may be responsible. Nonetheless, we can indeed say that judgments about obligation are "act-based" or "act-focused," in that they concern the assessment of agents' behavior (and the consequences thereof) relative to behavior in which they could otherwise engage or have engaged. Judgments about responsibility, by contrast, are "agent-based" or "agent-focused," in that

---

[10] See, e.g., Parfit (1984), p. 25; H. M. Smith (2018).
[11] This seems to be the position advocated in the examples given in Husak (2016), pp. 151 f. and 158 f., in which Juan causes harm and Juan* risks harm.

they concern the assessment of agents in light of the behavior in which they have engaged.

We can lose sight of this distinction if we are careless regarding how we express ourselves. It is unfortunate that philosophers and laypeople alike often talk of blameworthy *acts*. If what they mean is that the acts in question are *wrong*, then that is what they should say.[12] If, as seems often to be the case, what they mean is that the *agents* of the acts are to blame *for* the acts in question, then *that* is what they should say.[13] (There is a large literature on the so-called "moral worth" of acts that conflates these two types of evaluation. I will provide some comments on it in §9.2.2.)

That there is a distinction between an agent's being blameworthy for some act (or omission) and that act's being wrong does not itself imply that the two are to any extent independent of one another in the way that I have claimed they are. Even if the distinction is correct, it could still be that one is blameworthy for some act if and only if one's committing it was wrong. This is indeed the view that some philosophers advocate,[14] and perhaps there is some pressure to say that someone's behavior isn't "really" wrong unless its agent is to be condemned for engaging in it. But, if so, this is pressure that we would do well to resist. Consider Constance, a thoroughly conscientious person who takes her moral obligations very seriously indeed. She constantly tries very hard to ensure that she does the right thing on all occasions. In order to avoid doing wrong, she often engages in very careful investigation and deliberation; for she knows that, despite being well motivated, she is just as fallible as the next person and may nonetheless unwittingly do wrong. Unsurprisingly, she sometimes slips up and, despite her best endeavors, does indeed do what she so earnestly strives not to do: the wrong thing. Here, surely, the wrong thing is indeed "really" wrong, *morally*, in that it is precisely what Constance, who is the epitome of *moral* conscientiousness, was seeking to avoid. But, also surely, she is not to blame for what she did. Her mistake was a moral mistake, but it was an honest one.

2.1.4 Three kinds of moral judgments

I have distinguished between two kinds of moral judgments, those having to do with moral obligation and those having to do with (retrospective) moral

---

[12] Or instead they could say that *committing* these acts is wrong, or even that it is wrong *of* or *for* the relevant agents to commit these acts. I would recommend that they *not* say that the *agents* are wrong to commit these acts (despite the fact that this is a grammatically acceptable locution), since doing so serves only to blur the distinction at issue.

[13] See for example G. E. Moore (2005), pp. 97 f., in which Moore vacillates between talk of blameworthy acts and talk of blameworthy agents. Cf. Tannenbaum (2015), pp. 67 f., 74.

[14] See, e.g., Dahl (1967), pp. 420 f.; Wallace (1994), pp. 127, 135; Rivera-López (2006). Cf. Talbert (2017a), pp. 57, 60 for a closely related view.

responsibility. Judgments of the first kind are often called *deontic* judgments (from the Greek δέον, meaning that which is binding or right). There is, strangely, no common term for judgments of the second kind. As in previous works, I will call them *hypological* judgments (from the Greek ὑπόλογος, meaning held accountable or liable).

I have said that hypological judgments are agent-based or agent-focused. It's important to recognize that they are not the only kind of agent-based or agent-focused moral judgments that we make. We also make moral judgments about *character*, judgments that concern the virtues or vices that people may have and may display through their behavior. Judgments of this kind are often called *aretaic* judgments (from the Greek ἀρετή, meaning excellence or virtue).

As with the distinction between deontic and hypological judgments, so too with the distinction between hypological and aretaic judgments: it's a distinction that is often overlooked.[15] But it is a distinction that we should take care to make, for a number of reasons.

First, a person's character is composed of a variety of dispositions to think, feel, and act in certain ways. To qualify as traits of character, these dispositions must be relatively general, relatively long-term, and relatively deeply entrenched. It's clear, I think, that, if we can be morally responsible for anything, we can be morally responsible for behavior that does *not* manifest such traits. We can, that is, be responsible for behavior that is *un*characteristic. Consider Chloë, who goes to church every Sunday and makes sure to give generously when the collection plate comes around. It's not that she's well off. On the contrary, she's poor, and she is often tempted to steal from the plate rather than deposit money into it. But she resolutely resists temptation and does (what she regards as) her duty, even though doing so means having to scrimp and save just to get by. That's just the way she is. It's the way she's always been... until, one Sunday, when the plate comes around, rather than make her usual donation, she furtively snatches a five-dollar bill from it and quickly stuffs the bill in her pocket, looking around nervously to see if anyone has noticed.

I assume two things. First, Chloë's behavior was uncharacteristic, and, second, it is behavior for which she nonetheless can be, and may well be, morally responsible. You might dispute this conjunction of assumptions. As to the first, you might agree that Chloë's behavior was unusual, indeed unique, in that she had never before yielded to the temptation to steal, and yet deny that it was uncharacteristic, on the grounds that, even though it was characteristic of her to resist temptation, it was of course also characteristic of her to be tempted in the first place; this is what explains her behavior on this occasion, and so this is what renders her behavior characteristic on this occasion, too. But that "and so" seems

---

[15] See, e.g., Dahl (1967), p. 420, and the discussion of attributability in §2.3.1 below.

plainly mistaken. Yes, it was characteristic of Chloë to be tempted to steal, but the question isn't whether she's responsible for *that*. The question is whether she's responsible for *yielding* to temptation, and, since it was characteristic of her *not* to yield to it, it cannot also be correct to say that it was characteristic of her *to* yield to it.

At this point, you might question the second assumption, on the grounds that, if Chloë's behavior was indeed so uncharacteristic, so atypical, it cannot be properly imputed or attributed to her; there isn't the requisite connection between it and her for her to be responsible for it; it came out of nowhere. This line of thinking seems to be gaining popularity. It has been said that behavior that does not express one's "real" or "deep" self is behavior for which one cannot be morally responsible.[16] (There are different ways in which this idea has been developed. One's deep self is variously characterized as a function of one's character, or of one's evaluative commitments, or of what one cares most deeply about, or of what one identifies with.) This is hyperbolic. True, it may be difficult to explain Chloë's behavior (she might not understand it herself, lamenting, "I don't know what came over me. I'm so ashamed"), but that doesn't mean that no explanation exists. It's simply false to say that her behavior "came out of nowhere." *Part* of what explains it is the underlying temptation to steal. What's the *rest* of the explanation? Who knows? (Maybe it's to be found in the fact that, just as the collection plate reached Chloë, the clouds lifted and sunlight poured through the stained-glass window, bathing the plate in brilliant colors and rendering its contents especially attractive. But maybe not.) The lack of a ready explanation should not lead us to think that Chloë cannot be responsible for what she did.

Another, closely related point is this. Due to the fact that the way in which people behave seems to be strongly influenced by situational factors, there is growing skepticism about whether anyone in fact has *any* traits of character.[17] If warranted, such skepticism would undermine aretaic judgments entirely but, although it might also be relevant to whether certain hypological judgments that we tend to make are in fact justified, it would not itself suffice for a wholesale rejection of such judgments. We might be surprised to discover how easily a person's readiness to help others can be affected by, for example, how close he or she is to the fragrant smell of coffee,[18] but, again, that by itself shouldn't lead us to think that such a person therefore bears no responsibility for such behavior.

Finally, it seems reasonable to think that we can sometimes be morally responsible *for* having (or lacking) certain traits of character. A dramatic example is that of being to blame for having become addicted to some drug. Now if, as Aristotle

---

[16] See, e.g., Wolf (1987), p. 52; Watson (2004), pp. 267 ff.; Shoemaker (2015b), pp. 42 ff.
[17] See, e.g., Doris (2002), Zimbardo (2007).   [18] Cf. R. A. Baron (1997).

seems to have thought,[19] we are morally responsible for *all* our traits of character, then it would follow that hypological judgments must be distinct from aretaic judgments, for one's being to blame for one's first character trait could not itself reflect any prior character trait. But even if, as I think is clear (if only because ignorance can provide an excuse for the unwitting development of a trait), Aristotle's view is false, the mere possibility of its being true shows that the two types of judgment are distinct—unless, that is, it's possible for one to be to blame for something in virtue of that very thing, a matter to which I will now turn.

2.2 Blameworthiness

2.2.1 The basis of blameworthiness

I have said that, where there is blameworthiness (*moral* blameworthiness), it is *agents* who are to blame *for* something (an act, an omission, or a consequence thereof). We might say that agents are the *subjects* of blameworthiness and that what they are to blame for are the *objects* of blameworthiness. But we must also acknowledge another aspect or component of blameworthiness: its *basis*. Consider Heinrich again. He learned in 1956 of the risks posed by thalidomide. Partly as a result of his keeping quiet about these risks, Sally took a dose of Distaval in 1961 and subsequently gave birth to a child with phocomelia. I said in the last chapter that almost everyone would want to say that Heinrich was to blame for the child's condition, *C*. But *why* should we accept this verdict? *In virtue of what*, precisely, was Heinrich blameworthy for *C*?[20]

Some philosophers hold that one is to blame *for* something just in case one is to blame *on the basis of* that thing.[21] They claim, in effect, that the object and the basis of blameworthiness are one and the same. If this claim is to have any plausibility, it must be restricted to *direct* blameworthiness. Surely the basis of Heinrich's blameworthiness for *C* is not *C* itself. It is not *C* that makes Heinrich blameworthy for *C*. *C* occurred in 1961. The basis of Heinrich's blameworthiness for *C* is to be traced to 1956. That's when he made the decision not to divulge the pertinent information about thalidomide.

But this still leaves the question of *exactly* what it is that happened in 1956 that rendered Heinrich blameworthy for his behavior and for the consequences to

---

[19] Aristotle (1941), bk. III, ch. 5.
[20] I will treat "being worthy of blame" and "deserving blame" as synonymous. It is a common observation that, if some person *P* deserves something *X*, there must be some *basis* for this fact. (See, e.g., Feldman and Skow (2019), §3.) It is also commonly said that, in such a case, *P* is the *subject* and *X* is the *object* of desert. That's fine, but notice that this use of the term "object" differs from my use of it in this paragraph (a use that comports with others'—see, e.g., Khoury (2018)). There is a difference between what *P* is to blame for (namely, some wrongdoing) and what *P* deserves (namely, blame).
[21] See, e.g., Copp (1997), pp. 449 f.

which that behavior gave rise. A by-now-standard answer, one that stems from P. F. Strawson's seminal essay "Freedom and Resentment," is that it is the *quality of will* that informed Heinrich's behavior that accounts for his being blameworthy for it and its consequences.[22] I think that this answer is on the right track, but it must be developed carefully.

I said in the last chapter that it has traditionally been held that, to be blameworthy, a person must satisfy two conditions, one epistemic, the other agential. An agent's quality of will has to do with the first of these conditions, but to call the condition an *epistemic* one may be inadvisable; for there is more to someone's quality of will than what that person knows or believes. Indeed, the term "quality of will" is itself potentially misleading, with respect to both "quality" and "will."

Consider, first, "will." The title of Strawson's essay explicitly mentions freedom, and he begins the essay with a discussion of the relation between moral responsibility and determinism. The reader might be forgiven, therefore, for thinking, at least initially, that it is with the agential condition of moral responsibility that Strawson is primarily concerned and that, when he writes of "will," he is using that term as it is used in the context of discussions about freedom of will. But that is not so. In the context of such discussions, "will" means the same as, or close to the same as, "choice." Strawson's use of the term is much broader. He is primarily concerned with whether we show *good will* or *ill will* (or indifference) toward others, and in this context "will" encompasses a wide variety of attitudes that we take toward others through the choices we make or, indeed, the choices we do not make. "Benevolence" and "malevolence" come much closer to capturing what is at issue, although they are still too narrow, if only because Strawson is in fact concerned not only with the attitudes we take toward others but also with the attitudes we take toward ourselves. "Regard" and "disregard" serve better in this respect, although "disregard" blurs the distinction between ill will and mere indifference. Indeed, "regard" and "disregard" have an advantage over "good will" and "ill will," in that the latter terms are, as Strawson himself intended, most naturally understood as characterizing our attitudes toward *people* in particular, whereas the former have greater latitude. And, since it seems plain that we may be morally responsible for behavior that concerns not just people but any other object of moral import (a fact that many recent discussions of moral responsibility oddly overlook or, worse, deny), it may be a mistake to focus on quality of will in particular when investigating the mental condition requisite for moral responsibility, even when "will" is construed as broadly as Strawson intends it to be. "Quality of mind" would be a more general, and therefore perhaps more appropriate, expression.

---

[22] Strawson (1974), p. 14.

What I have just said about how to understand the term "will" as it is used in the expression "quality of will" matches pretty closely what Michael McKenna has to say,[23] but I part company with him regarding how to understand the term "quality." He says:

> I understand the relevant notion of quality here to be a matter of *value* or *worth*. It's not that the term *quality* is meant to pick out some positive feature, property, or characteristic of an agent's will—not in the way in which a ball can have the quality of being red or spherical. Rather, it is meant to call attention to the value or worth of an agent's regard for others. The relevant synonym, therefore, is not *property* but *worth*.[24]

I think this passage oversimplifies matters. As I have noted, it is with certain kinds of mental states that we are concerned here. These kinds must be identified *prior* to any moral evaluation of them, and it is my understanding that Strawson's use of the terms "good will" and "ill will" is intended, at least in part, to aid us in making this identification. As I see it, even if we agree that it is a good thing to show good will toward others, and a bad thing to show them ill will, this is a *substantive* claim. It surely makes sense (whether or not it would be correct) to say that it is a *bad* thing to show good will toward, say, villains. Thus, insofar as the "quality" of an agent's will has to do with whether that will is a good will or an ill will, it does *not* concern the value or worth of that will but rather its content; it has to do with whether the agent wishes someone well or ill. (Having said that, I should immediately add that it is certainly legitimate to use the expression "quality of will (or mind)" to refer to the value or worth of the will (or state or states of mind) in question. Indeed, it seems to me that the expression often does double duty, alluding both to mental states of a certain kind or kinds and to the value of those states.)

2.2.2 Diverse mental qualities

I have said that "quality of mind" may be a more appropriate expression than "quality of will" to refer to the basis of blameworthiness, but clearly this term is too broad as it stands. After all, there is much that one's quality of mind may comprise that has nothing to do with one's being blameworthy for anything. For example, if Sven is exquisitely sensitive, aesthetically, that fact about his quality of mind clearly provides no reason to declare him blameworthy. And even if Tessa's tastes are irredeemably vulgar, that fact still provides no reason to declare her blameworthy—not, at least, blameworthy in the way that concerns us.

---

[23] McKenna (2012), pp. 58 f.   [24] McKenna (2012), p. 59.

As I have repeatedly noted, the sort of blameworthiness at issue here is of course *moral* blameworthiness, and so we should focus on the *moral* quality of mind that one exhibits through one's behavior.[25] Consider, in this regard, what the *Model Penal Code* has to say about the different forms of *mens rea* (literally, a "guilty mind").[26]

In §2.02(2), the *Code* distinguishes four kinds of culpability, having to do with whether someone commits an offense *purposely*, or *knowingly*, or *recklessly*, or *negligently*. Each of these ways of committing an offense is said to constitute the grounds of culpability. Moreover, according to §2.02(5) of the *Code*, these grounds form a hierarchy, in that, *ceteris paribus*, purposely committing an offense confers greater culpability on an agent than does knowingly committing it, which itself confers greater culpability than does recklessly committing it, which in turn confers greater culpability than does negligently committing it.[27] The *Code* is, of course, concerned with *legal* culpability, but I expect that many would find its account of the kinds and degrees of *mens rea* applicable to *moral* culpability, too. For example, I expect that many would want to say that, *ceteris paribus*, negligently harming someone renders one blameworthy, but blameworthy to a lesser degree than does recklessly doing so, which itself renders one less blameworthy than does knowingly doing so, which in turn renders one less blameworthy than does doing so on purpose. Each of these ways of harming someone, it might be thought, reflects ill on the agent; each bespeaks a morally objectionable disregard for others, the manner in which such disregard is manifested being more and more objectionable as one moves up the hierarchy.

Two questions arise here. First, is it in fact the case that degree of blameworthiness increases as one moves up this hierarchy? Second, are there other states of mind, beyond the four listed, that can ground blameworthiness or alter the degree of blameworthiness? As to the first question, I have already provided some reason to question our common judgments in this area. Consider Karl from the last chapter. Many would declare him guilty of negligence, but the Origination Thesis, derived from the Argument from Ignorance, casts doubt on this verdict. As to the second question, it might be held, for example, that harming someone *gleefully* confers an even greater degree of blameworthiness on an agent than does "merely" doing so on purpose.

---

[25] I won't try here to provide an account of the distinction between moral and non-moral traits. (For discussion, see Zimmerman (2001), pp. 226 ff.) I hope that it is as clear to you as it is to me that neither aesthetic sensitivity nor aesthetic insensitivity qualifies as a moral trait.

[26] American Law Institute (1985).

[27] This statement is over-simple, in that it overlooks the fact that the law typically includes *mens rea* as an *element of* an offense. Thus, for example, if a statute defined theft in such a way that one could not commit this offense unless one knew that the property one was taking was not one's own, then it would not be possible to commit this offense either recklessly or negligently. (Cf. Husak (2016), pp. 99 ff.) I will ignore this complication here.

These are questions that I will address later. For the moment, I will simply note that, if one is to blame for some wrongful act or omission or consequence thereof, the quality of mind that renders one blameworthy is to be found in the attitude or attitudes that one exhibits in committing that act or omission. This claim is decidedly rough and is certainly in need of further development (regarding which, see Chapters 5–9). Nonetheless, as it stands, it is, I submit, plausible and also, I should think, quite unsurprising.

2.2.3 Control

Two further points that should be explicitly noted here are these.

First, although I have been focusing on blameworthiness, we should not forget the other modes of responsibility that I mentioned earlier: praiseworthiness and indifference-worthiness. As with blameworthiness, each of these other modes will have its basis in the agent's quality of will or mind.

Second, if there is an agential condition of responsibility, then, unless quality of will or mind somehow incorporates this condition, it would be a mistake to say that the basis of responsibility has *exclusively* to do with quality of will or mind. The exercise of control will also constitute part of this basis.[28]

2.2.4 The relation between the object and the basis of blameworthiness

I noted above that some philosophers hold that the object and the basis of blameworthiness are one and the same. I noted also that, if this claim is to have any plausibility, it must be restricted to *direct* blameworthiness. But is it plausible even then?

The answer to this question turns on what sort of thing can function as the object of direct blameworthiness. In this regard, consider the most recent renditions of Premises 4 and 7 of the Argument from Ignorance:

(4) one is morally to blame for something only if one was in control of that thing;

(7) if one is morally to blame for something over which one had only indirect control, then one's blameworthiness for it is itself only indirect.

---

[28] As I am construing the relevant terms, then, there is of course no inconsistency in saying that the basis of moral responsibility comprises *both* the agent's quality of will *and* the agent's exercise of control. Contrast Levy (2011), ch. 8, and Husak (2016), p. 164, among others.

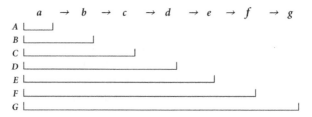

Figure 2.1 BILL AND JILL

Conjoined, these premises imply that one is directly to blame for something only if one was directly in control of it. Thus, on the assumption that this is so, the answer to the question we are considering can now be seen to turn on what sort of thing is such that one can be in direct control of it.

Consider the following case. Bill is in love with Jill. His love is unrequited. He becomes despondent, then enraged. One day he goes over to Jill's house, pulls out a gun, aims it at her, shoots, and kills her. In this miserable little story, many things happen over which (we may assume) Bill exercised control. One portion of this story can be represented as in Figure 2.1. In this figure, the arrows represent causation. *A*, which consists simply of *a*, is the minimal act, if it can be called an act at all, constituted by Bill's decision to kill Jill. (To be clear: by "Bill's decision" I here mean his *executive* decision to kill Jill *then and there*. I take this decision to be the locus of his *exercise of control* over the events depicted in the figure. Such a decision is of course often preceded by one or more *non*-executive decisions that form parts of plans to engage in the relevant behavior *later*. Moreover, if such a plan is sufficiently complex, it will involve certain preparatory components, the carrying out of which will require their *own* particular *executive* decisions. For example, in the story, Bill went over to Jill's house, pulled out his gun, and aimed it at Jill, and each of these acts will have involved its own particular exercise of control. None of these acts is depicted in Figure 2.1; each would require its own separate figure.) *B*, which consists of Bill's decision, *a*, causing the movement of his finger, *b*, is the act of Bill's moving his finger. (In Georg von Wright's terminology, *b* is the "result" of *B*.[29]) *C*, which consists of *a*'s causing *c*, is the act of Bill's pulling the trigger. *D* is the act of his firing the gun. *E* is the act of his causing the bullet to fly. *F* is the act of his shooting Jill. *G* is the act of his killing her (where *g* is, of course, the event of Jill's death). Note that, in light of the causal connections between *a* through *g*, Bill may be said to do *G* by doing *F*, *F* by doing *E*, and so on. In terminology that is familiar (but nonetheless sometimes used differently by different philosophers), *A* (or, possibly, *B*) is a *basic* act, while the

---

[29] von Wright (1971), p. 66.

others are *non-basic* acts. Figure 2.1 provides a graphic representation of this Russian-doll-like nesting of basic acts within non-basic acts within non-basic acts.[30]

As Figure 2.1 illustrates, an executive decision, as I conceive of it, occurs, not *prior to* the relevant act, but as *the initial part of* that act.[31] In a typical case, the decision will be relatively close, in both causal and temporal terms, to the results of those acts of which it is a part, but it can on occasion be quite distant from such results. (Think of a killing in which the death occurs only months after the pertinent executive decision to kill.) Moreover, an executive decision is typically one that the agent himself understands to constitute the initiation of action and to be the means by which he exercises control over consequent events.

The story of Bill illustrates how it is that control may be merely indirect. Whether Jill died was in Bill's control, but only because he was in control of the bullet's trajectory; moreover, he was in control of the bullet's trajectory only because he was in control of the gun's firing; and, of course, he was in control of the gun's firing only because, ultimately, he was in control of his decision to act. It is *a* that was in his direct control; the other results of his acts, *b* through *g*, were in his control, but only indirectly so. What of the *acts B* through *G* themselves? Since they were composed of a combination of *a*, which was in Bill's direct control, and some causal consequence of *a*, which was only in his indirect control, I think we should declare his control over them "hybrid."

Just as control may be either direct, indirect, or hybrid, so too may blameworthiness. If Bill is blameworthy for the events depicted in Figure 2.1, his blameworthiness for *a* is direct, whereas for *b* through *g* it is indirect, and for *B* through *G* it is hybrid. The claim that the basis of Bill's blameworthiness for *a* through *g* (and *A* through *G*) is the same as the object of his direct blameworthiness for what happened is, then, the claim that *a* (or *A*) is the basis of his blameworthiness. Is this plausible? It may seem so. I have said that I take *a* to be the locus of Bill's exercise of control over what happened. In making his decision, Bill exercised his control over both it and the other events depicted in Figure 2.1. Moreover, in making this decision, Bill did so with the purpose of killing Jill, thereby manifesting the highest degree of *mens rea* recognized in the *Model Penal Code*.

Nonetheless, I think we should deny that *a* itself constitutes the basis of Bill's blameworthiness in this case. According to the Origination Thesis, blameworthiness requires at some point knowing that one is doing something overall morally wrong. Such knowledge certainly speaks to one's quality of mind but, if Bill possessed this knowledge, it was something that was not itself contained in

---

[30] The kind of generation of non-basic acts out of a basic act represented in the figure is causal. As Alvin Goldman notes, there are other kinds of generation that may relate non-basic to basic acts. See Goldman (1970), ch. 2.

[31] Contrast Persson (2019), ch. 3, where it is claimed that executive decisions are passive, happening to the agent rather than being made to happen by the agent.

his decision to kill Jill. Hence that decision did not itself constitute the entire basis of his blameworthiness for what happened. Note that this point indicates that we should reject, not only the claim that one is directly to blame for something *just in case* one is to blame on the basis of that thing, but also the weaker claim that one is directly to blame for something *only if* one is to blame on the basis of that thing.[32]

2.3 The blame in blameworthiness

2.3.1 Thin blame (and praise)

Blameworthiness consists in the worthiness of *blame*, and we should now ask what blame is. This is a question that has recently garnered a great deal of attention, and I will address it in this section. It's worth noting that blameworthiness of course also consists in the *worthiness* of blame, and so we should also ask what worthiness is. This is a question that has received comparatively little attention. I will take it up in §2.4.

I said earlier that judgments about moral responsibility—hypological judgments—have to do with the evaluation of agents. Such judgments may be positive, neutral, or negative. When they are negative, they involve blame. Notice that, just as it is *agents* who are blameworthy for what they do or bring about, so too is it *agents* whom we blame for what they do or bring about. (Instead of saying "I blame Heinrich for the child's condition" we might say "I blame the child's condition on Heinrich," but the acceptability of the latter locution should not lead us to think that it is the child's condition, rather than Heinrich, that is being blamed.) To blame someone for something is, at least in part, to think poorly of that person in light of that thing. It is a form of appraisal. It is a judgment to the effect that the person in question doesn't measure up to some standard—at least as far as the something in question goes; after all, we can blame someone for something while also praising him or her for something else.

As I also noted earlier, there are non-moral forms of praise(worthiness) and blame(worthiness). When it comes to judgments about moral responsibility, the relevant appraisals are of course *moral* appraisals. In the case of blame of the sort at issue here, then, the judgment is that the person in question has failed to measure up to some *moral* standard. *Just* what that standard is, however, is a subtle and delicate question to which I will return below.

There is a thin sense of "blame" and "blameworthiness" in which to blame someone morally simply is to engage in such a negative appraisal of him or her

---

[32] This weaker claim is made in Khoury (2012), p. 195, and (2018), p. 1363.

and one's being blameworthy consists in one's being worthy of such an appraisal. In an earlier work, I gathered together a bunch of metaphors to give expression to this idea:

> Blaming someone may be said to constitute judging that there is a "discredit" or "debit" in his "ledger," a "negative mark" in his "report-card," or a "blemish" or "stain" on his "record"; that his "record" has been "tarnished"; that his "moral standing" has been "diminished." ... Someone is blameworthy if he is deserving of such blame; that is, if it is correct, or true to the facts, to judge that there is a "debit" in his "ledger" (*etc.*).[33]

I also claimed that there is a thin sense of "praise" and "praiseworthy" that matches the thin sense of "blame" and "blameworthy." That now seems to me rather doubtful. As Nomy Arpaly and Timothy Schroeder have observed, "credit" and "creditworthy" would be more appropriate terms, although unfortunately the latter already has a decidedly different meaning.[34]

John Martin Fischer and Mark Ravizza have aptly dubbed the kind of view of moral responsibility just sketched a "ledger view."[35] It is a view that is shared by many philosophers, including especially Joel Feinberg, on whose work I was drawing when I gave my account.[36] It is important to emphasize that, on the ledger view, metaphors of the sort that I have just used to characterize blame and praise (credit) are indeed simply metaphors. There is no presupposition that any such ledgers or records in fact exist, let alone that anyone is making entries into them. Moreover, the kind of ledger or record that is being imagined is, more particularly, a *hypological* one. After all, one may have the "record" of being a habitual wrongdoer, but that is a *deontic* matter that may have no bearing on what one is morally responsible for. So, too, one may have a long "record" of vicious activity, but that is an *aretaic* matter that again may have no bearing on what one is morally responsible for. Thus the question of *just* what the moral standard is that a blameworthy person has failed to measure up to is indeed a pressing one.

One worry about the kind of account I favor of the thin sense of "blame" has been raised by Justin Coates and Neal Tognazzini. They suggest that such an account, being "purely cognitive," is inadequate, on the basis of the observation that "if you are a co-conspirator in a crime, your partner might be perfectly justified in judging that you acted viciously or wrongly, while simultaneously congratulating you for these things rather than blaming you for them."[37] This is an

---

[33] Zimmerman (1988), p. 38.   [34] See Arpaly and Schroeder (2013), p. 160.
[35] Fischer and Ravizza (1998), p. 9, n. 12.
[36] See Feinberg (1970), pp. 30 f., 124 f. See also Glover (1970), p. 64; Morris (1976), p. 124; and Haji (1998).
[37] Coates and Tognazzini (2012), p. 200.

important point. The supposition that it is possible to judge something (or someone) to be in some way morally objectionable without thereby disapproving of it (or him or her) is controversial, but I suspect that it is correct. If so, we must add disapproval to my account of moral blame in the thin sense. As I understand it, disapproval can be "purely cognitive." At least, it need not be emotionally tinged, in the way in which the so-called reactive attitudes (shortly to be discussed) are usually taken to be.

My so-far-sketchy account of blame and praise (credit) in the thin sense has some affinities with what Gary Watson says when discussing that "face" of responsibility that he calls attributability.[38] So, too, for others who have followed Watson in their use of this term.[39] Watson says:

> In one way, to blame (morally) is to attribute something to a (moral) fault in the agent... [Such] kinds of blaming and praising judgments... invoke only... attributability conditions, on which certain appraisals of the individual as an agent are grounded. Because many of these appraisals concern the agent's excellences and faults—or virtues and vices—as manifested in thought and action, I shall say that such judgments are made from the *aretaic perspective*.[40]

I think it is a mistake, however, to say that appraisals of the kind in question constitute judgments that are made from an aretaic perspective, for two reasons.

First hypological judgments should be distinguished from aretaic judgments for the reasons I gave in §2.1.4. In particular, it is important to recognize that a fault *in* an agent need not be the agent's fault, in the sense that the agent need not be *at* fault regarding—i.e., need not be responsible for having—the fault.[41]

Second, Watson holds, correctly I believe, that aretaic judgments do not in general presuppose that the agent was in control of that for which he or she is being appraised. But, along with many others, I want to say (in keeping with Premise 4 of the Argument from Ignorance) that appraisals of the kind at issue here do presuppose this. In this regard, consider what Daniel Haybron has to say when contrasting the sort of evil embodied by Claggart, the master-at-arms in Herman Melville's *Billy Budd*, with the sort of evil embodied by Dorian Gray in Oscar Wilde's story. He puts the matter well:

> The purely evil individual [such as Claggart] is unquestionably vile, but he lacks an important fault: he does not give himself freely to evil, but is delivered to it.

---

[38] Watson (2004), pp. 263 ff.
[39] See, e.g., Scanlon (1998), p. 248, and (2008), p. 202; A. M. Smith (2005), p. 238; Shoemaker (2011a), p. 603.
[40] Watson (2004), p. 266.   [41] Cf. Rosen (2008), p. 608; Pink (2016), p. 163.

Claggart could not help but be a cruel man—that's just the way he *is*. Dorian Gray's cruelty, on the other hand, is entirely of his own making.[42]

On the assumption that Haybron's observation is accurate, Claggart, though clearly morally evaluable in light of his particular brand of cruelty, is not, I would say, morally responsible for it, whereas this cannot be said of Dorian Gray regarding the cruelty that characterizes him.[43] Here it is important to note that, as I and (I assume) Haybron are using the term, "cruelty" refers to a trait or set of traits that comprise the *disposition* to engage in certain forms of behavior and not to the *behavior* itself. I understand Haybron to be claiming that, even if both Claggart and Gray were in control of their behavior, only Gray was in control of forming the disposition in question. Even so, Claggart's disposition, as well as Gray's, is clearly a vice and, as Haybron says, Claggart is unquestionably vile in light of this vice.

2.3.2 Thick blame (and praise)

The view that there is such a thing as moral blame (and praise or credit) in the thin sense that I have just identified is sometimes regarded with apparent suspicion. Despite his own discussion of attributability, at one point in an earlier piece Watson himself has this to say:

> Merely to cite such judgments [i.e., judgments that attribute something to a moral fault in someone] is to leave out something integral to the...concept of moral responsibility...It is as though in blaming we were mainly moral clerks, recording moral faults...[44]

In a similar vein, T. M. Scanlon says this:

> [I]t might be said that to blame a person for something is to take that action as showing something negative about that person's character...By itself, however, this view does not explain the distinctive weight that moral blame seems to have. Unless we say more about why we are interested in this kind of character assessment, it may seem to be a pointless assignment of moral "grades."[45]

It may be, though, that, in the passage cited, Watson is simply reporting, and not also endorsing, the criticism contained in that passage. Moreover, it is important

---

[42] Haybron (1999), p. 143.
[43] See Chapter 9 below, however, for further discussion of this claim.
[44] Watson (2004), p. 226.   [45] Scanlon (2008), pp. 126 f.

to note Scanlon's qualifying phrase "By itself." In any case, however these remarks by Watson and Scanlon are precisely to be interpreted, it seems to me important to acknowledge that blame in the thin sense is genuine blame. For example, I am strongly inclined—as, I suspect, you are too—to blame Hitler for his contribution to the Holocaust.[46] My doing so involves my making a (disapproving) judgment to the effect that (a) the Holocaust was extremely bad, (b) Hitler's contribution to it was egregiously wrong, and (c) Hitler himself is extraordinarily reprehensible in light of his contribution. And, as far as I can tell, it involves no more than that. (This isn't to say that it's easy to ascertain just what such a judgment comes to. As will become apparent below, clause (c) is especially difficult to pin down.)

Often, however, moral blame certainly does involve quite a lot more than simply making some such judgment. Moral blame in the *thick* sense involves *reacting* to the person blamed in some way, a reaction that somehow is based on, incorporates, and reflects the judgment. So, too, for praise, when it goes beyond merely crediting someone with something. Talk of "reactions" in this context is now commonplace, thanks to the pervasive influence of Strawson's discussion of what he calls "the reactive attitudes."[47]

Precisely how the notion of a reactive attitude is to be understood is an important question to which I will attend below. For the moment, however, let us suppose that we already have the answer to this question. The question would still remain what the relation is, or is supposed to be, between the reactive attitudes and moral responsibility. It may seem that this second question should be addressed only after the first question has been answered but, for reasons that will emerge (take this as a promissory note), I will address it now. Strawson himself is often interpreted as offering an analysis of the concept of moral responsibility in terms of the reactive attitudes. It is controversial whether this interpretation is accurate and, if it is, just what the analysis is.[48] My concern here is not exegetical. I will simply inquire into whether some such analysis has merit.

Watson claims that Strawson claims that the reactive attitudes "are *constitutive* of moral responsibility."[49] On one reading, this suggests the following *Reactive-Attitude Analysis* of responsibility:

RAA1: *P*'s being morally responsible for *X* consists in someone's directing some reactive attitude toward *P* in respect of *X*.

---

[46] The Argument from Ignorance indicates that this inclination ought perhaps to be resisted. Consider the example of Sam at the end of the last chapter. For further discussion of this issue, see Chapters 8 and 9 below.
[47] Strawson (1974), p. 6.   [48] See De Mesel (2017) and Zimmerman (2017c) for discussion.
[49] Watson (2004), p. 220.

This proposal is clearly unacceptable, however. Regardless of just what kind of attitude a so-called reactive attitude should be said to be, it is easy to imagine cases in which someone is responsible for something although (perhaps because no one is aware of what he or she has done) that person is not the object of any reactive attitude in respect of it, and it is also easy to imagine cases in which someone is the object of a reactive attitude in respect of something although (because the attitude is misguided) that person is not responsible for it.

A much more plausible proposal is this:

RAA2: *P*'s being morally responsible for *X* consists in its being fitting for someone to direct some reactive attitude toward *P* in respect of *X*.

Such an analysis is often called a Strawsonian analysis. It may be the sort of analysis that Strawson himself intended, and certainly analyses along these lines have been proposed by several philosophers.[50] Whether in the end such an analysis is acceptable, however, is a difficult question.

One challenge to RAA2 is this. It seems reasonable to think that, if ever it is fitting to direct some reactive attitude toward some person *P* in respect of something *X*, that will be *because P* is responsible for *X*. *P*'s responsibility comes first, as it were, in that it underlies the fittingness of any reactive attitude toward *P*. But, if so, then it is hard to see how it could be correct to analyze *P*'s responsibility in terms of the fittingness of any such attitude, since doing so renders the former a function of the latter.[51]

One response to this challenge is simply to deny the premise on which it is based, namely, that, if it is fitting to direct some reactive attitude toward *P* in respect of *X*, that will be *because P* is responsible for *X*. There is precedent for this response in a parallel debate in the theory of value. There is a popular view about value that mirrors the analysis of responsibility given in RAA2. This view, often called the *Fitting-Attitude Analysis* of value, may be rendered as follows:

FAA: *X*'s being good [neutral, bad] consists in its being fitting for someone to show favor [indifference, disfavor] toward *X*.[52]

Here, "favor" and "disfavor" are intended as umbrella terms to cover a wide variety of positive and negative responses, and "indifference" covers responses intermediate between the two. FAA has been subjected to a number of challenges,

---

[50] See, e.g., Wallace (1994), pp. 76 f.; Fischer and Ravizza (1998), p. 7; Levy (2011), p. 194; McKenna (2012), pp. 34 ff.

[51] Cf. Feinberg (1970), pp. 30 f.; Schlossberger (1992), pp. 100 f. and 163 ff.; Haji (1998), pp. 3 f.; Watson (2004), pp. 265 f. and 316; Nelkin (2011), p. 29 f.

[52] See, e.g., Brentano (1969), p. 18; Ewing (1948), p. 152; Chisholm (1986), p. 52; Lemos (1994), pp. 12, 15; Scanlon (1998), pp. 96 f.

one of which mirrors the present challenge to RAA2. The objection is that, if it is ever fitting to favor X, that will be *because* X is good, and this is incompatible with the analysis given in FAA.[53] The best-known response to this objection has been to invoke one version of the so-called "buck-passing" account of value and say that, if X is the fitting object of favor, that will *not* be because X is good, but rather because X has some *other* property (the property, say, of being pleasant), and it is because X has *this* property that it is (both) good and the fitting object of favor.[54] In like fashion, one might invoke a buck-passing account of responsibility and say that, if P is the fitting object of some reactive attitude in respect of X, that will *not* be because P is responsible for X, but rather because P has some *other* property (the property, say, of having freely and deliberately harmed someone), and it is because P has *this* property that it is the case (both) that P is responsible for X and that it is fitting to direct some reactive attitude toward P in respect of X.

This response is attractive in its simplicity, but I'm afraid that it may be too simple. Suppose (to embellish an example from Stephen Darwall,[55] who himself borrows it from David Hume[56]) that you are on a crowded elevator, and the lady in front of you, who is wearing stiletto heels, suddenly takes a step back and treads directly on your foot. She is causally responsible for your experiencing a great deal of pain, but is she *morally* responsible for this? More particularly, is she *to blame* for your agony? Would you—should you—*resent* her for what she has brought about? The answer depends on further features of the case. If what she did was purely accidental—she was jostled, say, by the person in front of her—then resentment on your part would be out of place, unwarranted. But if it is clear that she stepped on your foot freely and deliberately, and with no provocation from you, that would be another matter entirely. In that case, you would indeed be justified in resenting her for what she did. (Or better—remember the Argument from Ignorance—you might well be justified in doing so.) Why? The answer seems clear: *because she's responsible*—more particularly, *she has no excuse*—for her behavior. But if this is so, then it is a mistake simply to dismiss the claim that it is fitting to direct some reactive attitude toward P in respect of X because P is responsible for X.

Another response to the present challenge to RAA2 is not to dismiss this claim but to interpret it as being perfectly consistent with RAA2 (and with a buck-passing approach). If the claim is interpreted as maintaining that the fittingness of directing a reactive attitude toward P in respect of X *is grounded in* P's responsibility for X, then this kind of ontological priority of *analysandum* over *analysans* is indeed difficult to reconcile with the kind of conceptual priority of *analysans* over *analysandum* that is apparently asserted in any such analysis. (Whether this

---

[53] See, e.g., Blanshard (1961), pp. 284 ff.
[54] See Ewing (1948), pp. 157 and 172; Scanlon (1998), pp. 97 f.   [55] Darwall (2006), p. 5.
[56] Hume (1998), p. 42.

difficulty can be overcome is a complicated matter that I won't try to resolve here.) But the claim need not be understood as implying any such ontological priority. Suppose that Bob and Carol are discussing something that they both recognize to be a circle. Bob asserts that the circle is equidistant at all points from some fixed point; Carol expresses doubts about this. Bob then says, "Look, it's equidistant at all points from some fixed point *because* it's a circle. That's just what it *is* to be a circle." What Bob says seems true, and it is of course perfectly compatible with the analysis at issue of what it is for something to be a circle. If it's this sort of "because" that is at work in the claim about responsibility and fittingness, then there is no need to think that accepting the claim requires rejecting RAA2.

But there is reason to doubt that it is this sort of "because" that is at work in the claim under discussion. Bob's explanation of what it is to be a circle presupposes that Carol *fails* to recognize that something's being a circle requires that it be equidistant at all points from some fixed point. But this sort of ignorance need not be presupposed in the present context. It seems perfectly coherent for someone to *acknowledge* that your resenting the lady on the elevator is fitting just in case she is to blame—i.e., she has no excuse—for what she did but nonetheless maintain that your resentment is fitting *because* she has no excuse for what she did. (Compare this claim with that of someone who holds that an act is morally right just in case *and because* it maximizes utility.)

Yet another response to the challenge is to agree that the claim in question is a claim about grounding and yet deny that it is at odds with the analysis given in RAA2, on the grounds that this analysis should not be construed as being of the classic "decompositional" kind according to which a complex concept (in this case, the concept of moral responsibility) is said to be *composed of* other concepts (in this case, the concepts of fittingness and of a reactive attitude) that enjoy priority over it. Rather, it should be understood as an analysis of the kind that purports simply to provide a "connection" between the relevant concepts without making any claim of conceptual priority of *analysans* over *analysandum* and is therefore not threatened by the possibility of there being an ontological priority of *analysandum* over *analysans*.[57] Whether this response succeeds will depend on just what kind of connection is envisaged. I leave it to those who advocate this position to provide the necessary details.

There is still another response to the challenge that deserves mention. It employs a divide-and-conquer strategy and goes as follows. Just as there are thin and thick senses of "blameworthy" and "praiseworthy," so too there are thin and thick senses of "morally responsible." The claim that it is fitting to direct some reactive attitude toward P in respect of X because P is responsible for X is to be understood as the claim that P is *thickly* responsible for X because P is *thinly*

---

[57] See De Mesel (2017), §4; García (2018), appendix.

responsible for X. That is, it is thick responsibility that *consists in* being the fitting object of a reactive attitude, and it is *in virtue of* being thinly responsible that one is the fitting object of such an attitude. Applied to the case of the lady in the elevator, the claim thus comes to this: she is (thickly) blameworthy (worthy of, say, your resentment) for what she did *because* she has no (thin) excuse for it (it is the occasion of a debit in her hypological ledger), and she has no (thin) excuse for it *because*, in turn, she engaged in it freely and deliberately and without provocation. This strategy has been suggested, whether explicitly or implicitly, by many philosophers. Talk of "thin" and "thick" responsibility is not common, but, ever since Watson's influential discussion of the two "faces" of responsibility, talk of "attributability" and "accountability" is widespread.[58]

Two cautionary points should be noted. First, just as with "responsibility," so too with "attributability" and "accountability": these terms can be, and have been, used in a variety of ways. In particular, they have not always been used to capture the distinction between what I have called thin and thick responsibility.[59] Second, those who hold that accountability is grounded in attributability often do not maintain that the former is grounded *wholly* in the latter. Let me elaborate.

Consider what Watson himself says about attributability and accountability. As I noted above, he claims that judgments of attributability are made from the aretaic perspective and, as such, do not presuppose that the person being judged was in control of that for which he or she is being judged. When it comes to judgments of accountability, however, Watson is (or seems) prepared to grant that such judgments do presuppose control on the part of the person judged.[60] But if so, then it seems that, on his view, accountability is not grounded wholly in attributability, whereas the present suggestion is that thin responsibility *suffices* for thick responsibility—that, for example, it is the control coupled with the quality of mind that she exhibited when she stepped on your foot that grounds and explains the debit in the hypological ledger of the lady in the elevator, and it is this debit that in turn grounds and explains the fittingness of your resenting her for what she did.[61]

I readily admit, though, that unless I clarify the metaphor of the ledger, it is hard to compare the merits of this view about the relation between thin and thick

---

[58] See Watson (2004), ch. 9. Cf. Darwall (2006); A. M. Smith (2008); Shoemaker (2011a); Nelkin (2016a).

[59] One example: John Fischer and Neal Tognazzini use the term "attributability" to refer to the property of being what they call "a sensible target" of ascriptions of moral responsibility, by which they mean that such ascriptions would not involve a category mistake (as would be the case if one ascribed moral responsibility to a dog, for example). See Fischer and Tognazzini (2011), pp. 383 ff. This comes close to saying that attributability consists in having the *capacity* to be morally responsible for something (regarding which see §2.1.1). Another example: Kurt Baier uses the term "accountability" to refer to this same capacity. See Baier (1970), pp. 103 f. Cf. Agule (2016), p. 2, n. 2.

[60] Watson (2004), pp. 271 f.

[61] Cf. Scanlon (2015), p. 89, n. 1, where the claim is made that "responsibility as attributability" suffices for "moral reaction responsibility."

responsibility with the view of Watson and others about the relation between attributability and accountability. Providing such clarification is therefore an important task, one that it might seem should be carried out before any attempt is made to provide an account of thick blameworthiness. But, again for reasons that will emerge (take this as a second promissory note), I doubt that this is in fact the case, and so I will now turn directly to an extended consideration of the question of what it is that thick blame and thick blameworthiness consist in.

2.3.3 Thick blame (and praise) and the reactive attitudes

According to RAA2, the conditions necessary and sufficient for thick blameworthiness have to do with the fittingness of certain reactive attitudes. Whether we should accept this view therefore turns on just what a reactive attitude is supposed to be.

It is an unfortunate fact that, despite the great deal of attention that the reactive attitudes have received in the literature on moral responsibility since Strawson's introduction of them, this question, far from having been settled, has seldom even been addressed. Writers seem often simply to assume that we all know what a reactive attitude is, but that is a bad mistake.

Strawson himself never states explicitly just what he takes a reactive attitude to be. He rests content with giving a general characterization of them, accompanied by a few examples. He describes them as

> the non-detached attitudes and reactions of people directly involved in transactions with each other;...the attitudes and reactions of offended parties and beneficiaries;...such things as gratitude, resentment, forgiveness, love, and hurt feelings.[62]

This and ensuing passages warrant close attention.

Strawson's characterization of the reactive attitudes is both broad and narrow. It is broad in that it encompasses not only attitudes of the sort just mentioned (gratitude, resentment, etc.), but also certain activities and practices (such as quarreling with someone[63] or certain forms of punishment[64]), which are not themselves attitudes, although they are of course reactions, ones that typically incorporate certain attitudes. This distinction between attitudes, on the one hand, and activities and practices that incorporate them, on the other, indicates that, even in what I have called the thick sense of "blame" and "praise," we should draw a distinction between what may be called weak and strong ways of blaming and

---

[62] Strawson (1974), p. 4.   [63] Strawson (1974), p. 9.   [64] Strawson (1974), p. 19.

praising. For example, I might feel resentment (weak) without showing or acting on it (strong); I might feel gratitude (weak) without showing or acting on it (strong); and so on.[65] (Even here I suspect a disanalogy between "blame" and "praise." It seems clear that blame in what I have called the thick sense can be weak. Even if I keep my resentment of you to myself, never showing it, let alone acting on it, that doesn't alter the fact that I blame you. It is less clear that genuine praise can be private in this way. Perhaps only public displays of approbation, perhaps even only a proper subset of such displays, are properly called instances of praise.)

Strawson's characterization is broad in another way, too, in that it encompasses not only what might be called "directed" reactions (such as resentment and punishment) which are taken toward someone, but also "undirected" reactions (such as the hurt feelings that he mentions) which, in themselves, have no such object or target.

Strawson's characterization is also narrow, however, in that it encompasses only those "non-detached" reactions that presuppose that the person toward whom—or, in the case of undirected reactions, the person with respect to whom—one is reacting is "a member of the moral community,"[66] someone who is "not outside the reach of personal relationships."[67]

Insofar as Strawson's account is understood as an account of the reactions of *blaming* and *praising* in particular (which is how it is often treated, although that presumably is *not* all that Strawson himself intended it to be[68]), it seems to me that, rich and insightful though it undoubtedly is, it is nonetheless questionable in certain respects. First, it seems *too* narrow. As Watson remarks,[69] and as I will elaborate later, some of the reactions that Strawson has in mind (such as "acquiesc[ing] in that infliction of suffering on the offender which is an essential part of punishment,"[70] punishment of a sort that Strawson himself characterizes as reactive) would seem not to require regarding the person in question as a co-member of the moral community with whom one is engaged in a kind of conversation (to use Michael McKenna's term[71]). Second, Strawson's account also seems *too* broad. In the case of what I have called undirected reactions, one is certainly reacting *to* something (otherwise one could not be said to be reacting at all), something, such as an attitude or bit of behavior, that is in some way intimately tied to someone, so that it would therefore seem acceptable to say that one is reacting *with respect to* the person in question; nonetheless, even if the reaction reflects some kind of assessment of that person,

---

[65] Cf. Shoemaker (2011a), p. 617.   [66] Strawson (1974), p. 17.   [67] Strawson (1974), p. 12.
[68] Love is not a form of praise; nor is forgiveness a form of blame, although it may presuppose blame.
[69] Watson (1982), p. 6, n. 7.   [70] Strawson (1974), p. 22.   [71] McKenna (2012).

one is not reacting *toward* him or her, and one's reaction would therefore seem not to qualify as either blame or praise in the thick sense.

If, as is commonly said and as I myself suggested in §2.1.1, the negative aspect of moral responsibility consists in moral blameworthiness (and the positive aspect in moral praiseworthiness or creditworthiness), then the observations just made pose another challenge to RAA2. First, if there are forms of moral blame (and praise) that consist in something other than (or even just more than) the adoption of an attitude, then moral responsibility might involve something other than (or more than) the fittingness of attitudes. Second, if there are negative (and positive) reactive attitudes that do not count as forms of moral blame (or praise), then such attitudes might be fitting even in the absence of moral responsibility.

With respect to the first point, it is very important to note that, as the discussion in Chapter 9 will make clear, the terms "praise" and "blame" are umbrella terms that cover a wide variety of reactions to people's behavior, even when they are restricted to reactions that incorporate *moral* appraisal in particular.[72] This fact is often overlooked, although Strawson himself acknowledges it, at least implicitly. For example, even if the attitudes of resentment and indignation have something in common and, partly in virtue of this fact, are both forms of blame, they are nonetheless distinct. Once the diversity of blaming reactions is recognized, though, it becomes an open question whether "blame" should be said to refer to attitudes alone. Strawson indicates, indirectly, that the answer to this question is "No." As I mentioned, he concerns himself, not just with attitudes, but also with reactions that go beyond the adoption of some attitude and include engaging in some activity, such as the activity of punishment. And I think he is clearly right to do so. Questions of thick blameworthiness run the gamut from the fittingness of modest pique to that of high dudgeon, and from the fittingness of a mild reprimand to that of capital punishment. Depending on just what the behavior at issue is, some reactions along this gamut may be fitting while others are not.[73] (Some, such as capital punishment, may never be fitting.) Since this is so, it is a mistake, when inquiring into the conditions of thick blameworthiness, to

---

[72] In this respect, "praise" and "blame" function very much like the terms "favor" and "disfavor" as they are employed in the fitting-attitude analysis of value.

[73] Michael McKenna claims, in (2012), pp. 143 f., and (2019), pp. 266 f., that, although punishment presupposes blame, it's a mistake to think of punishment as a form of blame, for two reasons. First, while blame is indeed liable to harm the person blamed, the blamer need not intend to cause harm, whereas punishment essentially involves such an intention. Second, although punishment presupposes blame, they are distinct because they concern different stages of the "conversation" between the relevant parties. I grant the first point (regarding which see Zimmerman (2011), ch. 1), but that can be accommodated simply by observing that some forms of blame differ from others with respect to what they essentially involve. The second point seems to me dubious. Even if a "conversation" between two parties is sufficiently extensive so as to contain all the stages that McKenna has in mind, it seems clear that blame of the sort that McKenna has in mind—e.g., resentment or indignation—need not cease before punishment begins; on the contrary, as I have noted, punishment may well incorporate such an attitude. (I should perhaps add that punishment is a form of thick moral blame only when it includes thin moral blame. Just as blame can be non-moral, so too can punishment.)

confine one's attention to the fittingness of reactive *attitudes*. I will therefore talk, more generally, simply of the fittingness of *reactions*, by which I mean to include, not only attitudes of the sort at issue, but also activities and practices that can serve, at least in part, to give expression to these attitudes. Thus I propose that we put RAA2 aside in favor of this *Reaction Analysis* of thick moral responsibility:

> RA1: *P*'s being morally responsible for *X* consists in its being fitting for someone to direct some reaction toward *P* in respect of *X*.

RA1 seems extremely plausible. In characterizing *respons*ibility in terms of the fittingness or worthiness of some *response* (of a sort that I am calling a reaction), it is supported by considerations of etymology (compare admirability, desirability, reprehensibility, and so on) and thus aligns perfectly with understanding praiseworthiness and blameworthiness to be particular forms of responsibility.[74] But, of course, RA1 is acceptable *only if* the second point just raised has received satisfactory treatment. Unless and until the kind of reaction at issue has been identified, we cannot be sure that negative (and positive) responses that do not count as forms of moral blame (or praise) have been excluded. So the question remains: What *is* blame in the thick sense? Precisely *which* negative responses fall under its umbrella and which do not, and why? Resentment, for example, presumably qualifies,[75] whereas hurt feelings do not, but what accounts for this? Let us now take a look at some proposals.

2.3.4 Thick blame as essentially emotional

According to Strawson and many others, blaming someone essentially involves having an emotion of some kind toward that person.[76] (They have what I call thick blame in mind, even if they don't call it that.) Resentment and indignation, for example, are emotions, and behavior that seeks to give expression to these emotions (shunning someone's company, say, or punishing someone) is to that extent emotional behavior. But, although it may be that thick blame is typically

---

[74] I should note, however, that it's not clear how much weight such etymological considerations can bear. It is difficult to see how the construal of responsibility as the worthiness of some response could be correctly applied to prospective responsibility or causal responsibility.

[75] Actually, I would urge caution here. Although resentment can of course be directed at people, it needn't be. We can resent facts, but I don't think we can blame facts. Suppose, for example, that I resent the fact that you have deceived me. Must it then be that I resent *you* for having deceived me? Must it be that I *blame* you for having deceived me? Could I not have forgiven you but still resent the fact? Fans of resentment as a paradigm of blame should address these questions.

[76] Strawson (1974), pp. 5 ff. Cf. Wallace (1994), p. 75, and (2011); Wolf (2011); Graham (2014); Menges (2017).

emotional, there is good reason to deny that it is essentially so. George Sher gives the following examples:

> [Someone] might view it as emotionally extravagant to allow himself to be bothered by each of the countless individuals whom he blames for violating moral norms; might believe it is pointless to remain angry at a dead person whom he still blames for a past misdeed; or might consider it unloving to want his errant daughter to undergo any suffering at all.[77]

Julia Driver offers another kind of example in support of the claim that blame need not be emotional:

> Caroline has been suffering from clinical depression. In her case, the depression is marked by severe lack of affect. She does not derive pleasure from her experiences, and does not feel much in the way of emotion at all, with the exception of the negative affect associated with her condition. She finds out that her accountant has stolen from her bank account. She doesn't feel angry, but she judges both that her accountant has transgressed and that anger on her part would be entirely appropriate (she may even wish that she could feel angry).[78]

Commenting on this example, Driver says: "This seems like a case of blaming the accountant, even though there is no actual emotion felt on the part of the blamer."[79]

In response to these purported counterexamples to the claim that blame is essentially emotional, one might say that they only concern blame in the thin rather than the thick sense. But, although this response invokes a distinction that Sher himself does not acknowledge, he nonetheless shows why it should be rejected. Unlike Caroline in Driver's example, who judges that anger on her part would be appropriate, the person in Sher's examples expressly repudiates this idea. Sher says of these examples:

> Because each belief implies that anger would be an inappropriate response to the person blamed, each seems flatly inconsistent with the belief that anger at him would be appropriate. Thus, just as we can find counterexamples to the claim that blame always involves a negative emotional response to the person blamed, so too we can find counterexamples to the claim that every instance of affectless blame is one in which the blamer at least believes that a negative emotional response to the person blamed would be appropriate.[80]

---

[77] Sher (2006), p. 91.   [78] Driver (2015), pp. 169 f.   [79] Driver (2015), p. 170.
[80] Sher (2006), p. 91.

This is a very important observation. We are seeking an informative general account of what the blame in thick blameworthiness consists in. Even if there is a kind of blame that is essentially emotional, as long as there are coherent judgments (as surely there are) of the form that P is thickly blameworthy for X—that is, that it is fitting to direct some pertinent negative reaction toward P in respect of X—that do not consist in judgments that it is, in particular, fitting to react with some negative emotion toward P in respect of X, then the claim that the blame in thick blameworthiness is essentially emotional must be rejected.

2.3.5 Thick blame as essentially involving certain dispositions

Sher himself offers a different account of blame, which goes as follows:

> To blame someone...is to have certain affective and behavioral dispositions, each of which can be traced to the combination of a belief that that person has acted badly or has a bad character and a desire that this not be the case.[81]

But, as Angela Smith has argued, this account is problematic, too. Smith asks us to imagine a mother who believes that her son has acted badly and desires that he not have done so, this combination of belief and desire giving rise to the mother's not only being disposed to react, but indeed reacting, with profound pity. Pity is not a form of blame; hence, Smith says, Sher's account does not succeed in providing a sufficient condition for blame. Nor, she says, does it provide a necessary condition, since it is possible to blame someone without desiring that that person have acted differently; for blaming someone, while no doubt requiring disapproval of his or her behavior, is compatible with being glad that this behavior took place.[82] I think that she is right on the first count, and perhaps also on the second.[83]

2.3.6 Thick blame as essentially calling for an answer

Smith in turn offers a quite different account of blame, one that rests in part on the thesis that moral responsibility is essentially interpersonal—yet another theme (along with quality of will and the reactive attitudes) made popular by Strawson. In his discussion, Strawson holds that the reactive attitudes involve seeing the person to whom they are directed "as a morally responsible agent, as a term of

---

[81] Sher (2006), p. 115. [82] A. M. Smith (2013), p. 35.
[83] Regarding the second: McKenna claims with some plausibility that disapproval of someone's behavior entails desiring that that behavior not occur (or have occurred), even though one might also desire that it occur (or have occurred). See McKenna (2012), p. 23, n. 22.

moral relationships, as a member of the moral community,"[84] and he appears to regard these expressions as synonymous.

This theme of moral responsibility as essentially involving a moral community has been echoed by many philosophers, including Scanlon, Watson, McKenna, and Smith herself, along with R. Jay Wallace, David Shoemaker, Derk Pereboom, and others.[85] Some of these philosophers (e.g., Wallace and McKenna) are, as it might be put, strongly Strawsonian, in that they draw a tight connection between the moral community and the reactive attitudes in particular, while others distance themselves to some extent from this idea, but they all emphasize the interpersonal nature of responsibility.

Consider, for example, Scanlon's well-known account of blame and blameworthiness:

> [T]o claim that a person is *blameworthy* for an action is to claim that the action shows something about the agent's attitudes toward others that impairs the relations that others can have with him or her... To *blame* a person is to judge him or her to be blameworthy and to take your relationship with him or her to be modified in a way that this judgment of impaired relations holds to be appropriate.[86]

Scanlon advocates conceiving of responsibility as what has come to be called *answerability*, a view that is once again shared by several others, including Watson, Darwall, and Smith.[87] Smith has developed and defended this view perhaps more than anyone else. Here is a representative statement of it from one of her works:

> To say that an agent is morally responsible for something... is to say that that thing reflects her rational judgment in a way that makes it appropriate, in principle, to ask her to defend or justify it.[88]

One feature of the responsibility-as-answerability approach, not in fact emphasized by Smith but stressed by others, is that it construes responsibility as a *triadic* relationship: an individual is answerable *to* others *for* something.[89] Stressing this feature serves to highlight the interpersonal nature of moral responsibility, on this

---

[84] Strawson (1974), p. 17.
[85] See Wallace (1994); Scanlon (1998) and (2008); Watson (2004); A. M. Smith (2005), (2008), (2012), (2013), and (2015); Darwall (2006); Shoemaker (2007), (2011a), and (2015b); Pereboom (2013).
[86] Scanlon (2008), pp. 128 f. See also Scanlon (2013).
[87] See Scanlon (1998), p. 272, and (2008), p. 193; Watson (2004), part III; Darwall (2006), pp. 82 f.; A. M. Smith (2005), (2008), (2012), (2015).
[88] A. M. Smith (2008), p. 369.
[89] See, e.g., Watson (2004), pp. 7 and 274; Darwall (2006), pp. 68 f.

conception. Accordingly, I suggest the following formulation of the *Answerability Analysis* of responsibility:

> AA: P's being morally responsible to Q for X consists in its being fitting for Q to call on P to answer for (i.e., to defend or justify) X.

We may think of AA as a particular version of RA1, inasmuch as calling on P to answer for X is one particular reaction among others that Q might direct toward P in respect of X. As Smith notes, if P does respond to Q's demand for P to defend or justify X, such a response "is the key to opening the door to the further moral responses that *may* (depending on the details of the case) appropriately follow upon the answer she gives."[90] On this view, then, responsibility is seen as involving a kind of *conversation* between members of a moral community, an aspect of responsibility emphasized not only by Smith but also by Darwall and, especially and in great detail, by McKenna.[91]

One immediate problem with AA is that there may be no person Q for whom it is in fact fitting to call on P to answer for X. It may be, for example, that no one knows the pertinent facts about P's relation to X, or that no one has the requisite moral standing or authority to direct the pertinent response (or set of responses) toward P in respect of X, and so on.

Smith in particular has addressed this problem (and others are aware of it[92]). It is for this reason that, in the passage just cited, she claims, not that it is *in fact* appropriate for someone Q to respond to P in the relevant way, but that it is *in principle* appropriate for someone Q so to respond. This is surely a sensible move to make, however exactly the qualifier "in principle" is supposed to be understood. (This is an issue to which I will shortly return.) Notice that AA would otherwise admit the possibility of a very peculiar and surely unacceptable form of moral luck, in that one could luckily escape being blameworthy just because no one was in fact in a position to engage in the pertinent blame. Notice, also, that it is therefore a move that *any* version of RA1 must make.

Another problem with AA, one shared by Scanlon's particular impaired-relations account of blame,[93] is that it seems unduly parochial. It appears to ignore responsibility for wrongdoing that does not involve other persons. Think of mistreating animals or destroying the environment. What does such behavior have to do with other members of a moral community?

---

[90] A. M. Smith (2015), p. 103. Why "defend *or* justify"? It might be that, although P cannot justify X, P can furnish an adequate excuse for X. Or it might be, of course, that P can neither defend nor justify X. P's success, or lack thereof, in answering for X will dictate the nature of Q's counter-response to P.
[91] See Darwall (2006), pp. 75 ff.; McKenna (2012), *passim*.
[92] See, e.g., Scanlon (2008), pp. 175 ff.
[93] An account that Smith herself explicitly endorses in A. M. Smith (2013), p. 43.

One response is to say that AA is not supposed to account for responsibility for such wrongdoing; it is supposed only to concern wrongs done to other persons. At times, Scanlon seems to suggest this response, as does Darwall,[94] but I have to say that it seems to me quite ill advised, since it belies the claim, to which their allegiance to AA commits them, that moral responsibility is *essentially* interpersonal.

A second response, one that is in keeping with AA, is to say that the obligation that we have not to mistreat animals or destroy the environment is one that we owe to other members of our moral community. Both Scanlon and Darwall suggest this response too,[95] but it faces difficulties. It's clear that I have a moral obligation not to mistreat my dog or destroy the local habitat, but is it so clear that I owe it to anyone else not to do these things? If I do, then of course these examples don't impugn AA after all. But if I don't, the view is in trouble. In the case of my dog, I think I probably do owe it *to him* not to mistreat him, but I'm not sure that that provides any support for the view. Even if the notion of a moral community is understood expansively, so as to include animals such as my dog, the fact remains that my dog cannot call on me to answer for my mistreating him. Maybe a proxy for my dog could do so, however, in which case the view might still be thought to apply to such a case. But even if so, this kind of account cannot be applied to destruction of the environment. Although I have an obligation not to destroy the local habitat, I don't owe it to the habitat not to destroy it, and it makes no sense at all to think of the habitat as a member of any moral community.[96]

Still another problem with AA is that it seems more suited to playing a role in an account of blameworthiness in particular than in an account of moral responsibility in general. As I noted above, such responsibility can on occasion take the form of praiseworthiness (or of indifference-worthiness), and, whereas it is often appropriate to call on someone to answer for some wrongful act, it is rarely, if ever, appropriate to call on someone to answer for doing what was right. Smith is aware of this problem. At one point she says this:

> This feature of negative moral appraisal [viz., calling upon an agent to answer for something] is more difficult to extend to its positive analogue, but I think we can say something like the following: positive moral appraisal, though it does not itself address a demand to its target, by its nature involves an acknowledgment

---

[94] See Scanlon (1998), pp. 178 ff. and (2008), p. 124; Darwall (2006), p. 28.
[95] See Scanlon (2008), p. 166; Darwall (2006), pp. 28 f.
[96] In making this claim, I am presupposing that we can have moral obligations *regarding* certain entities (including people) that we don't owe *to* these things, and hence that these things don't have a moral *right* to the fulfillment of the obligations, even though it would of course be morally *wrong* not to fulfill them. Cf. Feinberg (1980), pp. 143 ff. and 161 ff. (although Feinberg's emphasis tends to be on legal, rather than moral, rights and obligations).

that the agent has exceeded in some way the legitimate moral demands that apply to her.[97]

However, this response to the problem strikes me as inadequate. Smith appears to conflate two kinds of demand. First, there are the demands that *morality* makes of an agent, P. These consist in the moral obligations or duties that P has to behave in certain ways. (To call these demands is to speak metaphorically. Morality is not literally capable of demanding anything; only individual persons can do that.) Then there is the demand that *another person*, Q, makes of P when Q calls upon P to answer for having done something that apparently violated some obligation. (To call this a demand is to speak literally.) It is the latter kind of demand that is at issue in AA. That P has gone beyond what morality demands of her does not render it appropriate to demand that she answer for her behavior.

A final problem with AA is that, even if its application is restricted to blameworthiness, the fit is still awkward. If we substitute "blameworthy" for "responsible" in the statement of AA, we end up with the nonsensical phrase "P is blameworthy to Q for X." This is an indication that the connection between responsibility as understood in AA and responsibility understood as consisting in either praiseworthiness or blameworthiness (or indifference-worthiness) is indirect at best.

The diagnosis is not hard to come by. The phrase "P is responsible to Q for X" is intelligible only when the form of responsibility at issue is *prospective*; it implies that P owes it to Q to do something in respect of X. And, of course, this is precisely what AA maintains; it maintains that P owes it to Q to answer for X. But *why* does P have this prospective responsibility (if, indeed, P does have it)? The answer, I suggest, is that P owes it to Q to answer for X at least in part because P is a morally responsible agent (period), in the sense of being capable of being *retrospectively* morally responsible (more particularly, blameworthy) for X. As I see it, therefore, AA doesn't *provide* an account of retrospective moral responsibility; rather, it *presupposes* some such account.[98]

2.3.7 Thick blame as essentially conversational

One need not subscribe to AA itself, according to which responsibility just *is* answerability, in order to hold the view that responsibility *entails* answerability.

---

[97] A. M. Smith (2008), p. 381, n. 15.
[98] This presupposition may fail in certain cases of strict liability in which, in virtue of having performed some act, one person owes another something (maybe only an explanation; possibly some form of compensation), even though the former was not at fault, and is known not to have been at fault, in doing what he or she did. But such cases, if possible, serve only to underscore the distinction between retrospective responsibility and the kind of prospective responsibility in question.

McKenna's *conversational theory* of responsibility has this feature (although he doesn't couch it in terms of "answerability"). According to his view, one's being (retrospectively, morally) responsible for something consists in one's behaving in such a way that one initiates a kind of conversation with other members of the moral community, in that one's behavior renders one open to being addressed by these other members (this is the stage that corresponds to being called upon to answer for one's conduct), to which one's responding by giving an account of oneself constitutes the next stage in this conversation-like interaction (an interaction that might continue indefinitely through yet further stages).[99]

Since the conversational theory doesn't claim that responsibility just is answerability, it doesn't face the last objection that I raised against AA. But, like AA, it does seem to be open to the charge that it is unduly parochial, in that it is difficult to see how it can adequately account for responsibility for the mistreatment of animals and the environment.[100] Moreover, insofar as the theory construes blame in terms of a practice that involves an *exchange* between persons, it faces a new objection, namely, that it cannot account for blame that is purely *private*, as when one keeps one's resentment to oneself (whether deliberately or simply because one lacks the opportunity to vent one's resentment to the person at whom it is directed). This is an objection that has been pressed forcefully by Julia Driver and Manuel Vargas.[101]

McKenna is keenly aware of this objection. His response is that, although private blame is indeed possible, it is in effect a degenerate form of public blame. More particularly, his claim is that Q's privately blaming P for X is to be understood in terms of how Q would publicly blame P for X, were P present and in a position to respond appropriately to Q. Furthermore, Q's privately blaming P for X is fitting just in case it would be fitting for Q to blame P publicly, were P present and in a position to respond appropriately to Q.[102] But McKenna gives no reason (one that is independent of a prior commitment to the conversational theory) why we *should* construe private blame(worthiness) as a degenerate form of public blame(worthiness). Moreover, his particular proposal regarding how to do so seems flawed, and it is hard to see how any modification of it could prove satisfactory. Vargas puts the point very nicely. I can do no better than to quote him at length:

Consider the following two cases:

> DEAD: Joan and Alan are atheists. Alan commits suicide and Joan is stunned and angry...

---

[99] McKenna (2012), pp. 88 ff. Cf. also Mason (2019), ch. 5.
[100] McKenna is aware of the charge and responds to it in McKenna (2016), p. 248. I fail to see how his response preserves the thesis that moral responsibility is essentially interpersonal, however.
[101] Driver (2016); Vargas (2016).   [102] McKenna (2012), pp. 176 ff., and (2016), pp. 252 f.

GONE: Rogelio and Marion agree to meet for a musical performance, but arrive by separate transport. Marion is late and Rogelio is early to the performance. While waiting for the performance to start, and Marion to arrive, Rogelio begins to get agitated that Marion is not already there.

Let us suppose that Joan blames Alan for committing suicide, and that Rogelio blames Marion for not being there with him while he waits for the performance to start.

As innocuous as these judgments may seem, it is unclear how they can be accommodated on the conversational theory... According to the conversational theory, we understand the aptness of blame in terms of "what would be fitting or reasonable ways to manifest blame as a means of engaging the one who is blamed, were she present"... In DEAD and GONE, however, were the blamed person present in either case, the blaming agent would *not* blame—or, at least, such blaming would be inapt. Were Alan present, Joan would have no reason to blame him; were Marion present, Rogelio's blaming her would make no sense.

To be sure, we can generate cases where an agent's absence isn't a problem (e.g., Marion is blamed for being *late* as opposed to *not present*). But that is just to look in a different direction, away from the present difficulty. The root of the problem is that it appears that we will always be able to construct cases in which the antecedent of the counterfactual blocks the basis for blame... In cases where an agent's absence is the reason for blame, a simple counterfactual story about the suitability of blame—were the blamed agent present—is doomed to failure.[103]

McKenna responds to Vargas as follows:

As for the suicide case, it is not too hard to imagine that even for one who has no belief in survival beyond bodily destruction... she could still imagine—*per impossible* [sic]—confronting her friend who committed suicide and expressing her grief and anger. As for the case of Rogelio, it is not much of a departure to say of him that his *now* blaming Marion in her absence for being late *now* is to be understood in part in terms of how he would respond to her at some *later* time were she then present.[104]

But, again, no (independent) reason has been given for resorting to such *recherché* counterfactuals. Moreover, even if the counterfactual that McKenna suggests in the case of Rogelio does the job he requires of it, it is not at all clear that the one he suggests in the suicide case does so. When Joan blames Alan for committing suicide, she is presumably blaming him not simply for rendering himself not

[103] Vargas (2016), p. 232.   [104] McKenna (2016), p. 258.

present to her, but for rendering himself *permanently* not present to her. This is the difference between being gone and being dead. The antecedent of the suggested counterfactual, then, doesn't simply involve confronting someone later who is not present now; it involves confronting someone who is never present. This is a tall order. I am not claiming that counterfactuals with impossible antecedents should never be accepted—their truth conditions are notoriously controversial—but invoking them in order to salvage one's theory of blame and blameworthiness is a high price to pay.

If there were no better way to handle the issue of private blame(worthiness), we might have to resign ourselves to paying this price, but it seems clear to me that there is a better and more natural way to proceed here, one that relies on the distinction, noted earlier, between the weak and strong ways of thickly blaming someone. Let me illustrate this point by reference to resentment in particular. To resent someone in the weak way is simply to have or feel a certain emotion toward that person. To resent someone in the strong way is in some way to give expression to this emotion. These are distinct phenomena with their own distinct fittingness conditions; it may be fitting to have or feel a certain emotion and yet not fitting to give expression to it. Public resentment consists in public expression of one's resentment. Private resentment consists in either an expression of one's resentment in private (e.g., by throwing a dart, when all alone, at a target on which a picture of the person being blamed is pinned) or no expression of it at all.

2.3.8 Thick blame as essentially involving a moral community

It must be acknowledged, however, that, even if the foregoing considerations show both AA and the conversational theory in particular to be problematic, they don't directly threaten the general idea that one's being morally responsible for something essentially involves other members of some moral community. For even if non-human animals and the environment are not themselves members of any moral community, it could still be appropriate for other members of a (or the, or my) moral community to reproach me for mistreating them (or to praise me for treating them well). But other considerations do pose problems for this general idea, which I will call the *actual-moral-community approach*.

To begin with, there is the question whether there need be someone Q distinct from P for whom it is fitting (even in principle) to direct some reaction toward P in respect of X. In his discussion of the reactive attitudes, Strawson explicitly acknowledges that some such attitudes are "self-reactive" (rather than "other-reactive"), citing remorse as an example.[105] This seems quite right, and it is a point

---

[105] Strawson (1974), p. 15.

that has been echoed by others,[106] yet it would seem to put the idea that moral responsibility is essentially *inter*personal into question.

Jonathan Bennett has this to say on the matter:

> A self-reactive attitude does involve an important 'interpersonal' relation: remorse, for instance, can be represented as a confrontation—with an accusing glare on one side and downcast eyes on the other—between one's present self and some past self.[107]

Darwall approves of this passage,[108] but I find it forced: a "community" of one, composed of temporal slices of oneself! In any case, if all it takes is one person to make a moral community, then of course the claim that responsibility essentially involves such a community is true, but only trivially so.[109]

A more promising reply, I would think, is simply this. Responsibility's being essentially interpersonal doesn't preclude its also being essentially intrapersonal. It is therefore possible that, if ever some self-reactive attitude is fitting, then so too is some other-reactive attitude. True, only P can feel genuine remorse for what P has done, but it may be perfectly fitting for someone else, Q, to direct some related attitude toward P in light of what P has done.

Perhaps so, but we still need a reason to think that it *must* be the case that there be such another person, Q, for whom it is fitting to react negatively to P. One reason to think otherwise stems from considerations having to do with the *time* at which a blameworthy person is blameworthy.

Suppose that Martha committed murder on Monday in such a way that we would not hesitate to say that she was to blame for what she did. (She was in control of her actions, and her quality of will was defective in whatever way is required.) But suppose that on Tuesday Martha took leave of the moral community: she lapsed into insanity, or into a coma, or underwent some other kind of transformation that provided her with some kind of exemption from moral responsibility. (I will discuss exemptions further in §2.5.5.) Would it be fitting on Wednesday for Ralph (or anyone else) to direct some negative reaction toward Martha—that of reprimanding her severely, say—in light of her behavior on Monday? One answer is "Yes." But this is a troubling answer, since the target—or, rather, the nature of the target—of Ralph's attitude has changed drastically.[110] The other answer is "No." But then what does the actual-moral-community approach imply? Should we infer that, since it is not fitting for Ralph to reprimand Martha for the murder, Martha is not responsible for it after all? This is troubling,

---

[106] See, e.g., Watson (2004), p. 274; Scanlon (2008), pp. 154 f.; Duggan (2018).
[107] Bennett (1980), p. 44.   [108] Darwall (2006), p. 74.
[109] "Of course" is perhaps too strong. Perhaps one's temporal slices will fail to be interrelated in the appropriate way (whatever exactly that may be) to form a genuine community (whatever exactly *that* may be).
[110] Cf. Khoury and Matheson (2018).

too, since it introduces another very peculiar form of moral luck and, besides, seems at odds with the facts about Martha's control and quality of will on Monday; moreover, it overlooks the apparent fact that, had Ralph reacted sooner and reprimanded Martha for the murder prior to her lapse, his reaction would have been perfectly appropriate.

There may seem to be an obvious solution to this problem, and that is to take care to specify the times involved. Just as it would have been fitting for Ralph to reprimand Martha for her behavior at any time between the murder and the lapse, so too we can and should say that Martha was responsible for the murder during that same period of time, but not afterwards. This is a tempting response, but I don't think it solves the problem. For what if Martha's lapse had occurred *immediately* after her commission of the murder? There would have been no time for Ralph to adopt an appropriate reaction, in which case the actual-moral-community approach appears to imply that there was no time at which Martha was responsible for her behavior. But that contradicts the initial hypothesis that the manner in which Martha engaged in her behavior sufficed for her incurring responsibility for it.

Perhaps the best that can be said here on behalf of the actual-moral-community approach is this: Martha's behavior (and the control and quality of will associated with it) was such that it was in principle fitting for another member of her moral community to reprimand her immediately. That no one could in fact have reacted so quickly doesn't undermine this fact.[111]

But that reply doesn't get to the heart of the problem. What if Martha committed mass murder on a global scale, and there was no one left to reprimand her? Would she then have luckily escaped responsibility for her behavior after all? Surely not. That would be a grotesque conclusion to draw, and yet the actual-moral-community approach seems to mandate it. For if no person exists (other than Martha; but perhaps she committed suicide at the same time as committing mass murder), then there is and was no one for whom it is or was fitting, even in principle, to reprimand Martha.[112]

McKenna has discussed a similar case, one modeled on Daniel Defoe's *Robinson Crusoe*. He imagines Robinson living on a desert island, a member of no community, moral or otherwise, mercilessly beating his dog. Surely Robinson is blameworthy for his behavior; yet there is no one to blame him. McKenna replies that, in Defoe's story, Robinson was an Englishman who, though a castaway, "carried with him in his head, so to speak, the moral community of his earlier life... Were we to encounter him, there is no reason to think that we

---

[111] Cf. McKenna (2016), pp. 255 f.
[112] This observation poses a challenge not only to the view that negative moral responsibility consists in its being fitting for others to engage in blaming the agent but also to the view that such responsibility consists in its being fitting for the agent to feel guilty. Cf. Duggan (2018).

would not have (at least *pro tanto*) reason to blame him."[113] Maybe so, but this does not suffice as a defense of the actual-moral-community approach. Surely, Robinson's blameworthiness, like Martha's, is not contingent on our or anyone else's *actually* being in a position to blame him for what he has done. Nor is Robinson's blameworthiness contingent on his *having been* a member of some actual moral community, for it is conceivable that he developed the relevant moral capacities in total isolation from other moral agents. On the contrary, that a person P, whether isolated like Martha and Robinson or, like you and me, a member of some community, is responsible for something X has to do, not with its being fitting, whether in fact or in principle, for some other actual person Q to direct some reaction toward P in respect of X. It has rather to do with P's being *worthy* of such a reaction, and whether P is so worthy has to do, in turn, *only with* P and not with anyone else who happens to exist. Of course, someone else must in fact exist if P is in fact to receive the reaction he or she deserves (unless the reaction in question involves a self-reactive attitude or some other kind of self-directed reaction), but P's responsibility does not turn on his or her actually receiving it. The actual-moral-community approach is therefore mistaken.

It might be replied that human beings are *essentially* communal animals, and hence that it cannot after all be the case that anyone is responsible for anything in the absence of an actual community.[114] But even if it is essential to animals, of the sort with which we are acquainted, that they are born of other animals, it doesn't follow that it is essential to them that they are part of some *community*, let alone part of some *moral* community. But still, you might ask, could anyone be a *morally responsible agent* in the absence of such a community? If this is a question about what is *conceptually* possible (which it is; we're concerned with the *concepts* of moral responsibility in general and blameworthiness in particular), the answer is "Yes." As I just noted, it is conceivable that Robinson developed the relevant moral capacities in total isolation from others. This isn't to say, of course, that it is easy to imagine the details of his doing so. Those human beings we know who have these capacities presumably all relied on the help of role models to develop them, and it's hard to envisage an alternative way of attaining moral competence, but it doesn't follow from this fact that humans are essentially incapable of developing the relevant capacities in isolation from other humans.[115] But even if it should turn out for some reason that *humans* are indeed essentially incapable of doing this, it doesn't follow that it is conceptually impossible that some *person* do so. There is no reason to hold that only humans and other such animals can be conceived of as being persons with the capacity to be morally responsible for their

---

[113] McKenna (2012), p. 108.   [114] See De Mesel (2017), §3.
[115] Some recent research—e.g., Sloane et al. (2012); Smetana et al. (2013); Wynn and Bloom (2013)—indicates that human beings may have an innate moral sense, which in turn suggests, to me at least, that they may be capable of developing the relevant capacities in isolation from other people, at least to some extent.

behavior. There is a strong philosophical tradition to the contrary (consider Kant's moral theory[116]), and, whether it is correct or not, it is perfectly coherent.

In a final effort to defend the approach presently under consideration, it might be claimed that I have misrepresented the view of those who advocate understanding moral responsibility in terms of a moral community. I have interpreted them as insisting that it is inconceivable that anyone in fact be morally responsible for anything in the absence of an actual community of moral agents, but it might be said that all that they have intended is that the concept of moral responsibility cannot be understood without recourse to the *concept* of a moral community. That community need not *actually* exist.

One way to spell out this idea, which I will call the *hypothetical-moral-community approach*, is as follows:

RA2: *P*'s being morally responsible for *X* consists in its being the case that, if there were a person *Q* distinct from *P* who satisfied certain conditions *C*, it would be fitting for *Q* to direct some reaction toward *P* in respect of *X*.

I will leave it up to the advocate of the hypothetical-moral-community approach to specify what *C* would or might involve, although presumably *Q*'s being a member of the same moral community as *P* would have to be included in *C*.

For all that I have said so far, RA2 might be correct. My chief objection to RA2 is not that it is mistaken but only that it is highly misleading to say that moral responsibility essentially involves a moral community if all that is meant by that is that RA2 (or something close to it) is true. To say that moral responsibility essentially involves a moral community suggests very strongly that no one can be morally responsible for anything in the absence of an *actual* moral community, and it seems clear that this is what Strawson and others have typically had in mind when invoking the idea of a moral community.[117] Consider Scanlon: barring complications having to do with the dead or with fictitious characters, you cannot have relations, impaired or otherwise, with someone who doesn't exist. Consider Smith: you cannot be called upon to answer for your behavior by someone who doesn't exist. Consider McKenna: you cannot have a conversation, or a conversation-like interaction, with someone who doesn't exist. In general, it is highly misleading to declare moral responsibility "*essentially* interpersonal,"[118] if it is conceptually possible, as I have argued, that someone be morally responsible for his or her behavior even if no other person exists or has ever existed.

---

[116] See Kant (1964), p. 96 (B 65).
[117] Typically, but not necessarily. Cf. Darwall (2010), p. 146, n. 36.
[118] McKenna (2012), p. 110.

2.3.9 A conceptual circle

I want to stress that, the foregoing objections notwithstanding, I find the work of Strawson, Scanlon, and their followers to be in many ways interesting and enlightening. Their portrayals of the blaming practices in which we actually engage are often subtle and insightful. But even if what they have described is *typical* of blame, or even *paradigmatic* of blame (whatever that might mean, exactly; I am uneasy with the term), as long as it is not *essential* to blame, we are still left without an account of what the blame in thick blameworthiness consists in.

Given the wide variety of reactions, whether emotional or not, whether public or not, that seem to qualify as instances of thick blame, it may seem a fool's errand to seek some common feature that unites them all. Perhaps we should rest content with some family-resemblance account of blame. But let's not throw in the towel just yet. Here's an idea. Since it is with *moral* blameworthiness that we are concerned, we should limit our search for what counts as a "reaction" in the relevant sense to those responses that are morally tinged. Perhaps a unifying account of the reactions that qualify as blame in the thick sense can be formulated on this basis.

Wallace suggests the following analysis of thick blame: to blame someone thickly is to have some reactive emotion (such as resentment or indignation) toward him or her that comprises the judgment that that person has violated some moral obligation.[119] Although this proposal succeeds in identifying a feature of blame that renders it morally tinged (that feature of course being the judgment that some *moral* obligation has been violated), it seems to me nonetheless unacceptable. First, a relatively minor point: for reasons given earlier, it seems a mistake to say that blame is essentially emotional. Second, a far more important point: the proposal doesn't capture precisely the judgment that inheres in the relevant emotion. The reason is straightforward: it is possible to violate a moral obligation and yet have an excuse for doing so. Thus, when anyone who appreciates this fact engages in blaming someone, that person's blame will not involve only the judgment that the person blamed has violated some moral obligation, even if that is part of the relevant judgment.[120]

There is an obvious alternative candidate: thin blameworthiness. As I noted earlier, to blame someone thickly is to react toward that person in a way that incorporates a negative assessment of that person. For the reason just noted, that assessment cannot be a (merely) deontic one. On the contrary, the metaphorical ledger that such assessments concern is a hypological one. Given this fact, and also

---

[119] This account is extracted from Wallace (1994), pp. 51 and 63. I believe it accurately reflects his position.
[120] Cf. Rosen (2015), pp. 75 ff. Cf. also Graham (2014), p. 402—but contrast p. 407.

the fact that thick blame need not be emotional, the following amendment to Wallace's account suggests itself: to blame someone thickly is to direct some response toward him or her that comprises the judgment that that person is worthy of thin blame. This proposal fits nicely with the view mentioned earlier that thin blameworthiness suffices for thick blameworthiness, that is, that the correctness of the judgment in which thin blame consists suffices to render the person so judged worthy of some response that gives expression to that judgment. I wish to make two points about this proposal.

First, I think it is a mistake to claim that blaming someone thickly necessarily involves a *judgment* that the person blamed has failed to measure up to some standard. (This point of course also applies to the account that I have attributed to Wallace.) It sometimes happens that we blame people even when we recognize that we shouldn't. For example, I might harbor resentment toward someone, even though I know that my resentment is misplaced.[121] Such recalcitrant emotions are common. For example, Gertrude might feel survivor's guilt, in part because she cannot shake the sense that she has done wrong, all the while recognizing that she has in fact done nothing wrong and that her guilt is therefore misplaced. (This phenomenon isn't restricted to emotions. Optical illusions often persist even when one knows them to be illusory.[122]) We should therefore amend the proposal once again: to blame someone thickly is to direct some response toward him or her that comprises the representation of that person as worthy of thin blame.

The second point is far less easily handled. I said earlier that, unless the question of just what the standard is, to which someone who is worthy of thin blame has failed to measure up, has been answered, we have not been given an informative account of what judgments, or representations, of such blameworthiness amount to. We must now seek an answer to that question, since otherwise the account of thick blame(worthiness) presently under consideration cannot itself be assessed.

One answer that I find tempting is this: the negative assessment, in which judgments (or representations) of thin blameworthiness consist, is that the person being assessed is *thickly blameworthy*. *This* is the assessment that thick blame incorporates. I find this answer tempting because, as Rosen notes, it is "thoroughly plausible as a matter of phenomenology."[123] When applied to particular forms of blame, it implies, for example, that one cannot feel resentment or indignation toward someone without representing that person as meriting *that very reaction*. This is precisely what distinguishes such a reaction from mere

---

[121] Cf. Graham (2014), p. 393; Rosen (2015), pp. 71 f.; Carlsson (2017), p. 102, n. 19.
[122] Cf. Roberts (1988).
[123] Rosen (2015), p. 80. (Rosen doesn't employ the terms "thin blame(worthiness)" and "thick blame(worthiness)," however.) Cf. Pereboom (2014), p. 128; Nelkin (2016a), p. 183.

anger, which need involve no such representation and need not, more generally, be morally tinged.

But of course this answer, even if tempting, also comes at a high price: it is *circular*. Let me spell out this point in some detail. The account of thin blame(worthiness) that I proposed earlier can now be put more formally as follows:

(1) Q's blaming P thinly for X consists in Q's judging P to have a debit in his or her hypological ledger—that is, as having failed to measure up to some relevant hypological standard—in respect of X;

(2) P's being thinly blameworthy for X consists in its being correct to blame P thinly for X.

The account of thick blame(worthiness) presently under consideration is this:

(3) Q's blaming P thickly for X consists in Q's directing some negative response toward P in respect of X, a response that comprises the representation of P as being thinly blameworthy for X;

(4) P's being thickly blameworthy for X consists in its being fitting for someone Q to blame P thickly for X.[124]

No circle yet, but one immediately appears if we add the following:

(5) P's having a debit in his or her hypological ledger in respect of X consists in P's being thickly blameworthy for X.

To see the circle clearly, start with proposition 4, then move to 3 to 2 to 1 to 5—and back to 4. This circle has two important implications. The first is that propositions 1–5 cannot be treated as analyses of the classic "decompositional" kind, since no concept can be decomposed in terms of itself. The second is that the suggestion mentioned earlier as to how it is that thick blameworthiness is grounded in thin blameworthiness must be rejected.

With respect to this second point, return to the example of the lady in the elevator. I said that it seems correct to say that your resenting her for stepping on your foot, given that she did so freely and deliberately and with no provocation from you, is justified *because* she has no excuse for her behavior. The suggestion was that this claim be understood as follows: the lady's being thickly blameworthy (worthy, here, of your resentment in particular) for her behavior is grounded in her being thinly blameworthy for it (which in turn is grounded in her having

---

[124] For reasons given in §2.3.8, this account of thick blameworthiness should not be construed as implying that, for P to be blameworthy, there must *actually* be someone Q for whom it is or would be fitting to blame P.

engaged in it freely and deliberately and without provocation). But the circle undermines this account. Her being thickly blameworthy cannot be grounded in its being correct to judge her to be thickly blameworthy.[125] (Note that, given propositions 1–5, the claim that thin blameworthiness *suffices* for thick blameworthiness nonetheless remains true, as does the converse claim that the latter suffices for the former. This is because these propositions imply that P is thinly blameworthy if and only if it is correct to judge that there is a debit in his or her hypological ledger, and it is correct to judge that there is such a debit if and only if it is correct to judge that P is thickly blameworthy.)

Is there nonetheless a way to reconcile propositions 1–5 with the claim that your resentment is justified *because* the lady has no excuse? Perhaps it can be interpreted along the following lines. Excuses undermine blameworthiness. In principle, several distinct excuses are available—call them A–E. Thus, in order to determine whether the lady is blameworthy, you might want to go down this list to see if any of the potential excuses applies in her case. Does excuse A apply? You take a look and see that it does not. Does B? No. Does C? No. And so, too, for D and E. After you have completed your investigation, you reach the conclusion: the lady is to blame *because* none of A–E applies. This seems to me a correct conclusion to draw under the circumstances. The "because" doesn't signify grounding. It simply registers the fact that all the necessary conditions for blameworthiness have been satisfied. (Notice that something similar could be said in another version of the case of Bob and Carol. Suppose they're wondering, not whether the figure they're discussing is equidistant at all points from some fixed point, but whether it's a circle. Carol says that she doubts that it is, and so Bob undertakes an investigation. He fixes on what he takes to be the center of the circle and then measures its distance from each point on the circumference—well, not *each* point, since there are infinitely many of them—and establishes that each such point is the same distance from the center as all the other points on the circumference. He concludes by saying, "See, it's a circle because, as I've just shown you, each of the points on the circumference is equidistant from its center.")

---

[125] There is perhaps some similarity between my account of thick blameworthiness and David Shoemaker's in Shoemaker (2017), but just how his proposal is to be construed is unclear to me. On p. 508 he gives the following account of what he calls blameworthiness "in the realm of accountability," which I take to be what I have called thick blameworthiness:

> The blameworthy (in the realm of accountability) *just is* whatever merits anger (the angerworthy); that is, someone is blameworthy (and so accountable) for X if and only if, *and in virtue of the fact that*, she merits anger for X.

The italics are Shoemaker's. On pp. 494 f., he makes it clear that he focuses on anger simply for the sake of streamlining his discussion, acknowledging that there are several other "emotional responsibility responses." If he construes these responses as all falling under the umbrella of blame, then his account is circular, as mine is; for it amounts to saying that the blameworthy just is the blameworthy (surely an unexceptionable claim). Whether he intends this construal or not, there seems to me to be an unresolvable tension in his account, for he claims both that the blameworthy is identical to ("just is") the angerworthy while also apparently maintaining that the former is grounded in (obtains "in virtue of") the latter. As I understand these relations, they are incompatible with one another. Identity is symmetrical, whereas grounding is asymmetrical.

I leave it to you to decide whether what I have suggested does justice to the idea that your resentment is fitting because the lady has no excuse. Even if it does, the first point remains: propositions 1–5 cannot be treated as traditional analyses. Indeed, the circle is so small that one wonders whether it sheds any light at all on how to understand the blame in thick blameworthiness. Certainly, a non-circular account would be welcome, if one could be made to work.[126]

2.3.10 Breaking the circle

Gideon Rosen has offered an account according to which resentment does *not* necessarily represent the person at whom it is directed as worthy or deserving of *resentment*. He claims that what resentment requires instead is, among other things, representing the person in question as deserving of *suffering*. When plugged into the current framework (which is not a framework that Rosen invokes; he draws no distinction between thin and thick blame), Rosen's proposal amounts to replacing proposition 5 with the following:

(5*) *P*'s having a debit in his or her hypological ledger in respect of *X* consists in *P*'s deserving to suffer for having brought *X* about wrongly and with an objectionable quality of will.[127]

The conjunction of propositions 1–4 with proposition 5* does not form a circle and so does not raise either of the problems just discussed having to do with analysis and grounding. That is surely an attractive feature of Rosen's proposal.

But I'm afraid that the proposal is nonetheless unacceptable. Although the "retributive thought," as Rosen calls it, that *P* deserves to suffer for *X* is certainly *consistent* with resenting *P* for *X*, I doubt that it is *required*. Introspection on my own resentments doesn't reveal it, although introspection is of course fallible. But I think part of the reason why we should deny that the thought is required is that resentment can be *non*-moral, too. I might resent my doubles partner for failing to hold serve at a crucial juncture in the match, for example. In so doing, I find him deficient in a non-moral way, one that might correspond roughly to what Rosen has to say about wrongdoing and a poor quality of will. This certainly amounts to a kind of non-moral blame, but the thought that my partner deserves to suffer for his mistakes seems to be no part of it. Still, even if I am wrong about this and the retributive thought is essential to resentment after all, it seems to me very doubtful

---

[126] For a related discussion of circularity in reactive-attitude accounts of responsibility, see Coleman and Sarch (2012), pp. 125 ff.

[127] Rosen (2015), pp. 77 ff.

that it is essential to moral blame generally. If it isn't, then Rosen's account doesn't suffice for the task at hand.

There's another worry that comes from the opposite direction, and that is that the retributive thought, as Rosen characterizes it, isn't retributive enough. What I have in mind here can perhaps best be illustrated by focusing on retributive punishment in particular. It is often said that those who are guilty of certain crimes deserve to suffer for having committed them, but there's reason to think that this way of putting things doesn't fully capture the thought in question. Suppose that Carl commits a crime that (somehow) merits a form of incarceration that involves a certain degree of suffering, but that, before he can serve his sentence, a drunk driver runs into him and inflicts suffering on him to that very degree. Has Carl suffered as he deserves? Intuitively, the answer seems to be that he has *not* (although the authorities might nonetheless show mercy on him and waive his sentence—but probably not). This is because it seems that, on the retributivist approach, what Carl deserves is not simply to suffer to a certain degree, nor even simply to be *made* by someone to suffer to that degree, but rather to be made by someone to suffer to that degree *in a certain particular way*. What way? Presumably the answer is: by way of *punishment*. But why should this matter? The answer seems to be: because only punishment counts as the imposition of suffering *for* the commission of a crime, and it does this only because it constitutes a way of *thickly blaming* the offender for committing it.[128] If this is right, then the retributive thought, properly rendered, includes the thought that the person at whom it is directed is thickly blameworthy, and so Rosen's proposal does not succeed in breaking the circle after all.

There may be some way to break the circle successfully, but I'm not optimistic. (Redemption of the two promissory notes issued in §2.3.2: it is for this reason that I did not attempt to provide a detailed account of the reactive attitudes prior to examining the relation between them and moral responsibility or a detailed account of thin blameworthiness prior to examining the notion of thick blameworthiness.) If the circle cannot be broken, then we must accept that we cannot understand what it is to be blameworthy without understanding what it is to blame, and we cannot understand what it is to blame without understanding what it is to be blameworthy. This is a disappointing result, inasmuch as it precludes achieving the kind of insight that traditional conceptual analysis can provide.[129]

---

[128] Cf. Zimmerman (2011), pp. 16 ff.
[129] Value theory may be in a similar predicament. Recall the popular and plausible proposal I mentioned earlier:
FAA: x's being good [neutral, bad] consists in its being fitting for someone to show favor [indifference, disfavor] toward X.
As I noted, "favor," "indifference," and "disfavor" are here intended as umbrella terms that cover a wide variety of responses. For simplicity, let's focus on "favor" and "disfavor." Precisely what *kinds* of attitudes are they supposed to cover? Well, "positive" and "negative" ones, of course. But surely no

Some philosophers *seem* to accept this result without being disappointed by it. I stress "seem" because the evidence is not straightforward. The writings I have in mind are complex, and it's not absolutely clear that they commit the relevant author to the result in question, let alone to a lack of disappointment in it. Still, for what it's worth, both Smith and Scanlon seem to propose that we understand what it is for someone to be blameworthy partly in terms of that person's being judged to be blameworthy,[130] and Wallace and McKenna seem to be similarly committed, insofar as they propose that we understand *being* responsible in terms of *holding* responsible.[131]

If it's correct to say that Q cannot blame P for X without representing P as blameworthy for X, this will of course hold in those cases in which Q and P are identical, i.e., cases in which blame is self-directed. In such a case we might say that P *accepts* or *takes* responsibility for X, but, as is so often the case, we must be careful to explain what we mean, since these terms can be and often are used to mean something else.[132]

Even if Q cannot blame P without grasping what it is for P to be blameworthy, it of course does not follow that P him- or herself cannot be blameworthy without grasping what it is for P to be blameworthy. The latter is an implication of some theories of responsibility,[133] but it seems to me suspect. It may be that a certain subset of blaming reactions cannot be fittingly directed toward P unless P understands what it is to be worthy of blame (for example, it might be inappropriate to insist that P atone for his or her sins), but others might remain fitting (for example, it still might be appropriate to act *à la* Scanlon[134] and terminate one's friendship with P).[135]

---

proponent of FAA thinks that just *any* positive or negative attitudes will qualify. Consider, for example, the attitudes of belief and disbelief. These are intuitively positive and negative, respectively. It is, moreover, plausible to maintain that it is fitting to believe what is true (or, perhaps, what is evident) and fitting to disbelieve what is false (or, perhaps, what is evidently false). But no one would be tempted to say that a true (or evident) proposition is *good*, or that a false (or evidently false) proposition is *bad*. Hence neither belief nor disbelief will be among the attitudes that the proponents of FAA have in mind. So how are we to distinguish those attitudes that qualify from those that don't? It may be that the only way to do this is to identify the relevant attitudes by reference to the *value* of their objects. But that of course induces a circle. Cf. García (2018), appendix.

[130] See A. M. Smith (2013), p. 43; Scanlon (2008), p. 128. See also Driver (2015), p. 169; Peels (2017), pp. 18, 23 f.; Clarke (forthcoming a).

[131] Wallace (1994), pp. 91 ff.; McKenna (2012), pp. 34 ff. The kind of holding responsible that they have in mind is not the prospective kind (as when a boss holds an employee responsible for seeing to it that the customers are satisfied). It's the kind that consists at least in part in judging that the person in question has incurred retrospective responsibility for something.

[132] For example, they might be used prospectively to signal an intention to undertake an obligation. Also, Fischer and Ravizza (1998), ch. 8, contains an extended discussion of a technical notion of taking responsibility that is an alleged *precondition* of being retrospectively responsible.

[133] See, e.g., Fischer and Ravizza (1998), p. 211; McKenna (2012), pp. 81 ff.

[134] See Scanlon (2008), pp. 129 ff.

[135] For an interesting exchange on this issue, see Vargas (2016), pp. 233 ff., and McKenna (2016), pp. 258 ff.

2.4 The worthiness in blameworthiness

Let us now turn from *blame*worthiness to blame*worthiness*.

2.4.1 From fittingness to worthiness

As I have noted, just as there is a distinction between thin and thick blame, so too there is a distinction between thin and thick blameworthiness. In §2.3.9 I said that Q's blaming P thinly for X consists in Q's judging P to have a debit in his or her hypological ledger in respect of X, and that P's being thinly blameworthy for X consists in the correctness or accuracy of such a judgment. Now, whereas in many contexts whether a judgment is accurate has no moral significance, in this context it does. If Q judges incorrectly that there is a debit in P's hypological ledger, then Q does P an injustice, and this is true even if P is not adversely affected by the judgment. Likewise for thick blame, whether weak or strong (regarding which see §2.3.3), and the worthiness of such blame. If, for example, Q resents P when P is not worthy of resentment, then Q does P an injustice, irrespective of whether P is adversely affected by being the target of Q's attitude.[136] (Of course, if P is adversely affected by such a reaction, then the injustice is compounded.)

Like many others, I have used a wide variety of terms to give expression to the notion of blameworthiness, and so far I have done so indiscriminately. I have talked of P's being *worthy of* or *deserving* or *meriting* blame, of its being *fitting* or *appropriate* to blame P, and of blame's being *just, warranted, correct,* or *accurate*; others often talk in terms of blame's being *fair* or *apt*; and no doubt consultation with a thesaurus would quickly yield still further terms that would be fitting (or appropriate...) in this context. Fitting, yes, but not *equally* fitting. It is time to be more discriminating.

There may be a number of distinctions that could be drawn that would render one or more of the terms just mentioned more fitting for certain purposes than the others. Here I want to highlight one distinction in particular. When in the last section I criticized the actual-moral-community approach to responsibility, I stressed that P's being worthy of blame for X has to do *only with P* and not with anyone else who happens to exist. This is, I think, a very important point, although *just* what it comes to is hard to pin down. It cannot be that P's being blameworthy for X is a property that is *intrinsic* to P, not, at least, on those occasions on which X is itself not intrinsic to P—as when, for example, X is the action of harming another person, Q. (Still, I do think that it is correct to say that the *capacity* that P has to be blameworthy for X is intrinsic to P, no matter what X

---

[136] Contrast Graham (2014), pp. 390 ff.

might be. Of course, just what it is for a property of something to be intrinsic to that thing is itself a controversial question, one that I will not investigate here.[137]) What I had in mind when I said that P's being blameworthy for X has to do only with P was that this fact about P has its basis in some *personal quality* which, if not essential to P, is also not merely incidental and thus not contingent on how P just happens to be related to some other person, Q.[138] Whether it is *fitting* for someone Q to blame P, either thinly or thickly, is another matter, however, one that may well have as much to do with Q's personal qualities as with P's. (I concede that this is still very rough, but I hope not hopelessly so. I do not know how to make the point more precisely.)

As far as thick blame- and praiseworthiness are concerned, I entertained several proposals regarding how moral responsibility might be correctly analyzed in terms of the fittingness of certain attitudes or reactions. One that I declared "extremely plausible" in §2.3.3 was this:

RA1: P's being morally responsible for X consists in its being fitting for someone to direct some reaction toward P in respect of X.

As I have just reiterated, however, we should not take P's responsibility for X to be contingent on there actually being another person, Q, who is in a position to react appropriately to P, and so I urged in §2.3.8 that the underlying idea might be more perspicuously rendered as follows:

RA2: P's being morally responsible for X consists in its being the case that, if there were a person Q distinct from P who satisfied certain conditions C, it would be fitting for Q to direct some reaction toward P in respect of X.

But of course this proposal is still somewhat opaque, not only because it doesn't specify which reactions are the ones that qualify, but also because it doesn't specify just what the conditions in question are. The latter problem also afflicts Smith's proposal, cited above, that P's being responsible for X consists in its being appropriate "in principle" to ask P to defend or justify X.[139] This latter problem can, I think, be avoided entirely simply by dispensing with talk of what is fitting or appropriate and replacing RA1 and RA2 with the following:

RA3: P's being morally responsible for X consists in P's being worthy of some reaction being directed toward P in respect of X.

---

[137] For a useful discussion, see Humberstone (1996).
[138] McKenna (2019), p. 257, apparently accepts this claim, despite also claiming that moral responsibility is essentially interpersonal (regarding which see §§2.3.6–2.3.8). These claims are hard to reconcile with one another.
[139] A. M. Smith (2008), p. 369.

Instead of "being worthy of" the terms "deserving" or "meriting" are, I think, equally fitting here, but "fitting" and some of the other terms are *not*. To see just one advantage of the move to RA3, consider for a moment a problem that has recently been the focus of intense debate in the theory of value.

That problem has come to be called the Wrong Kind of Reason Problem,[140] since it was first raised in the context of a variation on the Fitting-Attitude Analysis of value that was mentioned above:

FAA: X's being good [neutral, bad] consists in its being fitting for someone to show favor [indifference, disfavor] toward X.

The variation in question was couched in terms of reasons rather than fittingness. It is known as the Buck-Passing Analysis of value and may be rendered as follows:

BPA: X's being good [neutral, bad] consists in X's having some property that provides a reason for someone to show favor [indifference, disfavor] toward X.[141]

The problem with BPA is that it seems clear that there can be a reason to direct some attitude toward X that does not correspond in the prescribed way to X's value. One can, for example, have a reason to respond favorably toward something bad. As a variation on a much-discussed case, suppose that a powerful demon threatens to inflict suffering on Sarah unless you respond favorably to Diana's distress; you will surely have some reason, and possibly a decisive reason, so to respond, but that fact doesn't somehow make Diana's distress a good thing. The reason you have to respond favorably is of the "wrong kind." This problem also afflicts FAA itself, since it seems clear that it can sometimes be fitting to respond favorably to something bad or not to respond favorably toward something good. Many attempts have been made to handle this objection.[142] The most natural solution seems to me to be this: replace talk of what there is *reason* to do or of what is *fitting* with talk of what X *deserves* or is *worthy* of; for it seems quite clear that, even if there is reason to favor Diana's distress and even if such favor is fitting, her distress is not worthy of such a response. The result is this Worthy-Attitude Analysis of value:

WAA: X's being good [neutral, bad] consists in X's being worthy of someone's showing favor [indifference, disfavor] toward X.

---

[140] See Rabinowicz and Rønnow-Rasmussen (2004), pp. 422 f.
[141] See Scanlon (1998), pp. 96 f.
[142] Among others: Parfit (2001); Rabinowicz and Rønnow-Rasmussen (2004); Olson (2004); Persson (2007); Danielsson and Olson (2007).

It's apparent that proposals such as those mentioned in the last section that offer analyses of moral responsibility in terms of fitting attitudes or reactions face the same challenge as FAA: sometimes a reaction of the "wrong kind" can be fitting. And it's apparent that this challenge is open to the same sort of solution. As Nomy Arpaly observes:

> If... an armed criminal enters a crowded room and shouts, "Give me some moral praise, or I shall kill everyone," it may be morally imperative to praise her, but that alone does not make her praise*worthy* for her action. The praise that we may be required to give her is... undeserved.[143]

The solution, in short, is to move from RA1 or RA2 to RA3.

Of course, this move doesn't solve *all* problems. The problem of specifying which reactions qualify, and which don't, remains. As far as that particular form of responsibility that is *blameworthiness* is concerned, however, there is a ready "solution" to this problem. Regarding not only thick but also thin blameworthiness, we can say:

RA4:   P's being blameworthy for X consists in P's being worthy of blame being directed toward P in respect of X.

I have put the scare-quotes around "solution," of course, because the only account of blame that I have offered (in §2.3.9) is itself given in terms of blameworthiness.

2.4.2 The ethics of blame

My proposal that we move from RA1 or RA2 to RA3 and RA4 should *not* be construed as a proposal to dispense with all talk of which reactions or judgments it might be fitting for someone Q to direct toward someone P in respect of something X. On the contrary, such talk can itself be perfectly fitting, as recent discussion of what has come to be called "the ethics of blame"[144] has made clear. There are several points worth noting briefly here.

First, whether it is fitting for Q to blame P, at least thickly and perhaps also thinly, for X would seem to turn in part on whether Q has the "moral standing" to do so.[145] Even if P is blameworthy for X, it would seem to be unfitting for Q to blame P for X if Q lacks the standing to do so. For example, Q may be guilty of the very same offense as P, without having acknowledged or atoned for this fact, in

---

[143] Arpaly (2003), p. 71.
[144] Scanlon (2008), pp. 166 ff. Cf. Adams (1985), pp. 23 ff., for a relatively early discussion.
[145] For a sustained critique of this claim, see Bell (2013).

which case it may be hypocritical for Q to blame P for X.[146] Or it may not be Q's "place" to blame P for X, because what P did was none of Q's "business."[147]

Second, whether it is fitting for Q to blame P, either thinly or thickly, for X would seem to turn in part on Q's epistemic situation. Even if P is blameworthy for X, it would seem to be unfitting for Q to blame P for X if Q lacks sufficient evidence of P's blameworthiness.[148] This point might be qualified by drawing a distinction between "objective" and "subjective" fittingness. It might be said that, if P really is blameworthy for X, then, while Q's lack of sufficient evidence of this fact renders it subjectively unfitting for Q to blame P for X, nonetheless it remains (or, given the first point, may remain) objectively fitting for Q to blame P for X. (Such a claim would be akin to the claim, mentioned in §2.1.2, that, in taking a dose of Distaval, Sally did something objectively wrong, even if what she did was also subjectively right.) If the fittingness of Q's blaming P for X turns in part on Q's epistemic situation, then the possibility also arises that it would be fitting for Q to blame P for X even if P is *not* blameworthy for X.[149] All the evidence might point to P's being guilty of murder, for example, even though P was in fact nowhere near the scene of the crime.

Third, whether it is fitting for Q to blame P, thickly if not thinly, for X might seem to turn in part on what has occurred since X occurred. Perhaps P has atoned for X, in which case P may be a candidate for forgiveness rather than blame. Or perhaps P has already received the punishment for X that he deserves, in which case it would be unfitting for P to be punished further for X. Or perhaps X happened long ago and by now Q should no longer be harboring the resentment that it was perfectly fitting for her once to have felt.[150] These points having to do with the passage of time are mundane, and yet they can be quite tricky. For example, it may be that Q's resentment of P is such that P remains just as worthy of it now as he was when X occurred, and yet it may be unfitting for quite independent reasons (reasons having more to do with Q than with P) for Q to continue to resent P. But if P has sufficiently atoned for X or already been sufficiently punished for X, then it may seem that it is unfitting for Q to (continue to) blame P thickly for X for reasons having to do with what it is that P is worthy of—and this is where things get a little tricky. I have said that thin blameworthiness consists in the correctness of a certain judgment to the effect that P has incurred a debit in his hypological ledger in virtue of having behaved in some way. It seems that such a judgment, if once true, will and must always be true; history can be forgotten but not erased. Yet I also claimed that thin blameworthiness suffices for thick blameworthiness. How, then, can it happen that P's thick

---

[146] Cf. A. M. Smith (2007), pp. 479 f.; Scanlon (2008), pp. 175 ff.; Wallace (2010); Coates and Tognazzini (2013), pp. 19 f.; King (2020), pp. 1425 ff.
[147] Cf. A. M. Smith (2007), pp. 478 f.; Coates and Tognazzini (2013), p. 21; King (2020), p. 1429.
[148] Cf. Coates (2016). Contrast Rosen (2015), pp. 69 f.   [149] Cf. King (2020), pp. 1423 f.
[150] Cf. Coleman and Sarch (2012), pp. 107 ff.

blameworthiness diminishes over time, or is even eradicated entirely, due to considerations having to do with atonement, punishment, or some other factor? The answer is that it *cannot*. Nonetheless, the following can be said. First, in many if not all cases, there will be a limit to either the degree or the amount of thick blame that P deserves. Punishment, for example, and other kinds of negative reactions can be excessive. If P has already received the punishment he deserves, then (barring a complication to be discussed in §2.5.2) he does not deserve—indeed, he deserves not—to receive *further* punishment; but this doesn't alter the fact that he *does* deserve the punishment he has already received. It is therefore a mistake to describe such a situation as one in which thick blameworthiness has diminished over time; for P's desert remains as it ever was. This point doesn't dispose of the puzzle posed by atonement, however. It seems to many that, even if P has *not* yet received the punishment (or other kind of negative reaction) that he deserves, still sincere repentance on his part renders him deserving of a reprieve rather than punishment. But this view, too, can be reconciled with the claim that thick blameworthiness cannot diminish over time. For it is perfectly possible for P to be blameworthy for X and yet praiseworthy (or, at least, worthy of a non-blaming reaction) for Y, and I know of no reason why this might not be true in the particular case in which Y consists in P's atoning for X. In such a case, it could turn out that the most fitting reaction, all things considered, is *not* to (continue to) blame P thickly for X.[151]

Fourth, whether it is fitting for Q to blame P, either thinly or thickly, for X would seem to turn in part on whether Q does, or is prepared to, blame others who are in the same "situation" as P. It is sometimes said that a person is blameworthy just in case blaming him or her would be fair,[152] but, insofar as fairness is a comparative matter having to do with treating "equals" equally, it can be unfair for Q to blame P for X, even if P is blameworthy for X, if Q does not, or is not prepared to, blame others who are "just like" P in the relevant respects.[153]

Fifth, whether it is fitting for Q to blame P, at least thickly and perhaps also thinly, for X would seem to turn in part on what would or might happen as a consequence of Q's blaming P for X. Some philosophers appear to hold the view that P is blameworthy for X just in case blaming P for X would have good (or the best) consequences.[154] That is an egregious mistake. But it is certainly not a mistake to take into consideration what the consequences of blaming P would be when trying to determine whether it would be right or fitting to blame P for X.[155] If the

---

[151] See Khoury and Matheson (2018) and Clarke (forthcoming b) for further discussion.
[152] See, e.g., Wallace (1994), pp. 15 f., 93 f.   [153] See Telech and Tierney (2019) for discussion.
[154] See, e.g., Moore (2005), pp. 97 f.; Schlick (1966), p. 61; Smart (1973), p. 54; Dennett (1984), p. 162.
[155] This point applies straightforwardly to thick blaming, which is typically a voluntary activity. Whether it also applies to thin blaming depends, I believe, on whether it, too, can be a voluntary activity.

consequences would be disastrous, that could well render it unfitting to blame P for X, even though P is blameworthy.[156] And, I suppose, it's also possible that, if the consequences would be wonderful, that might render it fitting to blame P for X, even though P is not blameworthy. (This latter claim should be distinguished from a related claim, namely, that it is sometimes justifiable to hold someone strictly liable for something. The term "strictly liable" can be, and is, used in a number of ways, one of which is roughly this: P is strictly liable to Q for some untoward past event X if and only if P owes Q some form of compensation in respect of X, regardless of whether P is to blame for X. It seems reasonable to say that it can happen that P owes Q compensation in respect of some such event X, and Q is justified in demanding this compensation, even though P is not to blame for X. But in such a case we should not say that, in making this demand, Q is *blaming* P for X, not, at least, if Q is not thereby representing P as blameworthy for X.)

Finally, just as Q's blaming P for X can be (un)fitting, so too can Q's excusing P for X be (un)fitting. If Q excuses P for X, then Q refrains from blaming P fully for X. (See §2.5.5.) As with Q's blaming P, whether it is fitting for Q to excuse P for X might depend on Q's moral standing, Q's epistemic situation, what has happened since X occurred, how Q reacts to others in the same situation as P, what would or might happen as a consequence of Q's excusing P, and perhaps on yet further considerations.[157]

2.4.3 Between blameworthiness and blamelessness

In distinguishing blameworthiness from the fittingness of blame, I have allowed both for the possibility that it is unfitting to blame a blameworthy person and for the possibility that it is fitting to blame a person who is not blameworthy. The former possibility is nonetheless consistent with the claim that, if a person is blameworthy, then it is fitting to blame him or her. That is because fittingness is what W. D. Ross calls a "parti-resultant" attribute, in that it "belongs to an act [or attitude] in virtue of some one component of its nature."[158] This means that something may be fitting in one respect while also being unfitting in another. Thus, if P is blameworthy for X but Q lacks the moral standing to blame P, then Q's blaming P for X will be unfitting (in virtue of Q's lack of standing) but also fitting (in virtue of P's blameworthiness). To put the point in terms of reasons: Q's lack of standing provides Q with *a* reason (or *some* reason) *not* to blame P, while P's blameworthiness nonetheless provides Q with *a* reason (or *some* reason) *to* blame P.

There is a middle ground between there being a reason to do something and there being a reason not to do it, and that is the possibility of there being no reason either way. So, too, there is a middle ground between its being fitting to do

---

[156] Cf. King (2020), p. 1424.   [157] Cf. Robison (2019).   [158] Ross (2002), p. 28.

something and its being unfitting to do it, and that is the possibility of its being neither fitting nor unfitting to do it. In like fashion, there is a middle ground between being deserving or worthy of receiving something and being deserving or worthy of not receiving it, and that is the possibility of lacking either form of desert or worthiness. It is easy to lose sight of this possibility. In everyday English we often say something along the lines of "I *don't deserve* to be treated in this way," when what we really mean is "I *deserve not* to be treated in this way." (Compare "I don't believe that," "I don't want to do that," and so on.) I think that it is extremely important that we *not* lose sight of this distinction. Compare blameworthiness with blamelessness or, equivalently, culpability with inculpability. It might seem that the latter simply consists in the absence of the former, but that is emphatically *not* the case. If P is charged with murder but was in fact nowhere near the scene of the crime, P's innocence does not consist simply in not being guilty of, or blameworthy for, the charge. (A chair or lamppost would be equally not guilty or blameworthy.) On the contrary, P's innocence, or blamelessness, consists in P's *deserving not* to be punished or otherwise blamed for murder. It is for this reason that it is important to recognize the third form of responsibility that I have called indifference-worthiness along with the other two forms, praise- and blameworthiness, that are commonly acknowledged. Indifference-worthiness doesn't simply involve the absence of praise- and blameworthiness; it involves the *presence* of a kind of worthiness, the worthiness of a response that *precludes* both praise (or credit) and blame.[159]

Once the middle ground between blameworthiness and blamelessness is recognized, it becomes an open question whether those whom we declare blameworthy really are blameworthy, even when we have all the relevant facts straight. "Worthy" always connotes a positive reason to do something,[160] and it may be that, instead of declaring someone blameworthy, we should instead declare him or her to be not blameless. Consider, for example, that particular form of negative reaction that is punishment. Is it really the case that an offender can deserve to be punished for committing some offense, or should we merely say that the offender does *not* deserve *not* to be punished for it? That is a question that, in my estimation, has received far too little attention.[161]

---

[159] Two caveats. First, since being blameless doesn't entail being praiseworthy (or creditworthy), the middle ground between blameworthiness and blamelessness should be distinguished from the middle ground between blameworthiness and praiseworthiness (or creditworthiness). Second, although blameworthiness (or culpability) is a form of moral responsibility, blamelessness (or inculpability) is not. Small children are inculpable even if they don't meet the conditions necessary for being morally responsible.

[160] Or almost always. As Mitchell Berman points out in Berman (2021), to say that a boat is seaworthy is not to say that there is a positive reason to put it to sea.

[161] For further discussion of this question, see Zimmerman (2011), ch. 3.

2.5 Degrees of blameworthiness

2.5.1 Maximal blameworthiness

Blameworthiness comes in degrees. P may be to blame for X and Q may be to blame for Y, and yet it may be that P is more to blame for X than Q is for Y. I know of no one, barring those who reject the possibility of blameworthiness altogether, who would deny this claim. (Note that the claim, as stated, allows both for the possibility that P is identical with Q and for the possibility that X is identical with Y. As for the former: imagine that P incurs blameworthiness on two occasions and is more blameworthy on the first than on the second. As for the latter: consider the case, discussed in the last chapter, in which the possibility was raised of there being many people to blame for the condition of Sally's child.)

I have said that blameworthiness is a form of (retrospective, moral) responsibility. If so, then, if blameworthiness comes in degrees, so does responsibility, at least in some of its forms. However, some philosophers deny that responsibility comes in degrees, treating it as an all-or-nothing precondition of blameworthiness rather than as a genus of which blameworthiness is a species.[162] This seems to me at odds with how we usually think of responsibility. I might have said, for example, that P bears more or greater responsibility for X than Q does for Y, and this would seem perfectly intelligible.[163] The only reason I can think of for denying that responsibility comes in degrees has to do with the fact that it has several forms—praiseworthiness and indifference-worthiness, as well as blameworthiness—and this gives rise to a twofold puzzle. First, how are we to compare P's degree of responsibility for X with Q's degree of responsibility for Y, if P is praiseworthy and Q is blameworthy? Second, how are we to compare P's degree of responsibility for X with Q's degree of responsibility for Y, if P is either praiseworthy or blameworthy and Q is indifference-worthy? As soon as this puzzle is posed, though, a solution suggests itself: assign positive numbers to degrees of praiseworthiness, negative numbers to degrees of blameworthiness, and zero to indifference-worthiness. This proposal might be made to work, but I would issue two caveats. First, a precise application of the proposal would require some unit of measurement that we currently do not have and, I suspect, have no hope of ever obtaining. Second, the proposal might be construed as implying that someone who is praiseworthy is "more responsible" than someone who is indifference-worthy,

---

[162] See, e.g., Baier (1970), p. 106, and Greenspan (2016), p. 266. See also, perhaps, Fischer and Ravizza (1998), pp. 6 f. I say "perhaps" because, although Fischer and Ravizza are sometimes interpreted as holding the view in question—see, e.g., Coates and Swenson (2013), p. 630, n. 2—it's not clear to me that this interpretation is correct. For what they say is that P is morally responsible for X *to the extent that* P is an appropriate candidate for some reactive attitude, and the phrase "to the extent" suggests degrees of responsibility.

[163] Cf. Coates and Swenson (2013).

who in turn is "more responsible" than someone who is blameworthy. I think there is little sense to be made of such a claim.

Regardless of just how we should handle the issue of degrees of responsibility in general, my concern in this section is with degrees of blameworthiness in particular. As I have just indicated, we ordinarily accept that blameworthiness comes in degrees, even if we have no precise way of measuring such degrees. (Recall the *Model Penal Code*, which surely accords with a common intuition: purposeful wrongdoing confers greater culpability on an agent, *ceteris paribus*, than does knowing or witting wrongdoing, etc.[164]) On the assumption that blameworthiness does indeed come in degrees, a number of questions arise.

One question that I don't recall having seen discussed before is this. Is there an upper limit to how blameworthy one can be? In principle, the answer would seem to be "No." If blameworthiness is in part a function of quality of will, and if there is no upper limit to how objectionable one's quality of will can be, then there would seem to be no upper limit to how blameworthy one can be. Consider, for example, the possibility, mentioned earlier, that the greater the degree of glee that one brings to wrongdoing, the worse, *ceteris paribus*, one's quality of will.[165] It seems plausible to say that, for any degree of glee that we imagine, a greater degree is imaginable.[166]

It might be responded that there nonetheless is a limit to how blameworthy someone can be. This limit corresponds to the greatest punishment imaginable: eternal damnation. But no matter how vividly[167] or enthusiastically[168] the torments of hell might be portrayed, it seems to me that it will always be possible to imagine them as being still worse. (Just add the dismay that comes from realizing that what's happening to you meets with God's approval. Or simply turn up the thermostat one notch.)

This question about whether there is an upper limit to blameworthiness may seem an idle one, and no doubt in many ways it is, but it serves to bring to our attention a point that I think is important, and that is that when people talk, as they often do, of someone's being "*fully* to blame" for something, it seems that they probably do not mean what the phrase at first blush suggests, namely, that that person is blameworthy to the maximum degree possible. So what *is* this phrase supposed to mean? I will return to this question shortly, when I discuss the nature of excuses.

---

[164] American Law Institute (1985), §2.02(5).   [165] Cf. McKenna (2016), p. 244.
[166] McKenna (2019, p. 267) claims that there is an upper limit to the kind of *harm* that can be caused by the kind of blame that he has in mind (a kind that is restricted to adopting certain attitudes). Perhaps that is in fact the case, but I don't see why we should say that it is necessarily the case. Moreover, even if it is necessarily the case, it doesn't follow that it is necessarily the case that there is an upper limit to the degree of *blame* of which one might be worthy.
[167] See Dante (2008).   [168] See J. Edwards (1789).

2.5.2 The two dimensions of blameworthiness

I suspect that, when it is said that P is more blameworthy for X than Q is for Y, almost always what is meant is that the blame of which P is worthy is greater or more intense than the blame of which Q is worthy. Perhaps, for example, P deserves a strong reprimand, whereas Q deserves only a weak one. Or perhaps P deserves severe punishment, whereas Q deserves only minor punishment. (These are of course examples of variations in degree of thick blameworthiness, but the idea is applicable to thin blameworthiness, too.[169] We may say that P is worthy of greater thin blame than Q just in case the severity of the judgment of which P is worthy in virtue of the debit in his or her hypological ledger is greater than the severity of the judgment of which Q is worthy in virtue of the lesser debit in his or her hypological ledger.) On this approach, then, degree of blameworthiness is understood as degree of *blame*worthiness; that is, it is understood to be a matter of *how much blame* one is worthy of.

But there is another approach possible—one that is seldom entertained[170] but is worthy of consideration—and that is that degree of blameworthiness is to be understood as degree of blame*worthiness*, that is, as a matter of *how worthy* one is of blame. (In this case, the idea may be applicable only to thick blameworthiness and not also to thin blameworthiness, which consists in the correctness of the relevant judgment. The notion of degrees of correctness is problematic.) That blameworthiness can vary in degree along two different dimensions is something that it shares with other, similar phenomena. Consider praiseworthiness, trustworthiness, admirability, and so on. In each case, there is something of which someone is worthy and which can vary in degree, but also that person can be more or less worthy of the thing in question. But now we face a puzzle. Aren't the two dimensions independent of one another? If so, what could count as *the* degree to which someone is blameworthy for something?

To get a better handle on this question, it will help to work with an illustration that involves one particular kind of blaming reaction. Let us suppose that Matt and Mary are both miscreants who have committed crimes that render them worthy of punishment. Suppose that it has been established (who knows how?[171]) that a punishment of ten years' incarceration is precisely the reaction of which Matt is worthy for the commission of his crime, whereas a punishment of five years' incarceration is precisely the punishment of which Mary is worthy for the commission of her crime.[172] Does it follow that Matt's being punished for, say, nine years or Mary's being punished for, say, six years would be something of

---

[169] Contrast Coates (2020), p. 239.   [170] Coates (2020) is a welcome exception to the rule.
[171] See Zimmerman (2011), pp. 88 ff.
[172] This assumption could be relaxed, so that the punishments, rather than having a precise duration, fall within a certain range of days behind bars, but that would make the ensuing discussion unnecessarily messy.

which neither person is worthy? No. They would be *less* worthy of these punishments, but they might still be worthy of them to some degree. I venture to say that in Matt's case, *given* the assumption that he is indeed worthy of a punishment of precisely ten years' incarceration, *any* punishment of ten years or less would be something of which he is worthy to some degree. *No* such punishment would be one of which he is not worthy, let alone one of which he is unworthy. Mary's case is different. We are imagining her receiving a punishment that is *excessive*. I suspect that what we should say here is that a punishment that is mildly excessive (say, five years and one day) could still be a punishment of which she is worthy to some degree. At some point, though, an increase in excess will result in a punishment of which she is not worthy, and some further increase will result in a punishment of which she is positively unworthy. (It may well be that she is positively unworthy of six years' incarceration. That is, it's not simply that she *doesn't deserve* to receive such a sentence; she *deserves not* to receive it.)

The approach to degree of worthiness just illustrated implies that, even if there is no upper limit to how much blame one can be worthy of, there is indeed an upper limit to how worthy one can be of blame. In Matt's case, what he is most worthy of is ten years' incarceration. In Mary's case, what she is most worthy of is five years' incarceration. (So saying is consistent with saying that Matt is nonetheless more worthy of his punishment than Mary is of hers, but this is a complication that we can safely ignore here.) In light of this fact, I suggest that we can in principle pinpoint "the" degree to which someone is blameworthy for something by presupposing that it is *maximal* worthiness that is at issue. In such a case, degree of blameworthiness will vary only according to how much blame the person is maximally worthy of.

2.5.3 Comparing and aggregating degrees of blameworthiness

I said above that, if P is to blame for X and Q is to blame for Y, it may be that P is more to blame for X than Q is for Y. That's true, but comparing degrees of blameworthiness is not a straightforward matter, in part because, as I emphasized in §2.3.3, "blame" is an umbrella term that covers a wide variety of reactions to people's behavior. Suppose, more particularly, that P is to blame to degree x for X and Q is to blame to degree y for Y. Then P is more to blame for X than Q is for Y only if $x>y$, and it will be true that $x>y$ only if x and y are degrees on the same scale of measurement. Moreover, it is plausible to think that, in this context, x and y are on the same scale of measurement only if the kind of blame of which P is worthy is in some way comparable to the kind of blame of which Q is worthy. But what it means to say that *different* kinds of blame are comparable is not at all clear to me. If P is worthy of resentment whereas Q deserves a reprimand, then, even if it makes sense to talk of different degrees of resentment and different degrees of reprimand, it's not clear how the degree to which P is to blame can be compared to the degree to which Q is to blame.

Suppose that Q is to blame to degree y for Y and that she is also to blame to degree z for Z. Will she then be to blame to degree $y+z$ for $Y\&Z$? Perhaps, but quite possibly not. Once again, unless the kind of blame of which Q is worthy for Y is comparable to the kind of blame of which she is worthy for Z, y and z would seem not to be on the same scale of measurement, in which case the expression "$y+z$" would seem to be nonsensical. But even if y and z are on the same scale of measurement, it may not be the case that Q is to blame to degree $y+z$ for $Y\&Z$. Imagine that Y and Z are crimes. Y (somehow) warrants five years' incarceration while Z warrants two years'. Perhaps, if Y and Z are wholly independent of one another, Q will deserve seven years' incarceration for the pair of crimes. But if the crimes are interrelated (committing a robbery while in possession of an illegal firearm, say), then there's no good reason, as far as I can see, to think that seven years' incarceration would be the appropriate sentence, *even if* it is granted that the individual sentences for X and Y, taken separately, are appropriate. And, of course, it might be wholly inappropriate to punish Q both for X and for Y *and* for $X\&Y$.

Yet another problem with comparing and aggregating degrees of blameworthiness has to do with the distinction between direct and indirect blameworthiness. Consider the case of BILL AND JILL, introduced in §2.2.4, in which Bill shot and killed Jill. Bill is directly blameworthy for his decision to kill Jill and thereby indirectly blameworthy for a number of consequences of this decision including, of course and especially, Jill's death. Suppose that Bill is blameworthy to degree x for his decision. Does it follow that he is blameworthy to that same degree for Jill's death, or might he be blameworthy to a lesser or greater degree for it? Suppose now that we have somehow arrived at an answer to this question: Bill is blameworthy to degree y for Jill's death (where y may or may not be equal to x). What would the degree of Bill's blameworthiness be for the compound event comprising both his decision and Jill's death: x, y, $x+y$, or something else? I propose an answer to this question in §5.1.4, one that certainly can be, and has been, disputed.

We are accustomed to holding people responsible not only for individual events in their lives but also for what happens over an extended period of time. Indeed, we sometimes hold them responsible for their entire (adult) lives. In light of the points made in the last two paragraphs, I think that such overall judgments, and the reactions that are based on them, are highly problematic, no matter how common they may be.

2.5.4 The basis of blameworthiness

None of what I have just said casts doubt on the intelligibility of the idea of one's being more or less to blame for a particular piece of behavior, but the question still remains, of course, of what can account for variation in the degree of one's blameworthiness for something. As we saw earlier, the *Model Penal Code* holds that, *ceteris paribus*, purposeful wrongdoing confers a greater degree of culpability on an agent than does knowing or witting wrongdoing, which itself confers a greater degree of culpability than does reckless wrongdoing, which in turn confers a greater degree of culpability than does negligent wrongdoing. Again, the *Code* is of course concerned with *legal* culpability, but I expect that many would find this account equally applicable to *moral* culpability or blameworthiness, on the grounds that the states of mind that accompany the wrongdoing all bespeak a quality of will that is objectionable, though decreasingly so as one moves down the list. I have some reservations, however.

My chief reservation has of course to do with blameworthiness for unwitting wrongdoing. This is the central topic of the book, and it concerns not only the propriety of blaming people for negligent wrongdoing but also the propriety of blaming people for reckless wrongdoing. These are issues that I will explore in later chapters. But I also have reservations about what the *Code* has to say regarding purposeful and witting wrongdoing. As an account of *moral* blameworthiness, I find it insufficiently discerning.

Consider the matter of purposely committing some moral wrong. There are two ways of understanding what such behavior amounts to, and the difference is very important. Consider Karl from the last chapter, whose failure to investigate thalidomide more thoroughly was, by hypothesis, morally wrong. Moreover, this failure wasn't accidental; it was intentional. Or consider Sam, whose repeated atrocities were, again, both morally wrong and, of course, intentional. Nonetheless, on the assumption that their behavior did not have its genesis in witting wrongdoing, the Argument from Innocence *absolves* these agents of the wrongs that they committed. This is because, although they purposely did what they did, and what they did was wrong, *they didn't purposely do wrong*. That is, *doing wrong* was not the purpose (or aim, or goal) of either of them.

It is controversial whether anyone ever does, or even can, have the purpose of doing something wrong. It is a possibility that is, or seems to be, rejected by some major thinkers, such as Plato, Kant, and Richard Hare.[173] I believe, but will not argue, that we should accept this possibility.[174] If we do, we should recognize two ways in which it might be realized. One might aim to do something wrong for the sake of doing something wrong, or one might aim to do something wrong for the sake of achieving some further goal.

Aiming to do something wrong for the sake of doing something wrong is extraordinary, and extraordinarily wicked. One might even call having such a

---

[173] See Plato (1961), *Meno* 77b–78b, *Protagoras* 358c, and *Gorgias* 468c; Kant (1985), p. 276; Hare (1952), pt. II.

[174] For a helpful discussion of this and closely related questions, see Milo (1984), chs. 6 and 7.

purpose satanic.[175] It seems safe to say that having this as one's purpose would constitute an aggravating factor with respect to the degree to which one is to blame. Even here, though, we should probably allow for greater or lesser degrees of blameworthiness, depending on just how serious the wrong in question is and also, perhaps, on just how gleefully one embraces the goal of doing wrong for the sake of doing wrong. I have to say that I wonder whether anyone has ever had this goal in mind. Consider Saint Augustine, who famously confessed to stealing pears from his neighbor's tree, addressing God with these words:

> Look at my heart, O God, look at my heart, which thou hast pitied in the depths of the abyss. Look at my heart; may it tell Thee now what it sought in this—that I might be evil without any compensation and that for my evil there might be no reason except evil. It was filthy and I loved it. I loved my own destruction. I loved my own fault; not the object to which I directed my faulty action, but my fault itself, was what I loved, my vile soul leaping down from Thy support into extinction, not shamefully coveting anything, but coveting shame itself.[176]

It seems that in this striking passage Augustine is reporting that his ultimate goal was, not simply to steal the pears, but to do wrong by virtue of stealing the pears. But we are not always the best judges of our motivations or purposes. A few paragraphs earlier, Augustine says that he was ashamed that he wasn't living "up" to the standard of his wanton companions:

> I became more vicious, so that I would not be vituperated and, when my conduct did not match the wickedness of my associates, I pretended to have perpetrated deeds which I had not performed, lest I would appear inferior because I was more innocent, lest I be considered viler because I was more chaste.[177]

This casts quite a different light on Augustine's behavior. It may be that he wasn't really aiming to do wrong for the sake of doing wrong, but rather was aiming to do wrong for the sake of earning the respect of his peers—a very common goal; not noble, certainly, but not satanic, either.[178]

If purposely doing wrong for the sake of some further goal is not satanic, should we declare it nonetheless to be an aggravating factor when comparing it with "merely" knowingly doing wrong? The answer to this question is not clear to me. It seems that Augustine thought that his companions wanted him to do wrong and that he was trying to impress them by doing just that. But suppose instead that he had thought that what would impress his companions was not the *wrongness* of his stealing his neighbor's pears but the *audacity* of his doing so, so that, in stealing

---

[175] Cf. Milo (1984), p. 7. [176] Augustine (1953), pp. 40 f. (the final paragraph in bk. II, ch. 4).
[177] Augustine (1953), p. 38. [178] Cf. Schmid (2018), p. 75.

the pears with the ultimate goal of earning his peers' respect, Augustine was (once again) perfectly *willing* to do wrong, but this time doing wrong was not part of his *purpose*. Would this fact diminish his blameworthiness for his behavior? Would it bespeak a less objectionable quality of will? I leave the question open, resting content with the observation that, if there is any such diminution, it is at best slight. As I see it, the key point to keep in mind is that, whether one aims to do wrong for the sake of some further goal or one aims at that goal "merely" knowing that one is doing wrong in doing so, one certainly *lacks* the purpose of *not* doing wrong. If one had *that* purpose, one would behave very differently. Had Augustine been intent on avoiding wrongdoing, he would not have stolen his neighbor's pears in an effort to impress his pals, regardless of just what he thought it was that would impress them.

2.5.5 Full blameworthiness

Consider Matt and Mary again. Matt is more blameworthy than Mary—indeed, precisely twice as blameworthy, given the spurious supposition made earlier about just what reaction each of them deserves. Yet there is a sense in which Mary is nonetheless *fully* blameworthy for the crime she committed. She has *no excuse*.

If one has an excuse, one has a defense against the charge that one has committed some offense (whether that offense is a legal one, as with Matt and Mary, or not). Consider again the case of BILL AND JILL. Suppose that Bill is charged with murder. How might he seek to defend himself against this charge? There are three distinct possibilities. He might deny that he killed Jill, claiming that the killing was in fact carried out by his identical twin, Bob. Or he might acknowledge that he killed Jill but claim that he was perfectly justified in doing so, since he was acting in self-defense. Or he might acknowledge that he killed Jill and also that he had no justification for doing so, but claim that he nonetheless is not to blame for doing so since he was high at the time on meth. The first kind of defense is commonly called a denial, the second a justification, and the third an excuse.[179] This taxonomy calls for some comment.

A defense is offered in an attempt to show that one is not guilty as charged, that one is not to blame for the occurrence of whatever untoward event is at issue. A denial, if accurate, surely constitutes an adequate defense (adequate in that it suffices for *its being the case* that one is not to blame; it may not be adequate in *convincing others* that one is not to blame). If indeed it was Bob and not Bill that killed Jill, then Bill is not to blame for Jill's death (unless he was complicit in it in some way; he might have egged Bob on, daring him to shoot, for example, or

---

[179] Cf. Husak (1987), ch. 7.

promising him a reward for doing so). This is not to say that there are no complications here. Although it is indeed the case that P cannot be to blame for X unless P committed or otherwise contributed to X,[180] there can sometimes be difficulties in identifying just what X is. Suppose that Stan is charged with stealing Harry's hat. He acknowledges that he took the hat without Harry's permission but denies the charge, on the grounds that he thought that Harry had abandoned it. Is the denial accurate? That depends on just what stealing should be said to consist in, an issue that is not straightforward.

If accurate, a justification also surely constitutes an adequate defense. If P was justified in doing A or contributing to X—if, that is, P did nothing wrong—then P cannot be to blame for A or X.[181] Once again, though, there can be complications. Killing in self-defense, for example, is a very tricky matter. Just what kind or level of threat is required for killing to be a "proportionate" response to the threat one faces? Just how "imminent" must that threat be? Must the threat be real, or would the fact that the person who kills in self-"defense" has very good evidence that it is real suffice (*ceteris paribus*) to render his or her action justified? And so on.

Even if one has done something wrong, however, one might not be to blame for what one has done. One might have an excuse. This fact lies at the heart of the Argument from Ignorance. Ignorance such as that displayed by Karl and Sam might render them blameless for the wrongs that they undoubtedly committed. It is not only ignorance that can provide an excuse for wrongdoing. Lack of control can, too. Consider the excuse that I just imagined Bill offering for killing Jill: that he was high on meth. You might not be very impressed by this, but let's not be too hasty. If Bill is to blame for having taken meth in the first place, then of course he might well be to blame for the behavior in which he engaged while high on the drug. I say only "might well," since there is the possibility that, at the time at which he took the drug, he was ignorant of the effect his doing so might have. His killing Jill might not have "fallen within the risk" of his decision to take the drug (regarding which, see the discussion of Principle D in the last chapter). But if Bill *isn't* to blame for taking the drug—because, say, it was forced down his throat by someone else—then he might well not be to blame for killing Jill as a result (given that he did indeed kill her *as a result* of taking the drug). Again, I say only "might well," for two reasons. First, his killing Jill might have been the result, not only of his having taken meth involuntarily, but also the result of his having voluntarily smoked some crack, just before he ingested the meth, and each drug might be such that it would have sufficed to render him lethally aggressive. In such a case, he might be to blame for having smoked the crack, and thereby be to blame

---

[180] Given, that is, the assumption, under which we are presently working (see Premise 4 of the Argument from Ignorance), that blameworthiness requires control. For further discussion, see Chapter 9 below.

[181] Given, that is, the assumption, under which we are presently working, that Premise 13 of the Argument from Ignorance is true. For further discussion, see §3.4.

for killing Jill, despite not being to blame for having taken the meth. Second, Bill might be directly to blame for killing Jill (or for the executive decision involved in his doing so), since, despite being high on meth, he might still have been in control of his behavior and have known that it was wrong. It is only if the drug robbed him entirely of such control or such knowledge that he would have been blameless for killing Jill.

"Entirely" suggests that ignorance and control can come in degrees, and it certainly seems plausible to say that they can. (I will investigate this idea further in the next two chapters.) Given that either or both of them can indeed come in degrees, the possibility arises that some excuses serve not to *eliminate* but to *reduce* blameworthiness.

Consider Susan. She is in the throes of an epileptic seizure and has no control at all over her movements; it is literally impossible for her to behave differently. Given that she is not to blame at all for her seizure (which she could be; she might have deliberately skipped her medication), she is not to blame at all for her behavior, even if it resulted in injury to someone standing nearby. Compare Susan with Tom. He is being tortured by captors and finds it very difficult, but not strictly impossible, to resist the impulse to divulge the information they seek. Given that Tom is not to blame at all for his predicament, it seems that he is not to blame for divulging the information as much as he would (or might) have been if he had done so fully voluntarily, but he might nonetheless be to blame to some degree.[182]

Now consider Sally from the last chapter. She was wholly ignorant of the properties of thalidomide and, given that she is not to blame at all for that ignorance, she is not to blame at all for her child's phocomelia. But what if she had had a suspicion, an inkling, that the drug might be harmful to her fetus? Then, it seems reasonable to say, she might be to blame to some degree for her child's condition, but perhaps not to the degree that she would have been to blame had she had full knowledge that thalidomide was teratogenic. (For further discussion, see Chapter 7.)

Perhaps there are excusing conditions other than lack of full control and lack of full knowledge,[183] but I will not pursue this issue (barring what I will have to say in the next paragraph). What I want to note here is simply this. If one lacks an excuse for one's wrongful behavior, then, I will say, one is "fully blameworthy" or "fully to blame" for it. Thus Mary is fully to blame for her crime, given that she was in full control of her behavior and that she knew full well that it was wrong (and that she had no excuse stemming from some other consideration), and this is so even

---

[182] Cf. Nelkin (2016b) for discussion.
[183] Some philosophers claim, for example, that autonomy is a necessary condition of moral responsibility, one that is distinct from the conditions of knowledge and freedom or control. See, e.g., Haji (1998), pp. 174 f.

though she is not as blameworthy as Matt and even if she would have been more blameworthy still had she committed her crime either gleefully or with the purpose of doing wrong. Had she had an excuse for what she did, that excuse would have been either "total" (i.e., one that was fully exculpatory, rendering her blameless) or "partial" (i.e., one that reduced but did not eliminate her blameworthiness).

I have heard the term "fully to blame" used differently, to give expression to the idea that one is *solely* to blame for some outcome. I would advise against such use of the term, since it suggests that *sharing* the blame for some outcome with someone else *reduces* the degree to which one is oneself to blame.[184] But that is surely a mistake. The idea seems to be that there is just so much blame(worthiness) to go around—the "pie" is just so large—and the more people involved, the smaller the share for each. But this is obviously false. Numbers by themselves do not furnish an excuse. One cannot reduce one's degree of blameworthiness just by getting others to join in one's misbehavior. The simple fact, for example, that Karl was one of many employees of Grünenthal doesn't provide him with any excuse at all for the condition of Sally's child.

Ever since the appearance of J. L. Austin's famous plea for excuses, the standard view seems to have been that justifications and excuses are mutually exclusive, in that, if P has a justification for X, then P has no excuse for X (there's nothing to excuse P *for*), and if P has an excuse for X, then P has no justification for X (because, again, there would otherwise be nothing to excuse P for).[185] This view seems to me to be at odds with our normal use of "excuse." One can of course have an excuse without offering one (and one can offer an excuse without having one), but, when one *does* offer an *ex*cuse, one does so in response to an *ac*cusation, and this often occurs when no wrongdoing has been conceded. Consider the following case, provided by Terrance McConnell:

> Suppose I am at a lake when a man drowns. Another accuses me of wrongdoing for failing to save the man. But I reply that I am not able to swim (or that the man was on the other side of the lake and I was not able to get there in time).[186]

It is surely clear in such a case that the appeal to inability does not presuppose any admission of wrongdoing. And yet it would be quite natural to describe the agent as offering his inability as an excuse for his failing to save the man from drowning,

---

[184] Consider the following claim made by L. Jonathan Cohen. Of a situation in which a hundred people let some person die, none of the hundred could have prevented the death by him- or herself, and it wasn't necessary for all one hundred to act for the death to be prevented, Cohen says: "[I]f there are a hundred independent defaulters... and one death, each carries a hundredth of the responsibility, not the whole of it... [E]ach carries only one hundredth of a murderer's guilt." (Cohen (1981), p. 75.)
[185] See Austin (1961), ch. 8. Cf. Sinnott-Armstrong (1988), p. 194, among many others.
[186] McConnell (1989), p. 438.

and also quite natural to say that, given that he was indeed unable to save the man, he did indeed have an excuse—a very good, fully exculpatory excuse—for not saving him.[187]

Are excuses compatible with denials? I think we should say that they are, inasmuch as, once again, a denial is made in the face of an accusation. Suppose that it was indeed Bob rather than Bill that killed Jill. When accused of the murder, Bill replies, "I have the perfect excuse. I wasn't even there!" I grant that this use of "excuse" smacks of overstatement, and perhaps also of sarcasm, but I see no harm in accepting it. If we do accept it, then we can say not only that P is fully blameworthy for X *only if* P has no excuse for X, but also that P is fully blameworthy for X *if* P has no excuse for X. (If we were to insist on using "excuse" more narrowly, as some philosophers do,[188] the second of these statements would require qualification.) And we can say, further, that P is partially to blame for X if and only if P has a partial (and not total) excuse for X.

It might be complained that what I have just said obscures the distinction between excuses and exemptions. Exemptions are conditions (such as early childhood or insanity, whether permanent or temporary) which render one incapable of being morally responsible—whether blameworthy or praiseworthy (or indifference-worthy)—for anything, whereas excuses, it might be said, are conditions that render one blameless (or only partially blameworthy) for something when one is nonetheless capable of being fully blameworthy for it.[189] That is certainly an important distinction to make but, again, there is sense, I think, in saying, for example, that a young child has a "perfect excuse"—namely, being a young child—for having spilled the milk. On this approach, then, exemptions do not preclude excuses; rather, the former constitute a subset of the latter.

---

[187] Cf. Husak (1987), p. 194.   [188] See, e.g., Peels (2017), p. 125.
[189] See Strawson (1974), pp. 7 f. Cf. McKenna (2012), pp. 74 ff.

3
Ignorance

This book is concerned with the relation between ignorance and moral responsibility. According to the Argument from Ignorance that I have presented, it appears that ignorance undermines such responsibility—in particular, it absolves one of blameworthiness—far more often than is commonly thought. This is because the argument culminates in the Origination Thesis, according to which all blameworthiness is rooted in *non*-ignorant, that is, *witting* wrongdoing, and such wrongdoing seems to occur relatively rarely. (Just *how* rarely it occurs is an issue that I will address in this and ensuing chapters.)

The most recent formulation that I have given of the Origination Thesis is this:

The Origination Thesis (Draft 2):
Every chain of moral blameworthiness is such that at its origin lies a piece of behavior for which the agent is directly morally blameworthy and which he or she knew, at the time at which he or she engaged in it, to be overall morally wrong.

Here, instead of saying that the agent was *not ignorant* of the wrongness of his (or her) behavior, I have said that he *knew* that his behavior was wrong. This way of framing the Origination Thesis may seem quite natural, but in fact caution is needed here, for the relation between (lack of) ignorance, on the one hand, and (lack of) knowledge, on the other, is perhaps not as straightforward as it first appears.

In this chapter I proceed as follows. In §3.1 I explain why it is that, in our inquiry into moral responsibility for ignorant wrongdoing, we should focus in particular on an agent's failure to believe that he or she is doing wrong.

In §3.2 I undertake an extended investigation into what it is to believe, and what it is to fail to believe, something. I begin with an examination of the relation between knowledge and belief, in the course of which I draw a distinction between belief and acceptance. Typically, acceptance is an attitude that one adopts intentionally, whereas belief is not. Nonetheless, it's clear that there is often a close association between belief and intentional behavior. Some philosophers claim that having a belief consists in having a disposition to engage in certain kinds of behavior, but it is notoriously difficult to specify precisely the kinds of behavior at issue. I briefly discuss some proposals. Regardless of the merit of these proposals, almost everyone acknowledges another connection between beliefs and dispositions, and that is that beliefs can themselves be merely dispositional, as opposed to being occurrently or consciously held. I investigate what this distinction consists in, paying particular attention to the role played by attention, which comes in degrees, as a result of which the type of consciousness or awareness involved in occurrent belief does, too. It is sometimes claimed that beliefs also come in degrees. This has to do with the degree of confidence that one has in a proposition. In this context, philosophers often talk of credences rather than beliefs. I discuss the nature of credences and examine the relation between them and "outright" beliefs. I then turn to the question of what it is to have beliefs that conflict with one another and with other belief-like attitudes. Finally, I discuss two ways in which one may fail to believe a proposition.

In §3.3 I address the distinction between acting from ignorance and acting merely in ignorance. Many philosophers claim that ignorance provides an excuse for wrongdoing only if one acts from, rather than merely in, ignorance of the fact that one is doing wrong. This is a claim that I think it would be wise to endorse.

Finally, in §3.4 I discuss two possible ways in which there might be blameworthiness without wrongdoing. The first concerns what I call accuses (as opposed to excuses). If one's quality of will can render one blameless even though one has done wrong, the question naturally arises whether one's quality of will can render one blameworthy even though one has done no wrong. I argue for an affirmative answer to this question. The second possibility is that one is to blame, not for doing something wrong, but rather for doing something suberogatory. (The category of suberogation is alleged by some philosophers to be the negative counterpart to that of supererogation.) I am inclined to deny the possibility of suberogation but, if even I am right to do so, that doesn't mean we can ignore it; for someone might believe that she is doing something suberogatory, in which case her quality of will would seem objectionable.

3.1 Knowledge and ignorance

It is often said that ignorance consists in lack of knowledge. Moreover, according to tradition (or legend[1]), knowledge consists in justified true belief. (The kind of knowledge at issue here is propositional knowledge, that is, knowledge *that* something is the case, rather than some other kind of knowledge, such as knowing how to do something or knowing someone by acquaintance, unless these are somehow reducible to propositional knowledge.) This traditional analysis is of course controversial. Each of justification, truth, and belief has on occasion been held *not* to be necessary for propositional knowledge,[2] and Edmund Gettier

---

[1] See Dutant (2015).   [2] For discussion, see Ichikawa and Steup (2017), §1.

famously demonstrated that the justification condition requires refinement if it is to be sufficient (*ceteris paribus*) for such knowledge.[3] Fortunately, we need not concern ourselves with most of these issues here. That is because, contrary to what is often said (and to what I have myself said in the past[4]), it is in fact a mistake to claim that ignorance consists in lack of knowledge. For, whereas it is certainly the case that ignorance of some proposition precludes knowledge of that proposition, lack of knowledge does not suffice for ignorance, for several reasons.

First, objects such as tables and chairs lack knowledge of any and all propositions, yet they are not ignorant of these propositions. To be ignorant of a proposition one must be capable of possessing propositional knowledge. (I won't venture to say what such a capacity itself consists in. Note, though, that I am not claiming that, to be ignorant of some proposition *p*, one must be capable of knowing *p* itself. That would clearly be far too restrictive a condition.)

Second, as Rik Peels has observed,[5] ignorance is ignorance of facts. Facts are (or may be taken in the present context to be) true propositions, and one cannot be ignorant of a proposition that is false. Suppose that Florence believes that the earth is flat. She obviously doesn't know that it is, because it isn't. But also, because it isn't, she's not ignorant of this "fact," either.

Third, as Peels has also observed,[6] it is doubtful that one is ignorant of a proposition that one doesn't know, if one's lack of knowledge is due, not to the proposition's being false or to one's failing to believe it, but rather to one's belief's lacking the requisite justification. Suppose that Harry believes, truly, that the house in which he lives was built in 1928, but suppose that he does so because he believes, falsely, that all the houses in his neighborhood were built then. Then he doesn't know that his house was built in 1928, but he doesn't seem to be ignorant of this fact, either.[7]

Let us say, then, that one is ignorant of a proposition just in case one is capable of possessing propositional knowledge and the proposition in question is true, but one fails to believe it. On the safe assumption that moral agents, agents capable of doing wrong and of being to blame, are also capable of propositional knowledge, it is therefore with such agents' *failure to believe* of some true proposition that it is true that we are at bottom concerned, and it is worth reformulating the Argument from Ignorance and the Origination Thesis to reflect this fact. Thus:

---

[3] Gettier (1963).   [4] In various places, including Zimmerman (1988), p. 75.
[5] Peels (2017), p. 166.   [6] Peels (2017), p. 167.
[7] Some people to whom I've proposed this example are inclined to say that Harry *is* ignorant of the fact in question. There's no need for present purposes to take a definitive stand on this issue. For, as Peels again has observed (2017, pp. 166 f.), "true belief does *not* provide an excuse, not even a partial one." He gives the example of someone who sets fire to a barn, believing truly, but without sufficient warrant for knowledge, that there is someone still inside. Cf. Rosen (2008), p. 596.

The Argument from Ignorance (Draft 3):
Suppose that

(1) (a) P committed A and (b) A was overall morally wrong, but (c) when P committed A, P **failed to believe** that A was overall morally wrong.

In general it's true that

(2) if one committed some act or omission that was overall morally wrong while **failing to believe** that it was overall morally wrong, one is morally to blame for it, and thereby morally to blame for any of its consequences, only if one is morally to blame for one's **failure to believe that it was overall morally wrong**.

Thus

(3) P is morally to blame for A, and thereby morally to blame for any of its consequences, only if P is morally to blame for P's **failure to believe** (call it F) that A was overall morally wrong.

It's also in general true that

(4) one is morally to blame for something only if one was in control of that thing.

Thus

(5) P is morally to blame for F only if P was in control of F.

Three further general truths are that

(6) one is never directly in control of whether one **fails to believe** something—that is, any control that one has over **failing to believe** something is always only indirect,

(7) if one is morally to blame for something over which one had only indirect control, then one's blameworthiness for it is itself only indirect, and

(8) one is indirectly morally to blame for something only if that thing was a consequence of something else for which one is directly morally to blame.

Thus

(9) P is morally to blame for A, and thereby to blame for any of its consequences, only if there was something else (call it X) for which P is directly morally to blame and of which F was a consequence.

But

(10) whatever X was, it cannot have been an act or omission such that (a) P committed it and (b) it was overall morally wrong and (c) when P committed it, P **failed to believe** that it was overall morally wrong, since otherwise the foregoing argument regarding A would apply all over again to X.

Thus

(11) whatever X was, it was either (a) not some act or omission that P committed or (b) not overall morally wrong or (c) something such that, when P committed it, P **believed** that it was overall morally wrong.

Two further general truths are that

(12) one has direct control over something only if that thing is an act or omission, and

(13) one is morally to blame for an act or omission only if that act or omission was overall morally wrong.

Thus

(14) whatever X was, it was an act or omission such that, when P committed it, P **believed** that it was overall morally wrong.

The Origination Thesis (Draft 3):
Every chain of moral blameworthiness is such that at its origin lies a piece of behavior for which the agent is directly blameworthy and which he or she **believed**, at the time at which he or she engaged in it, to be overall morally wrong.

For convenience, I will continue to characterize the Origination Thesis as the thesis that all blameworthiness is rooted in *witting* wrongdoing, but bear in mind from this point on that I do *not* mean by this that the agent *knows* that the behavior in question is wrong, since, in keeping with the foregoing remarks, I am not presupposing that the agent's belief that the behavior is wrong must meet the standard of epistemic justification required for knowledge.

There is a distinction between knowing *that* some proposition is true and knowing *whether* that proposition is true. The latter consists in either knowing that the proposition in question is true or knowing that it is false. So, too, there is a distinction between being ignorant *of the truth* of some proposition and being ignorant *of whether* that proposition is true. The latter consists in either being ignorant of the fact that the proposition in question is true or being ignorant of the fact that it is false. Notice that, even though it is impossible to know with respect to some proposition that one is ignorant of its truth, it is perfectly possible to know with respect to some proposition that one is ignorant of whether it is true. If some proposition is such that one neither believes nor disbelieves it, and one knows this, and one also knows that the proposition in question is either true or false, then, if one is rational, one will know that either the proposition is true but one fails to believe it or it is false but one fails to disbelieve it. This is all one needs to know in order to know that one is ignorant of whether the proposition is true. I will return to this point in §7.2.1.

3.2 Believing and failing to believe

Neither believing nor failing to believe is a simple matter. A proper assessment of the Argument from Ignorance and the Origination Thesis requires that we attend to each of these matters.

3.2.1 Knowledge and belief

I remarked above that it is sometimes held that (propositional) knowledge does not require belief. It is certainly true that people sometimes say that they don't believe something, even when it's clear that they know what they claim not to believe. Ichikawa and Steup consider the example of Walter, who comes home after work to find that his house has burned down. Walter says, "I don't believe it." But the "it" in question, namely, the fact that his house has burned down, is something that Walter knows, indeed knows all too well, to be true.[8]

This is not a convincing counterexample to the claim that knowledge requires belief. Walter has misspoken. It's obvious that he doesn't believe that his house is still standing, since otherwise he would not have reacted as he did. That he doesn't believe that his house is still standing does not of course entail that he does believe that it's not still standing, but, again, unless he had the latter belief, he would not have reacted as he did. Rather than his lacking this belief, what his remark indicates, as Ichikawa and Steup themselves note, is simply that he finds it hard to come to terms with the fact that his house has burned down. Indeed, in this regard, what he says is quite mild. Someone else in his position might well have said, "I *can't* believe it," thereby indicating that he finds it *very* hard, perhaps impossible, to come to terms with what has happened.

Suppose that Walter in fact cannot reconcile himself to what has happened. He is distraught, overwhelmed, unable to "move on." His friend, Nora, might say, "Poor fellow, he just can't accept the fact that his house has burned down." Unlike Walter, Nora has *not* misspoken. Some philosophers hold that belief and acceptance are one and the same,[9] but, as several others have recently emphasized,[10] they are not. (Or, to put matters less forcefully: there are common and important senses of the terms "believe" and "accept" that are distinct from one another. So, too, for the terms "disbelieve" and "reject.") As I am using the term, to accept a proposition is to take it as given, in order to achieve some desired outcome. It is an attitude that one typically adopts intentionally. One might accept a proposition for the sake of argument, for example, or in order to make plans for the future. In

---

[8] Ichikawa and Steup (2017), §1.2.   [9] See, e.g., Chisholm (1976), p. 27.
[10] See especially Cohen (1989) and Bratman (1992). See also B. Williams (1973), p. 140; Audi (2008), p. 413; Schwitzgebel (2015), §2.5.

contrast, in typical cases one cannot intentionally believe a proposition (although one can intentionally engage in some activity—undertake an inquiry, say—with the purpose of effecting a change in one's beliefs; I will discuss this issue more fully in §4.6). Note that, given this difference between acceptance and belief, it often happens that one accepts a proposition *because* one believes it. However, it can also happen that one fails to accept some proposition that one believes and fails to believe some proposition that one accepts. The case of Walter serves to illustrate the first of these possibilities. A case in which, whether compulsively or out of an abundance of caution, one double- or triple-checks the lock on a door that one knows to be secure, serves as another illustration of this possibility. An argument that proceeds by way of *reductio ad absurdum* serves as an illustration of the second possibility, as does a case in which I make plans on the basis of the assumption that you will be punctual, even though, given your habitual tardiness, I have no expectation that you will in fact turn up on time.

Colin Radford has offered another, much-discussed counterexample to the claim that knowledge requires belief.[11] Jean, a French-Canadian, professes ignorance of English history. Tom decides to test him on this and asks him a series of questions about the dates of certain significant events—when William the Conqueror landed in England, when Queen Elizabeth I died, and so on. To Jean's surprise, he answers several of these questions correctly, albeit very hesitantly, and he infers that he must at some time, many years before, have learned the relevant information, although he has no firm recollection of ever having done so. Radford claims that, when Jean gave the correct answers, he knew the relevant information but didn't believe it.

If we assume, as Radford clearly intends, that Jean's answers were not lucky guesses and do indeed indicate that he once learned the relevant information, we should surely agree that Jean did at some time know this information. Whether he knew it at the time that Tom quizzed him is perhaps less clear, although I suspect that many would say, along with Radford, that he did. But why say that, at that time, Jean knew it but didn't believe it? Jean's lack of confidence in his own answers indicates that he didn't believe *that he knew* the information in question, but that's another matter.[12] Radford himself allows for, indeed insists on, Jean's knowing this information nonetheless. I submit that there is just as much reason to insist on Jean's believing this information.

What it is perhaps most important to note, though, is that there is no need, for present purposes, to reach a definitive conclusion about whether knowledge requires belief. That is because, for the reasons given above, our present concern is not with whether one does something in the *knowledge* that it is wrong—that is, overall morally wrong—to do it, but simply with whether one does it in the *belief*

---

[11] Radford (1966).   [12] Cf. Cohen (1966), p. 11.

that it is wrong to do it. It was in order to emphasize this very point that I moved to the most recent formulations of the Argument from Ignorance and the Origination Thesis. If, contrary to what I believe, it were possible to do something knowing it to be wrong but *not* believing it to be so, this would not affect my central question, which is whether the *failure to believe* that what one is doing is wrong affords one an excuse for one's conduct. (It's true that, under such circumstances, the label "Argument from *Ignorance*" would be misleading, but, since I reject the possibility of such circumstances, I will stick with that label.)

3.2.2 Beliefs and dispositions

The question still remains, of course, what it is to believe something. This is a complicated and controversial question, on which there is an enormous literature. In the present context, I can only offer a few observations.

Philosophers have long noted a close association between belief and behavior. If you believe that it will rain later, you may well take an umbrella with you as you leave your house, whereas, if you believe that the sun will shine all day, you probably won't take an umbrella with you. This is a mundane, uncontroversial, but nonetheless helpful observation. How to improve on it in order to tighten one's grasp on the concept of belief, however, is highly controversial. The terms "may well" and "probably" that I just used are crucial, since clearly you might leave your umbrella behind even though you expect it to rain, and you might bring it with you even though you expect it not to rain. There is obviously no one-to-one correlation between belief and behavior; the link between the two is far more complex than that. Several philosophers have proposed that beliefs are *dispositions* to behave in certain ways, dispositions that may on occasion fail to be manifested, even under "favorable" conditions, due to the presence of some countervailing conditions. (Thus, even if you expect it to rain, you may leave your umbrella behind, if you also expect the wind to be so strong as to render the umbrella unusable, or if your umbrella is broken, or if you don't mind getting wet.) But, in light of such exceptions to the manifestation of the dispositions in question, it is extraordinarily difficult to identify precisely what the dispositions are (supposed to be) dispositions *to*. Perhaps the best that can be said in general along these lines is that one's believing some proposition *p* consists in being disposed to behave *as if p* were the case,[13] but just how this proposal is to be understood is far from clear. Suppose that today, having taken a look at the sky and noticed the gathering clouds, you took your umbrella with you when you left your house. Does this count as your acting "as if" it might rain? It may seem plausible to say so. But

---

[13] Cf. Marcus (1990).

suppose that your neighbor, Ned, likes to get wet. When today he took a look at that same sky and noticed those same clouds, he left his umbrella behind. Does this also count as his acting "as if" it might rain? It may seem plausible to say this, too. But don't you and Ned have the *same* belief, even though you are disposed to behave, and do behave, very *differently*? Unless the concept of behaving as if *p* were the case is clarified, the present proposal is difficult to assess.[14] Moreover, it seems plausible to think that, however the concept of behaving as if *p* were the case might be analyzed, it would remain possible that one have a disposition to behave in this way, not in virtue of believing *p*, but in virtue of something else—in virtue, say, of wanting to please one's friend, who very much likes it when one behaves as if *p* were the case.

In light of considerations of the sort just mentioned, many philosophers deny the "dispositionalist" view that beliefs are to be identified with dispositions to behave in certain ways. Several alternative accounts, which I will not discuss here, have been offered.[15] Despite being opposed to dispositionalism, almost all these accounts nonetheless endorse the idea that many, indeed most, of our beliefs are (merely) dispositional, although just what *this* idea comes to is, once again, controversial. The basic point, though, one that is highly relevant to my project in this book, is that, to believe that *p* is the case, one need *not* be currently considering (entertaining, adverting to, thinking about) *p*. For example, I expect that you believe that Paris is the capital of France, and that you believed this five minutes ago, too. Because I have just brought this fact to your attention, you may well be currently entertaining the proposition that Paris is the capital of France, but I bet you weren't thinking about it five minutes ago. Contrast this case with one that I raised in Chapter 1. Prior to consulting Wikipedia, I certainly did not believe that Astana was the capital of Kazakhstan (nor, of course, did I believe that it wasn't). If, prior to reading Chapter 1, you had this belief, then you were better informed than I was.

One account of the nature of belief, both occurrent and dispositional, that I find promising has recently been proposed by Rik Peels.[16] Peels notes that often, when we consider (entertain, advert to, think about) some proposition *p*, we think that *p* is indeed the case. (Note the difference between thinking *about* and thinking *that*; the former, though necessary, is not sufficient for the latter.) For example, when I think about Paris being the capital of France, I think *that* it is. This is *occurrent* belief. But, as just noted, not all belief is occurrent. Five minutes ago I believed that Paris was the capital of France, even though I wasn't considering this proposition. Peels distinguishes between two types of non-occurrent belief (neither of which he calls dispositional, although both of them involve having a disposition). Roughly, Peels holds that one *dormantly* believes *p* just in case one does not now

---

[14] Cf. Schwitzgebel (2015), §1.2.   [15] A useful overview may be found in Schwitzgebel (2015).
[16] Peels (2017), pp. 28 ff.

occurrently believe *p* but did occurrently believe it the last time one considered it and would now occurrently believe it if one were to consider it. (Let me stress that this is indeed rough, since, as Peels takes pains to acknowledge, there can be exceptional cases in which the counterfactual is false but one nonetheless has the relevant dormant belief. One might be distracted, for example, or under great stress, in which case, despite believing *p*, one might *not* think that *p* was the case even if one were to consider it.) Peels claims further (and again I am putting his proposal roughly) that one *tacitly* believes *p* just in case one neither occurrently nor dormantly believes it but it obviously follows, from one's own perspective, from propositions that one does occurrently or dormantly believe and one would now occurrently believe it if one were to consider it; for example (an example I borrow from Ingmar Persson[17]), *p* might be the proposition that birds do not wear boots.

There may be questions to be raised about the details of Peels's account, questions that there is no need to discuss here,[18] but one question that should be addressed is this: In allowing for the possibility that a dispositional belief be not dormant but tacit, is the account too expansive? Your believing five minutes ago that Paris was the capital of France will presumably qualify as a dormant belief, precisely because this is a proposition that you once considered and continue to endorse. But Peels's account attributes to you, and me, and everyone else beliefs in propositions that we have never considered. (His is not the only account to do so.[19]) There will presumably be *indefinitely*, quite possibly *infinitely*, many such propositions. Do we really have so many beliefs? Peels gives the following argument for the claim that indeed we do:

> People believe that they are less than two miles tall, that they are not bats, and that 2 is a smaller number than 999, even if they have never thought about these propositions. If you are not sure whether people believe these things, ask whether they *know* these things. There, it seems, the answer is surely positive. My neighbor knows that he is not a bat, even if he has never considered that proposition. But knowledge ... entails belief. Hence, people *believe* these things, even if they have never entertained the propositions in question ...[20]

One might reject this argument on the basis of denying the premise that knowledge entails belief. As I have said, though, I accept this premise. Nonetheless, I am inclined to resist Peels's argument. I am inclined to think that, in general, people do *not* know that they are less than two miles tall, that they are not bats, etc. It may

---

[17] Persson (2019), p. 26.
[18] Questions such as whether a dormant belief that *p* is the case can be formed only by way of considering *p* (regarding which see n. 23 below), what the criterion is for one proposition's "obviously following" from another, and the like.
[19] Again, see Persson (2019), pp. 26 f. Cf. Schwitzgebel (2015), §2.2, on "implicit" belief.
[20] Peels (2017), pp. 32 f.

well be, of course, that, were you to ask them whether they were less than two miles tall, they would immediately assent to this proposition (unless they suspected some sort of trick), but that, it seems to me, only shows that they would immediately form the belief upon being asked, rather than that they already have this belief—they have a *disposition to believe* the proposition but do not *dispositionally believe* it.

The distinction between a dispositional belief and a (mere) disposition to believe has been examined in detail by Robert Audi.[21] He claims that the distinction consists, at least in part, in the distinction between the accessibility of a proposition by a retrieval process that draws on memory and its accessibility only through a belief-formation process. When you assent to the proposition that Paris is the capital of France, you are accessing information that you already possess, information that is stored in your memory. When you assent to the proposition that 2 is a smaller number than 9999 (I have changed Peels's example slightly in order to fix on a proposition that, I assume, you had not already entertained and affirmed), you are not drawing on your memory. Or, to put the point more precisely, you are not drawing on your memory of the fact that 2 is a smaller number than 9999; you are, instead, drawing on your memory of *other* facts from which you immediately infer this proposition.

But, while I am inclined to deny that there can be tacit beliefs (as defined by Peels), I recognize that the case is not closed. Peels himself acknowledges the distinction between a disposition to believe and a dispositional belief.[22] He doesn't claim that every disposition to believe something qualifies as a tacit belief; he holds that one tacitly believes a proposition only if it obviously follows, from one's own perspective, from other propositions that one believes. This is what allows him to say that most people know, and hence believe, that they are not bats, even if they don't believe that they are not mammals of the order Chiroptera, and even though they would presumably assent to the latter proposition once they learned that that is how bats are classified zoologically. Moreover, I think it must be admitted that it does seem quite natural to say that most people do indeed know that they are not bats (and that birds don't wear boots, and that 2 is a smaller number than both 999 and 9999, etc.). To the objection, perhaps implicit in Audi's account of belief, that one cannot have a belief that one has not formed, and there is no occasion on which one forms the tacit beliefs that Peels identifies, Peels could, I think, respond as follows. First, it is perhaps somewhat misleading to say that people form beliefs at all, since this might be taken to suggest some voluntary activity on their part, and no one voluntarily forms beliefs, at least not directly. (See Premise 6 of the Argument from Ignorance. This premise is admittedly controversial; I will discuss it further in §4.6. I do *not* mean to suggest that Audi himself holds that beliefs are

---

[21] Audi (1994).   [22] Peels (2017), p. 36.

formed voluntarily.) It would be better to say that people acquire beliefs, or come to have them, or that beliefs form (or form themselves) in people. Second, Audi appears to presuppose that, in many cases at least,[23] one can come to have and retain a belief that p is the case only if one considers p and then stores it in one's memory. This presupposition immediately rules out the possibility of tacit beliefs in such cases, of course, but it is open to question. As Peels understands tacit beliefs, they constitute a proper subset of dispositions to believe. Such dispositions must presumably be acquired and retained in some way, but of course they need not be acquired by way of considering some proposition or retained by storing some proposition in one's memory. This observation also helps to dispel the worry that possession of a very large or infinite number of beliefs requires some vast storage capacity, inasmuch as, even if there are strict limits on what and how much we can remember, there seems to be no corresponding limit on what dispositions we can have. There seems to be no doubt, for example, that people in general have a disposition to agree that 2 is a smaller number than 999, a disposition (whether another disposition or the same disposition is a matter of debate) to agree that 2 is a smaller number than 1000, a disposition to agree that 2 is a smaller number than 1001, etc. ad infinitum.

In sum, it's clear that we have not only occurrent but also dormant beliefs. Whether we also have tacit beliefs is not so clear. I am inclined to think that we do not, but I acknowledge that there is reason to think otherwise.[24]

3.2.3 Occurrent beliefs

Dormant beliefs and, if there are any, tacit beliefs involve the disposition to have an occurrent belief. I have endorsed Peels's claim that occurrently believing some proposition p involves, in turn, considering (or entertaining, or adverting to, or thinking about) p. But what does *this* involve? This is yet another complicated and controversial question, on which I can again offer only a few observations. But offer them I must, since just how subversive of our everyday ascriptions of blameworthiness the Origination Thesis is may seem to depend in large part on whether the relevant beliefs must be occurrent—an issue that I will address in §6.2.1.

---

[23] Audi explicitly notes in his (1994), pp. 420 f., that it seems to be possible to acquire some beliefs (e.g., the belief that an ambulance passed by) through perception rather than consideration.

[24] There is a related, but different debate in the philosophy of mind about whether we have knowledge of the rules of grammar that we follow when we engage in linguistic behavior. Some theorists hold that we do have knowledge of these rules but that our knowledge is "tacit," in that what we know is inaccessible to us and, not being inferentially integrated with any of our beliefs, is itself not something that we believe but rather something toward which we have only a "subdoxastic" attitude. For discussion, see Macdonald (1995), Davies (1995), and Searle (1995). I will forgo any comment on this debate, except to note in passing that I have observed, on more than one occasion, small children misusing irregular verbs, treating them as if they were regular (saying, for example, "I hitted the ball," "He holded the bat," and so on). Such misuse seems to me to be evidence of a mistaken inference.

Consider again your belief that Paris is the capital of France. Five minutes ago (or, by now, ten or fifteen minutes ago), before I brought this belief to your attention, it was dormant. Now, I assume, it is occurrent. Earlier, you had the relevant information, but you were not thinking about it; now you are. It was, if I may put it this way, in your mind but not on your mind. What precisely is the difference?

Instead of saying that your belief that Paris is the capital of France is now *occurrent*, I might have said that you are now *conscious* or *aware* of this fact. This suggests an equivalence that some would deny, however. In a probing discussion of the difference in law between recklessness and negligence, Douglas Husak has the following to say:

> [C]*onsciousness* or *awareness* of a substantial and unjustifiable risk is the single factor that distinguishes recklessness from negligence. If the defendant *is* aware of the risk, he is reckless. If he is *not* aware, he is negligent as long as he *should* have been aware...
>
> When *is* a person aware of something? In particular, when is a person aware of a risk?... [T]he difference between the reckless and negligent defendant is simply a function of their beliefs: the reckless defendant, unlike the negligent defendant, *believes* that he is creating a substantial and unjustifiable risk...
>
> [However,] awareness (or belief) need not be *occurrent*...[I]t is clear that defendants need not have the explicit thought about the risk before their conscious minds in order to be reckless. In other words, reckless persons need not be saying to themselves "this is risky" when they act. Few of us would ever be reckless if we needed to rehearse such thoughts... Indeed, the number of beliefs we hold at any particular time would be very few if this test were adopted. For example, I would not believe the true proposition "My name is Douglas Husak" when concentrating on my writing. Phenomenologically, we rarely articulate propositions to ourselves in order to qualify as believing them. And for good reason. Persons who are keenly aware of a risk and seek to minimize it quickly learn not to be distracted from their task by mentally entertaining such propositions. For example, the experienced baseball player who bats with two strikes does not think to himself "I might miss the next pitch and strike out." Such thoughts would sap his focus from the job at hand: hitting the baseball if it is thrown over the plate. Yet I assume that no one would infer that this batter is unaware of and does not believe he is at risk of striking out... *Of course* he is aware of the risk...[25]

---

[25] Husak (2011), pp. 207 ff.

This rich passage raises a couple of issues that warrant explicit consideration.

First, Husak writes as if consciousness and awareness are one and the same.[26] But this is not the case. Awareness is veridical, whereas consciousness need not be. Crawling across the hot desert sand, you are conscious of water on the horizon. You are not aware of it, however, because what you see is a mirage. Also, awareness is an intentional attitude, but it is controversial whether consciousness must be intentional. (An attitude is intentional, in the present, technical sense, just in case it is directed toward some object.) To be aware is to be aware *of* something. Often, of course, when one is conscious, one is conscious of something. The question is whether it is possible to be conscious *without* being conscious of something. If, as many claim, to be conscious is to be the subject of *experiences*, that is, to be in a state that has a certain *phenomenal* character, then it seems plausible to say that consciousness need not be intentional; for it seems plausible to say that not all experiences need be experiences that are directed toward some object. (For example, you may be depressed but not depressed *at* anything.) However, if, as many others propose, consciousness is to be understood in terms of having *access to information*, then it must be intentional; the information in question will be the object toward which it is directed. These two conceptions of consciousness are not mutually exclusive, but they are distinct.[27]

My concern in this book is with whether one believes, at the time one does something, that one is doing wrong. This is a matter of having access to information. For my purposes, then, there will be no need to distinguish between consciousness and awareness on this score, and so I am happy to go along with Husak in this respect. Belief need not be veridical, of course, but insofar as my concern (like Husak's) is with ignorance of the *fact* that one is doing wrong, there will be no need to distinguish between consciousness and awareness on this score, either (for the time being, at least; I will return to this question in §3.4 below).

The second issue, regarding which I do differ with Husak, is this. He stresses what he takes to be an important distinction between consciousness or awareness, on the one hand, and occurrent belief, on the other. He appears to think of entertaining a proposition (something that is necessary for occurrently believing it) as a matter of focusing one's attention on it, of having it "at the forefront of one's mind."[28] As he observes, he does not have his own name at the forefront of his mind when he concentrates on his writing (or, at least, not usually; presumably he did do so when he gave his example). And, as he also observes, the batter knows that he had better not have the fact that he is at risk of striking out at the forefront of his mind if he is to succeed in not striking out. Nonetheless, Husak claims, the batter is clearly aware of this risk, and, I assume, Husak would say that he is clearly

---

[26] He is not alone in this. Cf. Sher (2009), p. 127; Levy (2014), p. 29.
[27] For discussion, see Siewert (2017) and Van Gulick (2017).
[28] See Husak (2016), pp. 195 f. Cf. Schwitzgebel (2015), §2.1.

aware of his own name. Another context in which, it might be claimed, one can be aware of something without attending to it is one in which one is listening to a complex piece of music.[29] Imagine that you are listening with your eyes closed to a recording of Beethoven's seventh symphony. The whole orchestra is engaged: strings, winds, etc. As you listen, you shift your attention from the strings to the winds and back again; then you listen even more closely to the strings, focusing on the cellos while bracketing the violins; and so on. It may seem plausible to say that, when you are attending to one set of instruments, you are not attending to the others, and yet all the while you are conscious or aware of them all.

I am not persuaded by such examples that one can be conscious or aware of something without attending to it.[30] Consider first what Husak says. In saying "...no one would infer that this batter is unaware of and does not believe he is at risk of striking out," he appears to be identifying awareness with (true) belief. But, given that beliefs can be dormant, this seems a mistake. No doubt Husak knows his own name even when he's not thinking about it, but is he really *aware* of it when he concentrates on his writing? Were you *aware* five (or ten, or fifteen, or twenty) minutes ago that Paris was the capital of France? It seems odd to say so. (Of course, had I asked you this question then, or had I interrupted Husak while he was writing and posed the relevant question to him, each of you would presumably have answered, correctly, that you were indeed aware of the matter at hand. But that answer would have been correct precisely because I had brought the matter to your attention.) It seems odder still to say that each of you was *conscious* of the relevant information. But then what about Husak's point that, if the batter had concentrated on not striking out, his doing so would have been self-defeating? We can grant this, while avoiding the view that awareness is simply a matter of (true) belief, if we make what I take to be a common and plausible observation: attention comes in *degrees*, and hence consciousness or awareness does, too. It seems plausible to say that, when he concentrates on his writing, Husak (usually) pays no attention at all to his own name. Likewise, before I raised the issue, you were paying no attention at all to the fact that Paris was the capital

---

[29] Cf. Watzl (2011), pp. 146 ff.

[30] For further discussion, see Jennings (2015). None of the (alleged) examples of consciousness without attention discussed in this article seem applicable to the particular case of being conscious of wrongdoing.

There is the converse question of whether someone can attend to something without being conscious of it. A dramatic, often-cited example of this alleged possibility is that of blindsight, which is the ability to detect and respond to visual stimuli despite the fact that, due to damage to one's primary visual cortex, one is not aware that one is seeing anything. There are cases in which people do indeed display this ability. (See Weiskrantz (1986) for discussion.) We can surely agree that in these cases the subjects are not aware of the stimuli. Whether they nonetheless attend to these stimuli is controversial, however; some (e.g., Wu (2014), pp. 110 ff.) contend that they do, while others (e.g., Prinz (2011)) claim that they don't. Unless there is some analogous phenomenon when it comes to attending to *non*-visual information, however (and I know of no suggestion that there is), I think we may safely ignore this possible instance of attention without consciousness.

of France. The case of the batter seems different, however. Although he is concentrating on the job at hand, he is nonetheless also conscious of the fact that he might strike out. (Consider Husak's own apparent admission that someone may be *more or less* keenly aware of a risk.) This observation also helps deal with the music example. Contrary to the claim that you are conscious of the entire orchestra and yet are attending to only one section of it, I suggest instead that no section is receiving your *full* attention precisely because you are conscious of, and thus *are* attending to, all the other sections, too, if only partially.

It is difficult to know how to flesh out this common observation about degrees of attention. One way to try to do so is to make use of certain metaphors. I have already employed a couple. I have talked of having certain information at the "*forefront*" of one's mind. This suggests, aptly I think, that certain other information may be on one's mind but lie somewhat further "back." When information is "on," as opposed to merely "in," one's mind, it is not just information to which one has access, it is information that one has accessed. It is something about which one is currently thinking, *even if* it is not "right up front." Another metaphor, employed by Husak himself and equally apt, is that of *focusing*. The batter focuses on the job at hand, but, as in any visual field, whether literal or metaphorical, there is not just a focal point but also a periphery, with some items lying closer to the former and others, of which one is perhaps only "dimly" aware, closer to the latter. Another, very closely related metaphor is that of a *center* of attention, a metaphor that might be embellished by saying that this center is surrounded by concentric circles.[31] (Husak himself talks of "concentration.") The "area" of attention is contained within the circumference of the outermost circle.[32]

---

[31] Cf. Watzl (2011).

[32] It is perhaps worth mentioning support for the thesis that awareness requires attention that is provided by the phenomenon of inattentional blindness. A dramatic, often-cited experiment that suggests that inattentive consciousness is *not* possible involved subjects watching a video in which six people, three wearing black shirts and three wearing white, moved from one spot to another, passing a pair of basketballs among themselves. The subjects were asked to count the number of passes made by those wearing white shirts. Doing so required careful attention. As the balls were tossed back and forth, a gorilla (or, rather, a person in a gorilla suit) entered the scene stage left, paused at center stage, turned to face the camera, thumped its chest, and then exited stage right. After having watched the video, half of the subjects, when asked whether they had seen the gorilla, replied that they had not. (See www.theinvisiblegorilla.com/gorilla_experiment.html. For discussion, see Simons and Chabris (1999).) Of course, no such single experiment can establish the truth of the *general* thesis that awareness requires attention. We can surely agree that these subjects did not attend to the gorilla. Whether they were aware of it, despite being unable to report on it afterwards, is controversial, however. Some contend that they may have been (e.g., Smithies (2011), pp. 254 ff.), others that they were not (e.g., Prinz (2011)). But even if they weren't, that still leaves the possibility that other people, in the same or another setting, might display awareness without attention. Nonetheless, the general thesis certainly seems plausible. It seems reasonable to say that those who both noticed the gorilla and managed to count the number of passes correctly succeeded in attending to both matters—not equally, perhaps, but that's precisely my point. (Whether we should say that in such a case one's attention is divided or multiplied is an interesting question.) Likewise, it seems reasonable to say that the batter in Husak's example attended primarily to doing the job at hand while also taking note of the fact that he might strike out.

Another complication here has to do with *self*-awareness. One can be aware of something without being aware that one is aware of it. (The term "conscious state" is often used in this context, but it is treacherous, I think, because ambiguous. There is a distinction to be drawn between a state *in* which one is conscious and a state *of* which one is conscious.[33]) The batter, for example, may not be aware that he is aware of the risk of striking out, while being quite aware that he is focusing, or attempting to focus, on hitting the ball if it is thrown over the plate. (Perhaps focusing "purely" on the job at hand—presumably the optimal state under the circumstances—would preclude such self-awareness, however.)

There is, it should be acknowledged, another way (consistent with the thesis that awareness requires some degree of attention, but also consistent with the denial of this thesis) to construe what happens in Husak's baseball scenario, and that is to say that the batter attends *first* to the risk of striking out and *then* to doing the job at hand. If the degree of focus needed to accomplish the job precludes devoting any degree of attention at that *same* time to the risk (or to anything else, including the fact that he is focusing on the job at hand), it would of course remain true that, at *some* time during his session at bat, the batter attended to the risk. Perhaps this construal of the scenario better accommodates Husak's allusion to the batter's being *keenly* aware of the risk of striking out, since a normal person cannot maintain keen awareness of one matter while focusing on another. In any event, notice how odd it would be if, when commenting later on his turn at bat, the player were to say, "You know, the thought of striking out never occurred to me." If that had indeed been the case, I think we should say that, far from being aware that he might strike out, the batter was oblivious to this possibility.

I am suggesting, then, that occurrently believing a proposition *p* consists in being conscious of or, in the case of true propositions, aware of the truth of *p*. This requires attending to *p* to some degree, but the degree may be minimal; for that is all that considering (entertaining, adverting to, thinking about) *p* requires.

3.2.4 Degrees of belief

An occurrent belief that *p* is the case involves attending to *p*. I have suggested that attention comes in degrees. It is often claimed that belief *also* comes in degrees. This is an entirely different matter, one that cuts across the issue that I have just been discussing. One can hold a dormant belief (such as the belief that Paris is the capital of France) with great confidence while holding an occurrent belief (such as the belief that one has just spotted an oasis in the desert) with considerable diffidence. In the latter case, one might even disavow having a belief altogether, saying only that one *suspects* that *p* is the case.

---

[33] Cf. Finkelstein (1999), p. 81.

Instead of degrees of belief or confidence, philosophers often talk of *credences*.[34] One common way of trying to regiment the discussion is to treat credences as falling within a numerical range from 0 to 1. A credence of 1 in p represents complete confidence, absolute certainty, that p is the case, while a credence of 0 in p represents complete confidence that p is *not* the case; credences between 1 and 0 thus represent uncertainty whether p is the case. This is a useful device, since it provides an intuitively appealing picture of how one can have, and how it can be reasonable to have, some degree of credence in a proposition while also having some degree of credence in its negation. But I would caution against too strong or uncritical a reliance on it, for two reasons.

First, it seems that in many, perhaps all cases there will be no fact of the matter as to *just* how strong one's credence in a proposition is. One's credence in a proposition may fall within some range—between 0.8 and 0.9, say—and yet not have any precise value within that range. It smacks of absurdity to claim, for example, that someone has a credence of precisely 0.83256 in some proposition. True, this absurdity might on occasion reside in the fact that no one can know that some credence has this precise strength, but on other occasions it seems to reside in the very idea of a credence having any precise strength. (Compare the claim that, regardless of whether there is a useful metric available to gauge strength of desire, one person has a desire for cake that is *precisely* as strong as another person's desire for ice cream.) The fact, as I see it, that credences can be imprecise raises some interesting questions.

One question, perhaps not too pressing, concerns the relation between credence and confidence. A precise credence of, say, 0.9 or a moderately imprecise credence between, say, 0.8 and 0.9 represents a fairly high degree of confidence in the proposition in question. Likewise, a precise credence of, say, 0.1 or a moderately imprecise credence between, say, 0.1 and 0.2 represents a fairly low degree of confidence in a proposition. But what degree of confidence should be associated with a massively imprecise credence between, say, 0.1 and 0.9? It would be misleading to say either that it is high or that it is low. It would also be misleading to say that it is middling, since that suggests a credence of, or close to, 0.5. Perhaps the best that can be said is that the degree of confidence is "broad," but I'm not sure whether that makes any sense. I'm inclined to think, therefore, that in this context talk of confidence may be misplaced. Some may take that to be a reason to deny that such massively imprecise credences are possible, but it seems plain to me that they are. (I give an example in the next paragraph.)

Another, far more pressing question concerns just how we should conceive of imprecise credences. According to one popular proposal, imprecise credences are

---

[34] Note that how *confidently* one holds a belief should be distinguished from how *firmly* one holds it. The latter has to do with how reluctant one is to give up the belief. For discussion, see Pojman (1986), pp. 154 f. and Moon (2017), p. 768.

representable, not (as precise credences are) by a single probability within the range of 0 to 1, but by a closed interval that comprises a set of probability functions that span that range.[35] But this convention seems to me to mask, and sometimes to misrepresent, the various ways in which credences can be imprecise. One may have an imprecise credence due to the fact that one's evidence is incomplete, or conflicted, or involves considerations that are in some respect incomparable, and the type of imprecision can vary accordingly and in a manner that is not accurately reflected in the proposed model. Consider, for example, a case in which you have good but incomplete evidence regarding a coin: you know that it is biased in such a way that, when tossed, it either lands heads 75% of the time or tails 75% of the time, but, whether because of lack of evidence or because of conflicting evidence, you don't know which of these biases it has. As a result, your credence regarding the proposition that the coin will land heads the next time it is tossed is imprecise. Is this credence properly represented by the interval [0.25, 0.75]? Presumably not, since, on the present approach, this represents a kind of credal indifference on your part across the range of probabilities contained in the interval. A better representation would seem simply to be the pair of numbers {0.25, 0.75}.[36] Or consider a case in which your evidence is very meager indeed: you know that the coin has some bias, but you have no idea what that bias is. Is your credence that it will land heads the next time it is tossed properly represented by the interval [0, 1]? Presumably not, for two reasons. First, this interval contains 0.5, which represents no bias at all. Second, this interval also contains both 0 and 1, which fall outside the range of relevant probabilities.

The second reason why I would caution against too strong a reliance on thinking of credences as being in some way representable as falling between 0 and 1 is that it suggests that one's credences regarding a proposition must sum to 1. Although this is arguably the case for someone who is fully rational,[37] there can be no guarantee that the credences of someone who is not fully rational will be so well behaved.

The expression "degrees of belief" strongly suggests that credences are degrees of *belief*, but in fact the relation between credence and what I, along with many others, will call *outright* belief is not at all straightforward.[38] One simple proposal about this relation is that one has an outright belief that *p* is the case if and only if

---

[35] For a helpful discussion of this idea, and of imprecise credences generally, see S. Bradley (2019).
[36] Both the example and the proposed representation are drawn from Mayo-Wilson and Wheeler (2016), p. 61.
[37] Note that this claim is compatible with the claim that not only precise but also imprecise credences can be rational, if the latter are representable by closed intervals. For example, rationality may require not only that, if one has a credence of, say, 0.9 in *p*, then one have a corresponding credence of 0.1 in ~*p*, but also that, if one has a credence, say, of [0.8, 0.9] in *p*, then one have a corresponding credence of [0.1, 0.2] in ~*p*.
[38] Alternative but, I think, less apt expressions are: "full belief," "plain belief," "belief flat out," "belief period," and "belief full stop."

one's credence in p is 1. This proposal seems clearly unacceptable, since it rules out the possibility of holding a belief with less than full confidence, a possibility that would appear to be frequently realized. Another proposal is that one has an outright belief that p is the case if and only if one's credence in p is greater than 0.5. But this proposal is unacceptable, too. Suppose, to borrow a well-known example, that you have just bought a lottery ticket. In all, 100 tickets have been sold. You believe (that is, you have an outright belief) that the lottery is a fair one, and so your credence in the proposition that you will not win the lottery is 0.99. Do you therefore believe that you will not win? Not necessarily. Given your belief that the lottery is fair, you also have a credence of 0.99 in each of the following propositions: Ticket 1 is not the winning ticket, Ticket 2 is not the winning ticket,..., and Ticket 100 is not the winning ticket. Call these propositions $P_1, P_2, \ldots$, and P_{100}, respectively. Now, suppose that your beliefs happen to conform to a norm, one that many philosophers endorse,[39] that requires that, if one believes some proposition p and also believes some proposition q, then one believes $p\&q$. Then, if you believed each of $P_1, P_2, \ldots$, and P_{100}, you would also believe $P_1 \& P_2 \& \ldots \& P_{100}$. But you *don't* believe this long conjunctive proposition. On the contrary, you are *certain* that it is *false* (that is, your credence in it is 0), since you are certain that one of the 100 tickets is the winning ticket. Hence you don't believe *any* of $P_1, P_2, \ldots$, and P_{100}, even though your credence in each of them is very high (0.99, which of course is much higher than 0.5).[40]

Credences are often said to consist in assignments of "subjective probability."[41] This might be taken to suggest that we say, not that one believes that p *is* the case, but rather that one believes that p is *probably* the case, if and only if one's credence in p is greater than 0.5. But this is problematic, too. I think that, on one understanding, this proposal is probably *correct* (that is, my credence in it is relatively high), but only if "believes" is understood as *not* referring to outright belief.[42] I say this for two reasons. First, an outright belief that p is the case requires that one grasp or understand p, and it seems likely that there are many individuals (small children, for example, and perhaps also some animals) that have credences but do not have any grasp of the concept of probability. Second, there are different kinds of probability. A commonly-acknowledged, even if somewhat obscure, threefold distinction is that between objective, epistemic, and subjective probability. It is clear that one's credences needn't align with one's beliefs about either objective or epistemic probabilities (whatever it is that these consist in, precisely). For example, one might acknowledge that only 10% of the people with the same medical condition from which one is suffering survive for more than a few weeks

---

[39] Though not all. See Foley (2009).
[40] Perhaps it is also possible for one to have an outright belief that p is the case even though one's credence in p is less than 0.5. Such a belief would no doubt be irrational, but that doesn't make it impossible.
[41] See, e.g., Huber (2009), pp. 4 ff.   [42] Contrast Moon and Jackson (2020).

(a matter of objective probability) and also acknowledge that there is no good reason to think that one's own case is exceptional (a matter of epistemic probability), while nonetheless being optimistic about—that is, having a high credence in—one's own long-term survival. Perhaps such optimism is irrational, but, as long as it is possible, it shows that the present proposal cannot be accepted, if it is either objective or epistemic probability that is at issue. That leaves subjective probability. Given that the subjective probability of a proposition is the measure of one's credence in it, this interpretation of the present proposal amounts to the claim that one's credence in p is greater than 0.5 if and only if one believes that one's credence in p is greater than 0.5. This, again, is clearly unacceptable, since one may be mistaken about how confident one is that p is the case.

In light of considerations such as the foregoing, I am inclined to believe that it is not possible to provide a satisfactory explication of credence in terms of outright belief or vice versa. Having a belief in a proposition of course does not preclude having a credence in it—on the contrary, the former presumably requires the latter; nonetheless, as we have seen, the latter does not require the former.

[Brief digression: It is perhaps worth taking note here of a somewhat mysterious phenomenon, and that is that, in certain contexts, making explicit mention of the fact that one believes some proposition serves to indicate that one's credence in it is not as high as it might otherwise seem. Suppose that you have just come from a meeting with Bob. A colleague asks you, "Where's Bob?" You reply, "He's in Room 216." Notice two things.[43] You have asserted that Bob is in Room 216; you have *not* asserted that you believe that he is in Room 216, although this belief is what is commonly known as a conversational implication of your assertion (that is, it would be reasonable, under the circumstances, for your colleague to infer that you do indeed have this belief). Now suppose that 15 minutes have passed, and another colleague comes along and asks, "Where's Bob?" This time you reply, "I *believe* he's still in Room 216." Notice two more things. This time, you have explicitly asserted that you believe that Bob is in Room 216, and your doing so serves paradoxically to indicate that you hold your present belief with *less* confidence than the belief you had 15 minutes ago. Of course, you could have given an even more cautious reply, such as "I'm *inclined to think* that he's still in Room 216," or "I *suspect he may* still be in Room 216," and the like.[44]]

The apparent independence of credence from belief raises an important question about my project in this book, a project that I have characterized as an

---

[43] Cf. G. E. Moore (2005), pp. 63 f.; B. Williams (1973), p. 138.

[44] Such hedging is common in many recent philosophical works, including this one (for confirmation, see the opening sentence of the previous paragraph). I recall Nicholas Rescher decrying this practice in private correspondence; he also published an editorial lamenting it (see Rescher (1984)). Although the practice can be irritating, it is, I believe (note again!), a mistake to call for its elimination. It signals the tentativeness with which one makes a claim, and it invites discussion. Feigning confidence is misleading and counterproductive.

examination of the relation between moral responsibility and the failure to *believe* that what one is doing is (overall morally) wrong. The question is whether this project, or my characterization of it, is too narrow, insofar as it doesn't take *credence* into account. This question may seem especially pressing when it comes to giving a satisfactory account of responsibility for *reckless* behavior, since, as Husak notes in the passage quoted above, such behavior is, by definition, behavior that involves running some kind of *risk*, and risk is to be understood in part in terms of probabilities. I will take up this important question in §7.1.4. For the time being, though, I will continue to portray my project as one that is concerned with belief about, rather than credence in, wrongdoing.

3.2.5 Conflicting beliefs

It is possible for someone to have conflicting beliefs. By this I mean that it is possible for one and the same person at one and the same time both to believe some proposition p and to believe some proposition q, even though it is impossible for it to be the case that $p\&q$ is true. (An analogous account of conflicts in intention and conflicts in desire can be given.) The impossibility in question might be merely empirical, or it might be something stronger. George has a conflict of the former kind if he believes that Len was in London yesterday while also believing that Len is in Paris today, when in fact all travel between the two cities has been closed off for over a week (the explanation of the conflict being that George doesn't know of the travel ban). Rhonda has a conflict of the latter kind if she believes that all squares are rectangles while also believing that no rhombuses are rectangles (the explanation of the conflict being that Rhonda isn't aware that rhombuses needn't have acute angles).

Might the conflict be strictly logical? That is, to put the question schematically, is it possible for there to be cases in which both Bp and $B\sim p$ are true for one and the same person at one and the same time? In a well-known article, Saul Kripke has argued that there is reason to think that the answer to this question is "Yes."[45] He gives the example of a Frenchman, Pierre, who speaks only French and, as a result of what others have told him, believes the proposition that he expresses by saying, "Londres est jolie." Subsequently, Pierre travels to England, learns some

---

[45] Kripke (1979). The question at issue should be carefully distinguished from the following questions:

(1) Is it possible for one and the same person at one and the same time to have both a non-zero credence in p and a non-zero credence in $\sim p$?
(2) Is it possible for $B(p\&\sim p)$ to be true?
(3) Is it possible for Bp and $\sim Bp$ both to be true?

The answer to the first question is clearly "Yes" and to the third clearly "No." I will leave the second question open.

rudimentary English, and takes up lodgings in an unattractive part of a city that, through conversation with the local inhabitants, he comes to know as "London." As a result, he sincerely assents to the proposition that London is not pretty, all the while apparently retaining his earlier belief that it is pretty. Is this a genuine case in which both Bp and $B{\sim}p$ are true? The matter is controversial. It's worth noting that, if it is, the explanation of the conflict in belief rests once again on the fact that the person who has the conflicting beliefs (in this case, Pierre) is ignorant of some crucial pertinent fact (in this case, that "Londres" and "London" refer to the same city).

Are there cases in which both Bp and $B{\sim}p$ are true whose explanation is *not* to be found in the person's being ignorant of some such underlying fact? Tamar Szabó Gendler has presented several kinds of cases that may seem to fit this description.[46] One that she discusses at length involves a person—call her Patty— who is near the edge of a precipice. She believes—she knows—that she is quite safe, since there is a high fence that prevents her from falling; nonetheless, she pulls anxiously away from the edge, thereby showing, it might be claimed, that she also believes that she is not safe. Such a situation is not at all uncommon. Other examples that Gendler gives include the common reluctance to eat fudge that is shaped like dog feces, even when one knows it to be fudge and not feces; the common experience of being terrified by what one sees on a movie screen; and the like. Perhaps we might also include the common tendency to speak back to the GPS in one's car (mine is called Emily).

Some commentators do indeed diagnose a conflict in belief in such cases.[47] Others offer a different diagnosis. Some, appealing to the thesis that "believes" is a vague predicate, claim that such cases involve a conflict between attitudes that, though akin to belief, do not fully qualify as such.[48] Gendler herself holds that such cases do *not* involve conflicting beliefs. On the contrary, she claims that they involve a conflict between a belief and another kind of attitude, one that she calls an "alief." As Gendler conceives of it, an alief is a mental state that is in several respects quite different from a belief. Among the differences are these: beliefs typically change in response to changes in evidence, whereas aliefs do not; and aliefs typically drive behavior "automatically," without the intervention of conscious thought and without the mediation of desires, whereas beliefs do not. Thus, although Patty believes that she is safe, she nonetheless alieves that she is not; she would revise her belief if she were to discover that the fence was damaged, whereas her sense that she is in danger persists despite her evidence. So too, although I believe that Emily is not a real person, I nonetheless alieve that she is a real person (especially when I get annoyed with her when she keeps saying

---

[46] Gendler (2008a) and (2008b).   [47] See, e.g., Borgoni (2015).
[48] See, e.g., Schwitzgebel (2010).

"Recalculating," the equanimity with which she does so serving only to add to my vexation). And so on for the other cases.

A particularly interesting kind of case in which Gendler claims that there is a conflict between a belief and an alief, one to which I will return briefly in §9.4, is that of someone—I'll call her Veronica—who is an avowed anti-racist. A white woman, she endorses racial equality with conviction, and frequently speaks out against those who hold racist views, and yet her behavior betrays the fact that she herself has strong racist tendencies. She automatically associates blacks with violence, tends to assume that they are intellectually inferior to her, and so on right down the line of wretched stereotypes, and she is usually quite unaware that she is doing so. On those rare occasions on which she catches herself out, she reacts to her own behavior with shame and bewilderment. According to Gendler, Veronica (whose case I have embellished a little) has a non-racist belief coupled with a contrary racist alief.

Not everyone accepts Gendler's assessment of cases such as Veronica's. Some critics point out that beliefs are not always responsive to evidence (a fact that Gendler herself acknowledges with the wry remark, "[T]hink about flat earthers, Roswellians, or your political opponents."[49]), whereas some automatic responses are (think of slamming on the brakes when a dog runs out in front of your car).[50] Some say that it can be appropriate to say of people like Veronica that they don't "really" believe "deep down" in racial equality.[51] Others say that such people do believe in racial equality but also "endorse" racial inequality in a "patchy" manner.[52] Still others say that such people do indeed have conflicting beliefs, one conscious and open to rational assessment and control, the other unconscious and rationally inaccessible.[53] It might seem important that this issue be settled, and indeed for some purposes (e.g., that of providing an accurate map of the mind) it surely is. For my purposes in this book, however, I don't think it matters one way or the other whether we say that Veronica's racist behavior is to be attributed to a belief of hers, to an alief, or to something else. This claim may surprise you. I will offer an explanation for it in §8.2, one that I will then go on to qualify in §9.4.

3.2.6 Failing to believe

Let me turn, finally, from believing to failing to believe. One fails to believe some proposition p just in case one does not believe it; that is, just in case $\sim Bp$.[54] There

---

[49] Gendler (2008b), p. 566, n. 26. Cf. Archer (2018). [50] Cf. Schwitzgebel (2010), p. 539.
[51] Cf. Schwitzgebel (2010), p. 539. [52] Cf. Levy (2017a), p. 13.
[53] Cf. Borgoni (2015). Cf. also Kornblith (2017), pp. 2586 f.; McHugh (2017), p. 2752.
[54] In saying this, I am presupposing that one currently exists. Notice that, for any proposition, it's true that Aristotle doesn't believe that proposition, but it would be odd to say that he fails to believe it.

are two basic ways in which it might be true that $\sim Bp$. First, one might *disbelieve* p; that is, $B\sim p$. Of course, as has just been discussed, it may be that its being true that $B\sim p$ is compatible with its also being true that Bp, but it seems safe to say that this is not the norm. On the contrary, the fact that it is true that $B\sim p$ is often what explains why it is the case that $\sim Bp$. Second, one might be *doxastically uncommitted* regarding p; that is, $\sim Bp$ & $\sim B\sim p$.[55] There are three types of such uncommittedness.[56] First, one may have some credence in the proposition and yet fail to believe it outright. In such a case one may be said to *suspect* that the proposition is true. (If one is rational, this suspicion will be accompanied by a complementary suspicion that the proposition is false.[57]) Second, one may have no credence whatsoever in the proposition, in virtue of never having considered it and thus being wholly *oblivious* to it. Third, one may have no credence in the proposition, despite having considered it, in virtue of being at a complete loss what to think about it—in which case I will say that one is *utterly baffled* by it.[58,59]

The most recent version of the Argument from Ignorance given in §3.1.1 is couched simply in terms of "failing to believe." No distinction is drawn between cases of disbelief and cases of doxastic uncommittedness, let alone between the different types of such uncommittedness. Do these distinctions matter? It may seem so. It may seem that whether one is blameworthy for ignorant wrongdoing can turn on whether or not one believes that one is doing the right thing, or merely suspects it, or is oblivious to or utterly baffled by the issue. Similarly, the most recent version of the Argument draws no distinction between the failure to have an occurrent belief that one is doing wrong, the failure to have a dormant belief that this is so, and the failure to have a tacit belief (if such a belief is possible) that this is so, and again it may well seem that this can matter as far as blameworthiness is concerned. I will take up these issues in Chapters 6 and 7.

---

[55] Cf. Chisholm (1976), p. 27; Peels (2017), pp. 165 ff.

[56] "Neutrality" would be a less awkward term than "uncommittedness," but it suggests a credence of 0.5, which of course is not necessary for one's neither believing nor disbelieving a proposition.

[57] In this context, I am taking "suspect" to mean the same as "have a (or some) suspicion," no matter how weak one's suspicion may be. In everyday usage, "suspect" is typically restricted to cases in which one's suspicion consists in having a credence greater than 0.5; where one's credence in a proposition is less than that, it would normally be said that one suspects that the proposition *may* be true. Also, it would not normally be said that one suspects a proposition to be true if one believes it outright.

[58] I suspect that utter bafflement (as I am using the term) occurs only rarely. A "credence" of [0, 1] may perhaps qualify as utter bafflement, being equivalent to one's having no credence at all, but a credence with a narrower range will not qualify as such.

[59] As to *suspension of judgment*: *if* we construe this as a way of failing to believe a proposition, I take it to consist in either suspecting that the proposition in question is true or being utterly baffled by it. I think, though, that suspension of judgment is typically construed as a way of failing to *accept* a proposition rather than of failing to believe it.

3.3 Acting from ignorance

Whenever one unwittingly does wrong, one commits the wrongdoing *in* ignorance of the fact that one is doing so. It is common to distinguish two ways in which this may happen. One acts *from* ignorance of the fact that what one is doing is wrong when one's ignorance *accounts* for one's wrongdoing; that is, the wrongdoing is to be *attributed* to one's ignorance; that is, one does what one does *because* of one's ignorance; that is, roughly, one would *not* commit the wrongdoing if one were not ignorant of the fact that it is wrong. In contrast, one acts *merely in* ignorance of the fact that what one is doing is wrong when one's ignorance does *not* account for one's wrongdoing; that is, the wrongdoing is *not* to be attributed to one's ignorance; that is, it is *not* the case that one does what one does because of one's ignorance; that is, roughly, one *would* still commit the wrongdoing even if one were not ignorant of the fact that it is wrong. This distinction can be traced to Aristotle, although it's not clear that he understood it precisely as I have just articulated it.[60] It's a distinction that many find significant, claiming that ignorance provides an excuse for wrongdoing only when the wrongdoing is committed from, and not merely in, ignorance.[61]

This view is plausible. Why should ignorance be thought to provide an excuse for wrongdoing if it is merely idle, supplying no explanation of one's behavior? Still, some remain unconvinced, claiming in turn that the fact that one would have engaged in the same behavior under counterfactual circumstances (circumstances in which one is not ignorant of the fact that the behavior is wrong) cannot be the grounds of one's culpability in the actual circumstances.[62] I think this is a mistake. As I see it, counterfactuals are highly relevant to the determination of actual culpability,[63] but the present view need not be cast in terms of counterfactuals anyway. All that's being claimed is that one's *actual* mental state of ignorance regarding one's wrongdoing furnishes an excuse only if it plays a certain role in the ancestry of that wrongdoing. If this view is correct, then the Argument from Ignorance requires further revision. (If it is not correct, then of course no revision is called for. But I'm inclined to think that it is correct, and caution dictates assuming that it is.) The following is perhaps a little rough (because "because" is a tricky term), but I hope it will do:

The Argument from Ignorance (Draft 4):
Suppose that

(1) (a) P committed A and (b) A was overall morally wrong, but (c) when P committed A, **P did so because** P failed to believe that A was overall morally wrong.

---

[60] Aristotle (1941), 1110b.
[61] See, e.g., Donagan (1977), pp. 128 ff.; Rivera-López (2006), p. 135.
[62] See Sarch (2014), p. 1059. Cf. Rosen (2008), p. 598, n. 14; Husak (2016), p. 224.
[63] See Zimmerman (2002).

In general it's true that

(2) if one committed some act or omission that was overall morally wrong **because one failed** to believe that it was overall morally wrong, one is morally to blame for it, and thereby morally to blame for any of its consequences, only if one is morally to blame for one's failure to believe that it was overall morally wrong.

Thus

(3) P is morally to blame for A, and thereby morally to blame for any of its consequences, only if P is morally to blame for P's failure to believe (call it F) that A was overall morally wrong.

It's also in general true that

(4) one is morally to blame for something only if one was in control of that thing.

Thus

(5) P is morally to blame for F only if P was in control of F.

Three further general truths are that

(6) one is never directly in control of whether one fails to believe something—that is, any control that one has over failing to believe something is always only indirect,

(7) if one is morally to blame for something over which one had only indirect control, then one's blameworthiness for it is itself only indirect, and

(8) one is indirectly morally to blame for something only if that thing was a consequence of something else for which one is directly morally to blame.

Thus

(9) P is morally to blame for A, and thereby to blame for any of its consequences, only if there was something else (call it X) for which P is directly morally to blame and of which F was a consequence.

But

(10) whatever X was, it cannot have been an act or omission such that (a) P committed it and (b) it was overall morally wrong and (c) when P committed it, **P did so because** P failed to believe that it was overall morally wrong, since otherwise the foregoing argument regarding A would apply all over again to X.

Thus

(11) whatever X was, it was either (a) not some act or omission that P committed or (b) not overall morally wrong or (c) **not** something such

that, when *P* committed it, **P did so because P failed to believe** that it was overall morally wrong.

Two further general truths are that

(12) one has direct control over something only if that thing is an act or omission, and

(13) one is morally to blame for an act or omission only if that act or omission was overall morally wrong.

Thus

(14) whatever *X* was, it was **not** an act or omission such that, when *P* committed it, **P did so because P failed to believe** that it was overall morally wrong.

The version of the Origination Thesis that is to be derived from this version of the Argument is rather cumbersome. It goes as follows:

> *The Origination Thesis (Draft 4):*
> Every chain of moral blameworthiness is such that at its origin lies a piece of behavior for which the agent is directly blameworthy and which **was such that either** he or she believed, at the time at which he or she engaged in it, **that it was overall morally wrong or he or she did not believe this but did not engage in the behavior because he or she did not believe this.**

That's quite a mouthful, but the gist of this version of the Thesis can be captured much more pithily, even if a little roughly. Let us say that wrongdoing that is committed merely in ignorance is wrongdoing that is *quasi-witting*. Then what the Thesis says is, roughly, that all blameworthiness is rooted in wrongdoing that is either witting or quasi-witting.

3.4 Blameworthiness without wrongdoing

As I mentioned above, ignorance is ignorance of facts. The particular form of ignorance with which this book is concerned is ignorance of the fact that one is doing something wrong. But must blameworthiness presuppose some such fact?

3.4.1 Accuses

I noted in the last chapter that it is possible to have an excuse for wrongdoing. Sally, whose child was born with phocomelia as a result of her taking a dose of Distaval, is surely not to blame for her child's condition. Whether she has an excuse for wrongdoing is perhaps not so clear, since there is some debate about whether behavior such as hers constitutes wrongdoing in the first place. But there are other cases in which it seems that such a verdict is well-nigh irresistible. In §2.1.3 I gave the case of Constance, who constantly tries very hard to ensure that she does the right thing on all occasions. Despite her best efforts, she nonetheless ends up sometimes doing wrong. On such occasions, she is surely not to blame; she has an excuse—a fully exculpatory excuse.

If there can be wrongdoing without blameworthiness, the question naturally arises whether there can be blameworthiness without wrongdoing. I think there can be. As I observed in Chapter 1, philosophers have traditionally identified two conditions, the dual satisfaction of which renders one blameworthy for one's behavior, one having to do with one's mental state, the other having to do with whether one was in control of one's behavior. As I noted in §2.2.1, nowadays the former condition is often couched in terms of one's "quality of will." I expressed reservations about such a use of this term, but let us put these aside for the moment. The question I want to raise is simply this: if it is possible for one to do wrong—something that is not only consistent with but, arguably, *requires* exercising control over one's behavior—and yet *fail* to exhibit the quality of will necessary for blameworthiness, why should it not also be thought possible for one to exercise control over one's behavior but *not* do wrong, while nonetheless *exhibiting* such quality of will? And, if this is possible, why should this not be deemed sufficient for one's being blameworthy for what one has done?

The possibility of being to blame for what one has done, even if one has done no wrong, used rarely to be entertained, let alone endorsed.[64] There is no term in common use to express this possibility. In an earlier work, I coined the term "accuse" (used as a noun, with a hard "s"), which I defined as the reason or grounds for imputing blameworthiness in the absence of wrongdoing,[65] and I argued that accuses are not only possible but indeed arise on occasion. What might count as such an occasion? Peter Graham provides the following case:

> Unbeknownst to Bob, Sue is about to detonate a bomb that will kill a thousand innocent people. The only way to prevent her from doing so is to kill her. Bob, for his own personal reasons, shoots her dead.[66]

According to Graham, Bob is blameworthy despite having done no wrong.

---

[64] Acknowledgment of this possibility is growing. Cf. G. E. Moore (2005), pp. 95 ff. (first published in 1912); Brandt (1958), pp. 38 f.; Donagan (1977), p. 112; Milo (1984); Parfit (1984), p. 25; Jackson (1986), pp. 362 f.; Thomson (1991), p. 295; Copp (1997), p. 448; Haji (1998), p. 146; Hieronymi (2008), p. 362, n. 12; Scanlon (2008), p. 125; Capes (2012); Khoury (2012), p. 198; Graham (2014), pp. 394 ff.; Levy (2014), p. 36; Shoemaker (2015a), p. 699.
[65] Zimmerman (1997a).   [66] Graham (2014), p. 394.

One reaction that you might have to Graham's case is to deny the claim that Bob did nothing wrong. Perhaps an objective view of moral obligation, of the sort I mentioned in §2.1.2, would declare Bob's behavior morally right, indeed morally obligatory, but, you might think, that just shows why we should reject such a view. Bob *had no reason to believe* that, in killing Sue, he was thereby saving a thousand innocent people from death, let alone that this was the only way to do so. You might think that, in light of this fact, what he did was therefore morally wrong after all, and so his also being to blame for what he did comes as no surprise.

To this, though, Graham could respond as follows.[67] All we need do is tweak the case a little so that Bob *is* aware of the threat that Sue poses to the innocent people, while letting it remain the case that he kills her for his own personal reasons. (We may imagine that he doesn't care at all about the innocent people. He simply sees an opportunity to get rid of Sue, whom he has hated ever since she was promoted over him.)

You might respond in turn by saying that we must take care to specify just what it is that Bob is to blame for. We shouldn't say that he is to blame for his action of *killing Sue*, precisely because this action wasn't wrong. But we can and should say that he is to blame for *killing Sue for his own personal reasons*, and *this* action was indeed wrong.[68] But I don't think this will do. Even if we agree that it was not wrong for Bob to kill Sue but it was wrong for him to kill her for his own personal reasons (a pair of claims that it would take some rather delicate theorizing to reconcile with one another), there seem to be cases that cannot be handled in this way. Suppose (this may take some stretch of the imagination) that Bob was so constituted that he *could not* kill Sue unless he did so for his own personal reasons. Then, on the present approach, he would be in a dilemma; he would be obligated to kill Sue and he would be obligated to refrain from doing so for his own personal reasons, and yet he could not do both of these things. I submit, but (as before[69]) I will not argue here, that this is an untenable result.

But then, you may well ask, if Bob isn't to blame either for killing Sue or for killing her for his own personal reasons, what *is* he to blame for? There are several possible answers. One is to say that he is to blame for doing what he *believed* was wrong. I don't think this will do, since Bob might not have had the belief in question. (This point is compatible with the Argument from Ignorance, as long as Bob is to blame for lacking the belief.) A second possibility is that what Bob is to blame for is not any *action* of his but an *attitude*. This is the approach recommended by Graham.[70] A problem with this approach is that it is difficult to see how it can be reconciled with the agential condition of control. Bob's hatred for Sue may be despicable, but how can he be to blame for having this attitude if it wasn't in his control? (This is not a purely rhetorical question. I will take it up in

---

[67] See Graham (2014), p. 395, including n. 13.
[68] Cf. Rosen (2015), p. 76. Cf. also Nelkin (2011), p. 107.   [69] See the very end of §2.1.2.
[70] Graham (2014), pp. 396 ff. Cf. Shoemaker (2015a), p. 699.

Chapter 9.) A third possibility is to draw on the distinction that I discussed in §2.2.4 between that for which one is to blame and that in virtue of which one is to blame. We might say that, in the case in question, Bob is not to blame *for* any action that he committed (let alone any attitude that he had), but he nonetheless is to blame *in virtue of* the quality of will that underlay his behavior. On this approach it is a mistake to think that, if one is blameworthy, one must be blameworthy for something, although it remains true that one must be blameworthy in virtue of something. I think that this approach has much to recommend it, but the idea is jarring and I won't press it here. I suggest instead that we embrace a final possible answer, which is to deny the presupposition and say that Bob is indeed to blame for killing Sue, even though that was the right thing for him to do. This no doubt sounds odd, but I think that it is nonetheless correct. Notice that accepting this answer does *not* require that we say that Bob is to blame for doing the right thing, an expression that may be taken to suggest, erroneously, that he is to blame for what he did *because* it was right.

No account of blameworthiness is complete unless it takes a stand on the possibility of accuses. If accuses are possible, then blameworthiness is likely incurred more often than is commonly supposed. This is a significant result, one that in a way runs counter to (although it is perfectly compatible with) the apparent implication of the Origination Thesis that blameworthiness is incurred less often than is commonly supposed. It is therefore important to try to determine whether accuses are possible and, if they are, which of the four approaches just outlined is correct. This point notwithstanding, it is in fact not important for *present* purposes to accomplish this task, for the Argument from Ignorance can be formulated in such a way that it remains neutral on the question of whether accuses are possible. The most recent version (Draft 4), which is explicitly couched in terms of one's *failing to believe* that one is doing wrong, lends itself easily to such a formulation. All that needs to be done is to delete any reference to the fact that one's behavior is indeed wrong, thereby leaving it open whether the belief in question, were one to have it, would be veridical. The result is the following simpler argument, the deletions being marked by bracketed ellipses:

The Argument from Ignorance (Draft 5):
Suppose that

(1) (a) *P* committed *A* [...] but (b) when *P* committed *A*, *P* did so because *P* failed to believe that *A* was overall morally wrong.

In general it's true that

(2) if one committed some act or omission [...] because one failed to believe that it was overall morally wrong, one is morally to blame for it, and thereby morally to blame for any of its consequences, only if one is morally to blame for one's failure to believe that it was overall morally wrong.

Thus

(3) P is morally to blame for A, and thereby morally to blame for any of its consequences, only if P is morally to blame for P's failure to believe (call it F) that A was overall morally wrong.

It's also in general true that

(4) one is morally to blame for something only if one was in control of that thing.

Thus

(5) P is morally to blame for F only if P was in control of F.

Three further general truths are that

(6) one is never directly in control of whether one fails to believe something—that is, any control that one has over failing to believe something is always only indirect,

(7) if one is morally to blame for something over which one had only indirect control, then one's blameworthiness for it is itself only indirect, and

(8) one is indirectly morally to blame for something only if that thing was a consequence of something else for which one is directly morally to blame.

Thus

(9) P is morally to blame for A, and thereby morally to blame for any of its consequences, only if there was something else (call it X) for which P is directly morally to blame and of which F was a consequence.

But

(10) whatever X was, it cannot have been an act or omission such that (a) P committed it [...] and (b) when P committed it, P did so because P failed to believe that it was overall morally wrong, since otherwise the foregoing argument regarding A would apply all over again to X.

Thus

(11) whatever X was, it was either (a) not some act or omission that P committed [...] or (b) not something such that, when P committed it, P did so because P failed to believe that it was overall morally wrong.

One further general **truth is** that

(12) one has direct control over something only if that thing is an act or omission. [...]

Thus

(13) whatever X was, it was not an act or omission such that, when P committed it, P did so because P failed to believe that it was overall morally wrong.

Given the deletion of any reference to the *fact* that one's behavior is wrong, a more accurate label for this argument would be "The Argument from the Failure to Believe." But I will stick with the original label, which is much more attractive.

This latest revision to the Argument from Ignorance requires no revision to the Origination Thesis, but I will nonetheless restate the latter under a new draft number so as to keep the numbers for Argument and Thesis aligned:

The Origination Thesis (Draft 5):
Every chain of moral blameworthiness is such that at its origin lies a piece of behavior for which the agent is directly blameworthy and which was such that either he or she believed, at the time at which he or she engaged in it, that it was overall morally wrong or he or she did not believe this but did not engage in the behavior because he or she did not believe this.

As long as "witting" is understood expansively, so that one engages in witting wrongdoing simply in virtue of doing what one believes, even if mistakenly, to be morally wrong, this version of the Thesis can once again be understood, roughly, as the thesis that all blameworthiness is rooted in wrongdoing that is either witting or quasi-witting.

3.4.2 Moral realism

Apart from the fact that it accommodates (but does not entail) the possibility of accuses, it may seem that Draft 5 of the Argument from Ignorance has a further advantage: it doesn't entail that there are any *facts* at all about whether someone has done something morally wrong. This is a feature that a moral non-realist might welcome.

I don't subscribe to such non-realism. I think that there are facts about moral right and wrong—and about moral praise- and blameworthiness—of which people are unfortunately all too often ignorant. If this weren't so, the Argument from Ignorance and the Origination Thesis would be devoid of almost all significance, it seems to me, although perhaps a non-realist might be able to put them to some use.

I won't try to defend moral realism here. That would be too great a digression. I will rest content with the observation that, if you have read the book up to this point, you probably have considerable sympathy for such realism yourself.

3.4.3 Suberogation

Some philosophers have claimed that there is a way in which one can be blameworthy without doing wrong that involves a departure from "common morality" that is perhaps less radical than that discussed so far, namely, the possibility of one's being to blame for *suberogatory* behavior.[71] Suberogation is to be understood as a kind of mirror-image of the more familiar phenomenon of supererogation. Whereas the latter consists in doing something that is *commendable* but which it is permissible *not* to do, the former consists in doing something that is *objectionable* or *indecent* but which it is nonetheless permissible *to* do.

It is well known that, despite the fact that common morality recognizes the possibility of supererogation (if not by that name, then by the description "going above and beyond the call of duty"), it is remarkably difficult to develop a plausible moral theory that accommodates this possibility. The possibility of suberogation, however, is far less often discussed in either of these contexts. And there may be good reason for this, since, mirror-image notwithstanding, the symmetry between super- and suberogation is not perfect. The mirror is distorted. For consider: the greater the extent to which an act goes beyond duty (on the assumption that this is indeed possible), the more supererogatory it is; its status as being something that it is permissible not to do is not thereby threatened. There is no parallel when it comes to suberogation. That is, it is not the case that, the greater the extent to which an act falls short of decency, the more suberogatory it is; on the contrary, its status as being something that it is permissible to do *is* thereby threatened, in that at some point it will presumably become impermissible or wrong. And it is arguable that this point is reached immediately, as it were, so that the status of being suberogatory is never attained. So why, exactly, should we accept the possibility of suberogatory behavior, let alone the possibility of being blameworthy for such behavior?

Consider some alleged examples of suberogatory behavior: a minor act of discourtesy, such as taking too long in a restaurant when you know that others are waiting for a seat,[72] or taking a seat on a crowded train, thereby preventing a couple from sitting together, when taking another, less convenient seat is an option;[73] or, more seriously, an odious act such as driving a competitor out of business when one's own business is flourishing,[74] or refusing to donate a kidney to one's brother, who will die without it, when doing so would not be particularly onerous.[75] These examples, offered by Roderick Chisholm and Ernest Sosa and by Julia Driver, undoubtedly have some intuitive appeal; nonetheless, I am inclined to think that it is a mistake to classify them as instances of suberogation. It is noteworthy that Chisholm and Sosa, in their article, and Driver, in hers, explicitly say that, in cases of the sort in question, the agent is acting "within his rights," from which they infer that the agent is doing nothing wrong. But that inference is questionable, for it seems plausible to hold that one can do wrong even though

---

[71] See, e.g., Haji (1998), p. 173; McKenna (2012), pp. 182 ff.
[72] See Chisholm and Sosa (1966), p. 326.   [73] See Driver (1992), pp. 286 f.
[74] See Chisholm and Sosa (1966), p. 326.   [75] See Driver (1992), p. 287.

one is acting within one's rights. One acts within one's (liberty-)rights in performing some act when no one has a (claim-)right against one that one not perform that act, that is, when, in performing that act, one violates no obligation that one *owes to* someone else.[76] But not all obligations, it seems, are obligations that are owed to someone. Consider Peter Singer's famous case of the child drowning in the pond.[77] Singer argues, plausibly, that you would do wrong to pass the child by, but at no point does he rest his argument on the contention that the child has a right to your help. So too, I submit, in the cases offered by Chisholm and Sosa and Driver, the behavior in question is indeed wrong, and not merely suberogatory, even though it involves no violation of anyone's rights.

There are difficulties, of course. Singer uses his case as the basis for an argument to the effect that very many of the acts that we would normally classify as supererogatory (such as donating a large proportion of one's assets to charity) are in fact obligatory, and many people, myself included, balk at this conclusion, although I confess it is not easy to tell just where Singer's argument goes wrong (if, as I hope, it does). One response to his argument that I do not endorse is to deny the initially plausible "datum" that it is wrong to pass the child by, on the basis of the claim that there are indeed no obligations that are not owed to someone, and you don't owe it to the child, or to anyone else, to rescue the child. Note that there may be room for someone who proposes this response to deny that rescuing the child would be supererogatory. In any case, it is certainly consistent to couple this response with the further claim that failing to rescue the child would be suberogatory.

In the absence of further investigation, then, I am in no position to insist that the category of suberogation is empty. What it is perhaps more important to note in the present context, however, is that, even if this category is empty, it of course remains possible for someone to think that it is not. Consider, then, Sabrina, who *believes* that what she is doing is suberogatory. Is she to blame for her behavior? There are three possible cases: first, Sabrina's behavior is in fact perfectly acceptable, that is, it is neither wrong nor suberogatory; second, her behavior is in fact suberogatory (and so not wrong); and third, her behavior is in fact wrong (and so not suberogatory). If accuses are impossible, then Sabrina is not to blame in either of the first two cases. If the latest version of the Argument from Ignorance is sound, then she is not to blame in the third case, either, unless her behavior is a consequence of some earlier episode of witting wrongdoing on her part (and let's assume that it isn't). But doesn't Sabrina, in all three cases, exhibit an objectionable quality of will, and shouldn't this suffice for her being blameworthy for her behavior (given that she was in control of it)?

---

[76] For a classic discussion of the relation between claim-rights, liberty-rights (and still other kinds of rights), and obligations, see Hohfeld (1919).
[77] Singer (1972), p. 231.

I confess to being unsure how best to respond to this question. One option is to answer "Yes," in which case the Argument from Ignorance needs still further revision. Another option is to answer "No," on the grounds that the quality of will in question, though morally objectionable, is not of the kind to render Sabrina morally blameworthy.[78] I am not prepared to endorse the second response, and so I concede that the Argument may need still further revision. However, since I suspect that the number of actual cases in which an agent believes that she is acting suberogatorily is likely to be very low, the issue strikes me as lacking any practical urgency. For this reason, I won't undertake any full-scale revision of the Argument in order to accommodate cases like Sabrina's. I simply ask you to keep in mind that it may be that every instance of "overall morally wrong" in both the Argument and the Origination Thesis should be replaced by "either overall morally wrong or suberogatory."

---

[78] Cf. Duggan (2018), pp. 299 ff., where it is argued that one can be "guiltworthy" but not blameworthy for suberogatory behavior.

4
Control

I noted in Chapter 1 that philosophers have traditionally maintained that one must satisfy two key conditions in order to be morally responsible—or more particularly, for present purposes, morally blameworthy—for something. One condition is epistemic, having to do with what one knows about the nature of one's behavior and its possible outcomes. I addressed this condition in the last chapter. The other condition, to which I now turn, is agential, having to do with whether one is or was in control of one's behavior and its outcomes.

My procedure in this chapter is as follows. In §4.1 I note that the kind of control in question is volitional control, the kind exhibited by an agent when he or she does something at will. Such control may be said to be bilateral in nature, in that it consists in having both the ability to see to it that some state of affairs obtains and the ability to see to it that it doesn't obtain. For example, if I am in control of my moving my finger in some way, then whether I do move it in that way is up to me; I can see to it that I do, but I can also see to it that I don't. Such control involves not only my having the general ability to move my finger in one way or another but also my having the opportunity to exercise this ability, and it has various dimensions which I go on briefly to describe: it may be direct or indirect (or a hybrid thereof), immediate or remote, complete or partial, basic or enhanced, and simple or intentional. There is a long history of attempting to account for the nature of volitional control in terms of statements along the lines of "If I were to try (or choose, or decide) to do such and such, then I would do such and such." I call these statements AB-conditionals, and I go on to conduct an extended inquiry into whether and to what extent such an account is acceptable.

In §4.2 I undertake a closer examination of one of the dimensions of control just mentioned, one that is especially germane to the relation between ignorance and moral responsibility: the simple-intentional dimension. I begin with a discussion of the relation between control and awareness. It is sometimes said that one cannot be in control of something without being aware of it. I argue that this claim is false, although a closely related claim may be true. I then consider the relevance of reasons-responsiveness to moral responsibility. Many philosophers hold that such responsiveness is necessary for one to be in control of one's behavior in the way that being morally responsible for one's behavior requires. I argue that this claim, as usually interpreted, is also false.

Next, in §4.3, I make some further observations about another of the dimensions of control that is especially germane to the relation between ignorance and moral responsibility: the direct-indirect dimension. Then, in §4.4, I inquire into how it is possible to have and exercise control over omissions. There are two kinds of omissions: acts of omission, and purely passive omissions. Accounting for control over acts of omission is as easy (and as difficult) as accounting for control over acts generally. Purely passive omissions present special problems of their own, however, and it is not clear to me whether it is possible to have or exercise direct control over them.

That control can vary in degree is a commonplace, but it is seldom noted that there are several ways in which it can do so. In §4.5 I discuss this matter. My discussion is relatively brief since, although blameworthiness also varies in degree (an issue I investigated in §2.5), and although I am working under the assumption that blameworthiness requires control, the Argument from Ignorance doesn't presume any particular relation between degree of blameworthiness and degree of control.

Finally, in §4.6 I turn to the question of whether and, if so, how we can control having the beliefs we have. It is clear that we can sometimes *indirectly* control our beliefs, but this poses no problem for the Argument from Ignorance, which claims only that we cannot ever *directly* control our beliefs. I explain how this claim, which appears to be accepted by the great majority of philosophers, follows straightforwardly from the account of direct control developed in §4.3. Some philosophers, however, hold that, on the contrary, we can sometimes directly control our beliefs (thereby committing themselves, if only implicitly, to an account of direct control that differs from mine). Usually this view is expressed in terms of believing certain propositions "at will." I argue that, even if my account of direct control is not presupposed, there is very good reason to deny that we can ever believe a proposition at will, except perhaps in some very special kinds of circumstances.

4.1 Volitional control

4.1.1 Doing something at will

I have called the control condition "agential," but it is not only agents that can control what happens. As Robert Nozick has observed, a thermostat controls the temperature in a room.[1] This is a simple example of non-agential control. An airplane's autopilot system provides a more sophisticated example. It is tempting to construe such control in terms of subjunctive conditionals. If the temperature were to transcend certain limits, the thermostat would restore it to a pre-set range.

---

[1] Nozick (1981), p. 315.

If the plane were to stray off course, or suddenly lose altitude or airspeed, the autopilot would fix the problem. And so on. Such conditionals ascribe certain capacities to the thermostat and to the autopilot. Of course, there are some familiar difficulties here. The conditionals that I have just given hardly suffice; they would need to be qualified considerably to capture the specific features of the control at issue, and even then there is the question whether they might misfire due to some mask or fink.[2] (Mask or fink? I will explain below what these terms mean in this context.)

Thermostats and autopilots are mere machines, not people, but people sometimes exhibit control of the same kind as machines like these. For example, by sweating or shivering, one controls one's body temperature. But people also often exhibit a kind of control that it seems mere machines cannot. A simple, mundane example is that of my moving my finger at will. A more sophisticated example is that of a regular pilot flying an airplane at will. The phrase "at will" is telling. It invokes an attribute (volition or, to use an archaic term, the "faculty of will"), one that agents possess but that non-agents do not, and it suggests that the conditionals associated with agential control in particular should be couched in terms related to this feature: if I were to will (or try, or choose, or decide) to move my finger, I would do so; if the pilot were to will (or try, or choose, or decide) to fly the plane, he or she would do so. Agential control is thus *volitional* control. A distinctive feature of such conditionals is that the antecedent makes reference to a mental attitude with intentional content, while the consequent makes reference to behavior that matches that content.[3] I will call such statements *Attitude-Behavior-conditionals*, or *AB-conditionals* for short. In the examples just given, the behavior that is mentioned is physical; in other cases (involving control over one's deliberations, for example) it may be mental. The idea that agential control is to be understood in terms of AB-conditionals is of course hardly new—it can be traced at least as far back as Hobbes[4]—and it is surely an attractive one. I want now to raise a number of points in pursuit of this idea.

4.1.2 The bilateral nature of volitional control

Agents are individual objects of a certain sort, but what sort of thing is it that agents control? The answer is not immediately obvious. Consider the examples just given of my moving my finger, and the pilot's flying the plane, at will. On the surface, these seem to be cases of one individual object (an agent) controlling another (a finger, a plane). But in each case closer inspection would seem to reveal that what is controlled is, more precisely, the movement of the object in question,

---

[2] Cf. Clarke (2009), pp. 324 ff.   [3] Cf. Shepherd (2014), p. 397.
[4] See Hobbes (1651), ch. 21.

so that what should be said to be in the agent's control is, strictly, not the object itself but some event that involves the object. Yet I don't think that that can be quite right, either.

The problem is that agential control is multifaceted. If I am in control of (my moving) my finger, then *how* or, indeed, *whether* I move it is "*up to*" me.[5] The "how" is, I think, reducible to the "whether," in virtue of which fact its many faces can be reduced to two. I will therefore call such control *bilateral*. Suppose that I can move my finger in 10 different ways. Then my being in control of how I move my finger is tantamount to its being the case that, for each of these 10 different ways in which I might move it, I am in control of whether I move it in that way. Still, the question remains what, precisely, the object of my control is and into what ontological category it is to be placed.

The answer to which I am inclined is this. There are a number of states of affairs involved in the example: my moving my finger in way 1, my moving my finger in way 2, etc. Such states of affairs are abstract objects that exist necessarily but obtain (if they obtain at all) only contingently.[6] To say that I am in control of whether I move my finger in way 1, or way 2, etc., is to say, somewhat more precisely, that each of the states of affairs in question is such that I can see to it that it obtains and I can also see to it that it does not obtain. (I don't pretend that this is fully perspicuous. The phrase "see to it that" is, in this context, a term of art that deserves scrutiny.) English furnishes a number of locutions that give expression to the fact that whether some state of affairs, S, obtains is in the control of some person or agent, P. There may be some subtle differences in meaning among these locutions, but for present purposes I will regard them as synonymous:

a. P is in control of whether S obtains
b. P is in control of S
c. P has control over (whether) S (obtains)
d. (whether) S (obtains) is under P's control
e. (whether) S (obtains) is in P's control

If control of the sort at issue is bilateral, and if it is to be understood (at least in part) in terms of AB-conditionals, then a *pair* of such conditionals will be involved. We might say, for example, that if I have agential control over my moving my finger in way 1, then not only is it the case that, if I were to decide to move it in this way, I would move it in this way, but it is also the case that,

---

[5] This, at least, is true of the sort of control that presently concerns me. John Fischer is well known for calling such control "regulative control" and distinguishing it from what he calls "guidance control" in Fischer (1994). I will remark further on guidance control in §4.2.2.

[6] Cf. Chisholm (1976), pp. 117 ff.

if I were to decide otherwise, I wouldn't move it in this way. Conditionals of this sort ascribe an *ability* to some agent (just as conditionals of the sort mentioned above ascribe a *capacity* to some machine). Agential control consists in having both the ability to see to it that some state of affairs obtains and the ability to see to it that it does not obtain. As is well recognized, though, in this context we should distinguish between what may be called *general* and *specific* abilities, and it is not just general but also specific abilities that are required for agential control.[7] If one has the specific ability to do something, then one has the general ability to do it,[8] but the converse does not hold, since one must also have the opportunity to exercise that general ability. For example, Usain Bolt has (or had) the amazing ability to run 100 meters in under 10 seconds, as do a few other people. This is just a general ability, though. Not even Bolt has the specific ability to run that fast if he is asleep, or debilitated by illness, or bound to a chair; and if he lacks the specific ability to do so here and now, then he is certainly not, here and now, in control of whether he does so.

4.1.3 Direct *vs.* indirect control and immediate *vs.* remote control

Just now, I characterized my control over my moving my finger in terms of a pair of conditionals having to do with my *deciding* whether to move it. I should explain why I appealed to deciding in particular in order to give expression to the volitional nature of agential control.

I intend the term "decide" to be understood in one way liberally but in another way conservatively. Some philosophers use it restrictively, applying it only to cases in which some "practical uncertainty" needs "settling."[9] I am using it more liberally. For example, when the time comes to choose dessert, one can decide to order the cheesecake, even if one has never seriously entertained any alternative. Nonetheless, what I have in mind in the present context is the kind of decision that may be called an *executive* decision—a decision to do something "here and now"—as opposed to the kind of decision to do something later that may fail to culminate in action due to the decision's having been forgotten or revoked. Consider again the miserable case, presented in Chapter 2, in which, enraged because his passion for Jill is not reciprocated, Bill shoots and kills Jill. I represented one portion of this story in Figure 2.1. As before, the arrows in this figure represent causation. *A*, which consists simply of *a*, is the minimal act

---

[7] Cf. Austin (1961), pp. 177 ff.; Nowell Smith (1960), pp. 87 ff.; Mele (2003), p. 447; Clarke (2014), pp. 88 ff.
[8] Typically, at least. For a possible exception, see Clarke (2014), p. 93.
[9] See, e.g., Mele (1992), pp. 158 f.; Clarke (2014), p. 63.

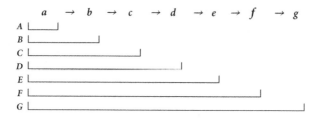

Figure 2.1 BILL AND JILL

constituted by Bill's executive decision to kill Jill then and there. B, which consists of Bill's decision, *a*, causing the movement of his finger, *b*, is the act of Bill's moving his finger. And so on for the remainder of *c–g* (where *g* is the event of Jill's death) and C–G (where G is the act of Bill's killing Jill). This figure helps to bring out the fact that agential control has a number of different dimensions.

One important dimension, upon which I have already commented in previous chapters and will comment further below, is that which consists in the distinction between *direct* and *indirect* control. In §2.2.4 I said that Figure 2.1 depicts the fact that Bill's control over *a* is direct, whereas his control over *b–g* is merely indirect, since he has control over them by way of, and only by way of, his control over *a*. (I also said that we may call Bill's control over B–G *hybrid*, inasmuch as it consists in a combination of his direct control over *a* and his indirect control over the consequences of *a*.) I will continue to talk in these terms, since it is convenient to do so, but I should note explicitly here that doing so is strictly inaccurate. After all, *a–g* and A–G are the names of certain *events*. In the last section, though, I said that, strictly speaking, it is *states of affairs* that are the sort of thing that can be in one's control. Being abstract, states of affairs cannot enter (directly) into causal relations, whereas events, as I am conceiving of them, can do so and, in the case of BILL AND JILL, do do so. So I need to explain what I mean when I talk in terms of an event being in an agent's control.

Consider *a*. This event is an instance of the state of affairs of Bill's deciding to kill Jill then and there. Call this state of affairs S(*a*). When I say that *a* is in Bill's control, what I mean, more exactly, is this: S(*a*) is in Bill's control (that is, Bill can see to it that this state of affairs obtains and also see to it that it does not obtain) *and*, moreover, *a* occurs (in virtue of the fact that Bill sees to it that S(*a*) obtains rather than that it does not obtain). Now consider *b*. This is an instance of the state of affairs of Bill's finger moving (more particularly, his right index finger, say). Call this state of affairs S(*b*). Then, to say that *b* is in Bill's control is to say, more exactly, that S(*b*) is in his control and *b* occurs. And so on.

A distinction distinct from, but closely related to, that between direct and indirect control is the distinction between what I will call *immediate* and *remote* control, where these terms signify a *temporal* relation between the items over which one has control.[10] Bill's control over *a* is immediate, whereas his control over *b–g* is remote, since these events occur later than *a* occurs. Of course, in this case *b–g* occur very soon after *a* occurs, but other consequences of *a* not mentioned in the story or depicted in the figure will have occurred only much later. Imagine, for example, Jill's fiancé dying of a broken heart six months after her death. The reason for declaring the direct-indirect distinction distinct from the immediate-remote distinction is that it seems possible for someone to be immediately but only indirectly in control of something. Suppose that Bill had promised Bert not to make any rash decisions when dealing with Jill. We may then assume that, in making the decision represented by *a*, Bill broke his promise to Bert. His control over both his decision and his broken promise was immediate, but, whereas his control over the former was direct, his control over the latter, which was a consequence of the former, was merely indirect.[11]

It is noteworthy that each of the results, *b–g*, over which Bill has indirect control, and each of the actions, *B–G*, over which he has hybrid control, might feature in AB-conditionals of the sort that I have mentioned: if he were to decide that the relevant state of affairs should obtain, it would, but if he were to decide otherwise, it wouldn't. But it is also noteworthy that, in the case under discussion, that event, *a*, over which he has *direct* control, will *not* feature in such a conditional. In particular, it is not the case that his control over *a* is to be understood in terms of the claim that, if he were to decide that $S(a)$ should obtain, it would. Since all control is anchored in direct control, it follows that volitional control *cannot* be understood wholly in terms of AB-conditionals of the sort at issue. This is an important point to which I will return. (It is also important to note that the phrase "decide otherwise" is ambiguous. I will return to this point, too, in §4.4.)

4.1.4 Complete *vs.* partial control

The direct-indirect dimension of control is sometimes confused with another, which consists in the distinction between what I will call *complete* and *partial* control. One has complete control over something only if its occurrence is not contingent on anything that is not within one's control; otherwise, one's control is at best partial. It appears that some philosophers have held that we have complete

---

[10] There is nothing sacrosanct about this construal of the terms. "Immediate" is often used to mean the same as "direct," for example, but the distinction between what *I* am calling direct control and immediate control must be captured somehow.

[11] A consequence, but not a *causal* consequence—a matter on which I will comment further in §4.3. Cf. Goldman (1970), pp. 26 f. on what he calls "simple generation."

control over our volitions,[12] but that is certainly a mistake. On the contrary, complete control is unattainable by anyone at any time. (If you doubt this, consider the simple fact that whatever control you enjoy over anything depends on your having been born—something that we may hope was in someone's control, but not yours.)

4.1.5 Basic vs. enhanced control

Another dimension of control worth mentioning here is that which consists in the distinction between what I will call *basic* and *enhanced* control. One has basic control over an event when it is *strictly* up to one whether the relevant state of affairs obtains, no matter how difficult one might find it to make one or other of the pertinent choices, whereas one has enhanced control over an event when one can make any of the pertinent choices with relative ease. One can thus have basic control without enhanced control, but not vice versa.

As illustration of this distinction, recall Susan and Tom from §2.5.5. Susan is subject to epileptic seizures. When in the throes of such a seizure, it is literally impossible for her to behave differently. She lacks basic control over her behavior, and thus lacks enhanced control over it, too. Tom's case is different. He is being tortured by captors and finds it very difficult but (I am stipulating) not strictly impossible to resist the impulse to divulge the information they seek. He therefore lacks enhanced control, but not basic control, over what he does. If he gives in to the temptation to divulge the information and later reports "I had no choice," we might well sympathize with him and, for that reason, not dispute what he says, but his claim would be strictly speaking false. So, too, for Betty, a bank teller, who hands over money to Rob when Rob points a gun at her and demands that she do so: there is a sense in which, being coerced to act as she does, Betty's behavior is not voluntary; nonetheless, strictly speaking, she has a choice whether to comply with Rob's demands (and, we may suppose, makes the right choice under the circumstances). Contrast this case with another in which Betty is in cahoots with Rob and knows that his threat is an idle one: in such a situation, her action is fully voluntary; she has not just basic but enhanced control over her behavior.

There is no doubt that the distinction between basic and enhanced control is morally significant. (Think of how our reaction to Betty would depend on whether we thought she was in league with Rob.) My characterization of this distinction has been decidedly rough, but I won't try to improve on it here. Since enhanced control entails basic control, we cannot understand the former without understanding the latter, and it is on the latter that I want to focus.

---

[12] See, e.g., Ross (1939), pp. 153 f., and Prichard (1949), pp. 31 ff.

4.1.6 Simple *vs.* intentional control

Yet another dimension of control is that which consists in the distinction between what I will call *simple* and *intentional* control.[13] Bill's control over the events depicted in Figure 2.1 is intentional, in that all of these events are ones that he intentionally brings about, but one can have control over events that is not intentional. Suppose that the bullet that Bill fired from his gun, having passed through Jill's body, struck and destroyed a clock on her mantelpiece. We can add the clock's destruction—call it *h*—to our account of what took place. Figure 4.1 represents this case. Let us assume that Bill had no idea that the clock was there. Then certainly its destruction was not intentional; nonetheless, it was in Bill's control. Since the clock's destruction was not intentional, Bill's control over it is clearly *not* to be understood even partly in terms of a pair of AB-conditionals having to do with a decision of his regarding its destruction. His control over *H* (and *h*) is therefore importantly different from his control over *A–G* (and *a–g*).

Although having a simple ability to do something, *X*, cannot be understood even partly in terms of an AB-conditional having to do with a decision regarding *X*, there is nonetheless good reason to think that this does *not* mean that the truth of some closely related AB-conditional isn't necessary for *all* indirect or hybrid control, whether intentional or simple. I say this because, even though not all action *is* intentional action, nonetheless, since all action is rooted in executive decisions which are themselves intentional, all action *requires* intentional action.[14] For this reason, although simple control over *X* does not require intentional control over *X*, it does require intentional control over something related to *X*. For example, Bill's simple control over the clock's destruction is contingent on his intentional control over the other, antecedent events in the example.[15] And so, if the truth of AB-conditionals is necessary for *intentional* indirect or hybrid control, then it is also necessary for *simple* indirect or hybrid control. For example, even if Bill's control

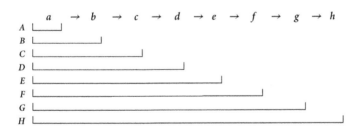

Figure 4.1 BILL AND THE CLOCK

---

[13] Cf. Mele (2003), pp. 448 f.   [14] Cf. Davidson (1980), p. 46. Contrast Persson (2019), p. 13.
[15] Cf. Davidson (1980), p. 71.

over the clock's destruction is not to be understood even partly in terms of its being the case that, if he were to decide to destroy the clock, he would destroy it, it may nonetheless be that his control over its destruction is to be understood partly in terms of its being the case that, if he were to decide to move his finger, he would move it.

4.1.7 AB-conditionals and indirect control

But, even if the example of BILL AND THE CLOCK does not provide a reason to deny that the truth of AB-conditionals is necessary for indirect or hybrid control, there might nonetheless be a good reason to deny this. This appears to be the lesson that J. L. Austin intends us to draw from the following famous example:

> Consider the case where I miss a very short putt and kick myself because I could have holed it. It is not that I should [i.e., would] have holed it if I had tried: I did try, and missed. It is not that I should have holed it if conditions had been different: that might of course be so, but I am talking about conditions as they precisely were, and asserting that I could have holed it.[16]

Austin claims that he could have holed the putt, and that seems plausible.[17] Moreover, had he holed it, he would presumably have done so intentionally. Thus it seems that the kind of control Austin had over holing the putt was intentional control. What, then, explains his missing it?

Austin suggests that there might be no good explanation in the offing. He says:

> [I]f I tried my hardest, say, and missed, surely there *must* have been *something* that caused me to fail, that made me unable to succeed? So that I *could not* have holed it. Well, a modern belief in science, in there being an explanation of everything, may make us assent to this argument. But such a belief is not in line with the traditional beliefs enshrined in the word *can*: according to *them*, a human ability or power or capacity is inherently liable not to produce success, on occasion, and that for no reason (or are bad luck and bad form sometimes reasons?).[18]

Again, this line of thinking seems plausible. Randolph Clarke suggests that Austin's example might be a case in which Austin's ability to hole the putt is

---

[16] Austin (1961), p. 166, n. 1.

[17] One indication of the plausibility of this claim is the fact that Austin kicked himself for missing the putt. This suggests that he thought that he ought to have holed it. If "ought" implies "can," then either Austin was mistaken in thinking that he ought to have holed the putt or he could indeed have holed it. Of course, whether the pertinent "ought" does imply the pertinent "can" is open to debate—but not here.

[18] Austin (1961), p. 166, n. 1.

masked by, say, a lapse of attention, and that that is why the AB-conditional at issue ("If I were to try to hole the putt, I would hole it") is false despite the fact that Austin had the pertinent ability.[19] (In this context, a mask is to be understood as something that blocks the exercise of an ability without removing that ability.) Even if that's right, though, the possibility remains that the truth of some *other* AB-conditional is necessary for Austin's having intentional control over his holing the putt.

One suggestion is that we should weaken the conditional, so that instead of "If I were to try to hole the putt, I would hole it," we have something like "If I were to try to hole the putt, I might hole it" or "If I were to try to hole the putt, I would probably hole it." But, although it is surely very plausible to say that the truth of these weaker claims is indeed necessary for Austin's having the specific ability to hole the putt intentionally, I think we can say more than this. An alternative suggestion is to look, not for a weaker version of the same AB-conditional, but for a different AB-conditional.[20] Suppose that Austin did in fact try his hardest to hole the putt but still missed it. Then clearly "If I were to try my hardest to hole the putt, I would hole it," is not the conditional we're looking for.[21] But here I think it's important to note that trying one's *hardest* is not the same as trying one's *best*. (Sometimes one can try *too* hard.) In any case, if Austin could indeed have holed the putt, it seems to me likely that there was, and must have been, some other *way* in which he could have tried to hole it such that, if he had tried in that way to hole it, he would have succeeded in holing it—and holing it intentionally.[22] I am inclined to think, therefore, that Austin's example does *not* give us a good reason to deny that the truth of an AB-conditional of the sort I have in mind ("If, in order to hole the putt, I were to decide to stand just so, and to move my putter just so, etc., I would hole it") is necessary for his having had control over holing the putt. Still, I acknowledge that this claim is controversial, since it is arguable that "there might be no end to what can mask [an ability]."[23]

I should also acknowledge that, whatever the merits of the claim that I have just made, it does not address the question whether the possibility of *finks* (entities that subvert an agent's ability in just the kind of circumstances in which that ability would typically be exercised) might provide a good reason to deny that the truth of AB-conditionals of the sort in question is necessary for indirect or hybrid control. What if Austin's golfing partner had been poised to yell "Fore!" if Austin had drawn back his putter in just the way necessary for him to hole the putt, a shout that would have so distracted Austin that he would have ended up missing the putt? Wouldn't Austin still have retained the ability to hole the putt? Here I think the answer is straightforward. Yes, Austin would have retained the general ability

---

[19] Clarke (2009), p. 328. [20] Cf. Chisholm (1964a), p. 24.
[21] Contrast Raz (2011), p. 247. [22] Cf. Moore and Hurd (2011), pp. 158 f.
[23] Clarke (2009), p. 325.

to hole the putt but, no, he would have lost the specific ability required for his having been in *control* over whether he holed it. Under the circumstances, it was *not* up to him whether he holed it (given that he was not in control over whether his partner was prepared to yell "Fore!").[24] Thus, I remain inclined to think that the truth of AB-conditionals of the sort I have been considering is indeed necessary for the possession of indirect or hybrid agential control.

4.1.8 AB-conditionals and direct control

Even if the truth of AB-conditionals of the sort I have been considering is necessary for the possession of indirect or hybrid control, though, it is clearly *not* necessary for the possession of direct control. As I observed earlier, Bill's direct control over his deciding to act cannot itself be understood in terms of AB-conditionals having to do with his deciding to decide. The reason is plain. Such a condition on direct control would be impossible to satisfy; for it would generate a regress of deciding, one that would require that the agent be capable of making a decision the intentional content of which was infinite, and no agent is ever capable of doing that.[25] Yet, I assume, some agents are sometimes capable of exercising direct control.

The problem here is perfectly general. I may be mistaken in holding that it is always an executive decision that functions as the initial part of an action and thereby constitutes the locus of an agent's exercise of control. Perhaps some other form of volition may play this role. To remain neutral on this matter, let us simply talk of "V-ing" in general, rather than of deciding in particular. The fact is that, whatever V-ing is, the possession of direct control cannot be understood in terms of a conditional of the form "If one were to V to V, then one would V."

It may be retorted that this just shows that it is a mistake to think that agential control requires control over one's volitions. But it seems clear that it *does* require such control. It may be the case both that, if I were to decide to move my finger, I would move it, and that, if I were to decide otherwise, I wouldn't move it. Still, I may have no control over my moving my finger—and I won't if, for example, I am in a coma.[26] In such a case, I lack hybrid control over my moving my finger precisely because I lack direct control over my deciding to move it—and this point would remain true, no matter what form of volition were substituted for deciding.

But even if it is agreed that direct control cannot require the truth of, and thus cannot be understood in terms of, AB-conditionals of the sort I have been

---

[24] Cf. Clarke (2009), p. 340.
[25] This is not to say that it is not *possible* to decide to decide. On the contrary, that can, and apparently sometimes does, happen. It is only to say that it cannot be the case that, *whenever* one makes a decision, one decides to make that decision.
[26] Cf. Chisholm (1964a), pp. 24 f.

considering, it remains possible that it is to be understood in terms of AB-conditionals of some *other* sort.[27] Perhaps, for example, my control over my deciding to move my finger is to be understood as consisting in the truth of the following pair of claims: if I were to *desire* to move my finger more strongly than I desired not to move it, I would decide to move it, and if I were to desire otherwise, I wouldn't. Or it might be that my control over my deciding to move my finger is to be understood as consisting in the truth of this pair of claims: if I were to *have a reason* to move my finger stronger than any reason I had not to move it, I would decide to move it, whereas if I didn't, I wouldn't.[28] Is such a proposal acceptable?

One objection to the claim that the truth of some such pair of conditionals *suffices* for my having control over my decision echoes the objection just considered, and that is that, if I am not in control of whether I have the relevant desire or reason, then I cannot after all be in control of my decision.[29] Here, though, the objection seems to me more dubious. I take it as a datum that, if I (am in a coma and therefore) cannot decide to move my finger, then I cannot move it (where "move" refers to a form of genuine agency; being in a coma does not preclude one's moving one's finger as a result, for example, of electrical stimulation of some portion of the brain). I don't take it as a datum that, if I (am revolted by the prospect and therefore) cannot summon a desire to move my finger, or if I (am opposed to the idea and therefore) cannot manufacture a reason to move my finger, then I cannot decide to move it. Let me explain.

It might seem that the objection should be summarily dismissed on the grounds that it presupposes the principle that there is no control without complete control, a principle which, as I noted in §4.1.4, is surely false. It is false because whatever control we have is always had in a *context*; there will always be a set of background conditions, almost all of which are not only presently outside of our control but never were in our control, and many of which are necessary for our having the control we have. For example, I am presently in control of whether I continue to write these words; among the background conditions necessary for my having this control is that there is air available in my location for me to breathe; and I am not, and have never been, in control of whether there is air available in my location.[30] But it would be a mistake to dismiss the objection on this basis, because the objection does *not* presuppose the principle just mentioned. Rather, it rests on something like the following principle: if one cannot do A unless p is true, and one cannot act so that p is true, then one cannot do A. This principle seems very

---

[27] Cf. Davidson (1980), pp. 68 f.
[28] Whether these claims count as AB-conditionals or as conditionals of some other sort depends on just what the relevant sort of reason is taken to be.
[29] Cf. Chisholm (1964a), p. 25.
[30] This is not of course to say that I have never been in control of whether I was in this location.

plausible.[31] It is this principle that is at work in the example about the coma: I cannot move my finger without deciding to do so; I cannot decide to do so (because I am in a coma); hence I cannot move my finger. So, too, in the example about my revulsion: I cannot decide to move my finger without desiring to move it; I cannot summon a desire to move it (because I am revolted by the prospect); hence I cannot decide to move it. What's wrong with this argument?

Peter van Inwagen, who is a chief proponent of the kind of principle employed in this argument, indicates that he would find nothing wrong with it and so would accept its conclusion. To put his view rather roughly, he holds that we are typically not presently in control of our present beliefs and attitudes and also that we have the power to do something only if we have some on-balance pro-attitude (or, at least, lack an on-balance contra-attitude) toward doing it.[32] On the supposition that in the present case the only pro-attitude that I might have toward moving my finger is a desire to move it, it follows that I cannot decide to move it. In support of his position, van Inwagen asks us to consider the following claim:

> C If P regards A as an indefensible act, given the totality of relevant information available to him, and if he has no way of getting further relevant information, and if he lacks any positive desire to do A, and if he sees no objection to *not* doing A (again, given the totality of relevant information available to him), then P is not going to do A.[33]

Van Inwagen claims that C is "something very like a necessary truth." To convince us of this, he asks us to imagine that P *does* do A, and he says:

> We ask him, "Why did you do A? I thought you said a moment ago that it was reprehensible." He replies:
>
>> Yes. I did think that. I still think it. I thought that at every moment up to the time at which I performed A; I thought that while I was performing A; I thought it immediately afterward. I never wavered in my conviction that A was an irremediably reprehensible act.... I didn't *want* to do A. I never had the least desire to do A.... [Nonetheless, it] is true without qualification that *I* did A, and it is true without qualification that I *did* A.
>
> This strikes me as absolutely impossible.[34]

---

[31] This principle resembles principle β, a key premise in van Inwagen's famous Consequence Argument against compatibilism. See van Inwagen (1983), pp. 93 ff. The principle has been criticized and may need tweaking.

[32] For some important details and qualifications, see van Inwagen (1989), pp. 405 ff.

[33] Van Inwagen (1989), p. 407, with slight changes in order to render the variables consistent with those used earlier in this chapter.

[34] Van Inwagen (1989), pp. 407 f.

Van Inwagen then proceeds to argue similarly for the impossibility of refraining from some action when performing that action is something that one wants very much to do and one has no countervailing desires. He eventually broadens this to accommodate all actions that seem to be "the obvious things to do in the circumstances."[35] He then concludes, in a manner strikingly reminiscent of C. A. Campbell,[36] that at best we are in control of what we do only in cases in which duty conflicts with inclination and cases in which one's alternatives are either evenly balanced or incommensurable; for only in these cases is it not obvious what to do.[37]

This is a startling conclusion. Most of us are surely inclined to think that our control over our behavior is far more extensive than van Inwagen allows. Surely I was not mistaken when I said a moment ago that I was in control of my continuing to write—that it was up to me whether to continue to do so—despite the fact that I was not in a state of equipoise of the kind that van Inwagen deems necessary for the exercise of control.

In an effort to undermine van Inwagen's position, John Martin Fischer and Mark Ravizza provide this criticism of C. They claim that C is not necessarily true, because it may be that P *can* generate a desire to do A and then act on this desire, even if P presently finds A indefensible (etc.) and in fact *will* not generate a countervailing desire and *will* not do A.[38] (Here "desire" is to be understood liberally, to cover all pro-attitudes, including X's taking himself to have a reason to do A in the absence of a desire, in some more restrictive sense, to do A.) But while it is correct to point out this lacuna in van Inwagen's argument, I don't think that this constitutes the most important or telling criticism of it. For one thing, if this criticism is itself to reinstate our common belief that our control over our behavior is extensive, it must be that our ability to generate desires that we do not presently have is itself extensive, and this seems quite doubtful (for reasons that it would be a distraction to explore here[39]). Secondly, and more importantly, I should think that van Inwagen might well plug the lacuna simply by restricting C's application to options over which P has *direct* control.[40] Here even Fischer and Ravizza would appear to be committed to conceding that one cannot do what one finds indefensible (etc.). I think that we should hesitate to concede this.

It might seem that we must concede this if we accept, as Fischer and Ravizza are prepared to do,[41] the claim that, necessarily, P intentionally does A (or intentionally refrains from doing A) only if P wants to do A (or wants not to do A). (Again,

---

[35] Van Inwagen (1989), p. 412. [36] Campbell (1951).
[37] Van Inwagen (1989), pp. 415 ff. Cf. Kane (1996), ch. 8.
[38] Fischer and Ravizza (1992), pp. 432 ff. Cf. Stump (1993), p. 248, n. 19.
[39] For discussion, see Zimmerman (1990) and van Inwagen (1994), §II.
[40] Interestingly, van Inwagen overlooks this move in his reply to Fischer and Ravizza in van Inwagen (1994).
[41] Fischer and Ravizza (1992), p. 432.

"want," like "desire," is to be understood liberally in this context.) For C's antecedent specifies that P has no desire to do what he finds indefensible. But we must be very careful how we construe the claim in question. It is safe to accept it, I think, only if we understand the relevant desire as something that is *constituted* by the intention and decision to do A. In this sense, the intention or decision to do A *itself* is (or includes) a pro-attitude toward doing A. But we should hesitate to accept the claim if we take the relevant desire to be something that *grounds* the intention and decision to do A. If we were to say that no one can do A intentionally without having some such *antecedent* (or, at least, *independent*) desire to do A upon which the intention and decision to do A is based, then perhaps Fischer's and Ravizza's way of trying to undermine C is the best that can be done. But I don't see why we should say this. Certainly doing A intentionally in the absence of any desire (broadly construed, and other than that which is simply constituted by the intention and decision to do A) is very puzzling; for it constitutes acting *irrationally*. As such, it is rationally *inexplicable*. But why should what is rationally inexplicable be thought *impossible*? Much of the existentialists' writings would appear to be evidence that it is certainly conceivable.[42]

One might at this point ask, with Susan Wolf,[43] why anyone would want to act irrationally, but that is not really the apposite question. The question is why anyone would want the *ability* to act irrationally, that is, want to *have* this ability even in the absence of wanting to *exercise* it. Wolf indeed recognizes that this is the issue but professes herself unable to see why anyone should value having such control. But the point surely is that it is *control*, so that, when someone does act rationally, he or she is not *forced* to do so; whether an agent acts rationally is *up to* the agent. In this connection, consider these questions posed by Jeffrie Murphy:

> Does not each person want to believe of himself, as part of his pride in his human dignity, that he is *capable* of performing...evil acts that would quite properly earn for him the...hatred of others? And should he not at least sometimes extend this compliment to them?[44]

Murphy raises these questions rhetorically. He is apparently mistaken in counting on his readers to share his view as to how the questions are to be answered, but I submit that there is good reason to answer them as he does.

You might disagree. You might find Murphy's position too expansive. Consider the words famously attributed to Martin Luther: "Here I stand. I can do no other."

---

[42] See, e.g., Sartre (1953), pp. 617 f.; Camus (1989). Contrast Velleman (1992b), §XIII. Contrast also van Inwagen (1994), p. 102, where the presupposition appears to be that even an existentialist *acte gratuit* must be grounded in some antecedent desire to perform an *acte gratuit*. While such an antecedent desire is of course possible, I don't see why we should take it to be necessary.

[43] Wolf (1990), p. 56.   [44] Murphy and Hampton (1988), p. 102.

Or consider these words of Ruth (from the *Book of Ruth*), as imagined by Eleonore Stump:

> I'm sorry, but it's unthinkable for me to abandon [Naomi] now. She was always good to me, and it would be heartlessly cruel to repay all her past kindnesses by deserting her just when she needs me most. I know all the prudential arguments in favor of leaving her, and I've thought and thought about them. But in the end it is plain to me that I just couldn't do such a thing. I *must* go with her.[45]

Murphy would apparently accuse Luther and Ruth of speaking falsely. Isn't such an accusation outrageous?

I'm not sure that it is. I'm inclined to side with Murphy on this and to declare Luther's and Ruth's claims hyperbolic. (Compare the claim famously attributed to George Washington that he couldn't tell a lie. Surely he could.) Nonetheless, I also have the contrary inclination to say that in at least some cases in which one finds an action "unthinkable"—or "inconceivable," or "beyond the pale"—one literally cannot (bring oneself to) perform that action. For present purposes there is no need to try to settle this question. I am perfectly willing to accept a compromise view, according to which actions that are in some sense beyond the pale for someone are literally unperformable by that person, as long as the area circumscribed by the pales is not taken to be so small as to include only those options regarding whose desirability the agent is in a state of equipoise.

Finally, you might be wondering why, if I am prepared to accept that I can decide to move my finger even if I do not have (and cannot directly summon) an independent pro-attitude toward moving my finger, I am not also prepared to accept that I can move my finger (where "move" refers to a form of genuine agency) even if I cannot decide to move it. The answer is straightforward. Decisions (*executive* decisions) are not independent of actions; they are the initial part of actions and, as such, essential to actions.

4.1.9 Control *vs.* freedom

We have been considering the question whether my control over my deciding to move my finger might be understood as consisting in the truth of a pair of conditionals such as: if I were to *desire* to move my finger more strongly than I desired not to move it, I would decide to move it, and if I were to desire otherwise, I wouldn't. In the last section I considered, and dismissed, an argument for thinking that such a pair of conditionals could not *suffice* for my having

---

[45] Stump (1993), p. 247.

control over my decision. Another objection targets the claim that such a pair of conditionals is *necessary* for my having such control. The objection is that no such "would"-conditionals are consistent with my *freely* deciding to move my finger; at best only "might"- or "would probably"-conditionals could be true.[46] In response, I will only say this. First, the incompatibilist view of freedom of will that inspires this remark is highly controversial (indeed, it's controversial whether incompatibilism requires assenting to the remark in the first place[47]). Secondly, and more importantly, in assuming that agents are sometimes capable of possessing and exercising *control*, I am *not* assuming that agents are ever capable of *free* will and action, in whatever sense or senses of these terms might be taken to be at issue in the perennial debate over free will. Nor am I assuming that they are not. It is, I think, obvious that we are agents, in the sense that we are capable of performing actions and sometimes actually do so, but I don't think it's at all obvious that we are free agents. I also take it to be clear, though perhaps less obvious, that volition is the hallmark of agency, but I don't think it's at all obvious that we ever enjoy freedom of will. And I take it to be clear that we sometimes possess and exercise control over our behavior (Look, here's proof: here is one hand, and here is another,[48] and I am controlling how they move), but I don't think it's at all obvious that such control is tantamount to freedom.

4.1.10 Possessing *vs.* exercising control

It will not have escaped your notice that, despite the rather laborious nature of the discussion so far, I have not come close to offering you a full account of the nature of volitional control. This is not due to coyness on my part. The unfortunate fact is that I can do no better. I have claimed that there is good reason to think that the truth of AB-conditionals of the form "if I were to decide to do such and such, I would do A, and if I were to decide otherwise, I wouldn't do A" is necessary but not sufficient for indirect and hybrid control, whether simple or intentional. I have claimed that these conditionals are neither necessary nor sufficient for direct control. I have considered whether certain other AB-conditionals might be necessary or sufficient for direct control, and I have left the matter open. And that is as far as my inquiry has taken me—not very far at all! Nonetheless, I will venture to use the little that I have accomplished as a basis for further inquiry into some aspects of volitional control that seem especially relevant to moral responsibility.

Before I do so, however, I should say something briefly about the distinction, which I have invoked on several occasions, between the *possession* and the *exercise* of control.

---

[46] Cf. Adams (1977) and van Inwagen (1997).   [47] Cf. Plantinga (1974), pp. 173 ff.
[48] Cf. G. E. Moore (1962), p. 144.

I noted earlier that one may have a general ability to do something and yet fail to do it because one lacks the opportunity to exercise that ability. If so, one lacks the specific ability to do that thing. Of course, one may have a specific ability to do something and still fail to do it because, for example, one chooses not to do it. If so, one will have failed to exercise one's specific ability. To exercise an ability to do something, whether that ability is general or specific, is simply to do that which one has the ability to do. If Bill has the ability to move his finger intentionally, then his moving it intentionally constitutes the exercise of that (intentional) ability. If he has the ability to destroy the clock, then his destroying it constitutes the exercise of that (simple) ability.[49]

Sometimes we talk of being able to exercise an ability to do something.[50] If the ability in question is general, then I think that what's meant by saying that one is able to exercise that ability is that one has the opportunity, and thus the specific ability, to do the thing in question. For example, to say that under the present circumstances Usain Bolt has the ability to exercise his general ability to run 100 meters in under 10 seconds is to say that nothing in the circumstances prevents him from exercising that ability. If the ability in question is specific, however, then, as far as I can tell, talk of being able to exercise it is redundant. For example, to say that under the present circumstances Bolt has the ability to exercise his specific ability to run 100 meters in under 10 seconds is to say no more than that he has that specific ability.

As noted earlier, control consists in having both a specific ability to see to it that some state of affairs obtains and a specific ability to see to it that that state of affairs does not obtain. Since specific abilities are the sort of thing that can be exercised, control is the sort of thing that can be exercised. Thus, if Bill is in control of whether he decides to move his finger and he does decide to move it, he will have exercised direct, intentional control over his decision. If he is in control of whether he moves his finger and he does move it, he will have exercised hybrid, intentional control over his moving it and indirect, intentional control over its moving. And if he is in control over whether he destroys the clock and he does destroy it, he will have exercised hybrid, simple control over his destroying it and indirect, simple control over its destruction.[51]

---

[49] Note that it can happen both that one has the ability to do something intentionally and that one does that thing, but that one's doing it constitutes the exercise, not of an intentional ability, but only of a simple ability. For example, if I unintentionally spill coffee on you, I will have exercised only a simple, and not an intentional, ability to spill it, even if I had the ability to spill it on you intentionally.

[50] Cf. Clarke (2017a), p. 70.

[51] The question arises: *When*, in this example, does Bill exercise his control over these various events? This is a good question, but I don't think we need to settle on any particular answer. One answer is that, for all the events in question, he exercises his control over them when and only when he makes his decision to act—that is, when and only when *a* occurs. Another answer is that he exercises his control when and only when both his decision and any other pertinent event occur—that is, in the

Sometimes we talk of its being up to us whether to exercise the control we have. Since control involves specific abilities, such talk is, I think, redundant. Suppose that it is up to me whether I move my finger. Then to say that it is "also" up to me whether to exercise my control seems infelicitous, insofar as it suggests, erroneously, that something more is being said than just that it is up to me whether I move my finger.

4.2 Simple *vs.* intentional control

4.2.1 Control and awareness

I have said that philosophers have traditionally held that there are two conditions that someone must satisfy, one agential and the other epistemic, in order to be morally responsible for something. This traditional view might be called into question on the grounds that the latter condition is not independent of but rather contained in the former.[52] For it is commonly claimed that one cannot be in control of something unless one is aware of it,[53] and this certainly seems plausible. Consider the plight of Priscilla, a contestant on a game show. She's just been told by the host, Howie, that "all" she has to do to win the fabulous grand prize is to enter the correct five-digit code on a keypad in front of her. If she does this within the next 60 seconds, the box next to the pad will open up and the prize will be hers. If she doesn't enter the correct code within that time, though, she won't win the prize. Priscilla's problem is that she doesn't know what the correct code is, and Howie won't tell her. The clock has already started and Priscilla frantically enters codes at random. Her time is quickly up and, to no one's surprise, the box remains shut. "I just couldn't do it," Priscilla says ruefully, while Howie mutters words of consolation with blatant insincerity.

Is what Priscilla said true? It seems so. She didn't know the correct code, and so she didn't know how to open the box and win the prize. There were, after all, 100,000 possible codes (don't forget 0-0-0-0-0), and she only had time to try a few. No wonder she lost!

---

case of *b*, when and only when both *a* and *b* occur; in the case of *c*, when and only when both *a* and *c* occur; and so on. Yet another answer is that he exercises his control during the entire period that spans his decision and the pertinent event—that is, in the case of *b*, the period that spans *a* and *b*; in the case of *c*, the period that spans *a* and *c*; and so on. And there are perhaps other answers worth considering. As far as I can tell, all of these answers are compatible with what I want to say about the exercise of control.

[52] Even Aristotle, who, as I noted in Chapter 1, is frequently cited as the source of the traditional view, often uses a single term ("voluntary") to cover both the agential and the epistemic conditions of responsibility.

[53] See Nagel (1976), p. 115; Sher (2009), pp. 146 ff.; Levy (2011), pp. 110 ff., and (2014), pp. 110 ff. Cf. Mele (2010).

But suppose that, after the show, Priscilla asks Howie what the correct code was. "Look, I'll show you," he says smugly, and proceeds to enter 3-1-1-4-8 on the keypad. ("My birthday," he confides with a wink.) The box springs open, revealing $1,000,000 in cash. "Oh," sighs Priscilla, now even more rueful than before, "I could have done that!"

Has Priscilla spoken truly this time? Again, it seems so. What could be easier than doing what Howie just did? But how could it be that Priscilla both could and couldn't open the box? The answer is obvious. There are two senses of "could" at work here. The sense in which Priscilla couldn't open the box is the sense in which Bill could (and did) shoot and kill Jill. The sense in which she could (but didn't) open the box is the sense in which Bill could (and did) destroy the clock on Jill's mantelpiece. In keeping with the terminology introduced in the last section, I will call the former the intentional sense and the latter the simple sense of "could."

It is one thing to distinguish these senses, though, and another to explain just what the distinction consists in. I cannot offer a full explanation (or maybe I can, but not intentionally). Consider the intentional sense. Unfortunately, Priscilla didn't know how to open the box, whereas, again unfortunately, Bill knew all too well how to shoot and kill Jill. Is that what "could intentionally" consists in: know-how? I think not, for two reasons—despite the fact that, as these cases show, the two are closely aligned. First, one can know how to do something without its being the case that one can do it intentionally; for one may have the requisite general ability but lack the requisite opportunity to exercise it (for example, I know how to ride a bike, but I cannot now ride one intentionally, because none is available[54]), or one may have the requisite knowledge but lack the requisite skill (for example, a tennis coach may know "in principle" how to hit an American Twist serve, and he may be successful in teaching this to his players, and yet he may be unable to hit such a serve himself[55]). Second, it seems that one can do something intentionally without knowing how to do it. Basic actions (understood as actions that one can intentionally perform without doing so by way of performing other actions) perhaps should not be said to be actions that one knows how to perform. It sounds odd to say, for example, that you know how to move your finger, if there is no means by which you move it. (Or, if that doesn't sound odd to you, consider *deciding* to move your finger. Do you know how to do that?[56]) And perhaps even some non-basic actions will be ones that one can perform intentionally without knowing how to perform them. Think of what you do when you've forgotten someone's name. You're trying hard to remember it. You're racking your brain. The name's on the tip of your tongue... Well, there are two

---

[54] Cf. Stanley and Williamson (2001), p. 416; Snowdon (2003), pp. 8 f.
[55] Here the distinction between "savoir faire" and "savoir comment faire," noted in Rumfitt (2003), seems pertinent.
[56] Cf. Snowdon (2003), p. 12.

possible outcomes: either you succeed or you fail. It seems plausible to say that, if you succeed in remembering the name, you have remembered it intentionally. But *how* did you succeed? What did the "racking" in question involve? If you're at all like me, on those occasions on which you do succeed, you've no clue how you managed to do so.

Return to the case of BILL AND JILL as represented in Figure 2.1. I have said that Bill exercised intentional control over all the events depicted in that figure (direct control over a, indirect control over b–g, and hybrid control over B–G). In so saying, I am assuming that none of the causal connections between a–g was "wayward" or "deviant." It is certainly possible for such deviancy to arise. If Bill's aim was terrible and he succeeded in killing Jill only because the bullet fired from his gun ricocheted off the sidewalk, then, although his firing the gun may have been intentional, his shooting Jill and killing her will not have been.[57] Still, if any of b–g had been brought about unintentionally, Bill would nonetheless have exercised some kind of control over them—just as he exercised control over h and H in Figure 4.1, despite being wholly unaware of the clock. I have borrowed the term "simple" in this context from Alfred Mele, who helpfully distinguishes between what he calls simple and intentional abilities (among other kinds of abilities),[58] although my use of this term may not match his exactly. According to him, one's performing an action suffices for one's having had the simple ability to perform it.[59] I am not endorsing—or denying—this claim.[60] Clearly, the simple control that I am claiming that Priscilla had over opening the box in front of her requires that she had not only the simple ability not to open it (an ability that she of course exercised) but also the simple ability to open it (an ability that she unfortunately didn't exercise). As far as I can tell, Mele is not committed to agreeing that Priscilla had the latter ability.

One might quibble with my use of the term "control" when all that is at issue is a combination of simple abilities of the sort just described. (Rik Peels, for example, prefers to talk in terms of "influence" rather than "control" in this sort of context.[61]) Isn't it misleading to say that opening the box was in Priscilla's control? I don't think so (although I am not wedded to the term), as long as it is made clear that only simple abilities are in play. There is, of course, a difference between Priscilla's case and Bill's. Bill had no knowledge of the clock on the mantelpiece, whereas Priscilla was keenly aware of the keypad, the box, and the prize within. But if, as it seems to me, Bill's destroying the clock is properly said to have been

---

[57] For classic discussions of this issue, see Chisholm (1964b) and Davidson (1980), p. 79.
[58] See Mele (2003).   [59] See Mele (2003), p. 448.
[60] In favor of endorsement: consider a situation in which Charlie says to Fred, "I bet you can't make that free throw." Fred will typically be taken to win the bet if and only if he makes the throw, regardless of whether his doing so is a fluke. In favor of denial: what general ability is it that is supposed to underlie the specific ability at issue? The ability to do what one in fact does? That has an odd ring to it.
[61] See Peels (2017), ch. 3.

"up to" him, even though he knew nothing about it, there seems to me to be at least as much reason to say that Priscilla's opening the box was "up to" her, given her knowledge of her situation.

If one can have simple control over something without having intentional control over it, then the claim that one cannot be in control of something unless one is aware of it is false. Nonetheless, I am inclined to think that a closely related claim is true, and that is that one cannot be in control of something, X, unless one is in control of something, Y, of which one is aware. (I say only "inclined" because of considerations that I raise immediately below and also in §4.4, where I discuss control over omissions.) This claim is supported by two observations. First, to repeat a point I made in the last section: all action requires intentional action. As I noted earlier, Bill's simple control over the clock's destruction is contingent on his intentional control over the other, antecedent events in the example—or, now to put the point more cautiously, contingent on his intentional control over at least his executive decision, a, that triggered the events that followed. The second observation is that one acts intentionally only if one is aware of what one is doing.

You might dispute this second "observation." Consider a protracted course of action, one in which one of the results occurs long after the relevant executive decision. (One example: in January, a terrorist buries a bomb that is timed to explode, and does explode, in December of that same year.) Suppose that the agent dies 'twixt decision and result. (The terrorist is killed in a drone attack in July.) In such a case, surely the agent has brought about the result intentionally, but just as surely the agent, being dead, is not aware of having done so. Fair enough. Let me therefore amend the observation: one acts intentionally only if one is aware of one's *decision* so to act. (When he buries the bomb, the terrorist is certainly aware of his decision to do so.)

You might still resist the second "observation," even when it has been amended in this way. Consider the following case provided by Randolph Clarke:

> [A]s I'm about to leave my office at the end of the workday, my wife calls to tell me that we're out of milk. My regular route home takes me right by a grocery store, and I tell her I'll stop and buy some. Between my office and the store, I start to think about a paper I'm writing on omissions. I continue to think about my work until I arrive home, where I realize that I've forgotten the milk.[62]

I will return to this case in Chapter 6, when I address the issue of responsibility for negligent behavior, but here I want to use it simply as an example of a phenomenon with which we are all familiar: doing something intentionally (such as driving) while paying attention to something else (such as a paper on omissions,

---

[62] Clarke (2014), p. 164.

or the news on the radio, and so on). Don't such cases of automatic action show that one can do something intentionally while nonetheless being oblivious to what one is doing, even to the decisions one is making? I suspect not. Given that, as noted in the last chapter, awareness or attention comes in *degrees*, it seems plausible to say that the behavior in question is not *fully* automatic. Although Clarke was thinking about his paper, he managed to drive home without having an accident, and that would seem to require his having paid at least some, even if only minimal, attention to staying on the right side of the road, braking when necessary, turning at corners, and so on.[63] Admittedly, it can be rather shocking to arrive home and not remember what you did to get there, but that doesn't mean that you weren't attending to driving while en route. (Driving-while-philosophizing is not, I hope, as dangerous as driving-while-texting tends to be.)

You might *still* resist. Even if we cannot drive intentionally without paying some attention to what we're doing, aren't there cases of relatively simple behavior in which we engage both intentionally and fully automatically, that is, wholly thoughtlessly? Suppose that you return home late at night. You tell yourself *not* to turn on the light because you don't want to wake your wife, and yet, as soon as you enter, that's just what you do! Habit has taken over, it seems, and, although you may plead with your wife, whose slumber you have so rudely interrupted, "I'm sorry! I'm sorry! I didn't mean to do that," surely you *did* have an intention to turn on the light—a "standing" intention, as it is sometimes called—one that ran counter to and somehow overrode your intention not to turn on the light and thereby explains why it is that you did turn it on. I think we can, and should, accept this explanation,[64] but I am nonetheless inclined to accept the second observation (amended). First, although it seems clear that you had an intention to turn on the light, it seems less clear that you turned it on intentionally. Second, even if we should say that you turned it on intentionally, your behavior is to be explained by reference to your habit, a habit that you presumably developed by way of repeated instances of consciously deciding to turn on the light. ("Presumably" is of course weaker than "necessarily." I leave it open whether the latter term applies.[65]) Insofar as this is the case, the second observation need not be abandoned but only once again amended, as follows: one acts intentionally only if one is, or at one time *was*, aware of one's decision so to act.

This second amendment to the second observation itself requires an amendment to the claim in support of which I have invoked the observation. That claim

---

[63] For a contrary view, see Levy (2014), p. 112.
[64] For a contrary view, see Douskos (2017), pp. 1140 ff.
[65] The question arises: Did you *decide* to turn on the light when you turned it on out of habit and contrary to your intention not to turn it on? Given that I am not restricting the term "decide" to cases in which some practical uncertainty is settled, I am inclined to say that you did make such a decision. (For a contrary view, see Mele (1992), p. 231.) I grant, though, that the idea of an unconscious decision is itself somewhat unsettling. If I am mistaken in this matter, then my account of action as being initiated by an executive decision must be qualified so as not to include purely routine or habitual action.

should now be rendered as follows: one cannot be in control of something, X, unless one is *or was* in control of something, Y, of which one is *or was* aware. (If the second observation is in the end to be rejected, then I suspect that this claim is to be rejected, too.) It might be thought that my (tentative) endorsement of such a link between control and awareness renders the Argument from Ignorance question-begging, but that is emphatically not the case. According to Premise 4 of that argument, one is to blame for something only if one was in control of that thing. In this chapter, I have suggested that, to exercise control over anything, one must exercise intentional control over some pertinent executive decision, which itself requires that either one be aware of that decision or one have been aware of some prior executive decision. (Again, this is no more than a suggestion, for reasons that will emerge in §4.4.) What follows from this is that one cannot be to blame for something unless one is or was aware of making some pertinent executive decision. It does *not* follow that one cannot be to blame for something unless one is or was aware of *the overall moral wrongness* of some such decision.[66] The other premises in the Argument from Ignorance are needed in order to reach that conclusion.[67]

4.2.2 Reasons-responsiveness

It might seem, however, that if another popular view of control is accepted, then Premise 4 does indeed threaten to render the Argument from Ignorance question-begging. On this view—call it RR—control requires *reasons-responsiveness*. Assume that RR is true. Then, if one cannot be responsive to reasons of which one is unaware, it follows that control requires that one be responsive to reasons of which one is aware. Moreover, if the kind of control required by *moral* responsibility itself requires responsiveness to *moral* reasons, it follows that this kind of control requires that one be responsive to moral reasons of which one is aware. From there it seems but a short step to the Origination Thesis, according to which blameworthiness (*moral* blameworthiness, of course) requires that at some point one be aware (or, at least, believe) that one's behavior is overall morally wrong.

Well, I'm not sure how short a step that in fact is, but let's focus on the steps that precede it, and let's do so by appealing to the best-known and most thorough account of reasons-responsiveness available, that provided by Fischer and Ravizza. On their view, reasons-responsiveness involves both being *receptive* to reasons and *reacting* to them. They give a very subtle account of each of these features,

---

[66] Contrast Rudy-Hiller (2017), p. 404.
[67] If accuses are possible (regarding which see §3.4.1), then, given that awareness is veridical, this conclusion must be weakened (as in Draft 4 of the Origination Thesis) so that it refers to belief rather than awareness.

according to which the kind of receptivity required is "regular" and the kind of reactivity required is "weak," in virtue of which the kind of responsiveness required is "moderate."[68] The upshot, very roughly, is that, if one is to have agential control over one's behavior, one must have both the general ability to engage in that behavior for certain kinds of reasons and the opportunity to do so, even if on occasion one does not avail oneself of that opportunity.

For several reasons, I am not convinced that agential control (of the sort with which I am concerned and which Premise 4 of the Argument from Ignorance invokes) requires this kind of reasons-responsiveness. First, it's very sophisticated. Consider certain non-human animals (my dog, for example) or young children. Don't they exercise agential (that is, volitional) control over at least some of their behavior? So it seems to me. Are they reasons-responsive in the sense employed by Fischer and Ravizza? Do they recognize reasons and react to them in the way that Fischer and Ravizza specify? Well, given only my very brief and rough presentation of their account, there is presumably no way to tell, but Fischer and Ravizza themselves deny that such agents are reasons-responsive in the sense that concerns them.[69] If that's right, then either I am mistaken in assuming that such agents sometimes exhibit agential control, or such control does not require the kind of sophisticated mentality that Fischer and Ravizza claim it does.

It may not be easy to know what to say about the kind of agency exhibited by dogs and young children, but I think it's pretty clear what we should say about psychopaths. Such agents (or some of them, at least) appear to be incapable of responding to moral reasons, and for this reason Fischer and Ravizza are prepared to say that they are not reasons-responsive in the sense that concerns them.[70] Yet it seems clear that such agents are perfectly capable of controlling how they behave, perhaps in virtue of being capable of responding to certain kinds of non-moral reasons. In any case, let me now simply stipulate that the kind of control at issue in Premise 4 of the Argument from Ignorance is the kind of control of which (such) psychopaths are capable. If such control involves a kind of reasons-responsiveness, so be it. Still the other premises in the argument (or premises like them) will be needed in order to arrive at the Origination Thesis.

I should stress that I agree entirely with Fischer and Ravizza that *moral* responsibility requires a grasp of certain *moral* concepts (and, in particular, that moral blameworthiness requires a grasp of the concept of overall moral wrongdoing—this is an implication of the Origination Thesis coupled with the claim that believing a proposition requires grasping that proposition), but I think it is a mistake to build this condition into an account of *control*. In this regard, the philosophical tradition that holds that there are indeed *two* conditions that must

---

[68] Fischer and Ravizza (1998), pp. 69 ff. [69] Fischer and Ravizza (1998), pp. 76 f.
[70] Fischer and Ravizza (1998), p. 77.

be satisfied for someone to be morally responsible for something, one agential and the other epistemic, seems to me preferable.

Another concern that I have with the view that agential control requires the kind of reasons-responsiveness specified by Fischer and Ravizza is that, in their account of what it is to be receptive to reasons, they talk in terms of "recogniz[ing] what reasons there are."[71] This strongly suggests (although at times they appear to disavow the suggestion[72]) that, to be morally responsible for one's behavior, one must be aware of certain moral reasons that pertain to that behavior. I suspect that this is a mistake. For reasons given in §3.4.1, I would counsel talking in terms of belief rather than awareness. It seems reasonable to suppose that someone who subscribes to a perverse ideology and fails to recognize the reasons that in fact pertain to the situations in which he finds himself can nonetheless be responsive to the reasons that he *believes* pertain to those situations in such a way as to exercise control over and incur moral responsibility for his behavior.[73]

It is worth noting further that, even if moral responsibility requires responsiveness to moral reasons, it's not clear that such responsiveness requires that one be aware of such reasons. Whereas some of those who subscribe to RR maintain that there is such a requirement,[74] others deny it. George Sher, for example, says that "[a]n agent who registers another's distress without bringing it to consciousness, and who unthinkingly adjusts his behavior to defuse the situation, may still be reason-responsive in the full sense."[75] This strikes me as a plausible claim. Notice that conjoining RR with a denial that reasons-responsiveness requires awareness of the relevant reasons is perfectly compatible with my suggestion that control requires that one be aware of making some pertinent executive decision, since awareness of making a decision doesn't itself require awareness of the reasons to which one is responsive in making that decision.

There is an important feature of the view proposed by Fischer and Ravizza that I have not yet mentioned but on which I must comment, and that is that, contrary to what I have been assuming, the kind of control that they think one must possess and exercise in order for one to be morally responsible for one's behavior is *not* bilateral. They draw a distinction between what they call *regulative* control and *guidance* control. The former kind of control is bilateral: one has such control over one's behavior just in case one can (that is, one has the specific ability to) engage in that behavior *and* one can behave otherwise. Traditionally, it has been held that moral responsibility for one's behavior requires that one have such control over it. The reason for which Fischer and Ravizza (along with many others) reject this

---

[71] Fischer and Ravizza (1998), p. 69.   [72] Fischer and Ravizza (1998), pp. 76 f.
[73] Cf. Haji (1998), pp. 75 ff., for an account of reasons-responsiveness that doesn't involve receptivity of the sort advocated by Fischer and Ravizza.
[74] E.g., Levy (2014), ch. 6.
[75] Sher (2009), p. 68. As this passage indicates, Sher talks of "reason-responsiveness" rather than "reasons-responsiveness," which is the more usual term.

traditional view is that they take so-called Frankfurt-cases to show it to be false. These kinds of cases, first introduced by Harry Frankfurt,[76] are supposed to be cases in which, due to the presence of some kind of impediment (either a counterfactual intervener or an actual "blockage" of some sort), an agent cannot in fact behave, or indeed decide to behave, in any way other than as he actually does but, being unaware of the impediment, behaves as he does for his own reasons and in such a way that the impediment is entirely "idle," playing no role whatsoever in the explanation of his behavior. Frankfurt maintains, as do Fischer and Ravizza, that in such cases the agent's lack of access to alternative possibilities of behavior provides no reason to say that the agent is not morally responsible for the behavior in which he actually engages. Now, those who, convinced by such cases, hold that moral responsibility doesn't require regulative control typically do *not* deny that such responsibility nonetheless requires control of some sort. Fischer and Ravizza are no exception. In giving their own particular account of guidance control, they draw a distinction between an *agent* being reasons-responsive and the *"mechanism"* that leads to the agent's behavior being reasons-responsive. This mechanism might be an ordinary process of practical deliberation, or it might consist in some form of compulsion or coercion that bypasses or subverts the agent's deliberation. In a Frankfurt-case, the agent is not and cannot be reasons-responsive, precisely because he cannot behave otherwise, but that doesn't mean that the mechanism that leads to his behavior cannot be reasons-responsive. On the contrary, if the agent does what he does as a result of engaging in ordinary practical deliberation, then the mechanism in question will be moderately reasons-responsive and the agent will thereby exercise guidance control over his behavior (as long as the agent also "owns" the mechanism, a matter having to do with the agent's history on which there is no need to comment further here[77]). Although the presence of the impediment means that the agent's behavior is not up to him, it doesn't mean that it isn't guided by and attributable to him, and that is *all* that is required, as far as control is concerned, for him to be morally responsible for his behavior.

Or so say Fischer and Ravizza (again very roughly—I have left out many important details). It is a controversial and very delicate question whether Frankfurt-cases do in fact succeed in showing the traditional view, that moral responsibility requires bilateral control, to be false. (Frankfurt's ground-breaking paper has given rise to an enormous and ever-burgeoning literature.) Since I have been presuming that the traditional view is true, it might seem that it is important for my purposes in this book to defend this view against the counterexamples to it that Frankfurt-cases allegedly provide. I think, though, that that is fortunately not the case.

---

[76] Frankfurt (1969).   [77] Fischer and Ravizza (1998), ch. 8.

Frankfurt-cases are supposed to be cases in which an agent has guidance control over his behavior but lacks bilateral control over it because of the presence of some idle impediment. It seems to me very natural to add that, if indeed the agent lacks bilateral control in such cases, this is so *only* because of the presence of the impediment. But, if this is so, it follows that in *non*-Frankfurt-cases the absence of bilateral control is sufficient for the absence of guidance control. And if it is granted that guidance control is necessary for moral responsibility, then, in *non*-Frankfurt-cases, so too will bilateral control be necessary for moral responsibility. Now, I take it to be clear that Frankfurt-cases are very special kinds of cases. If they ever occur, they occur only very rarely. But then, for all intents and purposes, we may continue to assume that, if control is necessary for moral responsibility, bilateral control is necessary for moral responsibility.

It may seem that what I have just said is badly mistaken. One of the main purposes of the extended investigation undertaken by Fischer and Ravizza is to make room for, and argue in favor of, the "semicompatibilist" view that moral responsibility is compatible with causal determinism even if such determinism rules out the possibility of bilateral control. Now, if causal determinism is true and in itself constitutes a kind of Frankfurt-case, then it is false to say that such cases occur only very rarely. If, on the other hand, such cases occur only very rarely but causal determinism is true and precludes bilateral control, then it is false to say that, when there is guidance control without bilateral control, this is the case *only* because of the presence of some idle impediment of the sort that is featured in Frankfurt-cases. In response, I wish only to point out that, in arguing for semicompatibilism, Fischer and Ravizza are of course explicitly concerned with whether a form of control that is tantamount to a robust kind of *freedom* is compatible with causal determinism.[78] As I said in the last section, however, that is *not* my concern here. Again, I take it to be clear that there is a perhaps modest but nonetheless important sense in which we sometimes, indeed very often, possess and exercise control—bilateral control—over our behavior, regardless of whether such control amounts to the kind of freedom that has preoccupied philosophers for millennia. Frankfurt-cases might be cases in which agents lack such control, but causal determinism certainly doesn't preclude it. (Don't misunderstand me. In saying that for all intents and purposes, if control is necessary for moral responsibility, then bilateral control is necessary for moral responsibility, I am not denying—or asserting—that a form of control that is tantamount to a robust kind of freedom is *also* necessary. Nor am I denying—or asserting—that this kind of freedom is compatible with causal determinism. I intend to stay well clear of that quagmire.)

---

[78] Fischer and Ravizza (1998), p. 17.

Finally, I want to comment very briefly on Fischer's and Ravizza's claim, to which I alluded earlier, that the exercise of guidance control is not only necessary but *sufficient* for the satisfaction of the control-condition for moral responsibility.[79] Unless the reasons-responsive mechanism at issue is or involves *volition* in particular—something that Fischer and Ravizza do not even mention, let alone insist upon—then it seems clear that guidance control is not tantamount to volitional control. Thus, if volitional control is necessary for moral responsibility, then the exercise of guidance control cannot be sufficient for satisfaction of the control-condition for such responsibility. One possible response to this observation, of course, is to deny that volitional control is necessary for moral responsibility. This is an issue that I will take up in Chapter 9. Here I wish merely to observe that a mechanism's simply being moderately reasons-responsive seems too weak a condition to fulfill the control-relevant role that Fischer and Ravizza appear to have in mind. As Verena Wagner has recently noted, fear is a mechanism that can be, and frequently is, moderately reasons-responsive, and yet it seems that even moderately reasons-responsive fear, far from providing an agent with the control necessary for being morally responsible for his behavior, can rob him of such control.[80]

4.3 Direct *vs.* indirect control

Return to the case of BILL AND THE CLOCK as represented in Figure 4.1. As I have noted on several occasions, it is Bill's executive decision, *a*, that was the locus of his control, by way of which his control extended to the remaining events. It is thus *a* over which he exercised direct control; his control over *b–h* was indirect, while over *B–H* it was hybrid. Wherever there is indirect or hybrid control, there must of course also be direct control, but whether the reverse is true is perhaps not so clear.

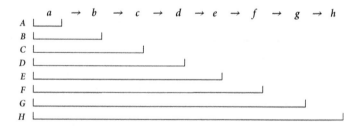

Figure 4.1 BILL AND THE CLOCK

---

[79] Fischer and Ravizza (1998), pp. 241 f., and (2000), p. 441, n. 1.
[80] Wagner (2017), pp. 2800 ff.

Imagine that Mavis decides to move her finger but that nothing happens as a result, since she has been suddenly stricken by total paralysis. Is such a scenario possible? Can an event have literally no consequences at all?

The answer may depend in part on just what is meant by "consequence." In Figure 4.1, *b–h* are all *causal* consequences of *a*. It seems to me at least conceptually possible that an event such as Mavis's decision to move her finger have no causal consequences, and so, in that respect at least, it seems that there could be direct control without indirect or hybrid control. But there are other kinds of consequences. That $2 + 2 = 4$ is a non-causal consequence of some sort (logical or metaphysical) of every proposition, and I think we should also say that it, or its obtaining, is a consequence of every event. But the matter is hardly pressing, since its obtaining is not in anyone's control. There is reason to think, however, that there are other kinds of non-causal consequences that can be in someone's control. Recall the supposition that Bill had promised Bert not to make any rash decisions when dealing with Jill. As a result of his decision to kill her, this promise was broken. Whether the promise was broken was within Bill's control, even though its being broken was presumably a non-causal consequence of his decision.[81] As another possible example of a non-causal consequence of his decision over which Bill exercised indirect control, suppose that his killing Jill prompted her sister, Gail, to campaign for tighter gun control. According to some philosophers of a libertarian bent, if Gail's activities were freely undertaken, they cannot have been caused by any prior events.[82] Nonetheless, they certainly occurred as a result of Bill's behavior and lay within his indirect control. Or suppose that Bill, enraged though he was, had decided *not* to kill Jill and thus, to his surprise and her profound relief, omitted doing so. According to some philosophers, omissions cannot have causal consequences.[83] Even if this is correct, both Bill's surprise and Jill's relief occurred as a result of his decision. In exercising direct control over it, he exercised indirect control over them.

The reason I say that these various events lay within Bill's indirect control, whether or not they were causal consequences of his decision, is that it was up to him whether the relevant states of affairs obtained (even if in some cases he was unaware of this fact). It was up to him whether they obtained because the events in question occurred as a result of his decision, and it was up to him whether to make this decision. Had he not made it, they would not have occurred. It is important to note here, though, that it seems possible that decisions sometimes have consequences that would have occurred even if the decisions themselves had not occurred. Suppose, for example, that Bob had seen Bill point his gun at Jill. Bob had a gun of his own and, in an effort to save Jill, fired it in Bill's direction. Being

---

[81] Cf. Goldman (1970), p. 27.
[82] See, e.g., Taylor (1966), pp. 109 ff.; Chisholm (1976), pp. 69 f.; Donagan (1977), pp. 46 f.
[83] See, e.g., Dowe (2001); M. S. Moore (2009), pp. 444 ff.

inept with firearms, however, Bob missed Bill and shot Jill instead, causing her to die at exactly the same moment at which her death occurred as a result of Bill's shooting her. If such a case of overdetermination is possible, it may seem to constitute a counterexample to Premise 4 of the Argument from Ignorance, which states that one is to blame for something only if one was in control of that thing. I have been assuming that the kind of control at issue is bilateral, but in this latest version of the Bill-and-Jill scenario it looks like it wasn't up to Bill whether Jill died when and where she did, since Bob's decision to take his shot at Bill ensured that she would die then and there anyway. Yet surely Bill (and possibly Bob, too) might well be to blame for Jill's death.

I agree that Bill might be to blame for Jill's death, even if her death was causally overdetermined, but there are at least two ways in which one might nonetheless seek to preserve the judgment that he had control over this event. One way is to adopt the Frankfurt-inspired strategy of identifying a kind of responsibility-relevant control other than bilateral control. (If one took this tack, one might have to relax the claim I made in the last section that "for all intents and purposes, we may continue to assume that, if control is necessary for moral responsibility, bilateral control is necessary for moral responsibility." How extensive this relaxation would have to be would depend on how frequently overdetermination occurs.) The other way is to note, as some opponents of Frankfurt have noted, that even if, when an event's occurrence is overdetermined, it is not within an agent's control *whether* the relevant state of affairs obtains, it may still be up to that agent *how* it obtains.[84] For example, that Jill died partly as a result of his shooting her would seem to have been in Bill's control, even if her dying was not. For present purposes, there is no need to try to settle just how cases of overdetermination should be handled, and so I won't pursue the matter further.

The version of the Bill-and-Jill case that involves Gail brings out an important point, and that is that the fact that some behavior (a decision, an action, an omission) is in one person's control does *not* preclude its also being in another's. If Gail would not have embarked on her campaign had Bill not killed her sister, then her behavior was a consequence of his behavior and lay within his control, even though her behavior presumably lay within her control, too. It can of course also happen that one's *own* behavior is a consequence of one's behavior. Recall Alice from Chapter 1. She suffered from Tourette's but declined to take her medication, as a result of which she slung racial slurs at Ben, offending him deeply. In this sort of context, philosophers often talk of *tracing* one's control over one's behavior at some later time to one's control over one's behavior at an earlier time, so that responsibility for one's behavior at the later time is correspondingly to be traced to responsibility for one's behavior at the earlier time. In

---

[84] See, e.g., Robinson (2019).

this way, Alice might be blameworthy for offending Ben in virtue of her being blameworthy for deciding to skip her medication. I will examine the idea of tracing responsibility further in §5.1.

4.4 Control over omissions

4.4.1 Acts of omission

Consider again the case of BILL AND THE CLOCK depicted in Figure 4.1. I have said that Bill had control (whether direct, indirect, or hybrid, and whether intentional or simple) over all the events depicted in the figure. But as I have also said, repeatedly, the kind of control in question is *bilateral*; whether the relevant states of affairs obtained was *up to* Bill. It's obvious that Figure 4.1 doesn't fully capture this fact, precisely because it represents only one side or aspect of Bill's control; it fails to represent the fact that he could have seen to it that the relevant states of affairs did *not* obtain, that is, that he could have *omitted* doing what he did. To complete the picture, a companion figure is needed. What should this figure look like?

One possibility is represented in Figure 4.2. This figure is supposed to be interpreted as follows. A^*, which consists simply of a^*, is Bill's executive decision *not* to kill Jill. B^*, which consists of his decision, a^*, causing his finger's *not* moving, $\sim b$, is his omitting to move his finger.[85] C^*, which consists of his decision, a^*, causing the trigger's *not* retracting, $\sim c$, is his omitting to pull the trigger. And so on down the line. Note that, in light of the causal connections between $a^* - \sim h$, if Bill had behaved in this way, he would have accomplished H^* (that is, he would have omitted destroying the clock) *by* accomplishing G^*, he would have accomplished G^* *by* accomplishing F^*, and so on.

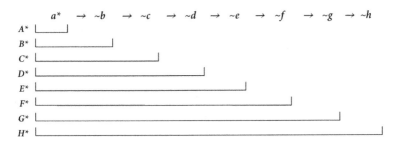

Figure 4.2 BILL'S ACTIVE OMISSION

---

[85] It is appropriate to call B^* an omission at least in part because Bill had the specific ability to move his finger. Not all not-doings are omissions, however. For example, whereas Usain Bolt has, presumably, often omitted to run 100 meters in under 10 seconds, I have never omitted to do so.

Figure 4.2 and my description of it raise two important questions. First, what sort of thing are $\sim b - \sim h$ supposed to be? Are they genuine entities, or are they mere absences? Second, if a^* and $\sim b - \sim h$ can be related by causation, is this the same type of causation that obtains among those entities, a and $b-h$, depicted in Figure 4.1? I won't try to answer these questions here, important though they are, for two reasons. First, how they are to be answered is a highly controversial matter, the investigation of which would lead us too far afield. (Some authors hold that omissions are absences and that they therefore cannot enter into relations of any sort.[86] Others hold that they are a kind of negative event that can only be related by a kind of "quasi-causation."[87] Still others hold that they are absences but that they can nonetheless be related by genuine causation.[88]) Second, and more significantly, there is no need to answer these questions here. The fact is, however they are to be answered, everyone agrees that the sort of situation represented in Figure 4.2 can arise, and that is all that I need for present purposes. Lest this seem too cavalier, let me simply point out that even the situation depicted in Figure 4.1 might well involve absences, negative events, prevention or double prevention, and the like. (Jonathan Schaffer claims that in such cases there are repeated instances of what he calls "causation by disconnection": nerve signals cause muscle contractions via blocking the presence of tropomyosin at certain sites; trigger pullings cause bullet firings via disconnecting the gun's sear, thereby allowing the spring to uncoil; heart piercings cause death via disconnecting the influx of oxygenated blood into the brain, thereby allowing oxygen starvation to run its course.[89]) In what follows, I will treat $\sim b - \sim h$ as genuine events related by genuine causation, but this is just a default position; I do not mean thereby to presuppose any particular answer to the two questions just raised. (Remember, too, that I am not presupposing that indirect control must operate via causation anyway. As I noted in the last section, the consequences that are at issue need not be *causal* consequences. Also, I should acknowledge that the possibility of over-determination arises in this sort of context, too. It may be that some of $\sim b - \sim h$ would have occurred even if a^* hadn't—perhaps Bill's gun would have backfired.)

I noted earlier that events such as $b-h$, over which Bill had indirect control, and actions such as $B-H$, over which he had hybrid control, might feature in AB-conditionals of the following sort: if he had decided that the relevant state of affairs should obtain, it would have, and if he had decided otherwise, it wouldn't have. I also noted that the phrase "decide otherwise" is ambiguous. One interpretation of that phrase is provided by the case of Bill's active omission. In Figure 4.2, it is A^* (or a^*) that constitutes his deciding otherwise, and the other events represented in the figure are what would have happened if he had so decided. Given that A^* was in his (direct) control, then those other events were

---

[86] See, e.g., M. S. Moore (2009), pp. 444 ff.   [87] See, e.g., Dowe (2001).
[88] See, e.g., Schaffer (2000).   [89] Schaffer (2000), pp. 286 ff.

also in his (indirect or hybrid) control. A^* is of course not an omission, but $B^* - H^*$ are. (More particularly, $B^* - G^*$ are *intentional* omissions;[90] H^* is an *unintentional* omission.) In this way, omissions, just like "regular" actions, can constitute the exercise of control.

The symmetry between Figures 4.1 and 4.2 masks an underlying asymmetry, one that has to do with the fact that, although moving one's finger entails its moving, the converse entailment doesn't hold. This raises the question whether it is possible to omit to move one's finger even though one doesn't bring about its not moving. Consider Figure 4.3. This simple figure is supposed to depict a situation in which, although Bill made the decision not to move his finger, this decision did not cause its not moving. This might have happened in one of two ways. First, $\sim b$ occurred, but its occurrence wasn't caused by a^*. Second, $\sim b$ didn't occur, because b did. Should we say in either case that Bill omitted to move his finger? Should we say that he intentionally omitted to do so? These are interesting and difficult questions, but we need not answer them here; for what is clear is that in Figure 4.3, although Bill may have exercised control over a^*, he certainly didn't exercise control over $\sim b$ (or b). That is, his decision not to move his finger may have been in his (direct) control, but its (not) moving was not in his (indirect) control, and so his (not) moving it was not in his (hybrid) control.

The kind of control exercised in Bill's active omission is a kind that is frequently exhibited. We may assume, for example, that when Heinrich failed to alert others to the dangers of thalidomide, when Karl failed to engage in further research on that same drug, and when Alice failed to take the medication that would have helped her manage the impulses associated with Tourette's, these were all instances of omissions like those involved in Bill's active omission—omissions that stemmed from the decision *not* to do something and that accordingly resulted in not doing that thing. In light of this decision, which is itself a form of activity, it seems appropriate to call intentional omissions of this sort *acts* of omission, even though, being omissions, they necessarily involve not-doing.

Some decisions are complex, comprising both a decision to do something and a decision not to do something. For example, I might decide to go to the museum and not to the theater. In such a case, both the action of going to the museum and the omission to go to the theater will be forms of intentional behavior, at least

$$a^* \not\to \sim b$$

Figure 4.3 Bill's inefficacy

---

[90] This once again requires, I think, that the links that bind a^* and $\sim b - \sim g$ not be "wayward." See §4.2.1. Cf. Clarke (2014), pp. 79 f.

under normal circumstances. Sometimes the decision to do something and the decision not to do something else are more intimately related. For example, I might decide to have the cheesecake *in order* not to disappoint my host.

Do all intentional omissions involve the activity of deciding? Randolph Clarke denies that they do, giving this example:

> Suppose that while standing admiring a well-shaped object, I see a sign in front of it saying, "Wet Paint/Do Not Touch." I comply with the instruction. There might be several things I do *while* refraining, but there need be no action I perform in order to prevent myself from touching the object. Having my arms at my sides before I saw the sign need not have been an action I was performing then. Having them there once I've read the instruction need not be, either.
>
> It might be suggested that a decision not to touch the object, made when I read the instruction, is the action by performing which I prevent myself from touching it. But I need not have made any such decision. We can come to have intentions by actively forming them in decision making. We can also come to have them nonactively, without actively forming them in making a decision. A decision resolves uncertainty about what to do, but sometimes there's no such uncertainty. When it's obvious what to do, or when one acts on a whim or by habit, one might come to intend without making a decision. My intention not to touch the freshly painted object might have been so acquired when I read the instruction not to touch it.[91]

I am inclined to deny what Clarke says here. His conception of decision-making strikes me as too restrictive. It seems to me that in many cases we make decisions even when there is no uncertainty that needs to be resolved. As I noted in §4.1.3, after finishing the main course I might decide to have the cheesecake, even if I have never seriously entertained not doing so. Or again, when I am driving home by a familiar route, I might make certain turns out of habit, "unthinkingly," but so saying seems to me consistent with saying that I decide, with little or no consciousness of doing so, to make the turns when and where I do. Clarke might concede this point, I suppose, but still insist that, in these cases, what I am calling a decision is not an instance of genuine activity; it merely involves coming to have an intention passively, rather than actively forming one. In any case, what is most important for present purposes is that Clarke maintains both that he was in *control* of his intentionally omitting to touch the object and that this control involved *no activity* on his part.[92] Is this a tenable view?

---

[91] Clarke (2014), p. 14. [92] Clarke (2014), pp. 96 ff.

4.4.2 Can control be purely passive?

In order to explore this question, consider the case of BILL AND JILL once again. I have just noted that one way to complete the picture of Bill's control over the events at issue is to couple Figure 4.1 with Figure 4.2. In the former figure, a represents Bill's (active) decision to kill Jill; in the latter figure, a^* represents his (actively) deciding otherwise. As I have observed, however, "decide otherwise" is ambiguous, and another way in which Bill might have decided otherwise is represented in Figure 4.4. The difference between Figures 4.2 and 4.4 consists, of course, in the difference between $A^* - H^*$, on the one hand, and $\sim A - \sim H$, on the other, and that difference is to be traced to the difference between a^* and $\sim a$, that is, to the difference between Bill's *deciding not* to kill Jill and his *not deciding* to do so. In Figure 4.4 it is the latter that constitutes his deciding otherwise.

In BILL'S PASSIVE OMISSION there was no activity on Bill's part at all. Prior to the occurrence of $\sim a$, he had not decided to kill Jill, and $\sim a$ was simply the event of his continuing not to decide to kill her. The ensuing events occurred because of $\sim a$ and, since $\sim a$ involved no activity, the omissions, $\sim A - \sim H$, that comprised both $\sim a$ and, where pertinent, some ensuing event, were purely passive. Unlike the omissions involved in BILL'S ACTIVE OMISSION, it would be a mistake to describe them as *acts* of omission.

The question arises: Were any of the events involved in BILL'S PASSIVE OMISSION in Bill's control? Since all control is rooted in direct control, the key question here is whether $\sim a$ was in his control. Now, of course, one way in which Bill could have seen to it that he didn't decide to kill Jill was by seeing to it that he did decide not to kill her. But that is precisely not what is at issue at this point. The question is whether a *purely passive* omission can be in an agent's direct control. From this point on, this is how I intend $\sim a$ to be understood: as Bill's not deciding to kill Jill, but *not* in virtue of his deciding not to do so.

I am unsure of the answer to this crucial question. When, in §4.1.8, I discussed the question of what direct control over an event such as a might consist in, I mentioned the possibility that it be understood in terms of a pair of conditionals such as these: if Bill had desired to kill Jill more strongly than he desired not to do

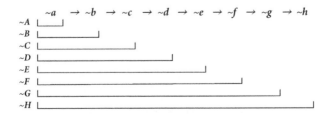

Figure 4.4 BILL'S PASSIVE OMISSION

so, he would have decided to kill her, and if he had desired otherwise, he wouldn't have. It's not clear to me how the corresponding formula for ~a should be phrased. Regarding the first conditional alone, there are two possibilities: first, if Bill had *desired not* to kill Jill more strongly than he desired to do so, he would not have decided to do so; second, if he had *not desired* to kill Jill more strongly than he desired not to do so, he would not have decided to do so. I also mentioned the possibility that control over an event such as *a* be understood in terms of having a reason, rather than a desire, to behave in a certain way. When applied to ~a, this idea yields still further conditionals for our consideration. Might Bill's control over ~a be understood in terms of any of these conditionals? I will leave the question open, primarily because, even if the truth of some such conditional proved to be necessary for Bill's having control over ~a, the question would remain whether it was also sufficient for such control. This matches the situation earlier regarding *a*. I raised the possibility that direct control over a decision to do something might be understood in terms of some such conditionals, but I certainly didn't insist on this. Nonetheless, it seems clear to me that we often *are* in direct control of our decisions, however such control is to be understood. Moreover, since I have no positive proposal to make regarding how direct control over events such as *a* is to be understood, I am in no position to rule out the possibility that we also have direct control over events such as ~a.

Here, though, the following objection might be made. One cannot have control that one cannot exercise, either by seeing to it that the relevant state of affairs obtains or by seeing to it that it doesn't. Thus, if Bill had control over whether he decided to kill Jill, then, trivially, he could "also" have exercised that control, and he would have exercised it if either he had decided to kill her (*a*) or he had decided not to kill her (*a**). But the *exercise* of control requires *agency*. Hence, ~a, being a purely *passive* omission, is not the sort of event that could have constituted the exercise of control, and so it is not the sort of event that could have lain within Bill's control (except indirectly, via the exercise of control over some other event—but that's precisely not what is supposed to be at issue here).

Although I have considerable sympathy with this objection, I'm afraid that it may simply beg the question at issue. The crucial premise is the claim that the exercise of "agential" control requires agency. Why accept this claim?[93] In §4.1.10, I contended that exercising an ability to do something consists simply in doing

---

[93] It is a claim that some philosophers apparently reject. Cf. Fischer and Tognazzini (2009), p. 551. It is noteworthy, though, that they provide no positive proposal regarding how it is that the exercise of control can be purely passive. Cf. also Rudy-Hiller (2017), pp. 412 ff., whose "capacitarian" account of control may be construed as implying either that the exercise of control doesn't require agency or that one can have control that one cannot exercise.

that which one has the ability to do. The corresponding claim in the case of omissions is this: exercising an ability not to do something consists simply in not doing that which one has the ability not to do. This claim does not presuppose that the exercise of an ability involves agency. Moreover, when we consider machines of the sort I mentioned earlier, such as a thermostat or an autopilot, it's clear that the exercise of control doesn't involve agency. True, it sounds a little odd to say that the thermostat exercises control over the temperature in a room, rather than simply that it controls the temperature, but that may be because we are accustomed to thinking of the exercise of control in intentional terms. It's also true that we might not normally draw a distinction between the thermostat's controlling the temperature and its being in control of the temperature. These terminological points notwithstanding, the fact remains that there is clearly a distinction between, on the one hand, the truth of a pair of subjunctive conditionals (such as, in the case of the thermostat: if the temperature were to transcend certain limits, the thermostat would restore it to a pre-set range, and if the temperature were to stay within these limits, the thermostat would remain "inactive") and, on the other hand, the truth of the consequent of one of these conditionals; and, I have suggested, it is partly in terms of just such a distinction that the distinction between the possession and the exercise of agential control is at least sometimes to be understood. Furthermore, we would normally not shrink from saying that the thermostat is not only in control of, but is indeed controlling, the temperature, even when the temperature remains within the specified limits and the thermostat therefore remains in passive mode. And if this is true of the thermostat, then perhaps the analogous claim is true of Bill in BILL'S PASSIVE OMISSION: he was in control of whether the relevant states of affairs obtained and exercised this control purely passively when, and simply in virtue of the fact that, the events in question occurred. I confess, though, that I struggle to understand how this could be the case.

Although my description of BILL'S PASSIVE OMISSION specifies that he didn't decide not to kill Jill, it doesn't specify that he didn't intend not to kill her. If he did have this intention, then Clarke would likely say that his omitting to kill Jill was intentional.[94] It is Clarke's view that we can have purely passive control not only over intentional but also over unintentional omissions. Consider again the case, presented in §4.2.1, of his failure to pick up milk on the way home. He maintains that he had both the ability to buy the milk—the *specific* ability, since he "had the general abilities *and the opportunity* needed" to get it[95]—and the specific ability not to buy it.[96] For this reason, he believes, he was in control of his unintentionally

---

[94] His verdict would depend on whether the causal connections involved were wayward. See n. 90 above.
[95] Clarke (2014), p. 166, emphasis added.   [96] Clarke (2014), pp. 89 f.

omitting to buy the milk. But how could this be? Did he *exercise* that control? Here I struggle even more to understand what the purely passive and, in this case, inadvertent exercise of control could consist in. At one point Clarke suggests that perhaps in such a case there is no *exercise* of control, even though one *possesses* the pertinent abilities.[97] Yet, as I just noted, it seems to be a truism that one cannot have control that one cannot exercise. Clarke might agree but say that, when it is in one's control whether to do some act or to omit doing it, it is only the doing of it that would constitute the exercise of one's control; unintentionally omitting to do it would not constitute such an exercise. But that would seem to imply that, in unintentionally omitting to do something, one is not controlling how one behaves, even though one is in control of how one behaves. That strikes me as impossible. Not only is it the case that one cannot have control that one cannot exercise, it is also the case, I think, that one cannot have control that one is not exercising.

In summary: it is clear that we can both possess and exercise control over intentional omissions and also over some unintentional ones. The case of BILL's ACTIVE OMISSION demonstrates that. Whether control can be purely passive is a question that I will leave open. I am skeptical that it can be, but I know of no definitive way to show that it cannot.

4.4.3 The locus of direct control

Finally, I wish to remark briefly on Premise 12 of the Argument from Ignorance. In every draft of the argument that has been given so far, that premise reads as follows:

(12) one has direct control over something only if that thing is an act or omission.

If one cannot have direct control over purely passive omissions, the phrase "or omission" is, in that respect, otiose. If what I have called acts of omission are indeed acts, then again this phrase is otiose. If what I have said about direct control in the previous section and elsewhere is correct, the term "act" should, strictly speaking, be replaced by the term "executive decision." These points notwithstanding, I will leave the premise as it stands. Since an executive decision is itself a form of activity, keeping the term "act" is not seriously misleading. Moreover, if one can after all have direct control over purely passive omissions, the phrase "or omission" must be retained.

---

[97] Clarke (2014), p. 166, n. 6. Cf. Clarke (2017a), p. 70, and Clarke (2020), p. 330.

CONTROL 177

4.5 Degrees of control

4.5.1 The extent of control

Consider again the case of BILL AND THE CLOCK depicted in Figure 4.1. Suppose that things had turned out very differently. Suppose, in particular, that a bird had intercepted Bill's bullet in its (the bullet's) flight toward Jill, thereby preventing her death and the destruction of the clock. This case is depicted in Figure 4.5. Of course, there is more to the case than what is represented in this figure. After all, bullets don't just evaporate. I simply want to emphasize that, in contrast with Figure 4.1, in Figure 4.5 none of *f–h* occur as a result of Bill's decision. Despite this dramatic difference between the two cases, there is a sense in which the degree of Bill's control over what took place was the same in both. I say this because, in both cases, all the events that occurred as a consequence of his decision, *a*, were in Bill's control only to the extent that *a* itself was; thus the presence or absence of events *f–h* does not affect the degree to which Bill exercised control over what took place. In both versions, *a* was the locus of his control; it exhausted his exercise of control; whether the ensuing events occurred was not in his control, except insofar as *a* itself was; or, to put the point in yet another way, whether the ensuing events occurred was not up to him, except insofar as *a* itself was, but "up to nature."[98]

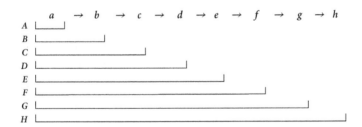

Figure 4.1 BILL AND THE CLOCK

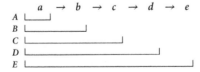

Figure 4.5 BILL AND THE BIRD

---

[98] Cf. Davidson (1980), p. 59.

178 IGNORANCE AND MORAL RESPONSIBILITY

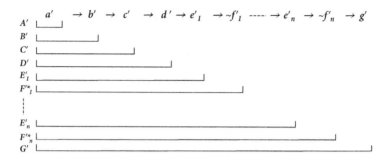

Figure 4.6 BILL'S PERSISTENCE

To appreciate the point that I'm trying to make, consider yet another twist on the original case, one in which Bill kills Jill by means of injecting a slow-acting poison rather than by shooting a fast-flying bullet. Let us suppose that he has an antidote to the poison that he could administer on any number of occasions, but that, on each of these occasions, he deliberately refrains from doing so. The case could then be depicted as in Figure 4.6. In this figure, a' is, as before, Bill's decision to kill Jill; b' is the movement of his finger; c' is the depression of the syringe; d' is the release of the poison; $e'_1 - e'_n$ are Bill's repeated decisions not to administer the antidote; $\sim f'_1 - \sim f'_n$ are the repeated incidents of the antidote's not entering Jill's body; and g' is, as before, Jill's death. We may assume that, in this version of the case, it is not only a' that is in Bill's direct control; so, too, are each of $e'_1 - e'_n$. In light of this fact, it would of course be a mistake to say that g' was in Bill's control only to the extent that a' was. On the contrary, he exercised control over g' on all those occasions, $e'_1 - e'_n$, on which he decided not to administer the antidote.

4.5.2 Whole control

I have talked of "the" degree to which Bill was in control of Jill's death, but that is misleading, since it is not only along the direct-indirect dimension of control that degree of control may (or, rather, may be thought to) vary.

Consider once again the case of BILL AND THE CLOCK depicted in Figure 4.1. There is a sense in which it was wholly, or fully, or entirely up to Bill whether any of the events depicted in the figure occurred. *Given* the background conditions, it was wholly up to Bill whether to make the decision (*a*) to kill Jill, and it was thus wholly up to him whether the subsequent events (*b–h*, and *B–H*) occurred. With respect to these subsequent events, it was true that, given the background conditions, they would occur if and only if Bill made the decision he did. Of course, all the events depicted in the figure are such that their occurrence was contingent on other events and states that lay beyond Bill's control; that's precisely what rendered his control over them merely partial. Nonetheless, given that these other events and states did occur (this is what I mean by "background conditions"), it was entirely up to Bill whether the events depicted in the figure occurred.

Not all cases in which an agent exercises control are like this. Consider that version of the Bill-and-Jill case mentioned in §4.3 in which, by virtue of his abortive attempt to save Jill, what Bob in fact managed to do was to shoot and kill her exactly when Bill did. In this version, it wasn't up to Bill at all whether Jill died when she did. So, too, for Bob. It might be said that, in such a case, it was nonetheless up to the group of Bill and Bob whether Jill died when she did, but I won't pursue this suggestion here.[99]

I noted earlier that, even if, because of Bob's bungling, it wasn't up to Bill whether Jill died when she did, it seems that it was still up to him whether she died partly as a result of his shooting her. Even so, whether she died *partly* as a result of his shooting her was something that was *wholly* up to him. Are there any kinds of case in which an event's occurrence is merely *partly* up to someone? It might seem that cases in which agents must cooperate with one another to achieve some result would be cases that meet this description, but I'm not sure that's right. Suppose that neither Bill's nor Bob's shot would have sufficed on its own to kill Jill; both shots were needed. Even so, *given* Bob's shot, Bill's sufficed and, *given* Bill's shot, Bob's sufficed. For each agent, the other's taking his shot counts as part of the background conditions. For this reason, I think that it is only in cases (if there are any) in which, given the background conditions, it is *not* true that an event *would* occur, but it *is* true that it *might* occur, if and only if an agent behaved in a certain way, that it can happen that that event's occurrence is partly but not wholly up to the agent.

If it is wholly up to Bill whether Jill dies and also wholly up to Bob whether she dies, then of course its being wholly up to someone whether some event occurs does not imply that it is solely up to that person that that event occurs. It can even happen that it is wholly up to one person whether it is wholly up to another person whether some event occurs. Perhaps Bob bought his gun from Bill the day before. Had Bill not sold the gun to Bob, Bob would not have been in a position to take the shot he took.

4.5.3 Awareness of circumstances

I have suggested that in the case of BILL AND THE CLOCK, although there is an important sense in which Bill's control over the events in question is only partial

---

[99] Cf. Postow (1977), pp. 51 f.; Conee (1983), pp. 422 f.

(since whether they occur is contingent on the occurrence of many events that are not, and never were, in his control), still there is an important sense in which each of these events is wholly in his control (since, given the background conditions, it is entirely up to him whether they occur). This is true even of *h*, the destruction of the clock on Jill's mantelpiece, of which Bill is wholly unaware. I know of no reason to think that one's degree of control can vary according to whether one's control is simple or intentional.

Nonetheless, awareness of one's circumstances can certainly increase the likelihood that one will exercise one's control in one way rather than another.[100] If Bill had known about the clock and wanted very much not to destroy it, he might have thought twice about taking his shot at Jill. So, too, regarding a case presented in §4.2.1: although whether to enter 3-1-1-4-8 on the keypad was equally up to Priscilla, whether she knew that that was the correct code or not, her knowing that it was would presumably have raised the probability considerably that she would exercise her control accordingly. So, too, with Veronica from §3.2.5: were she aware of the strong racist tendencies that prompt some of her behavior, she might well behave differently.

4.5.4 Reasons-responsiveness

Justin Coates and Philip Swenson contend that control varies in degree in a way that I have not yet acknowledged. They claim that the degree to which one is morally responsible for one's behavior is in part a function of the degree to which one controls one's behavior, and that the degree to which one controls one's behavior is a function of the degree to which the mechanism that issues in one's behavior is moderately responsive to reasons in the sense specified by Fischer and Ravizza.[101]

I agree that responsiveness to reasons can vary in degree (both in virtue of the degree to which there is receptivity to reasons and in virtue of the degree to which there is reactivity to reasons), and I don't wish to deny that the degree to which one is morally responsible, whether laudable or culpable, for one's behavior may turn in part on the degree to which one is responsive to (what one takes to be) moral reasons. But, for the reasons given in §4.2.2, I think it is a mistake to say that control is to be understood in terms of the kind of responsiveness to reasons specified by Fischer and Ravizza, and so I think it is a mistake to say that degrees of control are to be understood in terms of degrees of such responsiveness. However, as I also noted in §4.2.2, so saying is compatible with saying that control requires another kind of responsiveness to (perhaps merely apparent) reasons, a kind that a psychopath may be capable

---

[100] Cf. O'Connor (2009).   [101] Coates and Swenson (2013). Cf. also Levy (2017a).

of exhibiting, in which case control would presumably vary in degree in a manner that corresponds to variations in such responsiveness.

4.5.5 Difficulty

Return to Susan and Tom from §2.5.5. When in the throes of an epileptic seizure, it is literally impossible for Susan to control her movements. When being tortured by his captors, it is not literally impossible, but it is indeed very difficult, for Tom to resist the impulse to divulge the information they seek. Whereas Susan lacks basic control, and so also lacks enhanced control, over her behavior, Tom "merely" lacks enhanced control over his.

Impossibility doesn't come in degrees, but difficulty does, and so the degree to which one has enhanced control over one's behavior can vary. The greater the effort needed to resist his captors' demands, the lower the degree to which Tom has enhanced control over whether he divulges the information. Another way in which degree of difficulty can vary has to do, not with the effort that one must make to behave in a certain way, but with the sacrifice that behaving in that way would entail. As Dana Nelkin observes, little effort may be needed to throw oneself on a grenade to save one's fellow soldiers, but the cost of doing so is very high.[102]

It is sometimes difficult to tell whether behaving in some way is "merely" difficult for someone or literally impossible for that person. Throwing oneself on a grenade might require a great deal of effort after all—mentally, if not physically—and one might find that one "just can't" do it. Or consider again Martin Luther and Ruth, mentioned in §4.1.8. Did they "merely" have a low degree of enhanced control over their behavior, or was it, as they seem to suggest, strictly impossible for them to behave otherwise?

Given that difficulty comes in degrees, it is tempting to think that degree of blameworthiness varies with degree of enhanced control: the greater the degree of such control, the greater the degree to which one is to blame for one's behavior (given that one is to blame for it). Consider Betty, the bank teller from §4.1.5. As I indicated earlier, we would surely be inclined to blame her for handing over the money to Rob far more in the case in which she is in cahoots with him than in the case in which he is genuinely threatening to shoot her. Nonetheless, I suspect that it is a mistake to hold that degree of blameworthiness is directly correlated with degree of enhanced control. First, there appear to be exceptional cases in which the correlation doesn't hold. Betty's case could be such a case, even if Bob's threat is genuine; for, although it would be very difficult for her to defy Bob and resist

---

[102] Nelkin (2016b), p. 357.

doing what he demands, she might yield to the threat gladly rather than out of fear.[103] Second, as long as it is within one's basic control to do that which it is difficult to do, the question arises whether one knows or believes it to be morally wrong not to do it. If one does not, then one will (or may) have an excuse for not doing it, but the excuse will be grounded in what one knows or believes, and not simply in the fact that one has a low degree of enhanced control over what one does. If, however, one does know or believe it to be morally wrong not to do that which is difficult, then it's not clear whether or why any excuse would be forthcoming, despite the difficulty in question.[104]

4.5.6 Freedom

Philosophers often draw a tight connection between control and freedom. I noted in §4.1.9, however, that, in presupposing that we often control how we behave, I am not presupposing that we are ever capable of free will and action, in whatever sense or senses of these terms might be at issue in the debate about free will. Another way in which control and freedom can come apart is this. It seems reasonable to say that, the greater the number of options among which one is free to choose at any particular moment (however exactly "free" is to be understood), the greater one's degree of freedom is. Yet it certainly doesn't follow that one's degree of control is thereby augmented. On the contrary, at some point it may happen that, the greater the number of options available, the more difficult one finds it to choose among them, so that one's degree of enhanced control is diminished rather than augmented, and I suppose that it could happen that in some cases one is literally overwhelmed by the number of options available, so that one finds it not merely difficult but impossible to choose among them.

4.5.7 The relation between degree of blameworthiness and degree of control

A full account of the relation between blameworthiness and control would require a far more detailed account than I have attempted to provide of the relation between degree of blameworthiness and degree(s) of control. Fortunately, an assessment of the Argument from Ignorance doesn't require such an account. When degrees are introduced explicitly into the argument, all that Premise 4 comes to is this: one is to blame *to some degree* for something only if one was in

---

[103] Cf. Frankfurt (1969), pp. 832 f.; Nelkin (2016b), p. 365.
[104] Cf. Zimmerman (1988), pp. 104 ff.; Peels (2017), p. 137.

control *to some degree* of that thing. No further specification of the relation between degree of blameworthiness and degree(s) of control is required in order to reach the argument's conclusion.

4.6 Control over beliefs

4.6.1 Doxastic voluntarism

The reason for my extended inquiry in this chapter into the nature of control is, of course, that I have been working under the assumption that moral responsibility—more particularly, moral blameworthiness—requires control. In every formulation of the Argument from Ignorance given so far this assumption has been expressed as follows:

(4) one is to blame for something only if one was in control of that thing.

This premise is crucial to the argument. Although it has met with nigh-universal acceptance, it can be and, in recent years especially, has been disputed. This is a matter that I will investigate further in Chapter 9. Another crucial premise in the argument makes a substantive claim about what lies in our control. In its most recent formulation, the premise says this:

(6) one is never directly in control of whether one fails to believe something.

This premise can be and has been disputed, too. This is a matter that I will take up now.

The kind of control at issue in Premise 6 is *volitional* control. Those who claim that we sometimes have such control over our beliefs are often called doxastic voluntarists, whereas those who deny this claim are often called doxastic involuntarists. But we must be wary of such labels since, as I have noted in previous sections, volitional control has a number of different dimensions, and it is perfectly possible to be a doxastic voluntarist with respect to one dimension while being a doxastic involuntarist with respect to another. One dimension that is of particular importance in this context is that which consists in the distinction between direct and indirect control. Another important dimension is that which consists in the distinction between simple and intentional control.

The kind of control at issue in Premise 6 is also *bilateral* control. Thus, in the symbolism introduced in §3.2.5, to say (or deny) that one is in control of one's believing some proposition, p, is to say (or deny) that one can both see to it that Bp and see to it that $\sim Bp$, that is, that it is up to one whether it is the case that Bp or the case that $\sim Bp$. In keeping with what was said in §3.2.6, if one can see to it that $\sim Bp$, one might do so either by seeing to it that one disbelieves *p* or by seeing to it that one is uncommitted regarding *p*.

As I noted in §3.2.4, there is a distinction between outright belief and credence. In the most recent formulation of Premise 6, what is at issue is control over whether one believes something outright. This is what I will continue to focus on, but I should note explicitly here that I can see no good reason to think that, if a certain form of doxastic (in)voluntarism is true, it should not be extended so that it covers not only outright beliefs but also credences.[105]

4.6.2 Indirect control over beliefs

Almost everyone who considers the matter is a doxastic voluntarist concerning the possibility of having *indirect* control over one's beliefs (and other doxastic attitudes—note that in this context I am using the term "belief" to refer to an *attitude* and not to the proposition toward which an attitude is directed). It's easy to see why, since there are many ways in which such control might be exercised.

Perhaps the most obvious and most often cited way of indirectly controlling one's beliefs (and other doxastic attitudes) is to gather evidence.[106] Suppose that Betty asks me when the Boston Tea Party took place, and I respond, "I don't know, but I know how to find out! I'll text Harry."

Harry, who is a history buff, texts me back almost immediately.

"Harry says that the Boston Tea Party took place on December 16, 1773," I tell Betty.

"Do you believe him?" she asks.

"Absolutely," I say. "He's an expert on that kind of thing."

By means of texting Harry, I have moved from being uncommitted regarding the proposition that the Boston Tea Party took place on December 16, 1773 to believing that proposition. My believing it was in my control, indirectly, since the means by which I came to do so was in my control.

Things might have turned out differently, of course. Suppose that, as soon as I had texted Harry, I suddenly remembered that Carol had told me just the day before that his reputation as a historian was overblown and that the information he dispensed wasn't really all that reliable. In that case, I might well have remained uncommitted regarding the proposition in question, even after having received Harry's reply. Or suppose that I had suddenly recalled Denise's telling me that Harry was an inveterate liar. In that case, I might well have come to disbelieve the

---

[105] Roeber (2020), pp. 418 f., presents an argument for the compatibility of a certain form of credal involuntarism with a corresponding form of doxastic voluntarism. For reasons given below, I reject such doxastic voluntarism.

[106] Cf., among many others, Alston (1988), p. 270; Audi (2008), p. 414; Peels (2017), p. 117.

proposition. No matter. Whatever the outcome of my inquiry, I would have exercised indirect control over my doxastic attitude by way of exercising control over the inquiry itself.[107]

As I just noted, the kind of control in question is bilateral. If gathering some evidence is in one's control, then one can exercise that control by refraining from gathering it.[108] Suppose that I disliked Betty and had responded rudely to her question, "I don't know, and I don't care!" Then I would have remained uncommitted regarding the proposition in question, but nonetheless I would once again have exercised indirect control over my current doxastic attitude.

There are many similar ways in which one can exercise indirect control over one's doxastic attitudes. One can engage in deliberation,[109] or introspection,[110] or reflection,[111] or one can search one's memory,[112] or, even more indirectly, one can train oneself to become more careful and thorough when undertaking these kinds of activities.[113] (Or, of course, one can refrain from doing any of these things.) These familiar activities all involve controlling one's doxastic attitudes by mental means, but it's important to note that such control needn't involve such means. As Richard Feldman notes, if I have control over whether the lights in my office are on, then typically I will also have control over whether I believe that they are on.[114]

It will presumably not have escaped your attention that all the examples given so far of indirect control over one's doxastic attitudes are, more particularly, examples of *simple* indirect control over them. None of the attitudes in the examples were *intentionally* brought about (although of course the *means* by which they were brought about were intentionally undertaken). Some philosophers, such as William Alston and Rik Peels,[115] prefer to describe the relation that one bears to one's attitudes in such cases in terms of "influence" rather than "control," but, for reasons given in §4.2.1, I will stick with the latter term. In any case, it's important to note that indirect control over one's doxastic attitudes, though typically merely simple, need not be merely simple. Bernard Williams considers the possibility of intentionally getting oneself to believe some proposition (some *particular* proposition, such as, for example, the proposition that the Boston Tea Party took place on January 1, 2000) by means of submitting to hypnosis or ingesting some drug;[116] Alston mentions the possibility of somehow convincing oneself that one's love for someone else is requited;[117] and several

---

[107] This claim might be disputed in that version of the case in which my doxastic attitude remains unaltered even after I have heard back from Harry, but I think that, as long as I could have done something as a result of which my doxastic attitude would have changed, we should accept it.
[108] Cf. Paul (2015), p. 146; Peels (2017), pp. 118 ff.   [109] Cf. Paul (2016), p. 663.
[110] Cf. Peels (2017), p. 92.   [111] Cf. Rettler (2018), pp. 2218 ff.
[112] Cf. Alston (1988), p. 272.   [113] Cf. Peels (2017), pp. 92 f.
[114] Feldman (2000), p. 671. Cf. Peels (2017), p. 92.
[115] See Alston (1988), pp. 277 ff., and Peels (2017), pp. 89 ff.   [116] B. Williams (1973), p. 149.
[117] Alston (1988), p. 273.

authors have discussed the possibility of somehow deliberately inducing a belief that one doesn't currently have in order to reap a big reward.[118] Presumably, there is nothing conceptually incoherent about such examples (although, since any belief is embedded in a web of beliefs, realizing the possibility in question may be far more complicated than initially meets the eye[119]). Nonetheless, two points stand out. First, it seems that success in inducing the beliefs in these examples is likely to be elusive, since the means envisaged seem quite unreliable.[120] Second, the reasons for undertaking the inducement appear to be wholly divorced from any concern with believing what is true. But we shouldn't exaggerate the significance of these observations, accurate though they may be; for success in deliberately inducing some belief need not be unlikely and one's purpose in inducing it need not be divorced from any concern with believing what is true. Suppose that my goal is to believe only propositions that are true, that the lights in my office are off and I know this, but also that an eccentric billionaire has just offered me a rich reward for believing that the lights in my office are on. It's not hard to guess how I will respond to the offer.

4.6.3 Direct control over beliefs

None of what has just been noted contradicts the claim made in Premise 6 of the Argument from Ignorance. Again, what that premise asserts is that we are never *directly* in control of whether we believe something. On the account of control that I have proposed, this premise is clearly true. For confirmation, consider two cases already discussed. The first is that of BILL AND THE CLOCK, represented in Figure 4.1. As I have said repeatedly, in this figure it is A (or a), and *only* this event, over which Bill exercised direct control. His control over $b–h$ was indirect, while his control over $B–H$ was hybrid. The second case is that of BILL'S ACTIVE

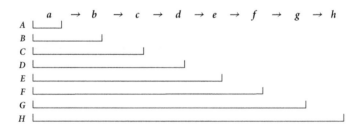

Figure 4.1 BILL AND THE CLOCK

---

[118] The source of this idea probably lies in Kavka (1983), where the attitude that one seeks to induce is an intention rather than a belief.
[119] Cf. B. Williams (1973), p. 151.   [120] Cf. Alston (1988), p. 276.

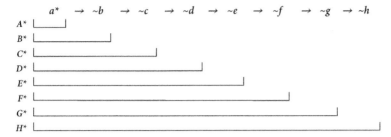

Figure 4.2 BILL'S ACTIVE OMISSION

OMISSION, represented in Figure 4.2. Had Bill behaved in the way represented in this figure, it is A^* (or a^*), and *only* this event, over which he would have exercised direct control. His control over $\sim b$ – $\sim h$ would have been indirect, while his control over B^* – H^* would have been hybrid. On the present approach, then (and putting aside for the moment the possibility of direct control over purely passive omissions), the locus of direct control—direct *volitional* control—is, and can only be, a *volition*. This is hardly surprising. (I might add that, on those occasions, if any, on which having volitional control over something is tantamount to enjoying the kind of freedom at issue in the debate over free will, the implication is that freedom of action is rooted in freedom of will. This is hardly surprising, either.)

What is the relevance of these observations to the question of whether we are ever directly in control of whether we believe something? Simply this. Volitions are not doxastic attitudes. Hence, if we only ever have direct control over our volitions, then we never have direct control over our doxastic attitudes. Any control that we may have over such attitudes, then, will be like the control that Bill had over the other events depicted in the figures: *not direct*.[121]

This conclusion may seem premature, since I have not yet addressed the relation between beliefs and purely passive omissions. Recall the case of BILL'S PASSIVE OMISSION, represented in Figure 4.4. In this version, there was no activity on Bill's part at all. In my earlier discussion, I left unresolved the question of whether Bill was in control of the events depicted. Suppose for the moment that he *was* in control of them. Would this verdict open up the possibility of one's having direct control over one's beliefs?

---

[121] Blake Roeber has recently proposed the following pair of definitions in Roeber (2019), p. 839:

(D₁) S Φ-d at will $=_{df}$ S decided to Φ and then carried out her intention to Φ by Φ-ing, in such a way that her intention to Φ was directly causally responsible for her Φ-ing;

(D₂) S had direct voluntary control over her Φ-ing $=_{df}$ S Φ-d at will and her will was free, in the sense that she had control over whether she decided to Φ in the first place.

He seems unconcerned with the fact that the claim that S had control over whether she *decided* to Φ in the first place would appear to imply that her control over her Φ-ing itself was *not* direct.

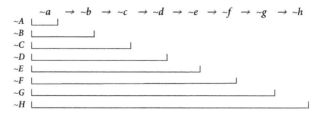

Figure 4.4 Bill's passive omission

On the account of control that I have proposed, the answer to this question is once again "No." On this account, if Bill had control over the events depicted, the only event over which he had direct control was ~a, that is, the event of his not deciding to kill Jill. This, too, is not surprising. Again, the kind of control at issue is *volitional, bilateral* control. When it comes to *direct* control, then, the two aspects of such control concern *a* and ~*a*. No other events qualify. Bill's control over whether *b* or ~*b* occurred, whether *c* or ~*c* occurred, and so on, was and could only be indirect; likewise, his control over whether *B* or ~*B* occurred, whether *C* or ~*C* occurred, and so on, was and could only be hybrid. This observation generalizes to all cases in which an agent exercises control. Given that, just as a volition (such as *a* or *a**) is not a doxastic attitude, so too a non-volition (such as ~*a*) is not a doxastic attitude, Premise 6 is once again confirmed: we are never *directly* in control of whether we believe something.

4.6.4 Believing at will

This confirmation of Premise 6 might strike you as altogether too quick. After all, doxastic voluntarism is a hotly debated issue on which there is a large literature. If my account of control closes the door on our having direct control over our beliefs in such peremptory fashion, perhaps that should be taken to show, not that Premise 6 is true, but rather that my account is to be rejected.

A great deal of the literature on doxastic voluntarism concerns the question of whether it is possible to believe something "*at will*." This of course is the very phrase that I used at the outset of this chapter when I embarked on my investigation of volitional control. One perhaps surprising implication of my account of such control is that *nothing* that one does at will can *ever* be in one's direct control. That's because, whatever counts as something that one does at will, one thing that one does *not* do at will is to *will* at will.[122] For example, even

---

[122] Typically, at least—but even the exceptions, if there are any, don't falsify the claim that one is never in direct control of what one does at will. As I noted in n. 25 above, it is possible to decide to decide, and if this were to happen, and if the decisions in question were both executive decisions, then we would have an instance of willing at will. As a possible example, suppose that, in an effort to impress

though it's correct to say that, in the case of BILL AND THE CLOCK, Bill did B (or brought about b) at will, it wouldn't be correct to say the same of A (or a). Again, though, this result might simply be taken as a reason to reject my account of control. I suspect that many people will want to say that, if ever anything is in our direct control, at least some of what we do or bring about at will is paradigmatic of the exercise of such control. Might there be some alternative, preferable account of direct control that incorporates this claim? If there is, and if this account accommodates the possibility of believing at will, then Premise 6 will be disconfirmed rather than confirmed.

Before looking into this matter, I want to acknowledge the fact that what we say in our everyday lives might well seem to presuppose that we can, and indeed sometimes do, believe some things at will. Consider the dramatic Senate confirmation hearing on Brett Kavanaugh's nomination to the U.S. Supreme Court. After Christine Blasey Ford presented her testimony, in which she accused Kavanaugh of a decades-old sexual assault, some people reacted to it by saying that they chose to believe what she said, while others said that they refused to do so. Later that same day, Kavanaugh gave his own testimony in which he strenuously denied Ford's charges, and again some people said that they chose to believe him, while others said that they refused to do so. Of course, what mattered for all practical purposes was how the Senate would vote, something that was not immediately obvious. As one columnist wrote, shortly after the hearing was over:

> But whether those who still control his fate will choose to believe Ford's compelling testimony or Kavanaugh's forceful denials remains to be seen.[123]

Doesn't the fact that such claims about what one may choose to believe are commonplace provide good reason for thinking that we do indeed sometimes have direct control over our beliefs? I suspect not.

In a recent, sophisticated study, John Turri, David Rose, and Wesley Buckwalter cite the results of several closely related experiments in which subjects were first presented with a short story and then asked to assess the protagonist's

---

Irma, Dennis promised her yesterday that he would take a high dive today. Now he's standing at the end of the diving board, dithering. The water is so far below him! He can see that Irma's getting impatient with him, and so he says to himself, "Look, stop being such a wimp! You know you're going to do it, so you might as well do it now," at which point he makes the decision to dive and dives. It seems to me that this could well be a case in which Dennis made a decision to decide to dive. Let us suppose that that is so, and let us call the decision to decide d_1 and the decision to dive d_2. On the account of control that I have proposed, and given that Dennis was in control of how he behaved, his control over d_1 was direct, but his control over d_2 by way of d_1 was not. (So saying leaves open the possibility that Dennis exercised direct control over d_2 *independently* of his control over d_1.) Thus, even though in this case we have an (apparent) instance of willing at will, still what is done at will is not within the agent's direct control.

[123] Russell Berman in *The Atlantic*: https://www.theatlantic.com/politics/archive/2018/09/christine-blasey-ford-brett-kavanaugh-testify-senate/571489/.

state of mind.[124] On the basis of a detailed analysis of these results, they claim that folk psychology accommodates the possibility of voluntary belief, even when the belief is summoned immediately and even when it is at variance with the available evidence. They conclude not only that believing at will is conceptually possible but also that there is some, perhaps good reason to think that it actually occurs. They say:

> Our results demonstrate that folk psychology countenances voluntary belief... It follows that conceptual arguments for [doxastic] involuntarism fail. Our results also provide evidence that psychological arguments for involuntarism probably fail too. Given minimal charitable assumptions about the competence manifested in ordinary folk-psychological judgments, our results make it likely that at least some belief (and disbelief) is voluntary. Overall, then, our results suggest that voluntary belief is not only possible but actual.[125]

I submit that this conclusion is premature.

There is no doubt that "the folk" commonly make claims that appear to presuppose that belief is sometimes within one's volitional control. The claims made in the wake of the Kavanaugh hearing confirm that fact. But I think we should be very cautious about what inferences we draw from it. After all, the folk (including you and me, of course) are frequently quite careless about how they express themselves, and they are also frequently confused. In saying this, I am not violating any principle of charity; nor am I committing the sin of armchair arrogance. I am simply being realistic. I can see no reason to take at face value claims about what people choose to believe or refuse to believe any more than claims about what it is hard to believe. Imagine the following dialogue:

> Martha: "Did you know that there are 100 billion neurons in the human brain?"
>
> George: "I find that hard to believe."
>
> Martha: "You should try a little harder, then."

I think it's plain that Martha's remark is at best a wry one. If she intends it to be taken literally, she's making a mistake.

I am not saying that Turri et al. are advocating simply taking the folk at their word. On the contrary, their discussion is appropriately circumspect. Nor am I saying that we should ignore the word(s) of the folk. That would indeed be arrogant. But in the end there is no substitute for a careful philosophical inquiry into how a commonplace claim is to be interpreted and whether, on some interpretation, it is a claim that should be accepted. After all, it is commonly

---

[124] Turri et al. (2018).   [125] Turri et al. (2018), p. 2529.

held that people are frequently to blame for their ignorant wrongdoing, but this entire book is devoted to a critical examination of that claim.

Recall the distinctions, noted in §3.2.1, between belief and acceptance and between disbelief and rejection. I noted that acceptance and rejection are attitudes that are typically adopted intentionally, and perhaps we may now add that they are typically adopted at will. But of course this gives us no reason to say that belief and disbelief, or the suspension of either one, is something that can be accomplished at will. Turri et al. are aware that the folk might be accused of confusing belief with acceptance (and disbelief with rejection) when making their claims about voluntary belief, and so one of their experiments was designed to address this issue. And this is what they say about it:

> The principal finding emerging from this experiment is that people continued to attribute voluntary belief when given the option of attributing "acceptance"... instead.[126]

Should we be impressed by this finding? I don't see why. If philosophers have routinely confused belief with acceptance,[127] is it any surprise that the folk would do so as well?

Another concern that might be raised about the findings of Turri et al. is that the folk might overlook the difference between the voluntary undertaking of a course of action from which a belief emerges and the direct voluntary acquisition of a belief. Turri et al. are aware of this concern, too, and another of their experiments was designed to address it. They found that

> ...people readily agreed that someone who professed to choose to believe forms the belief "immediately."[128]

Again, should we be impressed by this finding? Again, I don't see why. As I noted in §4.1.3, one can of course use the term "immediate" as a synonym of "direct," but that in fact is *not* how Turri et al. are using it. In their experiment, they explicitly state that by "immediate" they mean "without delay," and, as I noted earlier, when "immediate" is so understood, the distinction between direct and indirect control is itself distinct from the distinction between immediate and remote control. Once again, if philosophers have routinely confused the two

---

[126] Turri et al. (2018), p. 2528.
[127] As I believe but will not attempt to demonstrate here. Still, consider this. Descartes is often regarded as the high priest of doxastic voluntarism. Yet I take his method of doubt to be a strategy of withholding acceptance, not belief (although persistent pursuit of this strategy might indeed have the consequence that certain beliefs are undermined). Cf. Cohen (1989), p. 370.
[128] Turri et al. (2018), p. 2525.

distinctions,[129] is it any surprise that the folk would do so as well? Consider the train of events depicted in Figure 4.1. On my account, it is only over *a* that Bill exercised direct control; his control over the remaining events, *b–h*, was indirect, despite the fact that these events occurred (almost) immediately after *a*. (Bullets travel fast.) Even if my account of direct control is to be rejected in favor of some other account, one that implies that some of *b–h* were in Bill's direct control, surely no acceptable account will judge *all* of *b–h* to have been in Bill's direct control. The lesson to draw is simply this. No matter how *quickly* one forms a belief, there is no guarantee that one has formed it *directly*.

So let us turn from folk psychology to philosophical inquiry and address the question whether my account of control should be replaced by another account, one that declares that at least some of what we do or bring about at will is within our direct control and, perhaps, thereby accommodates the possibility of our being in direct control of some of our beliefs.

To answer this question, we must settle on an understanding of what it is to do or bring about something at will. In §4.1.1 I used the term "at will" expansively. I talked not only of one's moving a finger at will but also of a pilot's flying an airplane at will. The underlying idea, of course, was that these are typically things that are done *voluntarily*, whereas other things that one does (such as sweating or shivering) are not done voluntarily. I suspect that many would balk at such an expansive use of "at will." They would say that, whereas whatever is done at will is done voluntarily, the reverse doesn't hold. How might this asymmetry be captured?

One way to capture it would be to invoke the distinction between *basic* and *non-basic* action. A non-basic act is one that one performs *by* performing another act; a basic act is an act that is not non-basic. In the case depicted in Figure 4.1, for example, all of acts *C–H* were non-basic, since each of them was such that Bill performed it by performing some other act. What about *B* itself, namely, his act of moving his finger? Was it basic or non-basic? Philosophers differ on this question. The answer depends on whether Bill's decision, *A* (or *a*), was itself an act by means of which he performed *B*. If it was, then *B*, too, was non-basic. Many philosophers would however claim that *B* was a basic act, and perhaps they would do so precisely because they subscribe to the view that a basic act must be something that one performs at will and, as I have already conceded, Bill did not do *A* at will. Let's accept this view of basic action. The question then arises: Which of *B–H* did Bill do at will? Presumably *H* can be eliminated, on the grounds that whatever one does at will one does intentionally, and Bill did not intentionally destroy the clock. Should any of the remaining acts be eliminated? One answer—an answer that I think is implicitly adopted in many discussions of the issue and which

---

[129] As I believe but again will not attempt to demonstrate, although I should note that this confusion seems to arise on pp. 2524 f. of Turri et al. (2018).

I will explicitly adopt from this point on—is that it is only *B* that Bill performed at will. That is, as far as acts are concerned, all and only *basic* acts are *performed* at will.

Something similar may be said about omissions, although this is an issue that has received far less attention. We may say, and from this point on I will say, that, as far as omissions are concerned, only *basic* omissions are *committed* at will. Notice that I haven't said that *all* basic omissions are committed at will. Although we may indeed say that all basic *acts* of omission are committed at will, the fact is of course that some omissions are purely passive, and no such omission, not even a basic one, will be one that is committed at will. Thus, in the case depicted in Figure 4.2, we may say that B^* and only B^* is committed at will, whereas, in Figure 4.4, no omission, not even ~*B*, is committed at will.

Finally, as a corollary, I will say that all and only the *results* of those basic acts and basic omissions that are committed at will are themselves *brought about* at will. Thus in Figure 4.1 it is *b* and only *b* that is brought about at will, while in Figure 4.2 it is ~*b* and only ~*b* that is brought about at will.

Armed with this account of how "at will" is to be understood, we could then couple it with a complementary account of the distinction between direct and indirect control, one that differs from the account that I have proposed. We could say—as, I suspect, many would want to say—that, if one is in control of what one does, it is over one's *basic* acts and omissions (and, perhaps, their results), and *only* over these, that one exercises *direct* control. The question then arises: On this alternative account of control, would there be reason to say that one can on occasion exercise direct control over one's beliefs?

In a well-known article in which he accepts something close to this alternative account of control, William Alston answers this question with an emphatic "No."[130] He denies what he calls the "basic control thesis," according to which one can believe something at will. His denial is grounded not so much on an argument as on an appeal to introspection. He says:

> Can you, at this moment, start to believe that the U. S. is still a colony of Great Britain, just by deciding to do so[?] If you find it too incredible that you should be sufficiently motivated to try to believe this, suppose that someone offers you $500,000,000 to believe it, and you are much more interested in the money than in believing the truth. Could you do what it takes to get that reward? Remember

---

[130] Alston calls the kind of control with which he is concerned "voluntary" rather than, as I have done, "volitional." Although, in my attempt to settle on an understanding of "at will," I have just used the term "voluntary," I nonetheless prefer the term "volitional" to describe the kind of control at issue. I do so because "voluntary" is often used more restrictively than either Alston or I intend it to be understood in the present context. Recall the distinction between what in §4.1.5 I called basic and enhanced control. I noted that there is a sense in which, when Betty handed over the money at gunpoint to Rob, she didn't do so voluntarily. Nonetheless, she had volitional control over her behavior.

that we are speaking about believing at will... Can you switch propositional attitudes toward that proposition just by deciding to do so? It seems clear to me that I have no such power. Volitions, decisions, or choosings don't hook up with anything in the way of propositional attitude inauguration, just as they don't hook up with the secretion of gastric juices or cell metabolism... I very much doubt that any human beings are endowed with the power of taking on propositional attitudes at will.[131]

Alston goes on to note that his remarks pertain not only to beliefs about propositions that are obviously false but to all beliefs. One may *willingly* believe some obviously true proposition (such as the proposition that the study lights are on), but that of course doesn't mean that one believes it *at will*.[132] One's attitude toward it is, he says, no more within one's voluntary control than one's attitude toward the proposition that the U.S. is still a colony of Great Britain.

Alston's thesis seems clearly to be too sweeping. His claim is that we can never take on any propositional attitude at will, but surely we can. I have asked you on numerous occasions to do just that. "Suppose," I have said, "that [blah, blah, blah]." But supposition is one thing, belief another. Although I have often asked you to suppose something, I have never asked you to believe anything—at least, not at will. Nor will I do so. Along with Alston, it seems plain to me that I have no power to believe anything at will, and I strongly suspect that the same is true of you.

Alston's view about the non-voluntary nature of belief has been challenged. Matthias Steup, a prominent doxastic voluntarist, has recently accused Alston of overgeneralization. Even if we cannot believe at will that the U.S. is still a colony of Great Britain, the possibility remains, he says, that we can believe at will propositions that we don't regard as obviously false or obviously true. Steup claims that our inability to believe certain things at will is akin to our inability to engage in certain types of bodily behavior at will. For example, a normal person under normal circumstances can neither stick a knife in his hand nor walk in front of an oncoming truck. This fact doesn't entail that one is never in direct control of one's bodily behavior. Likewise, the fact that a normal person under normal circumstances cannot believe at will that the U.S. is still a colony of Great Britain doesn't entail that one is never in direct control of one's beliefs.[133] Steup goes on to argue that, in cases in which it is not obvious what to believe, what we can do, and typically do do, is to ponder the evidence and then *make up our minds* what to believe.[134]

Steup's position on what we can believe is strikingly reminiscent of van Inwagen's position, discussed in §4.1.8, on what we can do. Van Inwagen holds

---

[131] Alston (1988), p. 263.   [132] Cf. Pojman (1986), p. 162.   [133] Steup (2017), p. 2678.
[134] Steup (2017), pp. 2680 ff.

that our behavior is in our control only in cases in which the (practical) reasons that pertain to our situation don't make it obvious what to do. Steup holds that our beliefs are in our control, but only in cases in which the (epistemic) reasons that pertain to our situation don't make it obvious what to believe. The analogy is intriguing, but I find it unconvincing (and not because I have decided to do so). Even if it's true that a normal person under normal circumstances cannot walk in front of an oncoming truck (a claim that, like Martin Luther's, I suspect is hyperbolic), I doubt that our inability to believe obvious falsehoods is to be explained in similar terms. It may typically be the case that, when we ponder what to do, our deliberation is a voluntary activity within our control, but of course it doesn't follow that the conclusion of that deliberation—which, let us agree, consists in a decision to do one thing rather than another—is within our direct control. Nor does it follow that it isn't. Whether the decision is within our direct control is independent of whether the deliberation that issued in it was within our control, and so it is a question that must be decided separately. Likewise, it may typically be the case that, when we ponder what to believe, our deliberation is a voluntary activity within our control, but of course it doesn't follow that the conclusion of that deliberation—which, let us agree, consists in a doxastic attitude of some sort—is within our direct control. Nor does it follow that it isn't. Again, whether the doxastic attitude is within our direct control is independent of whether the deliberation that issued in it was within our control, and so it is a question that must be decided separately. It may be that, in the absence of any reason to decide these questions differently, the default position should be that they should be decided in the same way, but I submit that we do have such a reason, one to which Alston has drawn our attention: the evidence provided by introspection.[135]

I acknowledge that this reason may not seem particularly compelling, since what introspection on this issue reveals to me (and Alston) may not be what introspection reveals to you (or Steup). But I think we can do better. As Bernard Williams has observed, and as several philosophers have agreed, there seems to be something *conceptually incoherent* about believing at will. I think the case against the form of doxastic voluntarism advocated by Steup can be strengthened by pursuing this point.

4.6.5 The Argument against Believing at Will

At one point in his influential discussion of whether it is possible to decide to believe something, Williams compares believing at will with blushing at will. He says that he doesn't know whether anyone can blush at will but that, if no one can

---

[135] Cf. Pojman (1986), pp. 62 ff.; Peels (2017), pp. 159 ff.

in fact do so, that is simply a contingent fact. Believing at will is, he claims, quite different. He says:

> [I]t is not a contingent fact that I cannot bring it about, just like that, that I believe something, as it is a contingent fact that I cannot bring it about, just like that, that I'm blushing. Why is this? One reason is connected with the characteristic of beliefs that they aim at truth. If I could acquire a belief at will, I could acquire it whether it was true or not; moreover I would know that I could acquire it whether it was true or not. If in full consciousness I could will to acquire a 'belief' irrespective of its truth, it is unclear that before the event I could seriously think of it as a belief, i.e. as something purporting to represent reality. At the very least, there must be a restriction on what is the case after the event; since I could not then, in full consciousness, regard this as a belief of mine, i.e. something I take to be true, and also know that I acquired it at will. With regard to no belief could I know—or, if all this is to be done in full consciousness, even suspect— that I had acquired it at will.[136]

He goes on to conclude that "there is something necessarily bizarre about the idea of believing at will, just like that."[137] This passage has provoked much discussion.[138] I find it highly suggestive, but it is not entirely clear to me just what Williams's thesis is or what his argument for it is.

On one common interpretation, Williams's thesis is that it is *conceptually impossible* to believe something at will, where to believe something at will ("just like that") would be to perform a basic act analogous to Bill's moving his finger in the case depicted in Figure 4.1. Though agreeing that it is indeed conceptually impossible to believe something at will, Pamela Hieronymi has recently objected to Williams's discussion on the grounds that it is a mistake to think of believing at will as possibly being an act at all, whether basic or not.[139] To appreciate her point, consider Bill's act of moving his finger (i.e., act *B* in Figure 4.1). This consists in his bringing about his finger's moving (i.e., in his bringing about that event, *b*, that I have called the result of *B*). In this case, English tends to conceal the distinction between act and result, since the same verb ("move") is used to give expression to both. (It's true that in one case the verb is transitive, whereas in the other it's intransitive, but this distinction hardly leaps to the eye.) English is not always so unrevealing, however. For example, when one raises one's arm, one brings about one's arm's rising, and here the distinction is plain to see; one verb gives expression to the act, while another verb gives expression to its result. I take Hieronymi's

---

[136] B. Williams (1973), p. 148.   [137] B. Williams (1973), p. 149.
[138] Some especially useful discussions may be found in Winters (1979), Bennett (1990), Hieronymi (2009), and Benbaji (2016).
[139] Hieronymi (2009), p. 156.

point to be that "believe" can never be properly used to give expression to an act; at best it can be used to give expression to the result of an act, namely, the act of making oneself believe (or bringing it about that one believes) something. Since to do something at will is to act in some way, no one can possibly believe anything at will; at best one could make oneself believe something at will.

I think that Hieronymi is absolutely right about this, but her observation doesn't dispose of the underlying worry, which can now simply be reformulated as follows: Is it conceptually possible to make oneself believe something at will? Hieronymi appears to think that the answer to this question is also "No," but here I find what she says less persuasive. At one point she says this:

> If I have shown that believing is not an action, then I have also shown that it is not, properly speaking, the object of an intention.[140]

This strikes me as mistaken. If I raise my arm at will (and hence intentionally), then part of what I intend is that my arm rise—and I take myself to be speaking properly in saying this. Thus, if I were to make myself believe some particular proposition at will, then part of what I would intend is that I believe it.

Hieronymi gives another reason for thinking that it is conceptually impossible to (make oneself) believe something at will. She says:

> [I]f you believe p, you are committed to a positive answer to the question of whether p..., [whereas] if you x intentionally, or intend to x, then you are committed to a positive answer to the question of whether to x.[141]

These are of course different questions, and she goes on to say:

> You cannot become committed to an answer to a question by finding convincing reasons that you, yourself, do not take to settle *that* question... [Hence] you will not, by finding convincing reasons that you take only to show that [making yourself believe that p] is worth doing, therein become committed to the truth of p. Yet this is what you would have to do, to believe at will.[142]

By way of example, consider the question of whether to make yourself believe that the U.S. is still a colony of Great Britain. Taking yourself to have reasons (even as many as 500,000,000 reasons) in favor of a positive answer to this question does not help you in any way to settle the question of whether the U.S. is indeed still a colony of Great Britain. Yet, she claims, this is precisely what would have to be the case for you to believe this proposition at will.

---

[140] Hieronymi (2009), p. 166.   [141] Hieronymi (2009), p. 158.
[142] Hieronymi (2009), p. 165.

Hieronymi's argument is reminiscent of Williams's and, again, I find it highly suggestive; but, as before, it is not entirely clear to me just what the argument is. So instead of trying to figure out exactly what their argument (or arguments) is (or are), let me simply present an argument that seems to me to be suggested by what they say.

I say "simply," but, although it seems to me obvious that there is something conceptually fishy—or, as Jonathan Bennett puts it, "chokingly unswallowable"[143]—about believing a proposition at will (that is, more particularly, about making oneself believe a proposition at will), I have found it remarkably difficult to pin down precisely what makes it so. The best argument that I have managed to come up with is not very simple at all. Here is a first stab at it, where "p" ranges over all propositions:

The Argument against Believing at Will (Draft 1):

(1) Necessarily, if one believes p, then one regards p as given.

(2) Necessarily, if one intends to make oneself believe (i.e., bring it about that one believes) p, then one does not yet believe p.

Hence

(3) Necessarily, if one intends to make oneself believe p, then (a) one does not yet regard p as given but (b) one intends to bring it about that one regards p as given.

(4) Necessarily, if one intends to bring it about that one regards p as given, then one intends to bring it about that p is true as a means to regarding p as given.

(5) Necessarily, if one intends to make oneself believe p at will, then it is not the case that one intends to bring it about that p is true as a means to regarding p as given.

Hence

(6) Necessarily, it is not the case that one intends to make oneself believe p at will.

(7) Necessarily, one does something at will only if one intends to do it at will.

Hence

(8) Necessarily, it is not the case that one makes oneself believe p at will.

Let me first say something in support of the premises of this argument, after which I will entertain reasons for doubting them and the conclusions drawn from them.

---

[143] Bennett (1990), p. 90.

Premise 1 is intended to capture the idea that beliefs have, as it is now often put, a certain "direction of fit." When one believes something, one regards what one believes as a fact, as a given part of the world to which one's belief is a response, so that one's belief "fits" the world. The world thus has a kind of priority over one's attitude.[144] (In the passage cited above, Williams gives expression to this idea when he says that a belief is something that "purport[s] to represent reality." This way of expressing the idea seems to me not particularly felicitous, though, since it seems it could be used to characterize acceptance—regarding which see §3.2.1—as well as belief; yet acceptance need not have this direction of fit.) The direction of fit of belief, which is a cognitive attitude, is to be contrasted with the direction of fit of conative attitudes such as desire or intention. When one wants or intends for something to be the case, that thing is not regarded as a fact, as a *given* part of the world, but rather as something *to be made to be* a part of the world. The direction of fit is thus reversed. It's not that one regards one's attitude as fitting the world as it is; it's rather that one regards the world as being such that it should be altered to fit one's attitude. In this case, it is one's attitude that has a kind of priority over the world.

Premise 2 reflects this reverse direction of fit. If one already believed p, one's belief would be part of the world as it is, and there would thus be no call to change the world in this regard.

Given the competing priorities of world over attitude and attitude over world, there is obviously a tension that arises if one intends to have a belief, but it is a tension that can be accommodated if one works in stages in the manner depicted in Premise 4. The example given above of turning on the lights is a case in point. If I intend to make myself believe that the lights in my office are on, then I can accomplish this simply by turning them on. By this means, I will have brought it about that they are on and I can then respond to this fact by believing it—and will so respond, if I keep my eyes open. (What if the lights are in fact already on but, not being in my office, I merely suspect that they are rather than believe that they are? Can I intend to move myself from mere suspicion to outright belief by simply opening my door and taking a look? If so, then Premise 4 is false, since I won't have the intention to *bring it about* that the lights are on. I think it's pretty clear, however, that, precisely because I lack the belief in question, I don't *intend* to acquire it, but at most *hope* to do so, by means of opening the door and taking a look.)

The kind of means-end approach depicted in Premise 4 and illustrated in the example of the lights of course construes the act of bringing it about that one believes something as *non-basic*. But that's precisely not what's at issue in making

---

[144] Two especially useful discussions of direction of fit may be found in Humberstone (1992) and Velleman (1992a). It's worth noting that, despite the fact that "direction of fit" is a term of art, Humberstone and Velleman nonetheless differ regarding just how it is to be understood.

oneself believe something *at will*. Hence Premise 5. The only other premise in the argument is Premise 7, which I take to be uncontroversial.

As promising as this argument may be, however, it faces a number of difficulties. Let's begin at the beginning.

Consider, first, Premise 1. It seems plausible to say that no one can believe a proposition without regarding that proposition as true. That would seem to be a constitutive feature of belief. "Regard" is a term of art in this context, one that I borrow from David Velleman, who cautions:

> [T]o say that belief in *p* involves regarding *p* as true is not to say that it consists in a judgment whose object is the proposition "*p* is true." That way lies a vicious regress of propositional attitudes.[145]

To regard a proposition as true is to regard it as being such that it is the case rather than, as with conative attitudes, as being such that it should be the case.[146] But even if it is correct to say that believing a proposition essentially involves regarding it as *true*, it doesn't follow that believing a proposition essentially involves regarding it as *given*, in the sense at issue in Premise 1. For, even if it is true that beliefs have an attitude-to-world direction of fit and thus that an *enlightened* person who has an adequate appreciation of what his own propositional attitudes involve will recognize this fact, it is obvious that not everyone is always enlightened about such matters. For this reason, Premise 1 is perhaps too strong. *Must* believing some proposition involve regarding the world as having the kind of *priority* over one's attitude that is at issue here? I'm not sure how this question is to be answered.

Consider, now, Premise 2. It seems in general to be the case that one cannot intend to bring it about that some proposition is true if one already believes that that proposition is true. When this observation is applied to the particular case of intending to make oneself believe something, however, what follows is that, if one intends to make oneself believe *p*, then one does not yet *believe that* one believes *p*, and not that one does not yet believe *p* itself. To reach this further conclusion, something else is needed. Of course, the claim that one believes something only if one believes that one believes it would do the trick, but there is good reason to doubt this claim. Might there be some other way of bridging the gap in this case?

---

[145] Velleman (1992a), p. 8.

[146] I don't pretend that these brief remarks fully explain what regarding a proposition as true comes to. Velleman himself includes, among those propositional attitudes that involve regarding their objects as true, such attitudes as hypothesizing that *p*, fantasizing that *p*, and so on. Belief, he says, might be said to differ from these attitudes in that it involves regarding its object as *really* true. What he takes this to show is that "there is more than one way of regarding a proposition as true" (Velleman (1992a), p. 12). This is a subtlety that I will leave to one side.

I suspect not, precisely because, once again, one can be unenlightened about one's own attitudes.

Consider, next, the inference from Premises 1 and 2 to Conclusion 3. Here, too, a problem arises. Even if Premise 1 is true, someone who is unenlightened and doesn't recognize that it is true might fail to intend to bring it about that he regards some proposition as given, even if he does intend to make it the case that he believes that proposition.

The problems mentioned so far arise because it seems possible for an unenlightened person to have a propositional attitude while failing adequately to appreciate what having that attitude involves. (I suspect that it is at least in part because of this fact that, in the passage cited above, Williams qualifies his remarks by focusing on believing something "in full consciousness.") I regard these problems as minor, however, because I take it that fans of believing at will don't want to say that one can believe something at will only if one is unenlightened about some attitude that one has. All that is needed to fix the first three steps of the argument, then, is to restrict their application to persons who are appropriately enlightened.

A different kind of problem besets Premise 4, however; for this premise is plainly false, and it would remain so even if its application were restricted to those who are appropriately enlightened. Suppose that Oprah offers to give you $500,000,000 if you succeed in making yourself believe that the U.S. is still a colony of Great Britain and that she *doesn't* stipulate that you must accomplish this at will. You know that the proposition is false, but you also know (or think you know) that you can make yourself believe it simply by ingesting a certain drug. Under these circumstances you could surely intend to ingest the drug and thereby bring it about that you believe the proposition, even though you recognize full well that you cannot make the proposition true, and even though you have a perfectly adequate appreciation of what having the relevant intention and belief involves.

A key feature of the example just given is, of course, that you intend to *delude* yourself. You don't intend to make yourself *correctly* believe that the U.S. is still a colony of Great Britain. That would indeed require first making the proposition true, something that I have just said you recognize full well that you cannot do. (Not all cases are like this. As I mentioned earlier, you can indeed intend to make yourself correctly believe that the lights are on.) What we must do to get around the present problem, then, is to restrict the argument so that it concerns only correct beliefs.

Consider, then, this revised argument, where "enlightened" is to be understood in the manner indicated above:

The Argument against Believing at Will (Draft 2):
(1) Necessarily, if one **is enlightened and** believes p, then one regards p as given.

(2) Necessarily, if one **is enlightened and** intends to make oneself believe (i.e., bring it about that one believes) *p*, then one does not yet believe *p*.

Hence

(3) Necessarily, if one **is enlightened and** intends to make oneself believe *p*, then (a) one does not yet regard *p* as given but (b) one intends to bring it about that one regards *p* as given.

(4) Necessarily, if one **is enlightened and** intends to bring it about that one **correctly** regards *p* as given, then one intends to bring it about that *p* is true as a means to regarding *p* as given.

(5) Necessarily, if one intends to make oneself believe *p* at will, then it is not the case that one intends to bring it about that *p* is true as a means to regarding *p* as given.

Hence

(6) Necessarily, it is not the case that one **is enlightened and** intends to make oneself **correctly** believe *p* at will.

(7) Necessarily, one does something at will only if one intends to do it at will.

Hence

(8) Necessarily, it is not the case that one **is enlightened and** makes oneself **correctly** believe *p* at will.

This rendition of the argument seems to me pretty compelling, but there may still be a problem.

A key idea at work in both Premises 1 and 4 is that an adequate appreciation of what having a belief involves includes appreciating its direction of fit, so that an enlightened person will understand that, in general, *believing a proposition doesn't make that proposition true* (a point that, in this age of "fake news" and "alternative facts," it seems especially important to acknowledge), and thus also that, in order to bring it about that one correctly believes some proposition, one must aim to do so *by means of* bringing it about that the proposition is true. The problem is that there may be exceptions to this general truth; that is, there may be cases in which believing some proposition *does* make that proposition true, thereby ensuring the correctness of the belief itself. I will call cases of this sort cases of *self-verifying belief*.

[Brief digression: Before turning to possible cases of this sort, let me remark on one particularly prominent kind of case in which I think everyone agrees that believing a proposition does *not* make that proposition true. This is the kind of case that involves a proposition concerning the existence or nature of God. I have lost count of the number of times that I have been told that all I need to do to believe in God (which I take always to mean to believe at least that God exists and also usually to mean that God is omnipotent, omniscient, etc.) is to choose to do so. I take it that no one who has said this to me believes that God's existence and nature somehow depend on my having the belief in question. I have also often been told that my eternal salvation or lack thereof hangs in the balance. (Talk about pressure!) It seems to baffle those who have told me this when I reply that I cannot—literally cannot—do as they ask. I am baffled in turn when they assure me that I can, since after all that is what they did themselves. I can only surmise that they are misrepresenting what they did—or, if not, then, rather ironically, they are to be deemed unenlightened.]

One kind of case that might seem to be a case of self-verifying belief concerns propositions about one's own mental states. It has often been claimed that one cannot be mistaken about the present contents of one's consciousness—one's thoughts, feelings, sensations, and such.[147] If this claim is true, then if, for example, Pam *believes* that she is in pain, it follows that it's *true* that she is in pain. That we enjoy this kind of infallibility regarding our own conscious states is, of course, a controversial issue, but there is no need to investigate the matter here, since it is in fact irrelevant to our present concern. For even if we do have such infallibility, all that follows is that believing a proposition about one's present conscious states *suffices* for the truth of that proposition. It doesn't follow that the belief *accounts* for the truth of the proposition, and it is this that would be needed for the belief to *make* the proposition true.

A second possible kind of case of self-verifying belief concerns moral propositions in particular. A famous line of Hamlet's is that "there is nothing either good or bad, but thinking makes it so."[148] This line is subject to a number of interpretations, but one way to construe it is as the thesis that a moral proposition is true if and only if, and because, one believes it. If this thesis—I will call it the Conceited Thesis—were true, then the Argument from Ignorance and, along with it, this entire book would be scuttled, since both are based on the presupposition that it is possible not only to lack true moral beliefs (something that is perfectly consistent with the thesis) but also to possess false moral beliefs (something that is of course inconsistent with the thesis). I won't try to argue against the Conceited Thesis here. That would be too great a digression. Rather, as before,[149] I will rest content with the observation that, if you have read the book up to this point, you probably have little sympathy with the thesis yourself.

A third possible kind of case of self-verifying belief concerns the alleged capacity that confidence has to enable people to achieve what would otherwise be unachievable. We have all heard the fatuous claim that "anything is possible" as long as we believe in ourselves, but there may be a grain of truth buried inside it. In a famous passage, William James gives this example:

---

[147] For a thorough critical discussion of this and other closely related theses, see Alston (1971).
[148] *Hamlet* Act 2, Scene 2.   [149] Compare my brief remarks on moral realism in §3.4.2.

> Suppose... that I am climbing in the Alps, and have had the ill-luck to work myself into a position from which the only escape is by a terrible leap. Being without similar experience, I have no evidence of my ability to perform it successfully; but hope and confidence in myself make me sure I shall not miss my aim, and nerve my feet to execute what without these subjective emotions would perhaps have been impossible. But suppose that, on the contrary, the emotions of fear and mistrust preponderate; or suppose that, having just read the Ethics of Belief [a wry reference to Clifford (1877)], I feel it would be sinful to act upon an assumption unverified by previous experience,—why, then I shall hesitate so long that at last, exhausted and trembling, and launching myself in a moment of despair, I miss my foothold and roll into the abyss. In this case (and it is one of an immense class) the part of wisdom clearly is to believe what one desires; for the belief is one of the indispensable preliminary conditions of the realization of its object. *There are then cases where faith creates its own verification.* Believe, and you shall be right, for you shall save yourself; doubt, and you shall again be right, for you shall perish.[150]

Here James is claiming that believing certain propositions doesn't just suffice for their being true but indeed makes them true. He claims that the class of such propositions is "immense," but I am sure that this is a gross exaggeration. Still, it is perhaps possible that an enlightened agent should find himself (or, at least, take himself to be) in a situation of the sort that James describes and deliberately make himself believe that he can achieve a certain goal in order to make it the case that he can (and will) achieve it. If so, then the Argument against Believing at Will is unsound, not in virtue of relying on the claim that believing a proposition involves regarding that proposition as *true*, but rather in virtue of relying on the claim that, for someone who is appropriately enlightened, believing a proposition involves regarding that proposition as *given*. (That said, I should note that, contrary to what James himself maintains, it's not at all clear that, in the sort of case he is imagining, the agent would be making himself believe the relevant proposition *at will*. On the contrary, it would, I think, be far more likely that he would attempt to make himself believe it *by means of* some strategy such as, for example, the kind of visualization often advocated by sports psychologists.)

A final possible kind of case of self-verifying belief has recently been introduced by Rik Peels.[151] He calls cases of this kind Truth Depends on Belief cases, or TDB cases for short. He asks us to imagine a series of scenarios that involve a certain Dr. Transparent, a famous neuroscientist who has perfected mind-reading. In these scenarios there is a person—let's call her Rachel—to whom Dr. Transparent makes the promise that, if she comes to believe within a minute

---

[150] James (1967), p. 337.   [151] Peels (2015).

that he will give her $10, he will do so, and that, if she does *not* come to believe within a minute that he will give her $10, he will *not* do so. Dr. Transparent is trustworthy and can do what he says, and so Rachel realizes that whatever she believes will turn out to be true, that it will be true because she believes it, and that she has a choice in the matter. In one scenario, Rachel decides to believe that she will receive $10, and so that is what happens; in another, she decides to believe that she will not receive $10, and so *that* is what happens. Peels proceeds to discuss and reject various objections to the scenarios and concludes that TDB cases are conceptually coherent and thus that (in the terminology that I have introduced) it is quite possible after all for an enlightened person to intend to bring it about that he correctly regards a proposition as true *without* first making it true.

For my purposes in this book, it is not necessary to determine whether it is possible for belief to be self-verifying.[152] The reason is straightforward. I am concerned with the question of whether and, if so, how one can be in control of one's beliefs because of its relevance to the Argument from Ignorance. That argument is concerned, not with beliefs in general, but with beliefs having in particular to do with whether one is doing something overall morally wrong. Unless the Conceited Thesis is true, such beliefs are, as far as I can tell, never self-verifying. I can think of no scenario of the sort that either James or Peels brings to our attention in which such a belief would be featured, and I know of no other sort of scenario that would involve a self-verifying belief of this kind. On the assumption that the Conceited Thesis is false, all that must be done in order for the Argument against Believing at Will to provide the support needed for the purposes of Premise 6 of the Argument from Ignorance, then, is to revise the former argument one more time, as follows:

The Argument against Believing at Will (Final Draft):

(1) Necessarily, if one is enlightened and believes *p*, then, **unless one's belief is self-verifying**, one regards *p* as given.

(2) Necessarily, if one is enlightened and intends to make oneself believe (i.e., bring it about that one believes) *p*, then one does not yet believe *p*.

Hence

(3) Necessarily, if one is enlightened and intends to make oneself believe *p*, then, **unless one's belief is self-verifying**, (a) one does not yet regard *p* as given but (b) one intends to bring it about that one regards *p* as given.

(4) Necessarily, if one is enlightened and intends to bring it about that one correctly regards *p* as given, then, **unless one's belief is**

---

[152] For a critical discussion, see Antill (2020).

self-verifying, one intends to bring it about that *p* is true as a means to regarding *p* as given.

(5) Necessarily, if one intends to make oneself believe *p* at will, then it is not the case that one intends to bring it about that *p* is true as a means to regarding *p* as given.

Hence

(6) Necessarily, it is not the case that one is enlightened and intends to make oneself correctly believe *p* at will, **unless one's belief is self-verifying**.

(7) Necessarily, one does something at will only if one intends to do it at will.

Hence

(8) Necessarily, it is not the case that one is enlightened and makes oneself correctly believe *p* at will, **unless one's belief is self-verifying**.

This rendition of the argument seems to me very compelling, and I strongly commend it to you.

4.6.6 The Argument against Considering at Will

I said just now that the final draft of the Argument against Believing at Will provides all the support that is needed for the purposes of Premise 6 of the Argument from Ignorance. That is perhaps a little misleading, since the former argument is restricted to enlightened agents whose beliefs are not self-verifying, whereas Premise 6 of the Argument from Ignorance is not restricted in this way. But I won't undertake to reformulate Premise 6 to accommodate this restriction since, on the account of control that I have advocated, the premise is true as it stands. Remember that I investigated the question of whether it is possible to believe something at will only in order to convince those who reject my account of control that there are strong reasons to be suspicious of this possibility.

You may think that there's another reason to suspect that something has gone wrong with my investigation. Recall the distinction introduced in §3.2.2 between dispositional and occurrent belief. Suppose that Donna already dispositionally believes *p* but, because she isn't currently entertaining this proposition, doesn't occurrently believe it. Even if, for the reasons just given, she cannot have direct control over summoning the belief "from scratch," might she not still have direct control over transforming it from being dispositional to being occurrent? Surely she can do that. She simply has to consider the proposition.

On the contrary, there is nothing simple about effecting such a transformation, for several reasons. Note, first, that even if Donna could directly control whether she considers *p*, there is no guarantee that her considering *p* would transform her belief in it from being dispositional to being occurrent. As I noted in §3.2.2, to consider a proposition is to think *about* it, whereas to occurrently believe a proposition is to think *that* it is true; and even if, under "normal" circumstances, Donna has a disposition to think that *p* is true when she considers *p*, she might on occasion consider *p* and yet fail to think that it is true because her circumstances are abnormal (she may be distracted, say, or under great stress). For example, Donna may have recently married John Smith and changed her last name to his and yet, when asked whether she is Mrs. Smith, sincerely deny that she is.

Secondly, my account of control rules out the possibility of having direct control over considering a proposition just as surely as it rules out having direct control over believing a proposition. Again, on my account, one only ever has direct *volitional* control over one's *volitions* and, just as volitions are not beliefs (or other doxastic attitudes), so too they are not considerings.

Thirdly, even if my account of control is rejected in favor of an account according to which we have direct control over our basic acts and omissions (and, perhaps, their results), *still* it is clear that we cannot have direct control over bringing it about that we consider something that we are not currently considering. Since considering doesn't "aim at truth" in the way that belief does, no argument along the lines of the Argument against Believing at Will will work here, but none is needed. Consider instead this argument:

The Argument against Considering at Will:
(1) Necessarily, if one intends to make oneself begin to consider *p* at will, then one is considering making oneself begin to consider *p* at will.
(2) Necessarily, if one is considering making oneself begin to consider *p* at will, then one is considering *p*.
(3) Necessarily, if one is considering *p*, then one does not intend to make oneself begin to consider *p* at will.

Hence

(4) Necessarily, one does not intend to make oneself begin to consider *p* at will.
(5) Necessarily, one does something at will only if one intends to do it at will.

Hence

(6) Necessarily, one does not make oneself begin to consider *p* at will.

As far as I can tell, this argument is sound. Notice that the premises are explicitly concerned with *beginning* to consider *p* and with doing so *at will*. Intending to do anything *at will* requires considering doing it—hence Premise 1. Considering making oneself consider some proposition requires considering that very proposition—hence Premise 2. And as for Premise 3, perhaps it is possible, while considering some proposition, to intend to make oneself *continue* to consider it at will, but that of course is not the sort of case at issue here. If one is already considering a proposition, then one cannot intend to immediately *begin* considering it. (It is clearly possible to consider a proposition and intend to make oneself begin considering it *later*. This is what we do when we make reminders to ourselves, for example. But making reminders—putting an entry in one's calendar, say—is *a means by which* we make ourselves reconsider a proposition that has temporarily escaped our attention, and once again that is of course not what is at issue here.)

Finally, you might be wondering how I can embrace the claim that one can have direct control over deciding to do something and that deciding to do something requires that one consider doing it, and yet deny the claim that one can have direct control over considering doing something. The answer is straightforward. Unless one is *already* considering whether to do something, one cannot make a decision whether to do it. If, however, one *is* already considering whether to do something, then it may well be within one's direct control whether to decide to do it or not.

5
Culpable Ignorance

The Argument from Ignorance that I have presented in previous chapters culminates in the Origination Thesis, which holds that all blameworthiness or culpability is rooted in witting (or quasi-witting) wrongdoing, and thus that wrongdoing committed from ignorance of the fact that it is wrong can never be something for which one is *directly* to blame. This claim is of course compatible with holding that one can nonetheless on occasion be *indirectly* to blame for such wrongdoing. This possibility is in fact explicitly accommodated in the Argument's second premise, which in its most recent formulation (Draft 5) states:

(2) if one committed some act or omission because one failed to believe that it was overall morally wrong, one is morally to blame for it, and thereby morally to blame for any of its consequences, only if one is morally to blame for one's failure to believe that it was overall morally wrong.

In brief: blameworthiness for *wrongdoing* committed from ignorance is to be traced to blameworthiness for the *ignorance* (the failure to believe) that gave rise to that wrongdoing. This raises the question that I will pursue in this chapter: What does being blameworthy for such ignorance entail?

Philosophers frequently talk in this context of "culpable ignorance." Indeed, this has become standard, and I have accordingly employed the phrase in the title of this chapter. But in truth it is not well chosen, since it suggests that culpability attaches directly to a person's ignorance rather than to the person him- or herself *for* his or her ignorance. "Inexcusable ignorance" is more felicitous and thus the term that I will employ in this chapter, which proceeds as follows. In §5.1 I conduct an extended inquiry into whether and how one's being indirectly to blame for something is to be traced to one's being directly to blame for something else. According to the Argument from Ignorance, the distinction between direct and indirect blameworthiness tracks the distinction between direct and indirect control, and I inquire into what this claim means and why we should accept it. I then turn to the question of which consequences of behavior for which one is directly to blame should be said to be consequences for which one is indirectly to blame. It is very commonly held that, among the consequences of behavior for which one is directly to blame, only those that were foreseeable at the time at which one engaged in that behavior can be consequences for which one is indirectly to blame. I argue that this view needs qualification if it is to capture what its proponents intend. I then address a recent argument for the claim that one is never indirectly to blame for anything. I reject this claim but endorse the related claim that being indirectly to blame for some consequence of behavior for which one is directly to blame cannot increase the degree to which one is already to blame in virtue of having engaged in that behavior. Finally, I focus on indirect blameworthiness for ignorant wrongdoing in particular and respond to a number of objections that have been raised against employing the strategy of tracing in this context.

According to the Argument from Ignorance, ignorance of wrongdoing is an excuse for the wrongdoing that results, unless one is to blame for one's ignorance. In §5.2 I raise the question whether ignorance of wrongdoing is an excuse for the wrongdoing that results even when one *is* to blame for one's ignorance. I distinguish between two interpretations of this question and argue that, although the answer is "No" on one of these interpretations, it is "Yes" on the other. I end by addressing the question of whether ignorance can ever be inculpatory rather than exculpatory. I give reasons for denying that it can be but point out that, even if it can be, this fact is perfectly consistent with the position I have taken on the conditions under which ignorance provides an excuse for wrongdoing.

5.1 Tracing blameworthiness

5.1.1 Tracing and tracking

As I have just noted, Premise 2 of the Argument from Ignorance implies that blameworthiness for ignorant wrongdoing is to be traced to blameworthiness for the ignorance that underlay that wrongdoing. (This way of putting the point is rough, since it ignores the possibility of quasi-witting wrongdoing, regarding which see §3.3. For simplicity of exposition, I will continue to disregard this possibility in what follows.) The Argument goes on to imply that any blameworthiness one may have for one's ignorance must also be merely indirect. The relevant premises are these:

(6) one is never directly in control of whether one fails to believe something—that is, any control that one has over failing to believe something is always only indirect,

(7) if one is morally to blame for something over which one had only indirect control, then one's blameworthiness for it is itself only indirect, and

(8) one is indirectly morally to blame for something only if that thing was a consequence of something else for which one is directly morally to blame.

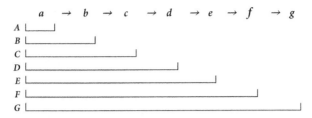

Figure 2.1 BILL AND JILL

I defended Premise 6 in §4.6. In this section I will attend to Premise 7. (Premise 8 is definitionally true.)

Premise 7 gives partial expression to the idea, one that goes back at least as far as Aristotle,[1] that the distinction between direct and indirect blameworthiness *tracks* the distinction between direct and indirect control; that is, if one is to blame for something, then one's blameworthiness for it is direct if and only if, and because, it was in one's direct control, and one's blameworthiness for it is indirect if and only if, and because, it was in one's indirect control. Consider once again the case of BILL AND JILL. In this case, Bill had direct control over a but merely indirect control over its consequences, $b-g$. Accordingly, on the present approach, if Bill is to blame for a, he is directly to blame for it, whereas, if he is to blame for $b-g$, he is merely indirectly to blame for these events. His control over $b-g$ was rooted in his control over a, and hence his blameworthiness for the former is correspondingly to be traced to his blameworthiness for the latter

This picture of the relation between blameworthiness and control is certainly attractive, but it faces a number of challenges.

5.1.2 Does tracing require tracking?

One question that deserves attention is this. Even if we grant both the distinction between direct and indirect control (as surely we should) and the distinction between direct and indirect blameworthiness (a somewhat more controversial matter, to which I will shortly return), why should we also grant that the latter tracks the former? Why might it not happen on occasion that one is directly to blame for something that is only in one's indirect control, or that one is indirectly to blame for something that is only in one's direct control?[2] This is a good question, since it seems clear that in other moral, or morally relevant, contexts

---

[1] See Aristotle (1941), 1113b.
[2] Cf. Montminy (2016), pp. 68 f., where it is argued that one can be directly responsible for something that is only in one's indirect control. Montminy's argument founders on the failure to recognize the category of hybrid control, regarding which see §2.2.4. See also Zimmerman (2008), pp. 182 f.

the direct-indirect distinction does not track the distinction between direct and indirect control.

Consider, for example, the distinction between final and non-final value. Suppose, for the sake of illustration, that pain is finally bad, i.e., bad for its own sake.[3] Then, all else being equal, something that causes pain—a blow to the head, say—will be non-finally (more particularly, instrumentally) bad.[4] In such a case, the badness of the blow will be derivative from the badness of the pain and thus indirect, whereas the badness of the pain will be original or non-derivative and thus direct. And notice that control might not enter the picture at all. It could do so (the blow could be one that is delivered during a fight), but it needn't (the blow could be caused by a falling rock).

Or consider the distinction, seldom discussed, between fundamental and incidental moral obligation. Here, it is plausible to think, control must be implicated (as the common claim that "ought" implies "can" suggests). By way of illustration, suppose that Dot is a doctor who is obligated to give her patient, Pat, an injection in order to improve his health. The case may be represented as in Figure 5.1. In this figure, L (l) is Dot's decision to inject the medication, M is her moving her finger (m is the movement of her finger), N is her plunging the syringe (n is the syringe's depression), O is her injecting the medication into Pat's body (o is the medication's entering his body), and P is her restoring Pat's health (p is the improvement in his health). As with the case of BILL AND JILL, it is the first of these events (L or l), and only the first, over which Dot exercises direct control; her control over $m-p$ is indirect, while her control over $M-P$ is hybrid. Yet, it is plausible to hold, what Dot is fundamentally, originally, and thus directly obligated to do is to perform P, that is, to restore Pat's health.[5] If we assume that each

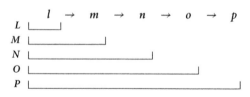

Figure 5.1 DOT AND PAT

---

[3] A more traditional way of putting this is to say that pain is *intrinsically* bad. But this suggests that the value that something has for its own sake must supervene entirely on its intrinsic properties, a claim that has been disputed. See Rabinowicz and Rønnow-Rasmussen (1999).

[4] Why all else being equal? Because otherwise the blow might have other consequences whose final goodness matches or outweighs the pain's final badness.

[5] This may be a mistake. Perhaps we should say that her fundamental obligation consists in performing some further act, F, such as showing respect for Pat or raising his level of welfare. On the distinction between fundamental and incidental obligation, see Ross (2002), p. 46.

of L–O is a necessary means to her doing P, then we can presumably say that Dot is obligated to do each of these things, too, but only incidentally, derivatively, indirectly. If this is so, then, even if moral obligation requires control, it will nonetheless be the case that what Dot is directly obligated to do is something that lies only in her indirect control, whereas what is in her direct control is something that she is only indirectly obligated to do.

Some philosophers would reject the view that I have just sketched about the nature of direct and indirect obligation, on the grounds that one cannot be indirectly obligated to do anything, and that what one is (directly) obligated to do is, and can only ever be, to make an executive decision to do something.[6] If this were so, then there would be no discrepancy after all between obligation and blameworthiness and their respective relations to direct control. But their argument itself rests on a mistake, I think, the mistake of confusing the distinction between direct and indirect control with the distinction between complete and partial control. They appear to hold that only executive decisions can be obligatory because only such decisions can, strictly speaking, be (fully) in one's control. But that is not so. As I noted in §4.1.4, complete control is unattainable by anyone at any time; decisions are just as vulnerable to the vicissitudes of nature (e.g., a sneeze that prevents one from making a decision that one was just about to make) as any other event that might lie within one's at-best-partial control. There is therefore no reason, on this score at least, to abandon our normal conception of moral obligation and say that it is not actions (or omissions), but only executive decisions, that we can ever be obligated to carry out. And if we stick with this conception, then we must acknowledge the distinction between direct (fundamental) and indirect (incidental) obligation. But then the question arises once again: Why should it be that the distinction between direct and indirect blameworthiness tracks the distinction between direct and indirect control, when the distinction between direct and indirect obligation does not?

The answer, I suggest, is this. As I noted in §2.1.3, judgments about blameworthiness, and about moral responsibility in general, are agent-focused, whereas judgments about moral obligation are act-focused. One's blameworthiness depends crucially on the quality of will that one displays at the time at which one exercises control and makes the decision to act, and it is therefore at this stage in the history of one's behavior that one's blameworthiness is rooted. One's moral obligations do not depend in this way on one's quality of will. On the contrary, they depend on the actual or probable outcomes of the various options one faces. Some of these outcomes are of fundamental significance, whereas others have only

---

[6] Cf. Prichard (1949), pp. 31 ff.; Ross (1939), pp. 153 f.; Khoury (2018), p. 1376. These authors talk in terms of "volitions" or "self-exertions" or "willings" rather than "executive decisions." I take these terms to be synonymous.

5.1.3 Foreseeability

The claim that one is indirectly blameworthy only for what was in one's indirect control of course does not imply that one is indirectly blameworthy for everything that was in one's indirect control. The latter claim is patently absurd, since it implies that one is to blame for all the good things that have happened as a result of one's exercise of control. Also unacceptable is the more restrictive claim that one is to blame for all the bad things that have happened as a result of one's exercise of control. Think of Sally from the first chapter. Her decision to take thalidomide resulted in her child's phocomelia—a tragic consequence. Yet surely Sally is not to blame for her decision and hence not to blame for this consequence of it. Unacceptable, too, is the still more restrictive claim that one is to blame for all the bad things that have happened as a result of an exercise of control for which one is directly to blame. The reason is that, as noted in Chapter 1, some of these things, despite being bad and despite having occurred as a consequence of an executive decision for which one is directly to blame, may not have "fallen within the risk" created by that decision.[7] Indirect blameworthiness, it seems, is restricted to consequences that were *foreseeable* by the agent at the time of the pertinent decision. This is a very common, and seemingly very plausible, claim. But exactly what is it for a consequence to be foreseeable?

One answer to this question, often given in legal contexts, is that a consequence is foreseeable just in case a (or, sometimes, the) reasonable person would have foreseen it. Whatever the merits of this answer for legal purposes (adopting it might facilitate administration of the law, for example[8]), it faces several problems when applied to the present context. One problem is simply that of determining what constitutes a reasonable person. Another problem is that of determining what such a person would foresee under whatever the relevant circumstances may be. But even if these problems can be resolved, the gravest problem remains, and that is that the reasonable-person standard is simply irrelevant to the question of whether and, if so, to what extent one is blameworthy for some decision or the consequences thereof, since one can blamelessly fall short of this standard. Simple Simon, for example, is not to blame, morally or otherwise, for trying to catch water in a sieve, even if a (or the) reasonable person would have foreseen the futility of doing so.[9]

The problem with the reasonable-person approach to foreseeability is, of course, that it fails to accommodate the basic point that, for a consequence to be

---

[7] Cf. American Law Institute (1985), §2.03(3).   [8] Cf. Prosser (1971), pp. 152 f.
[9] Cf. Keeton and O'Connell (1975), p. 85; Alexander et al. (2009), pp. 81 ff.

foreseeable by someone, it must be the case that *that* person *can* foresee it. But this rather obvious observation doesn't suffice to answer our original question of what it is for a consequence to be foreseeable, unless it is specified what sense of "can" is at issue.

It's safe to say, I think, that, if one actually foresaw a consequence, then one could have foreseen it, in any pertinent sense of "can." But, of course, what we're primarily concerned with in the present context is with one's being to blame for a consequence that one *didn't* foresee, even though it was foreseeable. I think that it will be generally agreed that such a situation cannot arise unless one is to blame for one's lack of foresight; that is, one's blameworthiness for the foreseeable-but-unforeseen consequence is to be traced to one's failure to foresee it. Now, there are perhaps many different senses of "can" that might be at issue when it is claimed that someone could have foreseen something, but, if culpably failing to foresee some allegedly foreseeable consequence is to be the occasion of one's being to blame for that consequence, and if (as stated in Premise 4 of the Argument from Ignorance) one is to blame for something only if one was in control of that thing, then it must be that one could have foreseen the consequence in that particular sense of "can" that expresses the specific ability involved in one's having control over something. (See §4.1.2.) Now, foreseeing a consequence consists in believing that it would or might occur as a result of some other event's occurring, and (as stated in Premise 6 of the Argument from Ignorance and as argued in §4.6.5), one is never directly in control of whether one fails to believe something. Hence one's being to blame for one's lack of foresight is to be traced in turn to one's being to blame for some prior piece of behavior, B, consisting in either doing something that caused one's lack of foresight or, more likely, failing to do something that would have prevented it (such as failing to keep one's eyes on the road while driving, for example[10]). If one is to blame for B, then B must have been an instance of wrongdoing; that is, it must have been something that one ought not to have done. (In saying this, I am for the time being putting aside the possibility of one's having an accuse for B, regarding which see §3.4.1.) This observation is of course perfectly in keeping with the common idea that one should have or ought to have foreseen certain consequences that one didn't foresee (one ought to have foreseen the accident that resulted from one's not keeping one's eyes on the road, for example). But here I think it's very important to point out something that is unfortunately frequently overlooked,[11] and that is that from the fact that one *ought* to have foreseen some consequence it doesn't follow that one is to *blame* for failing to foresee it. One might have an excuse! Indeed, the Argument from

---

[10] Cf. Rosen (2004), p. 301, on what he calls procedural epistemic obligations.
[11] See, among many others: M. Smith (2003), p. 31; Guerrero (2007), pp. 64, 66; Sher (2009), p. 87; Murray and Vargas (2020), pp. 831 ff., 840. For a welcome contrast, see Goldberg (2017), pp. 2885 ff.

Ignorance implies that one *will* have an excuse if one was inculpably ignorant of the wrongness of B.

Even given this clarification of the pertinent sense of "can," there remain complications with aligning blameworthiness for the consequences of one's behavior with those consequences that were foreseeable. I mentioned these complications in Chapter 1, but it will be useful to repeat them here. Consider again the condition, C, of Sally's poor child. As I noted in Chapter 1, it cannot reasonably be held that any of Grünenthal's employees could have foreseen that C itself would occur, since none of them knew or could have known of Sally, let alone that she was pregnant and thinking of taking Distaval. Any pertinent consequence that can plausibly be said to have been foreseeable by any of these employees must therefore be of a more general character, one that encompassed C but also other consequences relevantly similar to C. (For example, even if Heinrich could not have foreseen that C would occur as a result of failing to disclose the results of his research, perhaps he could have foreseen that the incidence of phocomelia would rise.) Moreover, as I also noted in Chapter 1, it would presumably be too restrictive to insist that, in order for any employee to be to blame for what happened, that person must have been able to foresee that this more general consequence *would* occur; that such a consequence *might well* occur would seem to suffice. These points are commonly recognized,[12] but they raise three problems that are less commonly acknowledged.

The first problem has to do with how to understand the "well" in "might well." I will postpone discussion of this issue until the next chapter.

The second problem has to do with matching that which was foreseeable with that for which one is to blame. I said earlier that it seems that indirect blameworthiness is restricted to consequences that were foreseeable by the agent at the time of the pertinent decision, and yet just now I also said that none of Grünenthal's employees could have foreseen C itself; they could at best have foreseen a more general consequence that encompassed C. But if we want to keep open the question of whether any of these employees is to blame for C itself, then we *cannot* after all say that indirect blameworthiness is restricted to consequences that were foreseeable by the agent. Perhaps this is not too big a problem, though. To fix it, perhaps all we need say is this: blameworthiness is restricted to consequences that were, at the time of the pertinent decision, either foreseeable by the agent or encompassed by consequences that were foreseeable by the agent. This would allow us to say that, if Heinrich was to blame for the increase in the number of cases of phocomelia that resulted from his decision to keep the results of his research to himself, then he was also to blame for C in particular.

---

[12] See, for instance, Fischer and Tognazzini (2009), pp. 537 f. and p. 546.

The third problem is seldom discussed.[13] It has to do with the fact that there would seem to be a limit to the proper employment of the strategy of generalization that was just used to justify holding Heinrich blameworthy for C even though he could not have foreseen C itself. As I said in Chapter 1, if further research by Grünenthal's employees would have revealed that taking thalidomide might well result in polyneuritis but *not* that it might well result in phocomelia, then, I suspect, most people would *not* be willing to say that C "fell within the risk" created by the decision not to pursue further research, even though there is a general consequence of this decision, namely, the occurrence of harm, which presumably the employees could have foreseen and which of course encompasses not only incidents of polyneuritis but also incidents of phocomelia and, thus, C itself.[14] That is why I said that the correct employment of the strategy apparently requires that one restrict its application to a certain "vicinity" beyond whose borders the occurrence of any particular consequence would be something for which one is not to blame. Without further development, this idea of course remains very vague, but I confess that I don't know how to sharpen it. That, as I said, is a problem. Just how big a problem it is is something that I will now briefly address.

5.1.4 Moral luck

I have been assuming throughout that there is good reason to draw a distinction between direct and indirect blameworthiness, but this assumption can be, and has been, challenged. Andrew Khoury has recently argued that one cannot be blameworthy for the consequences of one's behavior and hence, in effect, that there cannot be anything for which one is indirectly blameworthy. This is, of course, a very radical claim. It requires saying, for instance, not only that no one is to blame, but also that no one *could* be to blame, for the tragedy of thalidomide; that no one could *ever* be to blame for anyone's suffering; and so on. This view may seem preposterous, and yet Khoury's argument for it is straightforward. It is this:

(1) If some thing is not that in virtue of which one is blameworthy then one cannot be blameworthy for that thing.

---

[13] But not never. See M. S. Moore (1997), pp. 389 ff.
[14] Of course, just how to determine whether some consequence "falls within the risk" created by a decision is a difficult question about which even experts can differ. Consider, for example, the celebrated case of *Palsgraf v. Long Island Railroad Co.* (248 N.Y. 339 (1928)), in which the facts were these. While helping a man board a departing train, an employee of the company dislodged a package wrapped in newspaper that the man was carrying. The package, which contained fireworks, fell onto the rails and exploded. The shock rocked some scales standing some distance away, thereby causing the plaintiff injuries for which she sued. The judges on the New York Court of Appeals were divided 4 to 3 regarding whether the plaintiff's complaint should be dismissed.

(2) The consequences of one's actions are not that in virtue of which one is blameworthy.
(3) Therefore, one cannot be blameworthy for the consequences of one's actions.[15]

What should we make of this argument?

One concern that might be raised regarding this argument is that it begs the question at issue. As I noted in §2.2.1, some philosophers have held that the basis of blameworthiness (that in virtue of which one is to blame) and the object of blameworthiness (that for which one is to blame) are one and the same. But, as I also noted there, if this claim is to have any plausibility, it must be restricted to direct blameworthiness. It's clear, for example, that the basis of Heinrich's blameworthiness for the condition of Sally's child cannot simply be that condition itself. The same point applies to Khoury's first premise. But then, it may seem, that premise alone suffices for Khoury's conclusion.

Although I think there may be something to the charge that Khoury's argument begs the question, I am hesitant to endorse it. That is because what constitutes begging the question is a complex and delicate matter, in virtue of which the charge is often very difficult to adjudicate. (Even circular arguments can fail to be question-begging.[16]) I do find Khoury's first premise problematic for a different reason, though. In §2.2.4 I argued that the claim that the basis and the object of blameworthiness are one and the same should be rejected, even when that claim is restricted to *direct* blameworthiness. I won't repeat my argument here, but it applies equally to Khoury's first premise.

I am strongly inclined to think that Khoury's second premise is *true*, however. He bases it on the view that the basis of blameworthiness is the quality of will that informs one's behavior. If that is so, then, since nothing that occurs as a consequence of one's behavior can alter or affect the quality of will that informs that behavior, nothing that occurs as a consequence of one's behavior can alter or affect one's blameworthiness. I find this line of reasoning very appealing. Now it's true, as I pointed out in §2.2.3, that, unless quality of will is understood to comprise not just the mental but also the agential condition of moral responsibility, it would be a mistake to say that the basis of blameworthiness has *exclusively* to do with one's quality of will, and it might seem that this fact undermines Khoury's second premise; but I don't think it does, for a complementary line of reasoning can be offered regarding the agential condition. Let me explain.

In a famous paper about moral luck, Thomas Nagel asks, "How is it possible to be more or less culpable depending on whether...a bird [gets] into the path of one's bullet?" I take the answer to this question to be that this is *not* possible. Consider again, from §4.5.1, the case of BILL AND THE BIRD, represented in

---

[15] Khoury (2012), p. 195. Cf. also Khoury (2018), p. 1363.
[16] See Sinnott-Armstrong (1999) for helpful and insightful discussion.

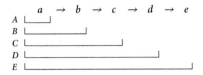

Figure 4.5 BILL AND THE BIRD

Figure 4.5. As I noted before, there is of course more to the case than what is represented in this figure. For present purposes, however, I will assume that what is left out is morally irrelevant, in that nothing further occurred for which Bill may plausibly be said to be culpable. (If the lives of birds have value, then this may be a mistake, but let's just put this concern to one side.) Question: Would there be any reason to declare Bill less culpable for what happened in BILL AND THE BIRD than for what happened in BILL AND JILL, depicted in Figure 2.1, in which he succeeded in killing Jill? Answer: Not that I can see. First, in keeping with Khoury's point, the absence in BILL AND THE BIRD of events f and g (the events of the bullet's piercing Jill's body and of Jill's death, respectively) does not affect or alter the quality of will that attached to his decision, a. Second, since all the events that occurred as a consequence of a were in Bill's control only to the extent that a itself was, the absence in BILL AND THE BIRD of events f and g does not affect or alter the extent to which Bill exercised control over what took place. True, in BILL AND JILL these events fell within the *scope* of his control, whereas in BILL AND THE BIRD they did not, but the *degree* to which Bill exercised control was the same in both cases (in *one* important sense of "degree of control"; for discussion, see §4.5). For this reason, and for the reason stated by Khoury, there is strong pressure to say that the *degree* to which Bill is to blame for what happened is the same in both cases. Thus, even if we reject Khoury's first premise (as I do) and allow for the possibility of indirect blameworthiness and thereby concede that the *scope* of Bill's blameworthiness in the original case (encompassing, as it does, all the events depicted in Figure 2.1) is greater than the scope of his blameworthiness in the modified case—so that, as we might put it, he is *to blame for more* in the former than in the latter—it seems nonetheless very plausible to maintain that he is *no more to blame* in the former (or, if that sounds objectionably lenient, that he is no less to blame in the latter), and thus that, more generally, one cannot, in Nagel's terminology, be *morally* lucky (or unlucky) in virtue of what happens to transpire as a consequence of the decisions one makes.

Once again, it may help to appreciate the point that I am trying to make if the case of BILL AND JILL is compared with the case of BILL'S PERSISTENCE, represented in Figure 4.6. I noted in §4.5.1 that, given the repeated opportunities that Bill has in BILL'S PERSISTENCE to administer an antidote to the poison that he has injected into Jill and his repeated decisions to refrain from doing so, his degree of control over

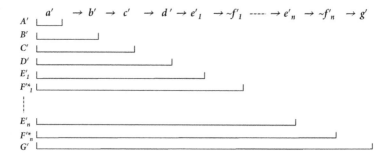

Figure 4.6 BILL'S PERSISTENCE

Jill's death in this case is greater than it is in BILL AND JILL. Given that his quality of will remains constant throughout, he incurs culpability afresh with each decision, and so his culpability for her death will be correspondingly greater, too.

In an earlier work, I summarized the view that there is no moral luck as far as responsibility is concerned as follows: "Degree of responsibility counts for everything, scope for nothing, when it comes to [the] moral evaluation of agents."[17] Khoury has himself objected to this statement (which is in tension with the first premise in his argument), on two grounds. He claims, first, that it is implausible to say that degree of responsibility counts for everything, and, second, that it is implausible to say that scope of responsibility counts for nothing.[18]

Regarding the first point: I have claimed that Bill is blameworthy to the same degree in both BILL AND JILL and BILL AND THE BIRD. Khoury agrees with this verdict. But, he says, there being no difference in Bill's blameworthiness in either case isn't merely a matter of Bill's being blameworthy to the same degree; it's also a matter of Bill's exhibiting the same quality of will. Another agent could exhibit a different quality of will, and thus be blameworthy in a different way, and yet be blameworthy to the same degree. Since one's being blameworthy is a function of the way in which one is blameworthy as well as the degree to which one is blameworthy, it's false to claim that degree of responsibility "counts for everything" in the moral evaluation of agents.

I think this objection misfires. There are two interpretations to be given to the phrase "the way in which one is blameworthy." On one reading, this refers to the *basis* of one's blameworthiness—the way in which one incurs blameworthiness; on another reading, it refers to the *mode of blame* of which one is worthy—the way in which one is to be blamed. Khoury intends the phrase to be understood according to the first interpretation (he holds fixed the mode of blame he takes into

---

[17] Zimmerman (2002), p. 568. The kind of moral evaluation in question is, of course, hypological rather than aretaic. See §2.1.3 for discussion.
[18] Khoury (2018), pp. 1361 ff.

consideration, namely, resentment); he is concerned with the basis of one's blameworthiness, which, as I noted, he takes to be the quality of will that one exhibits in one's behavior. Now, I am quite willing to concede that two agents can exhibit different qualities of will and yet be blameworthy to the same degree, but, if they are also worthy of the same mode of blame, then that, as far as I can see, exhausts the question of how they are to be evaluated morally: they are to be blamed in the *same* way and to the *same* degree. The fact that this evaluation has a different basis in one case than in the other doesn't feature in the evaluation itself.

But what if two agents are to be blamed in different ways? What if, for example, P is worthy of resentment whereas Q deserves a reprimand? Then, as I noted in §2.5.3, it's not clear how the degree to which P is to blame can be compared to the degree to which Q is to blame. Even so, it is presumably the case that P is to blame to some degree and that Q is also to blame to some degree, and, given that the mode of blame of which each is worthy has been established, once again that would appear to exhaust the question of how each of these agents is to be evaluated morally. Still, I concede that, given that there are different kinds or modes of blame and that someone can be worthy of one kind but not of another, I oversimplified matters (in a way that Khoury does not accuse me of) when I said that degree of responsibility counts for everything in the moral evaluation of agents. The kind of response of which they are worthy counts, too.

Oversimplified or not, my main aim in stating that degree of responsibility counts for everything in such evaluation was simply that of driving home the point that scope of responsibility counts for nothing. But this brings us immediately to Khoury's second complaint:

> If, in light of the rejection of... moral luck, we can retain the possibility of responsibility for external objects [i.e., objects that are the consequences of "internal" decisions] only at the cost of making such responsibility empty, why bother?[19]

This is a fair question. Here's my answer.

The idea that indirect responsibility is "essentially empty," as I have put it in previous work,[20] may be initially disconcerting, but one's unease with it should diminish when one recognizes that the emptiness of indirect responsibility is just one instance of a phenomenon that is exemplified elsewhere. Consider, for example, the distinction I mentioned earlier between final and non-final value. Suppose, as before, that pain is finally bad, i.e., bad for its own sake. Then, I said, something that causes pain will, all else being equal, be non-finally (more particularly, instrumentally) bad. Now consider these two scenarios. One is

---

[19] Khoury (2018), p. 1363.   [20] Zimmerman (1988), p. 55.

straightforward: Moe slaps Curly on the back of the head, causing him pain. The other involves an elaborate Rube Goldberg-type of apparatus: Larry lifts his finger, thereby rolling a ball down a chute, thereby setting a wheel in motion, thereby tripping a switch, thereby..., thereby releasing a paddle that delivers a slap to the back of Curly's head that causes exactly the same quantity and quality of pain to him as in the first scenario. Larry clearly does *more bad things* than Moe; all the actions mentioned are instrumentally bad. But, equally clearly, Larry does not do *more bad* than Moe;[21] the sum total of value in the world is reduced to the same extent in each scenario. Non-final value, being merely indirect, is thus essentially empty. Note that this point applies to positive value just as it does to negative value. Just as one person can do more bad things than another without doing more bad, so, too, one person can do more good things than another without doing more good. Suppose that pleasure is finally good, and then consider two different ways in which the same quantity and quality of pleasure might be caused, one straightforward, the other elaborate.

There is another way in which doing more good (or bad) things does not entail doing more good (or bad). Suppose that, in addition to pleasure (pain), knowledge (ignorance) is also finally good (bad). Then imagine that, in doing some act A, John brings about a trivial instance of each of these goods (bads), while, in doing some other act B, Jane brings about a substantial instance of just one of them. Then John does more goods (bads) than Jane,[22] but Jane does more good (bad) than John. This kind of case is quite different from the kind just mentioned. It is only non-final (indirect) goods and bads that are essentially empty. When it comes to final goods (bads), the more, the better (worse),[23] even if one good (bad), such as that brought about by Jane, can outweigh two goods (bads), such as those brought about by John.

We can couch the case of John and Jane in terms of reasons. John has *more reasons* (not) to do A than Jane has (not) to do B, yet Jane has *more reason* (not) to do B than John has (not) to do A. This fact does *not* point to any essential emptiness in the nature of reasons. Nonetheless, I believe that there *is* such a phenomenon: we can distinguish between direct and indirect reasons, and the latter are essentially empty. For example, one may have a direct reason (not) to cause pleasure (pain) and only an indirect reason to perform any of the means at one's disposal to accomplish this. As far as I can tell, however, the term "more reasons" as opposed to the term "more reason" cannot be used in any natural way to capture this distinction.

---

[21] Please pardon my English. "Do more bad" is a somewhat questionable phrase. "Do more evil" is less questionable, but "evil" itself carries connotations that I wish to avoid in this context.

[22] Once again, please pardon my English.

[23] This is an oversimplification. The claim should be restricted to *basic* final goods and bads. For clarification, see Zimmerman (2001), ch. 5.

Now consider the distinction, also mentioned earlier, between fundamental and incidental obligation. Suppose that Dot has two patients to whom she must administer an injection, Pat and Paul. Pat's case, as depicted in Figure 5.1, is relatively straightforward. Paul's case is quite different; Dot must make use of an elaborate method that involves many different steps. Suppose that in each case Dot does *none* of the things needed to ensure that either Pat or Paul receives the required medication. Then clearly she will have done *more wrongs* in the case of Paul than in the case of Pat. But, equally clearly, she will not have done *more wrong* in the former case than in the latter. Incidental obligation, being merely indirect, is essentially empty.

Should the essential emptiness of non-final value, of indirect reasons, and of incidental obligation lead us to reject the practice of making judgments in terms of these concepts? I see no reason to think so; indeed, it's hard to imagine how we could manage our lives without recourse to them. (Try eschewing such judgments as that it is good to donate to charity, wrong to beat a child, and so on.) So too, I think, for the concept of indirect moral responsibility. I see no need to follow Khoury and deny that we can ever be morally responsible for the consequences of our actions, especially when it's clear that we can be, indeed are, causally responsible for these consequences and it is at least arguable that the conjunction of moral with causal responsibility can render certain responses fitting that causal responsibility alone would not.[24] Nonetheless I concede that, in rejecting the possibility of moral luck, my view, though shared with several others,[25] is pretty radical, since it is in conflict with conventional "wisdom," according to which, for example, Bill would be far more culpable if he had succeeded in killing Jill than if he had tried to do so but, due to the passing bird, failed in his attempt.

I have said that in the case of BILL AND JILL, Bill is to blame for Jill's death. Clearly this is not true in the case of BILL AND THE BIRD, since in that case Jill didn't die. I have also said, however, that Bill is no more to blame in the former case than in the latter, since the degree to which he is to blame in both cases is exhausted by his blameworthiness for his decision. But then the question arises: To what degree is Bill to blame for Jill's death in BILL AND JILL? If he is no more to blame than he would have been if she hadn't died, then shouldn't we say that he is to blame to *no* degree for her death? But that would seem to imply that he is *not* to blame for it after all.

My answer is that we should *not* say that Bill is to blame to no degree for Jill's death. To use numbers in a purely ad hoc fashion, suppose that Bill is to blame to degree 10 for his decision to kill Jill. Then I propose that we also say that he is to blame to degree 10 for her death, for this captures precisely the degree to which he

---

[24] Cf. Scanlon (2008), pp. 148 ff.; Coleman and Sarch (2012), p. 116, n. 26.
[25] See, e.g., Feinberg (1970), ch. 2; Thomson (1989); Enoch and Marmor (2007); Alexander et al. (2009), ch. 5.

is to blame for what transpired. In order to fend off any suggestion that Bill's being to blame to degree 10 for Jill's death somehow compounds the degree (i.e., degree 10) to which he is already to blame for his decision, we need only note that he is merely *indirectly* to blame to degree 10 for the death, whereas he is *directly* to blame to degree 10 for the decision. The situation here is once again analogous to the situation elsewhere. Consider, for example, the case involving Moe and Curly. Suppose that Curly's pain was bad to degree 10. Then I propose that we also say that Moe's slap was bad to degree 10, since that captures precisely the degree to which what happened was bad.[26] To fend off any suggestion that the slap's being bad somehow compounds the degree to which the train of events was bad, we need only note that the slap was merely *instrumentally* bad to degree 10, whereas the pain was *finally* bad to degree 10.

Notice one distinct advantage of my view regarding the essential emptiness of indirect blameworthiness: the need to sharpen the notion of a "vicinity" of consequences for which one is to blame is far less urgent if blameworthiness for consequences is essentially empty than if it is not; for the failure in any particular case to map the borders of the relevant vicinity accurately need not result in any injustices, as long as the degree to which one is blamed is not thereby affected. Notice, though, one distinct limit to this advantage: if in fact the conjunction of moral with causal responsibility renders certain responses fitting that causal responsibility alone does not, then such a failure could still have significant repercussions, since causal responsibility itself extends to all consequences, both to those that lie outside of the relevant vicinity and to those that lie within its borders.

I don't pretend that these brief remarks prove conventional "wisdom" to be mistaken. It is arguable that the quotation marks should be removed and the wisdom acknowledged as genuine. If so, then, even though the distinction between scope and degree of blameworthiness would remain, nonetheless there would be a positive correlation between them: the greater the scope, the greater the degree. In this way, Bill would be properly declared more blameworthy for what happened in the original case in which he killed Jill than in the case in which he failed to do so because the bird got in the way. Anyone who takes this stand is of course faced with the task of determining just which consequences of that behavior for which one is directly blameworthy are indeed consequences for which one is indirectly blameworthy and which thereby serve to augment the degree to which one is blameworthy, and of explaining why this is so. This task is perhaps not so

---

[26] Complication: Moe's slap might also have caused Larry anguish, something that was, say, bad to degree 5. Then I suppose we should say that the slap was bad to degree 15, since *this* is what would now reflect how bad what happened was. Further complication: What if the slap had yet more bad consequences? Then we would have to re-calculate once again. (The device of addition that I have used for purposes of this illustration is of course questionable. For discussion, see Zimmerman (2001), ch. 5.)

daunting if the consequences in question are limited to those that are foreseen by the agent, but, for anyone who claims that the occurrence of foreseeable-but-unforeseen consequences also augments the degree to which one is blameworthy, the "problem of the vicinity" looms large.

5.1.5 Tracing culpability for ignorant wrongdoing

So far, I have used the term "trace" liberally. I have said that, if ever one is indirectly to blame for some consequence of one's behavior, one's blameworthiness for the consequence is to be traced to one's blameworthiness for the behavior. Philosophers often use the term more narrowly, restricting it to cases in which the consequence is *itself* some form of behavior. It is, of course, precisely such cases with which the Argument from Ignorance is concerned. In her classic paper, "Culpable Ignorance," Holly Smith introduced terminology in this context that has since become standard. In cases in which one is to blame for ignorant wrongdoing, the ignorant wrongdoing is something that Smith calls an "unwitting wrongful act,"[27] one's blameworthiness for which is to be traced to one's blameworthiness for one's ignorance; and one's blameworthiness for one's ignorance is in turn to be traced to one's blameworthiness for some prior act or omission which Smith calls a "benighting act."[28] This account accords perfectly with the Argument from Ignorance, although it is notable that Smith doesn't draw the conclusion that the benighting act must itself be a *witting* wrongful act.

Smith's paper is concerned with the *epistemic* condition of moral responsibility; she investigates how blameworthiness for *ignorant* wrongdoing is to be traced to blameworthiness for some prior piece of behavior. Those who favor the narrow use of the term "trace" do not restrict it to such cases, however. They are often, indeed usually, concerned with the *agential* condition of moral responsibility and invoke tracing in order to account for how blameworthiness for *out-of-control* wrongdoing is possible. Such wrongdoing might be unwitting, but it needn't be. The stock example is that of the drunk driver who cannot control his driving but is nonetheless to blame for it, since he is to blame for the drinking that led to it. This example is problematic, however, since, as many have remarked,[29] it's not clear whether such cases do typically involve behavior that, at the time at which it occurs, is strictly out of the agent's control. So, instead, let us consider a cleaner case, the case of Alice that I first presented in Chapter 1. She declined to take her medication for Tourette's and, as a result, hurled invective at Ben. Let me now simply stipulate that her decision not to take her medication was something that

---

[27] Here the term "act" is to be construed broadly, as encompassing omissions as well as acts in the strict sense.
[28] H. M. Smith (1983), pp. 547 f.   [29] See, e.g., Husak (2012).

was in Alice's direct control and which she knew to be wrong, whereas her hurling invective at Ben was, at the time it occurred, wholly outside of her control. Then, even if Alice was fully aware at the time that hurling invective at Ben was wrong, nonetheless her blameworthiness for this behavior can only be indirect; it is to be traced to her being to blame for her decision not to take her medication.

It's worth noting that, even if one is directly responsible for some later piece of behavior, that would not preclude tracing one's responsibility for it to some earlier piece of behavior for which one is directly responsible, so that one would *also* be indirectly responsible for one's later behavior. This point is often overlooked. Consider Beatrice who, like Alice, is subject to strong impulses to sling insults at others. In her case, though, the impulses are not irresistible. Like Alice, Beatrice has medication that helps eliminate these impulses; but it has a nasty taste, and so she is reluctant to take it. This morning, Beatrice decided to skip her medication. This afternoon, as Derek walked by, she had a strong impulse to insult him—strong, but resistible, though unfortunately not resisted. Let us assume that Beatrice is directly to blame for her decision to insult Derek. If that decision was a consequence of her earlier decision to skip her medication, then she may also be indirectly to blame for her later decision.

It might be objected that declaring Beatrice both directly and indirectly to blame for her decision to insult Derek involves an illegitimate form of double-counting, but that is not so, precisely because there were two occasions on which she incurred blameworthiness—those occasions of course being the time at which she made the decision to insult Derek and the earlier time at which she decided to skip her medication. Whether her being *twice* to blame for her later decision *increases* her blameworthiness for this decision is an interesting question. Those who, like myself, take indirect responsibility to be essentially empty will answer in the negative. Others may respond differently.

On the present approach, then, tracing in the narrow sense (tracing blameworthiness for later behavior to blameworthiness for earlier behavior) is simply a particular species of tracing in the broad sense (tracing blameworthiness for consequences in general to blameworthiness for behavior that led to these consequences). Given the possibility of indirect responsibility for consequences in general, there would seem to be nothing notable or surprising about the idea that one can be indirectly responsible for one's own behavior in particular. And yet this idea has recently been the target of several objections.

One objection, raised by Matt King in a pair of articles, is that tracing responsibility (in the narrow sense of "trace"—the only sense in which he uses the term) is theoretically dispensable, both in cases of out-of-control wrongful action and in cases of unwitting wrongful action.[30] He claims that an agent's blameworthiness

---

[30] King (2011) and (2017).

for such wrongful action can be fully accounted for by registering his or her blameworthiness for having behaved either recklessly or negligently in committing the benighting act that led to the later wrongful act, and hence that appealing to (narrow) tracing in this context is to make use of a special explanatory tool that serves no purpose. This objection misfires, though, precisely because appealing to (narrow) tracing is not to make use of some special explanatory tool; on the contrary, doing so simply involves applying the ordinary explanatory tool of tracing blameworthiness for consequences in general to that particular kind of case in which the consequence at issue consists in the agent's own wrongful behavior. (If some of those who invoke tracing in the narrow sense were to suggest otherwise, then I think King would be quite right to complain. But I'm not aware of anyone's making this suggestion.) I would add, moreover, that King's claim that all such cases involve either recklessness or negligence in the commission of the benighting act is mistaken. It is easy to imagine cases in which one commits a benighting act with the knowledge, and perhaps even the intention, that doing so will lead to one's committing a later wrongful act that is either unwitting or out of one's control (or both).

In objecting to resorting to the device of tracing (in the narrow sense), King does not claim that doing so is mistaken, but only that it is unnecessary, when accounting for an agent's blameworthiness for wrongful acts that were either unwitting or out of the agent's control. Although I just objected to his argument for this claim (on the grounds that he mistakenly takes proponents of tracing in the narrow sense to conceive of it as a special explanatory tool), the claim is nonetheless one with which I sympathize; for if, as I have argued, indirect responsibility is essentially empty, then one's being blameworthy for an unwitting wrongful act does not augment the degree to which one is already to blame for the benighting act that led to it. There are other philosophers, however, who have argued that resorting to the device of tracing (in the narrow sense—again, the only sense in which they tend to use the term) is not simply unnecessary but can in certain cases lead to mistaken assessments of responsibility.

One objection to this effect has been raised by Douglas Husak.[31] He is concerned with the degree of blameworthiness that advocates of narrow tracing assign to agents for unwitting wrongful acts committed as a result of some prior benighting act. (Husak focuses on cases in which the benighting "act" is a failure to inquire into the lawfulness of the behavior in which one eventually engages, but his concern has general application.) Husak asks us to compare two agents, whom I will call Wendy and Nathan. They both commit wrongful acts of the same kind, but, whereas Wendy does so wittingly, Nathan does so unwittingly as a result of some prior benighting act. Suppose that Wendy is blameworthy to degree 10 for

[31] Husak (2016), pp. 184 ff.

her wrongful act. What guarantee is there, Husak asks, that Nathan will likewise be blameworthy to degree 10 for *his* unwrongful act? If his blameworthiness for this act is to be traced to his blameworthiness for the prior benighting act, why assume that he will be blameworthy to degree 10 for that act? Isn't it on the contrary likely that he will only be blameworthy to a lesser degree for it, in virtue of the fact that in committing it he at best merely *risked* committing the later wrongful act? Suppose, then, that he was merely blameworthy to degree 5 for his benighting act. What reason could there then be to declare him blameworthy to degree 10 for his unwitting wrongful act?

Husak raises his objection in the context of a discussion of ignorance of law, and he directs it toward those who hold the view that agents such as Wendy and Nathan should be punished equally for their equally wrongful acts. He is surely right to question this view, but it's important to note that advocates of narrow tracing aren't committed to it. Certainly there is no reason to think that, if Wendy is blameworthy to degree 10 for her wrongful act, then Nathan must also be blameworthy to degree 10 for his. If, indeed, Nathan is only blameworthy to degree 5 for his benighting act, then, given my position on moral luck, I would say that he is also only blameworthy to degree 5 for the wrongful act that he committed as a result. Of course, a proponent of moral luck might want to say that Nathan is blameworthy to some higher degree for what transpired, but once again there is no need to think that his degree of blameworthiness must match Wendy's.

A second objection to narrow tracing has been raised by Craig Agule. It has to do with certain instances of what he calls Odysseus cases.[32] As the name implies, an Odysseus case is a case in which one incapacitates oneself in order to achieve some goal. The special sort of Odysseus case on which Agule focuses has the following features: first, in incapacitating oneself, one knowingly runs the risk of later committing some wrongdoing while one is incapacitated; second, one is not to blame for running this risk; and third, one commits the later wrongdoing. For example, one might justifiably consent to being anesthetized in order to undergo some necessary surgery, knowing that there is a risk of later committing some wrong (such as mistreating the nursing staff) while slowly emerging from the grip of the anesthetic, a risk that unfortunately turns out to be realized. Agule claims that in such a case one is not to blame for the wrongdoing that one commits while incapacitated, and yet the proponent of narrow tracing is committed to saying that one is to blame for this wrongdoing, since it was a foreseeable upshot of earlier behavior for which one is responsible.

This objection is mistaken. For the sake of argument, let's grant that one is morally responsible for incapacitating oneself. Then the proponent of tracing (whether narrow or broad) presumably is committed to saying that one is also

---

[32] Agule (2016).

morally responsible for one's later wrongdoing, since it was a foreseeable upshot of earlier behavior for which one is morally responsible. But recall from §2.1.1 that moral responsibility needn't take the particular form of blameworthiness. Even if the proponent of tracing agrees that one is responsible for one's later wrongdoing, he or she is surely not committed to saying that one is to *blame* for that wrongdoing, precisely because one is not to blame for the earlier behavior that led to it. On the contrary, an Odysseus case of this sort is just another case in which one has an excuse for doing something wrong. Indirect blameworthiness presupposes direct *blameworthiness*. If there is no direct blameworthiness for one's deciding to incapacitate oneself, then the proponent of narrow tracing can agree that there is indeed no indirect blameworthiness for any consequence of this decision (unless this consequence is also a consequence of something else for which one is to blame), whether or not such a consequence is itself an instance of wrongdoing.

Agule holds (incorrectly, as I have just argued) that invoking narrow tracing can lead to the mistake of declaring blameless agents blameworthy. Others have held that it can lead to the mistake of declaring blameworthy agents blameless. Manuel Vargas, in an article entitled "The Trouble with Tracing," offers a number of cases in support of this claim.[33] One such case involves a jerk called Jeff, whom Vargas describes as rude and inconsiderate about the feelings of others, but also as being unreflective about this moral failing, one that originated in a crucial formative period during Jeff's adolescence. When he was 15 years old, Jeff came to the realization that girls found him unattractive. In the belief that girls were only attracted to boys who exhibited what is in fact (although he didn't understand it to be) jerk-like behavior, Jeff deliberately undertook to become the sort of person who behaves in this way, and he succeeded in doing so with surprisingly little effort. Many years later it transpired that, as a middle-aged manager at a mid-sized company and with his jerk-like attitudes and habits deeply ingrained in his character, Jeff was faced with the task of laying off workers in order for the company to remain solvent. He went about doing so in his usual manner—rudely, inconsiderately, but unreflectively. Vargas claims that Jeff is to blame for firing the employees in the way he did, despite the fact that, having acted unreflectively, he was unaware at the time that it was wrong of him to do so. Moreover, Vargas says, Jeff's blameworthiness for this behavior cannot be traced to his blameworthiness for some prior piece of behavior at some suitable prior time, since the only time at which he exercised control over his developing into a jerk was a time at which he could not have foreseen that he would or might well treat his employees as he did.

John Martin Fischer and Neal Tognazzini, who are proponents of narrow tracing, agree with Vargas that Jeff is to blame for his later behavior, but they deny that tracing cannot account for this.[34] They point out that there are various

---

[33] Vargas (2005).   [34] Fischer and Tognazzini (2009).

ways in which the regrettable outcome of Jeff's hapless attempt to render himself attractive to girls might be characterized, among which are:

(Outcome 1) Jeff fires *those* employees who work for *that* company on *that* precise day in *that* precise manner.
(Outcome 2) Jeff fires some of his employees at some company or other at some point in the future in a despicable manner as a result of his jerky character.
(Outcome 3) Jeff treats some people poorly at some point in the future as a result of his jerky character.

And they claim that, the broader the characterization, the more plausible it is to think that Jeff could, even at 15 years old, have foreseen that he would or might well behave in the manner described. They conclude:

> We suggest that all tracing requires in this case is that Jeff could have reasonably foreseen Outcome 3 at the time he decides to acquire a jerky character. Why do we hold Jeff responsible for unreflectively firing his employees in such a despicable manner? We hold him responsible partly because he freely decided to become a jerk at some point in the past, and it is reasonable to expect Jeff's younger self to have known that becoming a jerk would in all probability lead him to perform jerky actions. Need Jeff have known that his becoming a jerk would specifically lead to the firing of *those particular employees* on *that particular day* in the future in order to be morally responsible for firing them in the way he did? Surely not. Need Jeff have known that he would fire *some employees* at *some point* in the future in order to be morally responsible for firing them when he did? Again, this would likely set the epistemic bar too high... When you choose to be a jerk, you can be held accountable for your subsequent specific acts of jerkiness—but you might not know in advance what they will be in all their particular glory![35]

This response seems to me quite right—as far as it goes; I would of course want to apply the Argument from Ignorance to Jeff's case as to any other, and if Jeff was not only unaware that he was acting wrongly when firing his employees as he did but also unaware that he was acting wrongly when undertaking to reform his character as he did, then I would conclude that Jeff is *not* to blame for either bits of behavior (unless some other relevant witting wrongdoing occurred yet further back in his history). The approach adopted by Fischer and Tognazzini is the same as that which I mentioned earlier when discussing the possibility of some of

---

[35] Fischer and Tognazzini (2009), p. 538.

Grünenthal's employees being to blame for the condition of Sally's child, even though they could not have known anything about Sally and her child in particular. (It's worth noting, though, that, in their response to Vargas, Fischer and Tognazzini pay no heed to the complication posed by the "problem of the vicinity.")

In an article entitled "More Trouble with Tracing," Seth Shabo has argued that, even if the response by Fischer and Tognazzini succeeds in disposing of Vargas's case about Jeff, there are similar cases that are impervious to this response. He asks us to consider the case of Greg who, like Jeff, is insensitive to the needs and interests of others, but whose insensitivity is the result, not of his ever having decided to become, or even to try to become, this way, but rather of his instinctively emulating the mannerisms of his socially dominant classmates, in virtue of which he came to regard others as falling into one of two classes, "big shots" and "nobodies." When asked to compile and submit a report to his company's board on which employees' positions should be eliminated, Greg does so in a manner that is typical, showing profound insensitivity to the "nobodies" involved. Shabo states:

> We ... have good reason to view Greg as blameworthy; his conduct, like Jeff's, is reprehensible, evincing a moral defect that grew out of his free, formative actions and habits.[36]

Shabo recognizes that in Greg's case there is an outcome similar to Outcome 3 in Jeff's case, namely:

> (Outcome 4) Greg imposes needless hardship on others at some point in the future, in part because of his indifference to the needs and interests of perceived social inferiors.[37]

But Shabo denies that this outcome was foreseeable by Greg at any point in his history, since, contrary to Jeff's case, there was no particular time at which the risk of this outcome should have been salient to Greg. Shabo maintains that Greg is nonetheless to blame for this outcome, even though it was unforeseeable, since it resulted from his failure to cultivate greater sensitivity to the needs and interests of others, something that he should have recognized he had an obligation to do.

In my view, Shabo's claim that Greg is to blame for Outcome 4 is unfounded. Even if it's true that Greg ought to have recognized the need to cultivate greater sensitivity to others rather than emulate the mannerisms of his classmates, he is not to blame for failing to do this, if, as is implicit in Shabo's description of the

---

[36] Shabo (2015), p. 997. [37] Shabo (2015), p. 997.

case, he was unaware of the wrongness of this failure (and this failure cannot itself be traced to some prior witting wrongdoing). This is the verdict of the Argument from Ignorance, and I see no reason to reject it. (That is perhaps stated too boldly. For further discussion, see Chapter 9.) More to the present point, however, it would be a mistake to think that either Vargas or Shabo has raised a problem with the strategy of tracing responsibility, despite what the titles of their articles might be thought to imply. What they have raised doubts about is the view that blameworthiness for some outcome requires the foreseeability of that outcome. Vargas doesn't draw a distinction between direct and indirect blameworthiness; he simply declares Jeff blameworthy for the way in which he treated his company's employees. Since he does not draw this distinction, he has done nothing to impugn it. He has at best shown it to be a mistake to invoke it when trying to account for Jeff's blameworthiness. Shabo does draw this distinction; he explicitly claims that Greg is indirectly blameworthy (Shabo says "derivatively blameworthy") for the way in which he treated his company's employees. In saying this, he is presumably committed to claiming that Greg's blameworthiness for this behavior *is* to be traced to some earlier event for which he is blameworthy, namely, his failure to recognize the need to become more sensitive to the needs and interests of others. Shabo seems to deny this; he claims that cases like Greg's involve "*untraceable* responsibility transmissions."[38] He uses this phrase because he denies that in such cases there is any particular time to which responsibility can be traced back. But this seems to me highly misleading. If Greg's alleged blameworthiness for the way in which he treated his company's employees is indeed indirect (derivative), then it *must* be traceable to his direct blameworthiness for something else. This, I take it, is a *conceptual* truth.[39] Shabo himself identifies the something else in question: Greg's omission to cultivate greater sensitivity to the needs and interests of others. Now, it can admittedly be very difficult to specify just when it is that an omission occurs (although it is of course the case that, if an omission occurs, it occurs at some time or times). In Greg's case, there is likely no single time that can be identified as *the* time at which it occurred. Even so, if this omission is to play the role of that for which Greg is directly blameworthy and in virtue of which he is indirectly blameworthy for his treatment of his company's employees, then, far from being refuted, the propriety of appealing to tracing is confirmed.

5.2 Exculpatory culpable ignorance

According to the Argument from Ignorance, and in the terminology introduced by Smith, one is to blame for an unwitting wrongful act (and its

---

[38] Shabo (2015), p. 1009.
[39] As I said at the outset of §5.1.1, Premise 8 of the Argument from Ignorance is *definitionally* true.

consequences) *only if* one is to blame for the ignorance that underlay it, and one is to blame for this ignorance only if one is to blame for the benighting act that led to it. This proposition only tells us when one *isn't* to blame for an unwitting wrongful act—one isn't to blame for it when the ignorance that underlay it was excusable; it doesn't tell us when one *is* to blame for an unwitting wrongful act. I think many would find it plausible to supplement this proposition with the further proposition that one is to blame for one's unwitting wrongful act *if* it was a foreseeable consequence of the ignorance that underlay it, and this ignorance was a foreseeable consequence of the benighting act that led to it, and one is to blame for that benighting act.[40] Combined, these propositions entail the thesis that excusable ignorance provides an excuse for an unwitting wrongful act, but inexcusable ignorance may not. (I say "may not" rather than "does not," since in some perhaps hard-to-imagine cases the unwitting wrongful act may not be a foreseeable consequence of the ignorance in question.) In this section I will distinguish between two interpretations of this thesis and argue that, although it is acceptable on one of these interpretations, it is unacceptable on the other.

5.2.1 Does ignorance of wrongdoing ever provide an excuse for wrongdoing?

I have repeatedly characterized the Argument from Ignorance as implying that ignorance of wrongdoing provides an excuse for wrongdoing far more often than is commonly thought. Yet if only *excusable* ignorance provides such an excuse, isn't it strictly false to say simply that ignorance *itself* can do so?

In response, let me make two observations.

First, even if it is the case that an excuse stemming from ignorance is in the offing only when the ignorance in question is itself excusable, it seems to me not seriously misleading to say that it is the ignorance that, under those conditions, provides the excuse. The situation here is in some respects similar to a situation in which we say that a short circuit caused a fire, even though we understand that there would have been no fire if the short circuit had occurred under different conditions (lack of oxygen, lack of flammable material, etc.).

Second, as I have just noted and will shortly argue, although the claim that only excusable ignorance provides an excuse for wrongdoing is indeed true on one interpretation, it is false on another. That is, on one interpretation, even inexcusable ignorance of wrongdoing provides an excuse for wrongdoing. On this

---

[40] This further proposition presumably needs qualification in light of the remarks made in §5.1.3 about some consequences encompassing others and about a vicinity of consequences. Consider such qualification implicit in what follows.

interpretation, the claim that ignorance of wrongdoing provides such an excuse is true without qualification.

5.2.2 The shadow cast by the benighting act

Return to the case of DOT AND PAT, and now imagine that the medication she gave him—call it *M2*—was, though quite effective in treating his condition, nonetheless inferior to another medication, *M1*, that could have been used instead. Then, given certain background assumptions, Dot's giving Pat *M2* instead of *M1* constitutes wrongdoing on her part. But suppose that she was unaware that this was the case, because she was unaware that *M1* was superior to *M2*. Does she have an excuse for treating Pat as she did?

On the view that only excusable ignorance excuses, the answer to this question will be: Perhaps, but only if Dot has an excuse for her ignorance. Suppose now that her ignorance stemmed from her failure to read a medical journal that she had not only a professional but also a moral obligation to read. Had she read this journal as she ought to have done, she would have learned that *M1* was superior to *M2* in cases such as Pat's and she would then not have committed the unwitting wrongdoing of giving him *M2*. Her decision not to read the journal thus constituted a benighting act, for which she might well be to blame. If she is to blame for it, and if her subsequent ignorance and unwitting wrongful act were foreseeable consequences of it, then, it is plausible to think, Dot is indeed to blame for giving Pat *M2* rather than *M1*.

It's important to note that there are other ways in which Dot's failure to read the journal could have led to her giving Pat *M2* rather than *M1*. Suppose that delivering *M1* to one's patient requires mastering a certain technique, which Dot of course didn't master but could and would have mastered if she had read the journal. Then her giving *M1* to Pat wasn't something that was, at the time at which she treated him, within her intentional control, and perhaps it wasn't even in her simple control. (On the distinction between simple and intentional control, see §4.1.6.) In this case, there is strong pressure to say that Dot's giving Pat *M2* rather than *M1 wasn't* wrong; since she hadn't mastered the requisite technique, giving him *M2* was the best that she could have done under the circumstances. If so, describing her behavior as an unwitting *wrongful* act is a mistake.[41] Even so, if this behavior was a foreseeable consequence of her benighting act, then it is something for which she would seem to be to blame. It might even have happened that, shortly before her treatment of Pat, Dot had learned of the superiority of *M1* but

---

[41] Cf. H. M. Smith (1983), p. 552, and (2017), p. 97. I would want to qualify this claim and say that Dot's giving Pat *M2* wasn't *immediately* wrong, though it may well have been *remotely* wrong. This is a subtlety that needn't detain us here. For discussion, see Zimmerman (1996), pp. 96 ff., and (2008), pp. 151 ff.

hadn't had time to master the technique required for its delivery. Then describing her giving Pat *M2* rather than *M1* as *unwitting* is also a mistake. Even so, if her doing so was a foreseeable consequence of her earlier benighting act, then her being blameworthy for this benighting act would seem to render her blameworthy for giving Pat *M2* rather than *M1*.

To hold Dot blameworthy for her treatment of Pat in virtue of her being blameworthy for her decision not to read the medical journal is of course to hold her *indirectly* blameworthy for this treatment. It is a separate question whether she is *directly* to blame for it (or, more particularly, for her decision to treat Pat in this way). There is surely very good reason to hold that Pat is *not* directly blameworthy for this. After all, she didn't believe that it was wrong to treat Pat in this way; on the contrary, she believed that it would have been wrong *not* to treat him in this way. The quality of will that informed her decision was thus above reproach.[42] There is therefore no reason to hold that there was a *fresh* incurrence of blameworthiness by Dot at the time she treated Pat beyond the blameworthiness that she had *already* incurred at the time she decided not to read the journal. Indeed, there is very good reason to deny that this is so, for notice that the case could be developed in such a way that Dot was positively *praiseworthy* for her treatment of Pat. Imagine, for example, that Pat was impoverished and that *M2* was very expensive; Dot knew that Pat couldn't afford the medication and, going well beyond the call of duty, decided to pay for it out of her own pocket.

It's important to note, as Smith herself has recently pointed out,[43] that the denial that Dot is directly to blame for her decision to give Pat *M2* rather than *M1* is *not* grounded in the denial of moral luck. Those who, unlike myself, accept the possibility of moral luck should agree that Dot was not *directly* blameworthy for her decision to treat Pat. What they may claim (and what I deny) is that this decision adds to the degree of blameworthiness incurred by Dot for her *earlier* decision not to read the journal.

Consider now the two interpretations of the thesis that excusable ignorance of wrongdoing provides an excuse for wrongdoing, but inexcusable ignorance may not. If one is not to blame for the ignorance that underlay one's wrongdoing, then one will not be to blame for this wrongdoing, either directly or indirectly (given that the act was not a foreseeable consequence of something else for which one is to blame). Thus excusable ignorance of wrongdoing does indeed provide an excuse for wrongdoing. However, if one is to blame for the ignorance that underlay one's wrongdoing, then, although (first interpretation) one may be *indirectly* to blame for this wrongdoing, nonetheless (second interpretation) one won't be *directly* to blame for it.

---

[42] Cf. H. M. Smith (1983), p. 559.   [43] H. M. Smith (2017), pp. 108 ff.

5.2.3 Inculpatory ignorance

I have just argued that there is a sense in which *all* ignorance exculpates. Yet it is often claimed that ignorance, far from being exculpatory, can *inculpate* an agent. If so, then my argument might seem mistaken.

Consider the case of BILL AND THE BIRD. Bill took a shot at Jill and missed. Clearly he is not to blame for killing Jill, because he didn't kill her. Nonetheless, he may well be to blame for his attempt on her life, and what partly explains his making this attempt is his mistaken belief that nothing would foil it. Some would say that his ignorance was inculpatory rather than exculpatory,[44] *even though* it itself was not something for which he is to blame.

Such cases pose no problem for my argument. I think that it's in fact a mistake to describe Bill's ignorance as inculpatory. *That* is not the basis of his being to blame. On the contrary, on the assumption that he is to blame, what rendered him blameworthy was his awareness of the wrongness of killing Jill, or even attempting to kill her, coupled with his having been in control of his attempt. But even if I'm wrong about this and we should say that Bill's ignorance inculpates him, my position is not threatened. My claim is that it is *ignorance of the fact that one is doing something morally wrong* that provides one with an excuse for wrongdoing. By hypothesis, Bill was *not* ignorant of this fact—his ignorance lay elsewhere—and so I am not committed to saying that he has an excuse for his behavior.

There are other kinds of cases, however, in which I think it comes closer to the truth to say that one's ignorance regarding wrongdoing can indeed be inculpatory rather than exculpatory. In §3.4.1, I argued for the possibility of what I called accuses, which consist in one's being to blame, despite not having done anything wrong, because one engaged in behavior that one *believed* to be wrong (and over which one exercised the requisite control). If such cases are indeed possible, then what renders one blameworthy is (in part) one's mistaken belief. Even in such cases, though, I find it misleading to say that it is one's ignorance that renders one blameworthy, since this suggests that it is the *falsity* of one's belief rather than the belief *itself* that is the basis of one's blameworthiness. Of course, if accuses are possible, then, as I noted in §3.4.1 when moving from Draft 4 to Draft 5 of the Argument from Ignorance, we shouldn't say, as I just did in the last paragraph, that it is *ignorance of the fact* that one is doing something morally wrong that provides one with *an excuse for wrongdoing*. Rather, what we should say is that it is *the failure to believe* that one is doing something morally wrong that renders one *blameless for one's behavior*, regardless of whether that behavior is in fact wrong.

---

[44] Cf. Alexander (1993) and (2017).

6
Negligence

In Chapter 1, I claimed that the Origination Thesis threatens to undermine all charges of negligence. In this chapter I explain why that is so.

In §6.1 I investigate the nature of negligence. I present the *Model Penal Code*'s well-known definition of negligence and explain why, when the issue is that of moral, rather than legal, responsibility for negligent behavior, this definition needs considerable modification. According to the definition I propose in its place, negligent behavior is wrongful behavior to whose wrongfulness the agent does not, but in some sense ought to, advert. Given that such inadvertence entails that the wrongdoing is committed unwittingly, the Argument from Ignorance has the implication that no one can be directly blameworthy for negligent behavior (unless this behavior is committed merely in, rather than from, inadvertence).

In §6.2 I investigate whether the implication just mentioned can be resisted, either on the grounds that inadvertence does not entail unwittingness, or on the grounds that direct blameworthiness can be properly ascribed to someone simply in virtue of the fact that he or she ought to have known better than to behave as he or she did. Regarding the first possibility, I acknowledge that inadvertence does not in general entail unwittingness, since one may lack an occurrent belief that one is doing something while nonetheless having a dispositional belief that one is doing it. Nonetheless, I argue that, in the particular case of negligent behavior, there is good reason to say that the agent does indeed fail to believe that his or her behavior is wrong. I also argue that, even if I am mistaken about this, the Argument from Ignorance can be recast in terms of occurrent belief in particular, thus preserving the conclusion that no one can be directly blameworthy for negligent behavior. Regarding the second possibility, I point out that, if the claim that someone ought to have known better than to behave as he or she did is understood as the claim that his or her ignorance is to be attributed to wrongdoing on his or her part, then, even if it is correct, it cannot suffice to establish that person's being to blame for what has occurred, since an excuse may be in the offing. I recognize, however, that the claim may be open to a different interpretation, discussion of which I postpone to Chapter 9.

6.1 Inadvertent wrongdoing

Among philosophers, it is for the most part philosophers of law who have been especially concerned with responsibility for negligent behavior. Their immediate concern has of course been with legal responsibility for such behavior (although many of them have also been concerned, whether explicitly or only implicitly, with moral responsibility for such behavior, on the grounds that such responsibility is necessary if the imposition of legal responsibility is to be morally justified[1]). In many cases, their discussions have focused on the definition of negligence given in the *Model Penal Code*, which goes as follows:

> A person acts negligently with respect to a material element of an offense when he should be aware of a substantial and unjustifiable risk that the material element exists or will result from his conduct. The risk must be of such a nature and degree that the actor's failure to perceive it, considering the nature and purpose of his conduct and the circumstances known to him, involves a gross deviation from the standard of care that a reasonable person would observe in the actor's situation.[2]

According to this definition, negligence has to do with risks of which one is unaware. Strictly, the first sentence of the definition does not imply this; for it could be that one *is* aware of that of which one should be aware. However, in focusing on the actor's failure to perceive the relevant risk, the second sentence makes it clear that the *Code* is indeed concerned with risks that are run *inadvertently*. Further confirmation of this is the fact that, immediately prior to its definition of negligence, the *Code* provides a definition of recklessness which, in contrast to negligence, it claims to involve *consciously* disregarding a substantial and unjustifiable risk. Some commentators reject this approach, claiming that it is possible for negligence to be conscious or advertent.[3] This is an issue that I will take up in the next chapter. In this chapter my concern is with behavior that involves risks to which one does not advert.

Although the *Code*'s definition of negligence perhaps suffices for purposes of the law, there are a number of problems with it when the issue of direct concern is whether and how one might be *morally* responsible for negligent behavior.

First, the *Code*'s definition is restricted to cases involving some "material element of an offense." It is of course with legal offenses that the Code is concerned, and "material element" refers to some harm or evil that the law

---

[1] See, e.g., Husak (2016), p. 36. Husak is in particular concerned with the criminal law. The relation between moral responsibility and legal responsibility in other areas of the law is perhaps not so straightforward.
[2] American Law Institute (1985), §2.02(2)(d).
[3] See, e.g., Hart (1968), pp. 137 and 259 f.; Brady (1996); Moore and Hurd (2011); Duff (2019).

seeks to prevent.[4] Whether one is morally responsible for negligent behavior is, however, a question that arises in non-legal as well as legal contexts, and so for present purposes this restriction in the *Code*'s definition should be lifted.

Second, the *Code* specifies that the relevant risk must be "substantial and unjustifiable." It's not clear to me just what work "substantial" is supposed to do here, but for our purposes it can and should be dropped. No doubt some risks are relatively high or substantial (and thus such that, as I put it in Chapter 1 and again in §5.1.3, they "might well" be realized), whereas others are relatively low or insubstantial. And no doubt, too, the higher the risk, the harder it is to justify running it. Nonetheless, from a moral point of view, it's clear that it is sometimes unjustifiable to run a risk that doesn't warrant being called substantial (and clear, too, that it is sometimes justifiable to run a risk that does warrant being called substantial). It is therefore a mistake to think that an insubstantial risk may be automatically dismissed as negligible or insignificant.

As a possible example of unjustifiably running a minor risk, consider again the case provided by Randolph Clarke that I cited in §4.2.1:

> [A]s I'm about to leave my office at the end of the workday, my wife calls to tell me that we're out of milk. My regular route home takes me right by a grocery store, and I tell her I'll stop and buy some. Between my office and the store, I start to think about a paper I'm writing on omissions. I continue to think about my work until I arrive home, where I realize that I've forgotten the milk.[5]

Clarke characterizes his failure to pick up milk as not being a "big deal," and that seems right. Nonetheless, he takes it to be wrongful behavior for which he is to blame. Some negligent behavior can be a very big deal, of course. As a possible example of such negligence, consider Ian's inadvertently leaving his two-year-old daughter, Emma, locked in a hot car for several hours with the windows closed, as a result of which the poor girl dies of hyperthermia. Such cases, which occur with alarming frequency, have recently garnered considerable attention.[6] Clearly, the seriousness of negligent behavior can vary between these extremes as well. Moreover, it can involve overt action rather than mere omission. As a possible example of not-so-seriously negligent action, consider a barber's absent-mindedly cutting your hair much shorter than you had requested. As a possible example of seriously negligent action, consider a surgeon's absent-mindedly operating on the wrong knee.

I have said that it's clear that it is sometimes morally unjustifiable to run certain risks, but here I should once again acknowledge the complication that some

---

[4] American Law Institute (1985), §1.13(10).   [5] Clarke (2014), p. 164.
[6] See Weingarten (2009), Husak (2011), Moore and Hurd (2011), H. M. Smith (2011), Talbert (2013), and Clarke (2017a) for discussion.

philosophers, in subscribing to an objective view of moral obligation, would balk at this claim. As I noted in §2.1.2, an objective view of moral obligation holds that one's obligations—and hence, by implication, what it is morally justifiable or unjustifiable for one to do—turn on what would *in fact* happen if one were to make one choice rather than another, *regardless* of whatever risks one might run in making this choice. On this view, whether one runs a risk of harm or evil is irrelevant to whether one is acting justifiably, as long as the risk is not realized.[7] Proponents of this view would thus claim that Clarke would have done nothing wrong, had it turned out that there was milk at home after all; that Ian would have done nothing wrong, had Emma miraculously not been harmed; that the barber and the surgeon would have done nothing wrong, had their inattentiveness not resulted in a mishap. This verdict may initially seem reasonable in the not-so-serious cases of the milk and the haircut, but I submit that it is patently false in the far more serious cases of the knee and the child, and parity of approach requires that we therefore reject it in the not-so-serious cases, too. The view that best captures these verdicts is, I believe, the view that one's moral obligations turn on the *evidence* that one has, at the time at which one makes one's choice, about the various possible outcomes of making that choice. On this view, one's moral obligation is in every case, not to do what would in fact turn out best, but rather to choose that option that constitutes one's "*best bet*," morally speaking, given one's epistemic circumstances and the options one faces—the option that it would be *most reasonable* to choose, were one motivated solely by moral conscientiousness. This is to put the point only very roughly, but I think it will suffice for present purposes.[8] We may assume that, in all the examples just given, it was the agent's best bet not to engage in the behavior in which he or she engaged, regardless of how things actually turned out; the behavior was too risky, irrespective of outcome. (It's worth noting that the failure to do what is one's best bet under the circumstances is not always a matter of doing something that is unduly risky; on some occasions it is a matter of doing something unduly cautious.[9])

A third problem with the *Model Penal Code*'s definition is that it measures negligence according to the standard of care that a "reasonable person" would observe in the situation in question. As I noted in §5.1.3, however, whatever reason there might be for the law to adopt such a standard, it is not a standard that we should adopt when trying to assess someone's moral blameworthiness, since one can blamelessly fall short of it. This observation might make the determination of blameworthiness for negligent behavior more difficult, since it requires a prior determination of which standard applies to the person being

---

[7] It might be suggested that running a risk of harm itself constitutes a kind of harm, so that even an objectivist can acknowledge risk-running as wrong-making. I think this suggestion cannot succeed, but I won't pursue the matter here. For discussion, see Thomson (1990), p. 244.

[8] I have developed and defended this view in detail in Zimmerman (2014).

[9] See Zimmerman (2014), p. 34.

assessed, but by itself it doesn't undermine such an undertaking. Even if the standard of care that applies to one person is not necessarily the standard that applies to another in the same situation, it remains perfectly sensible to say that someone has not met the standard that does in fact apply to him or her under the circumstances.

Fourth, however, there is a question about what the standard in question is supposed to be a standard of, for "care" can be construed in two different ways. On one understanding, it has to do with the *concern* that one shows, or fails to show, for those potentially affected (whether people, animals, or other objects of value) by one's behavior. On this understanding, it is, I think, simply false to say that negligent behavior must involve a deficit of care. It might, of course, but it might not. Some writers deny this, holding that inadvertence to a risk of harm to those potentially affected by one's behavior could only arise as a result of insufficient concern for their welfare.[10] But surely there can be extenuating circumstances, such as a catastrophe or an emergency, that can occasion such inadvertence even when one has sufficient concern for others' welfare. And even when such circumstances don't obtain, it seems clear that inadvertence need not be occasioned by insufficient concern, even in the most serious cases.[11] On another understanding, care has to do with the *attention* that one pays, or fails to pay, to one's behavior and its potential consequences. On this understanding, it is indeed true, but only trivially so, that negligent behavior must involve a deficit of care. The *Code* is concerned with risks of which one is not aware (that is, to which one pays no attention) but should be aware. In such cases, one's lack of awareness is perforce substandard. (On this understanding of a standard of care, however, it is difficult to make sense of what the *Code* might mean by a "gross deviation" from the standard. Although, as I noted in §3.2.3, it seems correct to say that awareness comes in degrees—one can be "fully" aware of some risks, for example, while only being "dimly" aware of others—it of course doesn't follow that unawareness also comes in degrees. And surely it doesn't. There are no degrees of paying no attention to something.[12])

Fifth, the *Code* doesn't specify what kind of standard it is that one's inadvertence fails to meet when one behaves negligently. If, as here, what is at issue is *moral* responsibility for negligent behavior, then the standard must presumably be a *moral* standard. But even then it's not clear what might be meant by saying that one should (or ought to) be aware of a risk of which one is unaware. There are two possibilities. If this is construed as a deontic judgment, the claim is that one's inadvertence constitutes, or is to be attributed to, some moral wrongdoing that

---

[10] See, e.g., Duff (1990), p. 163, and Husak (2011), p. 203.
[11] For discussion, see Weingarten (2009); King (2009), pp. 584 f.; H. M. Smith (2011), p. 119; Talbert (2011), pp. 150 f., and (2013), pp. 235 f.; Watson (2016), p. 399.
[12] Cf. Turner (1936), p. 40.

one is committing or has committed. If the judgment is construed as non-deontic (aretaic, perhaps), the claim is that one's inadvertence is morally deficient in a way that does not necessarily involve wrongdoing on one's part. I will explore each of these possibilities below. (On the distinction between deontic and other kinds of moral judgment, see §2.1.4.) For now, I will simply say that the inadvertence in question is to be understood as being morally substandard.

Finally, there is the question of just what it is that one fails to advert to when one behaves negligently. The *Code* is expressly concerned with one's inadvertence to some *risk*, and that is of course perfectly appropriate. But, as I noted in Chapter 1 when I introduced the character of Heinrich, the question of whether one is morally to blame for running a risk has to do, at bottom, with one's inadvertence to the *wrongness* of running that risk.[13]

In light of the foregoing observations, I propose that we replace the *Model Penal Code*'s definition of negligence with the following: one behaves negligently just in case (1) one's behavior is morally wrong,[14] (2) one does not advert, at the time at which one engages in it, to the moral wrongness of one's behavior, and (3) one's failure to advert to the moral wrongness of one's behavior is itself morally substandard. Note the following points.

First, unlike some other accounts of negligence, my definition does not imply that negligent behavior is behavior for which one is to blame (or so it seems—see §9.1.3 for discussion).[15] Nor does it imply that it is behavior for which one is not to blame. It is intended to leave the question open. My purpose in this chapter is to explore this question.

Second, my definition does of course imply that negligent behavior is behavior that is morally wrong. It thus implies that, even if one might have an excuse for negligent behavior, one cannot have an accuse for such behavior, since accuses, if possible at all, involve blameworthiness in the *absence* of wrongdoing. (See §3.4.1 for discussion.) Perhaps the definition should be amended in this respect, but I won't pursue the matter. I take the primary reason for thinking that accuses are possible is that it's possible deliberately to do something that one mistakenly believes to be morally wrong. On my account, negligent behavior cannot fit this description (or so it seems—see §6.2.1 for further discussion).

Third, the wrongful behavior in question may take the form either of action, strictly speaking, or of omission. Clarke's failure to pick up milk and Ian's failure to remove Emma from the car are omissions, but if a surgeon negligently operates on the wrong knee, the operation itself does not constitute an omission (although,

---

[13] Contrast Moore and Hurd (2011), pp. 152 f.   [14] That is, *overall* morally wrong. See §2.1.2.
[15] Contrast, e.g., Sverdlik (1993), p. 137; Clarke (2014), p. 160. (Joseph Raz maintains that it is a conceptual truth that negligent behavior is behavior for which one is responsible—see Raz (2011), p. 260—but in this context he does not take "responsible" to mean the same as "blameworthy.")

in performing this operation, the surgeon does of course omit to operate on the right knee—which might be the left knee, remember).

Fourth, on the understanding that wrongful behavior consists in failing to do what is one's "best bet," my definition accommodates the fact that one can behave negligently even if the risk that one is running isn't realized. Strictly speaking, the definition doesn't require that negligent behavior involve wrongly running a risk, since, as noted above, failure to do what is one's best bet may involve behaving in a manner that is unduly cautious rather than unduly risky. Perhaps the definition should be amended in this respect, too, but again I won't pursue the point. My underlying concern is with blameworthiness for inadvertent wrongdoing in general, regardless of whether the wrongdoing consists in behavior that is unduly risky.

Finally, although my definition doesn't explicitly address the issue, I think it's safe to say that it implies that all negligence involves omission. That's because it implies that all negligence involves wrongdoing and, as I see it (although the matter is controversial), all wrongdoing involves omission—the omission to do the right thing. This omission may in some cases be accomplished by virtue of performing some act, such as the act of cutting hair too short or performing surgery on the wrong knee, but in other cases it may not. Was there any particular act by virtue of which Clarke omitted to pick up milk or by virtue of which Ian omitted to remove Emma from the car? That seems doubtful, but the matter is difficult. Another difficult question is whether the substandard inadvertence involved in negligent behavior must itself involve an omission. If the inadvertence constitutes, or is to be attributed to, wrongdoing, then once again I take the answer to be that it must; but if the inadvertence is substandard in some other way, perhaps it needn't involve an omission. I say this because I take it that one has omitted to do something only if one had the specific ability to do that thing,[16] and that, whereas wrongdoing satisfies this requirement, other forms of moral deficiency might not. Once again, though, there is fortunately no need to settle this matter here.

I am now in a position to explain why it is that the Origination Thesis threatens to undermine all charges of negligence, by which I mean all claims that someone is *to blame* for having behaved negligently. The explanation is straightforward. Given that, when acting negligently, one fails to believe that one's behavior is morally wrong, the Origination Thesis implies that blameworthiness for negligent behavior is in every case to be traced to blameworthiness for some other piece of behavior that one did believe to be morally wrong (unless the negligent behavior is performed *merely* in ignorance of the fact that it is wrong). This rules out all blameworthiness for what, following Steven Sverdlik, we may call "pure"

---

[16] Cf. Clarke (2014), p. 90.

negligence, that is, negligent behavior blameworthiness for which is *not* to be traced to some prior benighting act.[17] Of course, it doesn't rule out blameworthiness for "impure" negligence, where such tracing can be carried out, but even in such cases a charge of negligence is, as I noted in Chapter 1, misleading, inasmuch as it should be replaced with the more perspicuous charge of recklessness, a charge that applies, moreover, not to the negligent behavior itself, but to the benighting act that generated it.[18]

6.2 Morally substandard inadvertence

It is natural that the revisionary implications regarding the propriety of charges of negligence that I have attributed to the Origination Thesis should meet with some resistance. There are two paths that such resistance might take.

6.2.1 Substandard inattention to what one already knows

Some writers reject the assumption that, when acting negligently, one fails to believe that one's behavior is morally wrong. They hold that typically, in cases of the sort we have been discussing, the agent *did* know better than to behave as he or she did. It's not the agent's *epistemic* state that was substandard; rather, what was substandard was the failure to *attend* to what he or she already knew. This position is based on the distinction, which I discussed in §3.2.2, between occurrent and dispositional belief. Since the agents in these cases don't advert to the fact that their behavior is morally wrong, they don't occurrently believe it to be so, but that is of course consistent with their dispositionally believing this. And if, as may seem likely, they do dispositionally believe this, then their wrongdoing, though inadvertent, is *not* unwitting. It would be astonishing if, for example, Ian didn't know that it was morally wrong to leave his daughter for hours on end locked in a hot car with the windows closed![19]

The view that the agents in these cases, and in others like them, do believe that their behavior is morally wrong, even if they don't advert to this fact, has some interesting implications. A relatively minor implication is that it opens up the possibility of accuses for such behavior. Another implication is that such behavior might properly be said to be reckless rather than, or in addition to, being negligent.[20] But by far the most important implication in this context is this:

---

[17] Sverdlik (1993), p. 141.　　[18] Cf. Moore and Hurd (2011), p. 180.
[19] For remarks along these lines, see Harman (2011), p. 450; Husak (2011), pp. 208 ff. and (2016), pp. 194 ff.; Amaya (2013), pp. 562 f.; Peels (2017), p. 194; and Biebel (2019), ch. 2.
[20] Cf. Husak (2011), pp. 208 ff.

even if the latest version (Draft 5) of the Origination Thesis is true, it doesn't rule out the possibility of one's being directly blameworthy for such behavior and thus doesn't threaten to undermine the ascriptions of blameworthiness that many find intuitively compelling.[21]

The distinction between occurrent and dispositional belief, though perhaps controversial in its details, is surely unassailable. Nonetheless, ascribing direct blameworthiness to agents for their behavior in cases of the sort under discussion, on the grounds that, when they engaged in it, they did know better than to behave as they did, is, I submit, a mistake. There are a number of reasons for thinking so.

First, it's not clear how a merely dispositional belief that one is doing something wrong could (along with the requisite control) ground blameworthiness in cases of this sort. This is a point I made in previous work, where I said:

> [W]hile beliefs presumably can be merely dispositional, it is, I suspect, occurrent beliefs about wrongdoing that are, with one possible exception, required for culpability; and such beliefs involve advertence. The reason is this. With one possible exception, if a belief is not occurrent, then one cannot act either with the intention to heed the belief or with the intention not to heed it; if one has no such intention, then one cannot act either deliberately on or deliberately despite the belief; if this is so, then the belief plays no role in the reason for which one performs one's action; and, I am inclined to think, one incurs culpability for one's action only if one's belief concerning wrongdoing plays a role in the reason for which one performs the action...
>
> The one possible exception is this: it may be that routine or habitual actions are performed for reasons to which one does not advert. It may also be that some people engage in deliberate wrongdoing in a routine or habitual, and hence inadvertent, manner. To the extent that this is so, the present considerations concerning advertence do not apply. But to the extent that this is not so, they do apply.[22]

My remarks in this passage have been criticized. Douglas Husak has pointed out that non-occurrent beliefs clearly can play a role in explaining why one does what one does. He gives the example of drinking water because one believes, non-occurrently, that doing so will quench one's thirst.[23] Rik Peels has made the same point with a different example.[24] They are surely quite right about this, and so part of what I said in the passage just quoted is plainly false—but only part. What's plainly false is, as they point out, the claim that one cannot act deliberately on a belief, if that belief is not occurrent; but this claim is in fact irrelevant in the present context (and thus not only one that I should not have made but one that

---

[21] Peels emphasizes this point in Peels (2017), pp. 193 ff. [22] Zimmerman (2008), p. 191.
[23] Husak (2016), p. 198. [24] Peels (2017), p. 195.

I need not have made). What matters for present purposes is whether one can do something deliberately *despite* the belief that it is wrong to do it, if that belief is not occurrent.

On one interpretation of this question, the answer is pretty obviously "Yes." (Compare the discussion of Saint Augustine in §2.5.4.) That interpretation is this: Can one do something deliberately, even though one has the non-occurrent belief that it is wrong to do it?[25] But this is not the interpretation I had in mind. As indicated in the passage just quoted, the question that concerned me was this: Can one do something, deliberately defying one's belief that it is wrong to do it, if that belief is not occurrent? I'm inclined to think that the answer to this question is "No," except possibly in cases of routine or habitual wrongdoing. I suppose, though, that someone who opposes me on the possibility of direct blameworthiness for inadvertent but witting wrongdoing might be quite willing to concede this point, holding that deliberately defying one's belief that one's behavior is wrong is not required for such blameworthiness; merely failing to heed that belief will suffice (*ceteris paribus*).

So let me now turn to a second reason for thinking that ascribing direct blameworthiness to agents in cases of the sort under discussion, on the grounds that they knew better than to do what they did, is mistaken. There is a crucial ambiguity in the claim that they knew that their behavior was morally wrong. In order to appreciate this ambiguity, let us focus on a particular case, that of Ian and Emma. There are a number of closely related propositions that Ian may or may not have believed, whether occurrently or merely dispositionally. Among them are the following:

1. Leaving a small child locked in a hot car for hours on end with the windows closed exposes that child to a serious risk of harm.
2. It is morally wrong (*ceteris paribus*) to expose someone to a serious risk of harm.
3. It is morally wrong to leave Emma locked in a hot car for hours on end with the windows closed.
4. Emma is in the car.
5. I am leaving Emma locked in the car with the windows closed.
6. I am exposing Emma to a serious risk of harm.
7. I am wrongly exposing Emma to a serious risk of harm.
8. I am wrongly leaving Emma locked in the car with the windows closed.

If Ian's case is typical of cases in which a parent forgets that his or her child is in the backseat, it seems safe to say that, at the time at which he left Emma in the car, he occurrently believed *none* of these propositions. Presumably, though, he did

---

[25] Cf. Rudy-Hiller (2018), §3.1.

dispositionally believe Propositions 1, 2, and 4, and possibly also Proposition 3, depending on just how the concept of dispositional belief is to be understood. Even so, it seems pretty clear that he did *not* have even a dispositional belief in any of Propositions 5–8 (although no doubt he would have believed them if they had been brought to his attention). I say this because we may assume that Ian had never explicitly entertained or considered any of these propositions, and so, on Peels's approach, none of them are propositions that he *dormantly* believed. The only other possibility is that they are propositions that Ian *tacitly* believed. In §3.2.2 I raised doubts about the very category of tacit belief, but, even putting these doubts aside, I cannot see how any of Propositions 5–8 can be properly said to "obviously follow, from Ian's perspective" from any of Propositions 1–4 or from any other propositions that Ian might have occurrently or dormantly believed. I take this to be a very significant point.

I have imagined someone saying that it would be astonishing if Ian didn't know that it was morally wrong to leave his daughter for hours on end locked in a hot car with the windows closed. It's not obvious to me that that is true. The proposition in question is *Proposition 3*, one in which Ian had at best a tacit belief, and if there is no such a thing as tacit belief, then Ian *didn't* know after all *that his behavior was wrong*. But the matter is moot, for, even if he did know this, it seems clear to me that he didn't know *that he was behaving wrongly*; that is, he didn't know, because he didn't believe, *Proposition 8*.[26] Given that he behaved as he did from ignorance of *this* proposition, he is, I submit, not to blame for what he did, unless he is to blame for his ignorance.

The distinction between the kind of *general* moral knowledge involved in knowing propositions such as Proposition 3 and the kind of *specific* moral knowledge involved in knowing propositions such as Proposition 8 is of first importance. It's a distinction that previous formulations of the Argument from Ignorance and the Origination Thesis have failed to render explicit. Let me now remedy this defect:

The Argument from Ignorance (Draft 6):
Suppose that

(1) (a) P committed A but (b) when P committed A, P did so because P failed to believe that **he or she was overall morally wrongly committing A**.

In general it's true that

(2) if one committed some act or omission because one failed to believe that **one was overall morally wrongly committing it**, one is morally to blame for it, and thereby morally to blame for any of its consequences, only if one

---

[26] Cf. Rosen (2004), p. 303.

is morally to blame for one's failure to believe that **one was overall morally wrongly committing it**.

Thus

(3) P is morally to blame for A, and thereby morally to blame for any of its consequences, only if P is morally to blame for P's failure to believe (call it F) that **he or she was overall morally wrongly committing A**.

It's also in general true that

(4) one is morally to blame for something only if one was in control of that thing.

Thus

(5) P is morally to blame for F only if P was in control of F.

Three further general truths are that

(6) one is never directly in control of whether one fails to believe something—that is, any control that one has over failing to believe something is always only indirect,

(7) if one is morally to blame for something over which one had only indirect control, then one's blameworthiness for it is itself only indirect, and

(8) one is indirectly morally to blame for something only if that thing was a consequence of something else for which one is directly morally to blame.

Thus

(9) P is morally to blame for A, and thereby morally to blame for any of its consequences, only if there was something else (call it X) for which P is directly morally to blame and of which F was a consequence.

But

(10) whatever X was, it cannot have been an act or omission such that (a) P committed it and (b) when P committed it, P did so because P failed to believe that **he or she was overall morally wrongly committing it**, since otherwise the foregoing argument regarding A would apply all over again to X.

Thus

(11) whatever X was, it was either (a) not some act or omission that P committed or (b) not something such that, when P committed it, P did so because P failed to believe that **he or she was overall morally wrongly committing it**.

One further general truth is that

(12) one has direct control over something only if that thing is an act or omission.

Thus

(13) whatever *X* was, it was not an act or omission such that, when *P* committed it, *P* did so because *P* failed to believe that **he or she was overall morally wrongly committing it**.

The Origination Thesis (Draft 6):
Every chain of moral blameworthiness is such that at its origin lies a piece of behavior for which the agent is directly blameworthy and which was such that either he or she believed, at the time at which he or she engaged in it, that **he or she was overall morally wrongly committing it** or he or she did not believe this but did not engage in the behavior because he or she did not believe this.

According to this draft of the Argument and the Thesis, it is a mistake to level a charge of pure negligence against Ian and other agents; that is, it is a mistake to hold them *directly* blameworthy for their negligent behavior.

I have said that I cannot see how Propositions 5–8 can be properly said to obviously follow, from Ian's perspective, from any other propositions that he might have believed, but I suppose this might be disputed. So let me now turn to a third and final reason for thinking that ascribing direct blameworthiness to agents in cases of the sort under discussion, on the grounds that they knew better than to do what they did, is mistaken. In none of the drafts of the Argument from Ignorance formulated so far has it been stipulated that the beliefs in question must be occurrent. Yet it seems to me that the argument would be just as compelling if this *were* stipulated. That is, to put the point roughly, just as acting from *ignorance* of the fact that one is doing something wrong is excusable, as long as one is not to blame for one's ignorance, so too acting from *inadvertence* to the fact that one is doing wrong is excusable, as long as one is not to blame for one's inadvertence. If so, then it follows that one cannot be *directly* blameworthy for acting from inadvertence to the fact that one is doing something wrong, even if one *does* know this fact.

To put the point more precisely, I am proposing, in addition to Draft 6, the following version of the Argument from Ignorance:

The Argument from Ignorance (Draft 7):
Suppose that

(1) (a) *P* committed *A* but (b) when *P* committed *A*, *P* did so because *P* failed to **occurrently** believe that he or she was overall morally wrongly committing *A*.

In general it's true that

(2) if one committed some act or omission because one failed to **occurrently** believe that one was overall morally wrongly committing it, one is morally

to blame for it, and thereby morally to blame for any of its consequences, only if one is morally to blame for one's failure to **occurrently** believe that one was overall morally wrongly committing it.

Thus

(3) P is morally to blame for A, and thereby morally to blame for any of its consequences, only if P is morally to blame for P's failure to **occurrently** believe (call it F) that he or she was overall morally wrongly committing A.

It's also in general true that

(4) one is morally to blame for something only if one was in control of that thing.

Thus

(5) P is morally to blame for F only if P was in control of F.

Three further general truths are that

(6) one is never directly in control of whether one fails to **occurrently** believe something—that is, any control that one has over failing to **occurrently** believe something is always only indirect,

(7) if one is morally to blame for something over which one had only indirect control, then one's blameworthiness for it is itself only indirect, and

(8) one is indirectly morally to blame for something only if that thing was a consequence of something else for which one is directly morally to blame.

Thus

(9) P is morally to blame for A, and thereby morally to blame for any of its consequences, only if there was something else (call it X) for which P is directly morally to blame and of which F was a consequence.

But

(10) whatever X was, it cannot have been an act or omission such that (a) P committed it and (b) when P committed it, P did so because P failed to **occurrently** believe that he or she was overall morally wrongly committing it, since otherwise the foregoing argument regarding A would apply all over again to X.

Thus

(11) whatever X was, it was either (a) not some act or omission that P committed or (b) not something such that, when P committed it, P did so because P failed to **occurrently** believe that he or she was overall morally wrongly committing it.

One further general truth is that

(12) one has direct control over something only if that thing is an act or omission.

Thus

(13) whatever *X* was, it was not an act or omission such that, when *P* committed it, *P* did so because *P* failed to **occurrently** believe that he or she was overall morally wrongly committing it.

(Regarding Premise 6, see not only the Argument against Believing at Will that I gave in §4.6.5 but also the Argument against Considering at Will that I gave in §4.6.6.) The version of the Origination Thesis that may be derived from this argument is of course the following:

The Origination Thesis (Draft 7):
Every chain of moral blameworthiness is such that at its origin lies a piece of behavior for which the agent is directly blameworthy and which was such that either he or she **occurrently** believed, at the time at which he or she engaged in it, that he or she was overall morally wrongly committing it or he or she did not **occurrently** believe this but did not engage in the behavior because he or she did not **occurrently** believe this.[27]

I have throughout described wrongdoing as "witting" if the agent who engages in it believes it to be wrong, and in §3.3 I described wrongdoing as "quasi-witting" if the agent doesn't believe it to be wrong but doesn't engage in it *because* he or she doesn't believe this, that is, doesn't engage in the behavior *from* ignorance of the fact (if it is a fact[28]) that his or her behavior is wrong. Let's now say that wrongdoing is "*overtly* witting" if the agent who engages in it *occurrently* believes it to be wrong, and "quasi-*overtly* witting" if the agent doesn't occurrently believe it to be wrong but doesn't engage in it *because* he or she doesn't occurrently believe this, that is, doesn't engage in the behavior from *inadvertence* to the fact (if it is a fact) that his or her behavior is wrong. Then Draft 7 of the Origination Thesis can be rendered more pithily, even if rather roughly, as follows: all blameworthiness is rooted in wrongdoing that is either overtly witting or quasi-overtly witting. Another, still pithier way to put the Thesis is this: all blameworthiness is rooted in *willing* wrongdoing. I suspect (but of course cannot prove—it's an empirical matter) that this thesis undermines a very large proportion of the charges of negligence that we customarily make. Agents such as Ian (and Clarke, and the

---

[27] Note that Draft 7 of the Origination Thesis is consistent with, but more restrictive, than Draft 6, in that the former yields a verdict of blamelessness in two kinds of case about which the latter is silent. One such kind of case is one in which, in the history leading up to the behavior for which the agent's blameworthiness is in question, the agent never adverts to behaving wrongly, and never acts merely in inadvertence to his (or her) behaving wrongly, but does at some point have the dispositional belief that he is behaving wrongly. The other kind of case is one in which the agent never has even the dispositional belief that he is behaving wrongly but does at some point act merely in ignorance of his doing so, although never merely in inadvertence to his doing so.

[28] See §3.4.1 on accuses.

other agents we have been discussing) clearly don't occurrently believe that they are behaving wrongly and clearly wouldn't behave as they do if they did occurrently believe this. The wrong that they do is committed *unwillingly*. According to the latest version of the Argument from Ignorance, they are therefore not directly blameworthy for their wrongdoing.

6.2.2 Substandard ignorance

Probably more common than the claim that agents in cases of the sort we have been discussing *did* know better than to behave as they did is the claim that they *ought* to have known better, and that *this* is the reason why they are to blame for their negligent behavior. Let's now look into this matter.

The charge that one ought to have known better than to behave as one did is typically made in circumstances in which it is thought that one could, and should, have adverted to what one was doing and that, if one had adverted to this, one would have realized that what one was doing was wrong. The "could" in this context refers to a mental capacity, the capacity to pay attention to one's own behavior.[29] This capacity may on occasion piggyback on some other mental capacity, such as the capacity to remember—that one's child is in the backseat, that one has promised to pick up milk on the way home, and so on.[30]

There is no doubt that we all have mental capacities of this sort, nor that we differ considerably with respect to the capacities we have. Some people, for example, have much better memories than others. Presumably these capacities are to be understood, at least in part, in terms of subjunctive conditionals (or, perhaps, in terms of "whole rafts" of such conditionals[31]), just as other capacities are. (Consider again, from §4.1.1, the capacity to fly an airplane and the capacity to adjust the temperature.) Just what the relevant conditionals should be said to be is a very difficult question, one that there is fortunately no need to investigate here, but one point that does bear stressing is that, as with capacities in general, so too with mental capacities in particular: their manifestation requires not only that one possess them but also that one have the opportunity to manifest them. For example, even if his mnemonic capacity had not been impaired, it would be false to say, in the relevant sense of "could," that Clarke could, let alone should, have remembered to pick up milk, if the reason that he forgot to do so was that he was distracted by a horrifying car crash, or an exploding bomb, or an apocalyptic news story on the radio.[32] In some cases it may be difficult to tell whether it is

---

[29] Cf. Hart (1968), p. 151; Murray and Vargas (2020), pp. 831 ff.
[30] Cf. Clarke (2014), pp. 166 f.; Rudy-Hiller (2017), p. 413.   [31] See M. Smith (2003), p. 27.
[32] See Clarke (2014), p. 166. Cf. Raz (2011), p. 246; Watson (2016), pp. 407 f.; Rudy-Hiller (2017), p. 413.

absence of capacity or absence of opportunity that renders a certain "could"-claim false (presumably not all distractions will qualify as depriving one of the opportunity to remember to pick up milk), but the distinction between capacity and opportunity nonetheless stands. Recall the difference (one of many differences) between Usain Bolt and me. He has the capacity to run very fast; when he is asleep, he lacks the opportunity to manifest this capacity, but he nonetheless retains it. I, on the other hand, have never had the capacity in question, let alone the opportunity to manifest it; even when I'm fully awake, I'll never pass you by in a blur (unaided; sometimes I drive quite fast). So, too, someone with a good memory retains this capacity even when unconscious. I, on the other hand, have a memory like a sieve, whether I am conscious or not.

There is an obvious similarity between the observations I have just made and the remarks I made in §4.1.2 regarding the nature of agential control, which I said consists in having both the specific ability (that is, the general ability conjoined with the opportunity) to see to it that some state of affairs obtains and the specific ability to see to it that that state of affairs does not obtain. The question naturally arises, therefore, whether someone who didn't advert, but could have adverted, to something was in *control* of (not) having adverted to it. If the answer is "Yes," then the door would seem open to charging this person with having done *wrong* in not adverting to the thing in question, and this in turn would raise the possibility of his or her being to *blame* for not having adverted to it and thereby also being to blame for any wrongful behavior to which the inadvertence gave rise.

It is certainly possible to be in control of whether one adverts to something, whether by way of exercising some other mental capacity, such as memory, or not. I can, for example, get myself to remember something—an appointment, for instance—by setting myself a reminder. (Sometimes I manage to get myself to remember something—a name, for instance—by a means that is wholly mysterious to me; I try to remember it and, as a result, I eventually do remember it, but I have no idea what the trying itself consists in.) In such a case the control is exercised only *indirectly*, though, and so any blameworthiness that attaches to one's inadvertence must be traced to blameworthiness for some prior benighting act. This won't do in the present context, since what we are investigating is the propriety of charges of *pure* negligence, that is, negligent behavior for which one is allegedly *directly* blameworthy. Can one exercise *direct* control over whether one adverts to something? According to the Argument against Considering at Will that I gave in §4.6.6, no one can do so.

It might be countered that the Argument against Considering at Will, even if sound, is not dispositive. The form of control with which the argument is concerned is *volitional* control. Even if one cannot exercise direct volitional control over whether one adverts to something, it remains possible that one can exercise direct control of some *non*-volitional sort over whether one adverts to something. Some philosophers claim that this is indeed the case,[33] and perhaps it is. There certainly are non-volitional forms of control, as I noted in §4.1.1. Thermostats and autopilots, for example, can be in control of certain events, control of a kind that is perforce non-volitional. Moreover, agents capable of exercising volitional control may also be capable of exercising some form of non-volitional control. Consider again the example of controlling one's body temperature by sweating or shivering. (This might be accomplished by means of an indirect exercise of volitional control—by means of stepping into a sauna or out into the snow, say—but that of course is not what's at issue here.) But even if it is possible to exercise direct non-volitional control of some sort over whether one adverts to something, this does not help support charges of pure negligence, precisely because the kind of control that appears to be, and has traditionally been taken to be, necessary for blameworthiness is volitional control, the kind of control that someone has when what happens is *up to* him or her. (See §4.1.2.) In my experience, whether something occurs to me is not directly up to me. (I venture to say that the same is true of you, too.) If it occurs to me, it does, and if it doesn't, it doesn't. I have no say (no direct say) in the matter.

Suppose that I am wrong about this. Suppose, that is, that it *is* possible to exercise direct, volitional control over whether one adverts to something. Even so, this does *not* help support charges of pure negligence. At best, it opens up the possibility of one's being directly blameworthy for one's *inadvertence*; it doesn't provide any reason to think that one can be directly blameworthy for the *behavior* in which one engages inadvertently. On the contrary, if one engages in this behavior *from* inadvertence, then, as before, one's blameworthiness for the behavior would seem to be *indirect*, tracing back to one's blameworthiness for one's inadvertence, which is what (allegedly) lay in one's direct control and perhaps constitutes the benighting act that initiated the relevant sequence of events. Why only "perhaps"? Well, as I observed in §5.1.3, from the fact that one has done *wrong* in not adverting to something it doesn't follow that one is to *blame* for one's inadvertence. Again, one might have an excuse! This possibility is precisely what gets the Argument from Ignorance rolling. According to it, one will indeed have an excuse for one's inadvertence to the wrongness of one's behavior if one was ignorant of the fact that one ought to have adverted to it (unless, of course, one is to blame for one's ignorance).

It might be retorted that, even if what I have just said is true, charges of pure negligence can still be justified. In order for such a charge to stick, it's not necessary for one to have had control (*volitional* control) over whether one *adverted* to the wrongness of one's behavior; all that's necessary is that one had control over one's *behavior*. Suppose that it was up to Ian whether he left Emma in

---

[33] See, e.g., Rudy-Hiller (2017), pp. 405 ff. on what he calls "capacitarian" control.

the car (something that I take to be necessary for his leaving her there to have been morally wrong), but suppose also that, even though he had both the capacity and the opportunity to advert to the fact that what he was doing was wrong, it was not up to him—he didn't have control over—whether he adverted to this fact. Then (I take it) his inadvertence was not itself something that either constituted or stemmed from wrongdoing on his part. Nonetheless, it could still be that he ought, in some *non*-deontic sense of "ought," to have adverted to the wrongness of his behavior, and this fact, conjoined with the fact that his behavior was indeed wrong, is sufficient to render him blameworthy for his behavior. Moreover, if the control he exercised over his behavior was exercised directly, then his blameworthiness for this behavior will itself be *direct*.

This is an intriguing line of thought. I will defer discussion of it until §9.1.

7
Recklessness

As I have noted in previous chapters, the *Model Penal Code* distinguishes between four kinds of culpability, having to do with whether someone commits an offense purposely, knowingly, recklessly, or negligently, and it holds that, *ceteris paribus*, degree of culpability diminishes as one moves down the list from one kind to the next.[1] Once again, it is of course with legal culpability that the *Code* is concerned, but its position reflects, indeed is presumably based on, a corresponding commonly-held view about levels of moral culpability. I argued in the last chapter that there is good reason to doubt this commonly-held view as far as culpability for negligence is concerned. In this chapter I take up the other categories of culpability addressed by the *Code*.

In §7.1 I discuss and endorse the view that the chief distinction between negligence and recklessness is that, whereas the former involves risky behavior to whose riskiness one does not advert,[2] the latter involves risky behavior of whose riskiness one is conscious. I note, however, that one can be conscious of taking a risk without being conscious of wrongly doing so, and one can risk doing harm without risking doing wrong. Failure to take note of these distinctions undermines much recent discussion of moral responsibility for reckless behavior. I also briefly address the distinction between acting recklessly and acting knowingly, and I comment on the issue of blameworthiness for purposely doing wrong.

In §7.2 I investigate the issue of moral responsibility for behavior that exhibits willful ignorance and other forms of motivated ignorance. Much of the discussion of this issue in the literature is hampered by a failure to distinguish motivated ignorance of some non-moral fact from motivated moral ignorance. I argue that, if this distinction is kept clearly in mind, there is no need to treat moral responsibility for motivated moral ignorance differently from moral responsibility for moral ignorance in general.

7.1 Conscious wrongdoing

The definition of recklessness given in the *Model Penal Code* goes as follows:

---

[1] American Law Institute (1985), §2.02(2). See ch. 2, n. 27 for qualification.
[2] Or, more generally, wrongful behavior to whose wrongness one does not advert. See §6.1.

A person acts recklessly with respect to a material element of an offense when he consciously disregards a substantial and unjustifiable risk that the material element exists or will result from his conduct. The risk must be of such a nature and degree that, considering the nature and purpose of the actor's conduct and the circumstances known to him, its disregard involves a gross deviation from the standard of conduct that a law-abiding person would observe in the actor's situation.[3]

Comparison of this definition with that cited at the beginning of §6.1 shows that, according to the *Code*, recklessness differs from negligence in three ways. First, the risk that a reckless agent runs is one of which he or she is conscious, whereas that is not the case with respect to the risk run by a negligent agent. Second, the standard from which the reckless agent deviates is a standard of conduct, whereas in the case of a negligent agent it is a standard of care. Third, the standard relevant to recklessness is one that a law-abiding person would observe, whereas that which is relevant to negligence is one that a reasonable person would observe.

I won't dwell on the second and third differences. As to the third: when it comes to moral, rather than legal, culpability, invoking a standard that is independent of the agent's actual capacities is as misguided in the case of reckless as in the case of negligent behavior, since, as I noted in §5.1.3 and §6.1, the agent may blamelessly fall short of it. As to the second difference: this is somewhat illusory, since in the case of negligence, too, the *Code* is concerned with the unjustifiability of the agent's conduct; it's just that it is also concerned with the substandard nature of the agent's inadvertence to the risk that he or she is running, an issue that of course does not arise in the case of recklessness, since the agent is *not* inadvertent to this risk.

It is this first difference, the difference between advertence and inadvertence to the risk that is being run, that is especially important and on which I will concentrate. It is, however, a difference that has been disputed. Some writers hold that one can act negligently even though one adverts to the relevant risk, and some hold that one can act recklessly even though one does not advert to the relevant risk.

7.1.1 Conscious negligence and inadvertent recklessness

Perhaps some people use the term "conscious negligence" simply to refer to recklessness, but others use it to refer to a category of wrongful behavior that

---

[3] American Law Institute (1985), §2.02(2)(c).

they take to be distinct from recklessness (and also, of course, from inadvertent negligence). James Brady discusses three possible grounds for doing so.[4]

On one approach, the distinction between recklessness and conscious negligence is marked in terms of the probability of the outcome that is risked. Recklessness involves a relatively high probability, whereas conscious negligence involves only a relatively low probability. As Brady notes, this approach seems flawed, since, in some cases in which someone consciously runs a low-probability risk, a charge of recklessness would seem clearly appropriate.[5] Imagine playing Russian roulette on someone sitting in front of you on the bus. Isn't that plainly reckless? Someone might say in reply that a 1-in-6 probability of death isn't sufficiently low to warrant the lesser charge of conscious negligence, but that simply raises the question, "How low is low enough?" To this question there is, I submit, no good answer. In many circumstances, risking a very grave outcome (a nuclear holocaust, say) will warrant a charge of recklessness, even if the probability of that outcome is very low indeed.

A second approach marks the distinction between (conscious) recklessness and conscious negligence in terms of the seriousness of the risk that is run, where this is understood to be a function of both the probability and the gravity of the outcome that is risked. (Given the gravity of a nuclear holocaust, risking such an outcome is very serious, even if the probability of its occurring is very low.) Michael Moore and Heidi Hurd, for example, express "considerable sympathy" for the idea that advertent risk-taking that is unreasonable, but not especially so (since the risk is not especially serious), should be classified as negligent rather than reckless, in virtue of which the agent is to be deemed culpable only to a relatively minor degree.[6] But this is once again problematic. As Brady notes, there are cases of (inadvertent) negligence that would normally be taken to confer greater culpability on the agent than cases of recklessness.[7] By way of illustration, consider two cases discussed in the last chapter. Compare Ian's inadvertently leaving Emma in the hot car to Clarke's behavior in the following twist on the original scenario: he didn't forget to pick up milk, but he did forget whether his wife had asked him to get 2 per cent or 1 per cent milk; rather than call her to find out what she wanted, he simply flipped a coin, hoping for the best. Of course, Moore and Hurd might respond that Clarke's behavior in this case, being only slightly unreasonable, didn't rise to the level of recklessness and counts only as an instance of conscious negligence. But then I think we need only raise the stakes to whatever level Moore and Hurd take to be required for the behavior to count as reckless. It would be surprising if this level warranted ascribing a degree of culpability to Clarke as high as that which would customarily (though, as I argued in the last chapter, mistakenly) be leveled at Ian. And if Ian's *inadvertent*

---

[4] Brady (1996). [5] Brady (1996), p. 327. [6] Moore and Hurd (2011), p. 149.
[7] Brady (1996), p. 332. Cf. Simons (2011), p. 111.

negligence involved a degree of culpability higher than Clarke's recklessness, it's hard to see why the charge of *conscious* negligence should be restricted to cases that involve only a lower degree of culpability.

A third approach marks the distinction between recklessness and conscious negligence in terms of the attitude one has to the risk that one consciously runs. If one is indifferent to the risk, not caring whether the outcome that is risked occurs or not, then one acts recklessly (provided that one satisfies the other conditions necessary for recklessness), whereas, if one is not indifferent to the risk, one acts negligently. (In this context, "not caring" is to be construed in terms of lacking concern for those potentially affected by one's behavior, rather than in terms of failing to pay attention to the potential consequences of one's behavior. See §6.1.) As Brady once again notes, however, this approach seems flawed too, since, in some cases in which someone is not strictly indifferent to the risk that is run, a charge of recklessness would still seem appropriate.[8] Imagine speeding down a busy high street in order to get home in time to watch that day's episode of *As the World Turns*. Isn't that plainly reckless, even if you would prefer not to hit anyone en route? In response, it might be said that your behavior betrays the fact that you are "practically indifferent," even if not strictly indifferent, to whether or not you run into, or over, someone. But what might this mean? One suggestion is that, although you prefer getting home in time for the show without hitting someone (T&~H) to getting home in time with hitting someone (T&H), you don't prefer getting home late without hitting someone (~T&~H) to getting home in time with hitting someone (T&H).[9] But that still seems too demanding. It would seem perfectly appropriate to charge you with recklessness even if you don't rise (or sink) to that level of callousness.

Notice that, if the difference between recklessness and negligence were to turn simply on whether one is practically indifferent to the risk that one runs, it would be possible not only to be consciously negligent but also to be inadvertently reckless.[10] But, just as a charge of recklessness would seem appropriate in certain cases in which the agent doesn't manifest such indifference, so, too, a charge of negligence, if ever appropriate (which I doubt—see the last chapter), would seem appropriate in certain cases in which the agent does manifest it. Suppose that, in the original scenario in which he forgot all about picking up milk, Clarke didn't care at all about whether he picked it up as promised—that that, indeed, was *why* he forgot to pick it up. If he is to be blamed at all for failing to pick it up, the natural charge would still be that he had behaved negligently. A charge of recklessness would seem quite out of place.

In the end, I think it matters little how we use the labels "negligence" and "recklessness." What does matter is that we take note of and attend closely to the

---

[8] Brady (1996), p. 328.   [9] Cf. Duff (2019), p. 652.
[10] Cf. Brady (1996), p. 332; Duff (2019), p. 659.

relevance of (in)advertence to culpability. Like the *Model Penal Code*, and in keeping with what I take to be usual, even if not universal, practice, I will continue to use the terms "negligence" and "recklessness" to help mark this distinction. And here I should add another note about terminology. Since occurrent belief requires advertence, if one inadvertently takes a risk, then one doesn't occurrently believe that one is taking it. So, too, if one inadvertently commits a wrong, then one doesn't occurrently believe that one is committing it. However, since advertence doesn't require belief, one can advert to risk-taking or wrongdoing that one doesn't occurrently believe one is committing. In order to refer to risk-taking or wrongdoing that one *does* occurrently believe one is committing, I will therefore talk in terms, not simply of advertent, but of *conscious* risk-taking and wrongdoing. (See §3.2.3.)

7.1.2 Acting recklessly vs. acting knowingly

The *Model Penal Code*'s definition of committing an offense knowingly[11] goes as follows:

> A person acts knowingly with respect to a material element of an offense when:
> (i) if the element involves the nature of his conduct or the attendant circumstances, he is aware that his conduct is of that nature or that such circumstances exist; and
> (ii) if the element involves a result of his conduct, he is aware that it is practically certain that his conduct will cause such a result.[12]

Unsurprisingly, in this definition, as in its definition of recklessness (and in contrast to its definition of negligence), the *Code* focuses on an attitude that the agent has (rather than lacks) toward a material element of some offense. In the case of recklessness, the attitude is said to consist in awareness of a substantial risk that some such element exists or will result, whereas, in the case of committing an offense knowingly, the attitude is said to consist in either awareness of, or awareness of the practical certainty of, some such element.

I find the *Code*'s procedure here rather odd. In distinguishing (as it should) between knowing, or being aware, that some material element of an offense obtains and knowing, or being aware, that there is a "practical certainty" that

---

[11] I use the phrase "committing an offense knowingly" rather than what might seem to be the more natural phrase "knowingly committing an offense" in order to suppress the suggestion that the offender knows that he or she is committing an offense, rather than simply knowing, with respect to what is in fact an element of an offense, that this element obtains. To appreciate the distinction, consider someone who knowingly kills another but doesn't know that killing another constitutes an offense.
[12] American Law Institute (1985), §2.02(2)(b).

some such element obtains, the *Code* seems to concede that the latter *doesn't* suffice for the former. This concession is quite correct, I think. The distinction between the latter and the former rests, at least in part, on the distinction between credence and outright belief (regarding which see §3.2.4). But then it seems inconsistent to say, with respect to the material elements of an offense, that one's being aware that it is (merely) practically certain that some result will occur *does* suffice for acting knowingly with respect to that result, an inconsistency that the *Code* appears to embrace explicitly when it goes on to say:

> When knowledge of the existence of a particular fact is an element of an offense, such knowledge is established if a person is aware of a high probability of its existence, unless he actually believes that it does not exist.[13]

The inconsistency may seem innocuous, amounting to no more than a stipulation that, for purposes of the law, the term "know" and its cognates are to be construed expansively. As I will explain in §7.2.2, however, I think the matter is not so straightforward. Be that as it may, for present purposes it seems reasonable simply to interpret the *Code* as holding that, insofar as the agent's attitude is concerned, committing an offense knowingly is a species—more particularly, a limiting case[14]—of committing an offense recklessly. In general, recklessness involves a credence in the proposition that some material element of an offense obtains or will obtain; in the case of "knowingly" committing an offense, the credence is especially high. Such an interpretation fits well with the view that, *ceteris paribus*, committing an offense knowingly confers greater culpability on the agent than committing an offense (merely) recklessly does: the higher one's credence, the greater one's culpability.

Another odd feature of the *Code*'s procedure is that, whereas it makes explicit reference in its definition of committing an offense recklessly to the unjustifiability of the agent's conduct, it makes no such reference in its definition of committing an offense knowingly. Whatever the *Code*'s rationale for this omission may be, I will not follow suit. My concern in this chapter is not just with being aware that one is taking a risk but, more fundamentally, with being aware that one is doing wrong. This is a distinction that is frequently overlooked, but it is of first importance.

7.1.3 Conscious risk-taking *vs.* conscious wrongdoing

All conduct is risky. You might choke on your cereal; the chair you're sitting in might collapse; you might have a heart attack while driving. Nonetheless, eating,

---

[13] American Law Institute (1985), §2.02(7).   [14] Cf. Alexander et al. (2009), p. 32.

sitting, and driving are, typically, perfectly morally justified. Some risks are more serious than others, of course, depending not only on how grave the outcome that is risked would be, were it to occur, but also on how likely it is to occur. But even very serious risks might be worth running. No doubt, the more serious the risk, the more difficult it is to justify running it, but, in the end, whether it is justifiable to run it will depend, as always, not only on the risk itself but also on what one's alternatives are. In general, whether it is morally justifiable to run a risk is a question of whether doing so constitutes, as I put it in §6.1, one's best bet, morally speaking, given one's epistemic circumstances and the options one faces. (This claim requires qualification in cases in which no alternative is a better bet than all others. In such cases, one's obligation is to choose some option to which there is no alternative that is a better bet.)

Suppose that Sandra runs a red light, and that doing so is *not* her best bet, morally speaking (that is, it's morally wrong), since the risk of harm that she poses, to herself as well as to others, is not warranted under the circumstances (there is no emergency, for example). There are two possibilities: either Sandra adverts to the risk that she's running, or she doesn't. If she doesn't advert to it, then she also doesn't advert to the fact that running it is morally wrong. Under these circumstances, Sandra will satisfy the first two conditions in the definition of negligence that I gave in §6.1. But, for reasons discussed in the last chapter, whether she satisfies the final condition (that is, whether her inadvertence to the wrongness of her behavior is morally substandard) is not a straightforward matter, let alone whether, if she does, she is to blame for her behavior.

But suppose that Sandra *does* advert to and is, moreover, conscious of the risk that she's running. Is she then acting recklessly? The answer depends on just how recklessness is to be defined. Consider this definition: one behaves recklessly just in case, in behaving as one does, one wrongly runs a risk of which one is conscious.[15] This seems a reasonable definition. (It departs in some ways from the definition provided in the *Model Penal Code*—it makes no reference to the material element of an offense, it doesn't require that the wrongness be substantial or gross, and it makes no reference to what a law-abiding person would do—but, as with the definition of negligence that I gave, there are good reasons for these discrepancies, given that our concern is with moral rather than legal responsibility for wrongful behavior.) On this definition, the answer is clear: Yes, Sandra is acting recklessly.

Even though Sandra is conscious of the risk that she's running, she might not advert to, and thus be aware of, the fact that running it is morally wrong. There are several ways this could happen. She might underestimate the probability of the harm that she risks. (To say that she is conscious of the risk is not to say that she

---

[15] As in the case of negligence, the wrongness at issue is *overall moral* wrongness.

assesses it accurately.) For example, she might expect the light to stay yellow longer than it actually does. Or she might underestimate the gravity of the harm that she risks. For example, she might mistakenly think that, at worst, she's risking only a fender-bender. Or she might misconstrue the nature of her other options. For example, although there is no emergency, she might think that there is, and so think that her other options are far less attractive than they really are. Or, of course, some combination of these possibilities might obtain. In any case, if Sandra isn't aware that it's wrong to run the risk she's running, the latest draft (Draft 7) of the Argument from Ignorance will apply, and its verdict, once again, will be that she is to blame for her behavior only if she is to blame for her failure to occurrently believe that it is wrong (unless her engaging in it isn't to be attributed to this failure).

It's important to note that, if Sandra doesn't advert to the wrongness of her behavior, then, according to the definitions that I have offered, she may be acting not only recklessly but also negligently. (Whether she is acting negligently will depend on whether her inadvertence is morally substandard.) Is this a problem? The *Code* implicitly denies that it is possible for someone to act both recklessly and negligently (with respect to the same offense on the same occasion), and this might seem a reasonable view. Once the distinction between conscious risk-taking and conscious wrongdoing has been recognized, however, it seems to me even more reasonable *not* to follow the *Code*'s lead in this respect, at least as far as *moral* responsibility for wrongful behavior is concerned. And so I see no need to amend my definition of recklessness on this score.

Another observation does point to the need for revision, however. Consciousness need not be veridical. One can be mistaken about the risks that one takes oneself to be running, and one can be mistaken about the wrongness of running them. Suppose that Mark makes a mistake of the latter kind: he believes that he is wrongly running a risk when in fact he is not. (This might be because he's not running a risk at all, or because he's running a risk that it's not wrong of him to run.) I am inclined to think that we should say that Mark is acting recklessly.[16] No doubt this inclination is due in part to the fact that I accept the possibility of accuses (regarding which see §3.4.1), and so I think it's possible for Mark to be blameworthy for his behavior even though he's not behaving wrongly; but the claim that he's acting recklessly is strictly independent of this view. In any case, I suggest that, in light of cases such as Mark's, we move to the following definition of recklessness: one behaves recklessly just in case, in behaving as one does, *either* one wrongly runs a risk of which one is conscious *or* one is conscious of wrongly running a risk.

---

[16] Cf. Alexander et al. (2009), p. 28.

7.1.4 Risking harm *vs.* risking wrong

Although the definition that I have just proposed differs in some respects from the one provided in the *Model Penal Code*, it seems to accord well with a common view that presumably underlies the *Code*'s definition and to which Alan Donagan gives expression in the following passage:

> Wrongs done through recklessness approximate to wrongs done in ignorance but not because of ignorance. A man who does a wrong through recklessness, who may well not know that he is doing it, is aware that what he does may involve wrongdoing, but does not reck it. It is true that there is a difference in culpability between doing something you know is wrong and doing something you think probably or possibly wrong; but it is not a great one. You voluntarily take the risk.[17]

What Donagan says here may seem sensible and straightforward, but in fact it conceals a conundrum that is rarely acknowledged.

The problem has to do with the distinction between risking harm (or some other kind of undesirable outcome—but let's stick with harm for the sake of illustration) and risking wrong. Consider these two questions, which should give you a glimpse into the issue that concerns me. I have said that much recklessness involves wrongdoing while perhaps some does not, but mightn't some behavior warrant being called reckless simply because it involves the *risk* of wrongdoing? I have also said that, when behaving recklessly, one may or may not be conscious of the wrongness of one's behavior (by which I mean, as I indicated in §7.1.1, that one may or may not occurrently believe that one is behaving wrongly), but mightn't some behavior warrant being called reckless simply in virtue of involving the *suspicion*, rather than the outright belief, that one is behaving wrongly?

In order to get a better grip on this problem, consider a couple of characters introduced by Douglas Husak.[18] The first is Juan, who routinely turns on the light in his office when he arrives at work in the morning. One day a terrorist rewires the mechanism so that a bomb will explode when the switch is flipped, leaving no evidence that he has done so. The next time Juan flips the switch, he detonates the bomb, thereby killing many innocent people. Husak claims that Juan is not at all to blame for causing their deaths. This verdict is surely plausible. Juan didn't know that, by flipping the switch, he would kill anyone and, in light of the lack of evidence that the switch had been rigged, he is presumably not to blame for his ignorance.

---

[17] Donagan (1977), pp. 129 f.   [18] Husak (2016), pp. 151 ff.

Husak contrasts Juan with another character whom he calls Juan*. The latter is aware that there are terrorists in the vicinity who have rigged a number of devices in order to trick people into unintentionally killing others. He attaches a 10 per cent probability to (by which I take Husak to mean that he has a credence of 0.1 in) the proposition that the switch has been rewired and will cause an explosion when it is flipped; he doesn't believe this proposition outright, but he suspects that it may be true. Despite his suspicion, Juan* goes ahead and flips the switch, thereby once again killing many innocent people. Husak claims that Juan* has acted recklessly and is to blame for causing the deaths, but not as much to blame as he would be if he had flipped the switch knowing that it had been rewired. This verdict echoes Donagan's claim about culpability, and it may seem reasonable, too, but there is reason to question it.

We should ask: Has either Juan or Juan* done anything morally wrong? Husak's answer is clear: They both have. What wrong? The wrong of killing innocent people.[19] Husak takes this to be the answer yielded by an objective account of moral obligation and wrongdoing, one to which he subscribes and according to which a certain form of conduct is wrongful just in case the moral reasons against it are stronger than the moral reasons in favor of it, such reasons being such that what they are and how they are balanced does not depend on the agent's beliefs.[20] As I have acknowledged (see §2.1.2 and §6.1), this is a common view about the nature of moral obligation and wrongdoing, but it is problematic. It doesn't capture what we would naturally want to say about agents such as Juan*— and by "we," I mean to include Husak and others who toe the objective line. Consider Juan** (not one of Husak's characters). He is in exactly the same situation as Juan* except that, as luck would have it, terrorists have *not* rigged the switch in his office. Thus, when he flips the switch, no bomb explodes and no one is killed. Isn't his behavior equally as reckless as Juan*'s? But, on the objective approach, what wrong has he done?

On the approach that I have advocated (which some call subjective but which, for reasons that I will shortly give, I would not), it's clear that Juan* and Juan** have run the same risk and thereby acted equally wrongly. In so saying, I am of course assuming that both Juan* and Juan** had a *better bet*, morally speaking, than to flip the switch. Note, however, that, this approach also implies that Juan, lacking any evidence that there were terrorists in the vicinity, did *not* do anything wrong; for, even though he killed many innocent people by flipping the switch in his office, we may assume that flipping it was, given his epistemic circumstances, not unduly risky and thus *not* such that some other option that he had was a better bet. This may be a rather disconcerting result, one that you would prefer to avoid.

---

[19] Husak (2016), p. 153.   [20] Husak (2016), p. 148.

One way to try to avoid it is to combine the two approaches in question and say both that, because he *in fact* caused the deaths of innocent people, despite lacking any evidence that he was at risk of doing so, Juan did indeed act wrongly, and that, because they *risked* causing the deaths of innocent people, Juan* and Juan** also acted wrongly. But this is problematic, for at least two reasons. First, it would appear that on this approach Juan* did a double wrong—the same wrong as that committed by Juan and also the same wrong as that committed by Juan**—even though there would seem to be strong pressure to say that he did no more wrong than Juan**. Second, the combined approach threatens to be incoherent. Consider the plight of Juan*** (also not one of Husak's characters), who is operating with the same evidence as Juan* and Juan** but whose switch has in fact been rigged in such a way that if he *doesn't* flip it when he enters his office a bomb will explode. On the combined approach, Juan*** is in an "impossible" situation, morally speaking; that is, there is no possibility of his avoiding wrongdoing. If he flips the switch, he wrongly runs the risk of the deaths of innocents; if he doesn't flip it, he wrongly fails to prevent deaths that he could easily have prevented. Such a situation is what is often called a moral dilemma. There are good reasons to think that moral dilemmas, so understood, cannot occur—that it cannot ever happen that one is in a situation in which one cannot avoid overall moral wrongdoing—but, whatever side we should take on this issue, surely we shouldn't say that, simply because his evidence is diametrically opposed to the facts, Juan*** cannot avoid wrongdoing.

Advocates of the combined approach might respond by saying that the problems I have noted arise only if we fail to distinguish between *kinds* of overall moral wrongdoing. One kind is objective, the other is not. We should say that Juan commits an objective wrong but not a non-objective wrong; that Juan** commits a non-objective wrong but not an objective wrong; that Juan* commits both kinds of wrong; and that Juan*** will commit one or the other kind, but not both, depending on what choice he makes. Perhaps so. Indeed, drawing such a distinction is very common, but doing so only invites the further question: Which of these two kinds of wrongdoing is pertinent to assessments of culpability? And here I think the answer is clear: Only the non-objective kind. Objective wrongdoing has no direct relevance.

In support of this claim, consider first what we should say about non-objective wrongdoing. If one (satisfies the control condition of moral responsibility and) does what one knows not to be one's best bet, morally speaking, one will be to blame for one's behavior, whereas, if one ignorantly does what is not one's best bet, one will not be to blame, unless one is to blame for one's ignorance (or one acts *merely* in ignorance). This observation yields the correct verdict in the cases we have considered. Given his epistemic circumstances, Juan's flipping the switch was not unduly risky, a fact of which we may assume he was aware, and so he is not to blame for flipping it. By contrast, if we assume that Juan* and Juan** were not only conscious of the risk they were running but also conscious of the fact that it was *unduly* risky, i.e., that running it was not their best bet, then they are to blame for flipping their switches. So, too, for Juan***, if he flips his switch.

Now consider what we should say about objective wrongdoing. If one (satisfies the control condition of moral responsibility and) does what one knows to be objectively wrong, one may nonetheless be entirely blameless for one's behavior, whereas, if one ignorantly does what is objectively wrong, one may be to blame for one's behavior, even if one is not to blame for one's ignorance. In support of this claim, consider a case of a kind that has recently been much discussed.[21] Jill has three drugs, A, B, and C, with which she can treat her patient, John. She knows that either A or C would cure John completely of his ailment and also that either A or C would kill him, but she doesn't know which would do which. She also knows that B would be slightly less effective than the best drug, whereas not giving John any drug at all would leave him considerably worse off. Under these circumstances, Jill's best bet is clearly to give John drug B—a fact of which, let me hereby stipulate, she is fully aware—and, if she does this, she certainly won't be to blame, even though she knows that doing so is objectively wrong, since either A or C would produce better results. (It might be countered that she doesn't know this, since in fact giving John drug B is *not* objectively wrong, given that producing the best results is not all that objective right and wrong turn on. Perhaps so, but the general point remains, since a case with the same structure can always be drawn up, no matter what account of objective wrongness is presupposed.) Suppose, however, that Jill gives John drug C, and this turns out to be the killer drug. Since she had no more confidence in the proposition that C would kill John than in the proposition that A would do so, she didn't believe outright that giving him drug C was objectively wrong, and we may assume that she's not to blame for failing to believe this. Yet she is certainly to blame for giving him this drug, given that she knew that doing so was not her best bet.

It is very important to note that, on the approach that I am advocating, it is perfectly possible for one to be mistaken about what one ought to do. I have stipulated that Jill knew that she ought to give John drug B, but in other cases ignorance about what one ought to do can easily arise. I am claiming that what one ought to do is what it is one's best bet to do. This is something that is determined by one's evidence, and one's beliefs may not comport with one's evidence. In such a case, one may well end up doing the wrong thing and yet have an excuse for doing it. In light of this fact, I am reluctant to describe my view as a subjective view, since it is often said that, if one does what is subjectively wrong, one is to blame for one's behavior.[22] I prefer to describe my view as a "prospective" view.[23]

---

[21] The original is given in Jackson (1991), pp. 462 f.   [22] See, e.g., Mason (2019), ch. 2.
[23] See Zimmerman (2014) for an extended discussion of the prospective approach.

Return to Juan and Juan*. Husak says that Juan* acted recklessly, whereas Juan did not. I quite agree, but I take this to be true because, in the relevant, prospective sense, Juan* acted wrongly, whereas Juan did not. Juan* took an *undue* risk, thereby failing to do what was his best bet. He risked harm that he ought not to have risked, thereby not merely risking wrong but actually doing wrong. Is Juan* to blame for what he did? On the assumption that he was in control of his behavior, my answer is that he is to blame for it if, and only if, he was aware that the risk he ran was an undue risk (or is to blame for not being aware of this). If he is to blame, how much is he to blame? I think this depends on how *seriously* wrong he took his behavior to be. If, as is reasonable, he believed his behavior to be wrong but not as seriously wrong as it would have been had the risk of causing deaths been higher, then he is to blame to a certain degree (I won't venture to specify what degree) but not as great a degree as he would have been had he believed the risk of causing deaths to be higher. Notice, though, that he might have mis-assessed the risk, or mis-assessed how seriously wrong it was to run it, or both. Husak describes Juan* as attaching a probability of 10 per cent to the proposition that the switch had been rewired and would cause an explosion when it was flipped. It could be that this was precisely what his evidence indicated, but it could also be that it constituted an over- or underestimation of the relevant probability. Of more immediate relevance is the degree of seriousness of wrong-doing that Juan* attached to the risk that he took himself to be running. If he underestimated this degree of seriousness, then his culpability is diminished (unless he is to blame for the underestimation). If he overestimated it, then, I would say (in consonance with my endorsement of the possibility of accuses), his culpability is augmented.

You might be inclined to agree with what I have just said but still think that something important is missing. In keeping with Husak's presentation of the case, I have described Juan* as having had a credence of 0.1 in the (non-moral) proposition that flipping the switch would cause an explosion, a credence that was clearly much too weak to support an outright belief in this proposition, but I have also described him as having been either aware or unaware of the (moral) fact that flipping the switch was wrong. Could it not be, though, that he had a credence in *this* fact that was *also* too weak to support his believing it outright, in which case it is misleading simply to describe him as having been either aware or unaware of it, since to do so is to overlook the fact that he *suspected* that it was or might be the case? And wouldn't such a suspicion suffice under the circumstances for his being to blame for reckless behavior?

This is a tricky question, far trickier than it may at first seem. Note the following.

First, merely having a suspicion that one is acting wrongly surely does not suffice (even in conjunction with satisfaction of the control condition for moral responsibility) for one's being to blame for one's behavior. If one has a credence of

0.1 that one is behaving wrongly, and one is rational, then one will have a credence of 0.9 that one is *not* acting wrongly. That hardly seems grounds for blame.

But, you might say, what if one's options are such that regarding one of them—call it A—one has a credence of 0.1, grounded firmly in one's evidence, that choosing it would be wrong, whereas, regarding each of the remaining options, one has an even lower well-founded credence that choosing *it* would be wrong? If one chooses A under *such* circumstances, wouldn't that be grounds for blame?[24]

Initially, it seems perfectly reasonable to think that such a situation could arise and that, moreover, the judgment that one would be to blame for one's choice is correct. And yet—and this is the tricky part—there is also good reason to think that the case has been misdescribed. Let me explain.

Suppose that you are inclined to the view, which many appear to hold, that in general one's best bet is to maximize expected value and thus that it is morally wrong to choose an option that does not maximize such value. This view is well suited to cases like that of Jill and John, for example. We don't need to assign precise numbers to the probabilities of the possible outcomes or to the values of these outcomes in order to be assured that Jill would fail to maximize expected value if she chose to do anything other than to give John drug B, a fact of which she herself is fully aware. But few cases are so straightforward. Suppose that you find yourself in a situation like that just described: you have a well-founded low credence that, in choosing A, you would fail to maximize expected value and, for each of your other options, an even lower credence that, in choosing it, you would fail to do so, but your evidence yields no definitive answer regarding which options would or wouldn't maximize expected value. You would like to improve your epistemic situation, but the time has come for you to choose. I think it's clear that, under the circumstances, choosing A would *not* be your best bet—from a moral point of view, it would *not* be reasonable for you to choose it—even though your evidence clearly doesn't warrant your believing that A would fail to maximize expected value. This means that the view to which you, and many others, are inclined is false. Although in some cases the right (or wrong) thing to do is to choose that option that would (or would not) maximize expected value, this is not, and cannot be, the case *in general*; and the reason that it cannot be the case in general is simply that on some occasions one's evidence is so paltry that it warrants no definitive judgments regarding what would, or would not, maximize expected value. Moreover—and this is crucial—this is a fact that we can assume that you yourself recognize, despite your inclination to accept the view in question. For you yourself will appreciate that, under the circumstances, choosing A is not your best bet. In other words, it's *not* the case after all that you have a credence

---

[24] Cf. Harman (2011), p. 449, and (2015), p. 63.

of 0.1 that choosing A would be wrong. On the contrary, you believe outright that it would be.

The lesson I draw from this observation is this. It is surprisingly difficult to find a case in which one has some degree of credence in the proposition that one is acting wrongly and yet lacks a belief outright either that one is doing so or that one is not doing so. Any case, such as the one just described, that initially appears to fit this description is one that, on further inspection, may well fail to do so. This is due to the fact that what does or does not constitute one's best bet—what it is, or is not, most reasonable for one to do, from the moral point of view—is a "moving target"; there is no fixed formula (such as that one's best bet is on every occasion to maximize expected value) that captures its protean nature, and this is a fact on which we would appear typically to rely, even if only unthinkingly, in our decision-making. Consider the plight of the conscientious person—you, let's say. You don't rest content simply with doing what *seems* to you *might* be your best bet; no, you make it your habit to try to figure out what *is* your best bet. However, if on a particular occasion the time to make a decision has come and you still haven't managed, to your own satisfaction at least, to figure out which option is your best bet, what choice will you make? Unless every option seems equally reasonable to you, you will shun some options in favor of one or more others. In so doing, you will have implicitly come to the conclusion that *under the circumstances*, circumstances in which you can no longer delay making a decision, the options that you shun are not merely possibly or probably the wrong thing to do but actually the wrong thing to do ("No, I won't—I mustn't—do that"), whereas the option or options that remain are not merely possibly or probably but actually permissible.

Or so it seems to me. Even if I'm right about this, however, it is of course true that what is typically the case may not always be the case. So let us now imagine that, for each of your options, you have some degree of credence in the proposition that choosing it would be morally wrong, but that for *none* of your options do you believe outright that choosing it would be morally wrong. Thus, whatever you do, you won't believe that you are acting wrongly. Is it nonetheless possible for you to be to blame for your behavior?

Perhaps so. Presumably a credence of 0.1 that you are acting wrongly won't suffice (along with your satisfying the control condition for moral responsibility) for your being to blame, but suppose that you have a much higher credence—say, a credence of 0.7—in this proposition. Would that suffice? It seems plausible to say that it would. Call any credence greater than 0.5 "substantial."[25] It seems plausible to say that a substantial credence that one is acting wrongly is sufficient

---

[25] Given the possibility of imprecise credences, it might be better to say that any credence within a range whose lowermost limit is greater than 0.5 is a substantial credence, but I'll put this subtlety to one side. See §3.2.4 for discussion.

(along with satisfaction of the control condition) for one's being to blame for one's behavior (given that one also has a substantial credence regarding some other option that choosing it would not have been wrong). It also seems plausible to say that, all else being equal, the higher the degree of credence, the more one is to blame for one's behavior (unless, perhaps, one also believes outright that one is acting wrongly). If this is correct, does it require that I revise any of the statements I have made?

One statement that might once again need revision is the definition of recklessness that I have offered. Instead of the definition that I gave at the end of §7.1.3, perhaps this is what we should say: one behaves recklessly just in case, in behaving as one does, *either* one wrongly runs a risk of which one is conscious *or* one is conscious of wrongly running a risk *or* one has a substantial occurrent credence that one is wrongly running a risk. This would allow for a diagnosis of recklessness in a case in which you have a credence of 0.7, but no outright belief, that you are wrongly running a risk.

But that is a minor matter. Of far greater importance, it may seem, is the need once again to revise the Argument from Ignorance and, along with it, the Origination Thesis, since, in their two most recent versions (Drafts 6 and 7), they concern only the belief (i.e., the belief outright) that one is acting wrongly and say nothing about having a substantial credence in this proposition without believing it. In fact, though, and perhaps surprisingly, *no* revision is called for on this score. This is because Drafts 6 and 7 of the Argument and Thesis are explicitly concerned with acting *from*, and not merely in, the failure to believe outright that one is acting wrongly. If one is behaving wrongly and has a substantial credence that one is doing so, then one is willingly doing wrong, regardless of whether one believes this proposition outright; one's wrongdoing is not to be *attributed* to one's failure of belief. Hence the possibility of having such a credence in the absence of an outright belief (a possibility whose coherence I question, given the protean nature of what constitutes one's best bet), leaves the Argument and the Thesis entirely unaffected.[26]

7.1.5 Purposely doing wrong

I have already addressed the issue of what degree of blameworthiness attaches to purposely doing wrong in §2.5.4. Here I will add just a few remarks.

---

[26] Compare risking harm with risking wrong. If one has a substantial credence, but no outright belief, that one is causing some harm—something that I concede is perfectly coherent—and one is indeed causing that harm, then one is willingly causing it; one's harm-causing is not to be *attributed* to one's failure of belief. This is true even if one would refrain from causing the harm if one believed outright that one was causing it. Hence the counterfactual account given in the first paragraph of §3.3 regarding what it is to do something from ignorance is indeed rough.

The definition of committing an offense purposely that is given in the *Model Penal Code* goes as follows:

> A person acts purposely with respect to a material element of an offense when:
>
> (i) if the element involves the nature of his conduct or a result thereof, it is his conscious object to engage in conduct of that nature or to cause such a result; and
>
> (ii) if the element involves the attendant circumstances, he is aware of the existence of such circumstances or he believes or hopes that they exist.[27]

This definition appears to presuppose, very plausibly, that committing an offense purposely requires either believing outright or, at least, having some degree of credence that one will succeed in doing so. Once again, though, this does *not* require in turn either believing outright or having some degree of credence that one will thereby be doing *moral wrong*, and that is of course my present concern.

Recall the distinction from §2.5.4 between purposely doing something, something that is in fact wrong, and purposely doing wrong. In the former case the wrongdoing may be wholly unwitting, in which case the Argument from Ignorance will apply. In the latter case the wrongdoing cannot be wholly unwitting.

Recall, too, the distinction between purposely doing wrong for the sake of doing wrong, which I characterized as satanic, and purposely doing wrong for the sake of achieving some further goal. The latter is to be contrasted with "merely" knowingly doing wrong (or believing outright or having some degree of credence that one is doing so) in the pursuit of some goal. This distinction is thought by some to be of great moral significance—consider, for example, the role it plays in the Doctrine of Double Effect—but it's not easy to see why we should agree. As I noted in §2.5.4, what does seem to be of great significance is the fact that, whether one purposely or merely knowingly does wrong in the pursuit of some goal, one certainly lacks the purpose of *not* doing wrong.

Suppose, however, that it is nonetheless true that purposely doing wrong in the pursuit of some goal does, *ceteris paribus*, confer greater culpability on the agent than merely knowingly doing so does. Even so, there is reason to doubt the *Code*'s approach to this issue. It apparently holds that committing an offense purposely always confers greater culpability on the offender than committing it merely knowingly does,[28] but this fits uneasily with the view that, the further a credence

---

[27] American Law Institute (1985), §2.02(2)(a).
[28] This is how I interpret §2.02(5) of the *Code*, which states that "[w]hen acting knowingly suffices to establish an element, such element is established if a person acts purposely" but conspicuously omits to state the converse.

that some material element of an offense obtains falls short of knowledge (or practical certainty) that it obtains, the lower one's degree of culpability; for one can do something purposely even when one is far from being practically certain that one will succeed. Consider Juan* again. He has a credence of 0.1 that flipping the switch will cause the deaths of many innocent people, in virtue of which, let us suppose, he attaches a certain degree of seriousness to the wrongness of flipping it. We can imagine that, if he had a credence of, say, 0.99 that the flipping would cause the deaths, he would attach a far higher degree of seriousness to the wrongness of the flipping. In either scenario, if he nonetheless goes ahead and flips the switch, then (given that he satisfies the control condition for moral responsibility) he will be to blame for doing so, but to a much greater degree in the latter scenario, in which he has a credence of 0.99, than in the former scenario, in which he has a credence of 0.1. Suppose now that we add to the former scenario, but *not* to the latter, that Juan*'s purpose in flipping the switch is to cause the deaths in question. Should we infer that, simply in virtue of this fact, his degree of culpability soars so high that it surpasses his degree of culpability in the latter scenario? That seems dubious to me. It might be retorted that, given how low his credence is in the first scenario, Juan* cannot have it as his purpose, but can only have it as his hope, that the flipping will cause the deaths, and hence that, even if, given this hope, his degree of culpability in the first scenario does not surpass his degree of culpability in the second, this fact does not impugn the *Code*'s approach. Perhaps so. I will leave the question open.

7.2 Motivated ignorance

True story: In search of what they imagined would be a "good time," Charles Demore Jewell and a friend rented a car and drove it from Los Angeles to Mexico. They were in a bar in Tijuana (it's not clear whether the good time had yet begun) when they were approached by a stranger who identified himself only as "Ray." Ray asked them whether they wanted to buy some marijuana. They declined to do so. Ray then asked them whether they would be willing to drive a car north across the border in exchange for $100. Jewell's friend declined this offer, too, but Jewell himself accepted it. While Jewell's friend drove the rented car back to Los Angeles, Jewell drove Ray's car. At the border crossing, a U.S. Customs agent discovered, hidden between the rear seat and the trunk of Ray's car, a compartment that contained 110 pounds of marijuana. (By then, the good time was definitely over.) Jewell was arrested and charged with knowingly importing a controlled substance. In his defense, Jewell testified that, although he thought that the car might contain contraband, he didn't know that it did. Indeed, he indicated that he had deliberately refrained from inspecting the car too closely precisely in order to remain ignorant about whether it contained contraband.

The Court was not impressed. It rejected Jewell's defense on the grounds that

> ... [t]he Government can complete their burden of proof by proving, beyond a reasonable doubt, that if the defendant was not actually aware that there was marijuana in the vehicle he was driving when he entered the United States his ignorance was solely and entirely a result of his having made a conscious purpose to disregard the nature of that which was in the vehicle, with a conscious purpose to avoid learning the truth.[29]

In support of this finding, the Court quoted the following passage from Glanville Williams:

> The rule that wilful blindness is equivalent to knowledge is essential, and is found throughout the criminal law... A court can properly find wilful blindness only where it can almost be said that the defendant actually knew. He suspected the fact; he realised its probability; but he refrained from obtaining the final confirmation because he wanted in the event to be able to deny knowledge. This, and this alone, is wilful blindness. It requires in effect a finding that the defendant intended to cheat the administration of justice.[30]

And the Court continued:

> The substantive justification for the rule is that deliberate ignorance and positive knowledge are equally culpable. The textual justification is that in common understanding one "knows" facts of which he is less than absolutely certain. To act "knowingly," therefore, is not necessarily to act only with positive knowledge, but also to act with an awareness of the high probability of the existence of the fact in question. When such awareness is present, "positive" knowledge is not required.

Did the Court provide good reason to find Jewell guilty as charged?

7.2.1 Varieties of motivated ignorance

To answer this question, let's start by exposing the underlying structure of Jewell's case.

If we take Jewell at his word, he didn't know that Ray's car contained contraband. Call this proposition p_1. Jewell didn't know p_1 at least in part because, although he suspected that it was true, he didn't believe it outright. Another

---

[29] *United States v. Jewell* 532 F.2nd 697 (9th Cir. 1976).   [30] G. Williams (1961), p. 159.

crucial feature of the case is that Jewell's continued ignorance of p_1 was contrived, in that he knew (or at least believed) that he could improve his epistemic situation but declined to avail himself of the means to do so; he could have inspected the car but chose not to. Although, being ignorant of p_1, Jewell of course didn't know that, by inspecting the car, he would come to know *that* p_1 was true, he did know (or at least believed) that he would (or would probably) come to know *whether* p_1 was true. (See §3.1 on the distinction between knowing-that and knowing-whether.) He thus took himself to be in control—indirect control (see §4.6.2)—of his doxastic state, and he chose to exercise this control by refraining from inspecting the car, his purpose being to remain ignorant of whether p_1 was true. In light of this fact, it is reasonable to adopt the Court's terminology and characterize Jewell's continued ignorance of whether p_1 was true as "willful." A word of caution, though. "Willful" typically carries a negative connotation—we readily talk, for example, of someone's "willful disregard" for some rule, whereas talk of "willful regard" sounds decidedly odd[31]—but we should guard against any such prejudgment, for fear of building culpability into the very idea of willful ignorance and thereby committing ourselves to the verdict that Jewell is to blame for his behavior. This verdict is precisely what is in question. It might be safer, then, to talk simply in terms of "deliberate" ignorance, a term that applies equally to all cases in which someone intentionally forgoes the opportunity to become better informed, whether for reasons that are morally suspect (as in Jewell's case) or not (as when a couple deliberately remain ignorant about the sex of their forthcoming child or a patient deliberately puts off learning the results of a recent biopsy).

Consider, now, this variation on Jewell's case—call it Variation 1. In this version of the case, Ray is not a stranger but a close friend. He doesn't offer to sell Jewell any marijuana. Instead he simply tells him that a mutual friend of theirs in the U.S. needs his car. He says that he is unfortunately tied up at the moment, and so he asks Jewell whether he would be willing to do him a favor and deliver the car on his behalf. He offers Jewell some money to pay for gas, but nothing beyond that. Jewell readily agrees. It occurs to him that there could be something fishy about Ray's request, but he regards Ray as a good friend and fully trustworthy and so dismisses this suspicion. Although he has a low credence in p_1, he doesn't believe it; indeed, he *dis*believes it, that is, he believes outright that it is *false*. As a consequence, although he is aware that he could check whether p_1 is true, he sees no need to do so; indeed, he thinks that there is a need *not* to do so, since

---

[31] This observation puts me in mind of a memorable plaque to be found on the grounds of Rugby School. The plaque reads:

This stone/commemorates the exploit of/William Webb Ellis/who with a fine disregard for the rules of football/as played in his time/first took the ball in his arms and ran with it/thus originating the distinctive feature of/the rugby game./A. D. 1823.

The delicious irony of this plaque is not lost on those schoolboys and -girls who daily pass it by, keenly aware that it is exceedingly unlikely that, if they were ever to show a similarly fine disregard for some school rule, their exploit would be celebrated in such grand fashion.

inspecting the car would show disloyalty to Ray. Unfortunately, Ray is not as good a friend as Jewell takes him to be. His car contains contraband.

In Variation 1, as in the original case, Jewell is ignorant of whether p_1 is true. But, as is not true in the original case, Jewell doesn't take himself to be ignorant of this, and so his declining to inspect the car doesn't constitute a deliberate attempt on his part to remain ignorant of it. It would therefore be quite misleading to call his continued ignorance *willful*. Still, his refraining from inspecting the car is deliberate, and he anticipates, and perhaps also has as part of his purpose, continuing to disbelieve p_1. Under these circumstances it seems appropriate to describe his continued ignorance as *motivated*. This description also applies to the original case. In that case, Jewell's continued ignorance was motivated by self-interest. In Variation 1 it is motivated by loyalty to Ray.

In both versions of the case considered so far, Jewell's doxastic state doesn't change, and as a result his epistemic situation also remains the same. In the original case, his initial doxastic state was that of suspecting but not believing p_1 ($Sp_1 \& {\sim}Bp_1$), and he deliberately maintained this state.[32] In Variation 1, his initial state is that of suspecting but nonetheless disbelieving p_1 ($Sp_1 \& B{\sim}p_1$), and he deliberately acts in such a manner that he anticipates, and perhaps even intends, that this state will be maintained. In these versions, whatever it is that motivates his failure to inspect the car, the lack of change in his doxastic state and in his epistemic situation is explained by that failure. But it is easy to imagine other versions of the case in which Jewell's doxastic state changes, as a result of which his epistemic situation deteriorates, and in these versions his failure to inspect the car cannot suffice as an explanation of where it is that he ends up either doxastically or epistemically. For example, he might initially suspect but not believe p_1 ($Sp_1 \& {\sim}Bp_1$) and end up disbelieving it ($B{\sim}p_1$), or he might even believe p_1 (Bp_1) initially but end up merely suspecting it ($Sp_1 \& {\sim}Bp_1$) or positively disbelieving it ($B{\sim}p_1$)—call these Variations 2, 3, and 4, respectively. In principle, there could be any number of reasons for such a shift in Jewell's attitude (hypnosis, a knock on the head, divine intervention, and so on), but, if we hold constant the feature that his failure to inspect the car is deliberate, the explanation for the shift will likely make reference to wishful thinking, self-deception, or the like, prompted once again by self-interest, loyalty, or some such motive.

7.2.2 The law on willful ignorance

Return to the original case of *United States v. Jewell*. There are several reasons to question what the Court had to say.

---

[32] Here I am using "suspect" to mean the same as "have a (or some) suspicion." See ch. 3, n. 57.

One glaring problem is this. The Court accuses Jewell of deliberate ignorance and yet holds that he satisfies the requisite *mens rea* of knowledge. This is untenable. If Jewell's being aware of the high probability that the car contained contraband suffices for what the law is content to recognize as knowledge, then the claim that he was ignorant of this fact must be withdrawn. If, however, Jewell was indeed ignorant of this fact (as surely he was), then the claim that he knew it must be withdrawn. "Almost" knowing something doesn't suffice for knowing it.

Despite the inconsistency in the Court's reasoning, you might nonetheless sympathize with its verdict. As the Court candidly admits, this verdict is based on the judgment that those who, like Jewell, deliberately avoid confirming some incriminating fact when engaged in what would otherwise be criminal behavior don't escape the culpability that those who need no such confirmation incur. It's clear that there are two ways in which the Court's verdict might be reached consistently. Either it can be stipulated that the term "know" and its cognates are to be construed in such a way that, for the purposes of the law, agents such as Jewell are to be deemed as indeed knowing the facts in question—in which case they cannot also be declared ignorant of these facts. Or it can be acknowledged that agents such as Jewell do not know the facts in question—in which case a new set of laws must be drafted in order to capture the particular *mens rea* that these agents supposedly exhibit.

I do not recommend taking the first option. Understanding the requirement of "knowledge" to be satisfied by an awareness of the high probability of some fact— a strategy apparently endorsed by the Court (and also, as I noted in §7.1.2, by the *Model Penal Code*)—won't do the job that's needed. As Douglas Husak points out, a modified *Jewell*-like case in which a stranger asks two tourists to transport one suitcase each across the border, assuring them that one of the suitcases is empty but declining to identify which suitcase that is, would not be a case in which either tourist assigns a high probability to the fact that he is importing a controlled substance, and yet both tourists would seem to exhibit the kind of willful ignorance that the Court is concerned to condemn.[33] Claiming that each of the tourists nonetheless "knows," as far as the law is concerned, that he is importing a controlled substance seems clearly to stretch the term too far. Moreover, one can of course imagine further iterations of the idea: three tourists with three suitcases, two of which are empty; four tourists with four suitcases, three of which are empty; and so on.[34]

The second option thus seems preferable: draft new statutes which purport to identify precisely the kind of *mens rea* that constitutes willful ignorance and which prohibit engaging with such ignorance in forms of behavior that are already prohibited when engaged in knowingly.[35] But whether even this option is

---

[33] Husak (2016), p. 219. Cf. Husak and Callender (1994), pp. 37 f.
[34] Cf. Alexander et al. (2009), p. 34.   [35] Cf. Husak and Callender (1994), pp. 68 f.

advisable depends on whether willfully ignorant agents are indeed culpable for the behavior in which they engage. The Court in *Jewell* maintains not only that they *are* culpable but also that they and their knowing counterparts are *equally* culpable. This claim clearly commits the Court to holding that willfully ignorant agents and their knowing counterparts are liable to equal punishment, but I think it's also clear that the Court intends more than just this. For liability to punishment can be based on a variety of grounds, and the Court appears to be especially concerned with one ground in particular: *mens rea*. At one point it quotes with approval the following passage written by J. Ll. J. Edwards:

> For well-nigh a hundred years, it has been clear from the authorities that a person who deliberately shuts his eyes to an obvious means of knowledge has sufficient *mens rea* for an offence based on such words as ... 'knowingly.'[36]

I therefore understand the Court to be claiming that willfully ignorant agents and their knowing counterparts are liable to equal punishment in virtue of manifesting equally depraved *mentes reae*.[37] Call this the Equal Culpability Thesis.[38] Should we accept this thesis?

7.2.3 The duty to inquire

Once it is acknowledged that willfully ignorant agents do not know what their knowing counterparts know, the Equal Culpability Thesis faces an immediate problem. Although it is no doubt true that, in typical cases, willfully ignorant agents act recklessly,[39] nonetheless, as I have repeatedly noted, the law holds that, *ceteris paribus*, reckless agents are *less* culpable than their knowing counterparts. Call this the Unequal Culpability Thesis. The only way to reconcile the two theses is to show that (to put the point ungrammatically), when recklessness takes the particular form of willful ignorance, *ceteris* is not *paribus*.

One way to try to show this is to invoke the view, mentioned in §7.1.2, that the law treats committing an offense knowingly as a limiting case of committing an offense recklessly. If the recklessness of willfully ignorant agents places them at this limit, then the Equal Culpability Thesis and the Unequal Culpability Thesis do not conflict. But this is surely a mistake. In general, the degree of credence that willfully ignorant agents have in the relevant proposition is *not* as high as that of

---

[36] J. Ll. J. Edwards (1954), p. 298.
[37] In adopting this interpretation, I join company with several other commentators. Cf. Husak and Callender (1994); Luban (1999); Sarch (2014) and (2016); Husak (2016); Yaffe (2018).
[38] I borrow this term from Husak and Callender (1994).
[39] Cf. Husak and Callender (1994), p. 42; Alexander et al. (2009), p. 34; Sarch (2014), pp. 1079 ff., and (2016), p. 281 n. 8 and pp. 302 ff.; Husak (2016), p. 221.

their knowing counterparts. Even if Jewell's degree of credence in p_1 was high, he recognized that he could (probably) raise it still further by inspecting the car. And certainly the degree of credence to be attributed to the tourists that their suitcase contained contraband was far below that of rationally supporting the belief outright that it did.

Another way to try to reconcile the two theses is to ascribe to willfully ignorant agents some reprehensible purpose that would elevate their degree of culpability to that of their knowing counterparts. But what purpose? Surely not the purpose of committing the offense in question. It was not Jewell's purpose to import a controlled substance. Nor, *pace* Williams, does it seem accurate to say that it is the purpose of willfully ignorant agents to "cheat the administration of justice."[40] After all, Jewell apparently believed that, if he managed to preserve his ignorance regarding the contents of Ray's car, he would have a genuine defense against the charge of knowingly importing a controlled substance and thus would *not* be breaking the law (or, at least, not that law) by driving the car across the border. Under these circumstances, the charge that he attempted to cheat the administration of justice seems to miss the mark. (Compare the strenuous efforts people often make to find legally permissible ways to avoid paying taxes.)

A third way to try to reconcile the Equal Culpability Thesis and the Unequal Culpability Thesis is to attribute an extra piece of wrongdoing to willfully ignorant agents, the culpability for which, when combined with their culpability for the offense that is also committed by their knowing counterparts, results in the two parties being equally culpable. Many commentators claim that, in typical cases at least, agents who exhibit willful ignorance in the commission of an offense have violated a prior duty to inquire into whether what they suspect to be the case is indeed the case.[41] Others hold that, even if some willfully ignorant agents don't have a positive duty to gather pertinent information, they at least have a negative duty not to screen themselves off from such information.[42] Let's apply this idea to Jewell's case. Suppose that, in light of the fact that he crossed the border while suspecting that he was importing a controlled substance, Jewell is culpable to degree m for this piece of reckless wrongdoing, whereas someone who crossed the border knowing that he was importing a controlled substance would have been culpable to a greater degree, n. Since $m < n$, Jewell is not as culpable as his knowing counterpart in light of this piece of wrongdoing *alone*. But there is also his prior failure to inspect the car to be taken into consideration. Suppose that this is a

---

[40] Cf. Husak and Callender (1994), p. 40, and Husak (2016), pp. 220 f., on the "motivational condition" that willfully ignorant agents allegedly satisfy.
[41] Cf. Husak and Callender (1994), p. 40; Hellman (2009), pp. 312 ff.; Sarch (2014), pp. 1078 ff., and (2016), pp. 297 ff.; Husak (2016), pp. 220 f.; Wieland (2017a), pp. 4480 ff. Also cf. on epistemic obligations generally, whether in legal or non-legal contexts, Clifford (1877), §1; Feldman (2000), pp. 688 ff.; Rosen (2004), pp. 301 ff., and (2008), pp. 601 ff.; FitzPatrick (2008), p. 604; Vanderheiden (2016), p. 305; and Peels (2017), ch. 3.
[42] Cf. Luban (1999), pp. 969 f.; Sarch (2016), p. 301.

separate wrongdoing for which he is culpable to degree l. Then (to engage in some spurious algebra) it seems in principle possible that $l+m = n$, in which case Jewell and his knowing counterpart will be equally culpable for their respective *courses* of action. (Notice that, in the case of the counterpart, there is no prior failure to inspect that we would need to concern ourselves with. Since he knew that the car contained contraband, he had no duty to inquire into whether it did.)

That it is possible for a willfully ignorant wrongdoer to be as culpable as his knowing counterpart in virtue of such a fact as that $l+m = n$ has been defended by Alexander Sarch.[43] Sarch does not insist that in all cases of this sort $l+m = n$, but only that this may sometimes be the case. (Indeed, on his approach, it would seem typically *not* to be the case. Sarch takes there to be many factors—having to do with ease of inquiry and the like—that can affect one's degree of culpability for violating a duty to inquire, and so it would be quite a coincidence if, nonetheless, $l+m$ were precisely equal to n.[44]) Even so, appealing to the duty of ignorant agents in situations such as Jewell's to seek (or, at least, not to screen themselves off from) information regarding whether their suspicions are accurate might seem sufficient to show that the Unequal Culpability Thesis is at least consistent with a qualified version of the Equal Culpability Thesis, according to which, *ceteris paribus*, willfully ignorant agents and their knowing counterparts are equally culpable.

I take such an approach to assessing the culpability of willfully ignorant agents such as Jewell to be highly suspect, however. For, contrary to what appears to be common opinion, it seems to me plain that such agents do *not* in general have an obligation to inquire into whether the facts are as they suspect them to be. They don't even have an obligation not to screen themselves off from information about these facts. Consider Jewell. Clearly, Jewell would have done nothing wrong if he had flat-out refused to drive the car. But notice that, had he chosen *this* option, there would have been no reason for him to inspect it at all! And so, I think, he indeed had no obligation to inspect it. What he *did* have an obligation to do was to inspect it *if* he was going to drive it. To bring this point out clearly, let "O" stand for "obligated," "d" for "drive," and "i" for "inspect." What I am asserting is this: $O(d \rightarrow i)$; that is, $O(\sim d \vee i)$; that is, $O\sim(d \& \sim i)$. What I am *denying* is this: Oi. And if Jewell had no free-standing obligation to inspect the car, then his failure to do so was not an extra piece of wrongdoing that involved an extra incurrence of culpability.[45]

---

[43] Sarch (2014), pp. 1088 ff., (2016), pp. 309 f., and (2019), pp. 168 ff.

[44] Sarch (2014), pp. 1086 f.

[45] I am also willing to assert this: $O\sim d$. What I mean by this is that, under the circumstances of the case (circumstances which included his not having inspected the car), Jewell ought not to have driven the car. If the circumstances had been different—in particular, if Jewell had inspected the car sufficiently thoroughly (I will leave open what "sufficiently" comes to in this context) and found no contraband—would it *then* have been the case that he ought not to have driven the car across the border? Maybe, maybe not. The answer depends on further details of the case.

You might agree with me that Jewell had the conditional obligation consisting in $O(d\to i)$ but still wish to claim that he *also* had the unconditional obligation consisting in Oi. But what would be the *basis* of this claim? Perhaps you would appeal to the fact that the condition, d, of the conditional obligation was satisfied—and of course it was: Jewell did indeed drive the car across the border. But, as is generally recognized, satisfaction of the condition of a conditional obligation does *not* necessarily engender the detachment of the corresponding unconditional obligation. Consider Martin. He likes to mistreat animals, and he's just managed to capture a stray cat. Among his options are these: he can refrain from torturing the cat; he can torture it briefly; he can torture it for an extended period of time. Surely, if Martin is going to torture the cat at all, he ought to torture it briefly rather than for an extended period of time. Suppose that, as is his wont, he is indeed going to torture it. Does it follow that he ought to torture it briefly? Certainly not! He ought not to torture it at all.

Sometimes, of course, an unconditional obligation *does* emerge via detachment from a conditional obligation. One kind of case in which this is so is one in which the agent *cannot avoid* the condition's being satisfied, and one way in which this can happen is this: the condition has *already been* satisfied. Consider Sonya. Like everyone, she has an (unconditional) obligation not to sin but also, let us assume, a (conditional) obligation to repent *if* she sins. Suppose that she has committed some sin. Prior to the commission of the sin, she had no obligation to repent; but, since the past cannot be undone, she does indeed now have an obligation to repent. In this way, the passage of time can account, in part, for the transformation of a conditional obligation into an unconditional obligation. But notice that this kind of account *cannot* be applied to Jewell's case, since in his case whether the condition, d, of his conditional obligation, $O(d\to i)$, was satisfied *was still up to him* at the time at which he was faced with the decision whether or not to inspect the car. Hence the detachment of an unconditional obligation to inspect it was not occasioned for the kind of reason presently under consideration, and I can think of no other reason that might be applicable, either.[46]

The kind of strategy employed by Sarch is one that requires identifying two independent instances of wrongdoing, one that occurs at the time of non-inspection, the other that occurs at the time of driving. Being independent, these two instances supposedly combine to render Jewell's total wrongdoing more serious than it would have been had just one of these episodes occurred, and this in turn is supposed to be what accounts for his overall culpability being computable along the lines of the formula $l+m = n$. But it's not easy to find a

---

[46] Similar remarks would apply to the detachment of an unconditional obligation for Jewell to inspect the car from the (alleged) conditional obligation for him to inspect it if he *intended* to drive it.

rationale that supports this strategy.[47] Certainly the attempt to account for his having an unconditional obligation to inspect the car by appealing to his having a conditional obligation to inspect it seems unpromising. Might some other approach work?

Well, consider this suggestion. Suppose that Jewell was the sort of person who, though quite willing to *risk* importing a controlled substance, would not have been willing to import it *knowingly* and so would not have driven the car across the border had he inspected it and discovered its contents. Then, in refraining from inspecting the car, he was forgoing the opportunity to reduce the likelihood of later wrongdoing on his part, and to forgo such an opportunity *itself* constituted a separate piece of wrongdoing in virtue of which he incurred increased culpability. What should we make of this?

I understand the suggestion to be that the reason that Jewell had an unconditional obligation to inspect the car was that he had not yet settled whether he was going to drive it. This suggestion is compatible with the fact that, as I pointed out earlier, Jewell's flat-out refusing to drive the car would have rendered inspecting it pointless, and it is also compatible with the fact that his being willing to drive it no matter what an inspection revealed would also have rendered inspecting it pointless. Thus it is compatible with the denial that, *in general*, agents in his sort of situation have a duty to inquire into whether the facts are as they suspect them to be. Moreover, the suggestion is in keeping with the view that *ceteris* is not *paribus* when it comes to comparing willfully ignorant agents with their knowing counterparts. Those agents who have deliberately forgone the opportunity to inquire into whether the facts are as they suspect them to be fall into two groups. In the first group are those who would have balked at committing the pertinent offense knowingly. Insofar as this is the case, they may be less culpable for committing the offense than their knowing counterparts, but the present suggestion purports to explain how this gap in culpability is narrowed, or possibly closed, in virtue of their having violated the prior duty to reduce the likelihood of their own later wrongdoing. In the second group are those willfully ignorant agents who had already settled on committing the pertinent offense and thus had no duty, and so violated no duty, to undertake an inquiry. The gap in culpability between them

---

[47] Notice that, even on my account, Jewell committed two wrongs: the wrong of not fulfilling the obligation consisting in $O{\sim}d$ (see n. 45 above) and the wrong of not fulfilling the obligation consisting in $O{\sim}(d\&{\sim}i)$. But, although these are two wrongs, they are not two *independent* instances of wrongdoing. After all, it seems very plausible to hold that, for any p and q, $O{\sim}p$ implies $O{\sim}(p\&q)$. (This principle implies that, whenever one does wrong, one commits an *infinite* number of wrongs! It doesn't follow that, whenever one does wrong, one's wrongdoing is infinitely serious. How *much* wrong one does is not dictated by how *many* wrongs one commits.) If so, then, even if Jewell hadn't had the opportunity to inspect the car, it would *still* have been the case that he had not only the obligation consisting in $O{\sim}d$ but also the obligation consisting in $O{\sim}(d\&{\sim}i)$, and so, even under these circumstances, he would still have committed the same two wrongs. Thus there is no reason, on this basis at least, to ascribe to Jewell under the actual circumstances of his case a greater degree of culpability than that which he would have incurred, had the opportunity to inspect the car not been available to him.

and their knowing counterparts is of course not closed in virtue of this non-violation, but, it may be claimed, there was in fact no gap to begin with, precisely because they were just as willing as their knowing counterparts to commit the offense.

For all that I have said, this suggestion might work. Note, though, two difficulties that it faces. First, it is surely not in general true that one is morally obligated to reduce the likelihood of later wrongdoing on one's part. If this were the case, we would all be morally required to commit suicide forthwith. Perhaps, though, some suitably qualified obligation to forestall later wrongdoing obtains in cases such as Jewell's. Second, even if such an obligation does obtain in such cases, there is certainly no guarantee that its violation raises the willfully ignorant agent's culpability to the same level as that of his knowing counterpart. He might have an excuse for violating it—perhaps an excuse grounded in *ignorance*![48] After all, who among us is aware of having this alleged, rather *recherché* duty?

7.2.4 Motivated non-moral ignorance

I have focused on *United States v. Jewell* in part because it is so well known, but primarily because it provides such a useful example of willfully ignorant behavior. It is important to remember, however, that the issue of responsibility for willfully ignorant behavior, and indeed for behavior that exhibits other forms of motivated ignorance, does not arise only in legal contexts. Although it is for the most part legal theorists who have addressed the issue up to this point, it has also recently captured the attention of moral philosophers who see motivated ignorance operating in a variety of non-legal contexts. Consider, for example, cases in which a politician, or military commander, or CEO deliberately contrives to maintain "plausible deniability" regarding the misdeeds of some subordinate. Or, in case you are tempted to think of motivated ignorance as someone else's problem, consider how often we turn a blind eye to the conditions in which animals are raised for eventual slaughter and consumption, how frequently we overlook the conditions in which factory workers in low-income countries labor to produce the cheap goods we buy, and so on. Indeed, when the issue is, as it is here, *moral* responsibility for behavior that exhibits motivated ignorance, there is a danger in focusing on legal cases, since the question that is typically of immediate concern in those cases is whether the accused is *legally* responsible for his or her behavior. I asked earlier whether the Court had provided good reason to find Jewell guilty as charged, but in truth that is not the question that I am really concerned with, since

---

[48] Cf. Rosen (2004), pp. 309 f., and (2008), p. 605, Husak (2016), pp. 179 ff., and Miller (2017), p. 1572, on the possibility of having an excuse for violating a duty to inquire in virtue of being ignorant of the fact that one has this duty.

in that context guilt is most naturally understood as a legal concept having essentially to do with liability to punishment by the state; and, as I noted earlier, such liability can be based on a variety of grounds, including moral culpability but also including considerations having to do with deterrence, incapacitation, and the like.[49]

So let me now turn directly to the question of moral responsibility for behavior that exhibits motivated ignorance. The first thing to note is that the Equal Culpability Thesis clearly does not hold in general. Whatever reason there may be to hold Jewell equally as culpable, morally, as his knowing counterpart, there would seem to be good reason to reach a verdict of *unequal* culpability between willfully ignorant agents and their knowing counterparts in other cases. Consider, for example, Husak's case of the tourists and the suitcases and the various iterations of this case. All else being equal, the greater the number of suitcases, the less reckless it would be to carry one of them across the border, until the point is reached at which, the number of suitcases being so large, carrying one across the border can no longer be properly called reckless at all. Thus, if (as is certainly possible, but is by no means necessary) degree of culpability tracks degree of recklessness in these iterations of the case, then the greater the number of suitcases, the lower the degree of culpability incurred for carrying one across the border, until at some point no culpability is incurred at all.

How, then, are we to judge degree of culpability in any particular case in which someone's behavior exhibits willful ignorance (or motivated ignorance more generally)? Well, here I would remind you of two crucial distinctions that are unfortunately all too often overlooked in discussions of this issue. The first is that between objective wrongdoing and what I have called prospective wrongdoing (see §7.1.4). The second is that between conscious risk-taking and conscious wrongdoing (see §7.1.3).

Philosophers who are sympathetic to the idea that ignorance of wrongdoing provides an excuse for wrongdoing often think that they must treat willful ignorance (and motivated ignorance more generally) as an exception.[50] This is because they subscribe, whether explicitly or implicitly, to an objective account of moral obligation and wrongdoing. Consider the original case of *Jewell*. Jewell suspected that Ray's car contained contraband, but he didn't believe outright that it did; hence he was ignorant of this proposition, which earlier I called p_1. Since he

---

[49] It is notable that, even though, in focusing on *mens rea*, the Court in *Jewell* appears to have been primarily concerned with moral culpability, it clearly also had deterrence in mind when it stated:

> Appellant's narrow interpretation of "knowingly" is inconsistent with the Drug Control Act's general purpose to deal more effectively "with the growing menace of drug abuse in the United States."... Holding that this term introduces a requirement of positive knowledge would make deliberate ignorance a defense. It cannot be doubted that those who traffic in drugs would make the most of it.

[50] See, e.g., Husak (2016), pp. 222 f., and Wieland (2019), pp. 1410 ff.

refrained from inspecting Ray's car, he remained ignorant of p_1 and, as a result, was also ignorant, at the time he drove the car, of the fact that he was importing a controlled substance—call this proposition p_2.[51] But, if his importing a controlled substance constituted wrongful behavior on his part, then he was also ignorant of the fact that he was wrongly importing a controlled substance—call this proposition p_3. Yet, these philosophers want to say, since his ignorance was willful, Jewell's ignorance of p_3 does *not* provide him with an excuse for his wrongful behavior. Thus willful ignorance constitutes an exception to the general rule that ignorance of wrongdoing excuses one's wrongdoing, one that these philosophers must now scramble to explain.

I think this is a mistake. No special explanation is necessary, for cases such as Jewell's are not an exception to the rule. Propositions p_1 and p_2 have no direct relevance to the issue at hand.

Even though Jewell was ignorant of the fact that he was importing a controlled substance, he was fully aware of the fact that he was *risking* importing a controlled substance—call this proposition p_4—and it is *this* that, on the prospective approach to moral obligation and wrongdoing, constituted wrongdoing on his part. And so the crucial question is this: Was Jewell aware that he was *wrongly* risking importing a controlled substance (call this proposition p_5)? It seems very reasonable to assume that he *was*. If so, no excuse is forthcoming on this basis. His willful ignorance doesn't excuse him, because it wasn't ignorance of the fact *that he was doing wrong*. Rather, it was ignorance of the *non*-moral fact that he was importing a controlled substance. So, too, for other cases of the kind mentioned earlier, in which one contrives to remain ignorant about the conditions in which the cheap products that one purchases were produced, or about the activities of one's subordinates, and so on. Ignorance about such facts in and of itself affords *no excuse whatsoever* for any wrongdoing in which one might engage.

Though improbable, it is of course possible that, despite being aware that he was risking importing a controlled substance, Jewell was not aware that he was wrongly doing so. (Similarly, and less improbably, it can happen that one is aware that, in buying certain goods, one is risking promoting perpetuation of the squalid working conditions in which they are produced and yet not believe that doing so is wrong—perhaps because one believes that to refrain from buying these goods would only result in the workers being shifted from low income to no income.)

---

[51] It might seem more accurate to say that Jewell, having been stopped at the border, didn't in fact import a controlled substance but merely attempted to do so. One problem with this description, though, is that it's not clear that one can be properly said to be attempting to do something that one hopes one is not doing. In any case, since the Court convicted Jewell of knowingly importing a controlled substance, I will assume that for present purposes it is correct to describe him as having imported such a substance, even though I take it to be incorrect to describe him as having knowingly done so.

If Jewell was not aware that his behavior was wrong, then he *does* have an excuse for his conduct after all—unless he is to blame for his ignorance or didn't act *from* this ignorance.

7.2.5 Motivated moral ignorance

Even though Jewell's case and other such cases that have been the focus of much of the discussion of motivated ignorance in the literature are not cases of motivated *moral* ignorance, such cases can nonetheless occur. Do *they* require special treatment?

They do not. Consider this artificially simple case. Fiona knows that a certain drug has two notable properties. First, it produces a temporary euphoria that is so intense that, second, it renders one wholly oblivious to the consequences of one's behavior. Aiming for ecstasy, she takes the drug and, high as a kite, shoves Charlie off his chair, breaking his arm. Since this is my case, I am free to stipulate—and I do stipulate—that the drug didn't somehow render Fiona unable to resist the urge to push Charlie; it simply rendered her blind to the fact that doing so risked causing him harm and thus blind to the fact that doing so was morally wrong. I submit that it is clear that Fiona is not *directly* culpable for her decision to push Charlie. (If you doubt this, consider a case in which Philippa is force-fed the drug in question, as a result of which she engages in behavior just like Fiona's.) Even so, Fiona may well be *indirectly* culpable for this decision, by way of being directly culpable for her decision to take the drug. Thus the case exactly fits the mold of a benighting act resulting in an unwitting wrongful act (regarding which see §5.1.5).

Fiona's ignorance of the fact that, in pushing Charlie, she was behaving wrongly is, of course, an instance of *moral* ignorance. It is, moreover, an instance of *motivated* moral ignorance; in acting as she did, she was motivated by her desire for euphoria. It would be a mistake to call it an instance of *willful* moral ignorance, though. Even though she was aware that the drug would render her oblivious to the consequences of her behavior, she wasn't *aiming* at such obliviousness, let alone aiming at being oblivious to the fact that, in light of these consequences, her behavior would be morally wrong. Still, we can imagine variations on the case in which Fiona *was* aiming at such moral obliviousness in addition to, or even instead of, the euphoria she anticipated.

As described, Fiona's case is a case of motivated *incidental* moral ignorance, not of motivated *fundamental* moral ignorance. (See Chapter 1 on this distinction.) But we can easily imagine a variation on the case that involves the latter. Simply suppose that the drug doesn't render one oblivious to the consequences of one's behavior but does render one oblivious to the moral rightness or wrongness of producing these consequences. Or, more dramatically, suppose that the drug distorts one's moral outlook in such a way that one takes it to be morally right, rather than morally wrong, to risk causing harm to others.

Fiona's case, though informative, is far-fetched. For a more routine kind of case, consider those variations on Jewell's case in which Jewell ended up positively believing that Ray's car did *not* contain contraband, even though initially he either suspected (Variation 2) or believed (Variation 4) that it did. On the supposition in each case that his initial state comported with his evidence, we may assume that, if, in either of these variations, Jewell had had to decide immediately whether to drive Ray's car across the border, he would have recognized the wrongness of doing so and thus have had no excuse for his behavior. This verdict matches the verdict that presumably holds in the original case. However, in contrast to the original case, in these variations we may assume that, in light of the change in his doxastic state that in fact took place, although Jewell wasn't ignorant, at the time he drove Ray's car, of the fact that he was risking importing a controlled substance, he *was* ignorant of the fact that he was *wrongly* doing so. How could this happen, if there was no change in his evidence? All too easily. We can imagine that, prompted by his loyalty to Ray, some form of rationalization, or wishful thinking, or self-deception enabled Jewell to suppress his suspicion (Variation 2) or his belief (Variation 4) that the car contained contraband and thereby to convince himself that what he wanted to be the case—namely, that the car did not contain contraband, so that in driving it he would be doing nothing wrong—was indeed the case. Given that Jewell acted *from* his ignorance of the fact that he was wrongly risking importing a controlled substance, he is not *directly* blameworthy for his wrongful behavior.

It remains possible, of course, that in these variations Jewell is nonetheless *indirectly* blameworthy for his wrongful behavior. The obvious occasion of his being so would be his being to blame for the means by which his ignorance regarding its wrongness was induced. Some philosophers appear to think that it is either definitely[52] or probably[53] the case that ignorance of wrongdoing that is produced via such a motivationally biased mechanism is ignorance for which one is to blame. I venture to say, on the contrary, that this is seldom the case. Given the Argument from Ignorance, one's being to blame in this way for one's ignorance and for the behavior that one performs from this ignorance requires that one be to blame for the operation of the mechanism, which in turn requires that one be in control of its operation. Moreover, one must be *aware of the wrongness* of causing or allowing the mechanism to operate, if one is to be directly to blame for its operation. That this could happen certainly seems psychologically possible, especially since awareness comes in degrees;[54] it is not difficult to imagine one's being

---

[52] See, e.g., Clifford (1877), §1.   [53] See, e.g., M. Baron (2017), pp. 64 ff.
[54] Cf. Husak (2016), pp. 214 f., and Lynch (2016), p. 521.

uneasily, if only dimly, aware that one is wrongly manipulating one's own doxastic states.[55] Nonetheless, I suspect that such manipulation is in fact quite rare,[56] and that it is even more rare that one should be aware of wrongly engaging in it. But I am content to leave it to others better informed than I am to diagnose when it is that this actually occurs. The point that I want to stress here is simply that, if blameworthiness for behavior that exhibits motivated ignorance of wrongdoing ever does arise in this way, its doing so is wholly in keeping with the Argument from Ignorance and the Origination Thesis.

---

[55] Does one's being only dimly aware that one is doing wrong render one less culpable than one would be if one were fully cognizant of this fact? I leave the question open.

[56] Cf. Johnston (1995) and Mele (2001).

8
Fundamental Moral Ignorance

Human beings are capable of unspeakable evil. Our history is rife with attempts at genocide. On a smaller but still unfathomable scale, mass shootings occur with alarming frequency. And then there are the daily, often hidden, innumerable instances of child abuse, rape, and other forms of violence and violation too ugly to contemplate. With a few bizarre exceptions (somnambulism, for example), no one can engage in such vile behavior unaware of what he is doing. Yet, I venture to say, in many, perhaps most cases the perpetrator is unaware that he is behaving wrongly.

Moral ignorance of this sort is deeply disturbing. It is not merely incidental, as it would be if it were attributable to some non-moral error, such as the proverbial slip of mistaking arsenic for sugar. It runs deeper, having its roots in some more fundamental moral error, such as the failure to appreciate the essential dignity of the person with whom one is dealing. Many instances of fundamental moral ignorance are egregious. Consider, for example, the twisted ideologies underlying the despicable behavior of Nazis, Islamic fundamentalists, and so on (and on and on). But it would be a bad mistake to think that it is only such people who exhibit such ignorance. On the contrary, fundamental moral ignorance is ubiquitous.[1] As W. D. Ross famously noted, even if one is fully aware of all the various morally relevant considerations (or *prima facie* duties, in Ross's terminology) that pertain to one's situation, there is no guarantee that one will know how to weigh them correctly in order to arrive at an accurate judgment about what one ought to do all things considered.[2] It may seem an exaggeration to call ignorance regarding how in some particular case one should assess the relative weights of, say, fidelity and beneficence "fundamental," but it is certainly not merely incidental, and I know of no better term. (It is obviously not the case that such ignorance always issues in behavior that is unspeakably evil.)

In this chapter I examine the exculpatory character of fundamental moral ignorance. In §8.1 I address the type of fundamental moral ignorance exhibited by psychopaths. In §8.2 I turn to the type of fundamental moral ignorance exhibited by conscientious wrongdoers. Finally, in §8.3 I discuss the possibility of wittingly doing wrong in the belief that one has sufficient reason to do so.

---

[1] Cf. Rosen (2004), pp. 304 f. Contrast Calhoun (1989), p. 395. [2] Ross (2002), p. 42.

8.1 Psychopathy

Despite, or perhaps because of, the large literature on the topic, there is no consensus on what causes or what constitutes psychopathy. Nonetheless, there is widespread agreement on some of the chief characteristics of psychopaths. As Matthew Talbert notes, it is generally agreed that psychopaths "are persistent wrongdoers whose behavior is characterized by egocentricity, lack of empathy, aggression, impulsivity, and lack of remorse, among other negative personality attributes."[3] As Talbert also notes, however, psychopaths can differ markedly with respect to the degree to which they manifest these characteristics.

At first blush, this description of psychopaths and their behavior may appear to have no obvious relevance to the present inquiry. The key trait that would seem to underlie all the others and to account for the psychopath's anti-social behavior is his lack of empathy, an affective deficit that is not typically taken to be among the excusing conditions that compromise either one's control over one's conduct or one's appreciation of its moral qualities. That Carrie couldn't care less about the suffering of her victims may explain why she doesn't behave differently, but it doesn't entail that she cannot behave differently or cannot appreciate the wrongness of her behavior.

One response to this remark is that, if one's lack of empathy makes it impossible for one to summon a desire to behave differently, and if one would behave differently only if one had a desire to do so, then indeed one cannot behave differently and so will have an excuse for behaving as one does (in virtue of failing to satisfy the *agential* condition of moral responsibility). This is an interesting argument, but I believe it fails for reasons given in §4.1.8.

Another response is that, if one's lack of empathy issues in an irresistible impulse to behave as one does, then, once again, one cannot behave differently and so will have an excuse for one's behavior. Maybe so, but, although this excuse may apply to some instances of psychopathic behavior,[4] I know of no evidence that the impulsiveness that is characteristic of psychopaths always involves impulses that are irresistible. (It is, of course, not easy to determine just when an impulse *is* literally irresistible, as opposed to "merely" being difficult to resist. See §4.5.5. Some philosophers contend that, strictly speaking, *no* impulse is ever irresistible.[5])

A third response is that, if one's lack of empathy renders one incapable of being motivated to avoid a certain form of behavior (behavior that is in fact morally wrong), then one cannot sincerely judge that such behavior is morally wrong and so will have an excuse for engaging in it (in virtue of failing to satisfy the *epistemic*

---

[3] Talbert (2016), p. 113. See Shoemaker (2007), p. 78, and Watson (2011), pp. 323 f., for fuller lists of the characteristics of psychopaths.
[4] Cf. Milo (1984), p. 63.   [5] Cf. Feinberg (1970), pp. 282 f.

condition of moral responsibility). However, although it may be true that the affective disorder that afflicts psychopaths renders them incapable of being moved by certain considerations,[6] the claim that judging an act to be morally wrong requires that one be motivated not to perform it is highly controversial and, I suspect, false as it stands.[7]

Nonetheless, there seems to me to be very good reason to think that psychopaths' lack of empathy *does* provide them with an excuse for their wrongful behavior, one that is grounded in their failure to satisfy the epistemic condition of moral responsibility. Regardless of the relation between this affective deficit and the capacity to be *moved* by certain considerations, it is plausible to think that this deficit renders them incapable of *grasping* the very concepts of moral right and wrong and hence of having any belief to the effect that they are engaged in wrongful behavior. This is a view defended by Antony Duff, who says:

> [T]here is a close logical connection between two commonly identified features of psychopathy: firstly, that it involves an incapacity for such emotional and moral responses as love, remorse, and concern for others... Secondly, that a psychopath, although not intellectually incompetent, is unable properly to understand the "nature and quality" of his acts, since he cannot grasp those emotional and moral aspects which are as much a part of them as their empirical features.[8]

I'm not sure just what Duff has in mind by a "logical connection." I doubt that it is conceptually or metaphysically impossible for someone who lacks certain, even all, emotions to grasp the concepts of moral right and wrong. Nonetheless, it certainly seems plausible to think that no human being who is incapable of the sort of emotional involvement with others described by Duff can arrive at an understanding of these concepts.

Like many others, Duff acknowledges that psychopaths typically can, and often do, behave *as if* they understood the difference between right and wrong. They can parrot the moral judgments made by others and apply them successfully to new cases.[9] This ability presumably rests on their understanding that there are certain forms of behavior of which others approve or disapprove, but it doesn't require that they understand the moral basis of these attitudes.[10] (Nor does it require that they attribute any other kind of normative basis to the judgments they mimic. It is often claimed that psychopaths are unable to draw the distinction between moral

---

[6] Cf. Shoemaker (2007), pp. 79 ff.   [7] For discussion, see Sayre-McCord (2017), §3.
[8] Duff (1977), pp. 191 f. Cf. Haksar (1965), pp. 136 ff.; Fingarette (1967), pp. 23 ff.; Murphy (1972), pp. 286 f.; Pritchard (1974), p. 632; Milo (1984), pp. 61 f.; and Levy (2007a), pp. 164 ff.
[9] Duff (1977), p. 196. Cf. Wallace (1994), p. 178.   [10] Cf. Alexander et al. (2009), p. 156.

and "merely conventional" transgressions.[11] This observation suggests that they nonetheless appreciate that merely conventional transgressions are indeed transgressions, such that there is some non-prudential reason, even if not a moral reason, to avoid committing them. I doubt that this suggestion is correct.) Thus, when psychopaths behave in ways that contravene the judgments that they parrot, this behavior is not to be construed as a rejection or defiance of these judgments, since that, too, would require an understanding of the moral concepts underlying them.[12]

It is often observed that psychopaths are not responsive to moral reasons.[13] Insofar as such responsiveness requires recognizing that the reasons in question are moral reasons, this observation is fully in keeping with the view that psychopaths lack moral understanding. Indeed, the inability to grasp moral concepts explains why psychopaths not only do not but cannot respond to moral reasons.[14]

It is also often said that psychopathy disqualifies those who suffer from it from being members of the moral community, for they are incapable of understanding the moral force of the demands that others make on them and it is therefore pointless to address these demands to them.[15] Whether this is so of course depends on what is meant by "the moral community." The term strikes me as dangerous, in that excluding psychopaths from the so-called moral community might be taken to suggest that a lack of moral understanding suffices for a lack of moral standing; but clearly we shouldn't infer, from the fact that psychopaths cannot appreciate the moral force of the demands made on them, that they don't deserve to be treated with the respect that is due to others.[16] Nor should we uncritically infer, from the claim that psychopaths are not members of the moral community, that they are not morally responsible for their behavior. (See §2.3.8.[17]) Their condition may well make it *pointless* to react in certain ways toward them (for example, to demand that they show sincere contrition for their misbehavior), but that in itself doesn't entail that they don't *deserve* to be blamed in some way (for example, to be resented, if only privately—see §2.3.7). Nonetheless, I of course agree that, given their lack of moral understanding, psychopaths are indeed incapable of appreciating the moral force of any demand that is made on them and of responding accordingly.

Having said that, I should now confess that my understanding of psychopathy is very meager. I have not studied the phenomenon in depth; what I know about it I have merely gleaned from the writings of others. Hence my remarks about

---

[11] For discussion, see Wallace (1994), p. 178; Fischer and Ravizza (1998), p. 79; Haji (2003); Levy (2007b); Vargas and Nichols (2007); Shoemaker (2011b); Watson (2011); and Greenspan (2016).

[12] Cf. Duff (1977), pp. 192 f. and 198; Levy (2007b), p. 135.

[13] Cf. Wallace (1994), p. 189; Fischer and Ravizza (1998), p. 79; Shoemaker (2011b), p. 117; Watson (2011), pp. 307 and 314; Talbert (2014), p. 277, and (2016), pp. 113 f.; and Nelkin (2015), pp. 375 ff.

[14] Cf. Watson (2011), p. 326, n. 16.

[15] Cf. Shoemaker (2007), p. 99; Watson (2011), p. 309; and Talbert (2014), p. 288.

[16] Cf. Levy (2007b), p. 136. Cf. also Lewis (1949).   [17] Cf. Talbert (2014), p. 288.

psychopathy are certainly not authoritative and should not be regarded as such. Indeed, I suspect that it is a mistake to claim without qualification that psychopaths' lack of empathy renders them incapable of moral understanding. It may well be, as Ishtiyaque Haji says, that there is "a spectrum of cases, with psychopaths incapable of reacting to any moral reasons at one end and those capable of reacting to any sufficient moral reason at the other."[18]

Be that as it may, the fact is that, for present purposes, it isn't necessary to determine the exact nature of psychopathy. All that I need note is that, *if* anyone (whether properly called a psychopath or not) lacks a sufficient understanding (whether due to a lack of empathy or not) of the concepts of moral right and wrong to be able to form any beliefs to the effect that he is behaving morally wrongly, *then* that person is not to blame for anything that he does. And even this claim must be qualified: such a person is not to blame for anything that he does, *unless* he is to blame for his lack of understanding or doesn't behave as he does *from* that lack of understanding.

Could someone be to blame for his inability to grasp the concepts of moral right and wrong? Conceivably. Imagine intentionally taking a pill that one knows will result in such a lack of understanding, believing this to be the wrong thing to do. Nonetheless, it seems to me exceedingly unlikely that anyone should ever in fact be to blame for his lack of moral understanding. According to some accounts, psychopathy probably has a genetic basis, and there is nothing that psychopaths could have done to prevent their disorder.[19] Other cases of moral incompetence in otherwise competent adults, whether qualifying as psychopathic or not, appear to be attributable to environmental factors equally beyond the agent's control. (Think of Susan Wolf's fictitious character of JoJo,[20] or of the real-life character of Robert Harris introduced into the philosophical literature by Gary Watson.[21]) Whether due to nature or nurture (or both), the fact (if it is a fact) that an agent's lack of moral understanding is not, and never was, in his control is sufficient to render him blameless for it. As to whether such a person's wrongdoing is to be *attributed to* his lack of understanding: presumably the answer is that it is (although there are obvious difficulties involved in trying to apply the counterfactual test, mentioned in §3.3, of "Would he have done what he did, if he had been aware that it was wrong?"). I thus infer that it is very likely that those who lack a sufficient grasp of the concepts of moral right and wrong are blameless for any moral wrongdoing that they commit; their condition affords them an exemption from blame (see §2.5.5). I will leave open the question of what "sufficient" comes to in this context. This is obviously a very important question (consider the thorny issue of whether and in what way children can be blameworthy), but I'm afraid I have nothing useful to contribute to it.

---

[18] Haji (2003), p. 77.   [19] Cf. Levy (2007b), p. 133.   [20] Wolf (1987).
[21] Watson (2004), pp. 235 ff.

8.2 Evil

In the newspaper article cited by Watson, Robert Harris is reported to have been planning to rob a bank. He spotted a parked car that he thought would be useful for the purpose. In the car were two 16-year-old boys eating lunch that they had just bought at a fast-food restaurant. Harris hijacked the car at gunpoint, got into the back seat, and told the boy behind the wheel to drive. After a while they pulled over and got out of the car. Harris then shot the boys, killing them both, and laughed about what he had done. Shortly thereafter he casually ate a hamburger that he had found in a bag containing the boys' lunch.[22]

This is a story of evil. At least, that's how Watson describes Harris's behavior, and I concur. The fact that, as a child, Harris suffered appalling abuse, in light of which his later behavior is perhaps to some extent understandable, doesn't confute that description. Some people use the term "evil" very liberally, so that it encompasses not only "moral evil" of the sort I take to be illustrated in Harris's case, but also "natural evil" such as that exemplified by a fawn's being horribly burned in a forest fire and suffering intense agony for days.[23] There are many other, narrower uses of the term. Here's just a small sampling:

> I define and use the word *evil* to mean behavior that deliberately deprives innocent people of their humanity, from small scale assaults on a person's dignity to outright murder.[24]
>
> Evil consists in intentionally behaving in ways that harm, abuse, demean, dehumanize, or destroy innocent others—or using one's authority and systemic power to encourage or permit others to do so on your behalf.[25]
>
> [E]vils are foreseeable intolerable harms produced by culpable wrongdoing.[26]
>
> [I]f an action is evil, it is an extreme culpable wrong.[27]

(These definitions of course concern only evil behavior or its consequences. We often talk also of evil desires, intentions, characters, persons, organizations, and so on.) Harris's behavior would seem to qualify as evil according to each of the first two definitions, but notice that, if, as some would claim, Harris's horrific upbringing rendered him inculpable for his later behavior, then this behavior doesn't qualify as evil according to either of the remaining two definitions. Notice also that not-so-serious wrongs can satisfy the accounts of evil given in the first three definitions, but not the account given in the fourth.

I don't want to get hung up on definitional matters. There may be certain purposes for which there is good reason to use the term "evil" as restrictively as the

---

[22] Watson (2004), pp. 235 ff. [23] Cf. Rowe (1979), p. 337. [24] Katz (1993), p. 5.
[25] Zimbardo (2007), p. 5. [26] Card (2002), p. 3. [27] L. Russell (2014), p. 4.

fourth definition does, but I take it that it is nonetheless perfectly legitimate for present purposes to describe behavior such as Harris's, and also far less serious behavior of that sort (such as dispassionately pulling the wings off flies), as evil, regardless of whether the agent is to blame for it. The sort of behavior I have in mind is behavior that is to be attributed to an agent's *lack of conscience*. Roughly speaking, I take an agent's conscience to consist in a set of beliefs regarding how he or she may or ought, morally, to behave under certain circumstances, conjoined with a disposition to act (in prospect) or react (in retrospect) in accordance with these beliefs. (If having such beliefs suffices for possession of the relevant disposition—something that, as I said in §8.1, seems to me dubious—then mention of the disposition is superfluous.) Thus a lack of conscience consists in either a failure to have such beliefs (due, perhaps, to a failure to grasp the pertinent concepts) or a failure to be disposed to act and react accordingly.

There is another, very important kind of evil behavior that is to be attributed to an agent's having a *misguided conscience*. In some cases such a conscience might involve merely incidental moral ignorance, but in many it will involve fundamental moral ignorance. Consider, for instance, the perverse consciences of Nazis, Islamic fundamentalists, etc., etc. Some writers deny that it was in fact the case that Hitler, for example, acted in accordance with his conscience,[28] and perhaps that is true. Be that as it may, it seems very plausible to think that, in many instances of evil behavior of the sort committed by Nazis and the like, the perpetrator of the evil is indeed acting in all "good" conscience; in fact, such a person may well take himself to be duty-bound to behave as he does. In her famous study, Hannah Arendt says that Adolf Eichmann claimed that "he would have had a bad conscience only if he had not done what he had been ordered to do,"[29] and she doesn't dispute this claim, noting that "the sad and very uncomfortable truth of the matter probably was that it was not his fanaticism but his very conscience that prompted Eichmann to do what he did.[30] Many commentators concur, applying this observation also to a host of other cases, such as the atrocities committed by those participating in the Crusades, the Spanish Inquisition, the Russian and Chinese Revolutions, the 9/11 attacks, and so on.[31] Of course, no one is claiming that the perpetrators of such evil always carry it out conscientiously, but only that that is likely often to be the case. As Arendt says, this is a very uncomfortable truth to acknowledge, but it is a truth nonetheless.

The question presently at issue is this. Does someone who, "in all good conscience," commits some evil, or any form of wrongdoing, have an excuse for his behavior?

---

[28] See, e.g., Arpaly (2003), pp. 101 f.   [29] Arendt (1977), p. 25.   [30] Arendt (1977), p. 146.
[31] See, e.g., Katz (1993), pp. 19 and 35; Baumeister (2001), ch. 6; Scarre (2004), ch. 9; L. Russell (2014), p. 78; and Fiske and Rai (2015), pp. xxii, xxv, 1, and 14.

In pursuit of an answer to this question, consider a case provided by Gideon Rosen:

> In the ancient Near East in the Biblical period the legitimacy of chattel slavery was simply taken for granted... [C]onsider an ordinary Hittite lord. He buys and sells human beings, forces labour without compensation, and separates families to suit his purposes. Needless to say, what he does is wrong. [He] is not entitled to do these things. But of course he thinks he is. Moreover, we may imagine that if he had thought otherwise, he would have acted differently.[32]

Rosen thinks it plausible to maintain that, in light of the fact that the institution of chattel slavery was taken for granted at the time, the Hittite was under no obligation to reflect on whether engaging in the practice was morally acceptable. But he recognizes that some might find this claim unduly complacent, and so he asks us to imagine that the Hittite carefully pondered the permissibility of his behavior and nonetheless reached the conclusion that it was morally legitimate. He says:

> Given the intellectual and cultural resources available to a second millennium Hittite lord, it would have taken a moral genius to see through to the wrongness of chattel slavery.
>
> The example is meant to show that blameless [fundamental] moral ignorance is a possibility. But I should add that in my view it also makes it plausible that insofar as he acts from blameless ignorance, it would be a mistake for us to blame the slaveholder... We may condemn the act. We may rail at the universe or at history for serving up injustice on so vast a scale. But in my view it makes no sense to hold this injustice against the perpetrator when it would have taken a miracle of moral vision for him to have seen the moral case for acting differently.[33]

I suspect that most people would find Rosen's assessment of the Hittite's blameworthiness wholly unacceptable. It is certainly disturbing. Some philosophers maintain that fundamental moral ignorance is never exculpatory.[34] Others hold a less extreme view but claim that, in cases of such abhorrent wrongdoing as the Hittite's, Rosen is exaggerating when he says that it would take a "miracle of moral vision," something that only a "moral genius" could manage, to see the error of one's ways.[35] On the contrary, they say, in such cases of egregious ignorance, the

---

[32] Rosen (2003), pp. 64 f. [33] Rosen (2003), p. 66.
[34] See, e.g., Aristotle (1941), bk. III, ch. 5; Milo (1984), p. 41; Harman (2011).
[35] See, e.g., Moody-Adams (1994), pp. 295 f.; Guerrero (2007), pp. 71 f.; Sher (2017), pp. 112 ff.

truth is "easily available,"[36] and it is likely that the ignorance consisting in the failure to recognize the truth is "affected,"[37] motivated by self-interest[38] and rooted in such vices as overconfidence, arrogance, dismissiveness, laziness, dogmatism, incuriosity, self-indulgence, and contempt.[39] This fact vitiates any excuse that might be tendered for the behavior in question.

Although I sympathize with this view, I believe it to be mistaken. First, it is surely false that all fundamental moral ignorance is attributable to some vice of the sort just mentioned,[40] even when it is deep and especially egregious.[41] Secondly, and for present purposes far more importantly, such ignorance may well provide an excuse for wrongdoing even when it *is* to be attributed to some such vice.

One argument for the claim that I have just made is grounded in the sobering observation, one that is now widely accepted in the wake of Arendt's testimony and the evidence provided by experiments of the sort conducted by Stanley Milgram and others,[42] that the vice or vices in question are ones to which we are all susceptible. It is a matter of luck whether one finds oneself in circumstances in which these vices are engaged, and blame shouldn't be allocated on the basis of such luck. However, although I am an opponent of moral luck as regards blameworthiness (see §5.1.4), I think this argument fails. Compare Valerie, who is filled with empathy for all living creatures, with Ron, an unabashed bigot, driven by fear and hate, who engages in vicious racist behavior. Even if (a big "if") it is only the luck of the draw that Ron wasn't raised in circumstances that would have led him to live a life as virtuous as Valerie's, and even if (another big "if," but one that I am inclined to accept[43]) that fact entails that he and Valerie are on a par hypologically, it doesn't follow that Ron is blameless; it may be that Valerie is blameworthy.[44]

A quite different argument for the claim that someone like Ron may well be blameless for his vicious behavior is ... the Argument from Ignorance! Even if Ron is fully aware that the victims of his bigotry are harmed by his treatment of them, as long as he is ignorant of the fact that his behavior is morally wrong he will not be to blame for it—provided that he acts *from* his ignorance and the ignorance is itself excusable. The fact (if it is a fact) that his ignorance has its source in some vicious motivation doesn't alter this verdict. (See §7.2.5.)

I want to reiterate that, regardless of whether Ron has an excuse for the way in which he treats members of the race(s) he despises, his behavior is certainly

---

[36] Sher (2017), p. 113.   [37] Moody-Adams (1994), p. 296.   [38] Calhoun (1989), p. 399.
[39] FitzPatrick (2008), p. 609. See also Mason and Wilson (2017), pp. 90 ff.
[40] Cf. Wieland (2017b), pp. 154 ff., and Johnson King (2020b).
[41] Cf. Calhoun (1989), pp. 393 ff.; Isaacs (1997), pp. 674 ff.; FitzPatrick (2008), p. 602, n. 27.
[42] Milgram (1974); Zimbardo (2007).
[43] Contrast, e.g., Arendt (1977), p. 278: "[T]here is an abyss between the actuality of what [Eichmann] did and the potentiality of what others might have done."
[44] Cf. Zimmerman (2002), p. 570, where I argue that agents such as Valerie and Ron may actually be *both* blameless (in virtue of certain facts about them) *and* equally blameworthy (in virtue of certain other facts about them).

morally wrong and, I would say, unquestionably evil. Indeed, insofar as this behavior is attributable to certain vicious traits of character, I would say that Ron is himself evil. These deontic and aretaic judgments are independent of, and perfectly consistent with, the judgment that Ron has (or may have) an excuse for his behavior grounded in his fundamental moral ignorance. (See §2.1.4.)

8.3 Amoralism

I have remarked on several occasions that the traditional view is that satisfaction of two conditions, one epistemic, the other agential, is both necessary and sufficient for one's being blameworthy for one's behavior. The details of these conditions are of course controversial, but it appears to be almost universally accepted that, if one has performed some act, knowing that doing so was overall morally wrong and that one could have done something else instead that wouldn't have been overall morally wrong, then that suffices for one's being blameworthy for what one has done.

Rosen demurs. He asks us to consider someone he calls an amoralist who performs some act, understanding full well that it is overall morally wrong but believing that its being so fails to constitute a sufficient reason not to do it. If this person is mistaken in his assessment, then he exhibits a kind of normative ignorance which, Rosen claims, renders him blameless for his behavior, provided that he is not to blame for his ignorance.[45]

The matter is difficult. Rosen's view presupposes that it makes sense to think of moral reasons competing with non-moral reasons in such a way that on some occasion the latter outweigh the former. I frankly don't know what to say about that. Even if this claim is correct, I'm not sure why we should think that one might be *morally* blameless for failing to do what one knows one has most *moral* reason to do. But I won't pursue the matter. Rosen's view countenances excuses for wrongful behavior beyond those strictly implied by the Origination Thesis that I have advocated, and I am sure that many will find the Thesis far too liberal as it is, once its implications regarding the exculpatory nature of both incidental and fundamental moral ignorance have been revealed. It is time to respond to challenges to the argument—the Argument from Ignorance—from which the Thesis is derived.

---

[45] Rosen (2003), p. 75.

PART III
CHALLENGES TO THE ARGUMENT FROM IGNORANCE

9
Varieties of Blameworthiness

I have on several occasions acknowledged the revisionary nature of the Origination Thesis. Perhaps this is nowhere more evident than in its implications regarding the exculpatory force of fundamental moral ignorance. The idea that someone like Adolf Eichmann might not be to blame for his execrable behavior surely sits uneasily with anyone who has even a smidgen of moral sensitivity. A very common reaction—one that I have encountered many times—is to declare this idea to be so far beyond the pale of credibility that it is outrageous even to take it seriously, let alone to endorse it. If that's what the Origination Thesis implies, then so much the worse for the Thesis and for any argument for it!

A similar, even if somewhat more muted reaction is often directed at the Origination Thesis's implication regarding negligence. After presenting a version of the Argument from Ignorance that issues in the conclusion that there is little or no negligent action (action that he takes to be such that one is blameworthy for it by definition[1]), Randolph Clarke has this to say:

> This line of thought relies on premises that have considerable intuitive appeal. Yet they aren't absolutely irresistible. And one reason to suspect them is the very fact that they lead to such a radical conclusion... Our everyday attributions of blameworthiness are fallible and sometimes mistaken. The mistakes are sometimes due to bias or ignorance of fact. But in the cases at hand, we're not dealing with either of these factors. The fact that certain proposed principles of responsibility nevertheless convict so many of our attributions of error is reason to suspect these principles. Moral practice is often wiser than theory.[2]

In like fashion, David Shoemaker describes arguments like the Argument from Ignorance as being "theory-drenched" (a term that I suspect is not intended as a compliment) and claims that there is no good reason to privilege the verdicts issued by such an approach over those contained in our everyday "responsibility practices."[3]

I understand and, to some degree, sympathize with this reaction, but I think it is a mistake to characterize the issue in terms of "theory" versus "practice." I take it

---

[1] Clarke (2014), p. 160.   [2] Clarke (2014), pp. 161 f.
[3] Shoemaker (2017), pp. 514 ff. Cf. also Mason (2019), p. 181: "[W]e should not let our theorizing take us too far from our actual practices."

that our everyday attributions of blameworthiness are ones that we presume to be firmly based on general principles, even if we typically don't bother to (try to) articulate these principles explicitly. These principles aren't divorced from practice; they underlie it and serve (supposedly) to justify it. The whole point of the Argument from Ignorance is that, once certain principles that underlie our practice are laid out explicitly and conjoined with one another, the surprising and, no doubt, disturbing result is that they undermine many of the verdicts that we mistakenly thought they supported.[4]

The principles to which I am referring are those contained in Premises 2 and 4 of the Argument from Ignorance—the principle that one is to blame for ignorant behavior only if one is to blame for one's ignorance, and the principle that one is to blame for something only if one was in control of that thing. These are the principles that drive the argument, and I take them to be central to our common conception of moral responsibility. Of course, we have seen that, upon inspection, both principles require refinement, the first especially. And, of course, the Argument from Ignorance rests on several other premises, too. However, only one of these remaining premises would seem to be at all controversial, namely, Premise 6, according to which our beliefs are never in our direct control. I discussed this premise at length in §4.6 and have nothing further to add here. In this chapter I consider challenges to Premises 2 and 4 that concern these premises' implications regarding blameworthiness for negligent behavior and for wrongful behavior committed from fundamental moral ignorance.[5]

The chapter proceeds as follows. In §9.1 I address an objection to the Argument from Ignorance that stems from the view that it is possible to be blameworthy for purely negligent behavior. This view challenges Premise 2 of the Argument in particular, since it denies that blameworthiness for negligent behavior requires blameworthiness for the inadvertence that underlies that behavior. Although the inadvertence must be morally substandard for the behavior to qualify as negligent, it needn't be something for which one is to blame in turn. My discussion of this challenge takes a detour through the territory of agent-regret and remorse, but I point out that, in the end, an assessment of whether the challenge succeeds requires taking a closer look at the question of precisely what constitutes the basis of blameworthiness.

In §9.2 I take up this question and investigate the relation between blameworthiness and quality of will. I discuss the increasingly popular view that whether one's will is morally commendable or objectionable turns on whether one cares for morality *de re* as opposed to caring for it *de dicto*. I propose a precise account of

---

[4] Cf. Rosen (2004), p. 298, and Levy (2017b).
[5] To my knowledge, none of the other premises—Premises 1, 7, 8, 10, and 12—has been challenged by other philosophers, except for Premise 7. I defend this premise in §5.1.2. In §4.4.3 I note that Premise 12 might need tweaking.

this distinction and then undertake a critique of the claim that having a good will consists in acting from a concern *de re* with doing the right thing. Conscientiousness, I claim, is at least part of what goes to make up a good will, and it consists in acting from a concern *de dicto* with doing what is right, though I concede that it is possible to be overly conscientious on occasion. Even so, the question remains whether acting from a desire *de re* to do something wrong suffices for blameworthiness. Some philosophers maintain that this is indeed the case, typically holding that one can be blameworthy not just for acting from such a desire but simply for having it, regardless of whether one is in control of having it. They thus reject Premise 4 of the Argument from Ignorance, and so the question becomes: How is the disagreement between those who accept this premise and those who reject it to be resolved?

In §9.3 I propose a compromise position, founded on the observation that there are many different kinds of blaming reactions. I note that there is good reason to think that someone may be deserving of some of these reactions while not being deserving of others. Moreover, these reactions may be divided into two classes: those the worthiness of which requires that the person blamed have been in control of that for which he or she is blamed, and those the worthiness of which does not require such control. I contend that the Argument from Ignorance is sound when it is restricted to those forms of blame that belong to the first class. I contend further in §9.4 that it is only these forms of blame that are such that the worthiness of them constitutes a form of moral responsibility.

9.1 Negligence

In §6.1 I proposed the following definition of negligence: one behaves negligently just in case (1) one's behavior is morally wrong, (2) one does not advert, at the time at which one engages in it, to the moral wrongness of one's behavior, and (3) one's failure to advert to the moral wrongness of one's behavior is itself morally substandard. I noted that the Origination Thesis threatens to undermine all charges that someone is to blame for having behaved negligently, since, given that, when acting negligently, one fails to believe that one is behaving wrongly, it implies that blameworthiness for negligent behavior is in every case to be traced to blameworthiness for some other piece of behavior that one believed at the time to be morally wrong (unless the negligent behavior is performed *merely* in ignorance of the fact that it is wrong). This rules out all blameworthiness for "pure" negligence, that is, negligent behavior blameworthiness for which is *not* to be traced to some prior benighting act. It doesn't rule out blameworthiness for "impure" negligence, where such tracing can be carried out, but even in such cases a charge of negligence is misleading, inasmuch as it should be replaced with the more perspicuous charge of recklessness.

This is a disturbing result, since charges of pure negligence are commonplace (even if the purity of the alleged negligence is often not explicitly noted). Many cases involving a lapse of attention—such as those, discussed in Chapter 6, involving forgetfulness or some other form of absent-mindedness—are typically thought to warrant such a charge. Other kinds of cases are also often thought to fit the bill. George Sher, who defends the possibility of blameworthiness for pure negligence, mentions, among others, cases of precipitate action and of sheer obliviousness to the possible consequences of one's behavior. As an example of the former, he gives the case of a panic-stricken homeowner shooting an intruder, only to discover that she has shot her son, who came home early for the holidays.[6] As an example of the latter, he gives the case of a woman's bewilderment when her rambling anecdote about a childless couple, a handicapped person, and a financial failure is not well received by an audience that includes a childless couple, a handicapped person, and a financial failure.[7] (Sher labels this case *Bad Joke*. I find it amusing, as he presumably intended. I wonder, though, whether the joke might not backfire on him—and also on me for repeating it here. Might not some of our readers find the case offensive, perhaps because they are themselves childless, or handicapped, or insolvent?)

9.1.1 Inadvertence and blameworthiness

At the end of Chapter 6 I mentioned a defense of the possibility of blameworthiness for pure negligence, discussion of which I deferred until this chapter. The defense goes as follows. Given that blameworthiness requires control, one can be blameworthy for having behaved negligently only if one was in control of one's behavior. In order for this behavior to qualify as negligent, it must have been behavior to whose wrongness one failed to advert at the time, and one's inadvertence must itself have been substandard. But it doesn't follow that one must have been in control of, let alone blameworthy for, one's inadvertence. On the contrary, the mere fact that it was substandard, conjoined with the fact that the behavior was wrong, suffices to render one blameworthy for the behavior. Given that this blameworthiness is not to be traced to blameworthiness for some prior benighting act, it will be direct, and so the negligence at issue will be pure.

Clarke has offered this defense in some recent work.[8] As he explicitly notes, it constitutes a rejection of Premise 2 of the Argument from Ignorance, since it holds that one needn't be blameworthy for one's inadvertence in order to be blameworthy for one's inadvertent behavior. In saying this, Clarke is of course not denying that one can be blameworthy for failing to advert to the wrongness of one's

---

[6] Sher (2009), p. 26.   [7] Sher (2009), p. 28.
[8] See Clarke (2014), pp. 161 ff., and (2017b), pp. 245 ff.

behavior. On the contrary, he acknowledges that this sometimes happens, in just the way depicted by Holly Smith's model of a benighting act causing or perpetuating one's inadvertence and thereby issuing in an unwitting wrongful act. But he insists that this need not be the case. Regarding his own example of his forgetting to pick up milk on the way home, he says that it was reasonable for him to entrust his plan to pick it up to memory, given that he is usually not forgetful about such matters, and that it would have "bordered on compulsion" for him to have entered a reminder on his phone, with an alert to be sounded at the estimated time of his approach to the store.[9] Thus, even though he could have taken such a precautionary measure, he wasn't obligated to do so, and his failure to do so doesn't qualify as a benighting act. Even so, he claims, his subsequent inadvertence was substandard and sufficient, under the circumstances, to render him blameworthy—directly blameworthy—for his failure to pick up milk.

I have two concerns about what Clarke has to say.

First, Clarke's position presupposes that, in cases of the sort under discussion, one exercises direct control over the behavior for which one is allegedly directly blameworthy. As I noted in §4.4.2, however, in cases like Clarke's that apparently require that the agent exercise direct control over a *purely passive* omission, it is not at all easy to see how this condition could be satisfied. This concern is not especially far-reaching, though, since there are other cases in which Clarke would presumably judge that someone is directly blameworthy for negligent behavior that don't require that this condition be satisfied. We may assume, for example, that the panic-stricken homeowner was in direct control of her decision to shoot the intruder.

My second concern goes deeper. It seems reasonable to think that, if Clarke's view is to be at all plausible, the standard that one's inadvertence fails to meet must be a moral standard. (See clause (3) of my definition of negligence.) How otherwise is the failure to meet this standard supposed to suffice, under the circumstances, for one's being morally blameworthy for one's inadvertent behavior? Yet, in many cases in which it is customary to level a charge of negligence against someone, it's not clear how this condition is supposed to have been satisfied. How, for example, was Clarke's failure to remember to pick up milk *morally* substandard? Clarke himself describes the failure as having been *cognitively* substandard.[10] Perhaps it was (although I'm not sure just what this means; presumably its having been uncharacteristic doesn't suffice for its meriting this description). But, unless his failure to remember was also morally substandard, there would seem to be no grounds for blaming Clarke for his failure to pick up milk.[11] Again, the mere fact (if it is a fact) that his failure to pick up milk was

---

[9] Clarke (2014), p. 165. See also pp. 172 f.   [10] Clarke (2014), p. 166.
[11] Cf. Talbert (2017a), pp. 57 ff.

morally *wrong* doesn't entail that he is morally to *blame* for it. Something more is needed, and presumably this something must itself be *morally* significant.

At one point, Clarke suggests that, even if there need be no ill will or even indifference implicated in mental lapses such as his, still such lapses constitute a failure to manifest good will, and this is sufficient, under the circumstances, both to render one's inadvertence morally substandard and to render one blameworthy for the behavior that results.[12] But this is implausible. Presumably, if one lacks both ill will and indifference, then one has good will, and having good will is obviously not itself morally substandard in any way. How, then, is the failure to manifest the good will that one has supposed to be morally substandard? I find the suggestion mysterious, precisely because no moral fault in the agent is implicated. It's also worth noting that lapses of the sort in question, far from constituting the failure to manifest good will, might involve its manifestation. Imagine that, instead of ruminating on his paper on omissions, Clarke had been thinking about what to buy his wife for her birthday.

9.1.2 Agent-regret and remorse

It might seem that some support for Clarke's position can be derived from Bernard Williams's discussion of what he calls "agent-regret." Consider this well-known case:

> The lorry driver who, through no fault of his own, runs over a child, will feel differently from any spectator, even a spectator next to him in the cab... We feel sorry for the driver, but that sentiment co-exists with, indeed presupposes, that there is something special about his relation to this happening, something which cannot merely be eliminated by the consideration that it was not his fault.[13]

In insisting that the driver was not at fault, Williams seems clearly committed to saying that the driver was not to blame for what happened, and so you may be wondering how Williams's remarks could provide any support for Clarke's claim that he (Clarke) *is* to blame for failing to pick up milk. But there are cases and cases.

It seems very plausible to think that Williams's lorry driver not only is not to blame for running over the child but also did nothing wrong in doing so. (Given that the driver presumably could have done something that would have prevented the accident—he could, say, have taken an alternative route, even though his evidence supplied him with no reason to do so—this verdict might be disputed by

---

[12] Clarke (2017b), p. 246. [13] B. Williams (1981), p. 28.

a proponent of an objective account of wrongdoing. However, for reasons given in §7.1.4, such an account is not to be recommended. We may assume that the driver took no undue risk in driving as he did.) Nonetheless, as Williams emphasizes in his discussion of the case, it is fitting for the driver to feel bad about his role in the unfolding of events; we would have "some doubt" about him if he failed to do so. It's hard to pin down just why this should be the case, precisely because the driver did nothing wrong; and yet it seems clear that it is indeed the case. It's worth noting, though, that, however fitting agent-regret may be, it doesn't follow that the driver *deserves* to feel bad about what happened.[14] (See §2.4.1.)

Regret is not remorse, although the latter includes the former. Even if it is fitting for the lorry driver to feel (a special sort of agent-) regret for running over the child, it's hard to see how it would be fitting for him to feel remorse for doing so, given that he indeed did nothing wrong. (What if he *believed*—falsely—that he had done something wrong? Then we might say that his feeling remorse would be "subjectively" fitting, even if not fitting to the facts.[15]) But now consider a case in which an agent *has* unwittingly done wrong. Recall Sandra, from §7.1.3, who wrongly ran a red light, and let's now suppose that she did so, not recklessly, but inadvertently, and that she, too, ran over a child. Doesn't it seem that it would be perfectly fitting for her to feel (not only regret but) remorse for what she did, *even if*, as in Clarke's case, there was no ill will, or even indifference, involved?

Joseph Raz claims that agents in situations such as Sandra's are indeed responsible, in a sense that he calls "responsible$_2$," for what they do.[16] In general, he says, we are responsible$_2$ for conduct that is the result of the functioning, whether successful or failed, of our powers of rational agency, and he adds:

> Actions due to malfunction of our capacities of rational agency result from failure to perform acts of which we are masters. In acknowledging our responsibility for these unintentional acts and omissions we affirm our mastery of these abilities, deny that we are disabled in the relevant regards. When others attribute to us responsibilities for such actions they acknowledge our mastery of those abilities, and hold us responsible for these results of their use.[17]

Raz is careful to note that accepting responsibility$_2$ for one's negligent conduct and its consequences is not merely a matter of acknowledging a duty to make amends to whomever one may have wronged.[18] It is, more fundamentally, a matter of embracing one's conduct as falling within one's "domain of secure competence."

Raz is also careful to note that he doesn't take responsibility$_2$ for one's negligent conduct (and its consequences) in itself to suffice for one's being to blame for it

---

[14] Cf. Clarke (2016), p. 128; Zhao (2020), pp. 288 f. [15] Cf. Conee (1982), p. 91.
[16] Raz (2011), p. 228.   [17] Raz (2011), p. 268.   [18] Raz (2011), p. 256.

(and them).[19] But he declines to say just what else he thinks is required, and so I'm not sure whether he would say that Sandra is to blame for her behavior (behavior that I'm pretty sure he would classify as negligent[20]). Recently, however, Elinor Mason, in what is perhaps the most nuanced discussion to date of agent-regret and remorse, has sought to explain why it is that agents like Sandra (and Clarke, in the example about the milk) are indeed to blame for their behavior and its consequences.[21]

Mason presents a case in which a woman called Perdita borrows a friend's sentimentally valuable necklace and loses it. The loss is not due to carelessness or any other form of ill will; it was just a "glitch" on Perdita's part. Nonetheless, Mason says, "...it seems plausible that Perdita should feel really bad about what she did, *even though* there was no bad will. She should apologize, she should try to make amends, but more than that, it is plausible that she should feel something in the region of remorse."[22]

In support of this claim, Mason asks us to imagine two versions of the conversation in which Perdita tells her friend that she has lost the necklace. In the first, Perdita expresses regret but not remorse, assuring her friend that what occurred was indeed just a glitch, there was no ill will involved, and so she is not to blame for what happened. In the second, Perdita expresses remorse, thereby taking responsibility—taking the blame—for what happened. Mason claims that there is something seriously amiss with Perdita's attitude in the first version. Although she owns up to the mistake she made, she refuses to "own" it. This is reminiscent of what Raz says about "mastery" over one's behavior, but Mason's account of the appropriateness of taking responsibility for one's glitches and their consequences differs from Raz's. Raz claims that taking responsibility in such cases is primarily a matter of maintaining self-respect.[23] Mason holds that this account is too self-centered and that, on the contrary, the reason that it is appropriate to take responsibility in such cases is that doing so helps sustain one's relationship with others. She says:

> Blame in personal relationships is a plea for recognition and acceptance of a wrong done... [In the second version of the conversation] Perdita shows her respect and love for her friend by accepting that the action is her own, and feeling remorse... Agent regret, at least in the thinnest sense, would not be enough. Thin agent regret does not fully answer the call of the injured party. A blame conversation is appropriate, though it is not the same as the sort of blame conversation that is appropriate in cases of ordinary blameworthiness [in which a bad will is implicated].[24]

---

[19] Raz (2011), pp. 251 f. and 265. Contrast Sher (2009), p. 88, and Rudy-Hiller (2017).
[20] Cf. Raz (2011), p. 244.   [21] Mason (2019), ch. 8.   [22] Mason (2019), p. 191.
[23] Raz (2011), pp. 245 and 268.   [24] Mason (2019), p. 195.

It may be that, once Perdita has expressed her remorse, the appropriate stance for her friend to take in this "blame conversation" is in fact not to blame Perdita but to forgive her, but it seems crucial that Perdita accept responsibility to begin with.

Mason's discussion is insightful. There is much in it that rings true and carries over to other contexts. Consider, for instance, J. L. Austin's example, presented in §4.1.7, of the golfer who has missed a very short putt. Austin imagines that the golfer had both the ability and the opportunity to hole the putt, and tried his hardest to do so, and yet failed to do so due to some glitch. Anyone who has played any sport will understand the golfer's berating himself, despite the fact that he tried his hardest to succeed. Moreover, if the golfer was a member of a team that lost the match because of his blunder, then we would expect him not only to scold himself but also to feel bad about having let the side down. This feeling would not simply be a matter of regret or frustration or anger or shame, although it might include any of these; it would be a matter of remorse. Perhaps the golfer's teammates would, and perhaps they should, seek to console him, but it seems important that the golfer initially take the blame for losing the match.

Perceptive though Mason's treatment of the issue undoubtedly is, it does not in my view succeed in showing how it is that agents such as Perdita (and Clarke, and Sandra) are to blame in any way for their behavior and its consequences. On the contrary, precisely because there is, by hypothesis, no ill will or indifference involved in such agents' behavior, they are blameless for what happens. This verdict can nonetheless be reconciled with Mason's observations about the appropriateness of such agents' taking responsibility for what they have done, as I shall now seek to show.

Let's begin with Williams's lorry driver, whom I'll call Larry. As Williams remarks, we would expect Larry to feel terrible about his having run over the child, a feeling that is akin to but nonetheless importantly different from the feeling that we would expect Larry's passenger to have. (In this context, "expect" has normative, and not merely descriptive, force.) We would be shocked if the passenger weren't deeply saddened by what he witnessed, but we would also be shocked if Larry were *merely* deeply saddened in the same way. He was, after all, not (merely) a spectator but (also) a participant in the events that transpired; he was himself an instrument of harm, and this fact, it seems, makes a difference to how he should feel.

But how, exactly, *should* Larry feel about what happened? What reaction, precisely, is it fitting for him to have? The answer, I believe, is that we expect him to feel, and show, *remorse* for having run over the child.[25] But this answer

---

[25] Williams rejects this answer, on the grounds that one can feel remorse only for what one has voluntarily done, and Larry didn't voluntarily run over the child. (B. Williams (1981), p. 30.) This strikes me as mistaken. I think it's probably true (cf. Thalberg (1963), p. 546) that one can feel remorse only for what one has done (or omitted)—or, better, for what one believes or suspects that one has done

immediately poses a puzzle. How can the expectation that Larry feel remorse for what he did be reconciled with the propriety of others' seeking to assure him that he is *not* to blame for what happened?

It will be instructive to compare Larry's case with Juan's. Juan, you will recall from §7.1.4, was in the habit of turning on the light when he got to work. On one fateful morning when he flipped the light-switch, Juan detonated a bomb that had been secretly installed by a terrorist and thereby killed several people in the vicinity. Juan had no reason whatsoever to think that his flipping the switch would cause such devastation. How should he feel about what happened?

I suspect that in this case we would *not* expect Juan to feel remorse for his having inadvertently killed so many innocent people. On the contrary, his participation in the events that led to their deaths was not only purely accidental but *obviously* so. Perhaps we would expect him to react differently from the way that we would expect a mere spectator to react, to feel a particular kind of regret that somehow reflects his having been causally involved in the bystanders' deaths, but one thing we presumably wouldn't, or at least shouldn't, expect him to do is to second-guess his flipping the switch (although we would understand it if he did so[26]). It's not only obvious to us that Juan did nothing wrong, but it's also obvious to us that it is, or should be, obvious to him that he did nothing wrong. This being the case, it is, or should be, obvious to all concerned that there is no occasion for remorse on Juan's part.

Larry's case is different. Although Williams stipulates that Larry was not at fault for running over the child, it is unlikely that that this would be immediately obvious to anyone who witnessed what happened, and this of course includes Larry himself. Under the circumstances, we *would* expect him to second-guess his own behavior; we would expect him, initially at least, to assume that he had done something wrong for which he is to blame; we would expect him to feel remorse. We would be dismayed if he immediately declared his innocence, and this is not simply because we would expect him to acknowledge the gravity of what occurred—after all, what happened in Juan's case was even worse—but rather because we would expect him to acknowledge that, in light of the gravity of what happened, there is a presumption of guilt that, to be defeated, requires proof, or at least strong evidence, of innocence. In Juan's case this presumption is, I submit, defeated immediately; that is why we would not expect Juan to feel remorse even initially. In a case such as Larry's, however, the presumption prevails, at least for a

---

(or omitted)—but of course Larry's case meets this restriction. The point is moot, however, since nothing of significance would be lost if we retreated from talk of *remorse* to talk of *guilt*, an emotion that Williams himself acknowledges is fitting in cases such as Larry's (B. Williams (1993), p. 93). I take feeling remorse for, or guilty about, some act or omission to be an essentially unpleasant emotion that incorporates the judgment, or at least the representation (see §2.3.9), that one is to blame for that act or omission. For a contrary account of guilt, see Zhao (2020).

[26] Cf. Kamtekar and Nichols (2019).

while. It is only after we have become convinced that Larry was not at fault that we would try to console him by assuring him that he wasn't, and it is only fitting that Larry should require more than we do to be convinced that he was not at fault.

In cases such as Perdita's (and Clarke's, and Sandra's) in which it seems clear that the agent has indeed done something wrong, the initial presumption of guilt is that much stronger and so that much more difficult to defeat. But if and when it becomes clear that the agent was not at fault, at that point remorse on his or her part and blame on the part of others is no longer fitting. Is blame ever fitting? The answer depends, I think, on how the cases are filled in. It seems reasonable to hold that in some such cases blame on the part of others is never fitting, even if remorse on the part of the agent initially is—that the evidential bar to be met regarding the agent's guilt is higher for others than it is for the agent him- or herself. It is very important to note, however, that, even if, given their epistemic circumstances, blame on the part of others is initially fitting, at *no* point is the agent blame*worthy*. (See §2.4.2.) On the contrary, given the stipulation that the agent was not at fault for the wrong that he or she did, he or she deserves at all times *not* to be blamed for it. (As to whether the agent deserves forgiveness: I will leave the question open. Forgiving someone is plausibly thought to involve more than just a victim's ceasing to blame a wrongdoer,[27] and so desert of the cessation of blame might not suffice for desert of forgiveness.)

9.1.3 Morally substandard inadvertence

Even though agents such as Perdita (and Clarke, and Sandra) have inadvertently done wrong, and even if, initially at least, it is fitting for them to take the blame for their behavior and also, perhaps, for us to blame them for it, it is, I have urged, in fact a mistake to declare them blameworthy for what they have done, and this is because their behavior cannot be attributed to a lack of good will on their part. It is to be attributed to their inadvertence, certainly, but this inadvertence was, by hypothesis, not morally substandard. This means that blaming them for their negligent behavior—a very common reaction in such cases—is doubly mistaken: not only are they not to blame for it, but the behavior doesn't qualify as negligent in the first place.[28]

Even if what I have just said is correct, however, it does not dispose of Clarke's objection to Premise 2 of the Argument from Ignorance, for Clarke could and, in the estimation of some,[29] should restrict his challenge to cases in which the agent's inadvertence *is* morally substandard. Consider Ian, from §6.1, who inadvertently left his daughter, Emma, locked in a hot car for hours with the windows closed.

---

[27] Cf. Hughes and Warmke (2017). [28] Cf. Talbert (2017b), pp. 22 ff.
[29] Cf. Talbert (2012), p. 101, and (2017b), p. 22.

Although, as I noted, his doing so need not have involved a deficit of care on his part (however exactly such a deficit is to be determined), it certainly could have done. Suppose, now, that it did. Then his inadvertence, being attributable to this deficit, would be morally substandard, and his behavior, Clarke would say, would not only qualify as negligent but also, in virtue of its morally objectionable basis, be behavior for which he is to blame. Moreover, this could well be the case even though Ian is *not* to blame for the inadvertence itself. As Clarke notes:

> [I]t isn't generally the case that blameworthiness for conduct arising from ill will or indifference requires blameworthiness for that quality of will. And I see no reason to think that it must do so in the case of unwitting wrongful conduct. Thus, even when an agent's failure to notice, think of, or remember something is due to an objectionable quality of will, direct blameworthiness for unwitting wrongful conduct is not ruled out.[30]

And so, Clarke would say, a charge of pure negligence could well be accurate in Ian's case and in many other cases, too.

To assess Clarke's view, we need to take another, closer look at the basis of blameworthiness.

9.2 Blameworthiness and quality of will

As I have observed several times, ever since Aristotle the traditional view has been that, to be blameworthy, one must satisfy two conditions, one agential, the other epistemic. In this book I have been engaged in an inquiry into both conditions, though my primary focus has been on the latter. As I noted in §2.2.1, however, to call the latter condition an epistemic one might well seem misleading, given (as I have conceded) that what is at issue is the quality of will that underlies one's behavior; for there is much besides what one knows, or even believes, that would appear to be relevant to determining whether one's will is morally objectionable. (I also noted in §2.2.1 that the term "will," even when construed expansively, may still be too restrictive, but for ease of exposition I will continue to use it here.) For example, if Ian's neglect of Emma was indeed attributable to a deficit of care on his part, then *that*, rather than anything to do with what he knew or believed, might well seem to be what's crucial to determining which reaction or reactions he deserves to receive from others (and should direct toward himself).

Some philosophers have recently contended that whether one's will is morally objectionable *never* has *anything*, at bottom, to do with one's epistemic state.

---

[30] Clarke (2017b), p. 247.

Perhaps the most prominent proponent of this view is Nomy Arpaly, who in several works has argued forcefully for the thesis that the moral quality of one's will essentially turns, not on what one knows or believes, but rather on what one desires. One example that she repeatedly uses to illustrate this thesis is that of Mark Twain's Huckleberry Finn, who cannot bring himself to return his slave friend, Jim, to his owner, even though he has the chance to do so *and* even though, on Arpaly's interpretation, he sincerely believes that he ought to do so. Arpaly contends that, in recognizing the fact that Jim is a fellow human being and acting on his desire to treat him as such, Huck is doing the right thing for the right reason and is therefore to be praised for his behavior, *despite* the fact that he believes that he is doing the wrong thing.[31] Even though he is unaware that he is doing so, he is in fact responding correctly to what matters morally, and so, Arpaly claims, his will is good. By contrast, someone like Ian, if indeed his behavior is attributable to a deficit of care, lacks a good will, while someone, such as a Nazi, who promotes an evil cause has a positively bad will, and so such agents are to be blamed for their behavior, *even if* they sincerely believe that they are doing the right thing.

9.2.1 Caring for morality *de re* vs. caring for morality *de dicto*

The view of praise- and blameworthiness that Arpaly espouses is one that is in many (but not all) respects shared by several others. It is a view that is often couched in terms of caring for morality *de re* as opposed to caring for it *de dicto*, terms that were introduced in this context by Michael Smith. Smith says:

> [C]ommonsense tells us that if good people judge it right to be honest, or right to care for their children and friends and fellows, or right for people to get what they deserve, then they care non-derivatively about these things. Good people care non-derivatively about honesty, the weal and woe of their children and friends, the well-being of their fellows, people getting what they deserve, justice, equality, and the like, not just one thing: doing what they believe to be right, where this is read *de dicto* and not *de re*. Indeed, commonsense tells us that being so motivated is a fetish or moral vice, not the one and only moral virtue... [I]t is constitutive of being a morally good person that you have direct concern for what you think is right, where this is read *de re* and not *de dicto*.[32]

Whether we should agree with what Smith says depends, of course, on just what he means by it.

---

[31] Arpaly (2003), pp. 9f. and 75 ff., and (2015). See also Arpaly and Schroeder (2013), pp. 178 f.
[32] M. Smith (1994), pp. 75 f.

In a commentary on Smith's view, Hallvard Lillehammer proposes a construal of the *de re-de dicto* distinction in terms of a difference in logical scope.[33] In so doing, he invokes W. V. O. Quine's classic discussion of the distinction.[34] In particular, Lillehammer suggests that the concern *de dicto* with doing what is right that Smith condemns is to be construed in terms of a person, P, desiring that, if some action is right, then P performs that action.[35] By this, I understand Lillehammer to mean the following:

DD1:   P desires that, for all right actions A, he or she performs A.

(I have substituted "he or she" for the second occurrence of "P" in order to fend off problems with referential opacity.) Lillehammer doesn't provide an explicit account of what it is to have a concern *de re* with doing what is right, but, given his claim about logical scope, I infer that this is what he has in mind:

DR1:   For all right actions A, P desires that he or she performs A.

(Problems with referential opacity remain here, of course, as Quine famously noted when discussing his concerns about quantifying into propositional attitude contexts. I will return to this issue shortly.) I should add that, like Smith, Lillehammer restricts his attention to desires that are non-derivative, that is, desires that such-and-such be the case for its *own* sake. (Lillehammer calls such desires "non-instrumental," a term also used by others.[36] Some use the term "intrinsic."[37]) The reason is straightforward. No one is tempted to say that it is morally good to care, for example, about behaving honestly, if one does so merely because one cares about appearing honest.

Lillehammer's interpretation of the distinction with which Smith is concerned has been endorsed by others,[38] but I think it's clear that it cannot be correct as it stands. (One problem, to which Lillehammer pays some attention, is that Smith actually couches his discussion in terms of a concern, whether *de dicto* or *de re*, with doing what one *thinks* or *believes* is right, rather than with doing what *is* right. This is a distraction that I won't pursue.) Surely no one has ever had the desire that is attributed to P in DD1. Suppose that Q, who is distinct from P, has made a promise, one that it is right for her to keep, and that P is aware of this fact. Then P's concern that the right thing be done may perhaps be construed as a desire that Q keep her promise, but it certainly doesn't consist in a desire that P keep Q's promise. Much more plausible than DD1 as an account of what Smith has in mind is this:

---

[33] Lillehammer (1997), p. 188.   [34] Quine (1956).   [35] Lillehammer (1997), p. 190.
[36] Cf. Markovits (2010), p. 230.   [37] Cf. Arpaly and Schroeder (2013), pp. 5 ff. and 162 ff.
[38] See, e.g., Dreier (2000), p. 621, and Carbonell (2013), p. 461.

DD2:   *P* desires that, for all actions *A* that it would be right for him or her to perform, he or she performs *A*.

But still there are problems. One has to do with the distinction between what is "*the* right" thing to do and what is "*a* right" thing to do. The former concerns what is obligatory, whereas the latter concerns what is permissible. There are thus two readings to be given to DD2:

DD2a: *P* desires that, for all actions *A* that it would be obligatory for him or her to perform, he or she performs *A*;

DD2b: *P* desires that, for all actions *A* that it would be permissible for him or her to perform, *P* performs *A*.

It may be that DD2a correctly captures the concern for morality that is to be attributed to some people, but I doubt that DD2b does. On the contrary, a concern with doing *all* that one is obligated to do is likely to be accompanied by a concern with doing, not all, but *only* that which it is permissible for one to do. That is:

DD3:   *P* desires that, for all actions *A* that he or she performs, it is permissible for him or her to perform *A*.

Perhaps either or both of DD2a and DD3 approximate Smith's conception of a concern *de dicto* with doing what is right, but questions remain. For example, is the desire at issue to be understood as long-standing, or might it be fleeting? Is it to be understood as being directed toward all actions that *P* might ever perform, or might it be directed only toward all actions that *P* might perform on some occasion or occasions? In either case, why must the desire be directed toward all actions that *P* might perform rather than toward only some? Indeed, it seems to me that the root idea at issue is that of performing some *particular* action from a concern *de dicto* with doing what is right, and I suggest that this be understood as follows:

DDo: *P*'s doing *A* from a non-derivative concern *de dicto* with doing what it is overall morally obligatory for him or her to do consists in *P*'s doing *A*

    (a)   in the belief that it is overall morally obligatory for him or her to do it, and

    (b)   with the purpose of satisfying a non-derivative desire to act in a way that it is overall morally obligatory for him or her to act;

DDp: *P*'s doing *A* from a non-derivative concern *de dicto* with doing what it is overall morally permissible for him or her to do consists in *P*'s doing *A*

(a) in the belief that it is overall morally permissible for him or her to do it, and

(b) with the purpose of satisfying a non-derivative desire to act in a way that it is overall morally permissible for him or her to act.

Consider, now, what it is to act from a concern *de re* with doing what is right. In addition to facing problems of the sort just discussed, DR1 faces two additional difficulties. The first is that of quantification into a referentially opaque context. The second is that of making sense of the notion of having a non-derivative desire to perform some action, that is, a desire to perform it for its own sake. Let me take these in reverse order.

Those who find value in acting from a concern *de re* with doing what is right do so because they find value in doing the right thing for the right reason, which they take to be a matter of being motivated to act as one does by the very reason in virtue of which one's action is right.[39] For example, if on some occasion what makes one's action right is that it is honest, then acting for the right reason would on this occasion consist in doing what one does *for the sake of acting honestly*. It wouldn't consist in doing what one does *for its own sake*—whatever that might mean.

Even with the requisite switch in focus regarding what it is for the sake of which one acts as one does, though, the problem of quantifying into a propositional attitude context remains. As Quine observes, one cannot account for there being someone whom Ralph believes to be a spy in terms of there being someone, S, such that Ralph believes that S is a spy; for the latter locution is insensitive to the fact that the content of Ralph's belief depends on how it is that he conceives of S. It may be, for example, that the man in question is someone whom Ralph has seen wearing a brown hat and has also seen at the beach, and yet Ralph is unaware that the men he has seen are one and the same. And it may be that, although Ralph believes that the man in the brown hat is a spy, he doesn't believe that the man at the beach is a spy.[40] In like fashion, one cannot account for there being some property that Rose wants her behavior to exemplify in terms of there being some property, F, such that Rose desires to behave in a way that exemplifies F; for the latter locution is insensitive to the fact that the content of Rose's belief depends on how it is that she conceives of F. It may be, for example, that, although Rose is

---

[39] Cf. Arpaly (2003), p. 72; Markovits (2010), p. 205; Harman (2011), p. 460; Arpaly and Schroeder (2013), p. 165.

[40] Quine (1956), p. 179.

aware that the property in question is her mother's favorite, she is unaware that it is also her father's favorite. And it may be that, although she desires to behave in a way that exemplifies her mother's favorite property, she doesn't desire to behave in a way that exemplifies her father's favorite property.

There is a solution to this problem. Consider wisdom. This is the property of being wise. It is also, let us assume, the property that is most frequently attributed to Solomon. But these two ways of referring to the property are very different. The phrase "being wise" expresses what, following Roderick Chisholm, I will call its *content*, whereas the phrase "most frequently attributed to Solomon" is a merely accidentally correct description of it.[41] Similarly, the property of respecting persons may be the property most frequently associated with Kant, but only the former locution picks out this property by reference to its content. I suggest that what those who find value in acting from a concern *de re* with doing what is right are celebrating is acting from a desire that concerns the content of some right-making property. More exactly, the following is what I take them to have in mind:

DRo: P's doing A from a non-derivative concern *de re* with doing what it is overall morally obligatory for him or her to do consists in there being some property, F, such that

(a) A exemplifies F,

(b) it is overall morally obligatory for P to do A in virtue of the fact that A exemplifies F, and

(c) while thinking of F in terms of its content, P does A

   (i) in the belief that A exemplifies F, and

   (ii) with the purpose of satisfying a non-derivative desire to act in a way that exemplifies F;

DRp: P's doing A from a non-derivative concern *de re* with doing what it is overall morally permissible for him or her to do consists in there being some property, F, such that

(a) A exemplifies F,

(b) it is overall morally permissible for P to do A in virtue of the fact that A exemplifies F, and

(c) while thinking of F in terms of its content, P does A

   (i) in the belief that A exemplifies F, and

   (ii) with the purpose of satisfying a non-derivative desire to act in a way that exemplifies F.

---

[41] Chisholm (1976), p. 166. The example is Chisholm's. Cf. Plantinga (1974), p. 31.

I should note that the phrase "while thinking of F in terms of its content" may not succeed in identifying precisely how P conceives of F. Suppose, for example, that the property of respecting persons is the same as the property of treating persons as ends in themselves. It could be that, while P takes himself to be acting in a way that respects persons, he doesn't think that he's acting in a way that treats persons as ends in themselves. No matter. *If* these properties are one and the same, then they have one and the same content. Regardless of how exactly P conceives of this content, as long as he is thinking in terms of it and acts accordingly, he will be acting from a concern *de re* with doing what is right (provided, of course, that it *is* a right-making property).

I should also note that, as my last parenthetical comment indicates, there is an asymmetry between DDo and DDp, on the one hand, and DRo and DRp, on the other. Whereas the former allow for the possibility that one act from a non-derivative concern *de dicto* that is erroneous (one's conscience may be misguided—see §8.2), the latter do not allow for the possibility that one act from a non-derivative concern *de re* that is erroneous. This is in keeping with the theme, stressed by Arpaly et al., of *doing the right thing* for the right reason. I will comment further on this asymmetry shortly.

9.2.2 Conscientiousness and doing something for the right reason

I understand acting morally conscientiously to consist in acting from a non-derivative concern *de dicto* with doing what is overall morally right, as explicated in DDo and DDp. We should distinguish between acting conscientiously and acting in accordance with one's conscience; the latter involves the belief that one is doing what is right but may not involve the desire to act in this way. Both, of course, are to be distinguished from acting in a way that contravenes one's conscience—acting "contra-conscientiously," as I will put it—which consists in doing something in the belief that one is acting overall morally wrongly.[42]

Conscientiousness is usually thought to be a virtue, and contra-conscientiousness a vice. Yet Arpaly denies this. As I have noted, she denies that Huckleberry is to be blamed, even though he acts contra-conscientiously, and she sees virtue, not in acting from a concern *de dicto*, but rather in acting from a concern *de re* with doing what is right. It is, she claims, when and only when one

---

[42] This account of conscientiousness and contra-conscientiousness is disputed by Peter Graham, who holds that it is possible to act conscientiously while believing that one is acting overall morally wrongly, if one believes that that is the only way to avoid the risk of acting in a way that is much more seriously overall morally wrong. (See Graham (2010), pp. 100 f.) In saying this, Graham is presupposing an objective account of moral obligation and wrongdoing, an account which I reject for reasons given in §6.1 and §7.1.4.

acts from the latter concern that one does the right thing for the right reason, which she identifies with the reason in virtue of which one's action is right. For example, regarding Kant's well-known case of a grocer for whom it would be prudent not to overcharge his customers,[43] she claims that doing the right thing for the right reason would consist in his treating them fairly for the sake of treating them fairly, rather than for his own sake.[44]

In denying that the grocer's treating his customers fairly would itself constitute doing the right thing for the right reason Arpaly is of course agreeing with Kant and also, no doubt, with common sense. Neither she nor Kant is denying that the grocer would be doing the right thing; on the contrary, the right thing for him to do *is* to treat his customers fairly. What she and Kant are denying is that treating his customers fairly is all that is required for him to do the right thing *for the right reason*. But Arpaly and Kant differ markedly regarding what else is needed. Kant famously claims that doing the right thing for the right reason requires that one act *from duty*, that is, from a non-derivative concern *de dicto* with doing what is right. Arpaly claims, to the contrary, that what is required is that one act from a non-derivative concern *de re* with doing what is right. If the grocer treats his customers fairly in order to maximize profits, then he does the right thing merely by accident. But if he treats them fairly for the sake of treating them fairly, then, she says, it is no accident that he does what is right; for he is thereby *responding* to the reason that makes his action right.[45] (It is interesting to note that reasons-responsiveness, so conceived, is here being understood to constitute satisfaction, not of the agential condition of moral responsibility, but of the condition having to do with quality of will.)

Initially, it may well seem plausible, even truistic, to hold that doing the right thing for the right reason consists in doing it for the reason that makes it right. Julie Markovits calls this the Coincident Reasons Thesis and formulates it as follows: one's action is morally worthy if and only if one's motivating reasons for acting coincide with the reasons morally justifying the action.[46] This rendition of the thesis not only captures the idea that acting from a non-derivative concern *de re* with doing what is right constitutes acting for the right reason but also provides an explanation of why acting from a non-derivative concern *de dicto* with doing what is right does *not* count as acting for the right reason. For the fact that it is right or justifiable to perform some act cannot, it seems, itself be a reason that justifies performing it, and so, if one is motivated to do something by the thought that it is right to do it, one's motivating reason won't coincide with the reason that makes one's action right.[47] Similarly, the fact that it is wrong to perform some act

---

[43] Kant (1964), Ak. 397. [44] Arpaly (2003), pp. 71 f. [45] Arpaly (2003), pp. 71 ff.
[46] Markovits (2010), p. 205. [47] Markovits (2010), p. 207.

cannot, it seems, itself be a reason not to perform it; on the contrary, the reason-constituting "buck" passes to that feature *in virtue of which* one's action is wrong.

Whether rightness and wrongness are buck-passing notions is in fact a vexed and complex matter. On reflection, it is not at all obvious that the fact that an act is right (or wrong) cannot itself constitute a reason to do (or not to do) it.[48] Fortunately, for present purposes there is no need to venture into this territory; for the Coincident Reasons Thesis should, I think, be rejected. Thus, even if it is correct to say that the reason to do (or not to do) some act resides not in that act's being right (or wrong) but in whatever feature it has that makes it right (or wrong), it may still be that being motivated by the fact that it is right (or wrong) is the, or at least a, right way, morally, for one to be motivated.

Arpaly claims that only acting from a non-derivative concern *de re* with doing what is right counts as being responsive to moral reasons and hence as doing the right thing non-accidentally, but I think this is a mistake. Unless one conceives of what one is doing *as* right, then one is not responding to the reason for which one's act is right *as* a moral reason. And if one is not responding to this reason *as* a moral reason, then to describe one's behavior as being responsive to moral reasons is quite misleading. Indeed, there is a sense in which one's behavior will, and must, be merely *accidentally* morally right.[49] Consider a situation in which morality and prudence coincide, not contingently as in Kant's case of the grocer, but essentially. Suppose, for example, that both morality and prudence require that one treat oneself with respect, and that Trudy treats herself with respect, not for the sake of doing what is right, but rather for the sake of doing what is prudent (she recognizes that so acting is indeed what prudence requires) *and* for the sake of treating herself with respect. In this case, that Trudy is doing what is prudent is no accident, but that she is also doing what is morally right is simply a fortunate coincidence, despite the fact that she has a non-derivative desire to act in a way that, unbeknownst to her, renders her act morally right.

So too, I would say, for Huckleberry Finn. If, in helping Jim escape, he's acting for a reason, one in virtue of which his act is morally right, it doesn't follow that he is responding to a moral reason. More particularly, if (in keeping with Arpaly's interpretation of the story) he doesn't recognize the reason for which he helps Jim escape *as* a moral reason, then he cannot be properly described as responding to a moral reason.[50] His behavior perhaps *accords* with moral reasons, but it isn't *responsive* to such reasons. Now, whether the reason for which Huck acts as he does is indeed both one in virtue of which his act is morally right and one that he doesn't recognize as a moral reason is not so clear to me. Arpaly describes him as responding to Jim's personhood,[51] but that might be an overly general description

---

[48] For insightful discussion, see Scanlon (2007), Darwall (2010), and Heuer (2010).
[49] Cf. Johnson King (2020a), pp. 188 ff.   [50] Cf. Fischer and Ravizza (1998), pp. 41 ff. and 69 ff.
[51] Arpaly (2003), p. 77.

of his motive, precisely because there's no reason to think that he is inclined to treat other persons like Jim in the same way. Moreover, if this is the correct description of his motive, then there's the sneaking suspicion (disavowed by Arpaly) that he is dimly aware after all of the moral rightness of treating Jim as he does, despite his protestations to the contrary. Jonathan Bennett, who agrees with Arpaly that Huck acts in a way that contravenes his conscience, contends that Huck behaves as he does out of sympathy.[52] This strikes me as a plausible interpretation, but it doesn't explicitly identify the motivating reason for which Huck acts. Perhaps it is simply the thought that, if he helps Jim escape, he'll make him happy. Or perhaps it is simply the thought that, if he doesn't help Jim escape, he'll make him sad.[53] And perhaps we can agree that promoting Jim's happiness or avoiding his sadness is a feature in virtue of which Huck's behavior is morally right. This coincidence between motivating and justifying reasons is fortunate, but it is, in an important sense, *just* a coincidence. By hypothesis, it's not one that Huck has in mind. Indeed, his motivating reason, so understood, is one that a *morally blind* person—someone with no grasp whatsoever of moral concepts, such as a young child or a temporarily benign psychopath—could act on. It's hard to see how acting for such a reason could itself confer *moral* credit on anyone.

Arpaly might respond that doing the right thing from a non-derivative concern *de dicto* with doing what is right is also no guarantee that the right thing isn't done by accident. She provides an example (one in which a person rightly refrains from killing another person from a concern *de dicto* with doing what is right, but only because the person he spares belongs to a certain ethnic group) that appears to show this.[54] But I draw two lessons from this observation. The first is that it may be that the only way to ensure that one does the right thing non-accidentally is to do it from a non-derivative concern both *de dicto* and *de re* with doing what is right. The second and, as I see it, far more important point is that this in some ways ideal state of affairs involves the intersection of two distinct moral domains, the deontic and the hypological. (See §2.1.3.) This fact is obscured by those who, in the manner of Kant but also in the manner of non-Kantians such as Arpaly and Markovits, seek to determine the conditions under which, as they put it, an *action* is morally *worthy*.[55] Whether an *action* is morally *right or wrong* is a deontic question; whether an *agent* is *worthy of praise or blame* is a hypological question. My concern in this book is with the latter question. This is where an agent's quality of will becomes relevant, and I submit that it is simply a distraction, one that invites confusion, to concern oneself with the rightness of someone's action when trying to figure out whether that person is to be praised for that action. It is

---

[52] Bennett (1974).
[53] On conceiving of reasons as expressible in terms of conditionals, see Persson (2019), ch. 3.
[54] Arpaly (2003), p. 74.
[55] Cf. Kant (1964), Ak. 398, 401; Arpaly (2003), pp. 67 ff.; Markovits (2010).

the agent's state of mind that matters in this regard, irrespective of the behavior that results from or accompanies it.

My last statement might strike you as preposterous. Surely, you might think, one can only be praiseworthy for doing what is right and blameworthy for doing what is wrong. Since whether one's act is right or wrong depends on more than just one's state of mind in performing it (if, indeed, it depends on this at all), whether one is praiseworthy or blameworthy for one's act will also depend on more than just one's state of mind in performing it.

In response, I agree that whether one's act is right or wrong is not simply a function of one's state of mind in performing it, but I deny that one can only be praiseworthy for doing what is right and blameworthy for doing what is wrong. On the contrary, it is perfectly possible to be praiseworthy for doing what is wrong and blameworthy for doing what is right. Or rather (since what I just said may seem to suggest, erroneously, that one can be praiseworthy for doing something *because* it is wrong and blameworthy *because* it is right), it is perfectly possible to be praiseworthy for doing some act, A, even though A is wrong, and it is perfectly possible to be blameworthy for doing some act, A, even though A is right. I addressed the latter possibility in §3.4.1, but let me now add this. It is apparent that Arpaly et al. are *themselves* committed to accepting the two possibilities in question.

To see this, consider the following account of praise- and blameworthiness proposed by Arpaly and her co-author Timothy Schroeder:

Praiseworthiness: a person is praiseworthy for a right action A to the extent that A manifests good will (or reverse moral indifference) through being rationalized by it.

Blameworthiness: a person is blameworthy for a wrong action A to the extent that A manifests ill will (or moral indifference) through being rationalized by it.[56]

In keeping with their view that a good or bad will has exclusively to do with the non-derivative desires that one has regarding the right- and wrong-making properties of actions, Arpaly and Schroeder proceed to elaborate this account as follows:

Praiseworthiness: a person is praiseworthy for a right action A to the extent that A manifests an intrinsic desire (or desires) for the complete or partial right or good (correctly conceptualized) or an absence of intrinsic desires for the complete or partial wrong or bad (correctly conceptualized) through being rationalized by it (or them).

---

[56] Arpaly and Schroeder (2013), p. 170.

Blameworthiness: a person is blameworthy for a wrong action A to the extent that A manifests an intrinsic desire (or desires) for the complete or partial wrong or bad (correctly conceptualized) or an absence of intrinsic desires for the complete or partial right or good (correctly conceptualized) through being rationalized by it (or them).[57]

Now, although they talk in terms of "praiseworthy for a right action" and "blameworthy for a wrong action," Arpaly and Schroeder nonetheless also talk in terms of "to the extent that" and of "partial right" and "partial wrong." They do so because they recognize that one might act for the sake of achieving something that renders one's action merely *pro tanto*, rather than overall, right or wrong, and they believe that, to the extent that this is so, to that extent one is praiseworthy or blameworthy.[58] Up until this point in this chapter, whenever I have spoken of an action's being morally right or wrong, it is with overall rightness and wrongness that I have been concerned. Often this has been only implicit in what I have said, but sometimes it has been explicit, as in the definitions I offered of acting from a non-derivative concern, whether *de dicto* or *de re*, with doing what is right. But such a restriction is unwarranted inasmuch as, as Arpaly and Schroeder stress, it is possible for one's concern with doing what is right to be merely partial. (To accommodate this possibility, I propose definitions that correspond to DDo, DDp, DRo, and DRp in which "overall" is replaced by "*pro tanto*."[59]) It is also possible, of course, for one to act from a concern with doing what is wrong. (Again, corresponding definitions can be given.) Now imagine that Gavin gives a gift to Pauline both for the sake of pleasing her and for the sake of arousing envy in Elaine; that he succeeds in achieving both these aims; and that, in virtue of this success, his gift-giving is both *pro tanto* right and *pro tanto* wrong. As I understand it, the view espoused by Arpaly and Schroeder implies that Gavin is both praiseworthy to some extent and blameworthy to some extent for his behavior. Hence, if what he does is overall morally right, he will nonetheless be blameworthy for doing it, and if what he does is overall morally wrong, he will nonetheless be praiseworthy for doing it. (This interpretation of Arpaly's and Schroeder's view requires that we construe "right action" and "wrong action" in their account of praise- and blameworthiness as meaning "*pro tanto* right action" and "*pro tanto* wrong action," respectively. If instead it is overall rightness and wrongness that they have in mind, then their account seems internally inconsistent.)

---

[57] Arpaly and Schroeder (2013), p. 170.
[58] Arpaly and Schroeder (2013), p. 166. Cf. Markovits (2010), pp. 237 ff.
[59] A *merely* partial concern *de dicto* with doing what is right involves having a non-derivative desire to act in a way that is *pro tanto* morally right while lacking such a desire to do what is overall morally right. This is a decidedly odd combination of conative states. I see no merit in it and will not comment on it further.

Some might consider the claim that it is possible to be both praiseworthy and blameworthy for doing one and the same thing to be obviously incorrect in virtue of being inconsistent. But there is no inconsistency here, as long as what is at issue is praiseworthiness in virtue of *some* aspect of one's quality of will conjoined with blameworthiness in virtue of some *other* aspect. An accurate moral assessment of a complex situation often calls for just such ambivalence.

Even though Arpaly's and Schroeder's account, as I have interpreted it, accommodates both the possibility of being praiseworthy for an action that is overall morally wrong and the possibility of being blameworthy for an action that is overall morally right, it is nonetheless committed to the claim that one can only be praiseworthy for doing what is at least *pro tanto* right and blameworthy for doing what is at least *pro tanto* wrong, a restriction that I find difficult to support even from their own point of view. Arpaly remarks, "To the extent that Huckleberry is reluctant to turn Jim in because of Jim's personhood, he *is* acting for morally significant reasons."[60] But suppose instead that it is Schmuckleberry who is on the raft with Jim, and that he is hopelessly but blamelessly confused not only about what morality requires of him but also about what will best help Jim. Responding to Jim's personhood, he turns Jim in. *If* a concern for Jim's personhood renders Huckleberry praiseworthy, I cannot see why that same concern wouldn't also render Schmuckleberry praiseworthy.[61] Yet since Jim's personhood does not in fact serve to justify turning him in, Arpaly and Schroeder are committed to assessing Huckleberry and Schmuckleberry differently. This strikes me as a mistake; that is, the asymmetry noted earlier between DDo and DDp, on the one hand, and DRo and DRp, on the other, would seem unwarranted. (If I'm right about this, then DRo and DRp require revision, something that I won't try to provide here.)

Although I think, for the reasons given above, that it is a mistake to say, on the supposition that he sincerely believes that it is overall morally wrong—and not even *pro tanto* morally right—to help Jim escape, that Huckleberry is responding to moral reasons when he nonetheless does help Jim escape, and although I said that it is therefore hard to see how his motivating reason confers any moral credit on him, I am in fact prepared to concede that it nonetheless does so. I am prepared to concede, that is, that virtue can be "unprincipled," as Arpaly puts it. ("Morally oblivious" would be an equally apt term.) This verdict is perfectly compatible with saying, as I do, that, in virtue of acting contra-conscientiously, Huckleberry is *also* to blame for his behavior. (He is, after all, *deliberately defying* what he takes to be the demands of morality—hardly a mark in his favor; indeed, surely a mark against him.[62]) This is just another instance in which ambivalence may be the correct stance to take. The point that I am keen to stress here is, once again, simply

---

[60] Arpaly (2003), p. 77.   [61] Cf. Johnson King (2020c), p. 420.
[62] Cf. Donagan (1977), p. 136.

that, contra Arpaly et al., it may still be that acting from a concern *de dicto* with doing what is overall morally right is, if not the only right way to be motivated, at least one of the right ways to be motivated.[63]

9.2.3 Moral fetishism

Even if Arpaly et al. have not shown that conscientiousness is not a virtue, it of course doesn't follow that it is a virtue. I said above that conscientiousness is usually thought to be a virtue, but again, even if this is true, it doesn't follow that it is. And is this true? What of Smith's contention that commonsense tells us that acting from a non-derivative concern *de dicto* with doing what is right, far from being virtuous, is a fetish—a *vice*?

At one point in his commentary, Lillehammer describes the moral fetishist (as conceived by Smith) as "a person whose *only* non-instrumental desire is a desire to do whatever is right."[64] This might well be what Smith has in mind. His remark in the passage, quoted at the start of §9.2.1, about caring non-derivatively about "just one thing" certainly suggests it, as does his subsequent discussion of Bernard Williams's well-known comments about the case of a man who is confronted by two persons in equal peril, one his wife and the other a stranger, only one of whom he can rescue, and who chooses to rescue his wife. Williams wryly remarks:

> [I]t might have been hoped by some (for instance, by his wife) that [the man's] motivating thought, fully spelled out, would be the thought that it was his wife, not that it was his wife and that in situations of this kind it is permissible to save one's wife.[65]

The latter motivation, Williams famously contends, "provides the agent with one thought too many." In commenting on this passage, Smith says:

> [The wife] would quite rightly hope that her husband's "motivating thought, fully spelled out" is that the person he saved was his wife. If any further motivation were required then that would simply indicate that he doesn't have the feelings of direct love and concern for her that she rightly wants and expects.[66]

I am not entirely sure what Smith means by these remarks.

One thing that Smith might be taken to suggest is that the man's having had a non-derivative concern *de dicto* with doing what was right precluded his also

---

[63] Cf. Hurka (2014) and Johnson King (2020a).
[64] Lillehammer (1997), p. 190; emphasis added.   [65] B. Williams (1981), p. 18.
[66] M. Smith (1994), p. 75.

having had a non-derivative concern for his wife, but that is simply not so. In general, it is perfectly possible to have non-derivative concerns for several things at once, and there is no reason to think that having the particular non-derivative concern *de dicto* with doing what is right should be incompatible with also having a non-derivative concern for something else.[67] On the contrary, the natural interpretation of Williams's description of the allegedly not-so-desirable motivating thought is that it reflects non-derivative concerns on the man's part *both* for his wife *and* for doing the right thing.

Another thing that Smith might be taken to suggest is that, if the man acted on a desire to save his wife *in order to* do what was right, then his concern for his wife was derivative and hence not non-derivative. But that, too, would be a mistake. In general, one can have both a derivative and a non-derivative concern for one and the same thing. (For example, I might want to do something that pleases my wife for the sake of pleasing her and also for the sake of pleasing my daughter.) Moreover, in the particular case of having a non-derivative concern *de dicto* with doing what is right, it's hard to imagine someone having such a concern without also having a non-derivative concern for what he or she takes to be the right-making features of actions. For example, if the man saved his wife in order to do what was right, then presumably he believed that saving her was the right thing to do. This belief will not have materialized out of thin air; it will presumably have had its basis in something like the thought that his wife was worth saving for her own sake. And it's hard (though admittedly not impossible) to imagine the man's conscientiously acting on this thought if he didn't care for his wife for her own sake.

Yet another thing that Smith might be taken to suggest is that, if the man acted on a desire to save his wife in order to do what was right, then, even if he had a non-derivative concern for his wife, this concern was not sufficient on its own to motivate his saving her, and so the concern with doing what was right was indispensable. But this once again seems to be a mistake. Motivational overdetermination seems just as possible in this context as in any other.

The foregoing observations notwithstanding, I acknowledge that Williams's pithy comment about the man's having one thought too many strikes a chord. It seems possible for someone to be *overly* conscientious, whether this is to be understood in terms of being solely or primarily or indispensably concerned with doing the right thing or in yet other terms. There are two ways to understand "overly" in this context: either as expressing an excess that is morally objectionable, or as expressing an excess that is non-morally objectionable. In the former case, the concern may be that one's attention to duty is crowding out the display of (other) moral virtues, such as kindness or compassion; or it may be that one's

---

[67] Cf. Olson (2002), pp. 91 f.

attention to duty is, ironically, getting in the way of one's actually doing one's duty. In the latter case, the concern may be that "the good life" involves a commitment to certain non-moral goals and ideals, as well as to certain moral ones, conjoined with a willingness in cases of conflict sometimes to sacrifice the latter in favor of the former. (Consider what Susan Wolf has to say about moral saints.[68]) This is all pretty rough and vague, but there is no need to try to be more precise here. The important point to note is that, however exactly they are construing *over*-conscientiousness, neither Williams nor Smith has done anything to impugn conscientiousness *as such*. The worries they raise, however precisely they are to be understood, clearly go well beyond anything contained in either DDo or DDp. After all, clause (b) of these definitions does *not* say "with the sole or primary or indispensable purpose of…" or anything else that implies that all conscientiousness is over-conscientiousness.

Once again, however, even if it is agreed that Smith has not shown that conscientiousness as such is a vice, it doesn't follow that it is a virtue. Does having a non-derivative concern *de dicto* with doing what is right always speak well of someone? I think that it does. Imagine that Eunice is uncertain whether to tell Tim the truth or to spare his feelings. She thinks hard about the question, weighing the pros and cons of each alternative. Eventually she decides that the overall right thing to do is to tell him the truth and proceeds to do so. Arpaly would concede that such deliberation reflects well on Eunice, but she would maintain that it does so only because it indicates that Eunice has the proper underlying concerns with telling the truth and sparing people's feelings.[69] But that doesn't seem right. Eunice is also concerned, and properly so, with figuring out which of these underlying concerns takes precedence over the other in the particular circumstances in which she finds herself. This "meta-concern" is a concern *de dicto* with doing what is overall morally right, and it is to Eunice's moral credit that she has it, even if it is also to her credit that she has the sort of underlying concerns of which Arpaly approves. A morally significant piece of the story would be missing if, without bothering to weigh the respective merits of her alternatives, Eunice simply plumped uncritically for one rather than the other.[70]

No doubt the cases in which it is hardest to find value in conscientiousness as such are those in which an agent has a radically misguided conscience. Markovits says that "there is something particularly sinister about agents who act terribly wrongly while claiming to have right on their side"[71] and claims that "Göbbels's persecution of the Jews is no less despicable because he believed he was acting rightly."[72] I of course agree with the latter verdict; it concerns Göbbels's behavior. And I agree that there is something profoundly disturbing about a conscience so

---

[68] Wolf (1982). [69] Arpaly (2015), pp. 147 ff.
[70] Cf. Sliwa (2015), p. 175; Aboodi (2017), pp. 225 ff. [71] Markovits (2010), p. 217, n. 35.
[72] Markovits (2010), p. 217.

badly twisted as the one that apparently prompted Göbbels to do what he did. (I'm not sure I'd agree that there is anything sinister involved, unless the thought is that hearkening to one's conscience tends to augment one's diligence in the pursuit of what one perceives to be one's duty.) Even so, the question remains whether, these points notwithstanding, the fact (if it is a fact) that Göbbels acted conscientiously itself speaks well of him. I'm inclined to think that it does—to think, that is, that this is yet another case in which ambivalence is called for, a case in which a relatively modest positive evaluation stands appropriately alongside some very weighty negative evaluations.[73]

Perhaps I am mistaken about this. Perhaps it is only conscientiousness-in-certain-circumstances that is a virtue, rather than conscientiousness as such. Or perhaps, although I find this incredible, not even conscientiousness-in-certain-circumstances is a virtue. No matter. Either view is consistent with the Argument from Ignorance, since that argument concerns *blameworthiness*, not praiseworthiness. What is *not* consistent with the argument is something else that Arpaly et al. hold to be true.

9.2.4 Ill will

Rejecting the claim that fundamental moral ignorance is an excuse, Arpaly asks us to

> ...consider what the "folk" think of the Nazis. Nazi war criminals are often assumed to have believed deeply in the rightness of their way—not only did they believe... that their actions were morally permissible but they also thought their actions morally desirable or required... In addition to the fact that Nazi war criminals are often used as the *default* example of *paradigmatic* evil, it is also true that, when some of them were still alive and hiding, it was considered worthwhile to do one's utmost to bring them to justice... Today, too, dictators cannot use their racist or nationalist views as excuses in the court of public opinion, and, similarly, terrorists cannot use their deep faith as an excuse in real courts.[74]

What Arpaly says is surely true. It's true that Nazi war criminals are often used as the default example of paradigmatic evil, and it's also true that dictators and terrorists cannot use their beliefs as an excuse, either morally or legally, if by this is meant that they cannot (in all likelihood) succeed in convincing others that their beliefs render them blameless for any atrocities that they have committed in light of them. Nonetheless, while I agree that such agents are evil (see §8.2), the

---

[73] Cf. Hurka (2014), p. 499; Johnson King (2020b), pp. 421 ff.   [74] Arpaly (2015), p. 155.

Argument from Ignorance commits me to saying, contrary to common opinion (and, no doubt many would say, to common sense), that they are not to blame for their heinous behavior, unless they are to blame for the ignorance from which it emanated.

Arpaly denies this, of course. She claims that the ill will displayed in such evil behavior renders its perpetrators blameworthy for their behavior, irrespective of whether they are ignorant of the fact that the behavior is wrong and, if they are, irrespective of whether they are to blame for their ignorance. In making this claim, she is rejecting Premise 2 of the Argument from Ignorance, according to which, roughly, one is to blame for some act that one committed from ignorance of the fact that it was wrong only if one is to blame for one's ignorance—a premise that many have thought "goes without saying."[75] She and Schroeder say:

> [W]e regard blameworthiness as a property people have for particular actions. Feelings, cognitions, and other mental attitudes... are best thought of as virtuous or vicious rather than praise- or blameworthy. But saying that someone has a character defect—a vice—is just as much... a condemnation as saying that he is blameworthy.[76]

Their view is that the kind of ill will exhibited in cases of the sort under discussion, ill will that essentially involves having a non-derivative desire for the wrong and the bad, suffices to render the agents in question blameworthy for their behavior. These agents are acting from a non-derivative concern *de re* with doing what is wrong, and that is all that counts. The fact, if it is a fact, that they are also acting from a non-derivative concern *de dicto* with doing what is right is irrelevant to their blameworthiness.

Others agree that Premise 2 is to be rejected. Elizabeth Harman, for example, says:

> Wrong actions that result from false moral beliefs are not thereby blameless; indeed, they may be loci of *original* responsibility... [T]he actions are not blameworthy *because* the beliefs are blameworthy.[77]

And Matthew Talbert says:

> I reject the premise that a morally ignorant wrongdoer is blameworthy only if her ignorance is culpable. Even if an unwitting wrongdoer's ignorance is not her fault, moral blame may be appropriate if her actions express contempt for those she injures... [I]t is quite possible both that a wrongdoer regards her behavior as

---

[75] Cf. Donagan (1977), p. 135.
[76] Arpaly and Schroeder (2013), p. 218. Cf. Arpaly (2003), p. 115.   [77] Harman (2011), p. 459.

permissible, and that, in an important sense, she is not "well-intentioned." If someone... treats others in ways to which she knows they object, then the fact that she regards this as permissible does not alter the fact that her actions express the judgment that these others do not merit much consideration, that their interests do not matter, that their objections can be overlooked. And if one is injured by a wrongdoer who is moved by judgments of this sort, then the attitudes and responses involved in moral blame are appropriate regardless of whether the wrongdoer is at fault for her moral ignorance.[78]

Although the example of the Nazi war criminals is a case of fundamental moral ignorance, and although it is such ignorance on which Harman and Talbert concentrate, it's important to note that ill will *à la* Arpaly can be exhibited in cases of merely incidental moral ignorance. For example, Arpaly would diagnose ill will (or, more precisely, moral indifference) in that version of the case in which Ian neglected Emma due to a deficit of care on his part. So, too, for many other cases of negligence.

It's not clear to me just why it is that the authors I have just cited pick on Premise 2 of the Argument from Ignorance. It is the ill will that they take to underlie the troublesome behavior that is the source of their blame of the agent for that behavior, and it would be odd if they withheld that blame in the event that no such behavior resulted. For example, if it is apparent that someone harbors the kind of contempt that concerns Talbert, why wouldn't resentment of him for it *therefore* be fitting, regardless of how he behaved? Suppose, for instance, that you're having a discussion with Donald, during the course of which he reveals to you his deep and abiding contempt for women. This surprises you, since you've seen no evidence of it before, but it's now become quite obvious. If you find such *contempt* contemptible, surely you wouldn't wait until Donald actually puts it into practice before you held *him* in contempt.

Arpaly and Schroeder say that people can be blameworthy for particular actions, but they deny that people can be blameworthy for feelings, cognitions, and other mental attitudes. Perhaps this is because they subscribe to the view that one can only be blameworthy for what is in one's control, and one cannot have (direct) control over the sort of mental attitudes they have in mind. (As noted in §9.1.1, it is this view that appears to explain Clarke's focusing on Premise 2 of the Argument from Ignorance, rather than Premise 4, in his discussion of negligence.) But, once again, this puzzles me. If it is the fact that Donald harbors contempt for women, the fact that Jasmine harbors hatred for Jews, and other such facts that account for such agents being blameworthy for the behavior that issues from their

---

[78] Talbert (2012), p. 101.

ill will, how is it that they are *not* to blame for the ill will itself? Arpaly and Schroeder admit that an attribution of ill will to someone constitutes condemnation of that person. How is such condemnation not a matter of blame?

If agents are to blame for their ill will, and if this is so regardless of their lack of control over it, then of course Premise 4 of the Argument from Ignorance is false. And it is indeed on this premise that most of those who reject the Origination Thesis (whether explicitly or only implicitly) have focused their attention.[79] A prominent example of this approach is to be found in Robert Adams's discussion of what he calls involuntary sins.[80] His account of what constitutes ill will (although he doesn't use that term) is very broad. The "sins" that he identifies as apt occasions for blame are many and varied. He writes not just of what he calls (in a manner reminiscent of Arpaly) "wrong desires," but also of "corrupt beliefs," of "cognitive failures," and of certain emotions, all of which he lumps under the general heading of "morally objectionable states of mind"; and he provides a whole slew of examples of such phenomena: anger (when excessive or otherwise inappropriate), jealousy, hatred, malice, contempt for other people, the lack of concern for others' welfare, self-righteousness, ingratitude, the failure to ascribe rights to others, the failure to be sensitive to others' feelings, Nazi ideology, and more.

The expansive account that Adams gives of morally objectionable states of mind (and, sometimes, of morally commendable ones such as gratitude) is one that has recently been embraced, in one form or another, by many other writers, especially, but not exclusively, by those who nowadays are often called "attributionists," according to whom agents are morally responsible for whatever expresses, or reveals, or reflects who they are as a person. Proponents of this approach observe that it is not just one's behavior but also, and more importantly, the attitudes, dispositions, and other personal traits that underlie this behavior that can reveal who one is as a person. A cutting comment, for example, may be symptomatic of a mean streak, a disparaging remark may reveal one's arrogance or envy, and so on, and, if the behavior is obnoxious, it's because of the obnoxious nature of the traits that underlie it. Moreover, if the traits are constitutive of who one is as a person, then one will be blameworthy both for the traits and for the behavior to which they give rise, *regardless* of whether the traits or the behavior are within one's control. Here is a representative statement of one version of this increasingly popular view provided by Angela Smith:

---

[79] Notice that there might still be reason to reject Premise 2 as well. Harman rejects both premises, for example. (Harman (2011), pp. 495 f.) Moreover, if it is possible for someone to do something wrong both from ill will and from ignorance of the fact that it is wrong, *without* the ignorance itself being attributable to the ill will, then finding that person blameworthy for the wrongdoing requires rejecting Premise 2.

[80] Adams (1985). Though increasingly popular, the thesis that "virtue and vice may...be involuntary" is certainly not novel. It is to be found in Hume (2007), bk. 3, pt. 3, sect. 4.

> [A] mental state is attributable to a person in the way that is required in order for it to be a basis for moral appraisal if that state is rationally connected in one of the relevant ways to her underlying evaluative judgment. This rules out most sensations and visual perceptions, random thoughts and mental images, appetitive desires, and "implanted" attitudes, since we do not expect these states to reflect or to be governed by our judgment. What gets ruled in, however, are ordinary cases of belief, intention, most desires, fear, indignation, admiration, and guilt, among others, as well as our moral perceptions and various patterns of unreflective thought and feeling which we take to be sensitive to and expressive of our underlying values and commitments. Since explicit choice or voluntary control is not necessary for these rational connections to judgment to obtain, this account implies that we can be responsible for our spontaneous attitudes and reactions no less than for our explicit practical and theoretical conclusions.[81]

Since Adams, Smith, and others[82] explicitly state that one can be to blame for mental attitudes other than desires, it may seem obvious that they reject the strict desire-based account of ill will proposed by Arpaly and Schroeder. But in some cases, at least, this is in fact not so obvious. Consider Harman's view, for example. She claims that one is *always* to blame for any false moral beliefs one holds that are not merely a matter of incidental moral ignorance.[83] She thus appears to be committed to saying that Huckleberry Finn is to blame, not (as I have urged) for doing what he believes to be wrong, but rather for believing that it is wrong to help Jim escape. Since Arpaly denies that one can be (directly) blameworthy for one's mental attitudes and also denies that Huck is to blame for his behavior, the difference between her view and Harman's may seem considerable. But appearances may be deceiving. As I have noted, Arpaly agrees that one's mental attitudes may be grounds for condemnation; and Harman holds her view on the grounds that fundamental moral ignorance always involves a failure to care adequately about what is morally significant. Thus it may be that the difference between them regarding Huck's blameworthiness simply turns on the question whether fundamental moral ignorance must involve a deficit of care; Harman claims that it must, whereas Arpaly presumably denies this.[84] And if the relevant notion of care is itself to be understood in terms of what one desires, then Harman may after all subscribe to a strict desire-based account of ill will, as Arpaly does.

Even if such a reconciliation can be successfully carried out in the case of Arpaly and Harman, however, I doubt that it can amongst attributionists generally. Smith's view, for example, would appear to constitute an evaluative-judgment-based,

---

[81] A. M. Smith (2005), pp. 262 f.   [82] Cf., e.g., Graham (2014) and (2017).
[83] Harman (2011), p. 460.
[84] Others who deny that fundamental moral ignorance must involve a deficit of care include Wieland (2017b), Hartford (2019), and Johnson King (2020b).

rather than a desire-based, account of ill will. And Adams's view seems to be quite eclectic with regard to what may form the basis of ill will. These disagreements notwithstanding, attributionists are united in rejecting the Origination Thesis, and again, in most cases even if not all, they do so because they are committed to rejecting Premise 4 of the Argument from Ignorance. They deny that blameworthiness requires (volitional) control.

9.3 The unique moral significance of voluntary wrongdoing

So where do matters now stand? The Argument from Ignorance depends crucially on the premise that blameworthiness requires control. Many attributionists (and others, too) reject this premise. How is this disagreement to be resolved?

Well, I've already made a concession that would appear to favor the *attributionists'* point of view. In defending the claim that a non-derivative concern *de dicto* with doing what is right is (plausibly said to be) a virtue, I said that I was prepared to agree that a non-derivative concern *de re* with doing what is right, such as that exhibited by Huckleberry Finn, is *also* to one's moral credit. But then, once this is granted, it's hard to see why it wouldn't also be the case that a non-derivative concern *de re* with doing what is *wrong*, such as that exhibited by the various villains mentioned by Arpaly, is to one's moral *discredit*, despite the (likely) fact that the desires implicated in such a concern are not within one's control. And if this is true, then why not grant that still other objectionable states of mind of the kinds discussed by Adams are to one's moral discredit, too? For example, regarding Nazi ideology in particular, Adams says:

> The beliefs ascribed to the graduate of the Hitler *Jugend* are heinous, and it is morally reprehensible to hold them (even if one has no opportunity to act on them). No matter how he came by them, his evil beliefs are a part of who he is, morally, and make him a fitting object of reproach.[85]

(Compare this comment by Richard Brandt:

> There are some things no decent person will believe to be right... and if we must defend our act by saying we believed what no decent person would believe, we may have condemned ourselves more than excused ourselves.[86])

---

[85] Adams (1985), p. 19.
[86] Brandt (1959), p. 473. Cf. also Schnall (2004), p. 308; Scarre (2005); Dimitrijevic (2011), chs. 3 and 4. Note that, as with Markovits's remark, quoted in §9.2.3, regarding Göbbels's persecution of the Jews, there is an unfortunate looseness in what Brandt says (a looseness also to be found in Scarre's

Adams makes it clear that, by someone's being a "fitting object of reproach," he means that that person is worthy of *blame*:

> Perhaps for some people the word 'blame' has connotations that it does not have for me. To me it seems strange to say that I do not blame someone though I think poorly of him... Intuitively I should have said that thinking poorly of someone... *is* a form of unspoken blame... Blaming is a type of response to faults in oneself or in others.[87]

I agree with Adams. It's clear that we often do engage, and quite reasonably regard ourselves as justified in engaging, in the moral appraisal not just of people's behavior, but also of the traits that underlie their behavior, and of the people themselves in light of their traits and behavior. Furthermore, we often tailor our interactions with these people to our appraisal of them, and, again, we regard ourselves, quite reasonably, as justified in doing so. For example, if our friend Phoebe were to engage in homophobic behavior, we would find her behavior reprehensible, we would find the attitude or set of attitudes underlying her behavior reprehensible, and we might even find Phoebe herself reprehensible. Moreover, on the basis of this appraisal, we might well refuse to have anything more to do with her. Our appraisal, and the reaction based on it, would strike us as wholly fitting, and this would be the case *regardless* of whether Phoebe was in control of her attitudes and the behavior to which they gave rise. So, too, in the case of cruelty, contempt, arrogance, envy, and all other such vicious traits, including those traits, such as inconsiderateness and insensitivity, that are perhaps best seen as consisting in the absence of some desirable attitude rather than in the presence of some undesirable attitude. Moreover, this observation would appear to apply with equal force to that particular state of mind that consists in being unaware that one is doing something morally wrong, at least on those occasions when such lack of awareness is morally objectionable (as, for instance, in the case of certain religious fanatics, and even in certain cases of merely incidental moral ignorance, when such ignorance is attributable to a deficit of care).

Again, I *agree*. Now, this concession may well seem fatal to my project in this book. After all, my project has been to expose what I take to be the revisionary implications of the Origination Thesis, the defense of which has rested squarely on the Argument from Ignorance, of which Premise 4 is an indispensable component. If, however, Premise 4 is false, as I have just now granted, then surely the

---

phrase "excusing the inexcusable," at least on one interpretation): it fails to distinguish adequately between the question whether an *agent* has an excuse—is not *blameworthy*—for something that he (or she) has done and the question whether the agent's *act* is morally *wrong*.

[87] Adams (1985), p. 21.

Argument collapses and, along with it, my project. That would seem to be rather an anticlimax, to put it mildly.

Well, yes and no. We can and, I believe, should insist on the truth of Premise 4 *in certain contexts*, while acknowledging its falsity in others. Let me explain.

I have just acknowledged that there is a wide range of ways in which someone can manifest ill will (broadly construed, so as to include not only "wrong desires" but also a variety of other objectionable states of mind), and hence I also acknowledge, in keeping with the Strawsonian approach introduced in Chapter 2, that there is a wide range of situations in which it would be fitting to react to someone by engaging in some form of blame—*moral* blame—toward him or her. Notice: *some form* of blame. As I noted in §2.3.3, blame (in the thick sense) comes in many forms. In addition to the much-discussed emotions of resentment, indignation, and guilt, there are various attitudes that one might adopt (possibly without emotion, possibly only privately) that, insofar as they reflect one's negative moral appraisal of someone, constitute a form of blame of that person. For example, simply ceasing to love someone might constitute a form of blame— again, *moral* blame—*given* that it incorporates and reflects such an appraisal. And there are various ways of dealing with someone which, *given* that they in turn incorporate such attitudes, also constitute a form of blame. These include not only punishment but also reprimands, displays of anger, termination of friendship, and the like.

No doubt there are difficulties in distinguishing precisely between some forms of blame (for example, between reprimanding and rebuking and reproaching someone), but suppose that we had somehow managed to draw the requisite distinctions and that we had drawn up a list of the various forms: $blame_1$, $blame_2$, $blame_3$, and so on. Then there would in principle be a corresponding list of forms of blameworthiness: worthiness of $blame_1$, worthiness of $blame_2$, worthiness of $blame_3$, etc. This list would capture what I take to be a very important fact, namely, that even when we confine our attention to moral blameworthiness, there are *varieties* of such blameworthiness. Now, just as there are instances of blaming someone that involve more than one form of blame, so too, no doubt, there are instances of blameworthiness that involve more than one form of blame. Nonetheless, it is surely also the case that *not all forms of blame are equally fitting under all circumstances*. On the contrary, some form or forms may be fitting while others are positively unfitting; in principle, someone may be worthy of $blame_1$ and/or worthy of $blame_2$ but not worthy of $blame_3$, and so on. For example, someone may deserve resentment but not disdain, or a reprimand but not punishment.

The recognition that there are varieties of moral blameworthiness not only allows us to refine our judgments about such blameworthiness by identifying which form or forms of blame are in play, but it also holds out the hope of resolving some disputes that might otherwise seem intractable. Consider again

Adams's comment about the graduate of the Hitler *Jugend*. In making it, he is disagreeing—or, at least, takes himself to be disagreeing—with the following remark by Alan Donagan:

> A graduate of Sandhurst or West Point who does not understand his duty to noncombatants as human beings is certainly culpable for his ignorance; an officer bred up from childhood in the Hitler *Jugend* might not be.[88]

This statement reflects Donagan's concern with how easy or difficult it would be to detect and correct errors in one's moral beliefs. He holds that whether one has some measure of control over one's beliefs is relevant to whether one is to blame for them, whereas Adams, of course, insists that sins are sins, voluntary or not.

Let's call the graduate of the Hitler *Jugend* Gerhardt. Whether Adams and Donagan disagree with one another about Gerhardt's blameworthiness depends on whether they have the same form or forms of blame in mind. I don't know the answer to this question, in part because (like many, indeed almost all, commentators) Donagan is not forthcoming about just what he takes culpability to entail. So let me take his place. The Argument from Ignorance commits me to saying that Gerhardt is to blame for his beliefs only if he was in control of having them, control that can at best have been only indirect. It certainly looks like Adams rejects this claim, but, again, whether he in fact does so turns on whether he and I have the same form or forms of blame in mind. And I think there's a good chance that we do *not*. For I should now confess, no doubt belatedly, that there is one form of (thick) blame that is of particular concern to me and that I have had implicitly, though by no means exclusively, in mind throughout my discussion of blame and blameworthiness in previous chapters: *punishment*. I understand punishment essentially to involve the intentional (and not merely anticipated) imposition of harm, something that I take to be *contrary to one's deserts* unless one was in control of that for which one is being punished.[89] This is, of course, a common view, and it is one that may well underlie the following comment by Adams:

> I do not believe that exactly the same responses are appropriate to involuntary as to voluntary sins. In particular, only voluntary acts and omissions are rightly *punished* by the state.[90]

Perhaps, then, the disagreement between us is merely apparent.

I have said that blame comes in many forms, but I haven't said how many. Nor will I venture to do so; the number may be indefinite. However many forms there

---

[88] Donagan (1977), p. 135.
[89] Cf. Zimmerman (2011), pp. 7 ff.; for qualification, see pp. 136 ff.
[90] Adams (1985), p. 21.

are, they may in principle be divided into two classes: those the worthiness of which requires that the person blamed have been in *control* of that for which he or she is blamed, and those the worthiness of which does *not* require such control. I will call all forms of blame that fall into the former class forms of blame$_c$ and all forms of blame that fall into the latter class forms of blame$_n$. On the presupposition that it is possible for someone to be blameworthy for something, three views may be distinguished regarding blame$_c$ and blame$_n$: all blame is blame$_c$; all blame is blame$_n$; some blame is blame$_c$ and some blame is blame$_n$. The first of these views has traditionally enjoyed widespread acceptance. I am not aware of anyone's having held the second view.[91] It is the third view to which I subscribe.

Once the distinction between blame$_c$ and blame$_n$ has been drawn, the Argument from Ignorance becomes subject to a number of interpretations. For example, Premise 4 can be understood in two ways, either as

(4$_c$)   one is to blame$_c$ for something only if one was in control of that thing

or as

(4$_n$)   one is to blame$_n$ for something only if one was in control of that thing.

The latter interpretation is obviously a non-starter; it is of course the former that is required for the Argument to go through. Matters become a little more tricky when we turn our attention to Premise 2, since that premise can now be understood in *four* different ways, which may be put (roughly) as follows:

(2$_{c/c}$) one is to blame$_c$ for committing some act from ignorance of its wrongness only if one is to blame$_c$ for one's ignorance;

(2$_{c/n}$) one is to blame$_c$ for committing some act from ignorance of its wrongness only if one is to blame$_n$ for one's ignorance;

(2$_{n/n}$) one is to blame$_n$ for committing some act from ignorance of its wrongness only if one is to blame$_n$ for one's ignorance;

(2$_{n/c}$) one is to blame$_n$ for committing some act from ignorance of its wrongness only if one is to blame$_c$ for one's ignorance.

Once again, it is the first of these interpretations that is needed for the Argument from Ignorance to go through. Here, though, the remaining interpretations cannot be summarily dismissed. On the contrary, although Premise 2$_{n/c}$ would seem to have nothing to recommend it, both Premise 2$_{c/n}$ and Premise 2$_{n/n}$ seem plausible.

---

[91] Philosophers who deny that we ever have (freedom-level) control over what we do but who nonetheless accept that blame plays an important role in our lives typically deny that we can be *worthy* of such blame. See, e.g., Pereboom (2014), ch. 6.

Consider Premise $2_{n/n}$ first. Suppose that we agree with Adams that Gerhardt's ignorance regarding how noncombatants should be treated constitutes a state of mind that speaks ill of him in such a way that, even though, since it is (by hypothesis) involuntary, he is not to blame$_c$ for it, he is nonetheless worthy of some form of blame$_n$ for it—reproach, say (which I am inclined to think is indeed a form of blame$_n$, although some might regard it as a form of blame$_c$). Such blameworthiness, not being predicated on Gerhardt's being to blame for something else, will be direct. It seems plausible to hold that this blameworthiness will carry over to any behavior that is attributable to his ignorance. That is, Gerhardt will be indirectly worthy of reproach for any such behavior because he is directly worthy of reproach for the ignorance from which he committed it. (This observation doesn't establish Premise $2_{n/n}$, of course, but it conforms to it.)

Now consider Premise $2_{c/n}$, and apply it once again to the case of Gerhardt. Imagine that Gerhardt has just dispatched Maria to the gas chamber, firmly believing that he was duty-bound to do so. Let's assume that, although he was not in control, even indirectly, of his ignorance regarding how Maria should be treated, he was in direct control of his decision to send her to the chamber. Let's again agree, with Adams, that Gerhardt is to blame$_n$ for his ignorance, even though he is not, and cannot be, to blame$_c$ for it. And let's agree that he is therefore to blame$_n$, indirectly, for his behavior toward Maria. The question remains whether Gerhardt is *also* to blame$_c$ for this behavior, something that is a live possibility precisely because he was in control of it. The Argument from Ignorance rules out a positive answer to this question. Premise 2—understood as Premise $2_{c/c}$—implies that Gerhardt is to blame$_c$ for his behavior only if he is to blame$_c$ for his ignorance; since he is only to blame$_n$ for his ignorance and *not* also to blame$_c$ for it, this premise implies that he is *not* to blame$_c$ for his behavior. But, someone might well protest, that just shows why Premise 2—understood as Premise $2_{c/c}$—should be rejected. Indeed, Adams himself might say this, in which case the disagreement between him and me is of course not merely apparent after all. Perhaps Adams thinks that, although Gerhardt doesn't deserve to be punished for his *ignorance* regarding how Maria should be treated, he nonetheless does deserve to be punished for *what he did* to her. More generally, it might be held that, whatever plausibility Premise 2 might seem to have should be attributed to its being understood as Premise $2_{c/n}$ rather than as Premise $2_{c/c}$. As such, it cannot do the work that the Argument from Ignorance requires of it, and so this argument is to be rejected. (This is one way to construe the remarks made by Talbert that I quoted in §9.2.4.)

This is an important challenge to the Argument from Ignorance. The idea underlying it can be generalized. Just as one can act from ignorance, so too one can act from cruelty, envy, anger, and so on. If one is in control of such behavior, then one may be to blame$_c$ for it. (Such blame may take the form of punishment, but it needn't.) Moreover, this may be the case even if one is *not* to blame$_c$ for the state of mind that prompts one's behavior. (Perhaps one will nonetheless be to blame$_n$ for this state of mind—cruelty and envy, for example, are morally objectionable—but perhaps one won't be to blame for it at all. Perhaps, for example, one's anger is fully justified, but one still ought not to act on it.) Thus the general claim that one is to blame$_c$ for acting from some state of mind M only if one is to blame$_c$ for M itself is clearly false. Why, then, accept this claim in the particular case in which M is the state of being ignorant of the fact that one is acting wrongly?

This is a good question, to which there is what I take to be a good answer. It's worth reminding ourselves that Premise 2 of the Argument from Ignorance certainly *seems* plausible, at least initially, whereas the corresponding claims about cruelty, envy, and so on have no intuitive pull at all. Why is this? Well, consider Martin (from §7.2.3), who likes to mistreat animals. Let's suppose that he cannot control *having* the cruel impulses that prompt his cruel actions but that he can control *acting on* these impulses. Then he would commonly be regarded as a prime candidate for blame, not (unless we're thinking in terms of blame$_n$) for having the impulses, but for *yielding* to them. I suggest that this idea of yielding carries with it the implication that Martin *knows better* than to act on his impulses. His sin, in Adams's terminology, is *voluntary*. Now, the term "voluntary" can be used in a number of ways, but what I mean by it—and what I take Adams to mean by it—is what Aristotle meant by it: one does something voluntarily just in case one does it wittingly *and* one is in control of doing it.[92] Note that it could be that one voluntarily does something that is wrong but doesn't voluntarily act wrongly, since one is unaware that the wrong thing one is doing *is* wrong. However, Martin, as I am imagining him, not only voluntarily tortures cats but voluntarily does wrong in doing so. *This* is what his yielding to his impulses consists in. (We wouldn't say of someone who likes to treat animals well and does so that he has *yielded* to his impulse to treat them well.) So, too, for cases in which one gives in to the temptation to indulge one's envy, anger, and so on. In such cases, one is to blame$_c$ for one's behavior in virtue of the fact that one's wrongdoing is voluntary. Note, though, that although the list of voluntary sins—yielding to impulses stemming from cruelty, envy, anger, "and so on"—is presumably a long one, one kind of wrongdoing that *cannot* be included in this list is doing something from ignorance of the fact that one is acting wrongly. Although the wrong act that one performs may be one that one voluntarily commits, one's commission of it cannot constitute voluntary wrongdoing, precisely because the wrongdoing is unwitting. In committing the act, one hasn't yielded to the temptation to do something that one recognizes to be wrong.

---

[92] Aristotle (1941), bk. III, ch. 1.

Voluntary wrongdoing has a unique moral significance. When one is aware that one can avoid doing something wrong (that is, *overall morally* wrong) but does it nonetheless, one exhibits a kind of ill will that is quite distinct from the kinds highlighted by Adams. The blame that one incurs for one's behavior (or, more particularly, for the decision to engage in that behavior) attaches *directly* to it. Notice that there is nothing to criticize in one's being aware that it is wrong to behave in a certain way. Rather, it is one's *choice* to behave in that way, *despite* being aware that it is wrong to do so and that one can avoid doing so, that is grounds for blame. One is *deliberately defying* the demands of morality, thereby manifesting a unique kind of morally objectionable contempt that is absent from any instance of unwitting or uncontrolled wrongdoing.[93] In such a case, the kind of ill will exhibited essentially involves not just a state of mind (to wit, wittingness of wrongdoing) but also the exercise of control. It thus comprises *both* of the conditions, one epistemic, the other agential, emphasized by Aristotle. It is plausible to hold that this particular kind of ill will renders one deserving of certain forms of blame (punishment, perhaps) that one would otherwise not deserve, indeed deserve not, to undergo.

As always, there are complications. One has to do with contravening a conscience that is misguided. In such a case, defying the demands of morality involves *believing* that one is acting wrongly but may not involve being *aware* that one is doing so. Huckleberry Finn is a case in point. In my view, this doesn't alter the fact that one is manifesting the unique kind of contempt in question. Another complication has to do with the distinction between *witting* and *willing* wrongdoing—regarding which see §6.2.1. Perhaps the kind of contempt at issue can be manifested in wrongdoing that is willing but not witting.

In brief and in sum, I am proposing one final reformulation of the Argument from Ignorance and the Origination Thesis (or, rather, one final pair of reformulations, one that includes "occurrently" and one that does not):

The Argument from Ignorance (Final Draft):
Suppose that

(1) (a) P committed A but (b) when P committed A, P did so because P failed to (occurrently) believe that he or she was overall morally wrongly committing A.

In general it's true that

(2) if one committed some act or omission because one failed to (occurrently) believe that one was overall morally wrongly committing it, one is morally to **blame**$_c$ for it, and thereby morally to **blame**$_c$ for any of its consequences,

---

[93] Cf. Husak (2016), p. 168.

only if one is morally to **blame**$_c$ for one's failure to (occurrently) believe that one was overall morally wrongly committing it.

Thus

(3) P is morally to **blame**$_c$ for A, and thereby morally to **blame**$_c$ for any of its consequences, only if P is morally to **blame**$_c$ for P's failure to (occurrently) believe (call it F) that he or she was overall morally wrongly committing A.

It's also in general true that

(4) one is morally to **blame**$_c$ for something only if one was in control of that thing.

Thus

(5) P is morally to **blame**$_c$ for F only if P was in control of F.

Three further general truths are that

(6) one is never directly in control of whether one fails to (occurrently) believe something—that is, any control that one has over failing to (occurrently) believe something is always only indirect,

(7) if one is morally to **blame**$_c$ for something over which one had only indirect control, then one's worthiness of **blame**$_c$ for it is itself only indirect, and

(8) one is indirectly morally to **blame**$_c$ for something only if that thing was a consequence of something else for which one is directly morally to **blame**$_c$.

Thus

(9) P is morally to **blame**$_c$ for A, and thereby morally to **blame**$_c$ for any of its consequences, only if there was something else (call it X) for which P is directly morally to **blame**$_c$ and of which F was a consequence.

But

(10) whatever X was, it cannot have been an act or omission such that (a) P committed it and (b) when P committed it, P did so because P failed to (occurrently) believe that he or she was overall morally wrongly committing it, since otherwise the foregoing argument regarding A would apply all over again to X.

Thus

(11) whatever X was, it was either (a) not some act or omission that P committed or (b) not something such that, when P committed it, P did so because P failed to (occurrently) believe that he or she was overall morally wrongly committing it.

One further general truth is that

(12) one has direct control over something only if that thing is an act or omission.

Thus

(13) whatever X was, it was not an act or omission such that, when P committed it, P did so because P failed to (occurrently) believe that he or she was overall morally wrongly committing it.

The Origination Thesis (Final Draft):
Every chain of **worthiness of moral blame**$_c$ is such that at its origin lies a piece of behavior for which the agent is directly **worthy of moral blame**$_c$ and which was such that either he or she (occurrently) believed, at the time at which he or she engaged in it, that he or she was overall morally wrongly committing it or he or she did not (occurrently) believe this but did not engage in the behavior because he or she did not (occurrently) believe this.

I noted above that the recognition that there are varieties of blameworthiness promises to help resolve certain disagreements regarding the circumstances under which someone is blameworthy, but to what extent it will in fact succeed in doing so is anyone's guess. Certainly the prospects are limited. Consider again that form of blame that is punishment. Arpaly says that Nazi war criminals, racist dictators, and the like "cannot use" their views as excuses for their behavior.[94] Similarly, George Sher says that the panic-stricken homeowner who shoots her son (in the example given at the outset of §9.1) "would definitely be blamed and might well be liable to punishment."[95] I agree with these remarks, if they are understood simply as predictions of the reactions that these agents would likely encounter from others. But if these remarks are intended, as they presumably are, as prescriptions regarding the reactions that it would be appropriate to direct toward these and other such agents, then I disagree with them (given that they don't satisfy the Origination Thesis). I doubt that simply drawing yet finer distinctions with respect to the various forms of blame would serve to resolve this disagreement. On the contrary, resolution is likely to be achieved, if at all, only after a detailed investigation has been undertaken into the question of which forms of blame match which forms of ill will. That is a daunting task and is certainly not one that I propose to tackle here. Consider what completing it would require.

First, the various forms of thick blame would need to be identified. I have mentioned several: resentment, indignation, disdain, contempt, reprimand, rebuke, reproach, withdrawal of love, termination of friendship, and punishment (plus the self-directed blame of remorse). Note that these and other such reactions count as forms of *moral* blame only if they incorporate and reflect a negative *moral* assessment of the person blamed. As I observed in §2.3.10, my resenting my doubles partner for having failed to hold serve is not a form of moral blame. In like

---

[94] Arpaly (2015), p. 155.   [95] Sher (2009), p. 26.

fashion, each of the other reactions just listed might be prompted by non-moral, rather than moral, concerns. (Note also that some other common reactions to perceived or suspected wrongdoing, even when prompted by moral concerns, won't count as forms of moral blame, either. Consider, for example, the expectation of remorse discussed in §9.1.2.) Note further that this list of reactions requires considerable refinement, in virtue of the fact that it is obviously incomplete[96] and of the fact that just how one form of blame (such as reprimand, for example, or contempt) is to be distinguished from another (such as reproach or disdain) may not be immediately clear.

Second, once the various forms of thick blame had been identified (a procedure that would include their classification as either weak or strong forms of blame—see §2.3.3), we would need to determine which forms fall into the class of blame$_c$ and which into the class of blame$_n$. In many cases this is likely to be a contentious issue. I have ventured the opinion that punishment is unjust unless the person punished was in control of that for which he or she is being punished, but I haven't tried to defend this claim. Nor will I. That is far too large a project to undertake here. I will merely note, as before, that it is a common claim that enjoys widespread support. (There is almost universal repugnance for strict criminal liability.) But I of course concede that there are dissenters. (Many utilitarians will reject the claim,[97] and some non-utilitarians will too.[98]) Moreover, I concede that how precisely the claim is to be interpreted is not immediately obvious.

On this last point, it's important to note that just what constitutes punishment is itself a controversial matter. I have said that I understand punishment essentially to involve the intentional, and not merely anticipated, imposition of harm, and I take this distinction to be morally significant: it's harder to justify the former than it is the latter. But once again this, too, can be and has been disputed. Why should the distinction matter if in either case the person is equally harmed? And why must there be harm at all (if, indeed, there is such a thing in the first place[99]), let alone the intentional imposition of harm? Can't punishment be beneficial rather than harmful?[100] Then there is the question, to which I alluded in §2.4.3, of just what the distinction between just and unjust punishment consists in. As I see it, it is not enough simply to note that someone who is blameless *doesn't* deserve *to* be punished; we should acknowledge, in addition, that such a person *does* deserve *not* to be punished. Unjust punishment is punishment *contrary* to

---

[96] Among those reactions that should be added to the list are remonstration, castigation, reprehension, reprobation, denunciation, censure, chiding, and scolding.

[97] Cf., e.g., Smart (1973), p. 54.

[98] Eugene Schlossberger, for example, claims that in principle it would be appropriate to mete out rewards and punishments according to the demands of "abstract justice," which dictates that the virtuous flourish and the vicious languish, irrespective of their exercising any control over being virtuous or vicious, although he admits that in practice there can be reason to deviate from this alleged ideal. See Schlossberger (1992), ch. 5. Cf. Ross (2002), ch. 2, app. 2.

[99] Cf. B. Bradley (2012).   [100] For discussion of this issue, see Zimmerman (2011), ch. 1.

one's deserts. But then what is just punishment? Is it merely punishment that is not unjust, that is, punishment that one *doesn't* deserve *not* to receive? Or is it, in addition, punishment that one *does* deserve *to* receive?

The questions just raised do not pertain only to punishment. Consider the view of blame proposed by Gideon Rosen on which I commented in §2.3.10. He claims that all forms of blame are "essentially hostile," involving both the "retributive thought" that the person blamed deserves to suffer in some way for having done that for which he or she is being blamed and the desire that he or she undergo such suffering.[101] This strikes me as far too restrictive a view of blame in general, but it certainly seems to capture a subset of forms of blame, regarding which the question arises whether anyone can in fact ever be worthy of such blame. Might it not simply be the case that some people are sometimes *not* worthy of *not* being subjected to such blame? Or might the truth lie somewhere in between, in that, although it might on occasion happen that one positively deserves to be the target of *weak* hostile blame, one can at most not deserve not to be the target of *strong* hostile blame?

The questions that I have raised should make it clear that the task of determining which forms of blame match which forms of ill will is indeed a daunting one that lies beyond the purview of this work. For what it's worth, though, perhaps I should record what I am inclined to say on the subject.

I am inclined to regard all forms of hostile blame—blame that presupposes the desert of suffering—as forms of blame$_c$, whether the blame be weak or strong. If ever anyone does deserve to (be made to) suffer for something, that person, I am inclined to think, must have been in control of that thing.

I am inclined to regard all forms of strong blame (such as, in addition to punishment, certain types of reprimand—for example, a public dressing-down—and certain displays of resentment) that involve the intentional imposition of either harm or suffering[102] as forms of blame$_c$. Can anyone ever in fact be worthy of such blame? I suspect so; but even if it is only ever the case that one can *fail* to deserve *not* to be the brunt of such blame, I am still inclined to think that this requires that one have been in control of that for which one is blamed.

I am inclined to regard all forms of weak blame as forms of blame$_n$, as long as the blame isn't hostile. Consider indignation, which, contrary to Rosen, I don't think necessarily involves either the thought that the person blamed deserves to suffer or the desire that he or she suffer. Does Gerhardt (the graduate of the Hitler *Jugend*) deserve our indignation? Does Phoebe (the homophobe)? I am inclined to answer "Yes" in both cases, even if neither person was in control of his or her beliefs or sentiments, precisely because indignation in and of itself involves no

---

[101] Rosen (2015), pp. 82 f.
[102] Note that the disjunction is required. Even very severe punishments need involve no suffering, whether mental or physical. Consider, for example, a painless, unanticipated execution.

form of adverse treatment.[103] Even here, though, there is need for caution. I find it interesting that attributionists tend to talk in terms of such blame being "fitting" rather than "deserved."[104] As I noted in §2.4.1, the latter term has a narrower scope than the former.

When it comes to strong blame that "merely" involves the anticipated (as opposed to intentional) imposition of harm or suffering, I find myself quite uncertain whether such blame is blame$_c$ or blame$_n$. Does Phoebe deserve to be given the cold shoulder by her (former) friends, when it's clear that this will badly hurt her feelings? Does she even fail to deserve not to receive such treatment, or is it merely fitting in some other way for her friendships to be modified or terminated? I am frankly at a loss as to what to say about such matters.

9.4 Blameworthiness without responsibility

In the last section, I conceded the thesis, advocated by attributionists (among others), that there are forms of blame, the worthiness of which does not require that the person being blamed have been in control of that for which he or she is blamed. Thus, for instance, it may be that Gerhardt is to blame in some way for subscribing to Nazi ideology or that Martin is to blame for his cruel disposition, even though neither man has ever been in control of the relevant morally objectionable state of mind. In contexts such as these, Premise 4 of the Argument from Ignorance fails to apply, and thus the argument is silent.

But there are contexts and contexts. The reach of attributionism is limited, for there are forms of blame, the worthiness of which *does* require that the person blamed have been in control of that for which he or she is blamed. Paramount among these, I contend, is punishment. Regarding such forms of blame the Argument from Ignorance is far from silent. If, as I contend, the Argument is sound, then the implications are indeed revisionary. For example, although Martin may deserve punishment for mistreating cats, Gerhardt does *not* deserve punishment for his mistreatment of Maria (given that he acted from ignorance regarding how she should be treated and that he is not worthy of blame—blame$_c$—for his ignorance); indeed, his blamelessness renders him deserving of *not* being punished. This conclusion may well be unwelcome, but I submit that it is correct.

The reach of attributionism is limited in another way, too. Attributionists claim that their view is a view about the nature of *moral responsibility*, but I suggest that this is a mistake. Let me explain.

Suppose that Sheila has broken her shoulder and is in a great deal of pain. Pain, as I understand it, is a kind of mental state, even though in this case, as in many, it

---

[103] Cf. A. M. Smith (2021), p. 341; P. Russell (2021), pp. 364 f.
[104] Cf. Adams (1985), p. 19; A. M. Smith (2021), p. 341.

can also be properly described as physical. And we may assume that in this case, as in many, such a mental state is bad. But it is not morally objectionable. (If Sheila broke her shoulder because Teresa tripped her, then what Teresa did may have been morally objectionable but, again, Sheila's pain itself is not.) Attributionists will agree with this assessment. Though bad, Sheila's pain is not attributable to her in the way that concerns them. It doesn't express or reveal who she is "as a person"—an important, though murky concept. Contrast Sheila with Phoebe, whose homophobia constitutes a state of mind that is not only bad but morally objectionable.

But we mustn't be too hasty. Even if Phoebe's homophobia is morally objectionable, it may still not be attributable to her in the requisite way. Like Veronica's racism (see §3.2.5) but unlike Ron's (see §8.2), it may be an attitude that is merely implicit and which conflicts with her considered judgment in such a way that we would be reluctant to say that it reflects who she "really" is. If so, then, even though moral condemnation of the trait may be perfectly fitting, condemnation of the person herself for possessing the trait may not.[105] More particularly, Phoebe may not be worthy of blame (blame$_n$) for her homophobia.

But even if Phoebe *is* worthy of blame$_n$ for her homophobia, as long as she is not also worthy of blame$_c$ for it, I think it's a mistake to say that she is responsible for it. As I noted in §2.1.4, judgments about moral responsibility (hypological judgments) are distinct from judgments about character (aretaic judgments). Phoebe's homophobia, Martin's cruelty, and Gerhardt's ideology may speak ill of them in such a way that they are worthy of blame$_n$ for having these traits, but to my ear it sounds distinctly odd to hold them morally *responsible* for these traits, given that there was nothing they could have done to prevent or eradicate them. These traits are faults of theirs, and so, as Adams says, it seems appropriate to blame them in some way for having them. But, as I noted in §2.3.1, *having* a fault is one thing, being *at* fault is another.[106] Or, to put the point slightly differently, the faults are of course *their faults* but, given their lack of control over them, not *their fault*.[107] They are worthy of blame$_n$ for them but not worthy of blame$_c$ for them, and it is, I think, only when one is worthy of blame$_c$ for something that one is properly held morally responsible (in a negative way) for it. I thus side with tradition in holding that control is essential to responsibility.

I will end with two observations. First, if there can be moral blameworthiness (worthiness of blame$_n$) without moral responsibility, then the chart presented in §2.1.1 of the taxonomy of responsibility—Chart 2.1—requires revision to reflect this fact. Second, however, my goal in this book has been to explore the relation between ignorance and moral responsibility in particular, rather than blameworthiness in general, and it is as a thesis about *responsibility* that I commend the Origination Thesis to you.

---

[105] Cf. H. M. Smith (2011), pp. 137 and 141 f.; Levy (2014), pp. 96 ff. Contrast, to some extent, Madva (2017).
[106] Cf. Levy (2005), p. 7. [107] Cf. Rosen (2008), p. 608; Pink (2016), p. 163.

Postscript

When I first embarked on the project of writing this book, I had envisioned including a final part in which I pursued the implications of the Origination Thesis for a variety of practices in which we routinely engage, including especially, but not exclusively, practices, such as punishment and conscientious objection, in which the law is implicated. For it is clear, I think, that the Thesis has many revisionary implications in this regard. What is not so clear is just what these implications are. It quickly became apparent to me, however, that I had enough on my plate as it was, without taking on the daunting task, mentioned at the end of §9.3, of trying to determine which forms of blame match which forms of ill will, let alone the further task of determining to what extent they do so. In a previous work I discussed what I take to be the Thesis's implications regarding punishment in particular, but I didn't pursue them in any great detail.[1] More recently, Douglas Husak has conducted an extended complementary inquiry into ignorance of law, and I commend his excellent book to you.[2] There is a great deal more work to be done, however, and I am hopeful that it will be done. Unfortunately, I cannot undertake it here.

---

[1] Zimmerman (2011), pp. 109 ff.   [2] Husak (2016).

Bibliography

Aboodi, Ron (2017). "One Thought Too Few: Where *De Dicto* Moral Motivation Is Necessary." *Ethical Theory and Moral Practice* 20: 223–37.
Adams, Robert M. (1977). "Middle Knowledge and the Problem of Evil." *American Philosophical Quarterly* 14: 109–17.
Adams, Robert M. (1985). "Involuntary Sins." *Philosophical Review* 94: 3–31.
Agule, Craig K. (2016). "Resisting Tracing's Siren Song." *Journal of Ethics and Social Philosophy* 10: 1–24.
Alexander, Larry (1993). "Inculpatory and Exculpatory Mistakes and the Fact/Law Distinction: An Essay in Memory of Myke Bayles." *Law and Philosophy* 12: 33–70.
Alexander, Larry (2017). "Ignorance as a Legal Excuse." In *Perspectives on Ignorance from Moral and Social Philosophy*, ed. Rik Peels (New York: Routledge): 205–16.
Alexander, Larry et al. (2009). *Crime and Culpability: A Theory of Criminal Law*. Oxford: Oxford University Press.
Alston, William P. (1971). "Varieties of Privileged Access." *American Philosophical Quarterly* 8: 223–41.
Alston, William P. (1988). "The Deontological Conception of Epistemic Justification." *Philosophical Perspectives* 2: 257–99.
Amaya, Santiago (2013). "Slips." *Noûs* 47: 559–76.
American Law Institute (1985). *Model Penal Code*.
Antill, Gregory (2020). "Epistemic Freedom Revisited." *Synthese* 197: 793–815.
Archer, Sophie (2018). "Why 'Believes' Is Not a Vague Predicate." *Philosophical Studies* 175: 3029–48.
Arendt, Hannah (1977). *Eichmann in Jerusalem: A Report on the Banality of Evil*. New York: Penguin.
Aristotle (1941). *Nicomachean Ethics*. In *The Basic Works of Aristotle*, ed. Richard McKeon (New York: Random House).
Arpaly, Nomy (2003). *Unprincipled Virtue*. Oxford: Oxford University Press.
Arpaly, Nomy (2015). "Huckleberry Finn Revisited: Inverse Akrasia and Moral Ignorance." In *The Nature of Moral Responsibility*, ed. Randolph Clarke et al. (Oxford: Oxford University Press): 141–56.
Arpaly, Nomy and Schroeder, Timothy (2013). *In Praise of Desire*. Oxford: Oxford University Press.
Audi, Robert (1994). "Dispositional Beliefs and Dispositions to Believe." *Noûs* 28: 419–34.
Audi, Robert (2008). "The Ethics of Belief: Doxastic Self-Control and Intellectual Virtue." *Synthese* 161: 403–18.
Augustine, Saint (1953). *Confessions*. Baltimore: Catholic University of America Press.
Austin, J. L. (1961). *Philosophical Papers*. Oxford: Clarendon Press.
Baier, Kurt (1970). "Responsibility and Action." In *The Nature of Human Action*, ed. Myles Brand (Glenview: Scott, Foresman): 100–16.
Baron, Marcia (2017). "Justification, Excuse, and the Exculpatory Power of Ignorance." In *Perspectives on Ignorance from Moral and Social Philosophy*, ed. Rik Peels (New York: Routledge): 53–76.

Baron, Robert A. (1997). "The Sweet Smell of... Helping: Effects of Pleasant Ambient Fragrance on Prosocial Behavior in Shopping Malls." *Personality and Social Psychology Bulletin* 23: 498–503.

Baumeister, Roy F. (2001). *Evil: Inside Human Violence and Cruelty*. New York: Henry Holt & Co.

Bell, Macalaster (2013). "The Standing to Blame: A Critique." In *Blame: Its Nature and Norms*, ed. D. Justin Coates and Neal A. Tognazzini (Oxford: Oxford University Press): 263–81.

Benbaji, Hagit (2016). "What Can We Not Do and Why." *Philosophical Studies* 173: 1941–61.

Bennett, Jonathan (1974). "The Conscience of Huckleberry Finn." *Philosophy* 49: 123–34.

Bennett, Jonathan (1980). "Accountability." In *Philosophical Subjects*, ed. Zak Van Straaten (Oxford: Clarendon Press): 14–47.

Bennett, Jonathan (1990). "Why Is Belief Involuntary?" *Analysis* 50: 87–107.

Berman, Mitchell N. (2021). "Blameworthiness, Desert, and Luck." *Noûs* doi.org/10.1111/nous.12405.

Biebel, Nathan (2019). *Epistemic Justification and the Ignorance Excuse*. Ph.D. thesis, Tulane University.

Blanshard, Brand (1961). *Reason and Goodness*. London: George Allen & Unwin.

Borgoni, Cristina (2015). "Dissonance and Doxastic Resistance." *Erkenntnis* 80: 957–74.

Bradley, Ben (2012). "Doing Away with Harm." *Philosophy and Phenomenological Research* 85: 390–412.

Bradley, Seamus (2019). "Imprecise Probabilities." *The Stanford Encyclopedia of Philosophy* (Spring 2019 Edition), ed. Edward N. Zalta, URL = <https://plato.stanford.edu/archives/spr2019/entries/imprecise-probabilities/>.

Brady, James B. (1996). "Conscious Negligence." *American Philosophical Quarterly* 33: 325–35.

Brandt, Richard B. (1958). "Blameworthiness and Obligation." In *Essays in Moral Philosophy*, ed. A. I. Melden (Seattle: University of Washington Press): 3–39.

Brandt, Richard B. (1959). *Ethical Theory*. Englewood Cliffs: Prentice-Hall.

Bratman, Michael E. (1992). "Practical Reasoning and Acceptance in a Context." *Mind* 101: 1–15.

Brentano, Franz (1969). *The Origin of Our Knowledge of Right and Wrong*. London: Routledge & Kegan Paul.

Brynner, Rock and Stephens, Trent (2001). *Dark Remedy: The Impact of Thalidomide and Its Revival as a Vital Medicine*. Cambridge, Mass.: Perseus Publishing.

Calhoun, Claudia (1989). "Responsibility and Reproach." *Ethics* 99: 389–406.

Campbell, C. A. (1951). "Is 'Freewill' a Pseudo-Problem?" *Mind* 60: 446–65.

Camus, Albert (1989). *The Stranger*, tr. M. Ward. New York: Vintage International.

Capes, Justin (2012). "Blameworthiness without Wrongdoing." *Pacific Philosophical Quarterly* 93: 417–37.

Carbonell, Vanessa (2013). "*De Dicto* Desires and Morality as Fetish." *Philosophical Studies* 163: 459–77.

Card, Claudia (2002). *The Atrocity Paradigm: A Theory of Evil*. Oxford: Oxford University Press.

Carlsson, Andreas Brekke (2017). "Blameworthiness as Deserved Guilt." *Journal of Ethics* 21: 89–115.

Chisholm, Roderick M. (1964a). "J. L. Austin's Philosophical Papers." *Mind* 73: 1–26.

Chisholm, Roderick M. (1964b). "The Descriptive Element in the Concept of Action." *Journal of Philosophy* 61: 613–25.
Chisholm, Roderick M. (1976). *Person and Object*. La Salle, IL: Open Court.
Chisholm, Roderick M. (1986). *Brentano and Intrinsic Value*. Cambridge: Cambridge University Press.
Chisholm, Roderick M. and Sosa, Ernest (1966). "Intrinsic Preferability and the Problem of Supererogation." *Synthese* 16: 321–31.
Clarke, Randolph (2009). "Dispositions, Abilities to Act, and Free Will: The New Dispositionalism." *Mind* 118: 323–51.
Clarke, Randolph (2014). *Omissions*. Oxford: Oxford University Press.
Clarke, Randolph (2016). "Moral Responsibility, Guilt, and Retributivism." *Journal of Ethics* 20: 121–37.
Clarke, Randolph (2017a). "Blameworthiness and Unwitting Omissions." In *The Ethics and Law of Omissions*, ed. Dana Kay Nelkin and Samuel C. Rickless (Oxford: Oxford University Press): 63–83.
Clarke, Randolph (2017b). "Ignorance, Revision, and Commonsense." In *Responsibility: The Epistemic Condition*, ed. Philip Robichaud and Jan Willem Wieland (Oxford: Oxford University Press): 233–51.
Clarke, Randolph (2020). "It's Up to You." *Monist* 103: 328–41.
Clarke, Randolph (forthcoming a). "Blame, Blameworthiness, and Desert."
Clarke, Randolph (forthcoming b). "Still Guilty After All These Years."
Clifford, W. K. (1877). "The Ethics of Belief." *Contemporary Review* 29: 289–309.
Coates, D. Justin (2016). "The Epistemic Norm of Blame." *Ethical Theory and Moral Practice* 19: 457–73.
Coates, D. Justin (2020). "Being More (or Less) Blameworthy." *American Philosophical Quarterly* 56: 233–45.
Coates, D. Justin and Swenson, Philip (2013). "Reasons-Responsiveness and Degrees of Responsibility." *Philosophical Studies* 165: 629–45.
Coates, D. Justin and Tognazzini, Neal A. (2012). "The Nature and Ethics of Blame." *Philosophy Compass* 7: 197–207.
Coates, D. Justin and Tognazzini, Neal A. (2013). "The Contours of Blame." In *Blame: Its Nature and Norms*, ed. D. Justin Coates and Neal A. Tognazzini (Oxford: Oxford University Press): 3–26.
Cohen, L. Jonathan (1966). "More about Knowing and Feeling Sure." *Analysis* 27: 11–16.
Cohen, L. Jonathan (1981). "Who Is Starving Whom?" *Theoria* 47: 65–81.
Cohen, L. Jonathan (1989). "Belief and Acceptance." *Mind* 98: 367–89.
Coleman, Jules and Sarch, Alexander (2012). "Blameworthiness and Time." *Legal Theory* 18: 101–37.
Conee, Earl (1982). "Against Moral Dilemmas." *Philosophical Review* 91: 87–97.
Conee, Earl (1983). Review of Donald H. Regan, *Utilitarianism and Co-operation* (Oxford: Clarendon Press, 1980). *Journal of Philosophy* 80: 415–24.
Copp, David (1997). "Defending the Principle of Alternate Possibilities: Blameworthiness and Moral Responsibility." *Noûs* 31: 441–56.
Dahl, Norman O. (1967). "'Ought' and Blameworthiness." *Journal of Philosophy* 64: 418–28.
Danielsson, Sven and Olson, Jonas (2007). "Brentano and the Buck-Passers." *Mind* 116: 511–22.
Dante Alighieri (2008). *The Divine Comedy*, tr. C. H. Sisson. Oxford: Oxford University Press.

Darwall, Stephen (2006). *The Second-Person Standpoint: Morality, Respect, and Accountability*. Cambridge, Mass.: Harvard University Press.

Darwall, Stephen (2010). "'But It Would Be Wrong.'" *Social Philosophy and Policy* 27: 135–57.

Davidson, Donald (1980). *Essays on Actions and Events*. Oxford: Clarendon Press.

Davies, Martin (1995). "Tacit Knowledge and Subdoxastic States." In *Philosophy of Psychology: Debates on Psychological Explanation*, vol. 1, ed. Cynthia Macdonald and Graham Macdonald (Oxford: Blackwell): 309–30.

De Mesel, Benjamin (2017). "Is Moral Responsibility Essentially Interpersonal? A Reply to Zimmerman." *Journal of Ethics* 21: 309–33.

Dennett, Daniel C. (1984). *Elbow Room: The Varieties of Free Will Worth Wanting*. Cambridge, Mass.: MIT Press.

Dimitrijevic, Nenad (2011). *Duty to Respond*. Budapest: Central European University Press.

Donagan, Alan (1977). *The Theory of Morality*. Chicago: University of Chicago Press.

Doris, John M. (2002). *Lack of Character: Personality and Moral Behavior*. Cambridge: Cambridge University Press.

Douskos, Christos (2017). "Habit and Intention." *Philosophia* 45: 1129–48.

Dowe, Phil (2001). "A Counterfactual Theory of Prevention and 'Causation' by Omission." *Australasian Journal of Philosophy* 79: 216–26.

Dreier, James (2000). "Dispositions and Fetishes: Externalist Models of Moral Motivation." *Philosophy and Phenomenological Research* 61: 619–38.

Driver, Julia (1992). "The Suberogatory." *Australasian Journal of Philosophy* 70: 286–95.

Driver, Julia (2015). "Appraisability, Attributability, and Moral Agency." In *The Nature of Moral Responsibility*, ed. Randolph Clarke et al. (Oxford: Oxford University Press): 157–73.

Driver, Julia (2016). "Private Blame." *Criminal Law and Philosophy* 10: 215–20.

Duff, R. A. (1977). "Psychopathy and Moral Understanding." *American Philosophical Quarterly* 14: 189–200.

Duff, R. A. (1990). *Intention, Agency, and Criminal Liability*. Oxford: Blackwell.

Duff, R. A. (2019). "Two Models of Criminal Thought." *Criminal Law and Philosophy* 13: 643–65.

Duggan, A. P. (2018). "Moral Responsibility as Guiltworthiness." *Ethical Theory and Moral Practice* 21: 291–309.

Dutant, Julien (2015). "The Legend of the Justified True Belief Analysis." *Philosophical Perspectives* 29: 95–145.

Edwards, J. Ll. J. (1954). "The Criminal Degrees of Knowledge." *Modern Law Review* 17: 294–314.

Edwards, Jonathan (1789). *The Eternity of Hell Torments*, 2nd edition, ed. C. E. De Coetlogon. London: R. Thomson.

Enoch, David and Marmor, Andrei (2007). "The Case against Moral Luck." *Law and Philosophy* 26: 405–36.

Ewing, A. C. (1948). *The Definition of Good*. New York: Macmillan and Co.

Feinberg, Joel (1970). *Doing and Deserving*. Princeton: Princeton University Press.

Feinberg, Joel (1980). *Rights, Justice, and the Bounds of Liberty*. Princeton: Princeton University Press.

Feldman, Fred and Skow, Brad (2019). "Desert." *The Stanford Encyclopedia of Philosophy* (Winter 2019 Edition), ed. Edward N. Zalta, URL = <https://plato.stanford.edu/archives/win2019/entries/desert/>.

Feldman, Richard (2000). "The Ethics of Belief." *Philosophy and Phenomenological Research* 60: 667–95.
Fingarette, Herbert (1967). *On Responsibility*. New York: Basic Books.
Finkelstein, David H. (1999). "On the Distinction between Conscious and Unconscious States of Mind." *American Philosophical Quarterly* 36: 79–100.
Fischer, John Martin (1994). *The Metaphysics of Free Will*. Oxford: Basil Blackwell.
Fischer, John Martin and Ravizza, Mark (1992). "When the Will Is Free." *Philosophical Perspectives* 6: 423–51.
Fischer, John Martin and Ravizza, Mark (1998). *Responsibility and Control*. Cambridge: Cambridge University Press.
Fischer, John Martin and Ravizza, Mark (2000). "Précis of *Responsibility and Control*." *Philosophy and Phenomenological Research* 61: 441–45.
Fischer, John Martin and Tognazzini, Neal A. (2009). "The Truth about Tracing." *Noûs* 43: 531–56.
Fischer, John Martin and Tognazzini, Neal A. (2011). "The Physiognomy of Responsibility." *Philosophy and Phenomenological Research* 82: 381–417.
Fiske, Alan Page and Rai, Tage Shakti (2015). *Virtuous Violence*. Cambridge: Cambridge University Press.
FitzPatrick, William J. (2008). "Moral Responsibility and Normative Ignorance: Answering a New Skeptical Challenge." *Ethics* 118: 589–613.
Foley, Richard (2009). "Belief, Degrees of Belief, and the Lockean Thesis." In *Degrees of Belief*, ed. Franz and Christoph Schmidt-Petri (Dordrecht: Springer): 37–47.
Frankfurt, Harry G. (1969). "Alternate Possibilities and Moral Responsibility." *Journal of Philosophy* 66: 829–39.
García, Andrés G. (2018). *Between Values and the World*. Ph.D. thesis, Lund University.
Gendler, Tamar Szabó (2008a). "Alief and Belief." *Journal of Philosophy* 105: 634–63.
Gendler, Tamar Szabó (2008b). "Alief in Action (and Reaction)." *Mind and Language* 23: 552–85.
Gettier, Edmund L. (1963). "Is Justified True Belief Knowledge?" *Analysis* 23: 121–23.
Glover, Jonathan (1970). *Responsibility*. London: Routledge & Kegan Paul.
Goldberg, Sanford C. (2017). "Should Have Known." *Synthese* 194: 2863–94.
Goldman, Alvin I. (1970). *A Theory of Human Action*. Princeton: Princeton University Press.
Graham, Peter A. (2010). "In Defense of Objectivism about Moral Obligation." *Ethics* 121: 88–115.
Graham, Peter A. (2014). "A Sketch of a Theory of Moral Blameworthiness." *Philosophy and Phenomenological Research* 88: 388–409.
Graham, Peter A. (2017). "The Epistemic Condition on Moral Blameworthiness: A Theoretical Epiphenomenon." In *Responsibility: The Epistemic Condition*, ed. Philip Robichaud and Jan Willem Wieland (Oxford: Oxford University Press): 163–79.
Greenspan, Patricia (2016). "Responsible Psychopaths Revisited." *Journal of Ethics* 20: 265–78.
Guerrero, Alexander A. (2007). "Don't Know, Don't Kill: Moral Ignorance, Culpability, and Caution." *Philosophical Studies* 136: 59–97.
Haji, Ishtiyaque (1998). *Moral Appraisability*. Oxford: Oxford University Press.
Haji, Ishtiyaque (2003). "The Emotional Depravity of Psychopaths and Culpability." *Legal Theory* 9: 63–82.
Haksar, Vinit (1965). "The Responsibility of Psychopaths." *Philosophical Quarterly* 15: 135–45.

Hare, Richard M. (1952). *The Language of Morals*. Oxford: Oxford University Press.
Harman, Elizabeth (2011). "Does Moral Ignorance Exculpate?" *Ratio* 24: 443–68.
Harman, Elizabeth (2015). "The Irrelevance of Moral Uncertainty." *Oxford Studies in Metaethics* 10: 53–79.
Hart, H. L. A. (1968). *Punishment and Responsibility*. Oxford: Clarendon Press.
Hartford, Anna (2019). "Moral and Factual Ignorance: A Quality of Will Parity." *Ethical Theory and Moral Practice* 22: 1087–1102.
Haybron, Daniel M. (1999). "Evil Characters." *American Philosophical Quarterly* 36: 137–48.
Hellman, Deborah (2009). "Willfully Blind for Good Reason." *Criminal Law and Philosophy* 3: 301–16.
Heuer, Ulrike (2010). "Wrongness and Reasons." *Ethical Theory and Moral Practice* 13: 137–52.
Hieronymi, Pamela (2008). "Responsibility for Believing." *Synthese* 161: 357–73.
Hieronymi, Pamela (2009). "Believing at Will." *Canadian Journal of Philosophy*, suppl. vol. 39: 149–87.
Hobbes, Thomas (1651). *Leviathan*.
Hohfeld, Wesley Newcomb (1919). *Fundamental Legal Conceptions*. New Haven: Yale University Press.
Huber, Franz (2009). "Belief and Degrees of Belief." In *Degrees of Belief*, ed. Franz and Christoph Schmidt-Petri (Dordrecht: Springer): 1–33.
Hughes, Paul M. and Warmke, Brandon (2017). "Forgiveness." *The Stanford Encyclopedia of Philosophy* (Summer 2017 Edition), ed. Edward N. Zalta, URL = <https://plato.stanford.edu/archives/sum2017/entries/forgiveness/>.
Humberstone, I. L. (1992). "Direction of Fit." *Mind* 101: 59–83.
Humberstone, I. L. (1996). "Intrinsic/Extrinsic." *Synthese* 108: 205–67.
Hume, David (1998). *An Enquiry Concerning the Principles of Morals*, ed. Tom L. Beauchamp. Oxford: Clarendon Press.
Hume, David (2007). *A Treatise of Human Nature*, ed. David Fate Norton and Mary Norton. Oxford: Clarendon Press.
Hurka, Thomas (2014). "Many Faces of Virtue." *Philosophy and Phenomenological Research* 89: 496–503.
Husak, Douglas N. (1987). *Philosophy of Criminal Law*. Totowa: Rowman & Littlefield.
Husak, Douglas N. (2011). "Negligence, Belief, Blame and Criminal Liability: The Special Case of Forgetting." *Criminal Law and Philosophy* 5: 199–218.
Husak, Douglas N. (2012). "Intoxication and Culpability." *Criminal Law and Philosophy* 6: 363–79.
Husak, Douglas N. (2016). *Ignorance of Law*. Oxford: Oxford University Press.
Husak, Douglas N. and Callender, Craig A. (1994). "Wilful Ignorance, Knowledge, and the 'Equal Culpability' Thesis: A Study of the Deeper Significance of the Principle of Legality." *Wisconsin Law Review* 1994: 29–69.
Ichikawa, Jonathan Jenkins and Steup, Matthias (2017). "The Analysis of Knowledge." *The Stanford Encyclopedia of Philosophy* (Fall 2017 Edition), ed. Edward N. Zalta. URL = <https://plato.stanford.edu/archives/fall2017/entries/knowledge-analysis/>.
Isaacs, Tracy (1997). "Cultural Context and Moral Responsibility." *Ethics* 107: 670–84.
Jackson, Frank (1986). "A Probabilistic Approach to Moral Responsibility." In *Logic, Methodology and Philosophy of Science VII*, ed. R. B. Marcus et al. (Amsterdam: Elsevier): 351–65.

Jackson, Frank (1991). "Decision-Theoretic Consequentialism and the Nearest and Dearest Objection." *Ethics* 101: 461–82.
James, William (1967). *The Writings of William James*, ed. J. J. McDermott. New York: Random House.
Jennings, Carolyn Dicey (2015). "Consciousness Without Attention." *Journal of the American Philosophical Association* 1: 276–95.
Johnson King, Zoë (2020a). "Accidentally Doing the Right Thing." *Philosophy and Phenomenological Research* 177: 186–206.
Johnson King, Zoë (2020b). "Don't Know, Don't Care?" *Philosophical Studies* 177: 413–31.
Johnson King, Zoë (2020c). "Praiseworthy Motivations." *Noûs* 54: 408–30.
Johnston, Mark (1995). "Self-Deception and the Nature of Mind." In *Philosophy of Psychology: Debates on Psychological Explanation*, vol. 1, ed. Cynthia Macdonald and Graham Macdonald (Oxford: Blackwell): 433–60.
Kamtekar, Rachana and Nichols, Shaun (2019). "Agent-Regret and Accidental Agency." *Midwest Studies in Philosophy* 43: 181–202.
Kane, Robert (1996). *The Significance of Free Will*. Oxford: Oxford University Press.
Kant, Immanuel (1949). *Critique of Practical Reason and Other Writings in Moral Philosophy*, tr. Lewis White Beck. Chicago: University of Chicago Press.
Kant, Immanuel (1964). *Groundwork of the Metaphysic of Morals*, ed. H. J. Paton. New York: Harper & Row.
Kant, Immanuel (1985). "Jealousy, Envy, and Spite." In *Vice and Virtue in Everyday Life*, ed. Christina Hoff Sommers (San Diego: Harcourt Brace Jovanovich): 272–79.
Katz, Fred E. (1993). *Ordinary People and Extraordinary Evil*. Albany: SUNY Press.
Kavka, Gregory (1983). "The Toxin Puzzle." *Analysis* 43: 33–36.
Keeton, Robert E. and O'Connell, Jeffrey (1975). "Why Shift Loss?" In *Responsibility*, ed. Joel Feinberg and Hyman Gross (Encino: Dickenson): 84–88.
Khoury, Andrew C. (2012). "Responsibility, Tracing, and Consequences." *Canadian Journal of Philosophy* 42: 187–207.
Khoury, Andrew C. (2018). "The Objects of Moral Responsibility." *Philosophical Studies* 175: 1357–81.
Khoury, Andrew C. and Matheson, Benjamin (2018). "Is Blameworthiness Forever?" *Journal of the American Philosophical Society* 4: 204–24.
King, Matt (2009). "The Problem with Negligence." *Social Theory and Practice* 35: 577–95.
King, Matt (2011). "Traction without Tracing: A (Partial) Solution for Control-Based Accounts of Moral Responsibility." *European Journal of Philosophy* 22: 463–82.
King, Matt (2017). "Tracing the Epistemic Condition." In *Responsibility: The Epistemic Condition*, ed. Philip Robichaud and Jan Willem Wieland (Oxford: Oxford University Press): 266–80.
King, Matt (2020). "Attending to Blame." *Philosophical Studies* 177: 1423–39.
Kornblith, Hilary (2017). "How Central Are Judgment and Agency to Epistemology?" *Philosophical Studies* 174: 2585–97.
Kripke, Saul (1979). "A Puzzle about Belief." In *Meaning and Use*, ed. A. Margalit (Dordrecht: D. Reidel): 239–83.
Lemos, Noah (1994). *Intrinsic Value*. Cambridge: Cambridge University Press.
Levy, Neil (2005). "The Good, the Bad and the Blameworthy." *Journal of Ethics and Social Philosophy* 1: 2–16.
Levy, Neil (2007a). "Norms, Conventions, and Psychopaths." *Philosophy, Psychiatry, and Psychology* 14: 163–70.

Levy, Neil (2007b). "The Responsibility of the Psychopath Revisited." *Philosophy, Psychiatry, and Psychology* 14: 129–38.
Levy, Neil (2011). *Hard Luck*. Oxford: Oxford University Press.
Levy, Neil (2014). *Consciousness and Moral Responsibility*. Oxford: Oxford University Press.
Levy, Neil (2017a). "Implicit Bias and Moral Responsibility: Probing the Data." *Philosophy and Phenomenological Research* 94: 3–26.
Levy, Neil (2017b). "Methodological Conservatism and the Epistemic Condition." In *Responsibility: The Epistemic Condition*, ed. Philip Robichaud and Jan Willem Wieland (Oxford: Oxford University Press): 252–65.
Lewis, C. S. (1949). "The Humanitarian Theory of Punishment." *The Twentieth Century: An Australian Quarterly Review* 3: 5–12.
Lillehammer, Hallvard (1997). "Smith on Moral Fetishism." *Analysis* 57: 187–95.
Luban, David (1999). "Contrived Ignorance." *Georgetown Law Journal* 87: 957–80.
Lynch, Kevin (2016). "Willful Ignorance and Self-Deception." *Philosophical Studies* 173: 505–23.
McConnell, Terrance C. (1989). "'Ought' Implies 'Can' and the Scope of Moral Requirements." *Philosophia* 19: 437–54.
Macdonald, Graham (1995). "Introduction: Tacit Knowledge." In *Philosophy of Psychology: Debates on Psychological Explanation*, vol. 1, ed. Cynthia Macdonald and Graham Macdonald (Oxford: Blackwell): 296–308.
McHugh, Conor (2017). "Attitudinal Control." *Synthese* 194: 2745–62.
McKenna, Michael (2012). *Conversation and Responsibility*. Oxford: Oxford University Press.
McKenna, Michael (2016). "Quality of Will, Private Blame and Conversation: Reply to Driver, Shoemaker, and Vargas." *Criminal Law and Philosophy* 10: 243–63.
McKenna, Michael (2019). "Basically Deserved Blame and Its Value." *Journal of Ethics and Social Philosophy* 15: 255–82.
Madva, Alex (2017). "Implicit Bias, Moods, and Moral Responsibility." *Pacific Philosophical Quarterly* 99: 53–78.
Marcus, Ruth Barcan (1990). "Some Revisionary Proposals about Belief and Believing." *Philosophy and Phenomenological Research* 50: 132–53.
Markovits, Julia (2010). "Acting for the Right Reasons." *Philosophical Review* 119: 201–42.
Mason, Elinor (2019). *Ways to be Blameworthy: Rightness, Wrongness, and Responsibility*. Oxford: Oxford University Press.
Mason, Elinor and Wilson, Alan T. (2017). "Vice, Blameworthiness, and Cultural Ignorance." In *Responsibility: The Epistemic Condition*, ed. Philip Robichaud and Jan Willem Wieland (Oxford: Oxford University Press): 82–100.
Mayo-Wilson, Conor and Wheeler, Gregory (2016). "Scoring Imprecise Credences: A Mildly Immodest Proposal." *Philosophy and Phenomenological Research* 93: 55–78.
Mele, Alfred R. (1992). *Springs of Action: Understanding Intentional Behavior*. Oxford: Oxford University Press.
Mele, Alfred R. (2001). *Self-Deception Unmasked*. Princeton: Princeton University Press.
Mele, Alfred R. (2003). "Agents' Abilities." *Noûs* 37: 447–70.
Mele, Alfred R. (2010). "Moral Responsibility for Actions: Epistemic and Freedom Conditions." *Philosophical Explorations* 13: 101–11.
Menges, Leonhard (2017). "The Emotion Account of Blame." *Philosophical Studies* 174: 257–73.
Milgram, Stanley (1974). *Obedience to Authority*. New York: Harper & Row.

Miller, Daniel J. (2017). "Reasonable Foreseeability and Blameless Ignorance." *Philosophical Studies* 174: 1561-81.
Milo, Ronald D. (1984). *Immorality*. Princeton: Princeton University Press.
Montminy, Martin (2016). "Doing One's Reasonable Best: What Moral Responsibility Requires." *Journal of the American Philosophical Association* 2: 55-73.
Moody-Adams, Michelle (1994). "Culture, Responsibility, and Affected Ignorance." *Ethics* 104: 291-309.
Moon, Andrew (2017). "Beliefs Do Not Come in Degrees." *Canadian Journal of Philosophy* 47: 760-78.
Moon, Andrew and Jackson, Elizabeth (2020). "Credence: A Belief-First Approach." *Canadian Journal of Philosophy* 50: 652-69.
Moore, G. E. (1962). *Philosophical Papers*. London: Allen & Unwin.
Moore, G. E. (2005). *Ethics*, ed. William H. Shaw. Oxford: Clarendon Press.
Moore, Michael S. (1997). *Placing Blame*. Oxford: Clarendon Press.
Moore, Michael S. (2009). *Causation and Responsibility*. Oxford: Oxford University Press.
Moore, Michael S. and Hurd, Heidi (2011). "Punishing the Awkward, the Stupid, the Weak, and the Selfish: The Culpability of Negligence." *Criminal Law and Philosophy* 5: 147-98.
Morris, Herbert (1976). *On Guilt and Innocence*. Berkeley: University of California Press.
Murphy, Jeffrie G. (1972). "Moral Death: A Kantian Essay on Psychopathy." *Ethics* 82: 284-98.
Murphy, Jeffrie G. and Hampton, Jean (1988). *Forgiveness and Mercy*. Cambridge: Cambridge University Press.
Murray, Samuel and Vargas, Manuel (2020). "Vigilance and Control." *Philosophical Studies* 177: 825-43.
Nagel, Thomas (1976). "Moral Luck." *Proceedings of the Aristotelian Society*, suppl. vol. 1: 115-35.
Nelkin, Dana Kay (2011). *Making Sense of Freedom and Responsibility*. Oxford: Oxford University Press.
Nelkin, Dana Kay (2015). "Psychopaths, Incorrigible Racists, and Faces of Responsibility." *Ethics* 125: 357-90.
Nelkin, Dana Kay (2016a). "Accountability and Desert." *Journal of Ethics* 20: 173-89.
Nelkin, Dana Kay (2016b). "Difficulty and Degrees of Moral Praiseworthiness and Blameworthiness." *Noûs* 50: 356-78.
Nowell Smith, P. H. (1960). "Ifs and Cans." *Theoria* 26: 85-101.
Nozick, Robert (1981). *Philosophical Explanations*. Cambridge, Mass.: Harvard University Press.
O'Connor, Timothy (2009). "Degrees of Freedom." *Philosophical Explorations* 12: 119-25.
Olson, Jonas (2002). "Are Desires *De Dicto* Fetishistic?" *Inquiry* 45: 89-96.
Olson, Jonas (2004). "Buck-Passing and the Wrong Kind of Reasons." *Philosophical Quarterly*, 54: 295-300.
Parfit, Derek (1984). *Reasons and Persons*. Oxford: Oxford University Press.
Parfit, Derek (2001). "Rationality and Reasons." In *Exploring Practical Philosophy*, ed. D. Egonsson et al. (Aldershot: Ashgate): 17-39.
Paul, Sarah K. (2015). "Doxastic Self-Control." *American Philosophical Quarterly* 52: 145-58.
Paul, Sarah K. (2016). "The Courage of Conviction." *Canadian Journal of Philosophy* 45: 647-69.
Peels, Rik (2015). "Believing at Will Is Possible." *Australasian Journal of Philosophy* 93: 524-41.

Peels, Rik (2017). *Responsible Belief: A Theory in Ethics and Epistemology*. Oxford: Oxford University Press.
Pereboom, Derk (2013). "Moral Responsibility without Desert." In *Free Will and Moral Responsibility*, ed. Ishtiyaque Haji and Justin Caouette (Newcastle upon Tyne: Cambridge Scholars Publishing): 213–28.
Pereboom, Derk (2014). *Free Will, Agency, and Meaning in Life*. Oxford: Oxford University Press.
Persson, Ingmar (2007). "Primary and Secondary Reasons." http://www.fil.lu.se/HommageaWlodek/site/papper/PerssonIngmar.pdf.
Persson, Ingmar (2019). *Reasons in Action*. Oxford: Oxford University Press.
Pink, Thomas (2016). *Self-Determination*. Oxford: Oxford University Press.
Plantinga, Alvin (1974). *The Nature of Necessity*. Oxford: Clarendon Press.
Plato (1961). *The Collected Dialogues*, ed. E. Hamilton and H. Cairns. Princeton: Princeton University Press.
Pojman, Louis P. (1986). *Religious Belief and the Will*. London: Routledge & Kegan Paul.
Postow, B. C. (1977). "Generalized Act Utilitarianism." *Analysis* 37: 49–52.
Prichard, H. A. (1949). *Moral Obligation*. Oxford: Clarendon Press.
Prinz, Jesse J. (2011). "Is Attention Necessary and Sufficient for Consciousness?" In *Attention: Philosophical and Psychological Essays*, ed. Christopher Mole et al. (Oxford: Oxford University Press): 174–203.
Pritchard, Michael S. (1974). "Responsibility, Understanding, and Psychopathology." *Monist* 58: 630–45.
Prosser, William L. (1971). *The Law of Torts*. St. Paul: West.
Quine, W. V. O. (1956). "Quantifiers and Propositional Attitudes." *Journal of Philosophy* 53: 177–87.
Rabinowicz, Wlodek and Rønnow-Rasmussen, Toni (1999). "A Distinction in Value: Intrinsic and For Its Own Sake." *Proceedings of the Aristotelian Society* 100: 33–52.
Rabinowicz, Wlodek and Rønnow-Rasmussen, Toni (2004). "The Strike of the Demon." *Ethics* 114: 391–423.
Radford, Colin (1966). "Knowledge—By Examples." *Analysis* 27: 1–11.
Raz, Joseph (2011). *From Normativity to Responsibility*. Oxford: Oxford University Press.
Rescher, Nicholas (1984). "The Editor's Page: The Egocentric Predicament." *American Philosophical Quarterly* 21: 277.
Rettler, Lindsay (2018). "In Defense of Doxastic Blame." *Synthese* 195: 2205–26.
Rivera-López, Eduardo (2006). "Can There Be Full Excuses for Morally Wrong Actions?" *Philosophy and Phenomenological Research* 73: 124–42.
Roberts, Robert C. (1988). "What an Emotion Is: A Sketch." *Philosophical Review* 97: 183–209.
Robichaud, Philip and Wieland, Jan Willem (2019). "A Puzzle Concerning Blame Transfer." *Philosophy and Phenomenological Research* 99: 3–26.
Robinson, Michael (2019). "Robust Flickers of Freedom." *Social Philosophy and Policy* 36: 211–33.
Robison, John (2019). "When and Why Is It Disrespectful to Excuse an Attitude?" *Philosophical Studies* 176: 2391–2409.
Roeber, Blake (2019). "Evidence, Judgment, and Belief at Will." *Mind* 128: 837–59.
Roeber, Blake (2020). "Permissive Situations and Direct Doxastic Control." *Philosophy and Phenomenological Research* 101: 415–31.
Rosen, Gideon (2003). "Culpability and Ignorance." *Proceedings of the Aristotelian Society* 103: 61–84.

Rosen, Gideon (2004). "Skepticism about Moral Responsibility." *Philosophical Perspectives* 18: 295–313.
Rosen, Gideon (2008). "Kleinbart the Oblivious and Other Tales of Ignorance and Responsibility." *Journal of Philosophy* 105: 591–610.
Rosen, Gideon (2015). "The Alethic Conception of Moral Responsibility." In *The Nature of Moral Responsibility*, ed. Randolph Clarke et al. (Oxford: Oxford University Press): 65–87.
Ross, W. D. (1939). *Foundations of Ethics*. Oxford: Clarendon Press.
Ross, W. D. (2002). *The Right and the Good*, ed. Philip Stratton-Lake. Oxford: Clarendon Press.
Rowe, William L. (1979). "The Problem of Evil and Some Varieties of Atheism." *American Philosophical Quarterly* 16: 335–41.
Rudy-Hiller, Fernando (2017). "A Capacitarian Account of Culpable Ignorance." *Pacific Philosophical Quarterly* 98: 398–426.
Rudy-Hiller, Fernando (2018). "The Epistemic Condition for Moral Responsibility." *The Stanford Encyclopedia of Philosophy* (Fall 2018 Edition), ed. Edward N. Zalta, URL = <https://plato.stanford.edu/archives/fall2018/entries/moral-responsibility-epistemic/>.
Rumfitt, Ian (2003). "Savoir Faire." *Journal of Philosophy* 100: 158–66.
Russell, Luke (2014). *Evil: A Philosophical Investigation*. Oxford: Oxford University Press.
Russell, Paul (2021). "*The Limits of Free Will*: Replies to Bennett, Smith and Wallace." *Ethical Theory and Moral Practice* 24: 357–73.
Sarch, Alexander (2014). "Willful Ignorance, Culpability, and the Criminal Law." *St. John's Law Review* 88: 1023–1101.
Sarch, Alexander (2016). "Equal Culpability and the Scope of the Willful Ignorance Doctrine." *Legal Theory* 22: 276–311.
Sarch, Alexander (2019). *Criminally Ignorant*. Oxford: Oxford University Press.
Sartre, Jean-Paul (1953). *Being and Nothingness*, tr. H. E. Barnes. New York: Washington Square Press.
Sayre-McCord, Geoffrey (2017). "Moral Realism." *The Stanford Encyclopedia of Philosophy* (Fall 2017 Edition), ed. Edward N. Zalta, URL = <https://plato.stanford.edu/archives/fall2017/entries/moral-realism/>.
Scanlon, Thomas M. (1998). *What We Owe to Each Other*. Cambridge, Mass.: Harvard University Press.
Scanlon, Thomas M. (2007). "Wrongness and Reasons: A Re-examination." In *Oxford Studies in Metaethics*, vol. 2, ed. Russ Shafer-Landau (Oxford: Oxford University Press): 5–20.
Scanlon, Thomas M. (2008). *Moral Dimensions*. Cambridge, Mass.: Harvard University Press.
Scanlon, Thomas M. (2013). "Interpreting Blame." In *Blame: Its Nature and Norms*, ed. D. Justin Coates and Neal A. Tognazzini (Oxford: Oxford University Press): 84–99.
Scanlon, Thomas M. (2015). "Forms and Conditions of Responsibility." In *The Nature of Moral Responsibility*, ed. Randolph Clarke et al. (Oxford: Oxford University Press): 89–111.
Scarre, Geoffrey (2004). *After Evil: Responding to Wrongdoing*. Aldershot: Ashgate.
Scarre, Geoffrey (2005). "Excusing the Inexcusable? Moral Responsibility and Ideologically Motivated Wrongdoing." *Journal of Social Philosophy* 36: 457–72.
Schaffer, Jonathan (2000). "Causation by Disconnection." *Philosophy of Science* 67: 285–300.
Schlick, Moritz (1966). "When Is a Man Responsible?" In *Free Will and Determinism*, ed. Bernard Berofsky (New York: Harper & Row): 54–63.

Schlossberger, Eugene (1992). *Moral Responsibility and Persons*. Philadelphia: Temple University Press.
Schmid, Hans Bernhard (2018). "The Guise of the Bad in Augustine's Pear Theft." *Ethical Theory and Moral Practice* 21: 71–89.
Schnall, Ira M. (2004). "Ignorance and Blame." *Philosophical Topics* 32: 307–29.
Schwitzgebel, Eric (2010). "Acting Contrary to Our Professed Beliefs or The Gulf between Occurrent Judgment and Dispositional Belief." *Pacific Philosophical Quarterly* 91: 531–53.
Schwitzgebel, Eric (2015). "Belief." *The Stanford Encyclopedia of Philosophy* (Summer 2015 Edition), ed. Edward N. Zalta, URL = <https://plato.stanford.edu/archives/sum2015/entries/belief/>.
Searle, John R. (1995). "Consciousness, Explanatory Inversion and Cognitive Science." In *Philosophy of Psychology: Debates on Psychological Explanation*, vol. 1, ed. Cynthia Macdonald and Graham Macdonald (Oxford: Blackwell): 331–55.
Shabo, Seth (2015). "More Trouble with Tracing." *Erkenntnis* 80: 987–1011.
Shepherd, Joshua (2014). "The Contours of Control." *Philosophical Studies* 170: 395–411.
Sher, George (2006). *In Praise of Blame*. Oxford: Oxford University Press.
Sher, George (2009). *Who Knew?* Oxford: Oxford University Press.
Sher, George (2017). "Blame and Moral Ignorance." In *Responsibility: The Epistemic Condition*, ed. Philip Robichaud and Jan Willem Wieland (Oxford: Oxford University Press): 101–16.
Shoemaker, David (2007). "Moral Address, Moral Responsibility, and the Boundaries of the Moral Community." *Ethics* 118: 70–108.
Shoemaker, David (2011a). "Attributability, Answerability, and Accountability: Toward a Wider Theory of Moral Responsibility." *Ethics* 121: 602–32.
Shoemaker, David (2011b). "Psychopathy, Responsibility, and the Moral/Conventional Distinction." *Southern Journal of Philosophy* 49 suppl. vol. 1: 99–124.
Shoemaker, David (2015a). "McKenna's Quality of Will." *Criminal Law and Philosophy* 9: 695–708.
Shoemaker, David (2015b). *Responsibility from the Margins*. Oxford: Oxford University Press.
Shoemaker, David (2017). "Response-Dependent Responsibility; or, A Funny Thing Happened on the Way to Blame." *Philosophical Review* 126: 481–527.
Siewert, Charles (2017). "Consciousness and Intentionality." *The Stanford Encyclopedia of Philosophy* (Spring 2017 Edition), ed. Edward N. Zalta. URL = <https://plato.stanford.edu/archives/spr2017/entries/consciousness-intentionality/>.
Simons, Daniel J. and Chabris, Christopher F. (1999). "Gorillas in Our Midst: Sustained Inattentional Blindness for Dynamic Events." *Perception* 28: 1059–74.
Simons, Kenneth W. (2011). "When Is Negligent Inadvertence Culpable?" *Criminal Law and Philosophy* 5: 97–114.
Singer, Peter (1972). "Famine, Affluence, and Morality." *Philosophy and Public Affairs* 1: 229–43.
Sinnott-Armstrong, Walter (1988). *Moral Dilemmas*. Oxford: Basil Blackwell.
Sinnott-Armstrong, Walter (1999). "Begging the Question." *Australasian Journal of Philosophy* 77: 174–91.
Sliwa, Paulina (2015). "Praise without Perfection: A Dilemma for Right-Making Reasons." *American Philosophical Quarterly* 52: 171–85.
Sloane, Stephanie, et al. (2012). "Do Infants Have a Sense of Fairness?" *Psychological Science* 23: 196–204.

Smart, J. J. C. (1973). "An Outline of a System of Utilitarian Ethics." In *Utilitarianism: For and Against*, by J. J. C. Smart and Bernard Williams (Cambridge: Cambridge University Press): 3–74.
Smetana, Judith G. et al. (2013). "The Social Domain Approach to Children's Moral and Social Judgments." In *Handbook of Moral Development*, ed. Melanie Killen and Judith G. Smetana (London: Routledge): 23–45.
Smith, Angela M. (2005). "Responsibility for Attitudes: Activity and Passivity in Mental Life." *Ethics* 115: 236–71.
Smith, Angela M. (2007). "On Being Responsible and Holding Responsible." *Journal of Ethics* 11: 465–84.
Smith, Angela M. (2008). "Control, Responsibility, and Moral Assessment." *Philosophical Studies* 138: 367–92.
Smith, Angela M. (2012). "Attributability, Answerability, and Accountability: In Defense of a Unified Account." *Ethics* 122: 575–89.
Smith, Angela M. (2013). "Moral Blame and Moral Protest." In *Blame: Its Nature and Norms*, ed. D. Justin Coates and Neal A. Tognazzini (Oxford: Oxford University Press): 27–48.
Smith, Angela M. (2015). "Responsibility as Answerability." *Inquiry* 58: 99–126.
Smith, Angela M. (2021). "Responsibility, Reactive Attitudes, and 'The Morality System'." *Ethical Theory and Moral Practice* 24: 333–45.
Smith, Holly M. (1983). "Culpable Ignorance." *Philosophical Review* 92: 543–71.
Smith, Holly M. (2011). "Non-Tracing Cases of Culpable Ignorance." *Criminal Law and Philosophy* 5: 115–46.
Smith, Holly M. (2017). "Tracing Cases of Culpable Ignorance." In *Perspectives on Ignorance from Moral and Social Philosophy*, ed. Rik Peels (New York: Routledge): 95–119.
Smith, Holly M. (2018). *Making Morality Work*. Oxford: Oxford University Press.
Smith, Michael (1994). *The Moral Problem*. Oxford: Blackwell.
Smith, Michael (2003). "Rational Capacities, or: How to Distinguish Recklessness, Weakness, and Compulsion." In *Weakness of Will and Practical Irrationality*, ed. Sarah Stroud and Christine Tappolet (Oxford: Clarendon Press): 17–38.
Smithies, Declan (2011). "Attention Is Rational-Access Consciousness." In *Attention: Philosophical and Psychological Essays*, ed. Christopher Mole et al. (Oxford: Oxford University Press): 247–73.
Snowdon, Paul (2003). "Knowing How and Knowing That: A Distinction Reconsidered." *Proceedings of the Aristotelian Society* 104: 1–29.
Stanley, Jason and Williamson, Timothy (2001). "Knowing How." *Journal of Philosophy* 98: 411–44.
Steup, Matthias (2017). "Believing Intentionally." *Synthese* 194: 2673–94.
Strawson, P. F. (1974). *Freedom and Resentment*. London: Methuen.
Stump, Eleonore (1993). "Intellect, Will, and the Principle of Alternate Possibilities." In *Perspectives on Moral Responsibility*, ed. John Martin Fischer and Mark Ravizza (Ithaca: Cornell University Press): 237–62.
Sverdlik, Steven (1993). "Pure Negligence." *American Philosophical Quarterly* 30: 137–49.
Talbert, Matthew (2011). "Unwitting Behavior and Responsibility." *Journal of Moral Philosophy* 8: 139–52.
Talbert, Matthew (2012). "Moral Competence, Moral Blame, and Protest." *Journal of Ethics* 16: 89–109.

Talbert, Matthew (2013). "Unwitting Wrongdoers and the Role of Moral Disagreement in Blame." In *Oxford Studies in Agency and Responsibility*, vol. 1, ed. David Shoemaker (Oxford: Oxford University Press): 225–45.
Talbert, Matthew (2014). "The Significance of Psychopathic Wrongdoing." In *Being Amoral*, ed. Thomas Schramme (Cambridge, Mass.: MIT Press): 275–300.
Talbert, Matthew (2016). *Moral Responsibility*. Cambridge: Polity Press.
Talbert, Matthew (2017a). "Akrasia, Awareness, and Blameworthiness." In *Responsibility: The Epistemic Condition*, ed. Philip Robichaud and Jan Willem Wieland (Oxford: Oxford University Press): 47–63.
Talbert, Matthew (2017b). "Omission and Attribution Error." In *The Ethics and Law of Omissions*, ed. Dana Kay Nelkin and Samuel C. Rickless (Oxford: Oxford University Press): 17–35.
Tannenbaum, Julie (2015). "Mere Moral Failure." *Canadian Journal of Philosophy* 45: 58–84.
Taylor, Richard (1966). *Action and Purpose*. Englewood Cliffs: Prentice-Hall.
Telech, Daniel and Tierney, Hannah (2019). "The Comparative Nonarbitrariness Norm of Blame." *Journal of Ethics and Social Philosophy* 16: 25–43.
Thalberg, Irving (1963). "Remorse." *Mind* 72: 545–55.
Thomson, Judith Jarvis (1989). "Morality and Bad Luck." *Metaphilosophy* 20: 203–21.
Thomson, Judith Jarvis (1990). *The Realm of Rights*. Cambridge, Mass.: Harvard University Press.
Thomson, Judith Jarvis (1991). "Self-Defense." *Philosophy and Public Affairs* 20: 283–310.
Turner, J. W. C. (1936). "The Mental Element at Common Law." *Cambridge Law Journal* 6: 31–66.
Turri, John et al. (2018). "Choosing and Refusing: Doxastic Voluntarism and Folk Psychology." *Philosophical Studies* 175: 2507–37.
Van Gulick, Robert (2017). "Consciousness." *The Stanford Encyclopedia of Philosophy* (Summer 2017 Edition), ed. Edward N. Zalta. URL = <https://plato.stanford.edu/archives/sum2017/entries/consciousness/>.
van Inwagen, Peter (1983). *An Essay on Free Will*. Oxford: Clarendon Press.
van Inwagen, Peter (1989). "When Is the Will Free?" *Philosophical Perspectives* 3: 399–422.
van Inwagen, Peter (1994). "When the Will Is Not Free." *Philosophical Studies* 75: 95–113.
van Inwagen, Peter (1997). "Against Middle Knowledge." *Midwest Studies in Philosophy* 21: 225–36.
Vanderheiden, Steve (2016). "The Obligation to Know: Information and the Burdens of Citizenship." *Ethical Theory and Moral Practice* 19: 297–311.
Vargas, Manuel (2005). "The Trouble with Tracing." *Midwest Studies in Philosophy* 29: 269–91.
Vargas, Manuel (2016). "Responsibility and the Limits of Conversation." *Criminal Law and Philosophy* 10: 221–40.
Vargas, Manuel and Nichols, Shaun (2007). "Psychopaths and Moral Knowledge." *Philosophy, Psychiatry, and Psychology* 14: 157–62.
Velleman, J. David (1992a). "The Guise of the Good." *Noûs* 26: 3–26.
Velleman, J. David (1992b). "What Happens When Someone Acts?" *Mind* 101: 461–81.
von Wright, Georg Henrik (1971). *Explanation and Understanding*. Ithaca: Cornell University Press.
Wagner, Verena (2017). "On the Analogy of Free Will and Free Belief." *Synthese* 194: 2785–2810.

Wallace, R. Jay (1994). *Responsibility and the Moral Sentiments.* Cambridge, Mass.: Harvard University Press.
Wallace, R. Jay (2010). "Hypocrisy, Moral Address, and the Equal Standing of Persons." *Philosophy and Public Affairs* 38: 307–41.
Wallace, R. Jay (2011). "Dispassionate Opprobrium." In *Reasons and Recognition*, ed. R. Jay Wallace et al. (Oxford: Oxford University Press): 348–72.
Watson, Gary (1982). "Introduction." In *Free Will*, ed. Gary Watson (Oxford: Oxford University Press): 1–14.
Watson, Gary (2004). *Agency and Answerability.* Oxford: Clarendon Press.
Watson, Gary (2011). "The Trouble with Psychopaths." In *Reasons and Recognition*, ed. R. Jay Wallace et al. (Oxford: Oxford University Press): 307–31.
Watson, Gary (2016). "Raz on Responsibility." *Criminal Law and Philosophy* 10: 395–409.
Watzl, Sebastian (2011). "Attention as Structuring of the Stream of Consciousness?" In *Attention: Philosophical and Psychological Essays*, ed. Christopher Mole et al. (Oxford: Oxford University Press): 145–73.
Weingarten, G. (2009). "Fatal distraction: Forgetting a child in the backseat of a car is a horrifying mistake. Is it a crime?" *Washington Post.* http://www.washingtonpost.com/wp-dyn/content/article/2009/02/27/AR2009022701549.html.
Weiskrantz, Lawrence (1986). *Blindsight: A Case Study and Implications.* Oxford: Oxford University Press.
Wieland, Jan Willem (2017a). "Responsibility for Strategic Ignorance." *Synthese* 194: 4477–97.
Wieland, Jan Willem (2017b). "What's Special About Moral Ignorance?" *Ratio* 30: 149–64.
Wieland, Jan Willem (2019). "Willful Ignorance and Bad Motives." *Erkenntnis* 84: 1409–28.
Williams, Bernard (1973). *Problems of the Self.* Cambridge: Cambridge University Press.
Williams, Bernard (1981). *Moral Luck.* Cambridge: Cambridge University Press.
Williams, Bernard (1993). *Shame and Necessity.* Berkeley: University of California Press.
Williams, Glanville (1961). *Criminal Law: The General Part*, 2nd edition. London: Stevens and Sons.
Winters, Barbara (1979). "Believing at Will." *Journal of Philosophy* 76: 243–56.
Wolf, Susan (1982). "Moral Saints." *Journal of Philosophy* 79: 419–39.
Wolf, Susan (1987). "Sanity and the Metaphysics of Responsibility." In *Responsibility, Character, and the Emotions*, ed. Ferdinand Schoeman (Cambridge: Cambridge University Press): 46–62.
Wolf, Susan (1990). *Freedom Within Reason.* Oxford: Oxford University Press.
Wolf, Susan (2011). "Blame, Italian Style." In *Reasons and Recognition*, ed. R. Jay Wallace et al. (Oxford: Oxford University Press): 332–47.
Wu, Wayne (2014). *Attention.* London: Routledge.
Wynn, Karen and Bloom, Paul (2013). "The Moral Baby." In *Handbook of Moral Development*, ed. Melanie Killen and Judith G. Smetana (London: Routledge): 435–53.
Yaffe, Gideon (2018). "The Point of *Mens Rea*: The Case of Willful Ignorance." *Criminal Law and Philosophy* 12: 19–44.
Zhao, Michael (2020). "Guilt Without Perceived Wrongdoing." *Philosophy and Public Affairs* 48: 285–314.
Zimbardo, Philip G. (2007). *The Lucifer Effect: Understanding How Good People Turn Evil.* New York: Random House.
Zimmerman, Michael J. (1988). *An Essay on Moral Responsibility.* Totowa: Rowman & Littlefield.

Zimmerman, Michael J. (1990). "The Range of Options." *American Philosophical Quarterly* 27: 345–55.
Zimmerman, Michael J. (1995). "Responsibility Regarding the Unthinkable." *Midwest Studies in Philosophy* 20: 204–23.
Zimmerman, Michael J. (1996). *The Concept of Moral Obligation*. Cambridge: Cambridge University Press.
Zimmerman, Michael J. (1997a). "A Plea for Accuses." *American Philosophical Quarterly* 34: 229–43.
Zimmerman, Michael J. (1997b). "Moral Responsibility and Ignorance." *Ethics* 107: 410–26.
Zimmerman, Michael J. (2001). *The Nature of Intrinsic Value*. Lanham: Rowman & Littlefield.
Zimmerman, Michael J. (2002). "Taking Luck Seriously." *Journal of Philosophy* 99: 553–76.
Zimmerman, Michael J. (2006). "Moral Luck: A Partial Map." *Canadian Journal of Philosophy* 36: 585–608.
Zimmerman, Michael J. (2008). *Living with Uncertainty: The Moral Significance of Ignorance*. Cambridge: Cambridge University Press.
Zimmerman, Michael J. (2010). "Responsibility, Reaction, and Value." *Journal of Ethics* 14: 103–15.
Zimmerman, Michael J. (2011). *The Immorality of Punishment*. Peterborough, Ontario: Broadview Press.
Zimmerman, Michael J. (2014). *Ignorance and Moral Obligation*. Oxford: Oxford University Press.
Zimmerman, Michael J. (2015a). "Moral Luck Reexamined." In *Oxford Studies in Agency and Responsibility*, vol. 3, ed. David Shoemaker (Oxford: Oxford University Press): 136–59.
Zimmerman, Michael J. (2015b). "Varieties of Moral Responsibility." In *The Nature of Moral Responsibility*, ed. Randolph Clarke et al. (Oxford: Oxford University Press): 45–64.
Zimmerman, Michael J. (2016). "Moral Responsibility and the Moral Community: Is Moral Responsibility Essentially Interpersonal?" *Journal of Ethics* 20: 247–63.
Zimmerman, Michael J. (2017a). "Ignorance as a Moral Excuse." In *Perspectives on Ignorance from Moral and Social Philosophy*, ed. Rik Peels (New York: Routledge): 77–94.
Zimmerman, Michael J. (2017b). "Omissions, Agency, and Control." In *The Ethics and Law of Omissions*, ed. Dana Kay Nelkin and Samuel C. Rickless (Oxford: Oxford University Press): 84–105.
Zimmerman, Michael J. (2017c). "Quality of Will and Moral Responsibility." In *Responsibility: The Epistemic Condition*, ed. Philip Robichaud and Jan Willem Wieland (Oxford: Oxford University Press): 219–32.
Zimmerman, Michael J. (2017d). "Strawson or Straw Man? More on Moral Responsibility and the Moral Community." *Journal of Ethics* 21: 251–62.
Zimmerman, Michael J. (2020). "Willful Ignorance and Moral Responsibility." In *Oxford Studies in Normative Ethics*, vol. 10, ed. Mark Timmons (Oxford: Oxford University Press): 56–80.

Index of Names

For the benefit of digital users, indexed terms that span two pages (e.g., 52–53) may, on occasion, appear on only one of those pages.

Aboodi, Ron 327n.70
Adams, Robert M. 84n.144, 154n.46, 331–4, 336, 338–40, 345n.104, 346
Agule, Craig xv, 56n.59, 228–9
Alexander, Larry 214n.9, 223n.25, 236n.44, 261n.14, 263n.16, 277n.34, 278n.39, 291n.10
Alston, William P. 184n.106, 185, 186n.20, 193–5, 203n.147
Amaya, Santiago xv, 244n.19
American Law Institute 9n.5, 44n.26, 90n.164, 214n.7, 238n.2, 239n.4, 256n.1, 257n.3, 260n.12, 261n.13, 272n.27
Antill, Gregory 205n.152
Archer, Sophie 124n.49
Arendt, Hannah 295, 297
Aristotle v, 12, 40–1, 126, 156n.52, 211, 296n.34, 312, 339–40
Arpaly, Nomy 49, 84, 295n.28, 313, 314n.37, 316n.39, 318–25, 327–33, 342
Audi, Robert xv, 106n.10, 111–12, 184n.106
Augustine 95–6, 246
Austin, J. L. 99, 141n.7, 146–7, 309

Baier, Kurt 56n.59, 89n.162
Baron, Marcia 287n.53
Baron, Robert A. 40n.18
Baumeister, Roy F. 295n.31
Bell, Macalaster 84n.145
Benbaji, Hagit 196n.138
Bennett, Jonathan 70, 196n.138, 198, 320–1
Berman, Mitchell N. 88n.160
Berman, Russell 189n.123
Bero, Steven xv
Biebel, Nathan xv, 244n.19
Björnsson, Gunnar xv
Blanshard, Brand 54n.53
Bloom, Paul 72n.115
Borgoni, Cristina 123n.47, 124n.53
Bradley, Ben 343n.99
Bradley, Seamus 119n.35
Brady, James 238n.3, 257–9, 259n.10
Brandt, Richard B. 129n.64, 333
Bratman, Michael E. 106n.10

Brentano, Franz 53n.52
Brynner, Rock 4n.2
Bykvist, Krister xv

Calhoun, Claudia 289n.1, 297nn.38,41
Callender, Craig A. 277nn.33,35, 278nn.37,38,39, 279nn.40,41
Campbell, C. A. 151
Camus, Albert 152n.42
Capes, Justin 129n.64
Carbonell, Vanessa 314n.38
Card, Claudia 294n.26
Carlsson, Andreas Brekke 75n.121
Castro, Yenni Milena xv
Chabris, Christopher F. 116n.32
Chisholm, Roderick M. 53n.52, 106n.9, 125n.55, 134–5, 140n.6, 147n.20, 148n.26, 149n.29, 158n.57, 167n.82, 317
Clarke, Randolph xv, 80n.130, 86n.151, 139n.2, 141nn.7,8,9, 146, 147nn.19,23, 148n.24, 155n.50, 159–60, 171n.90, 172, 175–6, 239–40, 242–3, 251–2, 258–9, 301, 304–9, 311–12, 330
Clifford, W. K. 204, 279n.41, 287n.52
Coates, D. Justin 49, 85nn.146,147,148, 89nn.162,163, 91nn.169,170, 180
Cohen, L. Jonathan 99n.184, 106n.10, 107n.12, 191n.127
Coleman, Jules 78n.126, 85n.150, 223n.24
Conee, Earl 179n.99, 307n.15
Copp, David 41n.21, 129n.64
Corlett, Angelo xv

Dahl, Norman O. 38n.14, 39n.15
Danielsson, Sven 83n.142
Dante 90n.167
Darwall, Stephen 54, 56n.58, 63–5, 70, 73n.117, 320n.48
Davidson, Donald 145nn.14,15, 149n.27, 158n.57, 177n.98
Davies, Martin 112n.24
De Mesel, Benjamin xv, 52n.48, 55n.57, 72n.114, Deery, Oisin xv

INDEX OF NAMES

Defoe, Daniel 71
Dennett, Daniel C. 86n.154
Dimitrijevic, Nenad 333n.86
Donagan, Alan 126n.61, 129n.64, 167n.82, 264–5, 324n.62, 329n.75, 336
Doris, John M. 40n.17
Douskos, Christos 160n.64
Dowe, Phil 167n.83, 170n.87
Dreier, James 314n.38
Driver, Julia 61, 67, 80n.130, 134–5
Duff, R. A. 238n.3, 241n.10, 259nn.9,10, 291, 292n.12
Duggan, A. P. 70n.106, 71n.112, 136n.78
Dutant, Julien 102n.1

Edwards, J. Ll. J. 278
Edwards, Jonathan 90n.168
Eichmann, Adolf 295, 297n.43, 301
Enoch, David 223n.25
Eriksson, John xv
Ewing, A. C. 53n.52, 54n.54

Feinberg, Joel 49, 53n.51, 65n.96, 223n.25, 290n.5
Feldman, Fred 41n.20
Feldman, Richard 185, 279n.41
Fingarette, Herbert 291n.8
Finkelstein, David H. 117n.33
Fischer, John Martin 30n.2, 49, 53n.50, 56n.59, 80nn.132,133, 89n.162, 140n.5, 151–2, 161–6, 174n.93, 180, 216n.12, 229–31, 292nn.11,13, 320n.50
Fiske, Alan Page 295n.31
FitzPatrick, William J. 279n.41, 297nn.39,41
Foley, Richard 120n.39
Ford, Christine Blasey 189
Frankfurt, Harry G. 164, 168, 182n.103

Gallimore, Richard xv
García, Andrés G. 55n.57, 79n.129
Gendler, Tamar Szabó 123–4
Gettier, Edmund L. 102–3
Glover, Jonathan 49n.36
Göbbels, Joseph 327–8, 333n.86
Goldberg, Sanford C. 215n.11
Goldman, Alvin I. 47n.30, 143n.11, 167n.81
Graham, Peter A. xv, 60n.76, 74n.120, 75n.121, 81n.136, 129–30, 318n.42, 332n.82
Greenspan, Patricia 89n.162, 292n.11
Grünenthal 3–4, 9, 11, 14–16, 32, 99, 216–17, 231
Guerrero, Alexander A. 215n. 11, 296n.35

Haji, Ishtiyaque xv, 30n.2, 49n.36, 53n.51, 98n.183, 129n.64, 134n.71, 163n.73, 292n.11, 293
Haksar, Vinit 291n.8

Hampton, Jean 152n.44
Hare, Richard M. 94
Harman, Elizabeth xv, 244n.19, 269n.24, 296n.34, 316n.39, 329–30, 331n.79, 332
Hart, H. L. A. 29n.1, 238n.3, 252n.29
Hartford, Anna 332n.84
Haybron, Daniel M. 50–1
Hellman, Deborah 279n.41
Herrera, Wilson xv
Heuer, Ulrike 320n.48
Hieronymi, Pamela 129n.64, 196–8
Hitler, Adolf 52, 295
Hobbes, Thomas 139
Hohfeld, Wesley Newcomb 135n.76
Huber, Franz 120n.41
Hughes, Paul M. 311n.27
Humberstone, I. L. 82n.137, 199n.144
Hume, David 54, 331n.80
Hurd, Heidi 147n.22, 238n.3, 239n.6, 242n.13, 244n.18, 258–9
Hurka, Thomas 325n.63, 328n.73
Husak, Douglas N. xv, 9n.5, 21n.8, 37n.11, 44n.27, 45n.28, 96n.179, 100n.187, 113–17, 122, 126n.62, 225n.29, 227–8, 238n.1, 239n.6, 241n.10, 244nn.19,20, 245, 264–6, 268, 277, 278nn.37,38,39, 279nn.40,41, 283n.48, 284, 287n.54, 340n.93, 347

Ichikawa, Jonathan Jenkins 102n.2, 106
Isaacs, Tracy 297n.41

Jackson, Elizabeth 120n.42
Jackson, Frank 129n.64, 267n.21
James, William 203–5
Jennings, Carolyn Dicey 115n.30
Jewell, Charles Demore 273–87
Johnson King, Zoë xv, 297n.40, 320n.49, 324n.61, 325n.63, 328n.73, 332n.84
Johnston, Mark 288n.56

Kamtekar, Rachana 310n.26
Kane, Robert 151n.37
Kant, Immanuel 33n.6, 73, 94, 317, 319–21
Katz, Fred E. 294n.24, 295n.31
Kavanaugh, Brett 189–90
Kavka, Gregory 186n.118
Keeton, Robert E. 214n.9
Khoury, Andrew C. 41n.20, 48n.32, 70n.110, 86n.151, 129n.64, 213n.6, 217–21, 223
King, Matt 85nn.146,147,149, 87n.156, 226–7, 241n.11
Koiv, Riin xv
Kornblith, Hilary, 124n.53
Kripke, Saul 122

INDEX OF NAMES 367

Lemos, Noah 53n.52
Levy, Neil 20n.7, 21n.8, 45n.28, 53n.50, 114n.26, 124n.52, 129n.64, 156n.53, 160n.63, 163n.74, 180n.101, 291n.8, 292nn.11,12,16, 293n.19, 302n.4, 346nn.105,106
Lewis, C. S. 292n.16
Lillehammer, Hallvard 314, 325
Luban, David 278n.37, 279n.42
Luther, Martin 152–3, 181, 195
Lynch, Kevin 287n.54

Macdonald, Graham 112n.24
Madva, Alex 346n.105
Magrin, Sara xv
Marcus, Ruth Barcan 108n.13
Markovits, Julia 314n.36, 316n.39, 319, 321, 323n.58, 327, 333n.86
Marmor, Andrei 223n.25
Mason, Elinor xv, 67n.99, 267n.22, 297n.39, 301n.3, 308–9
Matheson, Benjamin 70n.110, 86n.151
Mathlein, Hans xv
Mayo-Wilson, Conor 119n.36
McConnell, Terrance C. 99
McHugh, Conor 124n.53
McKenna, Michael xv, 30n.2, 43, 53n.50, 58, 59n.73, 62n.83, 63–4, 67–8, 71, 72n.113, 73, 80, 82n.138, 90nn.165,166, 100n.189, 134n.71
Mele, Alfred R. 141nn.7,9, 145n.13, 156n.53, 158, 160n.65, 288n.56
Menges, Leonhard 60n.76
Milgram, Stanley 297
Miller, Daniel J. 283n.48
Milo, Ronald D. 94n.174, 95n.175, 129n.64, 290n.4, 291n.8, 296n.34
Montminy, Martin 211n.2
Moody-Adams, Michelle 296n.35, 297n.37
Moon, Andrew 118n.34, 120n.42
Moore, G. E. 35n.7, 38n.13, 86n.154, 121n.43, 129n.64, 154n.48
Moore, Michael S. xv, 147n.22, 167n.83, 170n.86, 217n.13, 238n.3, 239n.6, 242n.13, 244n.18, 258
Morris, Herbert 49n.36
Munthe, Christian xv
Murphy, Jeffrie G. 152–3, 291n.8
Murray, Samuel 215n.11, 252n.29

Nagel, Thomas 156n.53, 218–19
Narváez, Alexander xv
Nelkin, Dana Kay xv, 53n.51, 56n.58, 75n.123, 98n.182, 130n.68, 181, 182n.103, 292n.13,
Nichols, Shaun 292n.11, 310n.26
Nowell Smith, P. H. 141n.7
Nozick, Robert 138

O'Connell, Jeffrey 214n.9
O'Connor, Timothy 180n.100
Olson, Jonas xv, 83n.142, 326n.67

Parfit, Derek 37n.10, 83n.142, 129n.64
Patarroyo, Carlos xv
Paul, Sarah K. 185nn.108,109
Peels, Rik xv, 21n.8, 80n.130, 100n.188, 103, 109–12, 125n.55, 158, 182n.104, 184n.106, 185, 195n.135, 204–5, 244n.19, 245, 247, 279n.41
Pereboom, Derk xv, 63, 75n.123, 337n.91
Perinetti, Dario xv
Persson, Ingmar xv, 47n.31, 83n.142, 110, 145n.14, 321n.53
Pink, Thomas 50n.41, 346n.107
Plantinga, Alvin 154n.47, 317n.41
Plato 94
Pojman, Louis P. 118n.34, 194n.132, 195n.135
Postow, B. C. 179n.99
Prichard, H. A. 144n.12, 213n.6
Prinz, Jesse J. 115n.30, 116n.32
Pritchard, Michael S. 291n.8
Prosser, William L. 214n.8

Quine, W. V. O. 314, 316

Rabinowicz, Wlodek 83nn.140,142, 212n.3
Radford, Colin 107
Rai, Tage Shakti 295n.31
Ravizza, Mark 30n.2, 49, 53n.50, 80nn.132,133, 89n.162, 151–2, 161–6, 180, 292n.11, 292n.13, 320n.50
Raz, Joseph 147n.21, 242n.15, 252n.32, 307–8
Reisner, Andrew xv
Rescher, Nicholas 121n.44
Rettler, Lindsay 185n.111
Rez, Anna xv
Rickless, Samuel xv
Rippon, Simon xv
Rivera-López, Eduardo 38n.14, 126n.61
Roberts, Robert C. 75n.122
Robichaud, Philip xv, 9n.5
Robinson, Michael 168n.84
Robison, John 87n.157
Roeber, Blake 184n.105, 187n.121
Rønnow-Rasmussen, Toni 83nn.140,142, 212n.3
Rosen, Gideon 20n.7, 21n.8, 36, 50n.41, 74n.120, 75, 78–9, 85n.148, 103n.7, 126n.62, 130n.68, 215n.10, 247n.26, 279n.41, 283n.48, 289n.1, 296, 298, 302n.4, 344, 346n.107
Ross, W. D. 33n.5, 87, 144n.12, 212n.5, 213n.6, 289, 343n.98

Rossi, Mauro xv
Rowe, William L. 294n.23
Rudy-Hiller, Fernando 161n.66, 174n.93, 246n.25, 252nn.30,32, 254n.33, 308n.19
Rumfitt, Ian 157n.55
Russell, Luke 294n.27, 295n.31
Russell, Paul 345n.103

Sarch, Alexander 78n.126, 85n.150, 126n.62, 223n.24, 278nn.37,39, 279nn.41,42, 280–1
Sartorio, Carolina xv
Sartre, Jean-Paul 152n.42
Sayre-McCord, Geoffrey 291n.7
Scanlon, Thomas M. 50n.39, 51–2, 53n.52, 54n.54, 56n.61, 63–5, 70n.106, 73–4, 80, 83n.141, 84n.144, 85n.146, 129n.64, 223n.24, 320n.48
Scarre, Geoffrey 295n.31, 333n.86
Schaffer, Jonathan 170
Schlick, Moritz 86n.154
Schlossberger, Eugene 53n.51, 343n.98
Schmid, Hans Bernhard 95n.178
Schnall, Ira M. 333n.86
Schroeder, Timothy 49, 313n.31, 314n.37, 316n.39, 322–4, 329–32
Schwitzgebel, Eric 106n.10, 109nn.14,15, 110n.19, 114n.28, 123n.48, 124nn.50,51
Searle, John R. 112n.24
Shabo, Seth 231–2
Shepherd, Joshua 139n.3
Sher, George 61–2, 114n.26, 156n.53, 163, 215n.11, 296n.35, 297n.36, 304, 308n.19, 342
Shoemaker, David 31n.3, 40n.16, 50n.39, 56n.58, 58n.65, 63, 77n.125, 129n.64, 130n.70, 290n.3, 291n.6, 292nn.11,13,15, 301
Siewert, Charles 114n.27
Simons, Daniel J. 116n.32
Simons, Kenneth W. 258n.7
Singer, Peter 135
Sinnott-Armstrong, Walter 99n.185, 218n.16
Skow, Brad 41n.20
Sliwa, Paulina 327n.70
Sloane, Stephanie 72n.115
Smart, J. J. C. 86n.154, 343n.97
Smetana, Judith G. 72n.115
Smith, Angela M. 50n.39, 56n.58, 62–6, 73, 80, 82, 85n.146, 331–2, 345nn.103,104
Smith, Holly M. xv, 9n.5, 37n.10, 225, 232, 234n.41, 235, 239n.6, 241n.11, 305, 346n.105
Smith, Michael 215n.11, 252n.31, 313–15, 325–7
Smithies, Declan 116n.32
Snowdon, Paul 157nn.54,56
Sosa, Ernest 134–5

Stanley, Jason 157n.54
Stephens, Trent 4n.2
Steup, Matthias 102n.2, 106, 194–5
Strandberg, Caj xv
Strawson, P. F. 28, 42–3, 52–3, 57–60, 62–3, 69, 73–4, 100n.189
Stump, Eleonore 151n.38, 153
Sverdlik, Steven 242n.15, 243–4
Swenson, Philip 89nn.162,163, 180

Talbert, Matthew xv, 38n.14, 239n.6, 241n.11, 290, 292nn.13,15,17, 305n.11, 311nn.28,29, 329–30, 338
Tannenbaum, Julie 38n.13
Tännsjö, Torbjörn xv
Taylor, Richard 167n.82
Telech, Daniel 86n.153
Thalberg, Irving 309n.25
Thomson, Judith Jarvis 129n.64, 223n.25, 240n.7
Tierney, Hannah 86n.153
Tognazzini, Neal A. 49, 56n.59, 85nn.146,147, 174n.93, 216n.12, 229–31
Turner, J. W. C. 241n.12
Turri, John 189–92
Twain, Mark 313

van der Vossen, Bas xv
Van Gulick, Robert 114n.27
van Hees, Martin xv
van Inwagen, Peter 150–1, 152n.42, 154n.46, 194–5
Vanderheiden, Steve 279n.41
Vargas, Manuel 67–8, 80n.135, 215n.11, 229, 231–2, 252n.29, 292n.11
Velasco, Alejandro xv
Velleman, J. David 152n.42, 199n.144, 200
Vesga, Alejandro xv
von Wright, Georg Henrik 46

Wagner, Verena 166
Wallace, R. Jay 38n.14, 53n.50, 60n.76, 63, 74–5, 80, 85n.146, 86n.152, 291n.9, 292nn.11,13
Warmke, Brandon 311n.27
Watson, Gary 40n.16, 50–2, 53n.51, 56–8, 63, 70n.106, 241n.11, 252n.32, 290n.3, 292nn.11,13,15, 293–4
Watzl, Sebastian 115n.29, 116n.31
Weingarten, G. 239n.6, 241n.11
Weiskrantz, Lawrence 115n.30
Wheeler, Gregory 119n.36
Wieland, Jan Willem xv, 9n.5, 279n.41, 284n.50, 297n.40, 332n.84

Williams, Bernard 106n.10, 121n.43, 185, 186n.119, 195–6, 198–9, 201, 306–7, 309–11, 325–7
Williams, Glanville 274, 279
Williamson, Timothy 157n.54
Wilson, Alan T. 297n.39
Winters, Barbara 196n.138
Wolf, Susan 40n.16, 60n.76, 152, 293, 327
Wu, Wayne 115n.30
Wynn, Karen 72n.115

Yaffe, Gideon 278n.37

Zhao, Michael 307n.14, 309n.25
Zimbardo, Philip G. 40n.17, 294n.25, 297n.42
Zimmerman, Michael J. 30n.2, 36n.8, 44n.25, 49n.33, 52n.48, 59n.73, 79n.128, 88n.161, 91n.171, 103n.4, 126n.63, 129n.65, 151n.39, 182n.104, 211n.2, 220n.17, 221n.20, 222n.23, 224.26, 234n.41, 240n.9, 245n.22, 267n.23, 297n.44, 336n.89, 343n.100, 347n.1

Index of Subjects

For the benefit of digital users, indexed terms that span two pages (e.g., 52–53) may, on occasion, appear on only one of those pages.

AB-conditionals 139–41, 143, 145–54, 170–1
ability 140–1
   exercise of 140–1, 146–7, 152, 155, 157–8, 174–5
     see also control, exercise of
   general vs. specific 140–1, 147–8, 155, 157–8, 161–4, 175–6, 215–16, 243, 253, 309
acceptance 106–7, 191, 199
   see also belief
accepting responsibility, see taking responsibility
accountability 27–8, 55–7, 77n.125
accuses 35, 128–33, 135, 161n.67, 215–16, 236, 242, 244–5, 251n.28, 263, 268
   see also blameworthiness, moral, relation to moral wrongdoing
act-evaluation 37–8, 213–14, 333n.86
acting from ignorance, see ignorance, moral, acting from
action
   basic vs. non-basic 46, 157–8, 192–3, 196–7, 199–200, 207
   intentional, see behavior, intentional vs. unintentional
   irrational 151–2
   morally worthy, see moral worth
   results of 46–7, 143, 159, 193, 196–7, 207
advertence 109–10, 112, 117, 257–60, 262–3
   see also consideration
agent-evaluation 37–8, 48, 213–14, 220, 333n.86, 334–5
agent-regret 306–11
alief 123–4
ambivalence 324–5, 327–8
amoralism 298
anger 61, 67–8, 75–6, 77n.125, 309, 331, 335, 338–9
answerability, see responsibility, moral, Answerability Analysis of (AA)
appropriateness, see fittingness
aretaic judgments 39, 49–50, 220n.17, 241–2, 297–8, 346
Argument against Believing at Will 195–206, 251
   Draft 1 198
   Draft 2 201
   Final Draft 205–6

Argument against Considering at Will 206–8, 251, 253–4
Argument from Ignorance 18, 22–3, 27, 32–3, 35, 44–5, 50, 52n.46, 54, 97, 103, 106–8, 111–12, 125–6, 130–1, 133, 135–6, 160–2, 167–8, 176, 182–3, 186–7, 203, 205–6, 209–10, 215–16, 225, 230–3, 236, 247, 249, 251–2, 254, 262–3, 271–2, 287–8, 297–8, 301–2, 304–5, 311–12, 328–40, 345
   Draft 1 19
   Draft 2 33
   Draft 3 104
   Draft 4 126, 131, 236
   Draft 5 131, 133, 209, 236
   Draft 6 247, 249
   Draft 7 249, 251, 263
   Final Draft 340
atonement 80, 84–6
   see also repentance
attention 109, 113–17, 159–60, 207–8, 241, 252, 259, 304
   see also inattention
attributability 27–8, 39n.15, 50–1, 55–7
attributionism 331–3, 344–6
awareness 114–17, 124n.52, 161, 163–4, 167–8, 238, 241, 260, 262–3, 266–70, 275–7, 285–8, 293, 340
   see also consciousness; control, and awareness; wrongdoing, moral, unwitting; wrongdoing, moral, witting

bafflement 124–5
begging the question 160–1, 174–5, 218
behavior
   intentional vs. unintentional 94, 101–2, 106–7, 145–7, 151–2, 155, 157–60, 170–2, 175–6, 185–6, 191–3, 197, 265, 274–5, 293–4, 333, 336, 343–5
   see also control, simple vs. intentional
   voluntary 86n.155, 111–12, 144, 156n.52, 191–2, 194–5, 309n.25
   see also wrongdoing, moral, voluntary

INDEX OF SUBJECTS

belief 79n.129
  at will 188–206
  conflicts of 122–4
  conscious *vs.* unconscious 124
  degrees of 98–9, 117–22
    see also suspicion
  dispositional 109–12, 206–7, 244–7, 251n.27
  dormant 109–10, 112–13, 115–17, 125, 246–7
  formation of 110–12
  nature of 106–25
  occurrent 109–10, 112–17, 125, 206–7, 244–7, 249, 251–2, 259–60, 262–4, 271, 340, 342
  outright 119–21, 124–5, 184, 199, 260–1, 264–5, 267–72, 274–6, 278–9, 284–5, 287
  relation to dispositions 108–12
  relation to knowledge 106–8, 110
  self-verifying 202–6
  tacit 109–12, 125, 246–7
  voluntary, *see* belief, at will
  see also acceptance; control, over beliefs; credence; disbelief; failing to believe
benighting acts 225–8, 232–6, 243–4, 253–4, 286, 303–5
best bet 239–40, 243, 261–2, 265–71
  see also obligation, moral, prospective view of
BILL AND JILL 46–7, 93, 96, 142, 158, 173, 211–13, 218–20, 223
  see also Figure 2.1
BILL AND THE BIRD 177, 218–20, 223, 236
  see also Figure 4.5
BILL AND THE CLOCK 145–6, 166–7, 169, 177–80, 186–9
  see also Figure 4.1
BILL'S ACTIVE OMISSION 169–71, 173, 176, 186–7
  see also Figure 4.2
BILL'S INEFFICACY 171
  see also Figure 4.3
BILL'S PASSIVE OMISSION 173–6, 187
  see also Figure 4.4
BILL'S PERSISTENCE 178, 219–20
  see also Figure 4.6
blame 31
  moral 48–81
    blame$_c$ *vs.* blame$_n$ 336–46
    consequences of 86–7
    ethics of 84–7
    fairness of 81, 86
    thick 51–81
      as calling for an answer 62–6, 73
      as conversational 58, 59n.73, 64, 66–9, 73, 308–9

      as emotional 60–2, 74
      as interpersonal 62–5, 69–70
      as involving a moral community 69–74
      as involving dispositions 62
      as involving impaired relations 63–4, 73, 308
      private 57–8, 67–9
      varieties of 220–1, 335–6, 342–5, 347
      weak *vs.* strong 57–8, 69, 81, 343–5
    thin 48–51, 76, 78
  non-moral 31, 48, 59n.73, 78–9
blamelessness, moral 6–7, 14, 20, 22–3, 27, 36–7, 87–9, 97–100, 214, 229, 236, 240–1, 251n.27, 257, 267, 293, 296–8, 309, 324, 328–9, 343–5
  see also excuses
blameworthiness 30–1
  moral 5, 33–4, 41–8, 81–101, 104–5, 126, 128, 131, 133, 160–3, 168, 183, 209–10, 215–17, 240–1, 243–4, 247, 249, 251, 313, 321–4, 328–31, 333, 340, 342
    agential condition of 12–14, 20, 42, 45, 129–31, 137, 156, 162–3, 218, 225–6, 266–8, 270–1, 273, 290, 298, 312, 319, 340
    see also control
    analysis of 74–80
    basis of 41–3, 45–8, 93–6, 130–1, 218, 220–1, 236, 312–45
    degrees of 85–6, 89–100, 182–3, 218–21, 223–5, 256, 258–9, 261, 264–5, 268, 270–4, 277–80, 281–3, 284, 287–8, 297n.44
    see also Equal Culpability Thesis; Unequal Culpability Thesis
    dimensions of 91–2
    direct *vs.* indirect 13–14, 17, 19–21, 33–4, 41, 45, 47, 93, 104–5, 126, 128, 131, 133, 209–14, 216–19, 223–6, 228–9, 231–2, 235, 244–7, 249, 251–5, 286–8, 304–5, 312, 329, 332, 338, 340, 342
    epistemic condition of 12, 20, 42, 129, 137, 156, 162–3, 225–6, 290–1, 298, 312, 340
    full 96–100
    hybrid 47
    object of 41, 45–8, 130–1, 216, 218
    relation to moral responsibility 345–6
    relation to moral wrongdoing 19–21, 32–7, 104, 126, 128–36
    see also Equivalence Thesis; excuses
    scope of 218–19, 224–5
    thick 56–7, 59–60, 62, 74–9, 81, 84–6, 91

blameworthiness (*cont.*)
    thin 56, 74–7, 79, 81, 84–6, 91
    time of 70–2, 85–6
    varieties of 301–46
    non-moral 31, 48

care 238, 240–1, 257, 259, 290–1, 308, 311–13, 326, 330, 332, 334
    lack of, *see* indifference
caring for morality, *de re vs. de dicto* 313–27, 329, 333
character 38–41, 51
    see also aretaic judgments
Chart 1.1 14
Chart 1.2 15–16
Chart 2.1 31, 346
Coincident Reasons Thesis 319–20
Conceited Thesis 203, 205
concentration 115–16
concern, *see* care
confidence 107, 117–21, 203–4, 267
    see also credence
conscience 294–5, 318, 320–1
    lack of 294–5
    misguided 295–7, 327–9, 340
conscientiousness 31, 239–40, 270, 295, 318–28, 347
consciousness 112–17, 163
    see also awareness; wrongdoing, moral, conscious
consideration 109–12, 117, 206–8
    see also entertainment; wrongdoing, moral, conscious
contempt 296–7, 329–31, 334, 340, 342–3
contra-conscientiousness 318–21, 324–5, 340
control 12–13, 45, 50, 70–1, 97–8, 129–31, 137–208, 212–13, 215–16, 218–19, 225–7, 253, 268, 287–8, 290, 293, 304, 331, 333–4, 336–40, 343–6
    and awareness 156–61, 179–80
    and freedom 42, 153–4, 165, 182, 186–7
    basic *vs.* enhanced 144–5, 181–2
    bilateral 139–41, 163–5, 167–9, 183–5, 188
    complete *vs.* partial 143–4, 178–9, 213
    degrees of 98–9, 177–83, 218–20
    direct *vs.* indirect 13–14, 17–19, 33, 45–8, 104, 126, 131, 141–3, 145–53, 158, 166–71, 173–4, 176–8, 183–9, 191–4, 206–8, 210–16, 225–6, 247, 249, 253–5, 274–5, 302, 305, 330–1, 336, 338, 340
    exercise of 13, 20n.7, 45–7, 129, 148, 151–6, 158, 160–7, 170–1, 174–80, 184–9, 191–3, 212–14, 218–19, 229, 236, 253–5, 274–5, 305, 340, 343n.98
    extent of 177–8, 218–19
    hybrid 47, 142–3, 145–8, 154–5, 158, 166–7, 169–71, 186–8, 211n.2, 212–13

    immediate *vs.* remote 143, 191–2
    locus of 46–7, 148, 166–7, 176–7, 186–7
    non-agential 138–9
    non-volitional 253–4
    over beliefs 104, 106–7, 111–12, 126, 131, 150, 183–207, 247, 249, 274–5, 302, 340
    over ignorance 17, 19, 33
        see also control, over beliefs
    over omissions 159, 169–77, 186–7
    possession of 153–6, 163–5, 174–6
    regulative *vs.* guidance 140n.5, 163–6
    scope of 218–19
    simple *vs.* intentional 145–6, 156–66, 169, 179–80, 183, 185–6, 234–5
    volitional 138–56, 162, 166, 183, 186–90, 207, 253–5, 332–3
    whole 178–9
conversation, *see* blame, moral, thick, as conversational
credence 117–22, 124–5, 184, 260–1, 265, 268–73, 275–6, 278–9
    imprecise 118–19, 270n.25
    substantial 270–1
    see also belief
creditworthiness, *see* praiseworthiness, moral
cruelty 50–1, 153, 334, 338–9, 345–6
culpability, *see* blameworthiness, moral
culpable ignorance, *see* ignorance, moral, culpable

decision 46, 93, 140–3, 148–54, 157–60, 163–4, 166–79, 186–7, 188n.122, 193–6, 208, 212–14, 216–21, 223–6, 228–9, 231, 235, 270, 281, 286, 305, 338, 340
    see also control, locus of
denials 96–7, 100
    see also excuses; justifications
deontic judgments 38–9, 49, 74–5, 213, 241–2, 254–5, 297–8, 321–2
desert 28, 41n.20, 49, 71–2, 78–9, 81, 83–8, 91–3, 96, 221, 292, 303, 306–7, 311–13, 335–6, 338, 340, 343–5
    see also fittingness; suffering, desert of; worthiness
desires 123–4, 151, 204, 294, 312–17, 322–3, 331–3, 335
    derivative *vs.* non-derivative 313–23, 325–7, 329, 333
determinism v, 42, 165
difficulty 98, 144, 181–2, 290
direction of fit 199–200, 202
disbelief 79n.129, 105–7, 124–5, 183–5, 190–1, 275–6
    see also belief
disdain 335, 342–3

INDEX OF SUBJECTS 373

Distaval 3–11, 14–15, 21–2, 35–6, 41, 85, 128–9, 216
Doctrine of Double Effect 272
doing something at will 138–9
  see also control, volitional
doing the right thing accidentally 319–22
doing the right thing for the right reason 312–13, 316, 318–25
DOT AND PAT 212–13, 234
  see also Figure 5.1
doxastic uncommittedness 124–5, 183–5
doxastic voluntarism, see control, over beliefs
duty to inquire 278–83, 296

empathy 290–3, 297
entertainment 109–10, 112–15, 117, 206
  see also consideration
Equal Culpability Thesis 278–80, 284
Equivalence Thesis 32–3, 35
evidence 36–7, 85, 97, 118–19, 123–4, 189–90, 204, 239–40, 264–70, 287, 306–7, 310–11
evil 50–1, 95, 152, 222n.21, 289, 294–8, 312–13, 328–9, 333
excuses 35–6, 40–1, 54–6, 64n.90, 74, 76–8, 87, 90, 96–100, 103n.7, 107–8, 128–9, 181–2, 215–16, 228–9, 242, 254, 267, 285, 287, 290–1, 295–8, 328–9, 333, 342
  see also denials; ignorance, moral, as an excuse; justifications
executive decisions, see decision
exemptions 70–1, 100, 293
  see also excuses

failing to believe 103–4, 107–8, 121–2, 124–6, 128, 131–3, 183, 209–10, 236, 243–4, 247, 249, 251, 262–3, 271, 340, 342
fault 50–1, 66n.98, 95, 306, 310–11, 329–30, 334, 346
Figure 2.1 46–7, 141–2, 145, 158, 218–19
  see also BILL AND JILL
Figure 4.1 145, 158, 166–7, 169–71, 173, 177–9, 186–7, 191–3, 196–7
  see also BILL AND THE CLOCK
Figure 4.2 169–71, 173, 186–7, 193
  see also BILL'S ACTIVE OMISSION
Figure 4.3 171
  see also BILL'S INEFFICACY
Figure 4.4 173, 187, 193
  see also BILL'S PASSIVE OMISSION
Figure 4.5 177, 218–19
  see also BILL AND THE BIRD

Figure 4.6 178, 219–20
  see also BILL'S PERSISTENCE
Figure 5.1 212–13, 223
  see also DOT AND PAT
finks 138–9, 147–8
Fitting-Attitude Analysis of value, see value, Fitting-Attitude Analysis of (FAA)
fittingness 53–7, 59–60, 62, 64, 67, 69–73, 76, 78, 79n.129, 80–9, 223–4, 306–7, 309–11, 330, 333–5, 342, 344–6
  see also desert; worthiness
focus 113–17
foreseeability 8–11, 36, 214–17, 228–35, 294
forgetfulness 159, 239, 246–7, 258–9, 304–6, 312
forgiveness 57, 58n.68, 85–6, 309, 311
Frankfurt-cases 163–5
freedom, see control, and freedom

good will, see will, good
guilt 4–6, 11, 15, 44, 71n.112, 75, 79, 84–5, 87–8, 96–7, 99n.184, 136n.78, 274, 283–4, 309n.25, 310–11, 332, 335
  presumption of 310–11
  see also blameworthiness, moral

Hitler *Jugend* 333, 335–6, 344–5
holding responsible 80
homophobia 334, 344–6
Huckleberry Finn 312–13, 318–21, 324–5, 332–3, 340
hypological judgments 38–41, 48–50, 76–7, 81, 85–6, 91, 213–14, 220n.17, 321–2, 346
  content of 74–81

ignorance 101–36
  moral 11–12, 19, 21, 33, 104
    acting from 126–8, 131, 133, 247, 249, 251, 271, 287, 293, 297, 337–40, 342, 345
    acting merely in 126, 128, 243–4, 251n.27, 264, 266–7, 271, 303
    as an excuse 4–23, 35–6, 126, 232–6, 283–6, 297
    control over, see control, over ignorance
    culpable 7, 16, 209–36, 287–8, 329–30, 336
    degrees of, see belief, degrees of
    deliberate, see ignorance, moral, willful
    fundamental 22–3, 286–7, 289–98, 301–2, 328, 330, 332
    incidental 22–3, 286–7, 289, 295, 298, 330, 332, 334
    inculpatory 236
    inexcusable, see ignorance, moral, culpable
    motivated 273–88, 296–7

ignorance (*cont.*)
    substandard 7, 15, 21, 252–5
    willful 273–86
    of law 347
    relation to knowledge 102–6
ill will, *see* will, ill
inadvertence 257–60, 304–7, 310
    acting from 249, 251n.27, 254
    acting merely in 251n.27
    substandard 241–55, 257, 262–3, 303–6, 311–12
    see also wrongdoing, moral, inadvertent
inattention 116n.32, 244–52
    see also attention
inculpability, *see* blamelessness, moral
indifference 42, 46n.29, 53–4, 83, 259, 306–7, 309, 312, 322, 330–1
indifference-worthiness 30, 32, 45, 65–6, 87–90, 100
indignation 59–61, 74–6, 332, 335, 342–5
inexcusable ignorance, *see* ignorance, moral, culpable
intentional behavior, *see* behavior, intentional *vs.* unintenional
irresistible impulse 12–13, 226, 290, 339

justifications 96–7, 99
    see also denials; excuses

know-how 157–8
knowing better v, 21, 244–6, 249, 252
    see also negligence; wrongdoing, moral, inadvertent
knowing that *vs.* knowing whether 105, 274–6
knowledge 260–1, 274–5, 277
    general *vs.* specific 247
    see also belief, relation to knowledge; ignorance, relation to knowledge

laudability, *see* praiseworthiness, moral
likelihood, *see* probability

masks 138–9, 146–7
memory 111–12, 185, 252–3
    see also forgetfulness
mens rea 44, 47, 277–8, 284n.49
Model Penal Code 44, 47, 90, 93–4, 237–42, 256–7, 259–64, 272–3, 277
moral blamelessness, *see* blamelessness, moral
moral blameworthiness, *see* blameworthiness, moral
moral community 27–8, 58–9, 62–7, 292
    actual 69–73, 81–2
    hypothetical 73
    see also blame, moral, thick, as involving a moral community
moral dilemmas 37, 130, 266
moral fetishism 313, 325–8

moral ignorance, *see* ignorance, moral
moral luck 64, 70–1, 217–25, 228, 235, 297
moral obligation, *see* obligation, moral
moral permissibility, *see* permissibility, moral
moral realism 133, 203n.149
moral responsibility, *see* responsibility, moral
moral rightness, *see* rightness, moral
moral standing 49, 64, 84–5, 87, 292
moral understanding 291–3, 298, 320–1, 336
moral worth 38, 319–22
moral wrongdoing, *see* wrongdoing, moral

negligence 15–17, 21–2, 44, 93–4, 113, 159–60, 226–7, 237–63, 301, 303–12, 330–1,
    definition of 238–44, 262, 303
    pure 243–4, 249, 253–4, 303–4, 312

obligation, moral 35, 74, 80n.132, 135–6, 315, 328
    all things considered 32–3, 289
    conditional *vs.* unconditional 280–3
    fundamental *vs.* incidental 212–14, 223
    objective view of 29, 36–7, 85, 130, 239–40, 265–7, 284–5, 306–7, 318n.42
    overall 32–3, 315, 317
    prima facie 32–3, 289
    pro tanto 32–3
    prospective view of 267–8, 284–5
    subjective view of 37, 85, 265, 267
    see also deontic judgments; responsibility, prospective; wrongdoing, moral
oblivion 28, 117, 124–5, 159–60, 286–7, 304, 324–5
omission 11–12, 32–3, 167–9, 213, 225n.27, 231–2, 242–3
    acts of 169–73, 176
    basic *vs.* non-basic 193
    intentional *vs.* unintentional, *see* behavior, intentional *vs.* unintentional
    purely passive 173–6, 187, 305
    see also control, over omissions
one thought too many, *see* moral fetishism
Origination Thesis 21–3, 27, 32–3, 44, 47–8, 101, 103, 105–8, 112, 128, 131, 133, 136, 161–3, 209, 237, 243–5, 247, 249, 251–2, 271, 287–8, 298, 301, 303, 331–5, 340, 342, 346–7
    Draft 1 21
    Draft 2 34, 101
    Draft 3 105
    Draft 4 128, 161n.67
    Draft 5 133, 245
    Draft 6 249, 251n.27
    Draft 7 251
    Final Draft 342
overdetermination 167–8, 170, 326

Palsgraf v. Long Island Railroad Co. 217n.14
permissibility, moral 315, 325, 328–30
   overall 315, 317
   see also rightness, moral
phocomelia 3–5, 8–11, 15, 41, 98, 128–9, 214, 216–17
   see also teratogen
polyneuritis 3–4, 9–10, 20, 217
praise 31
   moral 48–50, 52, 57–60, 69, 84
   non-moral 31, 48
praiseworthiness 30–1, 91
   moral 45, 48–9, 55–9, 65–6, 82, 84–90, 100, 180–1, 235, 312–13, 320–5, 327–9, 333
   non-moral 31, 48
prima facie duties, *see* obligation, moral, *prima facie*
probability 8, 11–12, 118–22, 153–4, 180, 213–14, 258–9, 261–5, 268–70, 274–5, 277–9, 282–3
problem of the vicinity 10–11, 217, 224–5, 230–1
psychopathy 162, 180–1, 290–4, 320–1
punishment 57–61, 79, 85–8, 90–3, 228, 277–8, 283–4, 335–6, 338–40, 342–5, 347

quality of will, *see* will, quality of

racism 124, 180, 297, 328, 342, 346
reactions 52, 57–60, 62, 64, 69–76, 80–2, 84–6, 88, 91–3, 96, 144, 292, 309–12, 332, 334–5, 342–3
reactive attitudes 49–60, 62–3, 69–72, 78n.126, 79
reasonable-person standard 214–15, 238, 240–1, 257
reasons
   direct *vs.* indirect 222–3
   moral 32–3, 161–3, 180–1, 265, 291–3, 298, 319–21, 324–5
   non-moral 162, 291–2, 298
reasons-responsiveness 161–6, 180–1, 292, 312–13, 319–21, 324–5
   RR 161, 163
rebuke 335, 342–3
recklessness 8, 11–12, 21–2, 36, 44, 93–4, 113, 121–2, 226–7, 243–5, 256–88, 303, 307
   definition of 238, 256–64, 271
remorse 69–70, 290–1, 302, 306–11, 342–3
repentance 85–6, 281
   see also atonement
reprimand 59–60, 70–1, 91–3, 221, 335, 342–4
reproach 69, 333–5, 338, 342–3
resentment 41–2, 54–61, 67, 69, 74–9, 81, 85–6, 92–3, 220–1, 292, 330, 335, 342–4
respect 292, 308, 317–18, 320

responsibility
   causal 5, 8, 11, 29–30, 32, 54, 223–4, 310
   moral 5, 27–101, 345–6
      Answerability Analysis of (AA) 63–7, 82
      as interpersonal, *see* blame, moral, thick, as interpersonal
      as involving a moral community, *see* blame, moral, thick, as involving a moral community
      buck-passing account of 53–5
      degrees of 89–90, 220–1
      indirect, essential emptiness of 221–7
      Reaction Analysis of 59–60, 64, 73, 82–4
         RA1 60, 64, 82, 84
         RA2 73, 82, 84
         RA3 82–4
         RA4 84
      Reactive-Attitude Analysis of 52–7
         RAA1 52–3
         RAA2 53–7, 59–60
      scope of 220–1
   non-moral 30–1
   personal 29–30
   prospective 29–32, 35, 60n.74, 66, 80n.131
      see also obligation, moral
   retrospective 29–32, 35, 38–9, 66–7, 80, 89–90
   vs. irresponsibility 31
   vs. non-responsibility 31
   see also blameworthiness; holding responsible; hypological judgments; praiseworthiness; taking responsibility
retribution 78–9, 344
rightness, moral 314–15, 317, 320–2, 325–9, 333
   overall 318, 323–4, 327
   pro tanto 323–5
   see also doing the right thing accidentally; doing the right thing for the right reason
rights 134–5
risk 9, 11–15, 20, 36–7, 41, 97–8, 113–17, 121–2, 214, 217, 227–8, 231, 238–43, 246, 256–64, 282, 284–7, 306–7, 318n.42
   risking harm *vs.* risking wrong 264–71
Robinson Crusoe 71–3

self-deception 276, 287
sin 80, 281, 331, 336, 339
strict liability 66n.98, 86–7, 343
suberogation 133–6
suffering, desert of 78–9, 344
supererogation 133–5

suspicion 36, 98, 117, 121, 124–5, 199, 264–5, 268–9, 274–6, 279–80, 282–5, 287

taking responsibility 80, 307–9, 311
teratogen 5–9, 14–15, 98
terrorism 159, 264–5, 310, 328–9
thalidomide, tragedy of 3–22, 32, 36, 41, 94, 98, 171, 214, 217
thinking about 109–10, 112–13, 115–17, 159–60, 306
   vs. thinking that 109–10, 206–7
Tourette Syndrome 12–13, 168–9, 171, 225–6
tracing 21–3, 41, 168–9, 209–32, 243–4, 253–4, 303–4
   narrow 225–32
tracking 210–14, 284

Unequal Culpability Thesis 278–80
United States v. Jewell 273–4, 276–8, 283–5
unwitting wrongful acts 225–8, 232–5, 286, 304–5, 312
   see also wrongdoing, moral, unwitting

value
   Buck-Passing Analysis of (BPA) 53–4, 83
   expected 269–70
   final *vs.* non-final 212, 221–4
   Fitting-Attitude Analysis of (FAA) 53–4, 79n.129, 83–4
   Worthy-Attitude Analysis of (WAA) 83
vice 49–51, 68–9, 296–8, 313, 318–19, 325, 327, 329, 331n.80, 334, 343n.98
   see also aretaic judgments
virtue 50, 313, 318–19, 324–9, 331n.80, 333, 343n.98
   see also aretaic judgments
voluntary behavior, *see* behavior, voluntary
voluntary belief, *see* belief, at will

will
   good 42–3, 306, 311–13, 322
   ill 42–3, 306–9, 312–13, 322, 328–33, 335, 340, 342, 344, 347

quality of 41–5, 62–3, 70–1, 78–9, 90, 93–6, 129–31, 135–6, 213–14, 218–21, 235, 312–33
   see also control, volitional
wishful thinking 276, 287
worthiness 71–2, 78, 81–9
   see also desert; fittingness
Wrong Kind of Reason Problem 83
wrongdoing, moral 6, 228, 321–3, 329, 333
   conscientious, *see* conscience, misguided
   conscious 256–73, 284
   defiant 246, 291–2, 324–5, 340
   gleeful 44, 90, 94–5, 98–9
   knowing, *see* wrongdoing, moral, witting
   ignorant, *see* ignorance, moral; wrongdoing, moral, unwitting
   immediate *vs.* remote 234n.41
   inadvertent 238–44, 263, 311
   on purpose 44, 90, 94–6, 98–9, 271–3
   overall 32–5, 47–8, 101, 104–5, 107–8, 121–2, 126, 128, 131, 133, 136, 160–3, 205, 209, 215–16, 242n.14, 247, 249, 251, 262n.15, 266, 298, 303, 305–7, 310–11, 318, 323–5, 340, 342
   overtly witting 251–2
   pro tanto 32–3, 323–4
   quasi-overtly witting 251–2
   quasi-witting 128, 133, 209–10, 251–2
   seriousness of 94–5, 239–40, 258–9, 268, 272–3, 281–2, 294–5, 318n.42
   unwilling 251–2
   unwitting 6, 27, 87, 94, 125–6, 190–1, 210, 225–35, 244, 272, 285–7, 289, 297, 304–5, 307, 312, 329–30, 334, 338–40
   voluntary 333–45
   willing 95–6, 251–2, 271, 282–3, 340
   witting 21–3, 27, 44, 90, 93–6, 101, 105, 128, 133, 135, 209, 225–8, 230–2, 236, 246, 251–2, 256, 260–1, 272–3, 277–9, 287–8, 298, 339–40
   see also blameworthiness, moral, relation to moral wrongdoing; deontic judgments